5 fifth edition

the psychology
of criminal conduct

D.A. ANDREWS / James **BONTA**

Carleton University Public Safety Canada

Routledge
Taylor & Francis Group

LONDON AND NEW YORK

First published 1994 by Anderson Publishing

Published 2015 by Routledge
2 Park Square, Milton Park, Abingdon, Oxfordshire OX14 4RN

and by Routledge
711 Third Avenue, New York, NY 10017, USA

First issued in hardback 2015

Routledge is an imprint of the Taylor & Francis Group, an informa business

The Psychology of Criminal Conduct, Fifth Edition

Library of Congress Cataloging-in-Publication Data

Andrews, D.A. (Donald Arthur), 1941-
    The psychology of criminal conduct / D.A. Andrews, James Bonta.-- 5th ed.
        p. cm.
    Includes bibliographical references and index.

    1. Criminal psychology. 2. Criminal behavior. I. Bonta, James II. Title.

    HV6080.A667 2010
    364.3--dc22   2010000283

Cover design by Tin Box Studio, Inc.   EDITOR Ellen S. Boyne
                                        ACQUISITIONS EDITOR Michael C. Braswell

ISBN 13: 978-1-138-12882-8 (hbk)
ISBN 13: 978-1-4224-6329-1 (pbk)

Preface to the Fifth Edition

It is a pleasure to introduce edition number five of *The Psychology of Criminal Conduct* (PCC-5). As in PCC-1 through PCC-4, we update research, theory, and applications in PCC-5. PCC-5 remains true to its original intent of developing a holistic and truly interdisciplinary general personality and social psychology of criminal conduct. We draw upon a variety of theoretical positions on variability in the criminal behavior of individual human beings but once again find particular value in general personality and cognitive-behavioral and cognitive social learning perspectives on human behavior in general and criminal behavior in particular.

We remain open to the full range of potential variables of interest from the biological through the personal, interpersonal, familial, structural/cultural, political/economic, and the immediate situations of action.

An outstanding change in criminology, forensic mental health, and criminal justice over the last 20 years has been the enhanced position of PCC academically and in practice. Indeed, applications of PCC have revolutionized corrections and forensic mental health in many areas of North America, Europe, Australia, and New Zealand. In applied terms, prevention and corrections have moved from "nothing works" through "what works" to "making what works work." All of this occurred in a political/judicial environment that was preoccupied with "getting tough."

We use the phrase "rehabilitative jurisprudence" to underscore the importance of crime prevention becoming once again a major focus within justice and corrections. For too long, crime prevention has been next to excluded because of a focus on due process, just desert, deterrence, "getting tough," and the fear of offenders being mollycoddled. We call for crime prevention efforts in the context of the normative structure of justice. Additionally, and more than ever before, PCC-5 calls for crime prevention to become a valued outcome of general educational, social, human, and clinical services.

The organizational and content changes in PCC-5 reflect a number of concerns. First, many colleagues and students have found earlier editions to be intellectually stimulating and professionally inspiring. That response we want to maintain and enhance. Yet some users of PCC have found PCC difficult and challenging in that so much attention was paid to quantitative research and to the analysis of competing intellectual traditions. Those concerns we addressed directly in PCC-4 and now in PCC-5. Detailed summaries of research and detailed discussions of

iv   The Psychology of Criminal Conduct

intellectual and discipline-based criticism are presented in Technical Notes that appear at the end of the text. The major content of the book may be appreciated without reading the Technical Notes.

As was PCC-4, PCC-5 is open to an audience broader than our original focus on the concerns of senior undergraduate students, graduate students, and professionals in psychology. We think that undergraduate students, graduate students, and practitioners in the domains of social work, sociology, education, health, youth and family studies, criminology, and youth and adult justice will profit from PCC-5. In addition, we are finding that many members of the general public have a tremendous interest in understanding antisocial behavior. Crime, after all, has always been a major interest within the news media and the arts and entertainment. We are finding now that extraordinary numbers of high school students, their parents, and members of the public find antisocial behavior to be not only interesting but fascinating. We receive e-mail requests for information regularly. (Yes, we agree, it is part an effect of the popularity of the "CSI" series and similar programs on TV). We hope that some members of the general public will check out PCC-5.

Fifteen chapters are organized into four sections of PCC-5. Part 1 includes an overview of the major knowledge base within PCC. Part 2 summarizes the knowledge through consideration of the "central eight" risk/need factors. Part 3 explores applications in the domains of assessment and crime prevention programming. Part 4 is a summary with conclusions in regard to the major issues in understanding criminal conduct.

Part 1: The Theoretical Context and Knowledge Base to the Psychology of Criminal Conduct. Chapter 1, not surprisingly, remains the introductory chapter, with special attention to where PCC fits within general human psychology and within criminology. We also continue to stress the seeking of a theoretical, research-based, and applied understanding of variation in the criminal behavior of individuals.

Chapter 2 is now built around the risk-need-responsivity (RNR) model of correctional assessment and crime prevention programming. The RNR model is a way of both summarizing knowledge and facilitating the effective application of knowledge. The approach is very unusual in that, by the end of Chapter 2, readers will be introduced to the concepts, principles, and research findings that will constitute the major material in our closing chapter. Indeed, much of the content of Chapter 2 is what the remaining chapters in PCC-5 are devoted to developing, testing, and reviewing in a critical rational and evidentiary manner.

Chapter 3 reviews the major theoretical understandings of criminal behavior as an introduction to our preferred general personality and cognitive social learning perspective. The personal, interpersonal, and community-reinforcement (PICI-R) perspective is outlined in Chapter 4.

Part 2: The Major Risk/Need Factors of Criminal Conduct. The five chapters in Part 2 explore the evidence in support of the major correlates of a criminal history and the major risk/need factors predictive of criminal futures. Chapter 5 surveys biological, personal, and social origins of differential patterns of criminal behavior. Chapter 6 emphasizes certain predisposition features that are sometimes labeled "antisocial personality" but that we prefer to call "antisocial personality pattern." Chapter 7 focuses on antisocial cognition and antisocial associates. Chapter 8 considers the social contexts of school/work, family/marital, and leisure/recreation. Chapter 9 explores substance abuse and criminal behavior.

Part 3: Applications. The applications reside in practical assessments of offenders, their classification not only in terms of risk/need but also in terms of a variety of subtypes. Prevention and rehabilitation are reviewed in detail along with the role of official punishment in justice and corrections.

Part 4: Summary and Conclusions. If the preceding 14 chapters were successful, you will find that Chapter 15 is nothing but a summary of the early chapters and a brief look ahead at where PCC may be heading.

DAA thanks Catherine for her love, support, and assistance in the development of PCC. Thanks to Rebecca and Adam. Best wishes to Ashley and Jaminha, and to Karen, Donna, Margo, Vicky, and David. Thanks to Paul Gendreau, Bob Hoge, Steve Wormith, Craig Dowden, and Annie Yessine. DAA has enjoyed working once again with Jill Rettinger and Rob Rowe.

PCC-5 is dedicated to the memory of Bob Watters. Bob was a dear friend of DAA's for 50 years, and as thesis advisor to James Bonta, he deeply stimulated JB's views on the influence of environmental contingencies and cognitions on behavior. His intelligence was inspiring, and his friendship was transformational. Willi, we trust you will enjoy some rest and some wonderful travel.

JB's comments. It is still remarkable to me that after more than 15 years and five editions that PCC continues to resonate within the criminal justice field. About the time we were preparing the first edition, I asked DAA, "What if we are wrong about the psychology of criminal conduct, RNR, etc.?" His usual answer to such a question was, "Well, we have to go by the evidence and change." As this book recounts, the evidence remains in our favor, although I am sure that the day will come when we will need to prepare for a significant re-think (perhaps in the sixth edition?).

First and foremost, I would like to thank my wife Christine for her support, patience, and love while I worked on this edition. Secondly, my thanks to my children, Carolyn (biologist) and Mark (MD), not only for their review of Chapter 5 but, along with my son-in-law Michael Johnson, for their enthusiastic encouragement during my work on the book. As noted in PIC-R, every behavior has both a reward and a cost. Writing

PCC-5 had its rewards but also its costs in that I could not spend as much time with my family. My thanks to them for helping me complete the project.

I have also been fortunate to work with our colleagues noted above by DAA. I would also like to acknowledge the remarkable collaborations that I have enjoyed with my fellow researchers at Public Safety Canada—Karl Hanson, Guy Bourgon, and Tanya Rugge.

Finally, DAA and JB would like to thank our longtime editor, Ellen Boyne, for her continued support through five editions of PCC.

D.A. Andrews
J. Bonta
2010

Preface to the Fourth Edition

It is a pleasure to introduce edition number four of *The Psychology of Criminal Conduct* (PCC-4). Of course we update research, theory, and applications within PCC-4, but PCC-4 remains true to its original intent of developing a holistic and interdisciplinary general personality and social psychology of criminal conduct. We remain open to the full range of potential variables of interest from the biological through the personal, interpersonal, familial, structural/cultural, political/economic, and the immediate situations of action.

An outstanding change in criminology, forensic mental health, and criminal justice over the last 15 years has been the enhanced position of PCC academically and in practice. Indeed, applications of PCC have revolutionized corrections and forensic mental health in many areas of North America, Europe, Australia, and New Zealand. In applied terms, prevention and corrections have moved from "nothing works" through "what works" to "making what works work." We look forward to expanding upon "rehabilitative jurisprudence" in a few years with PCC-5.

The organizational and content changes in PCC-4 reflect a number of concerns. First, many colleagues and students have found earlier editions to be intellectually stimulating and professionally inspiring. That response we want to maintain and enhance. Yet some users of PCC have found PCC difficult and challenging in that so much attention was paid to quantitative research and to the analysis of competing intellectual traditions. Those concerns we address directly in PCC-4.

PCC-4 places detailed summaries of research and detailed discussions of intellectual and discipline-based criticism in Technical Notes that appear at the end of each chapter. The major content of the book may be appreciated without reading the Technical Notes.

Additionally, we have opened up PCC to an audience broader than our original focus on the concerns of senior undergraduate students, graduate students, and professionals in psychology. We think that undergraduate students, graduate students, and practitioners in the domains of social work, sociology, education, health, youth and family studies, criminology, and youth and adult justice will profit from PCC-4. In addition, we are finding that many members of the general public have a tremendous interest in understanding antisocial behavior. Crime, after all, has always been a major interest within the news media and the arts and entertainment. We are finding now that extraordinary numbers of high school students, their parents, and members of the public find antisocial behavior to be not only interesting but fascinating. We get e-mail requests for information regularly. (Yes, we agree, it is part of the CSI effect.) We hope that some members of the general public will check-out PCC-4.

In terms of organization, Chapter 1 not surprisingly remains the introductory chapter, with special attention to where PCC fits within general human psychology and within criminology. We also continue to stress the seeking of a theoretical, research-based, and applied understanding of variation in the criminal behavior of individuals.

Chapter 2 stresses how the logic of various research designs determines how close we are coming to an understanding the causes of crime. It also includes a summary of the major research findings that are developed throughout the text. Chapter 3 describes the roots of general personality and cognitive social learning perspectives (the focus of Chapter 4) in psychodynamic and control theories, differential association, and general strain perspectives that broke free of social location.

Chapters 5 through 8 describe the major correlates of crime in a manner likely to appeal to a broader audience. Chapters 9 through 11 develop applications in prediction and crime prevention: What works and what does not. The general principles of PCC are applied in Chapter 12 to a variety of cases including substance abusers, violent offenders, the mentally ill, and sex offenders. Perhaps not surprisingly, the final chapter explores conclusions.

DAA thanks his family for their support: Thanks to Catherine, Karen, Donna, Margo, Vicky, Rebecca, Adam, Ashley, and Jaminha. Thanks to Annie Yessine for her help with theory in Chapter 4, her intellectual enthusiasm, and for her general critical eye. Thanks to Steve Wormith and Craig Dowden for suggesting so many interesting angles on the field over so many years. Thanks to Bob Hoge for insisting that young offenders not be conceptualized as "little criminals."

JB's comments: I am amazed that in this fourth edition that I am acknowledging my children for their academic contribution. I would like to thank my daughter zoologist, Carolyn, for her review of Chapter 5 and especially her comments on evolutionary theory. Also, with Chapter 5, my son "Dr. Mark" (MD) helped me with clarifying (hopefully) the discussion on genetic and neuropsychological explanations of crime. In addition to my children's helpful suggestions, Karl Hanson reviewed the section on sex offenders in Chapter 12 and parts of Chapter 9 (prediction of criminal behavior), and Toni Hemmati carefully read and commented on the case study in Chapter 9 (Resource Note 9.1). My thanks to both of them. Finally, my sincere appreciation for the support of my wife, Christine, in bearing with me through another edition of the book. Working on the book was very meaningful to me but it also required the work do be done on weekends and in the evenings. Now that it is done, she has me back again.

DAA and JB thank Ellen Boyne for her thoughtful and careful reading of the text.

For continuity, we reprint the Prefaces from the second and third editions.

D.A. Andrews
J. Bonta
2006

Preface to the Third Edition

The themes identified in the Preface to earlier editions remain important. (The previous preface is reprinted in this edition.) This third edition, however, was completed under conditions of some major changes in mainstream criminology. The psychology of criminal behavior is now readily evident in many mainstream textbooks and conferences. For example, there is a renewed interest in individual differences and an appreciation of the influence of personal, interpersonal, and structural factors. Developmental criminology continues to grow and contribute. Similarly, the literature on effective intervention including the effects of human service is becoming more sophisticated. The growing body of relevant research findings is represented throughout this third edition.

The text also includes some changes in organization of content. Chapter 2 now combines basic methodological concerns with overviews of the evidence regarding social origins and personality as covariates of criminal behavior. Chapter 2 also includes a brief narrative and quantitative overview of "what works" in terms of effective intervention. Systematic explorations of threats to validity are contrasted with more rhetorical approaches to criticism. Major theoretical approaches are now explored within only two chapters, with one chapter devoted to the general personality and social psychological perspective.

Applications of the psychology of criminal conduct remain a major focus in the third edition. Issues in practical prediction and effective intervention receive expanded coverage including the effects of official punishment and enhanced coverage of restorative justice models. Mentally disordered offenders, sex offenders, and psychopaths receive special attention along with domestic violence and substance abuse.

As in previous editions, the text concludes with consideration of contributions in the broader contexts of prevention, social change, and justice. The authors remain convinced that substantial progress is being made in understanding variation in the criminal behavior of individuals. At the same time, barriers to quality research and effective applications are a challenge.

Thanks to our editor Ellen Boyne for her thoughtful and careful review of the text and to our families for their continuous support and encouragement.

D.A. Andrews
J. Bonta
2002

Preface to the Second Edition

The content of this book reflects lecture notes and readings that were first compiled in the mid-1970s for an advanced undergraduate psychology course in criminal behavior. The course was designed with particular attention to understanding individual differences in criminal activity. The focus was on a conceptual and practical appreciation of the predictors of individual variation in criminal activity and of the effects of deliberate intervention on subsequent criminal activity. From the beginning, the authors have been involved as university-based instructors, as practicing psychologists in criminal justice settings and as consultants and researchers in human service and correctional agencies.

Our practice as psychologists, academicians, consultants and researchers served to support, strengthen and broaden our original conceptual and practical interest in understanding variation in criminal activity. Our experience as university-based instructors in the psychology of crime led us to extend our interests to include the social psychology of criminological knowledge. From the start, we were aware that mainstream sociological criminology and mainstream clinical/forensic criminology were not in tune with a general personality and social psychological approach to individual differences in criminal activity. We were not prepared, however, for the systemic nature and the depth and variety of the anti-differentiation, anti-prediction, anti-treatment and even anti-research bias that existed with the mainstream orientations.

With regard to mainstream sociological criminology, we quickly learned from our students who were exposed to sociology of deviance/crime courses that major portions of their learning involved denial of individual differences in criminality and denial of correlates of that variation. For example, many students entered our course believing that we are all equally criminal (that is, there is no variation in criminal behavior) and that any apparent variation was really a reflection of one's location in society (typically some variation on lower-class origins). Moreover, those students who had exposure to the sociology of deviance/crime already *knew* that deliberate intervention was not only criminogenic but morally deficient. These students *knew* that criminogenic processing also reflected too much processing (as they had learned from labeling theory) and too little processing (as they had learned from deterrence theory). Additionally, some of our students *knew* that the severity of criminal justice processing itself reflected not the seriousness of the offense but extra-legal considerations such as the personality of the judge or the social location of the offender and victim (their age, gender, race/ethnicity, class and/or geography). The problem for us (and some of our students) was that the actual research findings regarding variation in criminal activity and its processing contrasted dramatically with what mainstream criminology was teaching. Thus, this text includes direct comparisons between the antipsychological assertions of mainstream sociological criminology and the actual research findings within the psychology of crime. This second edition of the text welcomes the major changes evident in the last few years, as several of the social location theories are being reformulated and turned into social psychological perspectives.

In regard to mainstream clinical criminology, this text compares the research findings in the areas of prediction and intervention with what the psychiatric/clinical psychological tradition would suggest. The text finds, for example, that the experience of personal distress (alienation, anxiety, low self-esteem) is as weak as lower-class origins in the prediction of criminal behavior. Furthermore, we find that high-risk, egocentric offenders were not dropped on earth from alien spaceships, although mental disorder may well contribute to criminality. Once again, this second edition welcomes some major developments in clinical criminology as social psychological perspectives are gaining strength.

For these reasons, this text takes some time to explore the facts regarding individual differences in criminal activity and makes a distinction between accounting for that variation and accounting for variation in aggregated crime rates, variation in processing and variation in processing institutions. We often use the phrase "a general psychology of criminal conduct" rather than "psychology of criminal behavior" in order to underscore the differences between the psychology in this text and the psychology of crime that is so often presented in a distorted manner in many criminology textbooks. For example, the lack of reference to Freud, the facile dismissal of Glueck and Glueck, the continuing tendency to equate "psychological" with "pathological," the outrageous promotion of sociology and the disregard for evidence so apparent in mainstream criminology is rejected in the psychology outlined in this book. Even today, in mainstream sociological criminology, we find general criminological theories that have individual differences at their base and yet continue to deny personality, prevention, rehabilitation and the dynamic nature of human behavior.

We think it is time for a truly interdisciplinary general psychology of criminal conduct that is open to the full range of potential correlates including the personal, interpersonal, familial, structural/cultural, political, economic and immediate situations of actions. Faith in the explanatory power of inequality in the distribution of social wealth and power has reached ludicrous levels, as has faith in official punishment and the denial of the evidence regarding the potential of direct human service. It is time to break free of a self-consciously sociological criminology that for too long has denied human diversity, human service and any thought or evidence that might threaten professional or ideological interests. One route is the exploration and development of a general psychology of criminal conduct. Thanks to some papers by Travis Hirschi, Ronald Akers, Michael Hindelang, Gwynn Nettler and Francis Cullen, we know that criminology is not a monolithic monster devoted exclusively to the promotion of the class-based theories of anomie, subculture, labeling and critical/Marxism or to the variations on themes of official punishment embodied within labeling, deterrence and just deserts theory. There is a window opening in which full-functioning human persons may be represented in criminological theory and research, represented as something more than hypothetical fictions whose only interesting characteristics reflect social location as indexed by age, gender, class, geography and race/ethnicity. By bringing the psychology of human behavior back into criminology, some of the extremes of the punishment and processing themes of current criminal justice may come to be viewed as the natural products of any "truly social theory" that denied psychology.

We continue to look forward to the future because all indications are that we will see an explosion of research on the psychology of crime, crime prevention and corrections. We also think that the social psychology of criminological knowledge will have demonstrated how the rational empirical traditions of unsparing criticism and respect for evidence may contribute to a fuller understanding of the criminal offender.

Although this book is a product of years of research, professional practice and countless discussions with students, colleagues and friends, its completion depended upon the patience and support of our families. For this we would like to acknowledge and thank our partners and children: to Catherine Carvell, and Karen, Donna, Vicky, Ashley, Rebecca and Adam, and to Christine Bonta and Carolyn and Mark, our deepest thanks.

D.A. Andrews
J. Bonta
1998

Table of Contents

Chapter 3
Understanding Through Theory: Psychopathological, Psychodynamic, Social Location, and Differential Association Perspectives

Chapter 11
Prevention and Rehabilitation   345

Chapter 12
Creating and Maintaining RNR Adherence:
A Real-World Challenge   393

The Theoretical Context and Knowledge Base to the Psychology of Criminal Conduct

Chapter 1

An Overview of the Psychology of Criminal Conduct

The psychology of criminal conduct (PCC) outlined in this book seeks to describe and account for the fact that not all human beings are equally into criminal activity. People differ in the number, type, and variety of antisocial acts in which they engage, and they differ in when and under what circumstances they act in harmful ways. They also differ in when and under what conditions they reduce and may even cease their antisocial activity. In brief, this psychology seeks to account for variation in the criminal behavior of individuals.

If PCC has something of value to offer, it should be able to describe how people who are more into crime differ from those who are less into it. Better still, PCC should assist in predicting who will be more into it in the future and who will be less into it in the future. If PCC is very good, it should be able to suggest deliberate interventions that will reduce future crime and to offer warnings regarding actions that may increase crime. As will be seen, we will ask PCC to not only assist in predicting and influencing criminal activity but also to explain its occurrence in theoretical terms. That is, how do we explain the facts that some people are more into criminal behavior than others, that some get out of it and others do not, that some start early and may or may not continue, and that some start late and may or may not continue?

Do we need different explanations for different types of offenses (e.g., violent and nonviolent) and for different types of people (e.g., boys and girls, men and women, white and nonwhite) in different socioeconomic circumstances (e.g., the rich and the poor)? We will seek a general explanation, but if different PCCs are needed for different folks or for different antisocial acts, so be it. Less likely than a different PCC for each potential subtype of antisocial behavior and/or each subgroup of human beings, perhaps we may find that subtle shifts in the definitions of factors and/or the simple addition of specific considerations for selected subgroups may be sufficient. Specificity in the extreme is incompatible with the scientific objective of general understandings of human psychology. Finding uniformity under diverse conditions is a positive in science.

Indeed, this PCC seeks an understanding of variation in criminal behavior through applications of understandings of human behavior in general. Once again, however, specificity is valued when understanding is demonstrably enhanced.

As much as our approach to PCC values a general understanding of wide applicability, special interests are going to press for an appreciation of their concerns in particular circumstances. Such pressure is totally understandable, greatly appreciated, and likely to ultimately enhance the overall levels of understanding achieved, including general understandings. Human beings want their circumstances and aspirations to be appreciated. A dramatic example currently is in the domain of feminist criminology, wherein frequent references to "unique gendered contexts" and to the limits of male-centric theory are employed to challenge general understandings. When accompanied by systematic empirical research, explorations of unique contexts can only strengthen understandings, be they general or specific.

Definition of the Psychology of Criminal Conduct

The following constitutes a working definition of a psychology of criminal conduct:

> As a science, the psychology of criminal conduct is an approach to understanding the criminal behavior of individuals through: (a) the ethical and humane application of systematic empirical methods of investigation, and (b) the construction of rational explanatory systems.

> Professionally, a psychology of criminal conduct involves the ethical application of psychological knowledge and methods to the practical tasks of predicting and influencing the likelihood of criminal behavior, and to the reduction of the human and social costs associated with crime and criminal justice processing.

So defined, a psychology of criminal conduct is, in part, an intellectual exercise in the use of general psychological principles and methods. Therefore, the psychology of learning and cognition and the general principles of human development may be applied to the analysis of illegal behavior. At the same time, studies of criminal behavior may contribute to knowledge in psychology generally. For example, the study of socialization is a major element of the psychology of crime and is also a major concern in developmental psychology.

This general description makes two points. In the first place, PCC does not encompass the wide variety of interests that psychologists have in the area of criminology. Nor does it cover the many roles that psychologists play in criminal justice. Many psychologists, including the authors, are interested in the behavior of victims, legislators, voters, and the public in general. Similarly, many psychologists are interested in the behavior of police, judges, jurists, prison guards, probation officers, and practitioners in forensic mental health. Moreover, many psychologists in correctional practice probably spend more time dealing with the mental health needs of offenders than with criminality issues. All of these matters are interesting and important, but they are of concern in this text only insofar as they contribute to an understanding of individual criminal conduct.

Second, grounds have been established for making a distinction between psychology and the other disciplines and professions that share an interest in crime. Our focus is the criminal behavior of individuals. That focus is different from studies of bodily systems (biology), studies of variations in aggregate measures of crime rates and the structure of groups (sociology), and studies of the history and political economy of law and criminal justice. As important as these interests are for a general understanding of crime and criminal justice, they are outside the main focus of this text.

At the same time, many biologists, sociologists, social workers, political scientists, and economists share the interest in the psychology of criminal behavior. Their contributions to the psychology of criminal behavior are significant and will be represented throughout this text. Indeed, in the areas of the measurement of criminal behavior and in studies of the correlates of criminal behavior, many of the most important contributions of the last 20 years have been made by sociologists who conducted studies of the social psychological variety.

Values at the Base of PCC

We will describe antisocial activity and the objectives of PCC in detail shortly, but first some statements of values are required. The psychology of criminal behavior outlined in this book has certain values at its base. These values include a respect for human diversity and a respect for the complexity of human behavior. Respect for human diversity entails a respect for individual differences that extends well beyond the socially or biologically defined categories of ethnicity, race, gender, social class of origin, social class of achievement, or any other broad or narrow definitions of social arrangements. Individual differences are apparent in biology, personality, cognition, behavioral history, and immediate associates in the domains of home, school, work, leisure, and community. It is considered possible in this psychology of criminal behavior that variation is evident within and among the socially and politically defined categories of ethnicity, gender, socioeconomic status, social structure, culture, and political economy. Are all women the same? Of course not! Are all men the same? Of course not! Likewise, the poor are not all the same.

Respect for the complexity of human behavior means that this text is very suspicious of any account of human behavior that claims that individual differences in behavior may be attributed to any single type of variable, be it biological, psychological, social, or political-economic.

This psychology is holistic and interdisciplinary at its core by being open to the contributions of any discipline that assists in accounting for individual differences in the criminal behavior of individuals. It is also built to serve the interests of all who are interested in the criminal behavior of individuals, be they criminologists, sociologists, social workers, historians or practitioners in justice, corrections, youth services, or any other sector of society. It should be expected to serve the public as a whole (public well-being) along with individual members of the public, and along with any subgroup defined in psychological, socio-economic, and/ or political-economic terms.

This psychology is particularly uneasy with tests of social structure and culture that are based on assessments of age, race, ethnicity, and gender at the personal level when it is obvious that such so-called "social" variables are also biological and personal variables. Moreover, social contexts such as neighborhoods are frequently described in socioeconomic terms when it is obvious they may also vary in their age, ethnic, cultural, and/or personality composition as well as in the roles, statuses, and supports available to members. Neighborhoods may well differ in proportion of residents on welfare, but they may also differ in proportion of residents with attitudes supportive of criminal activity. In the search for the "social" and "personal" correlates of crime, both should be assessed and compared in terms of their association with criminal activity. In PCC, personal socioeconomic status (for example, having above-average income) and socioeconomic status of the neighborhood (for example, living in a neighborhood in which more than 70 percent of the residents have above-average incomes) are two different variables that may be associated with personal criminal activity. Similarly, personal attitudes toward crime and dominant attitudes in the neighborhood are distinct variables in PCC.

Additionally, respect for complexity means that while we seek complete and total understanding, we value an enhanced, albeit incomplete, understanding. With respect for complexity, we need to be able to conclude not only that a particular variable is associated with crime but how strongly it is associated with crime. We must be able to conclude, for example, that the poverty level of an area of a city is not only linked with crime but is more (or less) strongly linked than is an assessment of personal attitudes favorable to crime. We need to be able to conclude how much consideration of both variables enhances our level of understanding over and above that provided by consideration of only one variable. Respect for human diversity and for complexity combine to place additional value on a quantitative understanding of crime. How well can we predict? How much can we influence crime? How close are we to 100 percent predictive accuracy? How close are we to influencing criminal activity with complete certainty? How close are we to total understanding in quantitative terms?

Respect for personal autonomy is a key aspect of ethical practice. Recent contributions in clinical/forensic psychology (e.g., Birgden, 2004) have alerted us to our previous failure to highlight such a value. Perhaps that is why many clinical/forensic psychologists have appeared uneasy with the psychology of crime and more at ease with medically oriented perspectives. Now, beyond valuing collaborative relationships between clinicians and offenders, we think respect for personal autonomy should be underscored in a field of practice in which so much emphasis is placed upon structure, discipline, accountability, and state-sanctioned imposition of restrictions and punishment.

This psychology of criminal behavior also respects unsparing criticism of theoretical assertions and research findings. Unsparing criticism is a major source of advancement. At the same time, all criticism, including criticism of theoretical and research-based assertions, is best combined with respect for evidence. Additionally, a reduction of the costs of both crime and criminal justice processing are viewed as highly desirable. We are particularly interested in reducing the costs of crime by reducing criminal victimization in the first place.

In brief, and for reasons that will become clear in the pages that follow, we want the psychology of crime explained in this text to stand separate from the weak psychology represented in the mainstream sociological criminology and mainstream clinical/forensic psychology of the 1970s, 1980s, and even into the 1990s. While we do not deliver as many words as we used to do on relatively weak positions, readers will see that we do locate current understandings in their intellectual context through respect for intellectual history. Frankly, even in the new millennium, there are small sections of forensic mental health and small sections of sociological criminology that remain out of touch with the basic PCC approach. Notably, however, and very positively for this fifth edition of *The Psychology of Criminal Conduct*, both mainstream sociological criminology and mainstream clinical/forensic psychology have continued to move in the direction of the values underlying PCC. Once again, and as what was true from the beginning, PCC is eager to embrace the best of what sociological criminology and forensic mental health have to offer.

This text continues to suggest that there exists a general personality and social psychology (that is, a GPSP) within PCC that has conceptual, empirical, and practical value within and across social arrangements, clinical categories, and various personal and justice contexts. Even more specifically, the most powerful social psychology is suggested to be cognitive social learning perspectives. Thus, we will refer to a general personality and cognitive social learning (GPCSL) perspective on human behavior, including criminal behavior.

The psychology of criminal conduct (PCC) seeks a rational and empirical understanding of variation in the occurrence of criminal acts and, in particular, a rational empirical understanding of individual differences in criminal activity. The first task of this chapter is to introduce this objective of PCC from the perspective of achieving a "rational empirical understanding." It will be found that rational empiricism seeks a variety of understandings of the phenomenon of interest. The second task is to locate PCC within the concerns of the broader fields of study represented by criminology, general human psychology, and criminal justice. The third task entails a brief look at the systematic challenges to a PCC that exist within mainstream sociological criminology. We will see that the rational empiricism of PCC, unlike now, had been under severe attack for years by criminologists who placed higher value on social theory and political ideology than on rationality and/or respect for evidence.

Objectives of the Psychology of Criminal Conduct (PCC)

The objective of the psychology of criminal conduct (PCC) is to understand variation in the delinquent and criminal behavior of individuals. First, the meaning of "variation in criminal behavior" is explored; then we review the meaning of the term "understand" in the tradition of rational empirical inquiry.

The Focus: Variation in Criminal Conduct

Criminal behavior refers to acts that are injurious and prohibited under the law, and render the actor subject to intervention by justice professionals. The specific acts included are many. They are subject to some temporal and cultural variation. Historical and cross-cultural research, however, reveals that most societies have formal procedures for the negative sanctioning of acts of theft, robbery, and physical assault. Variation in the occurrence of acts injurious to others is the primary focus of the psychology of crime, even though antisocial acts may not always be prohibited under the law, and under some temporal and cultural circumstances may even be prescribed (for example, killing the enemy under the conditions of war). With a general perspective, it makes sense to explore the idea that variation in both types of injurious behavior may be predicted, influenced, and explained by the same general psychology of human conduct.

Variation in the occurrence of antisocial behavior at the individual level is of two types. First, people differ in the number, type, and variety of criminal acts in which they engage. This variation is typically referred to as **inter-individual** differences in criminal behavior. In addition, variation is found over time and across situations for particular individuals. This variation is called **intra-individual** variation. Some preliminary illustrations of these individual differences in criminal conduct will increase appreciation of what it is that the psychology of criminal conduct seeks to understand and explain. Examples of individual differences are presented below, and they illustrate the variation in the **criterion** or **dependent variable** (i.e., criminal behavior) within PCC.

Casual Observation of Others. Casual observation will readily establish that, within almost any group, people may be differentiated according to their criminal histories. For example, within your circle of acquaintances and friends, you may be aware that some have been arrested, convicted, fined, placed on probation, or incarcerated, while others have not. Additionally, you may have information that some within your circle violate some laws rather regularly (officially identified or not) while others do so much less frequently (if at all). Some may be particularly active in violating the laws governing the distribution of mood-altering substances, others may have difficulty conforming to laws governing property rights, while still others may violate laws designed to protect the dignity and integrity of the physical person.

Self-Observation. Reflecting upon your own behavioral history you may find that you have engaged in acts subject to the label "criminal." You may also find that your criminal activities were concentrated in a particular period of your life, or to have occurred under certain circumstances but not under others. For example, some people report that they are much more likely to violate rules when they have been drinking alcohol than when they are sober.

Systematic Observation. Systematic observation yields more detailed (and, typically, more interesting) information on the criminal conduct of individuals. Portions of Chapter 1 are devoted to illustrations of individual differences in criminal conduct. These differences are found through systematic exploration of victim reports, self-reports, and reviews of official records. Here are a few introductory examples based on a few classic reviews of official records These studies are described in more detail in Technical Note 1.1. (For this and all other Technical Notes, consult the Technical Notes section at the back of the book.) The Technical Note provides example after example of variation at the individual level. The note was prepared to illustrate the basic facts in more detail than some (but not all) readers may want.

1. It was found that 23.1 percent (6,545) of the 28,338 people born in 1958 and residing in Philadelphia from age 10 to 18 years had an official record of arrest by age 18. Their total number of recorded offenses was 20,089. The delinquents with two or more offenses represented 12.1 percent of the total sample or 52.6 percent of the delinquent sample (3,440/6,545). This subsample of delinquents accounted for 16,984 recorded offenses. Thus, 12 percent of the subjects were responsible for 84.5 percent of the total number of recorded offenses (16,984/20,089).

2. David Farrington (1997) and his colleagues have been following a sample of 411 London working-class males since 1961-62,

when the boys were about eight years of age. Data sources include interviews with parents, teachers, and the boys themselves, as well as reviews of official records of convictions. Farrington's 1997 report is based on 404 of the men whose criminal records were complete up to age 40.

- Overall, 40.1 percent of the sample had a criminal conviction up to age 40. The most frequent of the offenses recorded were nonviolent (a total of 643 nonviolent compared with 117 violent offenses).

- Six percent of the sample had six or more convictions. These "chronic offenders" accounted for one-half of the total number of convictions.

- Three percent of the boys were first convicted of a violent offense as children (age 10-16), 9.1 percent as young adults (17-24), and 7.9 percent as older adults (25-40).

- Ninety-six percent of officially convicted youths also self-reported convictions. In an earlier report (Farrington, 1983), fewer than 1 percent of the youths claimed convictions that were not officially recorded.

Surveys of the findings of many research studies similar to the ones described in Technical Note 1.1 have established a few of the basic facts regarding the criminal behavior of official offenders—facts that have been established in many areas of the world. Individual differences in criminal behavior are substantial.

1. Individual differences in criminal activity are apparent in many ways. They may be inferred from knowledge of aggregated crime rates based on both official records of crime and surveys of victims. They are discovered more directly by systematic surveys of criminal histories (officially defined or self-reported) and by systematic studies of criminal futures (officially defined or self-reported).

2. Individual differences in criminal activity are apparent within samples of people differentiated by country of origin, gender, age, race, social class, and any other means of differentiating subgroups of humanity.

3. While victim- and self-reported crime rates are much higher than rates based on official records, the demographic correlates of criminal activity remain very similar for different measures of criminal activity. The standard demographic correlates include being young, being male, being nonwhite, and being disadvantaged socioeconomically.

4. Official recidivism rates vary with the specific measure of official processing employed (for example, arrested versus convicted versus incarcerated) and with length of the follow-up period.

5. Repeat offenders, a small subset of all offenders, account for a disproportionate amount of total criminal activity. Careful study of criminal careers over the life span reveals, however, that the nexus of early, frequent, serious, and violent offending contains a small number of cases.

PCC has much to understand and explain given the facts of differences in the criminal behavior of individuals.

Definitions of Criminal Behavior. "Criminal behavior" suggests a large number and variety of acts. Specific meanings vary according to the concerns of users of the phrase as well as with historical and social contexts (Mannheim, 1965). This text will draw upon four definitions of criminal behavior and will be most concerned with those acts that fit within the domains of all four definitions. These four definitions are as follows:

1. *Legal:* Criminal behavior refers to actions that are prohibited by the state and punishable under the law.

2. *Moral:* Criminal behavior refers to actions that violate the norms of religion and morality and are believed to be punishable by supreme spiritual beings.

3. *Social:* Criminal behavior refers to actions that violate the norms of custom and tradition and are punishable by the community.

4. *Psychological:* Criminal behavior refers to actions that may be rewarding to the actor but that inflict pain or loss on others. That is, criminal behavior is antisocial behavior.

Criminal acts, no matter which of the four above-noted definitions are employed, are part of a more general class of behavior that social psychologists have been calling "problem behavior" or "deviant behavior" since the 1970s (e.g., Jessor & Jessor, 1977; Ullmann & Krasner, 1976). Thereby, the essence of deviant acts is that their occurrence places the actor at risk of being targeted for interventions by figures of authority, control, regulation, and assistance. Problematic acts may occasion the intervention of parents, teachers, religious leaders, and neighbors. They may place the actor at risk of being attended to by mental health professionals, or by an army of regulators of business, labor, professional practice, government, and civil and human rights.

The psychological definition of crime as antisocial behavior is best combined with the broader definition of "problem behavior." If not so combined, some of the nondeviant practices of dentists, surgeons, and teachers would surely be judged criminal. Thus, with thanks to Ullmann and Krasner (1976), our working definition of criminal behavior is as follows:

> Criminal behavior refers to antisocial acts that place the actor
> at risk of becoming a focus of the attention of criminal justice
> professionals within the juvenile and/or adult justice systems.

No definition of criminal behavior is totally satisfactory. For example, the norm-based definitions have led to a number of dramatizations of certain trivial truths. In the 1960s, it was fashionable in some circles to note that we are all "criminal" because we all violate some rules some of the time. According to this position, criminality is not a variable but a constant; that is, we are all equally "criminal." Note how the very possibility of a PCC is discounted by this position. Of course, the position was scientifically naive because not all rules are laws, and not all people violate the same rules (or laws) at the same rates or under the same circumstances.

At another extreme, the legal, moral, and social definitions imply that there would be no crime in the absence of legal, religious, and social norms. At a minor level, this is true. However, the injuries and losses suffered by victims would not be eliminated by the abolition of criminal codes and social norms. Two of the positive functions of the psychological definition (i.e., criminal behavior as antisocial behavior) are to prevent us from overdramatizing some of the trivial implications of norm-based definitions of deviance and to prevent us from losing touch with characteristics of offenders and the pain of victims.

"Acts of force or fraud in pursuit of self-interest," the psychological definition of crimes provided by Gottfredson and Hirschi (1990:15), is particularly interesting in this regard. These authors, as will be discussed in the theory chapters, developed their conception of the nature of criminal acts in such a way that the personality characteristics associated with criminal propensity follow directly from the nature of criminal acts. For example, criminal acts are said to provide immediate and easy gratification of desires; thus, weak self-control is an obvious personal source of variation in criminal activity.

An apparently serious problem remains. How can we claim to account for individual differences in a class of behavior that is, at the core definitional level, so subject to cross-cultural, subcultural, and temporal variability? How can we have a science of activities whose quality appears to be so dependent upon the evaluation of an audience? Indeed, how can we seek to account for individual differences in criminality when no act is intrinsically criminal? A review of Technical Note 1.2 will show that these issues have been found to be more threatening in rhetoric than in reality (e.g., Wellford, 1975).

Types of Understanding Sought

The understanding of criminal behavior sought by PCC is empirical, theoretical, and practical. In brief, this means that psychology seeks explanations of criminal conduct that are consistent with the findings of systematic observation, rationally organized, and useful to people with practical interests in criminal behavior. These three interrelated aspects of understanding criminal conduct are stressed throughout the text.

An Empirical Understanding. Empirically, PCC seeks knowledge not only of the observable facts regarding the nature and extent of individual variation in criminal conduct, but also knowledge of the biological, personal, interpersonal, situational, and social variables associated with or correlated with criminal behavior. These are termed *covariates* and include the correlates of individual differences in a criminal history and the predictors of the criminal futures of individuals. For reasons related to a practical understanding (see below), the predictors are called risk factors, and when those risk factors are dynamic (subject to change), they are called dynamic risk factors (or criminogenic needs). Perhaps most importantly, PCC seeks knowledge of the causes of the criminal conduct of individuals. Causal (or functional) covariates consist of observation-based knowledge that offers the potential to influence the likelihood of a criminal act through deliberate intervention. Knowledge of causes comes primarily from experimental studies. These three types of covariates— correlates, predictors, and causal or functional variables—may, once again, be found in biology, personality, attitudes and beliefs, aptitudes and skills, learning history, family, peer relationships, broader social arrangements, and the immediate situation of action.

As an illustration, gender is a well-known covariate of criminality. In the Philadelphia 1958 birth cohort (Technical Note 1.1), 23.1 percent of the total cases had an official record by the age of 18 years. However, among males, the delinquency rate was 32.6 percent compared with 14.0 percent among females. This simple example illustrates an enhanced empirical understanding of criminal behavior. It appears that being male is a risk factor for delinquency. That is not to say, however, that all males were arrested at least once by age 18, nor that no females were arrested. A meaningful association or covariation may be established without it being perfect. Empirical knowledge that yields perfect prediction is an ideal to be sought, but empirical knowledge that yields an improvement in predictive accuracy over that achieved by chance is not to be devalued.

Resource Note 1.1 discusses the **correlation coefficient** as a general measure of the magnitude of covariation. The particular type of correlation coefficient most frequently employed in research and in this text is the Pearson Product Moment Correlation Coefficient (also known as r). The r statistic takes a value of 1.00 when the level of association or predictive accuracy is 100 percent. For example, if all men (100%) had a criminal record and no women (0%) had a record the correlation between gender and a criminal history would be 1.00. On the other hand, if the percent of men and women with criminal records were equal (for example: 20% and 20%, 50% and 50%, or 70% and 70%), the r would be 0.00. Generally, the magnitude of the r reflects the difference in percent criminal for one group relative to another—it reflects the simple difference in percentage values. In the paragraph above, that simple difference was 32.6 minus 14.0 (that is, 18.6 percentage points or an r of .186). All correlation coefficients may be interpreted as reflecting such a difference. Resource Note 1.1 reveals that the simple difference in percentage points provides a meaningful way of comparing the strength of association (or the level of covariation) among variables. Please do not underestimate the importance of quantifying the magnitude

Resource Note 1.1

Measurement of Level of Covariation: The Pearson Product Moment Correlation Coefficient and Rosenthal's Binomial Effect Size Display

Covariation is important in this text. One of the most frequently used ways of quantifying level of covariation is the *Pearson Product Moment Correlation Coefficient* (or the Pearson r). Taking values between 0.00 and 1.00, r expresses the magnitude of a linear relationship between two variables. A linear relationship is one that may be described by a straight line: That is, for example, as the observed level of one variable increases, so does the observed level of the other. The correlation coefficient will take a negative value if there is an inverse relationship: That is, as the observed level of one variable increases, the observed level of the other variable decreases.

The correlation coefficient may be used to describe the findings of many types of studies. Often, the results of research on the potential covariates of criminal activity will be reported in terms of the percentage of one group (for example, men) who reoffend (no/yes) relative to the percentage of another group (for example, women) who reoffend (no/yes). Sometimes research results will be reported in terms of the covariation of a multilevel variable (such as verbal intelligence)

and a multilevel measure of criminality (such as number of new offenses). At other times, research may be reporting how a two-level variable such as gender (men/women) is associated with the average number of offenses. The findings of all of these examples of research may be defined in terms of a Pearson Product Moment Correlation Coefficient (r).

Robert Rosenthal (1984) has shown how the findings from diverse studies may be compared. *The binomial effect size display* assumes that 50 percent of the cases are at one level of the potential covariate and 50 percent are at the other level (for example: 50 percent of the cases are men and 50 percent are women; 50 percent are below average in verbal intelligence and 50 percent are above average in verbal intelligence). Rosenthal's binomial effect size display additionally assumes that 50 percent of the cases are criminal (or had relatively many new offenses) and 50 percent are not criminal (or had relatively few new offenses). Under these conditions, the r is the simple difference in percentage points between the two groups. One group is assumed to be at

Resource Note 1.1 (continued)

higher risk for criminal behavior than the other. Thus, for example, if being female is considered lower-risk, and being male is considered higher-risk, the findings may be as follows:

If the correlation is 1.00:
Lower-risk
(being female)   000% criminal
Higher-risk
(being male)   100% criminal
                 100-minus-000
                 = 100

If the correlation is 0.00:
Lower-risk   50% criminal
Higher-risk   50% criminal
                  50-minus-50 = 00

If the correlation is .10
Lower-risk   45% criminal
Higher-risk   55% criminal
                  55-minus-45 = 10

If the correlation is .60
Lower-risk   20% criminal
Higher-risk   80% criminal
                  80-minus-20 = 60

An inverse relationship, looks as follows:

If the correlation is −.60
Lower-value   80%
Higher-value   20%
                  20-minus-80
                  = −60.

Given knowledge of the value of the correlation coefficient, it is an easy matter to compute the criminality rates for the lower-risk and higher-risk groups. Employing the binomial effect size display, the proportion criminal in the higher-risk group is 0.50 plus the r divided by two, and the proportion criminal in the lower risk group is 0. 50 minus the r divided by two. For example, if the correlation is .40, then r divided by two is 0.20. Thus, with $r = .40$, the proportion criminal in the higher-risk group is 0.70 (0.50 plus 0.20) and the proportion criminal in the lower-risk group is 0.30 (0.50 minus 0.20).

The binomial effect size display approach also may be employed to summarize the effects of experimental studies wherein, for example, equal numbers of cases are randomly assigned to treatment and control groups. For example, if success is reduced re-offending and the correlation between treatment and re-offending is 0.20, then the recidivism rate in the treatment group is 40 percent (50 minus 10) compared with 60 percent in the control group (50 plus 10).

By computing correlation coefficients, researchers are in a position to state not only whether they established covariation but also the level of covariation. Researchers are also in a position to compare the relative strength of various correlates. The binomial effect size display approach provides a convenient and easily interpretable representation of the magnitude of covariation.

of covariation (or of predictive accuracy). As will be seen, PCC took great strides forward by being able to differentiate among risk factors according to their magnitude of association with criminal behavior.

Of course, correlation does not prove causation. The correlational, predictive, or causal status of covariates, regardless of the level of covariation (or predictive accuracy) achieved, depends upon the way in which the observations are conducted. Because the differences among the types of covariates are so important, this text includes a review of the different research designs that yield information on different types of covariates. An empirical focus also suggests that PCC must be concerned with the reliability and validity of assessments of criminal behavior and the potential covariates of criminal conduct. Thus, the text will be attending to issues of the quality of measurement. Finally, PCC is concerned with the reliability and validity of any conclusions made regarding the nature and level of associations established between potential covariates and criminal conduct. Therefore, presently we review some standard threats to the validity of conclusions that may be drawn from systematic research.

A Theoretical Understanding. The search for theoretical understanding is a search for general, rational, simple, emotionally pleasing, and empirically accurate **explanations** of variation in criminal behavior. General explanations are ones that apply to a number of specific observations. For example, a general theory of criminal conduct will account for variation in both violent and nonviolent offenses, and will do so for men and women of different ages, races, nationalities, and socioeconomic origins.

Rational explanations are ones that withstand logical analyses, both internally and externally. A good theory is expected to be internally and externally consistent. **Internal consistency** refers to how well the assumptions and explanatory variables fit together within a theory. **External consistency** refers to how well a theory fits with other scientific theories. For example, a theory of criminal behavior may make internally consistent use of certain biological assumptions, but it would be less than satisfactory if those assumptions were at odds with reasonably well-established theory in the broader biological sciences.

Simple explanations are ones that make relatively few assumptions. Less objective, but not unimportant, "good" theories are also ones that make personal sense, provide a sense of unity, and give us the emotional "rush" often associated with great literature and other great works of art. It is also expected that the language of a "good" theory will respect human dignity and will not be disrespectful of individuals or groups.

The most important aspect of theoretical understanding, however, has to do with predictive accuracy. Empirically defensible explanations are explanations that are consistent with the findings of systematic research; that is, the correlates, predictors, and causal variables identified in the theory are validated by systematic observation. There are four major empirical tests of the adequacy of a theoretical understanding of criminal behavior. One involves an understanding of how the various risk factors are associated with each other. For example, how does an inherited temperament such as "being a hot head" lead to disturbed familial relationships, which may in turn lead to association with criminal others? The second involves the ability to predict accurately variation in criminal behavior. For example, do assessments of temperament, family relationships, and criminal associates actually predict criminal activity, on their own and in combination? The third involves the potential to influence criminal activity by way of deliberate interventions that focus on the causal variables suggested by the theory. For example, does the delivery of intervention programs aimed at improving family relationships actually reduce criminal futures? A fourth aspect of empirical defensibility links with the standard of a "general" understanding. In brief, does the research evidence regarding the ability to predict and influence criminal behavior generalize to people who differ in gender, ethnicity, or other personal and/or social considerations? PCC does not assume answers to such questions or declare the uniqueness of particular groups. Rather, PCC seeks out the evidence by exploring the accuracy of prediction and the effects of intervention with different types of people under different circumstances.

Resource Note 1.2 provides a very brief overview of theories of criminal conduct. This overview will render some of the research findings provided in the introductory chapters more theoretically meaningful, even before Chapters 3 and 4 outline the theories in more detail.

A Practical Understanding. A practical understanding is guaranteed if the empirical and theoretical base of the psychology of criminal behavior is sound. Such a guarantee is possible because knowledge of predictors and causes brings with it the potential (although perhaps not the inclination) to influence the occurrence of criminal behavior in the

---

Resource Note 1.2

Overview of Theories of Criminal Behavior: A Brief Look Ahead to the Theory Chapters

The major theories of criminal activity have been classified in various ways by various authors. With some recognition of alternative classification systems, this text finds the following classification of value: psychodynamic, social location, differential association, and social learning/social cognition.

1. *Psychodynamic theory*, with roots in the psychoanalytic perspective of Sigmund Freud, is a source for much of current theory. The major contribution resided in Freud's description of the structure of human personality. The key structures of personality are ego and superego, which interact with the immediate environment and the demands of id for immediate gratification. Superego and ego develop as the child interacts with the zenvironment and, for most children, that immediate environment constitutes the family. Psychological maturity involves

a fully developed ego and superego and is characterized by the ability to delay gratification for longer-term gain, to love and be loved, and to be socially productive. A strong superego is the psychological representation of societal rules and a strong ego is a set of coping and defense skills by which demands for immediate gratification may be delayed for longer-term gain.

KEY THEORETICAL IDEA: Criminal behavior reflects psychological immaturity and particularly weak self-control in specific situations.

MAJOR RISK FACTORS: Impulsivity, disturbed interpersonal relationships, low levels of success in school and at work, weak superego (little guilt, reckless disregard for conventional rules and procedures, early misconduct, antisocial attitudes), weak ego (limited skill across a wide domain of skills),

Resource Note 1.2 *(continued)*

aggressive pleasure-seeking, readily angry, problems in the family of origin.

MAJOR IMPLICATIONS FOR PREVENTION: Strong on intermediate targets (see major risk factors above), weak on style and mode of service.

Psychodynamic theories are very much alive today, most notably in the form of social control theories such as those of Travis Hirschi (1969, 2004; Gottfredson & Hirschi, 1990). The most important development of psychodynamic theory, however, must be seen as the work of Sheldon Glueck and Eleanor Glueck (1950), who introduced the importance of temperament, attitudes, and family. To this day, multifactor theories are being developed that clearly reflect the work of Glueck and Glueck (1950).

The psychodynamic tradition is also evident in the development of frustration–aggression theory from the Yale school in the 1930s (Dollard et al., 1939), through the broadband social learning formulations of the 1970s and 1980s (Bandura, 1989), through the general personality and social psychology of the 1990s and the new millennium (see below).

2. *Social location theories* of crime suggest that criminal behavior reflects where one is located in the social system. Typically (although not necessitated by logic), the importance of social location is said to reflect inequality in the distribution of societal wealth, power, and prestige. The typical indicators of social location for most social theorists are social class, age, race/ethnicity, and gender. Thus, being poor, being young, and being a member of a disadvantaged ethnic group may all contribute to motivation for crime. Being female, a position of disadvantage in a patriarchal society, however, apparently does not contribute to motivation for crime.

KEY THEORETICAL IDEA: Criminal behavior reflects personal distress (strain) that may be linked with socially structured inequality in the distribution of wealth and power. Once again, the strain interpretation is a preference of social theorists and not a logical requirement (opportunity, weak social control, and over-representation of weak superego types are also possible structural factors).

MAJOR RISK FACTORS: Lower-class origins, low levels of success at school and work, feelings of alienation (as opposed to feelings of being mistreated), perception of limited opportunity in combination with desire for conventional success, being a gang member, adoption of lower-class values.

MAJOR IMPLICATIONS FOR PREVENTION: Open up educational and vocational opportunities, but weak on how to do it.

Robert Merton's (1938) anomie theory asserted that crime was not the expression of untamed impulses (as in psychodynamic/control theory) but an innovative route to conventional success for those who found legitimate routes blocked by virtue of their lower-class status. Subcultural developments within social location theories suggested that lower-class offenders were not innovating but conforming to criminal values and taking advantage of criminal opportunities.

Social location theories are in crisis today because the magnitude of the association between measures of inequality and individual criminal conduct is too slight to give the theories any serious consideration as a psychology of criminal conduct (see Chapter 2). Unfortunately, attention must be given because criminology textbooks continue to suggest that they remain important. Consider, however, the limited value of a near exclusive focus on young lower-class men who have been conventionally socialized and yet blocked in their pursuit of conventional success. Robert Agnew (1992) has severed ties to traditional strain theory and presents instead a general social psychology of

Resource Note 1.2 *(continued)*

criminal conduct reflecting the social learning models of anger and aggression.

3. *Differential association theory*, like psychodynamic theory, actually has a powerful psychology of human behavior at its base. That psychology is symbolic interactionism, wherein what people think is very important, and any particular situation may be defined as one in which it is "OK" to violate the law. The attitudes, values, beliefs, and rationalizations that may support such a definition are learned through differentials in exposure to procriminal and anticriminal patterns. The major part of the learning occurs in association with others. Sutherland's (1939; Sutherland & Cressey, 1970) differential association theory was made stronger when Burgess and Akers (1966: Akers, 1973) reformulated it by introducing the principles of operant conditioning from behavioral psychology. Ronald Akers called that reformulation "social learning theory."

KEY THEORETICAL IDEA: Criminal behavior is an expression of differentials in the reinforcement and punishment of criminal and noncriminal alternative behavior.

MAJOR RISK FACTORS: Antisocial attitudes, antisocial associates.

MAJOR IMPLICATIONS FOR PREVENTION: Strong on intermediate targets but weak on how to do it until integrated with behavior theory.

4. *A general personality and social psychology* of human behavior of wide applicability emerged in the late 1980s and 1990s and progressed into the new millennium. Criminal behavior is one class of behavior to whose analysis this general model appears particularly valuable. The general model is perhaps best described as a social learning/ cognitive behavioral/social cognition theory. With the contributions of the Yale school (for example: Dollard et al., 1939), Albert

Bandura (1989, 2001), Walter Mischel (1968, 2004), and Donald Meichenbaum (1977), with contributions from general social psychology (for example: Ajzen & Fishbein, 1980, 2005) and with developments in understanding the major dimensions of personality (for example: Digman, 1990), it is possible for psychologists to suggest that if one is interested in predicting and/or influencing the occurrence of any particular human act, it is of value to assess and/or try to influence one or more of the following sets of variables—attitudes, associates, behavioral history, or personality. The "Big Four" themselves (i.e., attitudes, associates, history, and personality) may be influenced and or moderated by conditions in the major domains of family, school and work, leisure, and neighborhood.

KEY THEORETICAL IDEA: The chances of a criminal act (a) increase with the density of rewards signaled for criminal behavior and (b) decrease with the density of signaled costs of criminal behavior. These signaled rewards reflect personal control through antisocial attitudes, interpersonal control through the social support for crime provided by antisocial associates, nonmediated control established by a history of reinforcement of criminal behavior, and/or personal predispositions.

MAJOR RISK FACTORS: Antisocial attitudes, antisocial associates, antisocial behavioral history, antisocial personality, problematic conditions in the domains of home, school, work, and leisure.

MAJOR IMPLICATIONS FOR PREVENTION: Strong on intermediate targets and strong on style and mode of service.

The general personality and social psychological approach, as demonstrated in Chapter 4, does still have a variety of competing perspectives on the essential causal variables (see Chapter 4).

context of corrections and prevention. In this sense, offenders and potential offenders, victims and potential victims, and all participants in prevention and criminal justice service may gain from a psychology of criminal behavior. In this text, special attention will be paid to those theories and empirical investigations that show the greatest practical potential.

Empirical Understandings and Research Designs

Empirical Knowledge of Covariates

Empirically, having established variation in the criterion of criminal conduct, PCC seeks knowledge of the covariates of that variation in criminal behavior. The covariates of interest in PCC are observable aspects of the universe, whether those aspects are "biological," "psychological," or "social." Again, we stress that it is an empirical focus on variation in criminal conduct of individuals that is the key to PCC, rather than disciplinary or political preferences regarding the potential covariates that ought to be observed.

The covariates of criminal conduct may be of several types, depending upon how the observations of covariation are conducted. As noted in Table 1.1, these types include the correlates, predictors, dynamic predictors, and causes of variability in criminal conduct. For reasons that will become clear, we will often refer to "causal" variables as "functional variables," or as variables of "functional significance." Furthermore, the correlates are linked with cross-sectional research designs, predictors with longitudinal research designs, dynamic predictors with multiwave longitudinal research designs, and functional variables with experimental designs (see Table 1.1). Also important are moderator variables. Moderator variables are variables that interact with covariates on criminal behavior. For example, "Social Support for Drug Use" may interact with "Attitudes Favorable to Drug Use" in such a way that attitudes are strongly associated with drug use when social support for use is high but only weakly linked when social support for use is low (Technical Note 1.3 provides a more detailed discussion). Moderator variables are a formal way of recognizing the complexity of human behavior—often, the correlates of criminal behavior "depend" upon other variables and/ or the social context.

When it comes to the application of our knowledge of covariates, we will be using the language of risk, need, responsivity, and strengths. We will discuss responsivity later, but for now we concentrate on risk, need, and strengths.

Risk. Risk factors refer to characteristics of people and their circumstances that are associated with an increased chance of future criminal activity. For example, favorable attitudes toward crime are

Table 1.1
Type of Covariate, Type of Clinical Variable, Research Designs, and Criterion Variables

Covariate Type	Clinical Type	Research Design	Criterion	Comments
Correlate	Risk/Need Factor	Cross-sectional	Criminal past	Post-diction, not prediction
Predictor	Risk Factor	Longitudinal	Criminal future	Emphasis on problematic
	Strength Factor	Longitudinal	Criminal future	Relative emphasis on the positive
Dynamic Predictor	Need Factor	Multiwave Longitudinal	Criminal future	May be less or more stable
	Stable Need	Multiwave Longitudinal	Criminal future	Slow changing (more stable)
	Acute Need	Multiwave Longitudinal	Criminal future	Fast changing (less stable)
Functional	Intervention	Experimental	Criminal future	Deliberate induction of change, in a controlled manner

Notes: a) Cross-sectional designs yield information on potential risk/need factors. Knowledge of true risk factors must be based on longitudinal studies and knowledge of criminogenic need factors must be based on multiwave longitudinal and/or experimental studies.

b) Example of risk and strength factors: Very low levels of reward and satisfaction at work is a potential risk/need factor (increasing crime), very high levels of reward and satisfaction is a potential strength factor (reducing crime), while intermediate levels of reward and satisfaction are the base rate of recidivism against which the increases or decreases are measured.

c) Strength factors may also be dynamic but changes in strength factors have not been well researched as yet.

linked with increased chances of criminal behavior compared to mixed ("so-so") attitudes toward crime or with attitudes unfavorable to criminal activity. The clinical (or practical) applications of knowledge of risk factors are many. In correctional agencies and facilities and in forensic mental health settings, issues of risk of reoffending are crucial to decisions of early release (e.g., parole or discharge), of level of supervision in community supervision programs, and of level of custody in the classification of prisoners. Generally, lower-risk cases are candidates for early release and low levels of supervision, while higher-risk cases are candidates for higher levels of supervision. Additionally, as will be seen in later discussions of prevention and correctional treatment programs, risk is also a major factor in the allocation of treatment services. According to the risk principle of case classification, more intensive services are best allocated to moderate and higher-risk cases, while low-risk cases have a low probability of recidivism even in the absence of treatment services. The applied value of risk assessments will be developed in the subsequent chapters.

Need. It has been traditional in corrections to identify problematic circumstances as "needs." Andrews, Bonta, and Hoge (1990) suggested that it would be even more valuable to differentiate between criminogenic need and noncriminogenic need. Criminogenic needs are dynamic risk factors, risk factors that can change. With change, we see changes in the chances of criminal activity. Changes in noncriminogenic needs are not followed by changes in the chances of criminal activity. Thus, the designation "dynamic risk factor" (or "criminogenic need") suggests possible intermediate targets of change for treatment services when an objective is reduced reoffending. The designation of noncriminogenic needs does not imply that dealing with that type of need will impact upon a criminal future. Of course, there are many reasons beyond crime control to try to reduce problematic circumstances. Providing shelter to the homeless and reducing emotional distress are worthy on their own even if only a minor factor in the analysis of crime. Focusing on noncriminogenic needs of importance to the offender may enhance motivation to participate in treatment.

Strength. Strength factors are sometimes called "protective" factors. Generally, strengths refer to characteristics of people and their circumstances that are associated with reduced chances of criminal activity. For example, attitudes toward crime may be assessed as being very negative toward crime, as relatively neutral, or as very positive toward crime. If negative attitudes are associated with low rates of crime relative to neutral attitudes, negative attitudes are a strength factor. If positive attitudes are associated with high rates of crime relative to neutral attitudes, positive attitudes are a risk factor. With this approach to risk and strengths, they can only be identified when factors are assessed at least three levels (weak, neutral, strong). If we simply compared "weak/neutral" with "strong" (or, "weak" with "neutral/strong") we would not know if we were dealing with a risk factor or a strength factor. When strengths are assessed with validity, they may increase the predictive accuracy (the magnitude of r) that is achieved by an assessment of risk factors only. Moreover, consideration of strengths allows for a more positive and complete picture of people than does simply a focus on risk.

Strengths have also been defined as "resilient" factors with an emphasis on protecting one from the effects of risk factors. This interpretation, however, remains very weak because of the inconsistent ability to demonstrate empirically that the effects of risk factors do actually vary with strength level. The findings may be clarified in the future, but for now we prefer the terms "strength" and/or "protective" factors.

In summary, clinically, assessments of risk suggest the level of services that should be introduced while assessments of criminogenic needs suggest appropriate intermediate targets when reduced recidivism is an objective of service. With the advent of assessments of strengths, the identification of those most likely to reoffend may be enhanced. Similarly, the selection of intermediate targets may be expanded beyond reducing criminogenic need to include enhancing the strengths of the case. Resource Note 1.3 illustrates the potential of considering both risk and strengths. In practical prediction in applied correctional settings, the vale of adding strengths is still under exploration.

The Research Designs

A focus of this chapter is the importance of the structure of research designs in the establishment of covariation. The chapter does not include a comprehensive review of the many potential sources of error in measurement, operationalization, and conceptualization. However, potential errors of measurement and conceptualization may inflate estimates of covariation, deflate estimates of covariation, or have no effect on level of covariation, depending upon the specifics of the threats.

Resource Note 1.3

Strength Factors

Our introductory examples of strength factors are drawn from the Pittsburgh Youth Study, a longitudinal study that began in 1987 (Stouthamer-Loeber et al., 2002). In the cited publication, the researchers predicted persistent serious delinquency over six years of assessment. "Persistent and serious" young male offenders reported (or were reported to have engaged in) one or more of the following offenses for at least two of the six assessment years: theft, selling drugs, robbery, physical attack, and/or rape. The authors have chosen to call their "strength" (or "protective") factors "promotive" factors, but here we use the term "strength." The potential risk and strength factors were based on child, caretaker, and teacher reports assessed in year one of the study. The potential risk/strength factors were scored as -1 (a strength, approximately 25% of the children), 0 (neutral, middle 50% of the children), or +1 (a risk, approximately 25%). If a score of -1 is associated with lower mean delinquency scores than a score of 0, that factor is called a strength factor. If a score of +1 is associated with a higher mean delinquency score, that factor is a risk factor. With this approach, it is possible that any particular factor may be a strength factor and/or a risk factor. The predictive factors explored included a set of indicators of personality (e.g., ability to feel guilt), behavioral history (e.g., cruel to people), attitudes favorable to antisocial behavior, family relations (relationship with parents, supervision), and demographics such as age and social class.

A few of the findings are as follows, with the children first assessed at age seven years. The ability to feel guilt was both a risk factor and a strength factor, decreasing the chances of crime when high and increasing the chances of crime when low. Relationship with parents was a strength factor but not a risk factor. Poor reading skills were a risk factor but not a strength factor. In correlation terms, risk factors are positively associated with delinquency while strength factors are negatively associated with delinquency. According to the Pittsburgh researchers, the risk and strength components make independent contributions to the prediction of persistent and serious delinquency (that is, considering both increases the level of the correlation coefficient compared to either alone). If you add the two scores together across the range of relevant factors, the probability of serious delinquency increases directly with the overall score. In Figure 1.1, some of the findings from the second sample of the Stouthamer-Loeber et al.(2002) study (13- to 19-year-olds) are summarized. The negative values reflect a disproportionate number of strength factors while the positive values reflect a disproportionate number of risk factors. Clearly, the percent of children becoming persistent serious delinquents is very slight among those children with multiple strengths but approaching near certainty among those with relatively high risk scores and low protective scores.

Resource Note 1.3 *(continued)*

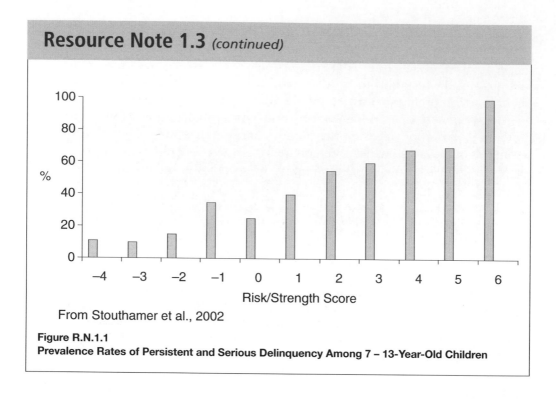

From Stouthamer et al., 2002

Figure R.N.1.1
Prevalence Rates of Persistent and Serious Delinquency Among 7 – 13-Year-Old Children

The research approaches reviewed here are in the systematic quantitative tradition. Qualitative approaches to research also play important roles in PCC, such as building tentative models (initial conceptualization of variables and the relationships among variables). Once applied and tested through quantitative research, researchers may return to a qualitative study in order to explore whether the model possesses the "ring of truth." There is, for example, nothing like a good case study to inspire the feeling that we really understand the phenomenon of interest.

Although case studies frequently have been used as "proof" for favored theoretical positions, their methodological shortcomings are so severe that they provide little beyond generating hypotheses for experimentation or illustrating a phenomenon. When we provide a case study in this text, it is meant only to illustrate a finding already established by systematic research, not to serve as the research evidence itself.

The Correlates of Crime: Differentiation Among Groups Known to Differ in Their Criminal History

Knowledge of correlates comes from cross-sectional observations of individuals known to differ in their criminal history. Cross-sectional studies tend to be of two types: extreme groups and surveys. In the extreme groups approach, individuals are selected for observation precisely because they are known in advance to differ in their criminal histories. For example, a sample of high school students may be compared with a sample of juvenile probationers, or a group of first offenders compared with a group of repeat offenders. The empirical issue here is to discover which of the potential covariates studied do, in fact, distinguish between offenders and nonoffenders. Alternatively, in the survey approach, a representative sample of individuals from some specified population is selected for systematic observation. One of the variables studied is the level and/or type of criminal activity in which the individuals have engaged. Other variables assessed are potential covariates of that criminal history. Here too, the task is to identify the variables that correlate with a criminal past. In brief, correlates are covariates of a criminal past.

Cross-sectional designs are the most frequently used in the analysis of criminal behavior. They tend to be less expensive to implement and provide information much more quickly than alternative approaches. Two of the most important and most cited studies in the whole of PCC and criminology are those of Sheldon Glueck and Eleanor Glueck (1950) and Travis Hirschi (1969). We will see how important their research was in the theory chapters (Chapters 3 and 4). Here, their findings are compared on a potential risk/need factor basis. The studies differed in many ways, yet their findings were remarkably similar and have been supported in many subsequent studies (see Table 1.2).

Table 1.2
Comparison of the Risk/Need Findings of Two Classic Cross-sectional Studies

	Cross-sectional Classics	
	Glueck & Glueck (1950)	Hirschi (1969)
Personality		
Energetic and easily bored	Y	Y
Lacking in self-control	Y	Y
History of Antisocial Behavior		
Multiple rule violations	Y	Y
Antisocial Attitudes		
Procriminal attitudes	Y	Y
Antisocial Associates		
Delinquent associates	Y	Y
School		
Dislike for school	Y	Y
Family		
Poor family relations	Y	Y
Poor parental supervision	Y	Y

Note : Y (Yes), N (No)

Predictor Variables: True Prediction in a Longitudinal Design

Knowledge of predictors of criminal behavior comes from observations conducted within a longitudinal study. In a longitudinal study, hypothesized predictor variables are examined in relation to subsequent or future criminal activity. Relative to cross-sectional and survey studies, longitudinal research has the advantage of ensuring that the covariation established is truly prospective. That is, we may feel reasonably confident that the criminal behavior was not responsible for the covariation, because the assessment of criminal behavior was based on events that followed assessment of predictor variables. Logically, "causes" must precede their "effects." In cross-sectional and survey designs, when we observe an association between two variables, we can never be sure what came first (e.g., does a muscular body type lead to criminal behavior, or does criminal activity produce a muscular figure?).

For purposes of illustrating the practicality of longitudinal designs, a concrete example of the ability to forecast future crime follows. Sally Rogers (1981) developed a simple, six-item risk scale that reflected certain well-known risk factors for criminal behavior. These six predictors (or risk factors) were: being male, being young (under 24 years of age), having a criminal record, having delinquent associates, aimless use of leisure time, and having a family that relies on social assistance. Rogers worked with a representative sample of 1,104 Ontario probationers whose official reconvictions were monitored during probation and for two years after completing probation. On the basis of interviews while on probation, each probationer was assigned a score of "1" for each risk factor that was present. Thus, the risk scale could take values from "0" (no risk factors present) to "6" (all factors present). That official reconvictions increased with scores on the risk scale is obvious upon inspection of Table 1.3. The practical implications of such levels of predictive validity are an important focus of PCC.

Table 1.3
Reconviction Rates by Intake Risk Level

Risk Score	Recidivism Rate	N
6	94.2%	(of 17)
5	76.9%	(of 108)
4	62.7%	(of 109)
3	42.9%	(of 220)
2	24.2%	(of 397)
1	9.4%	(of 181)
0	5.6%	(of 36)
Total Sample	35.8%	(of 1,104)

From Rogers, 1981

Dynamic Predictors: Dynamic Risk Factors, More and Less Stable

Definitive knowledge of dynamic predictors comes from multiwave longitudinal studies. Observations are made on at least three occasions in a multiwave longitudinal study. The first occasion involves the initial assessment of potential predictors, and the second involves a reassessment of these potential predictors. Some of the more dynamic aspects of body, psyche, and social arrangements may change over time. For purposes of establishing dynamic predictors, changes observed between the initial assessment and the reassessment are examined in relation to the third assessment, namely that of criminal conduct, which follows at some later date.

Dynamic predictors (dynamic risk factors) are ones on which assessed change is associated with subsequent criminal behavior. Some dynamic risk factors are relatively stable in that change occurs over a matter of weeks, months, or even years. Examples of such dynamic risk factors are enhanced interpersonal relationships at home, school, or work as well as reductions or increases in association with criminal others. Some dynamic risk factors are much less stable and may change almost instantaneously. These fast-changing dynamic risk factors are often called acute dynamic risk factors and typically reflect immediate situations or immediate circumstances (such as hanging out with a drug user tonight) and/or immediate emotional states such as anger, resentment, or desire for revenge (Hanson & Harris, 2000; Quinsey, Coleman, Jones & Altrows, 1997; Zamble & Quinsey, 1997). We begin with the more stable dynamic risk factors.

As an illustration of dynamic predictors, Andrews and Wormith (1984) found that intake assessments of probationers on a paper-and-pencil measure of antisocial attitudes called "Identification with Criminal Others" predicted criminal recidivism. With dynamic predictors, we are interested in the changes in scores between the first and second assessments and future recidivism. Andrews and Wormith (1984) found that probationers who identified with offenders to a moderate degree on intake and subsequently reduced their identification six months later had a recidivism rate of only 10 percent. Those who maintained moderate levels of identification with offenders (i.e., no change over the six months) had a recidivism rate of 38 percent. Those whose identification with offenders increased during probation had a recidivism rate of 57 percent. In summary, while all of these probationers were judged at moderate levels of risk for recidivism at intake, over a six-month period the risk levels decreased for some, remained the same for others, and increased for still others. The important point is that the changes from intake to retest were linked with criminal outcomes.

The identification of simple predictors in single-wave longitudinal studies shows that individuals may be reliably assigned to groups with different levels of risk for future criminal activity. The discovery of dynamic predictors confirms that risk levels are subject to change and that these dynamic predictors may serve as treatment goals. For example, in many probation agencies, a primary objective is to provide treatment services and supervision to probationers in such a way that the lower-risk cases remain low-risk and that the higher-risk cases become lower-risk ones. Thus, the dynamic predictors may serve as a focus for a probation officer's efforts in bringing about change.

An understanding of dynamic predictors is very important within PCC, because a psychology of criminal behavior rejects outright an exclusive focus on the more static aspects of individuals and their situations. Indeed, when PCC practitioners and researchers uncover highly stable predictors, they immediately begin to think in terms of what may be the dynamic correlates of that stable predictor. For example, we will see that past antisocial behavior is a major predictor of future antisocial behavior. But, thinking dynamically, perhaps an appropriate intermediate target of change would be to build up alternatives to criminal behavior in high-risk situations.

In practice, and as reviewed above, simple predictors are often called risk factors. Dynamic predictors of criminal conduct (that is, dynamic risk factors), on the other hand, are often called *criminogenic need* factors. The term "need" is used for the practical reason that it carries with it the hope that if criminogenic need factors are reduced, the chances of criminal involvement will decrease. However, our use of the term "need" is a highly specific one. We do not imply that all "unpleasant" conditions represent criminogenic need factors, nor that any or all of the covariates of crime are in any way "bad" or "unpleasant" on their own. Risk factors and need factors are simply predictors of future criminal conduct.

Reassessments over a period much shorter than six months or more (e.g., monthly, weekly, or even daily) may lead to the discovery of acute dynamic risk factors that will predict criminal occurrences over the very short term. If a parolee begins to talk with considerable resentment and anger over how things are going (at home or on the job), risk of recidivism may be considered to have increased at least for the short term.

Just as knowledge of predictor variables leads us closer to knowledge of causes than do simple correlates, so does knowledge of dynamic predictors yield a still higher level of empirical understanding. PCC, however, seeks more than knowledge of dynamic predictors. PCC seeks an understanding that offers the potential not to simply forecast criminal events but to influence the chances of criminal acts occurring through deliberate intervention.

Causal/Functional Variables

The causes of crime are most convincingly established not through the determination of correlates and predictors, but through functional variables, demonstrations of the effects of deliberate interventions. As the conditions of intervention approximate experimental ideals, confidence in the functional status of any particular variable increases. The classical experimental design maintains control over variables that would compete for causal status. These controls are typically introduced by rendering the competing variables either constant or random, while examining the potential effects of the functional variable of primary experimental interest. Thus, PCC is concerned with the introduction of control groups, random assignment to groups, and the employment of other research techniques that increase confidence in conclusions regarding the causal significance of the covariates of criminal conduct (see Resource Note 1.4).

Resource Note 1.4

The Classical Experimental Design

Two research designs allow us to reach conclusions regarding functional (causal) validity: the A-B-A type of design (Hersen & Barlow, 1976) used in single-subject research and the classical experimental design (Campbell & Stanley, 1963). In the study of criminal behavior, the classical experimental design is most frequently used, typically in studies evaluating the effectiveness of intervention programs.

The central features of the experimental design are:

1. A minimum of two groups: An experimental group exposed to the hypothesized functional variable and a control group not subjected to the hypothesized functional variable.

2. Random assignment of subjects to groups.

3. Posttesting on the criterion variable of both groups at the same point in time.

Such a design controls for bias from subject selection factors through random assignment. The use of a control group and posttesting of experimentals during the same time period controls for maturation (i.e., growing older) and history factors (i.e., naturally occurring experiences between the intervention and posttests), because these factors would be expected to influence the control subjects in the same manner as the experimental subjects. Given that attention was also paid to objective measurement and experimenter bias, and that the results are tested for statistical significance, any difference found between the experimental and the control groups at posttest may be attributed to the intervention or the hypothesized functional variable.

Illustrating the power of the experimental design is an experiment by Michael Chandler (1973). Chandler evaluated a treatment program designed to teach role-taking skills to juvenile delinquents. He reasoned that the inability of some delinquents to take into account the perspective of another individual indicated a deficit in socialization and that this egocentrism resulted in social conflicts.

Forty-five delinquent boys, aged 11-13, were randomly assigned (controlling for

Resource Note 1.4 *(continued)*

subject selection) to one of three conditions. The experimental condition consisted of the treatment intervention. Treatment involved graduate students who trained the boys to write film skits that involved real-life social situations. The idea was to encourage the delinquents to think about the various perspectives of all the actors in the skits. Their skits were recorded and observed by the experimental subjects, and discussions about the viewpoints of the others were led by the graduate students.

The second group also wrote and filmed skits, but the skits were documentaries about their neighborhoods or cartoons. No attempt was made to encourage perspective-taking. This control group was intended to control for any possible effects from simply receiving special attention from the therapists (i.e., the graduate students). A third group received no treatment whatsoever.

All of the delinquents were administered a test of role-taking ability before any intervention. The three groups did not differ significantly in their scores on the perspective-taking test. A pretest provides the opportunity to test whether, in fact, random assignment procedures do result in experimental groups and control groups being equivalent on relevant variables at the time of the pretest. In this study, random assignment was effective in producing groups that were indistinguishable statistically in egocentricism scores.

At posttest (10 weeks later), the average test scores were 5.5 for the experimental group, 8.6 for the "attention" group, and 8.0 for the control group (the lower the score, the less egocentric). Statistical tests showed that the lower scores for the experimental group were not likely the result of chance.

Can we attribute the lower scores on the measure of egocentrism for the experimental group to some specific experience or maturational influences? Probably not, because we would expect similar influences to be operating on the other two groups. In this study, we can also discount the possibility that simply giving attention to the experimental group, regardless of the content of the intervention, was a factor. Since the three groups differed only with respect to perspective-taking skills training, we can reasonably conclude that this training directly influenced egocentrism scores (i.e., functional validity).

Finally, we must ask the question whether changing perspective-taking skills is relevant to criminal behavior. Chandler followed the delinquents for a period of 18 months following the treatment.

At follow-up, police and court records showed that the average number of offenses for the "attention" group was 2.1; for the no treatment group, 1.8. These differences were statistically unreliable. However, the experimental group differed significantly: they had an average of 1.0 offenses. Compared to their average number of offenses before treatment (1.9), this was a significant reduction. No similar reductions were found for the other groups.

Chandler demonstrated that perspective-taking skills have functional validity with respect to criminal behavior. By deliberately and systematically intervening (i.e., providing treatment), egocentrism decreased and so did delinquent behavior. In this manner, Chandler affirmed the vitality of correctional rehabilitation. The fact that some correctional treatment programs can "work" and that we can demonstrate this fact experimentally is one of the major themes of this text.

Approximations of the ideals of true experimentation are difficult to achieve even under highly controlled laboratory conditions with non-human animals. The difficulties are compounded when attempts are made to study human behavior that is as socially significant as criminal behavior. Certainly, psychologists are not about to play with increasing the chances of criminal conduct just to prove some theoretical point within PCC.

Some social agencies, however, are formally called upon to intervene in the lives of individuals with the expressed and socially approved purpose of controlling their criminal conduct. These agencies are also expected to perform their duties in effective, efficient, fair, and just ways. It is this concern with the effective, efficient, and ethical control of criminal behavior that not only permits, but actually demands, active experimentation of the highest quality. Thus, throughout this text, contributions to the effectiveness of correctional and prevention programming are primary concerns. Controlled evaluations of practice are not only "practical," they permit a high-level exploration of the causes of crime.

In summary, much of our understanding of the covariates of criminal behavior is dependent upon the research methodology used in studies. This methodology limits our level of understanding and reminds us of the importance of empirical research to building knowledge. For all of this, the literature reviews conducted by Michael Gottfredson and Travis Hirschi (1990) suggest that the findings of cross-sectional studies and the findings of longitudinal studies have been highly compatible. The validity of potential risk factors identified in cross-sectional studies of a criminal past have tended to be confirmed in longitudinal studies of risk factors.

On the other hand, the number of multiwave longitudinal studies of potential criminogenic need factors is so low that we are not yet in a position to assert with high degrees of confidence that the potentially dynamic risk factors meet the required standards of dynamic predictive criterion validity. Moreover, as rare as multiwave longitudinal studies may be, ultimate tests of "criminogenic need" are even more rare, because these ultimate tests demand that "criminogenic need" be established within the structure of an experimental design. For the strict determination of criminogenic need, what we need to show is that: (1) deliberate interventions produce changes on the potential need factor, (2) deliberate interventions produce changes in criminal conduct, and (3) the magnitude of the association between intervention and criminal behavior may be reduced through the introduction of statistical controls for change on the potential need factor (Andrews, Bonta & Hoge, 1990).

Moderator Variables

It is important to note that PCC readily recognizes the complexity of human behavior and demands that the general validity of conclusions be explored under a variety of conditions. Most obviously these days, it is important to be able to demonstrate whether a conclusion from research is valid for people who may vary in age, gender, race, and socio-economic class. Similarly, it is important to show whether methodological issues such as randomization, sample size, and deviations from the ideals of research design are associated with increases, decreases, or null effects on effect size estimates. Any variable is a potential moderator. Yet, the actual moderator variables are those that do influence how, for example, one variable correlates with criminal behavior. Many tests of moderator variables follow in this chapter. For example, we will show that the effects of official interventions with offenders vary with whether the intervention included human service. We will show that the effects of correctional treatment programs depend upon what the targets of change are and what behavior change techniques are used.

A Preliminary Note on Meta-Analyses

Almost every student and practitioner, and certainly every professor, is familiar with the "literature review." Scholarly journals are devoted to articles that review areas of interest, and every dissertation and research report begins with a review of the literature. The traditional literature review has been narrative in nature, and the qualities of the reviews depend very much upon the expertise and thoroughness of the author(s). The reviewer is relatively free to select studies and unfettered to attend to those results viewed as relevant. Thus, it is not uncommon for two independent reviews of a particular literature to reach very different conclusions.

Meta-analytic reviews permit a more unbiased analysis of the literature, and they provide a quantitative estimate of the importance of the results. Although meta-analyses have been used for more than 20 years, their use has exploded in the last 15 years. Many now regard meta-analysis as the standard approach for reviewing the literature. In essence, the results from individual studies are converted into a common metric or statistic referred to as the effect size. The effect size allows more direct comparisons of the results from various studies and the averaging of effect sizes across studies.

As an illustration, let us take estimating the relationship between intelligence and crime. One study may report the results using a t test (a statistic measuring the differences in the means of two groups), another may use the Pearson correlation coefficient (r), and a third study may report the percentage of low IQ and high IQ individuals in a group of offenders and nonoffenders. How can we best compare the results? In the traditional, narrative literature review, reviewers must make a judgment of the relative importance of the three studies. Reviewer A may emphasize the results from Study 2 and discount the results from the other two studies. Reviewer B may prefer the results based upon the t test and minimize the other statistics. We can see how this approach may lead to different conclusions.

In a meta-analysis, the results from the three studies would all be converted into the same statistic or effect size. Often the effect size used is the Pearson correlation coefficient (see Resource Note 1.1). In our illustration, the t score would be converted to r, as would the percentage differences (recall how easily percentage differences can be transformed using Rosenthal's Binomial Effect Size Display; Resource Note 1.1). Consequently, we can compare the effect sizes from the three studies and by averaging them can more accurately estimate the "true" relationship between intelligence and crime. Because many studies are conducted in various locations with different samples and time periods, the generalizability of the results from meta-analyses is enhanced.

One may also search for moderators of the mean effect size. For example, the results from cross-sectional studies may (or may not) differ from the results of longitudinal studies. Similarly, the findings may vary depending upon whether the measure of criminal behavior is based on scores on a self-report paper-and-pencil questionnaire or measures of official processing such as arrest or conviction. There has long been a position in mainstream criminology that the "psychological" covariates of crime "really" reflect the social locator variables of age, race, gender, and/or socioeconomic class. In primary studies, and then in meta-analytic reviews of primary studies, we can explore whether mean effect sizes vary with age, gender, and so on.

At a number of points in the text, we will refer to the results from different meta-analyses. For the reasons outlined, we place more confidence in the results from a meta-analysis than from the traditional literature review. Indeed, we are interested in the results of individual "primary studies" (the separate studies that compose the collection of studies reviewed). Yet, we would never put too much faith in a single study. We look for the overall effect evident from analyses of many primary studies. Replication of findings is a convincing feature of science.

The Location of PCC in Psychology and Criminology

Our overall conclusions will be relatively strong and encouraging with regard to research and theoretical development within PCC. Our conclusions will also be positive regarding practical applications of PCC. At the same time, references to the many gaps in knowledge within PCC will be encountered throughout the text. These gaps must be bridged if the above-stated objectives of PCC are to be reached. We will also stress the threats to validity associated with different types of research designs and how they are evident within particular studies. In other words, this text will underscore the healthy skepticism insisted upon by a rational empirical approach. As noted by Frederick Crews (1986), the characteristics of a community of rational empiricists include an interest in understanding some phenomenon (e.g., variation in the criminal behavior of individuals) along with the enhancement of that understanding through both unsparing criticism in combination with respect for evidence.

Many irrational, anti-psychological, and anti-empirical impediments to the development of PCC are reviewed in this text. Interestingly, until very recently, the barriers to the development of PCC were most frequently encountered within the broad field of academic criminology itself. First, however, we locate PCC within the broader fields of psychology and criminology.

PCC and General Human Psychology

PCC is both a subfield of a truly interdisciplinary criminology and a subfield of human psychology. Being a subfield of psychology makes PCC a part of a vast scientific and professional discipline. As a science, psychology is concerned with producing empirically defensible explanations of behavioral phenomena. Professionally, psychologists are involved in the effective application of psychological knowledge at the individual, small group, organizational/broader community, and societal levels of action. Many psychologists combine professional and scientific interests because they have been trained according to a "scientist-practitioner model."

Criminal behavior has been a long-term (but not always mainstream) interest within psychology as a whole. In view of the great variety of interests and orientations within general human psychology, however, a psychological analysis of criminal behavior will be multifaceted. The many areas of interest in human psychology include human development, sensation and perception, learning and cognition, memory and information processing, motivation and emotion, personality and individual differences, assessment and evaluation, history and philosophy, clinical and applied, social and community, and biological and physiological psychology. This complex list includes areas of study sampled by almost all introductory textbooks in psychology. Thus, a psychology of criminal conduct seeks a richer and deeper understanding of criminal behavior than could possibly be found by concentrating on variables such as age, gender, race, and social class (until recently, the favored variables within sociological criminology). Similarly, PCC does not limit itself to clinical factors, to considerations of psychopathology, or to legal variables such as seriousness of the offense, culpability, aggravating factors, or mitigating factors (the favored variables of forensic mental health). In brief, a psychology of criminal conduct will insist that the analysis of criminal behavior consider biological, personal, interpersonal, familial, and structural/cultural factors as well as consider the individual in particular immediate situations and in the broader social context.

The theoretical orientations within human psychology are equally diverse. While this text emphasizes the contributions of social learning perspectives, this emphasis should not suggest that human psychology is successfully unified by that particular orientation. The psychology of human behavior in general, like the psychology of criminal behavior in particular, draws upon some combination of seven major orientations. These orientations to the exploration of human nature and individual differences are as follows:

1. *Biological* perspectives tend to emphasize relatively enduring soma-based predispositions (e.g., constitution and genetics), dynamic biological processes (e.g., the physiology of classical conditioning and/or hormonal activity), the neuropsychology of emotion and self-regulation, and events with major somatic implications (e.g., the effects of alcohol on bodily functioning, and/or brain injury).

2. *Trait* perspectives tend to emphasize relatively enduring behavioral, cognitive, and affective predispositions (e.g., extraversion, intelligence, emotionality, self-control) without necessarily requiring particular assumptions regarding the biological, psychological, or social bases of these traits. Typically, however, the inheritability of major temperamental factors is of interest and explored.

3. *Psychodynamic* perspectives emphasize what many people still think of as the "truly psychological." Psychodynamic perspectives search for understanding through an appreciation of the personal psychological motivations and controls of overt behavior.

4. *Sociocultural* perspectives within psychology emphasize the effects of family, peers, and community on individual behavior. These theories tend to be socialization theories whereby individual differences in personal behavior, cognition, and emotions are linked to differences in the training provided by different families, peer groups, and social institutions. Other sociocultural perspectives place an emphasis on the contextual contributions of gender, class, and ethnicity. The term "multi-systemic" has become popular over the last decade because it captures the idea of being part of multiple social systems while more readily recognizing not simply the socio-cultural but also the immediate contingencies of action (e.g., what activities are being encouraged/discouraged and /or enabled/restricted).

5. *Radical behavioral* perspectives concentrate on how the immediate behavior-environmental contingencies are responsible for the acquisition, maintenance, and modification of individual behavior. The effects of the immediate environment depend very much upon how the environment reinforces, punishes, and ignores behavior.

6. *Humanistic* and *existential* perspectives may be differentiated from the above according to three concerns. The first is the emphasis placed upon "free choice" and "personal responsibility." The second is the emphasis placed upon perceptions of the self and the world as "perceived" and "interpreted" by the self. The third involves an attraction to the notion that the experience of interpersonal warmth, openness, and acceptance are associated with a pattern of personal "growth" that is both psychologically and socially positive.

7. *Social learning/cognitive behavioral/social cognition* perspectives may be differentiated from all of the above orientations by virtue of the additional emphasis placed upon learning by observation, the role of cognition, and the importance of considering the person in combination with particular situations. General social psychological perspectives tend to emphasize personal attitudes and beliefs, perceptions of the expectations of others, self-efficacy beliefs, and the demands of particular situations.

8. A *general personality and cognitive social learning perspective* on human behavior. While certainly not accepted by all psychologists, we think that general human psychology is well served today by general personality and social learning/social cognition perspectives. These approaches recognize that there are fundamental dimensions of personality on which most if not all human beings may be located. It is also widely recognized that these fundamental dimensions of personality have biological underpinnings, and several are heavily influence by heredity. As the human being develops from infant through young adult through old age, biological potentials are shaped through interactions with the environment. If you want to predict behavior in the immediate situation of action, you must understand the situation in psychological terms. What is the emotional significance of the situation (pleasing, anger-generating)? Are certain outcomes (pleasing or not pleasing) for particular behaviors (prosocial or antisocial) being signaled in that situation? If you want to predict behavior over the moderate or longer term, we will see that certain variables are key (we will call them the **"Big Four"**). They include cognitions supportive of a particular behavior. "Cognition" refers to attitudes, values, beliefs, rationalizations, and identities supportive versus nonsupportive of the behavior. A history of engaging the particular behavior is another of the major factors. Association with others who approve of the behavior (social support) is the third factor. Fourth is temperament or personality predisposition for the behavior.

9. Psychology is forever growing. Hence, in the near future, we may expect that PCC will be drawing upon developments in "positive

psychology" and/or "post-modern" psychology and/or "feminist" psychology and/or "personal transformation" psychology and/or "culturally specific" psychology and/or "biologically universal" and/or "relational" psychology, and others not yet even on the horizon.

These interests and orientations within general human psychology are diverse. Fortunately, at least four unifying principles may be identified within this broad mix of interests and orientations:

1. An interest in understanding the thoughts, emotions, and behavior of individuals. A focus is on individuals with an interest in the full range of human thought, feeling, and action.

2. An openness to the full range of potential covariates of individual behavior, and to the full range of the moderators and mediators of those covariates (i.e., soma, psyche, interpersonal, social, cultural, political, economic, and the immediate situations of action).

3. Commitment to a rational empirical approach to knowledge construction.

4. The seeking of empirical knowledge, the construction of theoretical systems, and the application of psychological knowledge and opinion are subject to ethical and professional guidelines and to other norms that may vary with particular social contexts.

PCC and Criminology

Criminology is the broad interdisciplinary exploration of crime and criminal justice. As will be noted, however, textbook or official criminology has tended to be sociological. Until very recently, this sociological bent has been explicitly anti-psychological. The outline and boundaries of the field of criminology have shifted somewhat over the last three decades. In the late 1960s, Donald Cressey and David Ward (1969:xii) prefaced their reader, *Delinquency, Crime, and Social Process*, with the following outline of the two key issues within criminology. One is the statistical distribution of criminal and delinquent behavior in time and space ("Why is the delinquency rate of this group, city, or nation higher than the delinquency rate of that group, city, or nation?"). The second issue is the process by which individuals come to behave criminally or in a delinquent manner ("How did Johnny happen to go wrong?").

The second issue (explaining individual differences in criminal behavior) is the primary focus of PCC. The defining element of PCC is the focus on individual criminal conduct, whereas the defining element of a social science of crime rates is a focus on aggregated crime rates. These focal concerns are not conflicting but simply different. Moreover, from a logical perspective, aggregated crime rates are direct reflections of individual differences in criminal conduct. Technical Note 1.3 develops these ideas and issues some warnings regarding the problem of inferring knowledge of the correlates of individual criminal behavior from knowledge of the correlates of aggregated crime rates.

Social Context as a Moderator of Individual Differences

This text attends whenever possible to the social, political, economic, and historical contexts within which individual differences in criminal behavior are established. In particular, information on the generalizability of the correlates of individual differences in criminal behavior is sought. Although some correlates may be limited to particular social arrangements, many correlates are highly stable across social arrangements. A few preliminary examples follow.

Certain personality variables have proven to be relatively major correlates of the criminal conduct of adolescents even when social location varies according to geography, historical period, class of origin, race, age, and gender. John Hagan, A.R. Gillis, and John Simpson (1985) have shown that a propensity for risk-taking was a major correlate of the self-reported "common" delinquency of high school students in Toronto. Many other investigators have confirmed that risk-taking and sensation-seeking are correlates of a criminal history (e.g., Eysenck, 1977), but here we use the Hagan study to illustrate the general, versus limited, nature of this personal correlate of criminal conduct.

Hagan and his colleagues (1985) assessed a taste for risk-taking by looking at responses to two items on a self-report questionnaire. Students were asked to indicate their levels of agreement with the statements: "I like to take risks" and "The things I like to do best are dangerous." Dear reader: How about you? Do you have a strong taste for risk? Answer each question on a five-point scale from "Not at all true of me" (scored 0) to "very true of me" (scored 4).

They found that a taste for risk was associated with self-reported delinquency. More importantly, the study confirmed that an above-average taste for risk was associated with relatively high levels of criminal activity, regardless of the social class of family of origin or the gender of the young people studied. The positive correlation between a personal taste for risk and self-reported delinquent behavior was found among both the sons and daughters of owners, managers, workers, and the unemployed.

Hagan et al. (1985) also found that young men, regardless of their scores on the personality measure, reported more criminal activity than did young women. The effect of gender was evident among the offspring of owners, managers, and employees. This finding provides another example of the generality of correlates of delinquency. It, however, also appeared that the gender-delinquency link was not found among the children of the unemployed—at least not once a taste for risk was statistically controlled for. This very tentative qualification suggests that class of origin may moderate the correlation between gender and criminal behavior. This is an illustration, albeit weak, of how social class may influence the way other variables correlate with criminal conduct.

As weak as the moderating effects of social class were, the direct effects of social class on delinquent behavior were not only weak but also opposite in direction to that predicted by the class-based theories of criminal behavior. The adolescent offspring of managers, workers, and unemployed heads of household were not only statistically indistinguishable from one another in their levels of criminal behavior, but their level of criminal activity was slightly lower than that of the sons and daughters of owners. This trend is in direct opposition to those class-based theories that suggest that lower-class origin is a major risk factor for delinquency.

A final illustration of the interaction of social location and personal factors is an example of the recent rediscovery of the importance of neighborhood. Per-Olof H. Wikström and Rolf Loeber (2000) showed that variation in the socioeconomic neighborhood context had implications for the validity of assessments of risk that reflected impulsive personality, antisocial attitudes, antisocial associates, and problematic family relationships (recall the risk factors suggested by a general personality and social psychological perspective). The correlation of risk with serious youthful offending was approximately .70 within the more advantaged neighborhoods while the correlation was not statistically greater than .00 within the most disadvantaged neighborhood. Stated another way, even the young men who were at low risk for antisocial behavior according to their personality, attitudes, and immediate interpersonal environment were actually put at risk when they lived in a highly disadvantaged neighborhood.

On the other hand, high-risk young people offended at relatively high rates regardless of socioeconomic context. Note, that the contribution of personal risk overall was much greater than the contribution of disadvantaged neighborhood overall (a correlation coefficient of .69 between personal risk and serious youthful offending compared to a correlation coefficient of .28 for neighborhood and serious youthful offending). The above noted correlation coefficients were gammas, and gammas yield somewhat higher values than Pearson rs. Overall, it is becoming very clear that the risk factors for criminal behavior are very similar across different neighborhoods. Moreover, one of the major characteristics of disadvantaged neighborhoods is the proportion of individuals scoring high on personal risk factors (Stouthamer-Loeber, Loeber, Wei et al. 2002).

In summary, PCC is interested in how social arrangements may moderate the personal correlates of criminal behavior. PCC also seeks knowledge of personal moderators of the effects of social context on individual behavior.

The Social Research on Aggregated Crime Rates

As you have seen, within PCC a major distinction is drawn between studies of aggregated crime rates and variation in the criminal behavior of individuals. Not all criminologists are as sensitive to the distinction as we are. Our suggestion is not that one concern is more important than the other. Our concern is that the correlates of aggregated crime rates not be thought to be the same as the correlates of the criminal conduct of individuals. Technical Note 1.3 explores the problem of the "ecological fallacy" in some technical detail. The basic message is straightforward: If you want to understand variation in the criminal behavior of individuals, study individuals and do so with a full range of potential factors from the biological, personal, interpersonal, community, and structural-cultural arenas.

Objections to the Goals of PCC

Our brief description of the goals and methods of PCC may appear noncontroversial, and perhaps even rather mundane and banal. Who would argue against the importance of individual differences, and against rationality, regard for evidence, and practicality? Not many, one might think, because the alternatives would surely involve seeking an understanding of criminal conduct that is irrational, empirically false, useless, and dismissive of the characteristics of individuals. Nevertheless, many criminologists have argued—and a few continue to argue—in ways that are anti-person, irrational, anti-empirical, and anti-application. Consider the following assessments of mainstream sociological criminology of the 1970s and 1980s and even into the new millennium:

- From the beginning, the thrust of sociological theory has been to deny the relevance of individual differences to an exploration of delinquency, and the thrust of sociological criticism has been to discount research findings apparently to the contrary. "Devastating" reviews of the research literature typically meet with uncritical acceptance or even applause, and "new criminologies" are constructed in a research vacuum (Hirschi & Hindelang, 1977:571-572).

- In most sociological treatments of crime and delinquency, genetic explanations are either ignored or ridiculed (Rowe & Osgood, 1984:526).

- An objective of the psychology of crime is to understand personal covariates of criminal activity, whereas an objective of major portions of mainstream criminology is to discredit such an understanding (Andrews & Wormith, 1989:290).

- Sociology possessed a conceptual scheme that explicitly denied the claims of all other disciplines potentially interested in crime (Gottfredson & Hirschi, 1990:70).

- Advances in personality theory and assessment . . . have had little influence on research conducted by criminologists . . . Indeed, *Criminology* has published only four articles on the role of personality factors in crime since the journal was founded in 1964 (Caspi et al., 1994:165).

- The reason that most criminologists continue to resist the incorporation of biological factors into their understanding of criminal behavior is ideological. As part of their liberal academic tradition, criminologists tend to resist attempts to blame individuals . . . preferring instead to blame society and its institutions (Ellis & Hoffman, 1990:57).

- . . . [there is a] . . . skepticism within criminology and other social sciences about our ability to make accurate and reliable predictions of dangerousness and recidivism (Hannah-Moffat & Shaw, 2001:18).

The changes in mainstream textbook criminology and indeed in the content of the major criminology and criminal justice journals have bordered on the astounding in the 1990s and to the present millennium. The two major empirical concerns of PCC—prediction and influence—are now mainstream. What were once called the major sociological theories of crime have almost uniformly been revised into social psychological theories. Within criminal justice, whole state, provincial, and even some national correctional systems have been transformed through attention to the principles of PCC. All of this will be explored in this text.

At the same time, some small portions of criminology and criminal justice are struggling openly with PCC and continue to advance the anti-prediction, anti-treatment, and anti-PCC themes. Technical Note 1.4 explores the nature and sources of objections to PCC studies and applications.

A Look Ahead

Part 1 of the text includes four chapters. The theoretical context and the empirical base of PCC is summarized. Part 2 surveys the major risk/need domains, including examples of intervention programs that incorporate the intermediate targeting of the major domains. Part 3 is a detailed review of applications of PCC in the areas of prediction and effective intervention. Part 4 presents a summary and conclusions.

Part 1. Following the introductory material of Chapter 1, Chapter 2 plunges the reader into two major sets of research findings that provide the testing grounds for the value of PCC. What is known about the ability to predict criminal futures and what is known about the ability to intervene and actually influence the occurrence of criminal activity? Chapter 2 opens with the risk-need-responsivity (RNR) model of correctional assessment and correctional treatment. Chapters 3 and 4 review the major theoretical explanations of crime.

Chapter 2 is very unusual in that prior to detailed descriptions of theory and classic research studies, it directs the reader to summaries of the findings in regard to the key issues of: (a) the prediction of criminal conduct and (b) the ability to influence the occurrence of criminal conduct. The two key issues are reviewed in the context of the risk-need-responsivity (RNR) model of correctional assessment and rehabilitation. The idea is that armed with an overview of the current state of research findings readers will be in a much better position to grasp the significance of particular theories and particular research studies. In Chapter 2, the integration of the objectives of theoretical, empirical, and practical understandings is sought.

Throughout Chapter 2, and in every subsequent chapter, generality and specificity are considered in regard to types of human beings, types of settings, and socioeconomic and cultural contexts. In brief, are the risk/need factors the same for females and males? Are they the same in follow-ups of prisoners and probationers? Are the principles of effective crime prevention the same for females and males, for young offenders and adult offenders, for ...... ? Do the same theories of criminal conduct apply to males and females, to.... ?

Chapters 3 and 4 summarize the dominant theoretical perspectives on criminal conduct. A variety of perspectives are compared with a general personality and social psychological perspective. The social psychology of particular value is a cognitive social learning perspective.

Part 2. Chapters 5 through 9 explore potential sources of variability in criminal behavior that in total have been major preoccupations for years within mainstream criminology. In Chapter 5, biological origins are reviewed along with genetics and the mediating variable of temperament (or personality as it emerges through the interaction of biology and the environment). Socioeconomic class of origin (social origins) was the number-one causal variable in sociological criminology for years. We will suggest that genetics, personality, and class of origin are well-established risk factors for criminal activity but only temperament/personality will enter our "Big Four" set of major risk/need factors (Chapter 6).

Chapter 7 explores antisocial attitudes and antisocial associates. Chapter 8 extends the discussion of the person in a variety of social contexts, including family of origin, marriage and romantic attachments, school/work, leisure/recreation, and neighborhoods. The focus of Chapter 9 is on substance abuse and crime.

Part 3. Chapters 10 through 14 are concerned with applications of PCC through practical prediction and prevention and rehabilitative programming. Chapter 12 outlines a major challenge in applications of the PCC knowledge. This particular challenge exists in the psychotherapy arena generally. Tightly controlled programming in the context of short-term demonstration projects reveal positive effects that greatly exceed those found in regular programming. "Regular" programming is also referred to as "routine" programs and/or "real world" programs. Chapter 13 is a detailed analysis of the effects of official sanctioning on reoffending when human service is not introduced. Chapter 14 extends applications of PCC with special groups including the mentally ill and sex offenders, and understanding violence in its many forms (sexual, domestic, etc).

Part 4. Chapter 15 assesses the extent to which PCC achieves the objectives that were outlined in Chapter 1.

Worth Remembering

1. The objective of PCC is to understand variation in the criminal behavior of individuals.

    The understanding sought is empirical (research based), theoretical (explanatory), and practical (applied).

2. There are substantial individual differences in criminal behavior that are evidenced through a variety of research approaches from around the world in a variety of biological and social contexts such as those associated with age, race, gender and socioeconomic class.

3. A very handy and powerful way of describing the strength of the covariates of criminal behavior is the Pearson r. It is not without limitations, however, and additional approaches are introduced from time to time.

    The r is readily interpreted through the Binomial Effect Size Display (BESD). BESD is the difference in the percentage of cases criminal in one condition (e.g., high-risk) compared to the percent criminal in another condition (e.g., low-risk).

4. PCC has a vast storage of knowledge to draw upon from general human psychology and in particular from a general personality and cognitive social learning psychology.

5. PCC is a major part of criminology, but the dampening of anti-psychological bias in mainstream sociological criminology took many years to be achieved.

6. There is a direct connection between individual differences in criminal behavior and aggregated crime rates, but one must be cautious interpreting findings at the aggregate level with reference to individual differences.

7. Our particular concern in this text, the psychology of criminal conduct (PCC), is but one aspect of psychology's concern with crime, criminal justice, and antisocial behavior in general.

8. Psychology is not the only discipline with an interest in criminal behavior. Other disciplines have an interest in criminal behavior but, when the focus is understanding variation in the criminal behavior of individuals, the issue is the one of primary concern within PCC. PCC seeks a general, holistic, and truly interdisciplinary understanding of variation in the criminal behavior of individuals that all disciplines, professionals, and the public may find valuable.

The Empirical Base of PCC and the RNR Model of Assessment and Crime Prevention Through Human Service

Chapter 1 outlined the purposes, objectives, and methods of PCC. Chapter 2 provides an outline of the current state of knowledge in regard to three major sets of issues. One is empirical understandings of the predictors of criminal conduct. Our emphasis is the best validated of the major, moderate, and mild risk/need factors. Another is empirical understandings of the ability to influence the occurrence of criminal activity. The third is a summary of the applied value of this knowledge base as it may be outlined and rendered practical through a model of correctional assessment and rehabilitation. That model is widely known as the risk-need-responsivity (RNR) model of correctional assessment and rehabilitative programming. We begin with the RNR model (see Table 2.1).

The RNR Model of Correctional Assessment and Treatment

The principles of RNR extend well beyond risk, need, and strength factors. A useful model of active intervention must be established within a normative and organizational context. The RNR model is also strongly attached to general personality and cognitive social learning perspectives on human behavior. It is not limited to models of justice and official punishment because those models do not rest on a solid psychology of human behavior. A broad personality and social psychological model of human behavior will help to shape the identification of risk/need factors, the characteristics of effective behavioral influence strategies, and the characteristics of effective approaches of staffing and management.

The implications of the RNR model extend to all efforts at crime prevention through the delivery of clinical, social, and human services to individuals and small groups. The model is very specific about several key clinical issues including (a) who should be offered more intensive rehabilitative services (the risk principle of RNR), (b) what are the most appropriate intermediate targets of service for purposes of an ultimate reduction in criminal behavior (the criminogenic need principle of RNR),

Table 2.1

The Risk-Need-Responsivity (RNR) Model of Effective Correctional Assessment and Crime Prevention Services

Overarching Principles

1. **Respect for the Person and the Normative Context:** Services are delivered with respect for the person, including respect for personal autonomy, being humane, ethical, just, legal, decent, and being otherwise normative. Some norms may vary with the agencies or the particular settings within which services are delivered. For example, agencies working with young offenders may be expected to show exceptional attention to education issues and to child protection. Mental health agencies may attend to issues of personal well-being. Some agencies working with female offenders may place a premium on attending to trauma and/or to parenting concerns.
2. **Psychological Theory**: Base programs on an empirically solid psychological theory (a general personality and cognitive social learning approach is recommended).
3. **General Enhancement of Crime Prevention Services**: The reduction of criminal victimization may be viewed as a legitimate objective of service agencies, including agencies within and outside of justice and corrections.

Core RNR Principles and Key Clinical Issues

4. **Introduce Human Service**: Introduce human service into the justice context. Do not rely on the sanction to bring about reduced offending. Do not rely on deterrence, restoration, or other principles of justice.
5. **Risk:** Match intensity of service with risk level of cases. Work with moderate and higher risk cases. Generally, avoid creating interactions of low-risk cases with higher-risk cases.
6. **Need:** Target criminogenic needs predominately. Move criminogenic needs in the direction of becoming strengths.
7. **General Responsivity:** Employ behavioral, social learning, and cognitive behavioral influence and skill building strategies.
8. **Specific Responsivity:** Adapt the style and mode of service according to the setting of service and to relevant characteristics of individual offenders, such as their strengths, motivations, preferences, personality, age, gender, ethnicity, cultural identifications, and other factors. The evidence in regard to specific responsivity is generally favorable but very scattered, and it has yet to be subjected to a comprehensive meta-analysis. Some examples of specific responsivity considerations follow:
   a) When working with the weakly motivated: Build on strengths; reduce personal and situational barriers to full participation in treatment; establish high-quality relationships; deliver early and often on matters of personal interest; and start where the person "is at."
   b) Attend to the evidence in regard to age-, gender-, and culturally responsive services.
   c) Attend to the evidence in regard to differential treatment according to interpersonal maturity, interpersonal anxiety, cognitive skill levels, and the responsivity aspects of psychopathy.
   d) Consider the targeting of noncriminogenic needs for purposes of enhancing motivation, the reduction of distracting factors, and for reasons having to do with humanitarian and entitlement issues.
9. **Breadth (or Multimodal):** Target a number of criminogenic needs relative to noncriminogenic needs.
10. **Strength:** Assess strengths to enhance prediction and specific responsivity effects.
11. **Structured Assessment:**
    a) Assessments of Strengths and Risk-Need-Specific Responsivity Factors: Employ structured and validated assessment instruments.
    b) Integrated Assessment and Intervention: Every intervention and contact should be informed by the assessments.

12. **Professional Discretion:** Deviate from recommendations only for very specific reasons. For example, functional analysis may suggest that emotional distress is a risk/need factor for *this* person.

Organizational Principles: Settings, Staffing, and Management

13. **Community-based**: Community-based services are preferred but the principles of RNR also apply within residential and institutional settings.
14. **Core Correctional Staff Practices:** Effectiveness of interventions is enhanced when delivered by therapists and staff with *high-quality relationship skills* in combination with *high-quality structuring skills*. Quality relationships are characterized as respectful, caring, enthusiastic, collaborative, and valuing of personal autonomy. Structuring practices include prosocial modeling, effective reinforcement and disapproval, skill building, problem-solving, effective use of authority, advocacy/brokerage, cognitive restructuring, and motivational interviewing. Motivational interviewing skills include both relationship and structuring aspects of effective practice.
15. **Management**: Promote the selection, training, and clinical supervision of staff according to RNR and introduce monitoring, feedback, and adjustment systems. Build systems and cultures supportive of effective practice and continuity of care. Some additional specific indicators of integrity include having program manuals available, monitoring of service process and intermediate changes, adequate dosage, and involving researchers in the design and delivery of service.

Sources: Andrews, 1995, 2001; Andrews, Bonta & Hoge, 1990; Andrews & Bonta, 1994, 2006; Andrews, Zinger et al., 1990a; Bonta & Andrews, 2007; Gendreau, 1996.

---

and (c) what styles, modes and strategies of service are best employed (the general responsivity and specific responsivity principles).

The Core RNR Principles and Key Clinical Issues

In 1990, together with our colleague Robert Hoge, we presented three general principles of classification for purposes of effective correctional treatment: the (1) risk, (2) need, and (3) responsivity principles of effective correctional treatment (Andrews, Bonta & Hoge, 1990). Since then, as Table 2.1 demonstrates, we have added others. Because they are the core clinical principles—the source of the name RNR—we highlight human service delivery and adherence with the core clinical principles.

The Principle of Human Service. The typical legal and judicial principles of deterrence, restoration, just desert, and due process have little to do with the major risk/need factors. It is through human, clinical, and social services that the major causes of crime may be addressed.

The Risk Principle. There are two aspects to the *risk principle*. The first is that criminal behavior can be predicted. We began to provide the evidence that criminal behavior can be predicted in Chapter 1 and continue the process in the next section of Chapter 2 and throughout the text. The second aspect of the risk principle involves the idea of *matching levels of treatment services to the risk level of the offender*. This matching of service to offender risk is the essence of the risk principle and is the bridge between assessment and effective treatment. More precisely, higher-risk offenders need more intensive and extensive services if we are to hope for a significant reduction in recidivism. For the low-risk offender, minimal or even no intervention is sufficient.

Although the risk principle appears to make a great deal of common sense, sometimes theory and practice do not always agree. Some human service workers prefer to work with the motivated lower-risk clients rather than with the high-risk, resistant clients. After all, it is personally reinforcing to work with someone who listens and tries to follow your advice.

The largest known test of the risk principle was conducted by Christopher Lowenkamp and his colleagues (Lowenkamp, Latessa & Holsinger, 2006). Ninety-seven residential and nonresidential programs in the state of Ohio were reviewed as to how well they adhered to the risk principle. Information was collected on the length of time in a program, whether more services were offered to higher-risk offenders, and the delivery of cognitive behavioral programs to offenders. Providing intensive services to higher-risk offenders was associated with an 18 percent reduction of recidivism for offenders in residential programs and a nine percent reduction for offenders in nonresidential programs.

Table 2.2 provides some further examples of what happens when treatment is—or is not—matched to the risk level of the offender. In each of the studies, reductions in recidivism for high-risk offenders were found only when intensive levels of services were provided. However, when intensive services were provided to low-risk offenders, they had a negative effect. This detrimental effect is not found in all studies. In general, there is a very small positive effect (phi = .03; Andrews & Dowden, 2006). A meta-analytic review of 374 experimental tests of correctional treatment that explores the risk and other RNR principles will be summarized at the end of this chapter.

The Criminogenic Need Principle. Many offenders, especially high-risk offenders, have multiple needs. They "need" places to live and work

Table 2.2
Risk Level and Treatment (% Recidivism)

Study	Risk Level	Level of Treatment	
		Minimal	Intensive
O'Donnell et al. (1971)	Low	16	22
	High	78	56
Baird et al. (1979)	Low	3	10
	High	37	18
Andrews & Kiessling (1980)	Low	12	17
	High	58	31
Bonta et al. (2000a)	Low	15	32
	High	51	32
Lovins et al. (2007)	Low	12	26
	High	49	43

and/or they "need" to stop taking drugs. Some have poor self-esteem, chronic headaches, or cavities in their teeth. These are all needs or problematic circumstances. The *criminogenic need principle* draws our attention to the distinction between criminogenic and noncriminogenic needs, a point that we introduced when discussing dynamic risk factors in Chapter 1. Criminogenic needs are a subset of an offender's risk level. They are dynamic risk factors that, when changed, are associated with changes in the probability of recidivism. Noncriminogenic needs are also dynamic and changeable, but they are weakly associated with recidivism.

Our argument is that if treatment services are offered with the intention of reducing recidivism, changes must occur on criminogenic need factors. Offenders also have a right to the highest-quality service for other needs, but that is not the primary focus of *correctional* rehabilitation. Addressing noncriminogenic needs is unlikely to alter future recidivism significantly unless doing so indirectly impacts on criminogenic needs. Typically, noncriminogenic needs may be targeted for motivational purposes or on humanitarian grounds. We may help an offender feel better, which is important and valued, but this may not necessarily reduce recidivism.

The reader will note that criminogenic needs are actually represented by the Central Eight as outlined in the next section of this chapter. Noncriminogenic needs often fall among factors considered important in sociological and psychopathological theories of crime (as described in Chapter 3).

As an illustration of the link between criminogenic needs and criminal behavior, we select the criminogenic need of criminal attitudes. All theories— labeling theory, control theory, differential association, and so forth—in some way or another give respect to the role of criminal attitudes in criminal behavior (Andrews, 1990). Assessments of procriminal attitudes have repeatedly evidenced significant associations with criminal behavior among adult criminals (Andrews, Wormith & Kiessling, 1985; Bonta, 1990; Simourd, 1997; Simourd & Olver, 2002; Simourd & Van de Van, 1999; Walters, 1996) and young offenders (Shields & Ball, 1990; Shields & Whitehall, 1994).

There is also evidence for the *dynamic* validity of procriminal attitudes (see Table 2.3). Increases in procriminal attitudes are associated with increased recidivism, and recidivism decreases when the offender holds fewer procriminal beliefs and attitudes. In contrast, traditional clinical treatment targets, such as anxiety and emotional empathy, fail to demonstrate dynamic predictive validity. Continued research and development into the assessment of criminogenic needs will have enormous impact on the rehabilitation of offenders and the development of our conceptual understanding of criminal behavior.

The General Responsivity Principle. The *responsivity principle* refers to delivering treatment programs in a style and mode that is consistent with the ability and learning style of the offender. The *general responsivity principle* is quite straightforward: Offenders are human beings, and

Table 2.3
Three-Year Recidivism Rates by Six-Month Retest of Procriminal Attitude (N)

Intake Risk Level	Retest Risk Level			
	Low	Moderate	High	Overall
High (38)	7	43	40	29
Moderate (58)	10	37	57	33
Low (56)	10	20	67	16
Overall (152)	10	34	52	19
	(72)	(53)	(27)	(152)

From Andrews & Wormith, 1984

the most powerful influence strategies available are cognitive-behavioral and cognitive social learning strategies. It matters little whether the problem is antisocial behavior, depression, smoking, overeating, or poor study habits—cognitive-behavioral treatments are often more effective than other forms of intervention. Hence, one should use social learning and cognitive-behavioral styles of service to bring about change. These powerful influence strategies include modeling, reinforcement, role playing, skill building, modification of thoughts and emotions through cognitive restructuring, and practicing new, low-risk alternative behaviors over and over again in a variety of high-risk situations until one gets very good at it.

The Specific Responsivity Principle. There are many specific responsivity considerations. For example, an insight-oriented therapy delivered in a group format may not "connect" very well for a neurotic, anxious offender with limited intelligence. Offender characteristics such as interpersonal sensitivity, anxiety, verbal intelligence, and cognitive maturity speak to the appropriateness of different modes and styles of treatment service (Bonta, 1995). It is under the responsivity principle that many of the psychological approaches to offender assessment may have their value (Van Voorhis, 1997). By identifying personality and cognitive styles, treatment can be better matched to the client.

There have been a number of personality-based systems developed to guide the treatment of offenders. For example, the Conceptual Level system (Hunt & Hardt, 1965) was developed for use with juvenile delinquents and describes four stages of cognitive development (from egocentric thinking to an ability to think of problems from many different perspectives). Young offenders are assessed and categorized into one of the four conceptual level stages and then matched to different degrees of structured treatment. What is important in the Conceptual Level system and other similar systems (e.g., I-Level; Jesness, 1971) is the idea of differential treatment. That is, a certain treatment strategy and/or therapist are matched to the characteristics of the offender. Table 2.4 summarizes

Table 2.4
The Specific Responsivity Principle

PICO: Mean Follow-Up Months Incarcerated (Grant, 1965)

	Psychodynamic Casework		
Client Type	No	Yes	p
Amenable	4.8	2.1	*
Nonamenable	4.8	5.5	ns

Camp Elliott: Estimated Success Rates (Grant, 1965)

	Level of Structure		
Client Type	Low	High	p
High Maturity	.72	.60	*
Low Maturity	.46	.60	*

Recidivism Rates of Probationers (Andrews & Kiessling, 1980)

	Supervision by Citizen Volunteers		
Client Type	No	Yes	p
High Empathy	.80	.00	*
Low Empathy	.48	.42	ns

Mean # of New Offenses (Leschied, 1984)

	Level of Structure		
Client Type	Low	High	p
High Conceptual Level	nr	nr	nr
Low Conceptual Level	1.54	.47	*

p = probability; ns = not significant; nr = not reported

Adapted from Andrews et al. (1990)

a number of studies that found differential effects on outcome depending upon the type of treatment provided and the characteristics of the client, including a study that used the Conceptual Level system.

Only a few of the possible variables that come under the responsivity principle have been studied in any detail. Theories of personality and crime suggest a host of possibilities that have barely been considered by researchers in corrections. The issue of amenability or motivation to treatment is an important area of research. James Prochaska and his colleagues (Prochaska, DiClemente & Norcross, 1992) describe methods that a therapist can use to increase the client's motivation to change. Their work has been in the area of addictions, but some of the principles of "motivational interviewing" have relevance to general offenders (Ginsberg et al., 2002; Kennedy & Serin, 1999; Ogloff

& Davis, 2004) and sex offenders (Wilson & Barrett, 1999). Increasing motivation may be particularly important with high-risk offenders who tend to drop out of treatment. If we are to adhere to the risk principle, then we must ensure that high-risk offenders remain in treatment (Wormith & Olver, 2002).

Additional Clinical Principles

Principle 9 (**Breadth**) highlights the importance of targeting multiple criminogenic needs when working with high-risk cases. The higher the risk, the more criminogenic (dynamic risk factors) become evident. Thus, addressing only one or two criminogenic needs among high-risk offenders does not go as far as targeting the multiple criminogenic needs of these individuals.

Principle 10 (**Strength**) has implications for both the accurate prediction of recidivism and for specific responsivity. In regard to prediction, recall the discussion of strengths in Chapter 1. To date, however, there are few examples in the practical world of risk assessment that actually demonstrates improved accuracy when considerations of strengths and risk are combined.

Principle 11 (**Structured Assessment**) underscores the evidence that the validity of structured assessments greatly exceeds that of unstructured professional judgment. In order to adhere to the risk principle, one must reliably differentiate low-risk cases from higher-risk cases, and structured risk assessments do a better job at this than unstructured judgments of risk.

Principle 12 (**Professional Discretion**) recognizes that professional judgment on rare occasions may override structured decisionmaking. However, this principle also stresses that the use of professional discretion must be clearly documented.

Overarching Principles

Principle 1 is overarching because any intervention is expected to respect the norms of the broader and narrower communities of which it is a part. This is as true for correctional activities as it is for the delivery of recreational, dental, medical, or any other services. Ethicality, legality, decency, and cost-efficiency are widely appreciated standards of conduct. All forms of human, social and clinical services are subject to evaluations in regard to ethicality, legality, and some other norms. It is equally true, as indicated in Principle 1, that there is some setting-specificity in the normative context. For example, it is perhaps fair to say that an ethic of caring is more readily evident in some forensic mental health settings than in some prison settings.

The normative principle is not to be confused with the active "ingredients" of service. The active ingredients for reduced offending are adherence with the core principles of human service, including the principles of risk, criminogenic need, and responsivity. Under certain conditions, adherence with relevant norms will have a positive impact on treatment outcome. For example, addressing noncriminogenic needs may well enhance motivation for participation in treatment and/or enhance an offender's ability to participate more fully in treatment.

Principle 2 recommends that psychological understandings of crime be drawn upon. If you are interested in the criminal behavior of individuals, be sure to work from theoretical perspectives on the criminal behavior of individuals. In particular, general personality and cognitive social learning (GPCSL) theoretical perspectives are recommended. GPCSL perspectives are unsurpassed in their power and wide applicability. Their power resides in (a) the identification of effective clinical practices and interpersonal influence strategies of wide applicability, (b) the specification of major risk, need, and responsivity factors in the analysis and prediction of criminal and noncriminal alternative behavior, (c) a ready integration with biological/neuropsychological perspectives as well as broader social structural and cultural perspectives, and (d) the flexibility to incorporate new conceptions and strategies (such as motivational interviewing). GPCSL is reviewed in detail in Chapter 4.

Principle 3 extends the RNR model of crime prevention to health and other agencies outside of justice and corrections.

Organizational Principles

Principles 13 through 15 stress the importance for policy and management to support the integrity of RNR programming. Staff cannot deliver programs and services in adherence to RNR without the support of their own organization and those of other agencies (mental health, social services, etc.) that can support the rehabilitation of offenders. Note that the relationship and structuring skills inherent in staff practice draw directly upon GPCSL-based interpersonal influence strategies and behavior change approaches.

Alternatives to RNR

Alternatives to the RNR model have been suggested. For example, Ward, Melzer, and Yates (2007) have forwarded a Good Lives Model (GLM). This model posits that personal well-being is attained through the "human goods" of enjoyable friendships, work that is valued, and sexual satisfaction. Is this a better alternative to the GPCSL-based RNR approach to work with moderate and higher-risk offenders? A Good Lives Model would suggest the following:

1. Offer intensive crime prevention services to low-risk offenders. Our response: Why? They have a low probability of reoffending even without service.

2. Rely on punishment. Our response: Official sanctions will not reduce criminal offending unless human services are delivered in adherence with the principles of RNR.

3. Rely on increasing the personal well-being of the offender. Our response: That is a valid humanitarian aspect of RNR, but it will not reduce criminal offending unless the services are otherwise and additionally in adherence with the principles of RNR. There is no reason to expect reduced reoffending if the criminogenic needs of moderate and higher-risk cases are not reduced.

GLM's conceptualization of rehabilitation suggests that living a fulfilling life is incompatible with crime. Another motto is that enhancing personal well-being automatically results in reduced criminogenic needs. These slogans utterly miss the importance of the contingencies of human action that are stressed within GPCSL perspectives.

Consider the importance of living the most fulfilling life possible through achievement of satisfactions associated with friendship, enjoyable work, loving relationships, creative pursuits, sexual satisfaction, positive self-regard, and intellectual challenge. A simple exercise is to count the ways in which the achievement of such satisfactions could readily increase crime: (1) friendship and loving relationships (with criminal others that increase criminal associates and may also weaken friendships with noncriminal others and foster the acquisition of antisocial sentiments); (2) enjoyable work (the often quick and easy route to rewards and the sometimes exciting pursuit of a criminal career); (3) creative pursuits/intellectual challenge (the joy of beating the system); (4) positive self-regard (personal pride in criminal achievements); and (5) sexual satisfaction (through exploitation of children and/or sexual aggression).

Interventions are supportive of crime if the interventions do not shift the supports for crime in a direction unfavorable to crime (or a shift in the direction of risk factors becoming strength factors). As you proceed through PCC, you will discover example after example of well-intentioned family programs, vocational programs, and substance abuse programs all failing to reduce criminal recidivism unless the contingencies are shifted through adherence with the principles of RNR.

Summary

In the context of GPCSL, crime cannot be understood without understanding whether the personal, interpersonal, and community supports for human behavior are favorable or unfavorable to crime. When the contingencies of human action are ignored, actions based on the rhetoric of official punishment, fundamental human needs, and positive goals can be criminogenic. It is not sufficient to highlight personal well-being or to highlight the accumulation of rewards and satisfactions. It must be made explicit that the contingencies should be supportive of noncriminal alternative routes to rewards. That is what adherence with the principles of RNR is designed to support. Now an overview of the research findings in regard to risk/need factors will be outlined, as will be some research findings in regard to applications of the RNR model.

The Major and Moderate Risk/Need Factors

The Best Validated of Risk/Need Factors

What are the major risk/need factors in the analysis of criminal behavior, and how strongly are they associated with criminal behavior, on their own and when acting in combination? Most often we will use the Pearson correlation coefficient (r) as the measure of strength of association (or effect size). We should be able to rank order potential risk/need factors in terms of the strength of their covariation, or at least form sets of major, moderate, and minor risk factors. Here you will be introduced to the *"Central Eight"* risk/need factors, which incorporate the *"Big Four."* The "Big Four" are proposed to be the major predictor variables and indeed the major causal variables in the analysis of criminal behavior of individuals.

As a preamble to the forthcoming discussion, it will help if you recognize where your authors were coming from when they began doing meta-analyses in the late 1980s. As social psychologists of knowledge will explain, the conclusions drawn from research must in part reflect the decisions made by primary researchers, the meta-analysts themselves, and by reviewers of the meta-analytic reviews. Some of the values underlying our version of PCC were outlined in Chapter 1. While trying to remain open to all types of potential risk/need/strength factors, we are not favorably predisposed toward the social location perspectives, the early forensic mental health perspectives, or deterrence and some other justice perspectives. In part this reflects our understanding of the research literature, including the weak power of the social location, mental health, and deterrence variables found in our own early research and early reviews of the literature.

Before the meta-analytic explosion of the 1990s, the authors (Don Andrews, Jim Bonta, and colleagues such as Robert Hoge, Stephen Wormith, and Paul Gendreau) had a decent handle on the state of both sets of research studies (risk/need factors and correctional treatment). Our group already "knew" by the early 1980s, from our own research and from narrative reviews of the literature by members of our group and by others, that social class of origin and personal emotional distress and mental disorder were minor risk factors at best. We "knew" that various measures of antisocial personality pattern, antisocial attitudes, antisocial associates, a history of antisocial behavior, substance abuse, and problematic circumstances at home and at school or work were all risk factors for criminal behavior. "How could one read Glueck and Glueck (1950), Hirschi (1969), and subsequent longitudinal studies and continue to declare the relative importance of mental illness and class of origin," we thought. "How could one read the literature on the effects of official punishment and correctional treatment and believe that punishment works and treatment does not work," we wondered. And then the meta-analyses began to appear on the academic scene: PCC was energized, and much of what was mainstream sociological criminology and mainstream forensic mental health collapsed and then reformed all in a short period of about 15 years. Deterrence and other justice models, such as restoration, may also now be in the process of transformation through the welcoming arms of therapeutic jurisprudence (Andrews & Dowden, 2007).

In the early 1980s, the first version of the Level of Service Inventory–Revised (LSI-R) was in use in the province of Ontario, Canada (Andrews, 1982, 1994; Andrews & Bonta, 1995). That offender risk/need assessment instrument was built to be scored by probation and parole officers through interviews with offenders and relevant others (e.g., family members) and through reviews of correctional agency and police or court files. The instrument was composed of a set of risk/need items that fell in the domains of antisocial attitudes, antisocial associates, criminal history, substance abuse, family/marital, school/work, leisure recreation, financial problems, accommodation problems, and personal/emotional issues that included signs of antisocial personality problems mixed in with mental health issues. This was our first structured outline of the Central Eight risk and need factors.

The risk/need section of the newer version of the LSI-R (LS/CMI or Level of Service/Case Management Inventory; Andrews, Bonta & Wormith, 2004) has been reduced to the Central Eight (including antisocial personality pattern) with a supplementary sampling of history of violence and aggression. The LS/CMI and the youth version (YLS/CMI: Hoge & Andrews, 2002) are also now gender-informed instruments in that a wider range of noncriminogenic needs are sampled for purposes of program planning. Research over the years with the Level of Service (LS) instruments has greatly sharpened our appreciation of the power of the Central Eight and in particular the predictive power of the Big Four.

All in all, our research and experience up to the 1990s set us to see the world in terms of major, moderate, and minor risk/need factors. That model has generally been supported by the meta-analyses summarized below. We included this introductory piece, however, to alert the reader to the fact that while we were shaped to discuss the Central Eight, other researchers may choose to describe the major and minor risk/need factors in different ways.

To our knowledge, with perhaps a few exceptions in critical (Marxist/socialist) criminology, critical feminism, and feminism in portions of sociological criminology, there are few investigators or scholars who would deny the overall pattern of results that are described herein. We return to those exceptions presently.

Some researchers do not impose any theoretical order on the findings. They tend to be pure "empiricists" who seek risk assessments composed of the smallest number of assessed factors needed to maximize predictive accuracy. Typically, statistical techniques are employed to select that minimum number of predictive factors. In Chapter 10, these types of risk assessment approaches will be called "second generation" because they tend to ignore dynamic risk factors (or criminogenic needs). On the other hand, the LS instruments, as noted above, are called "third generation" instruments because they carefully survey the major criminogenic needs, or "fourth generation" because in addition to the survey of needs (criminogenic and noncriminogenic) they structure case planning in a manner that is in adherence with the RNR model. As will be seen in Chapter 10, the best of the second-generation instruments do very well as risk assessment instruments, but they are otherwise of very limited value in selecting appropriate intermediate targets and other aspects of service planning. To our knowledge, supporters of second-generation assessments do not deny the evidence that we will be reviewing. Simply expressed, primarily they are interested in efficient risk assessment and not the planning of crime prevention services with moderate- and higher-risk cases.

Other researchers may not refer to the Big Four or the Central Eight but do impose different labeling or classification systems. For example, antisocial personality and criminal history may be combined to form a measure of "antisociality," "antisocial potential," or for that matter, Hare's (1991) assessment of "psychopathic personality."

Some prefer to say that all of the Central Eight are the expression of a single factor. Hirschi (2004) called that single factor "weak self-control." These alternative labeling approaches will be introduced throughout the text. To our knowledge, investigators who prefer alternative descriptive labels do not deny the evidence that we outline. As noted above, to our knowledge, with perhaps a few exceptions in critical and feminist portions of sociological criminology, there are few investigators or scholars who would deny the evidence. We will take a fresh look at the issue of gender differences shortly.

For now, we want readers to appreciate the state of the evidence on risk/need factors very early in the textbook without arguing about the fine points of measurement and conceptualization. We will develop the theoretical, measurement, and methodological issues as we proceed through the story of PCC.

A Narrative Summary of the Central Eight

Table 2.5 provides a narrative summary of the Central Eight risk/need factors, beginning with the Big Four and followed by the moderate four. Note that the table also specifies dynamic aspects of each risk factor

Table 2.5
Major Risk/Need Factors: The Central Eight

The Big Four

1. **History of Antisocial Behavior**. This includes early involvement in a number and variety of antisocial activities in a variety of settings, such as in the home and out of the home. Major indicators include being arrested at a young age, a large number of prior offenses, and rule violations while on conditional release. Place little weight on the seriousness of the current offense or the amount of injury imposed by the current offense. The latter is an aggravating factor at the time of sentencing, but that is not the same as being a risk factor. In risk assessment, place the emphasis on early onset and number and variety of offenses.
   Strength: Antisocial behavior is absent or so rare that procriminal contributions to antisocial attitudes will be minimal.
   Dynamic need and promising intermediate targets of change: A history cannot be changed, but appropriate intermediate targets of change include building up new noncriminal behaviors in high-risk situations and building self-efficacy beliefs supporting reform ("I know what to do to avoid criminal activity and I know that I can do what is required").

2. **Antisocial Personality Pattern**. In everyday language: impulsive, adventurous pleasure-seeking, generalized trouble (multiple persons, multiple settings), restlessly aggressive, callous disregard for others (see Glueck and Glueck's research in Chapter 3). Other classifications and descriptions of Antisocial Personality Pattern include:
   Defined according to the Multidimensional Personality Questionnaire (Caspi, Moffitt et al., 1994; Patrick, Curtin & Tellegen, 2002). Weak Constraint (low on traditionalism, or endorsing high moral standards; low on harm avoidance, or low on avoiding excitement and danger; low on self-control; low on being reflective and planful). Negative Emotionality (aggression, or causes discomfort in others; alienation and feels mistreated; stress reaction dominated by anger and irritability). Note that Positive Emotionality is not a major correlate of delinquency (the indicators of positive emotionality include being happy, having positive self-esteem, and being sociable).
   Defined according to the Five Factor Model (Miller & Lynman, 2001; Digman, 1990): Low Agreeableness (hostile, spiteful, jealous, self-centered, indifferent to others, antagonistic) and Low Conscientiousness (lack persistence, impulsive, weak planning, weak constraint, criminal values). The following are not major correlates: extraversion (as defined by sociability), openness to experience, and neuroticism (except for items that suggest irritability).
   Defined according to the Seven Factor Model (Cloninger et al., 1993): Novelty Seeking (intense exhilaration/excitement in response to novelty). Low Self-Directedness (self-determination and willpower). Low Cooperativeness (tending to be antagonistic and hostile, not agreeable). Harm avoidance, persistence, and self-transcendence (spirituality) are not associated with antisocial behavior.

Defined according to the four facets of Hare Psychopathy Checklist (Hare, 2003): The strongest facet is a history of antisocial behavior (as noted above). The weaker facets are the personality aspects of interpersonal glibness, shallow affect and lack of guilt, parasitic lifestyle.

Defined according to the LS/CMI (Andrews, Bonta & Wormith, 2004). Indicators of psychopathy and/or anger problems. Early and diverse antisocial behavior. Criminal attitudes. Generalized trouble in multiple domains.

Strength: High restraint, thinks before acting, highly agreeable.

Dynamic need and promising intermediate targets of change: The dynamic aspects of personality are weak self-control skills, weak anger management skills, and poor problem-solving skills, and the intermediate targets, of course, are to build up those skills.

3. **Antisocial Cognition**. This set of variables includes attitudes, values, beliefs, rationalizations, and a personal identity that is favorable to crime. The cognitive-emotional states associated with crime are anger and feeling irritated, resentful, and/or defiant. Specific indicators would include identification with criminals, negative attitudes toward the law and justice system, a belief that crime will yield rewards, and rationalizations that specify a broad range of conditions under which crime is justified (e.g., the victim deserved it, the victim is worthless).

    Strength: Rejects antisocial sentiments; personal identity is explicitly anticriminal and prosocial.

    Dynamic need and promising intermediate targets of change: The antisocial cognitions are subject to change through reduction of antisocial thinking and feeling and through building and practicing less risky thoughts and feelings

4. **Antisocial Associates**. This risk/need factor includes both association with procriminal others and relative isolation from anticriminal others. This risk/need factor is sometimes called "social support for crime."

    Strength: Close and frequent association with anticriminal others; no association with criminal others.

    Dynamic need and promising intermediate targets of change: This factor is dynamic, and the appropriate intermediate targets are again obvious: reduce association with procriminal others and enhance association with anticriminal others.

The Moderate Four

5. **Family/Marital Circumstances**. The key to assessing both family of origin for young people and marital circumstances for older people is the quality of the interpersonal relationships within the unit (parent-child or spouse-spouse) and the behavioral expectations and rules in regard to antisocial behavior, including monitoring, supervision, and disciplinary approaches. In assessments of youths, the two key parenting variables are nurturance/caring and monitoring supervision. On the part of the young people themselves, look for the young person caring about the parent and caring about the parent's opinions. In the case of marriage (or its equivalent), look for a high-quality relationship (mutual caring, respect, and interest) in combination with anticriminal expectations ("Do you know where your spouse is?"). The risk factor is poor-quality relationships in combination with either neutral expectations with regard to crime or procriminal expectations.

    Strength: Strong nurturance and caring in combination with strong monitoring and supervision.

    Dynamic need and promising intermediate targets of change. Reduce conflict, build positive relationships, enhance monitoring and supervision.

6. **School/Work**. Yet again we place a major emphasis on the quality of the interpersonal relationships within the settings of school and/or work. Generally, the risk/need factors are low levels of performance and involvement and low levels of rewards and satisfactions.

    Strength: Strong attachments to fellow students/colleagues along with authority figures in combination with high levels of performance and satisfaction at school/work.

    Dynamic need and promising intermediate targets of change: Enhance performance, involvement, and rewards and satisfactions.

7. **Leisure/Recreation**. Low levels of involvement and satisfactions in anticriminal leisure pursuits.

    Strength: High levels of involvement in and satisfactions in anticriminal leisure pursuits.

Table 2.5 *(continued)*

Dynamic need and promising intermediate targets of change: Enhance involvement and rewards and satisfactions.

8. **Substance Abuse**. The risk/need factor is problems with alcohol and/or other drugs (tobacco excluded). Current problems with substances indicate higher risk than a prior history of abuse.
   Strengths: No evidence of risky substance abuse, and sentiments tend to be negative toward substance abuse.
   Dynamic need and promising intermediate targets of change: Reduce substance abuse, reduce the personal and interpersonal supports for substance-oriented behavior, enhance alternatives to substance abuse.

Note: The minor risk/need factors (and less promising intermediate targets of change) include the following: personal/emotional distress, major mental disorder, physical health issues, fear of official punishment, social class of origin, seriousness of current offense, and other factors unrelated or only mildly related to offending.

(that is, the criminogenic need factors) as well as appropriate intermediate targets of change when an ultimate interest is reduced future offending. The positive extremes are listed as strengths. Each factor is thereby formulated to encourage adherence with the risk, criminogenic need, and strength principles of RNR.

The specification of a history of antisocial behavior notes the importance of not equating risk of offending with seriousness of the current offense. The indicators of risk are early involvement, an extensive history, a variety of antisocial activities (property plus violent offences), and rule violations even while under supervision (e.g., parole violations).

A major error in risk assessment is to score seriousness of the current offense as a risk factor. It is not a major risk factor. It is an aggravating factor in sentencing (in the sense that the more serious the injury imposed by an offense, the more severe the penalty). Just desert and risk of reoffending reflect different concerns.

The descriptions of antisocial personality factors uses everyday language as well as the more precise language associated with certain well known personality classification and dimensional systems. You will learn more about those systems in subsequent chapters, and you do not need to feel that you must have an in-depth appreciation for each system now. An antisocial personality pattern in regard to risk/need typically involves at least two relatively independent dimensions. One is weak self-control and a lack of planning. The second is negative emotionality (in the sense of irritability, feeling mistreated, and being antagonistic).

It is important to note that the trait measures of antisocial pattern assess these predispositions as relatively stable, enduring factors. However, self-control and negative emotionality may also be assessed as acute dynamic factors. Acute changes, such as an angry outburst, are highly important in a GPCSL understanding of variation in criminal activity.

Finally, the personality research is also very helpful in identifying factors that have very little to offer in understanding individual differences in criminal activity. Considering so many misunderstandings of crime and criminals that are widely and actively promoted, it is quite helpful to attend to those aspects of personality that are not associated with criminal activity in a major way. These weak factors include happiness, self-esteem, sociability, spirituality, openness to experience, feelings of anxiety and worry, and psychopathology. We will be returning to these issues throughout the text because misunderstandings of crime and criminals are so common. It appears that some happy people are offenders, and many are not offenders; some sad people are offenders, and many sad people are not; and so on. You should feel free to provide your own examples.

Some of these noncriminogenic factors may well be specific responsivity factors. You may approach and work with sad people in ways that are different from the ways you work with happy people. Some sad offenders may be so sad that they are unable to focus on treatment. Some happy offenders may be so happy with their being and circumstances that they show little interest in making any changes. Why would they want to reduce criminogenic needs when their criminal activity is obviously contributing to their well-being?

Meta-Analyses of Risk/Need Factors

Resource Note 2.1 summarizes an early meta-analysis conducted primarily at the University of New Brunswick by Paul Gendreau, Claire Goggin, and Chantel Chanteloupe. It was a primitive meta-analysis in many ways, but its overall pattern of results has now been replicated by many reviewers. You will note for purposes of categorization, in those early years, studies of antisocial attitudes and antisocial associates were pooled in a single category. Similarly, antisocial personality pattern and history of antisocial behavior were pooled. Thus, the Big Four were represented by only two categories. In the early study, parent characteristics (e.g., father's criminal history) and family structure (e.g., single-parent home) were pooled with studies of family cohesiveness and parenting practices.

Inspection of Resource Note 2.1 reveals that the pattern was clear. Lower-class origins and personal distress/psychopathology were minor risk factors compared to the other sets of variables. This was true for males and females, whites and blacks, and for younger and older persons. The pattern was evident whether cross-sectional or longitudinal designs research were used and whether criminal behavior was defined by self-report or by official records. Whatever way you cut it, attitudes/associates and personality/history were most strongly correlated with criminal behavior.

Resource Note 2.1

The University of New Brunswick/Carleton University Meta-analysis of Predictors of Criminal Behavior: Highlights of Findings

This ongoing project (Gendreau, Andrews, Goggin & Chanteloupe, 1992) involves a survey of all studies of the correlates of crime published in the English language since 1970. The studies were uncovered through automated library searches, surveys of key review articles, and follow-ups on reference lists of the studies in hand.

Approximately 1,000 studies had been listed, 700 studies located, and 372 studies subjected to content analysis and meta-analysis. These 372 studies yielded more than 1,770 Pearson correlation coefficients, each of which reflected the covariation of some potential correlate of individual criminal conduct with some measure of criminal conduct.

Reflecting the general personality and social psychological perspective underlying this text, particular risk/need factors were assigned to seven categories. These categories were: (1) lower-class origins as assessed by parental educational and occupational indices and neighborhood characteristics, (2) personal distress indicators, including "psychological" measures of anxiety, depression, and low self-esteem as well as more "sociological" assessments of anomie and alienation, (3) personal educational/vocational/economic achievement, (4) parental psychological status and functioning as well as family cohesiveness and parenting practices, (5) antisocial temperament, personality, and behavioral history, (6) antisocial attitudes and antisocial associates, and (7) other variables not obviously fitting within the first six categories.

The mean correlation coefficients for each of the first six categories of risk/need factors were as follows (with number of coefficients in parentheses):

1. Lower-Class Origins   .06 (97)
2. Personal Distress/   .08 (226)
   Psychopathology
3. Personal Education/   .12 (129)
   Vocational Achievement
4. Parental/Family Factors   .18 (334)
5. Temperament/   .21 (621)
   Misconduct/Personality
6. Antisocial Attitudes/   .22 (168)
   Associates

The rank ordering of the six sets of risk/need factors has proven to be very robust across various types of subjects (differentiated according to gender, age, and race) and across methodological variables (such as self-report versus official measures of crime and longitudinal versus cross-sectional designs). The robustness of these findings is illustrated in the following table:

In summary, the research findings reveal that lower-class origins and personal distress are *minor* risk factors for criminality relative to indicators of antisocial propensity drawn from assessments of family, personality, attitudes, and interpersonal association patterns.

Mean Correlation Coefficient by Type of Risk/Need Factor and Various Control Variables (N)
Type of Risk/Need Factor

	1		2		3		4		5		6	
Overall	.06	(97)	.08	(226)	.12	(129)	.18	(334)	.21	(621)	.22	(168)
Gender												
Male	.04	(58)	.09	(157)	.11	(180)	.16	(180)	.18	(461)	.21	(113)
Female	.03	(12)	.08	(19)	.13	(7)	.16	(43)	.23	(38)	.23	(12)

Resource Note 2.1 (continued)

Mean Correlation Coefficient by Type of Risk/Need Factor and Various Control Variables (N)
Type of Risk/Need Factor

	1		2		3		4		5		6	
Age												
Juvenile	.03	(49)	.09	(66)	.10	(40)	.18	(151)	.22	(142)	.23	(63)
Adult	.05	(49)	.09	(105)	.12	(60)	.11	(64)	.18	(301)	.19	(50)
Race												
White	.05	(20)	.09	(102)	.10	(56)	.20	(148)	.19	(235)	.24	(77)
Black	.07	(7)	.05	(6)	.17	(5)	.12	(22)	.22	(23)	.29	(10)
Measure of Crime												
Self-reported	.00	(28)	.08	(31)	.10	(19)	.14	(94)	.20	(58)	.25	(42)
Official	.06	(40)	.10	(140)	.12	(81)	.18	(121)	.19	(385)	.19	(71)
Design												
Longitudinal	.11	(47)	.08	(152)	.14	(89)	.17	(179)	.21	(423)	.20	(118)
Cross-sectional	.03	(50)	.08	(74)	.08	(40)	.19	(156)	.19	(198)	.27	(50)

1) Lower-Class Origins 2) Personal Distress/Pathology 3) Personal Education/Vocational Achievement
4) Parental/Family Factors 5) Temperament/Misconduct/Personality 6) Antisocial Attitudes/Associates

Linda Simourd, at Carleton University at the time, was particularly interested in adolescent criminality and gender (Simourd & Andrews, 1994). She drew a fresh set of studies, each of which assessed both young men and young women with the same instruments. As summarized in Table 2.6, it is stunning how similar her findings were to the University of New Brunswick findings. The similarity is evident in regard to the relatively weak strength of class of origin and personal distress and the stronger validity of personality. Linda Simourd added some improvements to the analysis. She hypothesized that the parenting skills of nurturance/caring and monitoring/supervision were more important than family structure (single-parent status, etc.) and parental history

Table 2.6
Mean r by Gender (k = number of primary correlations)

		Female	Male	Total
(1)	Lower-Class Origins	.07	.06	.05 (38)
(2)	Personal Distress/Psychopathology	.10	.09	.07 (34)
(3)	Family Structure/Parent Problems	.07	.09	.07 (28)
(4)	Minor Personality Variables	.18	.22	.12 (18)
(5)	Poor Parent–Child Relations	.20	.22	.20 (82)
(6)	Personal Education/Vocational Achievement	.24	.23	.28 (68)
(7)	Temperament/Weak Self Control/Misconduct History	.35	.36	.38 (90)
(8)	Antisocial Attitudes/Associates	.39	.40	.48 (106)

Adapted from Simourd and Andrews, 1994

variables. Note that the mean *r*s for the latter variables were no greater than those for personal distress while parent-child relations were much more strongly associated with youthful offending. Linda Simourd also strengthened the personality/history set by putting factors such as extroversion in the minor personality set. The personality set then only included personality factors such as psychopathy, weak self-control, anger, and resentment, with substantial gains in the mean effect size. The pattern was virtually identical for the boys and for the girls. Remember, the correlations do not imply that the boys and girls are equally involved in criminal activity or that they score in similar ways on measures of the risk/need factors. Indeed, if young women are less involved in criminal behavior than are young men, we expect that young women will score as lower-risk on average on at least some of the factors than do the young men.

Table 2.7 is interesting because it summarizes the findings of eight separate meta-analyses, including the two noted above. This is possible because each meta-analysis made use of the Pearson *r* as the measure of effect size and hence we can report on the grand mean effect size for each of the Central Eight risk/need areas and we can compute separate grand means for the Big Four and the residual four of the Central Eight. We also report a grand mean for a set of risk/need factors that we label minor a priori on the basis noted in our introduction to this section. Not all of the meta-analytic studies computed the *r* values in exactly the same way but that is controlled for in that the minor variations were constant within meta-analytic studies.

CI is the Confidence Interval that gives the range of values that are likely to occur around the mean effect size. Typically, the CI is set at 95 percent, meaning that 95 percent of the time the true mean falls within that interval. The grand mean *r* for the Big Four was .26, and 95 percent of the time the true mean would fall between .22 and .30 (the CI range). The grand mean for the moderate set was .17 with a CI of .13 to .20. The mean for the minor set was .03 (CI = −.02 to .08). The latter CI includes .00, hence the mean of .03 is not significantly different than .00, which indicates that on average there is no relationship between the potential predictor variables and criminal behavior.

This pattern of results is rather powerful evidence for the predictive power of the Big Four (and the Central Eight) relative to lower-class origins, personal distress, and fear of official punishment. The CIs are nonoverlapping and thus the three means are significantly different statistically. However, only one meta-analytic study included leisure/recreation as a potential risk/need factor, and that study was Number Five, which included the Central Eight subscales of the LS/CMI (as noted above). Obviously, more work is needed on leisure /recreation as a member of the Central Eight.

The Predictive Validity of Composite Assessments of the Central Eight

The applicability of the findings reviewed in Tables 2.3 through 2.7 is a major theoretical, empirical, and practical issue. The LS/CMI is a comprehensive offender assessment instrument and will be described more fully in Chapter 10. The first section of the LS/CMI provides a General Risk/Need score, which is the sum of scores on assessments of the Central

Table 2.7
The Correlation (*r*) Between Criminal Behavior and the Central Eight, Personal Emotional Distress, and Lower-Class Origins: Mean Estimates from Eight Meta-Analyses

			Meta-analytic Review					
	One	Two	Three	Four	Five	Six	Seven	Eight
History of Antisocial Behavior								
	.21p	.38p	.16	.26	.35	.22	.28	.16
Antisocial Personality Pattern								
	nt	nt	.18	19	.31	.12	.34	.33
Antisocial Attitudes								
	.22p	.48p	.18	nt	.21	nt	.15	.36
Antisocial Associates								
	nt	nt	.21	.37	.27	nt	nt	.28
Grand Mean of Big Four Risk/Need Mean Estimates (.26, 95% CI = .22/.30, k = 24)								
	.22	**.43**	**.18**	**.27**	**.29**	**.17**	**.26**	**.28**
Family/Marital								
	.18	.20	.10	.19	.16	.10	.14	.33
Education/Employment								
	.12	.28	.13	.19	.28	.04	.17	.21
Substance Abuse								
	nt	nt	.10	.06	.24	.11	.22	.06
Leisure/Recreation								
	nt	nt	nt	nt	.21	nt	nt	nt
Grand Mean of Moderate Risk/Need Mean Estimates (.17, 95% CI = .13/.20, k = 23)								
	.15	**.24**	**.11**	**.15**	**.22**	**.08**	**.18**	**.20**
Lower-Class Origins								
	.06	.05	.05	.10	nt	.00	nt	nt
Fear of Official Punishment (Deterrence)								
	nt	nt	nt	nt	nt	nt	nt	−.25
Personal Distress / Psychopathology								
	.08	.07	.05	nt	.14	−.04	.02	−.08
Verbal Intelligence								
	nt	nt	.07	.11	nt	.01	nt	nt
Grand Mean of Minor Risk Factor Mean Estimates (.03, 95% CI = −.02/.08, k = 16)								
	.07	**.06**	**.07**	**.11**	**.14**	**−.01**	**.02**	**−.17**

p: pooled estimates for attitudes / associates and for history/personality; nt: not tested.

Notes: The meta-analytic studies: One: Gendreau, Andrews, Goggin & Chanteloupe (1992); Andrews & Bonta (2003:75–76). Two: Simourd & Andrews (1994). Three: Gendreau, Little & Goggin (1996). Four: Lipsey & Derzon (1998). Five: from data in Andrews, Bonta & Wormith (2004). Six: Bonta, Law & Hanson (1998); Seven: Hanson & Morton-Bourgon (2004). Eight: Dowden & Andrews (1999ab); Andrews & Bonta (2003:310).

Eight risk/need factors. The scores may be grouped into five levels of risk/need from Very Low to Very High. The scores have been found to link with reoffending in U.S., Canadian, Singaporean, and U.K. samples of men and women and various other groups (Andrews et al., 2004). Inspection of Table 2.8 reveals the recidivism rates for offenders from Ontario, Canada. Overall, in the total sample, the recidivism rates increased directly with LS/CMI risk/need scores (the correlation of risk and reoffending was .44). The recidivism rates are presented as percentages at each level of risk/need. Examining the first row, it is evident that 9 percent of the 151 probationers scoring very low-risk recidivated, 20 percent of the 169 low-risk cases recidivated, through to 100 percent of the two very high-risk cases.

In two of the meta-analyses already reviewed in this chapter, we have seen that the predictive validity estimates were virtually identical for male and female samples. Still, it is not at all unusual in the feminist and critical criminology literature to read that the predictive validity of the Central Eight does not hold up for various combinations of age, gender, and poverty. Indeed, it is sometimes said that the predictive value of members of the Central Eight *really* reflect the predictive power of age, gender, and socio-economic inequality. These challenges demand serious consideration and will be considered throughout the text. For now, and very briefly so, we explore the applicability issue with the LS/CMI General Risk/Need scale that we mentioned has helped to shape our views regarding prediction.

Table 2.8 presents the association between LS/CMI risk/need and the recidivism of female and male probationers, for young and adult offenders, and for those who rely on social assistance and those who are

Table 2.8
Percent Reoffending by Intake LS/CMI General Risk /Need Level for Subgroups of 561 Probationers Based on Gender and Poverty (n).

	Risk Level				
Very Low (0–4)	Low (5–10)	Medium (11–19)	High (20–29)	Very High (30+)	r with Recidivism
Total Sample					
09 (151)	20 (169)	48 (196)	72 (43)	100 (2)	.44
Female Offenders					
05 (37)	11 (27)	37 (24)	78 (9)	—(0)	.50
Male Offenders					
10 (114)	22 (142)	49 (172)	71 (34)	100 (2)	.41
Young Offenders					
09 (32)	31 (39)	59 (51)	87 (16)	100 (2)	.52
Adult Offenders					
09 (119)	17 (130)	44 (145)	63 (27)	—(0)	.38
Poverty: Relies on Social Assistance					
09 (11)	25 (24)	47 (72)	77 (22)	—(0)	.39
Does Not Rely on Social Assistance					
09 (140)	19 (145)	48 (124)	67 (21)	100 (2)	.43

not economically dependent on the state. The values in the table come from a re-analysis of the original LSI databank (Andrews & Bonta, 1995). Generally, the assessment scores were predictive of criminal futures within the total sample and within subgroups defined by gender, age, and social class.

Table 2.8 was intended to be descriptive and illustrative. Later in the text (Chapter 10), we will explore the issues of wide applicability meta-analytically, and do so in detail. The evidence is that LS general risk/need predicts the criminal recidivism of female offenders at least as well as it does that of male offenders. In other words, LS risk/need is a gender-neutral predictor of criminal recidivism, even though it is well-established that, on average, male offenders are more likely to reoffend than are female offenders.

Indeed, generally, boys are more likely to engage in antisocial activity than are girls, and the gender difference in criminal activity extends into adolescence and adulthood. Still, gender similarities in the predictive validity of some risk/need factors far outweigh gender differences. If males are more into offending, it suggests that, on average, they score higher on risk/need factors than do females. It does not imply that there are gender differences in what constitutes risk/need factors.

Likewise, gender differences in scores on particular domains of need do not imply gender differences in the predictive validity of those particular domains. For example, it is often noted that women experience more incidents of sexual abuse and greater levels of emotional distress than do men. However, that does not mean that there are gender differences in the validity of assessments of victimization or anxiety in the prediction of offending.

Few, if any, scholars and/or practitioners would deny the existence of some gender-specificity in risk/need factors. Male-specific factors are predictive only with males. Female-specific factors are predictive only with females. Empirically, however, the establishment of gender similarities and differences in the predictive validity of risk/need factors must actually be based on studies of gender similarities and differences in which the findings with samples of females and males are actually compared. Gender-specificity is sometimes implied by the use of terms such as "gendered," "gender-informed," or "gender-responsive" without the actual testing of gender differences in the predictive validity of the risk/need factors.

Fascinated by the ability to identify examples of gender-specific risk/need factors, we gathered together all the meta-analyses we could find and sought to uncover gender differences in the validity of risk/need factors. The risk/need factors explored in particular are from a set of "gender-informed" (GI) factors. "Gender-informed" factors are ones suggested by gender-informed theoretical perspectives on crime. Three social location factors (age, ethnicity, and social class) are suggested to be of importance by critical feminists in particular. "Critical feminism" is based on critical criminology wherein the label "critical" refers to Marxist (and sometimes socialist) perspectives. Emotional distress, victimization, poverty, and housing problems are suggested to be important risk/need factors by some critical feminists, by some sociological feminists, and within some humanistic perspectives on female offenders. The seven factors are not exhaustive of all possible GI factors but they constitute a reasonable sample of factors.

Inspection of Table 2.9 reveals no evidence of female-specificity in the risk/need factors reviewed. All factors were minimal-to-mild risk/need factors for females and for males. Being younger is a stronger risk factor for males than for females, and abuse history is a stronger risk factor for females than for males. Salience indicates that a factor is predictive with both males and females but stronger with males (male-salient) or stronger with females (female-salient). Technical Note 2.1 identifies the eight meta-analyses that are summarized in Table 2.9.

Of course, there will be some exceptions under some circumstances, but the available evidence is that despite myriad differences between females and males, many of the best-established risk/need factors are gender-neutral in their predictive validity. This appears to be the case with GPCSL-based risk/need factors (e.g., LS/CMI general risk/need as in Table 2.8) and with some risk/need factors identified within gender-informed perspectives (as in Table 2.9).

A major task of the remainder of the textbook is to reveal how the knowledge regarding risk/need factors grew and to outline the theoretical and practical applications. There is however, another story remaining to be told. How is it possible that the objectives of PCC were so seriously challenged within mainstream sociological criminology? How is it possible that the same objections and challenges are currently being raised by some sociological criminologists in regard to female offenders?

Table 2.9
Mean Predictive Validity Estimate for Gender Informed Risk/Need Factors by Gender: Overall Mean r was Averaged Over Mean Estimates Found in up to Eight Meta-Analyses

	Female	Male	A Gender-Neutral Factor?
Being Younger	.06	.15	Yes, but Male Salient
Being Non-White	.07	.06	Yes
Lower-Class Origins	.06	.07	Yes
Emotional Distress	.11	.12	Yes
Abuse History	.13	.06	Yes, but Female Salient
Poverty	.19	.16	Yes
Housing	.16	.16	Yes

Note. See Technical Note 2.1 for a fuller presentation of the eight meta-analyses summarized here.

The evidence regarding the correlates of criminal behavior was apparent as early as 1950 and verified over and over again even up to the 1970s. Even within forensic mental health (the domain of clinical social workers, psychiatrists, and psychologists), the belief was that you cannot predict serious crime. If what has just been reviewed is an accurate rendering of the evidence, how is it that the evidence was missed for so long? We are not asking about the reasons underlying the discounting of PCC outlined in Technical Note 1.3. We are talking about the specific knowledge-destruction techniques that must have been employed for PCC to be discounted while social class theory thrived in mainstream criminology and mental illness models thrived in forensic mental health. We will return to this point in later chapters. Now we turn to the research literature on an understanding of the ability to influence criminal offending through applications of the RNR model of correctional treatment.

Experimental Investigations of the Effectiveness of Correctional Treatment: A Quick Look at What Works and Research Support for the RNR Model

The issue of the effectiveness of correctional programs has been a controversial one. Before RNR, many within criminology had taken the position that, simply put, "nothing works." These criminologists appear to have known a priori that a focus on individual offenders could not work. Hence, they endorsed without criticism program evaluations that failed to establish the effects of human service and severely criticized studies that appeared to find evidence in support of particular approaches to counseling or supervision.

For mainstream criminology, human service could be rejected outright a priori because it was inconsistent with their myths. The myths were that individual differences in criminal activity are trivial, any important variability reflects social location and social inequality, criminal behavior is essentially unpredictable, and "nothing works" except perhaps a reduction in socioeconomic inequalities.

Having rejected direct human service, many in mainstream criminology and criminal justice fell into the active endorsement of official punishment in controlling the criminal conduct of individuals (to be reviewed in Chapter 13). Here we take just a brief look at the cumulative findings of the treatment effectiveness literature.

First, note that we have been unable to find any review of experimental studies that reveals systematically positive effects of official punishment on recidivism. That is, there is no evidence, beyond incapacitation effects, that official punishment reduces recidivism. In contrast, studies of direct service have been conducted in the context of a variety of conditions of judicial sanctioning, such as diversion, probation, and custody. In dramatic contrast to the effects of official punishment, reduced recidivism was demonstrated in 40 to 80 percent of the studies. The reviews of controlled studies of human service programs in corrections began to appear in the literature in the 1950s.

In a review published in 1954, Bernard Kirby was able to locate only four studies of correctional counseling that approximated experimental ideals. Three of the four studies produced findings that were favorable to the notion that direct and controlled interventions were responsible for decreases in criminal behavior. By 1966, Walter Bailey was able to find 100 studies of correctional effectiveness in the research literature; nearly 60 percent (13 of 22) of the better controlled studies found evidence in support of the idea that type of intervention was related to outcome. In 1972, Charles Logan reviewed the literature. Our inspection of his tables showed that at least 18 studies focused on counseling procedures, involved the use of experimental and control groups, and employed objective outcome indices. At least 50 percent of these studies found evidence in support of counseling.

Martinson (1974) and Lipton, Martinson, and Wilks (1975) examined more than 230 studies. A minimum of 40 percent and up to 60 percent of the studies yielded results consistent with a conclusion that some treatments work. Reporting in 1979, Paul Gendreau and Robert Ross found 95 reasonably well-controlled studies published between 1973 and 1975. Eighty-six percent of the studies reported some significant levels of reduced criminal behavior as the result of treatment. Again, in 1987, they reached essentially the same conclusions based upon studies published between 1981 and 1987. In 1989, Mark Lipsey reported on the findings of more than 400 studies of correctional effectiveness, wherein 60 percent reported positively.

How could "nothing works" prevail and punishment be promoted when, at a minimum, the research evidence suggested that at least some programs appeared to be working for some offenders under some circumstances? The evidence was not consistent with the myths of sociological criminology. The myths were: (a) the roots of crime are buried deep in structured inequality, (b) individual differences and personal variables are trivial or just a reflection of social class, and (c) correctional treatment/rehabilitation cannot possibly work because the psychology of criminal behavior is misguided. The problem is theoreticism. *Theoreticism* entails accepting or rejecting knowledge, not on the basis of evidence, but on the basis of personal and professional interests and/or on the basis of political ideology.

The meta-analyses have proved to be less readily dismissed than the narrative reviews. The Carleton University meta-analyses of effective correctional treatment and many other meta-analyses will be reviewed in detail later in the chapters on prevention and rehabilitation. For now, we present a brief summary to give an overview of the findings and to see how research design, methodological issues, and knowledge-destruction approaches may be explored in meta-analyses. Technical Note 2.2 summarizes the anti-rehabilitation themes that allowed dismissal of the positive pattern of results evident even in the narrative reviews.

The Carleton University databank (Andrews, Dowden & Gendreau, 1999) includes information on 374 controlled experimental tests of the effects on recidivism of various judicial and correctional treatment interventions. Every test represents an approximation of the ideals of the true experimental design in that there is an intervention and a comparison group, and group members are followed forward in time for a specified time period. A measure of recidivism is taken on the intervention and comparison group in each study and the differences computed within the many studies are expressed by a common measure of effect size (in our case, the Pearson correlation coefficient, which is also known as the phi coefficient when two groups are compared on a binary outcome such as no-yes in regard to reconvictions). Variability in effect sizes may be explored through investigation of study, methodological, and treatment variables as potential moderators of the sources of variability in effect size. Recall that we have already seen that the specific targets of change selected were a major source of variability in effect size.

Overall, the 374 tests yielded a mean effect size of .08, with a dramatic range of effect sizes varying from –.43 (a 43 percentage-point increase in recidivism, according to the Binomial Effect Size Display (BESD; Resource Note 1.1) to .83 (an 83 percentage point reduction in recidivism). What can we do in the face of such variability? First, note that on average, the least valid conclusion is that nothing works. Rather, in 374 tests, the mean effect is not .00 (no effect on average) and it is not a negative value, which would indicate, on average, an increase in reoffending. What was found, on average, was a mild decrease in reoffending. Using the BESD, on average, the recidivism rate in the intervention group was 46 percent [(50 – 8)/2], and 54 percent [(50 + 8)/2] in the comparison group. The mild positive effect encourages exploration of the sources of variability in effect size. What can account for the more negative, the more neutral, and the more positive findings represented in the research literature? Only a small sampling of variables is explored here because later chapters will focus on official punishment and human service/treatment in more detail.

The Effects of Severity of Sanctions

Among the 374 tests were 101 tests of the effects of increases in the severity of official punishment. These tests compared, for example, longer versus shorter periods of community supervision, longer versus shorter periods of incarceration, a custody disposition versus a community-based disposition, and formal arrest versus a warning. The overall mean effect of increases in the severity of the penalty was a very mild increase in reoffending (mean $r = -.03$, range $-.32$ to $.22$, 95% confidence interval (CI): $-.05$ to $-.03$). Once again, there is considerable variability, but 95 percent of the time the true mean value resides in the narrow negative range of $-.03$ and $-.05$.

The Effects of Correctional Treatment. Among the 374 tests were 273 tests of the effects of human service in the justice contexts of community supervision, custody, and diversion from the justice system. The human service programs studied included academic and vocational programs, skill-building programs, family therapy, substance abuse treatment, and anything that identified itself as a correctional treatment program as opposed to an official punishment. The mean effect size was $.12$ (range $-.43$ to $.83$, CI $= .09$ to $.14$.) The value of $.12$ is mild but positive, and the confidence intervals do not even overlap with those for official punishment. On average, employing the BESD, the average recidivism rate for the treated offenders was 44 percent [(50 $-$ 12)/2] and 56 percent for the comparison group, a 12 percentage point difference.

Testing RNR Principle # 4 (Introduce Human Service)

As noted above, the mean effect of increases in the severity of sanctions was a mild increase in reoffending ($-.03$, CI $= -.05$ to $-.03$). In contrast, the mean effect of service delivery was a mild decrease in reoffending ($.12$, CI $= 09$ to $.14$). For purposes of reduced offending, introduce human service into the justice context. That is, adherence with the human service principle was associated with reduced reoffending (see Figure 2.1).

The Effects of Clinically Relevant and Psychologically Informed Human Service: Adherence to the Three Core Principles of Risk-Need-Responsivity (RNR)

The three core principles support delivering human service to higher-risk rather than lower-risk cases (**risk principle**), targeting dynamic risk factors (**the criminogenic need principle**), and using generally powerful influence and behavior change strategies (**general responsivity principle**: use behavioral/social learning/cognitive behavioral strategies rather than unstructured, nondirective, or "get tough" approaches). Inspection of Figure 2.2 reveals that adherence with the risk principle—that is, delivering human services to higher risk cases—results in a larger mean effect size than does nonadherence with the risk principle. The figure also reveals that adherence with the principles of need and general responsivity each yield higher mean effect sizes than does nonadherence.

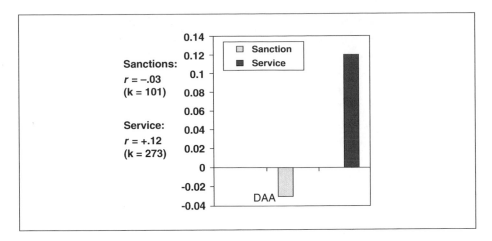

Figure 2.1
Mean Effect Size (r) by Principle of Human Service (k = 374)

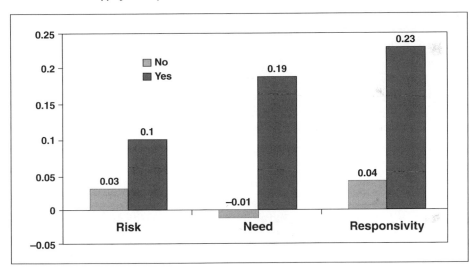

Figure 2.2
Mean Effect Size (r) by Adherence to Principles (k = 374)

The meta-analytic researchers computed a simple four-level index of overall adherence with risk, need, and general responsivity. A score of "0" was assigned to those programs that were pure punishment without any human service or to human service programs that were not in adherence with any of the three core principles. A score of "1" was assigned to those tests of treatment that were in adherence with only one of the three principles. A score of "2" indicates adherence with two of the three, and a score of "3" indicates human service that is in full adherence with risk, need, and general responsivity.

When human service is delivered in corrections and that service adheres to the principles of risk, need, and general responsivity (RNR), the mean effect size was .26 in 60 tests of treatment. When only two of the three human service principles are met, the mean effect size drops to .18 (in 84 tests). With conformity to only one of the three principles, the mean effect size is a mere .02 (106 tests). When no human service is introduced and/or human service is delivered in a manner inconsistent with each of risk, need, and responsivity principles, such as a high-intensity psychodynamic therapy targeting self-esteem, the mean effect size is –.02 (124 tests). Figure 2.3 provides a graphic representation of the effects on reduced recidivism of RNR adherence. It appears that nonadherence with RNR may actually be increasing crime and that the hope for crime prevention resides in the delivery of treatment services consistent with the major principles of effective correctional treatment. This is a serious conclusion and needs to be subjected to very serious critical review. You will be presented with considerations of RNR adherence throughout the text as various contextual and potential moderator variables are explored.

For now, Figures 2.4 through 2.6 illustrate the same basic findings with female offenders and male offenders, with young offenders and adult offenders, and in follow-ups of prisoners and offenders in community corrections.

Figure 2.7 presents a different but very important finding. It speaks to the importance of integrity in service delivery. Integrity refers to adherence with our fourteenth (staffing) and fifteenth (managerial) RNR principles. It is apparent that without adherence to the core clinical principles of RNR, the integrity of service delivery does not matter at all. You can't make up for nonadherence to the core principles through the selection, training, and clinical supervision of therapists (or counselors or officers). Figure 2.8 summarizes the increases in crime prevention effects through cumulative levels of RNR adherence.

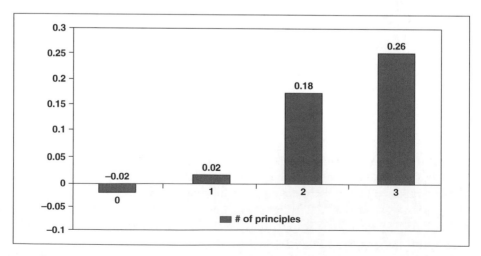

Figure 2.3
Mean Effect Size (r) by Adherence to the Number of Principles

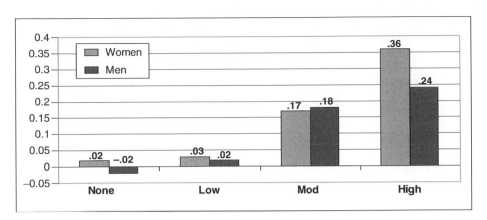

Figure 2.4
Mean Effect Size (r) by RNR Adherence and Gender

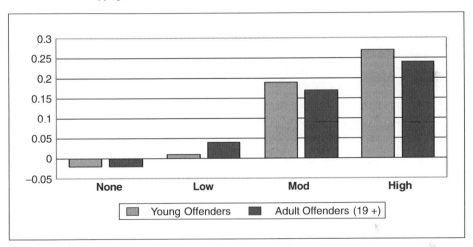

Figure 2.5
Mean Effect Size (r) by RNR Adherence and Offender Age

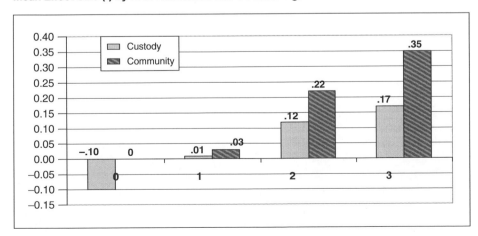

Figure 2.6
Mean ES (r) by RNR Adherence and Correctional Setting (Custody/Community)

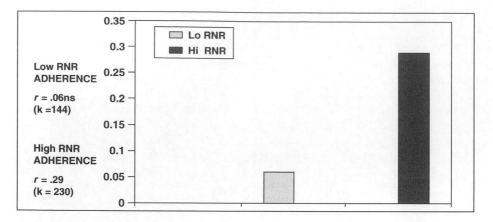

Figure 2.7
The Correlation of Effect Size with Adherence to Staffing and Management Principles by Level of Adherence with the Core Clinical Principles of RNR

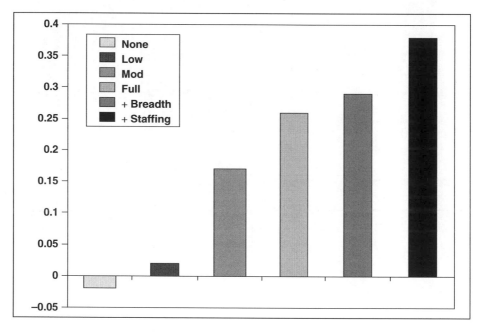

Figure 2.8
Mean ES by Increasing Levels of RNR Adherence

We have used the Carleton University findings to introduce the basic results regarding the effects of official punishment and of correctional treatment. As will become clear as you progress through the text, the evidence comes from many additional sources. James McGuire (2004) lists 42 meta-analyses of the effects of correctional treatment on recidivism published since the late 1980s.

Mark Lipsey (2009) has independently reviewed the literature on effective interventions with young offenders. He finds support for the human service or therapeutic principle, for the risk principle, for the importance of program integrity, and for behavioral and cognitive behavioral strategies. Unfortunately, his tests of general responsivity were limited to only some of the service programs, and he did not code for the need principle. Much more remains to be said about correctional treatment and will be developed throughout this book. We now turn to Chapters 3 and 4, which deal with the development of knowledge through theory and theoretically relevant research.

Worth Remembering

1. The risk-need-responsivity (RNR) model of correctional assessment and treatment is based on a general personality and cognitive social learning perspective on human behavior, including criminal behavior and the major risk, need, and responsivity factors involved in crime prevention through the delivery of human and social services.

2. The Big Four risk/need factors are antisocial personality pattern, history of antisocial behavior, antisocial attitudes, and antisocial associates. The Central Eight includes the Big Four along with substance abuse and problematic circumstances in the domains of family/marital, school/work, and leisure recreation.

3. It is possible to produce similar but differently organized lists of risk/need factors. The designation of the "Big Four" and the "Central Eight" is a means of assisting in the organization of knowledge, but the designations are subject to change in the face of new evidence and/or theoretical considerations.

4. The available meta-analytic evidence strongly supports the predictive validity of the Central Eight risk/need factors.

5. Traditional narrative reviews of the literature and more recent meta-analyses of the correctional treatment literature support the relative power of correctional treatment in comparison with severity of punishment. The research literature also supports the power of adherence to the human service principles of risk, need, and general responsivity.

6. As suggested in Chapter 1, our approach to PCC places considerable emphasis upon seeking general understandings of criminal conduct while attending very carefully to issues of specificity in regard to types of human beings (e.g., boys and girls, men and

women) and types of settings (e.g., custodial and community corrections). Such attention was illustrated in this chapter and will be found throughout the text.

7. Three great stories are involved with the material reviewed in this chapter. The first story, contained in the Technical Notes associated with this chapter, was the torturous attempts to destroy the very possibility of a PCC through intellectual games involving the definition of crime. The second and third stories were the specific knowledge-destruction techniques used to dismiss the very possibility of (1) the prediction of crime and (2) successful rehabilitation.

Recommended Readings

We have two articles that we would suggest for further elaborations on the major points made in this chapter. The first is Mark Lipsey and Francis Cullen's (2007) review of the effectiveness of offender rehabilitation in the *Annual Review of Law and Social Science*. Their review summarizes 19 meta-analyses on the effectiveness of sanctions and compares them with eight meta-analyses of rehabilitation programs. Their conclusions are virtually identical to ours—treatment works! The second article, in *Victims & Offenders*, follows a similar approach to reviewing the literature. Paula Smith, Paul Gendreau, and Kristin Swartz (2009) also use the findings from a number of meta-analyses to affirm the effectiveness of services over sanctions. Moreover, they reinforce the RNR principles as key to effective intervention.

In summary, the research findings reveal that lower-class origins and personal distress are *minor* risk factors for criminality relative to indicators of antisocial propensity drawn from assessments of family, personality, attitudes, and interpersonal association patterns. The findings applied very widely across gender, age, and race; by self-reported versus officially recorded crime; and by type of research design.

Understanding Through Theory: Psychopathological, Psychodynamic, Social Location, and Differential Association Perspectives

A theory of criminal conduct is weak indeed if not informed by a general psychology of human behavior. The psychological base for the more empirically defensible theories of crime and delinquency include the psychodynamic perspective of Sigmund Freud, the radical behavioral perspective of B.F. Skinner, and the cognitive behavioral perspectives of Albert Bandura, Walter Mischel, and Donald Meichenbaum. Likewise, a general cognitive social psychology has emerged that reflects, for example, the symbolic interactionism of George Herbert Mead, the self-efficacy work of Albert Bandura, and general developments in the social psychology of attitudes and behavior (Ajzen, 1996; Ajzen & Fishbein, 1980, 2005). Now, entering the second decade of the new millennium, it is clear that models of self-regulation are paramount: "To do anything, the self has to keep its own inner house in order, such as by organizing its actions toward goals, avoiding swamps of emotional distress, obeying laws, and internalizing society's standards of good (both moral and competent) behavior" (Baumeister & Vohs, 2004:xi). The new models that incorporate self-regulation may serve a highly integrative function in regard to the contributions of psychodynamic, behavioral, social learning, and cognitive perspectives.

By the end of Chapters 3 and 4, theoretical and research studies of crime and delinquency will have been found to be converging on a general personality and social psychological framework that is empirically rich and of considerable practical value to those interested in reducing the harm caused by criminal conduct.

The outlines of this high-consensus theoretical framework were drawn in Europe by the 1900s, and the outline was significantly advanced in the 1940s in the United States (e.g., Glueck & Glueck, 1950). The framework continued to develop in Australia (e.g., Mak, 1990), the United Kingdom (e.g., Farrington, 1995), Canada (e.g., LeBlanc, Ouimet & Tremblay, 1988), and the United States (e.g., Sampson & Laub, 1990). The converging constructs are found in general psychodynamic and control models (Glueck & Glueck, 1950; LeBlanc et al., 1988), integrated differential association/behavioral perspectives (Akers, 1973, 1985), bonding perspectives (Hirschi, 1969; Linden, 1987), personality and self-control perspectives (Hirschi, 2004), and general social learning perspectives strongly influenced by Bandura (Jessor & Jessor, 1977; Patterson, 1982). Now, general personality and cognitive social learning perspectives appear most powerful.

Empirically, the weakest of the theories of criminal behavior were based on psychopathology and social location perspectives. On the other hand, psychodynamic perspectives, historically, are at the heart of empirically defensible criminological theory. We begin, however, with psychopathological perspectives. Quite frankly, we want this discussion out of the way so that we may move directly to the progress evident in the psychodynamic, symbolic interaction, behavioral, personality, and social learning/cognitive behavioral pathways toward an empirically defensible theory with considerable practical value.

Psychopathological Perspectives

Psychopathological perspectives perform very poorly when evaluated according to the standards of an adequate theory. Rarely is there a rationally organized set of principles that may be evaluated according to their internal consistency, external consistency, parsimony, and so on. In fact, we cannot find an example that we think even approximates the minimum standards of a theory. Rather, in early clinical forensic mental health (clinical psychology, clinical psychiatry, and social work), there has simply been the position that assessments of mental disorder conducted by clinical professionals will assist in understanding criminal behavior. Typically, this understanding would be evident by the ability to predict criminal recidivism and, in particular, to predict violent behavior.

How well do clinicians perform in their professional judgments of the probability of antisocial outcomes? As will be reviewed in the chapter on prediction (Chapter 10), the mean predictive validity estimates (correlation coefficients) for professional clinical judgment are in the area of .03 to .12 (as summarized in Andrews, Bonta, and Wormith (2006) and the reviews by James Bonta, Karl Hanson, and their colleagues). Beyond forensic mental health, professional judgment has a weak record generally. Systematic structured assessment instruments *not* concentrating on psychopathology readily yield mean predictive validity estimates (r) of .35 and higher (as broadly reviewed in Chapter 2 and as will be reviewed in detail in Chapter 10).

In regard to the ability to influence antisocial outcomes through programs based on psychopathological models, the evidence is equally bleak. Recall from Chapter 2 (and to be developed in more detail in Chapter 11), the effective intervention programs were those consistent with the principles of human service, risk, need, and general responsivity. None of these conditions need make any major use of psychopathological perspectives. Two important exceptions are noteworthy. First, mental disorder may be a major specific responsivity factor within the RNR model. Second, the clinical talent that resides within forensic mental health may come to be mobilized in pursuit of effective crime prevention.

Forensic mental health has recently undergone a major intellectual revival because of the demonstrated predictive validity of assessments of substance abuse and, most importantly, because of the predictive validity of the Psychopathy Checklist–Revised (PCL-R: Hare, 1991; see Chapters 2 and 8). In the analysis of youthful crime, diagnoses based on the American Psychiatric Association manual, such as Attention-Deficit Hyperactivity Disorder, Oppositional Defiant Disorder, and Conduct Order, have predicted juvenile delinquency (American Psychiatric Association, 1994). The criteria for the diagnoses of conduct disorder constitute a survey of a history of antisocial behavior including fighting, stealing, fire setting, truancy, and other items. The criteria for the other two youthful disorders reflect impulsivity, inattention, anger, and resentment. You have already seen that indicators such as these predict criminal recidivism, and they do so without invoking notions of pathology.

In regard to viewing substance abuse as mental illness, we expect there was an alcohol-crime link long before alcoholism came to be viewed as a disease, and diagnosed or not, the alcohol-crime link exists. There will be more on this in Chapter 9.

Recall from Chapter 2, and as you will see in more detail later, the PCL-R does predict recidivism and violent offending at levels well above that achieved by unstructured clinical judgment. However, how does the PCL-R do relative to assessments of the "Big Eight" as introduced in Chapter 2? As a risk/need scale, PCL-R is an assessment instrument that focuses on antisocial personality pattern and a history of antisocial behavior. The quick answer is easy: The mean predictive validity estimate for the PCL-R is in the area of .25 while the mean predictive validity for the LSI-R is .37 (Gendreau, Goggin & Smith, 2002). We saw in Chapter 2 that the mean predictive validity of LS/CMI general risk/need (based on the Big Eight) is .41.

The more prolonged answer requires attention to the construction of the Violence Risk Assessment Guide (VRAG; Quinsey et al., 1998). The detailed clinical records and psychosocial histories of various selected samples of more than 600 mentally disordered offenders were subjected to exhaustive review. In addition, quantitative indices were explored in relation to violent recidivism. The major predictors were not psychiatric history, clinical diagnoses, or clinical symptoms. The major risk factors were early involvement in crime, criminal history, alcohol abuse, aggression, impulsivity, trouble in school and at work, psychopathy (PCL-R) and other personality disorders, and scores on the Level of

Service Inventory–Revised (LSI-R). Each of these make considerable sense given the literature on the Central Eight factors reviewed in the last chapter.

VRAG is a weighted composite of PCL-R scores, elementary school maladjustment, being young at time of Index offense, nonviolent offense history score, separated from either parent when under age 16, never married, alcohol abuse, meeting criteria for any personality disorder, and failure on prior conditional release. Finally, three items were surprising to some people. Meeting the American Psychiatric Association's Diagnostic and Statistical Manual-III (DSM-III) criteria for schizophrenia is scored as a *protective* factor (that is, it is negatively correlated with violent recidivism), as are serious victim injury and having a female victim in the Index offense. The predictive validity estimate for the VRAG was a very impressive *r* of .45. More recent meta-analytic evidence suggests a mean *r* of .39, which is still very impressive (Andrews et al., 2006).

The performance of the three "protective" factors noted above helps us to understand why clinical judgments have performed so poorly in forensic mental health. Briefly put, clinicians tended to make their judgments on the basis of the seriousness of psychiatric disorder and the seriousness of the offense that brought the individual to the attention of the court and/or clinic. Both, in fact, are negatively associated with a criminal future.

What about the PCL-R and personality disorder items? Do they support the mental health perspective? Well, not really. We have already noted that the PCL-R may be considered a high-quality assessment of a history of antisocial behavior as well as an assessment of antisocial personality pattern (impulsivity, restless aggressive energy, easy to anger). Moreover, Vernon Quinsey and his associates (Quinsey, Book & Skilling, 2004; Quinsey, Harris, Rice & Cormier, 1998, 2006) have already proposed that the PCL-R may be replaced by an eight-item survey of child and adolescent indicators including elementary school maladjustment, teenage alcohol problems, childhood aggression rating, history of school suspension/expulsion, an arrest under age 16, parental alcoholism, and living with both parents to age 16 (except for death of parents), and more than three conduct disorder symptoms as defined in DSM-III (which is a checklist of a history of antisocial behavior). The items of the DSM-III could be replaced without reference to formal mental disorders. We also expect that with a host of nonclinical risk factors available, the VRAG references to "schizophrenia," "personality disorder," "female victims," and "serious damage to victim of the Index offense" could easily be replaced without damaging predictive validity.

As the creators of the VRAG acknowledge, VRAG is a very high-quality contribution to the applied task of sorting folks on the basis of potential for future violence. VRAG, however, is of little use in explaining criminal behavior in theoretical terms. For example, what are the unique treatment implications of a VRAG if we view the items as potentially causal? Cure psychopathy? Encourage future violence against women? Turn the personality disordered into people with schizophrenia? In brief, this is simply silly and of little help in the pursuit of an understanding of criminal conduct.

What about the striking examples of the persons suffering from depression killing family members and then killing themselves? What about the dramatic accounts of persons diagnosed as schizophrenic who receive messages from their radio or from their kitchen toaster that they should kill someone before they themselves are killed? We are not denying the suffering of the mentally ill. Nor are we denying that some symptoms may well, for example, contribute to antisocial cognitions. For example, seeing the world as a hostile place and thinking that one must act aggressively for self-protection, diagnosed or not, is an example of antisocial cognition. We are suggesting that a solid theory of criminal behavior will be more helpful to the field of forensic mental health than the field of forensic mental health has been to the development of PCC. For example, in Chapter 6, an RNR-based analysis of psychopathic personality is employed to sharpen understandings that may lead to effective interventions (see also Wong & Hare, 2005 and Thornton & Blud, 2007).

For all of that, and once again, forensic mental health (FMH) has something that has been sadly lacking in the field of corrections. FMH has a deep connection to the ethos of patient care and a deep respect for clinical skills. In the final chapter of this book, a plea is made for FMH to come to view the reduction of criminal victimization as a primary objective of clinical intervention.

As it is now, crime prevention is viewed as restrictive within FMH while enhanced well-being is viewed in a more positive light. Building rewards and satisfactions for noncriminal alternative behavior may come to be judged more positively within FMH. Skeem, Louden, Polaschek, and Camp (2007) illustrate the power within FMH when assessment and treatment contribute to the blending of care and control. Considerable order in the outcomes of sex offender treatment programs has been found when adherence with the principles of the RNR model is considered in meta-analytic reviews (see the work of Karl Hanson, Guy Bourgon, and colleagues as described in Chapter 14). In recent years, the interests and approaches within FMH and PCC are not simply converging but strengthening each other.

Of course, putting understanding criminal behavior aside, the political-economic and humanitarian issues surrounding the treatment and management of the mentally ill in the justice system are huge. And we return to that in Chapter 14. Also more fully explored in Chapter 14 is a systematic survey of: (1) risk/need factors among the mentally ill, and (2) mental illness as a specific responsivity factor.

Psychodynamic Conceptions of Human Behavior

Freud's perspective on human behavior was rich, detailed, and deeply human, and we encourage everyone to take the time to read his 1915 introductory lectures on psychoanalysis (Freud, 1953). It is a highly literary perspective—one informed by biology, anthropology, and an appreciation of Western culture and the arts. The theory was also very speculative. Many of Freud's specific ideas have not survived systematic empirical exploration, and yet, in its broader outlines, as will be shown, Freudian theory anticipated many elements of current theory.

Freudian theory postulates that behavior is a function of four main "structures." One of the structures is external to the individual (the immediate situation of action), and three of the structures are internal. The internal structures are id, ego, and superego. Behavior in any particular situation is to be understood in terms of how the ego manages the external situation, the forces of the id, and the demands of the superego.

Freud offered many suggestions regarding how the ego and superego developed and functioned. Basically, the emergence of the ego and superego depends upon the interaction of biologically determined growth patterns with the environment. The most crucial developmental periods are early and middle childhood, and the major determinants reside in the context of familial relationships.

Id. According to Freud, human beings have strong aggressive and sexual drives that are biologically based. The psychological storehouse of this aggressive-sexual energy is the id, and the id operates according to the pleasure principle. The pleasure principle summarizes human nature in the form of seeking immediate gratification. Gratification always means the maximization of pleasure and the minimization of pain in the immediate situations of action. Aggression is particularly evident when basic needs (e.g., to suck, eat, experience warmth, and sexual relief) are frustrated. This basic frustration-aggression hypothesis contributed to important behavioral and social learning theories (as reviewed later in this chapter).

In Freudian theory, the motivation of all behavior reflects the sexual and aggressive forces of the id. In this sense, Freudian theory is a proto-type for what criminologists call "control theory" or "containment theory." The motivation for rape, murder, suicide, and theft is within us all. For all practical purposes, however, individual differences in criminal behavior are not a reflection of basic motivation. Rather, individual differences in criminal behavior are (indeed, all behavior is) the result of the differences in the external realities faced by individuals and in the abilities of the ego and the superego to perform their control functions. As the person matures, the internal structures of the ego and the superego emerge from the id.

Ego. The ego emerges from id as the developing child confronts an external environment that selectively reinforces, punishes, or ignores certain behavioral expressions of basic needs. The fully developed ego has the capacity to consciously (and unconsciously) regulate or manage the demands of id in accordance with the demands of the immediate external situation. That is, the ego operates in accordance with the reality principle, which prescribes that gratification may be delayed for longer-term gain.

The child learns that unbridled biting and expulsion of feces are not appreciated by the immediate environment. In fact, most everything the infant/child finds delightful is subject to the judgments of a highly selective environment. Eating and drinking are dependent upon the presence and will of others to nourish (and, increasingly, only at certain times of day). Urination and defecation are judged proper only in certain locations. Limits are placed on access to the physical warmth of parents, and playing with one's genitals becomes so problematic that such play comes to be restricted to only the most private settings.

Selective environments (i.e., "training" experiences) like these are frustrating for the child. The natural response, according to Freud, is to protest and act aggressively. However, these displays of aggression also are subject to a selective environment. Parents do not like being hit, and they do not enjoy temper tantrums. Fortunately, the selective environment is interested in more than placing limits on highly pleasurable behavior. The training also involves encouraging children to master their environment, to be independent, and to cooperate with others.

Through such training, the executive and coping skills of the ego begin to emerge. The ego's task is to maximize pleasure and minimize discomfort while balancing the demands of the id and the external situation. Conscious ego functions include rational analysis of the situation, consideration of alternative courses of action, and the selection of a course of action that maximizes pleasure and minimizes pain. Ego, unlike id, recognizes that sometimes the delay of immediate gratification is associated with long-term gains.

The many unconscious functions of the ego, the "defense mechanisms," are highly important. They are unconscious because the ego does not recognize that the "justified" behavior is in fact an attempt to satisfy the sexual or aggressive needs of the id. The process must be unconscious; otherwise the satisfaction of the id would be impossible. Thus, for example, rape is possible because "she wanted it" (defense mechanism of "rationalization") or because "she wanted me" (a "projection").

Superego. An additional task of the ego is to manage the demands of the superego. The superego emerges from the ego as a result of the selective reactions of the environment to certain behaviors, and through identification with intimate authority figures. For Freud, this identification process is the single most important determinant of moral conduct, and it is largely determined by the age of six or seven. The superego consists of two elements: the conscience and the ego-ideal. The conscience contains internalized representations of conduct that are subject to punishment. The ego-ideal is the mental representation of conduct that is positively valued by the environment.

For boys, identification with the father is the solution to the "Oedipal" conflict. Faced with a desire for intimate contact with their mothers and recognizing that their fathers are quite powerful, being "just like daddy" may one day earn them a privileged relationship with someone like mommy. Girls are faced with the "Electra" conflict. Aware, like their mothers, that they do not have a penis (which they desire), girls identify with their mothers in the hope that, because they are just like mommy, someone like daddy will eventually come along.

With these Oedipal and Electra conflicts resolved through identification with the same-sex parent, the developing person enters the latency period. The child is able to get on with the tasks of developing basic social and life skills, and acquiring knowledge of the world. The basic sources of energy are sublimated so that sexual and aggressive drives are channeled into socially constructive ways. Thus, with the development of the superego, the opportunity arises for still further strengthening of the ego.

In sum, the id operates according to the pleasure principle, while the ego operates according to the reality principle. The superego operates according to a severe moralistic principle whereby moral lapses of commission or omission are subject to the experience of intense guilt. The ego thus manages the demands of the id, external reality, the conscience, and the ego-ideal.

Adolescence represents a particularly risky period for criminal activity because, with puberty, the sexual instincts are reawakened and remain at relatively high levels until dampened by advancing age. By puberty, however, a more mature ego has developed that can manage the id, the superego, and the opportunities and barriers provided in immediate situations of action.

Psychological Maturity. If the developmental process proceeds well, a mature adult emerges. For Freud, maturity is reflected in the ability to delay immediate gratification, to love and be loved in the context of a long-term sexual relationship, and to be socially productive. Without question, Freud's conception of the mature person coincides with what is often called "middle-class morality." This coincidence may not, however, rule it out of order. One may place a high value on personal creativity and self-actualization without dismissing the relevance of "conventional" concerns for other people—and the protection that rules may provide for the integrity of others.

Value judgments put aside, the empirical fact is that each of Freud's three indicators of "maturity," when absent in individuals, are risk factors for criminal conduct. That is, weak self-control, marital instability, and an unstable employment record are each well-established predictors of criminal conduct in adult samples.

There is another side to Freud's conception of maturity that is often missed in discussions of psychoanalytic theory. One of the consequences of a strong superego is a hyper-conventionality, which, while often incompatible with criminal conduct, produces high levels of personal misery. Freudian theory is explicit on the point that the very socialization experiences that may control criminal conduct may also be responsible for neurotic misery. In other words, clinicians who are Freudians are as much, if not more, concerned with freeing individuals from the prison of conventional controls as they are with controlling violations of conventional codes.

The extraordinary psychological significance that Freud assigned to weaning, toilet training, and early sexual advances toward opposite-sex parents are among the features of Freudian theory that have not survived systematic research. In family life, however, issues of feeding, toilet training, and management of intimate personal relationships are indeed preoccupations at times. Freudian notions of the importance of moment-to-moment, day-to-day, and more sustained environmental conditions have received some consistent empirical support. These notions are developed below.

Environmental Barriers to Development

In classical Freudian theory, the development of a mature ego and superego depends upon conditions of warmth, care, and attention, in combination with supervision, direct training, and direct modeling for purposes of both skill development and moral development. In Freudian theory, a number of conditions are associated with problematic development. One is extreme neglect and the outright abuse of the developing child. Neither a strong ego nor a strong superego may be expected to develop under such conditions.

A second problematic condition is that of extreme permissiveness or unconditional warmth and affection. While a strong ego may evolve, the superego will be weak except insofar as the parents have incidentally demonstrated clear conceptions of "right" and "wrong."

A third problematic developmental condition involves patterns of child rearing in which the moral training occurs without a background of warmth and affection. Children from these families may be oriented to rules but may not possess a positive orientation to people. These are just some of the variations in early childhood experience that a Freudian perspective suggests may be important.

In brief, over and over again, the major family of origin variables associated with youthful offending are weak parental nurturance/caring and poor parental monitoring, supervision, and discipline. Recall from

Chapter 2 that those are the key parenting variables within risk assessments based on parenting in the family origin.

The Immediate Environment, the Situation of Action, and the Psychological Moment

A strength of the general personality and cognitive social learning perspectives is that they recognize the importance of both: (1) the person in the immediate situation of action, and (2) background predisposition factors. Attention to the immediate situation of action suggests the immediate causes of human behavior, while the background dispositional factors suggest what leads some people to circumstances in which the probability of a criminal act may be high. Background dispositional factors attempt to account for "criminality," that is, to identify the factors responsible for variation in criminal conduct over a broad time frame. This variation, however, reflects a history of particular people in a variety of immediate situations of action.

In psychodynamic theory, the immediate causes of crime are both situational and personal. Criminal acts are to be understood in the context of the person in immediate situations. Figure 3.1 presents a summary of the immediate causes of antisocial behavior according to psychodynamic theory, wherein the person is represented by the superego, the ego, and the id. The immediate environment may be distinguished according to the temptations they provide and the external controls present.

Thus, understanding and predicting individual criminal conduct requires a knowledge of superego strength (e.g., attitudes, values, and beliefs regarding

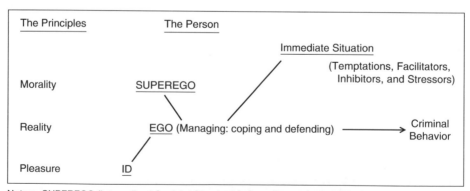

Notes: SUPEREGO (Internalized Societal Standards): Conscience plus ego-ideal.
         EGO: Coping, defending, *and* "interpreting."
         ID: An antisocial constant in Freud.
         SITUATION: In part selected by the person, in part a function of family of origin, and in part a function of broader social arrangements.

Figure 3.1
The Psychological Situation (or Psychological Moment) in Traditional Psychodynamic Theory

rule violations), knowledge of the self-regulation/self-control and problem-solving skills and processes possessed by the ego, and knowledge of the facilitating and inhibiting aspects of the immediate environment.

The psychodynamic perspective also has much to say on background predispositional factors. These are reviewed below as a variety of routes to crime and as a psychodynamic typology of offenders.

Types of Offenders in Psychoanalytic Theory

Freudian theory suggests many different routes to crime. Here we sample some of the more frequently traveled routes, drawing upon the work of Mannheim (1965). This summary of types of offenders does not cover the most inclusive of the Freudian types because they have already been described. Recall that the psychologically immature are characterized primarily by impulsivity and the inability to delay gratification as well as instability in both their family and vocational lives. The psychologically immature present some combination of what is described below as weak superego and weak ego.

The Weak Superego Type. Some people engage in frequent and serious criminal behavior because they lack internalized representations of those behaviors that are punished and reinforced in conventional society. Thus, their behavior, whether prosocial or antisocial, is subject only to the need for immediate gratification and the demands of the immediate external situation. These indicators of a weak superego may be defined independently of the criterion of criminal behavior and include the following:

1. Reckless disregard for conventional rules and procedures;

2. Antisocial cognitions/procriminal sentiments (lack of a conscience);

3. Little evidence of a life plan and weak conventional ambition (lack of an ego-ideal);

4. Little evidence of guilt (lack of a conscience);

5. The early appearance of persistent and generalized conduct problems (the superego is supposedly formed by the age of eight);

6. Expressions of bravado, flirtatiousness, and exhibitionism (early conflicts stemming from the seduction of the opposite-sex parent are unresolved);

7. Conflict with authority figures (again, early conflicts and frustrations have not been resolved);

8. A basic separateness from other people that reflects essential isolation, lovelessness, and a desperate loneliness.

Perhaps the best known description of a "weak superego" type comes from Hervey Cleckley's *The Mask of Sanity* (1982), which is a classic work in the psychiatric/clinical tradition. It has been so influential and so closely tied to the image that his list of characteristics has come to be known as the "Cleckley checklist for psychopathy." These characteristics are: superficial charm; good intelligence (not intellectually handicapped); absence of delusions and other signs of irrational thinking (not psychotic); absence of nervousness (not neurotic); unreliability; untruthfulness and insincerity; lack of remorse or shame; inadequately motivated antisocial behavior; poor judgment and failure to learn from experience; pathological egocentricity and incapability for love; general poverty in major affective relations; specific loss of insight; unresponsiveness in general interpersonal relations; fantastic and uninviting behavior with drink (and sometimes without); impersonal, trivial, and poorly integrated sex life; and failure to follow any life plan. The Hare Psychopathy Checklist-Revised (PCL-R), an objective measure of psychopathy, was mentioned at the beginning of this chapter and in Chapter 2, and the PCL-R will be reviewed in detail in Chapter 6.

It should not be a surprise that systematic empirical research consistently supports the predictive validity of assessment instruments that tap into the content described above for weak superego and psychopathy.

The Weak Ego Type. A weak ego implies immaturity, poorly developed social skills, poor reality testing, gullibility, and excessive dependence. In psychoanalytic terms, the weak ego types are less under the control of superego than of the id and the immediate environment. For weak ego types, criminal behavior may represent stumbling into trouble (misreading the external environment), having a temper tantrum, or following the leader.

The "Normal" Antisocial Offender. These offenders have progressed through the psychosexual stages of development without any particular problems. Psychologically, they match the ideal of the full-functioning mature adult. However, a mismatch with the ego-ideal is evident. The superego is procriminal as a result of identification with a criminal parent, and the ego has incorporated a mastery of criminal skills.

The Neurotic Offender. Freudian theory suggests a number of ways in which neurotic conflicts may translate into criminal behavior. The "criminal from a sense of guilt" is the most interesting, though perhaps not the most frequent. This type is driven by an unconscious desire to be punished for past crimes. An overactive superego may be seeking punishment for prior sins that, even if not actually committed, were either contemplated or the focus of a wish-fulfilling fantasy.

Frequently represented in samples of neurotic offenders are people who use criminal acts as a means of managing specific frustrations or emotional disturbances, or as a way of impacting on disturbed family relations. For example, some "neurotics" may use criminal activity to gain the attention of, or to punish, their parents.

Many clinicians have noted that the offenses of some offenders have elements that appear to exceed those necessary for the achievement of certain concrete goals. For example, obtaining money is an obvious explanation of the behavior of a purse snatcher. Yet, understanding this behavior may benefit from a deeper analysis when the stealing is associated with increases in sexual arousal.

Other Types. The psychoanalytic perspective recognizes a number of other routes to crime. Among those routes are the following:

1. The psychotic and intellectually challenged are at risk for violations of the law. This may be a logical extension of the incapacities that underlie definitions of being psychotic or being intellectually challenged. If one is out of contact with reality or so intellectually disadvantaged as to be unable to manage one's affairs, illegal acts may occur as just another of many transgressions of conventional rules.

2. The situational offender responds to extreme and isolated circumstances such as having stumbled upon the infidelity of a trusted spouse or being confronted with some other particularly "unjust" or "enraging" situation.

3. The perception of injustice is a particularly interesting route to crime within psychoanalytic theory. Those who are persistently criminal as a result of a sense of injustice also possess a hatred of their fathers. In brief, the state has been equated with the hated father.

4. Psychoanalytic thinkers, like most others who have attempted to map the routes to crime, have attended to the role of alcohol and other drug use (and abuse). Some drugs for some people may enhance motivation for crime and reduce internalized controls.

5. The accidental offender may have stumbled into crime because of particularly unlucky circumstances. Within psychoanalytic theory, even crimes of negligence or "slips" may reflect unconscious motivation.

According to psychoanalytic theory, the possible routes to crime are many and diverse. With respect for another medical father of criminology, we will take a brief look at the typology of Lombroso, who was a physician in Italian prisons during the late 1800s. Lombroso was not a Freudian, but he and Freud had similar intellectual backgrounds. Freud saw all human beings as born criminals, with most of us socialized out of it before coming of age. Lombroso was interested in offenders in particular and thought that the observation and measurement of individual offenders should be an important component of criminology. His ideas, summarized in Chapter 5, were heavily influenced by evolutionary theory, but shifted over his working life toward an emphasis on environmental factors in response to criticism, further observation, and reflection.

The vast majority of criminals, according to Lombroso, were of the "occasional" type: the pseudocriminal who is essentially nonevil and relatively harmless, who is either responding to extreme socioeconomic pressures or whose acts are crimes of passion. Lombroso also identified a group of habitual offenders whose criminal activity reflected a procriminal upbringing as well as association with criminals, and another group whose criminality reflected mental disease or insanity. Lombroso, however, is best known for his work on the atavistic or "born" criminal. The born criminal, said to represent about 35 percent of all criminals, was described as a genetic throwback to primitive human or prehuman evolutionary types. The psychology of the born criminal had both motivational and control elements in the form of exceptionally strong animalistic drives and exceptionally weak internal controls, respectively. In psychoanalytic theory, there is little interesting variation in the desire to achieve pleasure and avoid pain (it is a basic part of human nature) and almost all of the variation of interest resides on the control side (and depends upon the interaction of the biopsychological organism and the environment).

Lombroso provided a list of psychosocial factors associated with born criminality. Many of the items on the "Lombroso checklist" bear a strong resemblance to the psychoanalytic concept of the superego (and to the content of questionnaires and rating scales currently used in the prediction of recidivism): moral immaturity, cruelty, idleness, vanity, high tolerance for physical pain, use of criminal argot, and the wearing of tattoos (the latter may be less relevant today, as your authors have been presented with a stunning array of tattoos displayed on the bodies of their students and colleagues).

The intellectual base for a vigorous pursuit of the variety of routes to crime had been established by the 1920s through the work of Freud and Lombroso. Two intellectual giants, both medically trained, one preoccupied with psychology and the other with biology, had each suggested that understanding criminal conduct would be significantly advanced through the development of perspectives that recognized the importance of both the egocentric pursuit of gratification and the development of internal controls. The perspectives of each also noted that some criminal activity may reflect benign psychological inadequacies, atypical situational pressures, conformity within a criminal subculture, and even self-righteous and deliberate responses to a perceived social injustice. Freud and Lombroso may have disagreed in regard to the importance of variation in the pursuit of pleasure, but they agreed on the importance of variation in control. Recall, however, from Chapters 1 and 2, the problematic status of biology and psychology in mainstream sociological criminology:

> Due to historic misfortune sociology captured the field in the 1920s. The contributions of biology and psychology have been minimized (Jeffery, 1979:7).

> In most sociological treatments of crime and delinquency, genetic explanations are either ignored or ridiculed (Rowe & Osgood, 1984:526).

These promising leads were systematically missed for years in criminology. Later in this chapter we will review the most explicitly anti-psychological of criminological theories (the class-based anomie, subcultural, labeling, and conflict/Marxist perspectives) and they are found to be the least empirically defensible theories in the whole of PCC. With a focus on social learning theory, we will outline differential association theory, which was sociological in conception but did not become empirically defensible or of any practical value until integrated with social learning and social cognition theory.

Next, however, this chapter concentrates upon developments of the psychodynamic perspective. However, readers are reminded that the authors of this text do not believe that classic psychoanalytic thought represents the current state of psychological knowledge.

Psychodynamic Thought and Recent Psychological Advances

The psychoanalytic approach is largely a matter of history in psychology although it remains alive and very hot in literary criticism and the humanities. As we shall see here and in later chapters, current psychology has concepts and procedures that have significantly advanced, altered, and successfully replaced the psychoanalytic perspective. Several of these advances are briefly noted:

1. Freud, in contrast to Lombroso, did not hypothesize individual differences in the innate strength of the id or in the capacity for ego or superego development. Yet, current personality theorists who conceptualize individuals as having enduring personality characteristics or traits have drawn upon convincing evidence that children vary in their propensity for rule violations and their ability to learn. For example, in Chapter 2, Low Agreeableness and Low Conscientiousness were two dimensions of personality most strongly associated with criminal conduct.

2. Behavioral genetics and physiological psychology have pointed to the importance of inheritance, cortical arousal, the classical conditioning of anticipatory fear responses, and the neuropsychology of self-regulation. The early avoidance-learning models of socialization (e.g., Eysenck, 1977; Eysenck & Gudjonsson, 1989) appeared to be particularly relevant to some types of persistent and serious criminal behavior. Developments in the neuropsychology of self-regulation are of recent interest and of considerable value (Baumeister & Vohs, 2004). A focus of Chapter 5 is heredity as one of the origins of the major risk/need factors.

3. There have been advances in theory and research on the importance of environments in the selection of acts that are reinforced, punished, or ignored. Principles of learning (e.g., operant conditioning) are better understood now than they were in Freud's time.

4. Current theory and research in social learning and cognition has much to offer regarding the variables associated with modeling, identification, and learning by way of observation.

5. Current social learning and cognitive theory specifies some of the processes of behavioral self-control. Research has detailed the specific skills of self-control and recognized the importance of personal standards of conduct. That is, self-regulation may be guided by attitudes, values, and beliefs that may be either anti-criminal or procriminal.

6. Developments within social psychology include perspectives on how attitudes, values, and beliefs supportive of a specific action may combine with perceived social support for that action, and thereby yield highly accurate predictions of specific behavioral acts.

7. Freud emphasized that the person must always deal with the external environment, but he thought that the major elements of personality were formed very early. While not denying the importance of early learning and experience, social learning theory considers the person in the contemporaneous environment to be of overriding behavioral significance.

In summary, the Freudian model of human behavior, for all of its speculative components, encompasses many people's notions of what it is to be human. Human beings seek pleasure and avoid pain, and that pursuit is governed by the demands, constraints, and opportunities of the immediate situation and by the internal controls that are developed through socialization experiences.

Reformulations of Psychodynamic Theory

The most important development in a psychodynamic theory of delinquency and crime must be that of Sheldon Glueck and Eleanor Glueck (1950). Their "tentative causal formula," reflecting Freudian theory as well as their empirical findings, is among the best validated of all predictive models of criminal behavior.

Glueck and Glueck thought the roots of criminality were more deeply and personally rooted than either 1940s practice or theory recognized. They accepted that underprivileged urban neighborhoods were criminogenic for young males, but they also expected that the families and individuals residing in underprivileged areas were far from being uniform in their attitudes and abilities:

> The varieties of the physical, mental, and social history of different persons must determine, in large measure, the way in which they will be influenced by social disorganization, culture conflict, and the growing-pains of the city (p. 6).

Arguing for a fair sampling of the various aspects of a complex biopsychosocial problem, Glueck and Glueck proposed that research and theory should focus upon personal and environmental variables. This focus was fundamental to psychoanalytic thinking, according to which all human behavior is to be understood in terms of "the point of contact between specific social and biologic processes as they coalesce, accommodate, or conflict in individuals" (p. 7). Quoting from Freud's introductory lectures:

> Economic conditions . . . can do no more than set their [people's] instinctual impulses in motion—their self-preservative instinct, their love of aggression, their need for love and their impulse to attain pleasure and avoid pain (p. 9).

Glueck and Glueck had a clear idea regarding the environmental and situational factors that might be criminogenic. They explicitly noted the many exciting opportunities and the lack of controls in some neighborhoods. Their "tentative causal formula" emphasized weak internal controls (a weak superego) resulting from poor parenting practices and parental modeling, and temperamental/constitutional predispositions toward the expression of aggressive energy and the pursuit of self-interest. Perhaps it is best if Glueck and Glueck (1950: 281–282) provide their own summary of their perspective on male delinquency:

> Physically: Delinquents are essentially mesomorphic in constitution (solid, muscular).
>
> Temperamentally: restlessly energetic, impulsive, extroverted, aggressive, destructive.
>
> Attitudinally: hostile, defiant, suspicious, stubborn, adventurous, unconventional, nonsubmissive to authority.
>
> Cognition: direct and concrete rather than symbolic, less methodical in problem-solving.
>
> Familial: reared in homes of little understanding, affection, stability, or moral fiber by parents usually unfit to be effective sources for emulation needed for the construction of a well-balanced and socially normal superego.

In the exciting, stimulating, but little-controlled and culturally inconsistent environment of the underprivileged area, such boys readily give expression to their untamed impulses and their self-centered desires by means of various forms of delinquent behavior.

Some of the language used by Glueck and Glueck is offensive, but readers are reminded that they were committed to reducing behavior harmful to others and to enhancing the quality of services for those at risk for antisocial behavior. They were disturbed by the differential in societal resources devoted to the punishment of offenders relative to the resources devoted to the reduction of harm.

Note that Glueck and Glueck's causal formula did not make reference to two of the strongest correlates of delinquency in their research: delinquent associates and misconduct in school. For them, patterns of companionship and behavior problems in school were expressions of more fundamental personal and familial variables. School and community, however, were viewed as major settings for intervention by Glueck and Glueck.

In addition to developing psychodynamic theory, the Glueck data suggested that certain theories of delinquency were simply not capable of accounting for much of the variability in officially defined delinquent behavior within disadvantaged urban neighborhoods:

1. Culture conflict: Intergenerational culture conflict was uncovered in more than 50 percent of the families but culture conflict was unrelated to delinquency.

2. Social class: Within the narrow range sampled, economic circumstances, educational levels of parents, and occupational levels of

parents were all incapable of accounting for much of the variability in delinquency. Economic considerations were not even a major emotional issue for the boys.

3. Limited access to services: The families of delinquents had more, not fewer, contacts with social service agencies. Quality of service, as our review of the treatment literature will reveal, is more important than number of services.

4. Physical health: Physical and general health problems were not associated with delinquency.

5. Conventional ambition: Conventional ambitions on the part of parents and the boys were negatively, not positively, associated with delinquency. It was clear that personal or parental endorsements of conventional success standards could not account for delinquency.

6. Feelings of failure in conventional pursuits: Preoccupation with personal and academic failure was more characteristic of nondelinquents than of delinquents. Indeed, delinquents disliked school because it was confining and controlling, while it was the nondelinquents who disliked school because of feelings of failure. Emotional conflicts regarding school, future prospects, finances, and material surroundings occurred with a low frequency within both groups of boys and generally were weakly associated with delinquency.

7. Marxist/conflict perspectives: Overall, those confined in the "prisons" of convention (family, church, school, and work) were less likely to be delinquent than were "nonprisoners" of convention. Clearly, delinquency was most evident among those who were most free of the "prison" of convention. They were the boys who took to the streets and unsupervised playgrounds, who ventured outside of their neighborhoods and who rejected age-based norms regarding smoking, sexual conduct, and school attendance. The price paid by the prisoners of conventional morality was suffering an increased risk for neurotic misery and hyper-banality.

8. Psychopathology: Glueck and Glueck were very clear that the major personality correlates were not simply pathological traits. Rather, the correlates were impulsiveness, a strong taste for adventure, a lack of conscientiousness, hostility, and anti-authority attitudes. Psychopathological antisociality was slightly more evident within the delinquent sample, while psychopathological neuroticism was slightly more evident within the nondelinquent sample of boys.

9. Personal distress theories of delinquency were not supported by Glueck and Glueck. The Glueck and Glueck data suggested that many young people harbor feelings of insecurity, anxiety, powerlessness, and of not being appreciated or loved. These near

constants of the human condition, however, were unrelated to delinquency.

Overall, Glueck and Glueck recognized multiple routes to illegal conduct, and any of the potential causes implied in the weak theories (described as 1 through 9 above) may well apply to some individuals on some occasions. Their "tentative causal formula," however, was more widely applicable. According to them, some delinquency may be explained by any one of the major psychological, familial, and neighborhood factors, but the probability of delinquency increases as the various contributors are combined.

The theoretical contributions of Glueck and Glueck rest solidly on their psychodynamic underpinnings and on their research findings. Their 1950 study is the classic piece of cross-sectional research in the whole of criminology to this day. At the very least, the flavor of their approach and their data should be appreciated. The research study involved comparisons between 500 delinquent boys recruited from two training schools in the Boston area and 500 nondelinquent boys recruited from schools in the same neighborhoods. The delinquents and nondelinquents were matched on age (generally from 10 to 17 years, mean age of 14), IQ, and ethnic origin.

Data were collected through social history interviews with the boys, their relatives, and others (such as social workers and teachers). Social welfare, court, and correctional records and school files were reviewed, as well as medical examinations, psychiatric interviews, psychological tests, anthropometric analyses of photographs of the boys, and teacher-completed checklists.

The findings of Glueck and Glueck are selectively summarized in Tables 3.1, 3.2, and 3.3. Table 3.3 may most usefully be perused with attention to our nine-point summary of variables that were not highlighted in Glueck and Glueck's causal formula. It is remarkable! In 1950, Glueck and Glueck had already shown that the factors favored within sociological criminology (class of origin and their very weak conceptualizations of anomie/strain) were of very limited differentiation value. Likewise, the variables favored within forensic mental health (psychopathology and emotional distress) were of limited value.

The Glueck and Glueck causal formula is sometimes criticized because those variables that actually differentiated between delinquents and nondelinquents were identified as causal. Since 1950, however, many other researchers have conducted independent tests of similar models of proposed causal significance (e.g., Laub & Sampson, 1988; Sampson & Laub, 1990). Perhaps the best known of the theories derived from the psychodynamic model are the control theories of Walter Reckless and of Travis Hirschi. The next section of this chapter explores these variations on psychodynamic themes.

Table 3.1
Temperament/Personality, Cognitive Skills, Antisocial Attitudes, Antisocial Associates, and School: Percent of Delinquents and Nondelinquents with a Factor Present

	Delinquents	Nondelinquents	Difference
Temperament/Personality			
Mesomorphy dominant	60	31	29
Extreme restlessness	60	30	30
Inattention	48	19	29
Vivacity, liveliness	51	23	28
Self-control	39	66	−27
Conscientiousness	9	54	−45
Cognition			
Mean Verbal IQ	88.6	92.0	ns
Common sense: Marked	29	39	−10
Methodical approach to problems: Absent	79	65	14
Antisocial Attitudes			
Marked submissiveness	27	80	−53
Defiance	50	12	38
Ambivalence to authority	41	20	21
Conventional ideas, behavior	8	32	−24
Adventurousness	55	18	37
Hostility	80	56	24
Antisocial Associates			
Gang member	56	1	55
Chums largely with delinquents	98	7	91
School			
Poor grades	41	8	33
School misbehavior	96	17	79
Never truant	5	89	−84
Persistently truant	63	0	63
Mean grade in which first misbehavior occurred	4.36 (of 478)	7.38 (of 86)	

ns = not significant

Adapted from Glueck & Glueck, 1950

Variations on Psychodynamic Themes in Control Theories

Control or containment theories produced by sociological criminologists concentrate upon explaining why people do not commit crimes rather than explaining why people do commit them. Following Freudian theory, control theories are socialization theories. They are theories that focus upon how people come to develop strong ties to convention and resist the temptations to steal and aggress.

Walter Reckless (1967) followed Freudian theory in suggesting that there were both inner and outer sources of control. The external controls were social pressures to conform, and the strength of these controls would

Table 3.2
Family and Parenting: Percent of Delinquents and Nondelinquents with a Factor Present

	Delinquents	Nondelinquents	Difference
Family of Origin			
Mother's family of origin			
Criminality	55	36	19
Father's family of origin			
Criminality	40	32	12
Mother's history			
Mental retardation	33	9	24
Criminality	45	15	30
Father's history			
Emotional disturbances	44	18	26
Criminality	66	32	34
Siblings' history			
Criminality	65	26	39
Stability of Living Arrangements with Parents			
Raised continuously by one or			
both parents	54	88	−34
Out-of-home placements	71	9	62
Affective Quality of Family Life			
Cohesiveness of family			
Marked	16	62	−46
Affection of father for boy Warm	40	81	−41
Affection of mother for boy			
Warm (even if overprotective)	72	96	−24
Supervision/Discipline/Standards of Conduct			
Poor conduct standards	90	54	36
Supervision of children by mother suitable	7	65	−58
Mother's discipline of boy firm but kindly	4	66	−62
Father's discipline of boy firm but kindly	6	56	−50
Social service agency involvement (mean)	11.7	6.9	***

Adapted from Glueck & Glueck, 1950

increase with a sense of belonging to anticriminal groups. These groups include the family, social clubs, schools, and religious organizations. "Inner containment" is Reckless's term for what psychologists call self-control, conscience, or superego. Reckless listed five indicators of inner control:

1. Positive self-concept that involves not only self-esteem but also seeing one's self as conventional as opposed to criminal;

2. A commitment to long-range, legitimate goals;

3. Setting realistic objectives;

4. High tolerance for frustration;

5. Identification with lawfulness and respect for the law.

Table 3.3
Other Factors Suggested by Other Theories: Percent of Delinquents and Nondelinquents with a Factor Present

	Delinquents	Nondelinquents	Difference
Socioeconomic Class of Origin			
Economically Dependent	29	12	17
Reasons for Financial Assistance			
Illness of breadwinner	16	16	ns
Recession/seasonal unemployment	39	59	−20
Unwilling to assume responsibility	45	25	20
Reason First Left Home			
Delinquency	32	0	32
Ran away	31	0	31
Death/separation/divorce	14	55	−41
Financial problems	8	17	−9
Sources of Emotional Conflict			
Lack of monetary resources	4	2	ns
Material surroundings	3	0	ns
Father	23	5	18
Mother	15	2	13
Problems of identification			
with adult male	30	12	18
Anomie/Strain/Personal Distress/Powerlessness			
Sources of Emotional Conflict			
Educational expectations	10	7	ns
General prospects	5	2	ns
Reasons for Marked Dislike of School			
Unable to learn	33	50	−17
Feels inferior	14	28	−14
Resents restriction or control	24	5	19
Lack of interest	22	10	12
Shyness	10	19	−9
Uncritical of self	29	11	18
Fear of failure and defeat	44	63	−19
Enhanced feeling of insecurity/anxiety	14	29	−15
Feeling of helplessness and powerlessness	42	54	−12
Feeling of resignation	5	3	ns
Depressive trends	3	1	ns
Feeling of being able to manage own life	73	64	9
Feeling of not being taken seriously or not counting	59	64	−5
Feeling of not being wanted or loved	92	97	−5
Marked vague/unconscious feeling			
of insecurity/anxiety	89	96	−7
Psychopathology			
Psychopathic	24	6	18
Neurotic	25	36	−11

ns = not significant

Adapted from Glueck & Glueck, 1950

Reckless's list fails to incorporate certain key indicators, such as guilt and generalized disregard for conventional rules, and misses completely the restless energy and aggressive pursuit of self-interest that the psychodynamic image contains. From the perspective of sociological theorizing, the major theoretical significance of Reckless's theory was that the social networks of young people constituted something more than socioeconomic status and subcultural membership. He also gave ascendancy to internal control and to the recognition of individual differences in socialization.

Travis Hirschi's *Causes of Delinquency* (1969), a classic cross-sectional study, contained his variation on the psychodynamic/Glueck and Glueck themes. The present summary will focus upon a selection of the theoretical issues explored by Hirschi. Comparisons will be made with Glueck and Glueck's *Unraveling Juvenile Delinquency* (1950), because both books are important in understanding criminal behavior.

There are a number of theoretical points of convergence between the two studies. Most notably, both studies are grounded in control theory. In both *Unraveling* and *Causes*, it is accepted that the crucial explanatory issue is "why don't we violate the law?" rather than "why do we violate the law?" In brief, it is conformity rather than deviance that must be explained.

Psychoanalytically, Glueck and Glueck accepted that antisocial behavior was an expression of basic sexual and aggressive energy. Thus, delinquency was an expression of untamed impulses, or of immorality in the absence of external controls. Hirschi saw little value in postulating an id, but was quite willing to assume that there are individual differences in morality without concerning himself with the nature of criminal motivation.

For Hirschi, the moral ties consist of attachment, commitment, involvement, and belief in the validity of the law:

1. Attachment to (or caring about) the opinions of family, teachers, and peers is the social psychological version of the "ego ideal" portion of the superego.

2. Commitment to conventional pursuits involves increasing the risk of losing one's investment should deviance be detected. Thus, commitment serves the same theoretical role as does the ego, that is, the operation of the reality principle in the control of rule violations. The Freudian ego, however, involves the operation of self-regulation skills, problem-solving, and various conscious and unconscious processes.

3. Involvement in conventional pursuits reduces delinquency simply by the limited time available for deviant pursuits. Similarly, the development of absorbing moral substitutes for crime was a

particular recommendation within Glueck and Glueck's list of principles of prevention programming.

4. Belief in validity of the law refers to individual differences in the extent to which people believe they should obey the rules. Thus, belief serves the same theoretical function as the superego and antisocial attitudes (the "conscience" portion of the superego).

The second point of convergence between the Hirschi study and the Glueck and Glueck study involves rejection of the central causal significance of social class. The Glueck and Glueck theory drew upon Freud, to whom class meant little unless individual differences entered the prediction formula. Able to draw upon the post-1940s research evidence, Hirschi "knew" that class was at best a weak correlate of delinquency. He also was aware that the logical structure of social class theories was very weak.

Third, both Hirschi's theory and Glueck and Glueck's theory were underwhelmed by differential association theory. We have already seen that Glueck and Glueck chose not to include delinquent associates (the single strongest correlate of delinquency that their work had uncovered) in their list of causal variables. Similarly, Hirschi's downplaying of the role of delinquent associates proved to be the empirically weakest of his theoretical positions. (Reanalyses of Hirschi's data have confirmed that having delinquent associates is a major correlate of delinquency; Matseuda, 1982.)

In terms of research, *Causes* illustrates the methodological advances that had occurred since *Unraveling*. Hirschi surveyed both official and self-reported delinquency. He carefully selected a representative sample of delinquents and nondelinquents by working with a high school cohort from a community. Most of Hirschi's delinquents were not persistent and serious official offenders. Typical of a limitation of much of the cross-sectional research in the 1960s and 1970s (with only a few exceptions), assessments of potential correlates of delinquency were totally dependent upon self-reports provided on paper-and-pencil questionnaires. A comparison of the findings from *Causes* and *Unraveling* is interesting in view of the conceptual overlap and the dramatic differences in methods of inquiry.

Table 3.4 reveals that the Glueck and Glueck findings regarding the empirical importance of (1) parental supervision, (2) the boy's identification with his father, and (3) delinquent companions were each supported by Hirschi's study. Similarly, findings regarding the importance of verbal intelligence and attitudes toward school were replicated and extended by Hirschi in 1969. Hirschi did not include traditional assessments of personality beyond sampling a few of what the Glueck and Glueck analysis had called "adventurous activities" and some attitudinal/belief items (e.g., involvement with smoking, alcohol, and girls correlated with delinquency).

Table 3.4
Delinquency Rates by Family, Peer, and Other Characteristics

Predictor/Question	% Delinquent	N
Mother's Supervision (Does your mother know where you are/whom you are with when you are away from home?)		
0 Never	55	11
1	41	29
2	29	236
3	20	252
4 Usually	12	698
Affectional Identification with Father (Would you like to be the kind of person your father is?)		
0 Not at all	38	138
1	22	172
2	17	387
3	11	404
4 In every way	16	121
Delinquent Companions (Have any of your close friends even been picked up by the police?)		
0 Four or more	45	208
1	44	62
2	21	99
3	21	164
4 None	7	520
Verbal Aptitude Scores (DAT)		
0 Very High	10	21
1	13	140
2	14	319
3	22	452
4 Very Low	21	224
Attitudes Toward School (Do you like school?)		
0 Dislike	49	72
1	25	101
2 Like	9	580
Educational Aspirations (How much schooling would you like to get eventually?)		
0 Less than college	56	172
1	47	240
2 College graduation	40	825
Age at which Cigarette Smoking Began		
0 Before age 13	48	154
1 Age 13–15	32	117
2 After age 15	28	29
3 Don't smoke	12	952
Involvement in Adult Activities (smoking, drinking, dating)		
0 Smokes, drinks, dates	78	154
1	65	17
2	62	149
3	61	73
4	40	270
5 Not one of the 3	25	535

Feeling Bored (Do you even feel that "there's nothing to do"?)		
0	Often	51	313
1		43	619
2		40	246
3	Never	38	78

Attitude Toward the Law: (It is all right to get around the law if you can get away with it.)		
0	Strongly agree	41	49
1		45	93
2		29	219
3		15	493
4	Strongly disagree	9	426

Lack of Self-Control (I can't seem to stay out of trouble no matter how hard I try.)		
0	Strongly agree	63	46
1		66	104
2		49	176
3		44	621
4	Strongly disagree	25	251

Respect for Authority (I have a lot of respect for the police.)		
0	Strongly agree	45	89
1		33	98
2		22	325
3		13	496
4	Strongly disagree	12	273

Adapted from Hirschi, 1969

In addition, Table 3.4 reveals that egocentric attitudes toward law violations, deficits in self-control, disrespect for authority, and boredom were each associated with delinquency. While these data were not presented, Hirschi also noted that mesomorphs (self-described as "well-built," as opposed to fat, skinny, or average) were more likely to have committed delinquent acts.

Overall, the correlates were highly consistent with the image of delinquents provided by *Unraveling*: energetic and easily bored, mesomorphic, below average in verbal aptitude, lacking in self-control, exhibiting a generalized violation of age-based norms, and having dislike for school, poor family relations, poor parental supervision, procriminal and anti-authority attitudes, weak conventional ambitions, and delinquent associates.

The importance of the near identical pattern of results in the two studies cannot be overemphasized. Critics of the Glueck and Glueck findings noted that they reflected the correlates of frequent and serious crime committed by serious criminals, and hence were not of general significance. Critics of the Hirschi findings noted that they reflected the correlates of minor and trivial antisocial acts committed by schoolchildren, and hence were not of general significance. Unless you are not at all interested in individual differences in youthful crime, in our opinion these strikingly similar findings from two dramatically different studies are very impressive.

As we shall soon see, however, Hirschi's four-factor theory places an overemphasis on ties to convention, an underemphasis on ties to crime (only antisocial attitudes are included and antisocial associates are excluded) and relegates the temperamental/personality variables such as self-control, taste for adventure, and aggressivity to background factors with unspecified linkages with ties to either crime or convention.

More Recent Variations on Psychodynamic Themes

In 1990, in collaboration with Michael Gottfredson (Gottfredson & Hirschi, 1990), Travis Hirschi returned once again to basic psycho-dynamic principles (the Glueck and Glueck work is cited, but Freud is not mentioned at all). Ties to convention are minimized, and procriminal attitudes are minimized; what is emphasized is what Freud called psychological maturity, that is, self-control or the ability to avoid the temptations of the moment. Gottfredson and Hirschi's (1990) "general theory of crime" suggests that low self-control is the personality variable that accounts for stable individual differences in criminal behavior. They flirted with the construct of "criminality," but felt that the word connoted compulsion rather than lack of restraint. They also considered the construct "conscience," but decided that "conscience" was too connected to the notion of compulsive conformity (in Freudian theory, it is the construct of ego-ideal, not conscience, that connects with allegiance to "doing good"). More generally, on several occasions they note their discomfort with constructs such as "aggressivity" or "psychopathy."

It is fascinating to read how Gottfredson and Hirschi dealt with what has always been a serious problem in psychodynamic (and behavioral) perspectives on crime: Is there a single construct underlying the undeniable predictive validity of the set of personality variables identified, for example, by Glueck and Glueck (1950)? If there is, what is it? Can it be assessed in a manner independent of assessments of the criterion of criminal behavior and, more generally, how can we best measure it? If there is not a single construct that will serve the function of capturing "psychological immaturity" or "psychopathy" or "weak ego/weak superego," how many different constructs are involved and how do we best assess them?

Gottfredson and Hirschi took on this task in a brave and somewhat innovative manner. The least innovative, but still courageous, aspect of their approach is that they actually make a choice and declare that there is only one construct: "self-control." The choice of the term "self-control" is a brave one because the task of describing the construct and building a single-assessment approach that would tap it in a reliable and valid manner represents a major unresolved set of problems in psychology to this day (cf. Baumeister & Vohs, 2004; Webster & Jackson, 1997). Innovatively, perhaps, they purport to derive the elements of self-control directly from the nature of criminal acts. Interestingly, too, a majority of elements of their self-control construct coincide with some of the empirically best established correlates of criminal conduct.

The elements of their construct of low self-control are as follows:

1. The tendency not to defer immediate gratification. They speak of a "tendency" rather than an "ability." Hence, they appear willing to operationalize this element of self-control by assessments of a behavioral history of deferment as opposed to an analysis of the process of deferment. The link with criminal acts is said to be the fact that criminal acts provide immediate gratification.

2. The tendency to lack diligence, tenacity, or persistence in a course of action. Once again, behavioral history rather than an analysis of process (in this case, of conscientiousness) is suggested to be sufficient for assessment of an element of self-control. The link with criminal acts is said to be the fact that criminal acts provide easy/simple gratification of desires.

3. Tending to be adventuresome, active, and physical (as opposed to cautious, cognitive, and verbal). Criminal acts are described as exciting, risky, or thrilling.

4. A history of unstable commitments to work, marriage, family, and friends. We think shortsightedness is being referred to here, but once again it appears that the construct is assessed through behavioral history rather than directly. In order to link these aspects of behavioral history with criminal acts, criminal acts are said to provide few or meager long-term benefits.

5. Minimal cognitive, academic, and manual skill, and devaluation of cognitive, academic, and manual skill. Criminal acts are said to require little skill or planning.

6. Being self-centered and indifferent or insensitive to the suffering and needs of others. This is said to link with criminal acts because criminal acts are antisocial acts (i.e., harmful to others).

There are a number of interesting issues here. First, although this was an opportunity to introduce antisocial attitudes, values, and beliefs as a trait, Gottfredson and Hirschi chose not to do so. Rather, they chose to work with the constructs of empathy and egocentrism. Interestingly, they entered one of the ongoing debates in psychology: in brief, to what extent are the constructs of egocentrism, callousness, and emotional empathy in any sense overlapping? Also interesting is that Gottfredson and Hirschi were careful to qualify this element of low self-control by noting that people with low self-control may well be charming and generous because they have learned how easily such behavior generates rewards. This qualification recalls ongoing debates regarding the defining elements of psychopathy, that is, dealing with the fact that some offenders are interpersonally "nice" and some are "not nice."

The above-noted six factors appear to be the defining elements of Gottfredson and Hirschi's (1990) construct of self-control. In a summary statement (p. 90), they characterize people with low self-control as impulsive (#1 above), insensitive (#6), risk-taking (#3), shortsighted (#4, we think), physical as opposed to mental (#3 and/or #5, perhaps), and non-verbal (#3 and #5 again, perhaps). Within our understanding of the elements of their construct of self-control and their summary of that construct, Element #2 (conscientiousness) does not even appear in their summary statement, and there is ambiguity with regard to what traits fit within which categories. This, of course, is the classic problem that personality-oriented researchers and theorists have always faced.

A major source of variation in self-control suggested by Gottfredson and Hirschi is ineffective child-rearing. Indicators of ineffectiveness follow the Glueck and Glueck research findings and "tentative causal formula" to a close degree: weak attachment of parent to child, poor parental supervision, poor conduct standards (parents' failure to recognize deviance), and ineffective punishment. The authors of the general theory recognize, like Glueck and Glueck, that not all children are equally lovable or equally subject to supervision, but they leave individual differences of the temperamental/constitutional variety an open question.

In this first statement of their general theory, Gottfredson and Hirschi (1990) did not present original research. Nor did they review the psychological literature on the construct of self-control, the assessment of self-control, or even the links between assessments of self-control and criminal conduct. Thus, the conceptual and measurement problems noted in our outline of their elements of self-control had yet to be faced. They did make it clear, however, that the massive body of empirical research on personality is consistent with their theory but does not meet their standards of relevant evidence. In particular, they were concerned that some of the personality measures (e.g., socialization and psychopathy scales) reflect content that directly samples a history of antisocial acts.

Assessments of antisocial personality pattern are among the strongest of risk factors (Chapters 6 and 10). Directly relevant to low self-control theory, Travis Pratt and Francis T. Cullen (2000) revealed meta-analytically not only that antisocial attitudes and antisocial associates were risk factors in addition to low self-control but that they made incremental contributions to the prediction of criminal behavior. The effect size (correlation coefficient) was .44 with only indicators of low self-control entering the prediction formula but increased to .59 with the addition of antisocial attitudes and antisocial associates. In regard to the theory being "general," the measures of low self-control correlated with the delinquency of males and females, the younger and older, general samples and offender samples, and with both delinquent and nondelinquent antisocial behavior.

Hirschi's Self-Control Variation on Psychodynamic Theory

Travis Hirschi (2004) has rethought his position once again. "Self-control" in the early 1990s was "the tendency to avoid acts whose long-term costs exceed their monetary advantages." Apparently the human organism "knows" long-term costs in advance of the moment of action. So now, for Hirschi (2004:543), "self-control" is "the tendency to consider the full range of potential costs of a particular act." Now cause (low self-control) and effect (criminal activity) are at least contemporaneous. This is to be preferred over an effect that precedes the cause.

Please consider the following items in the new Hirschi (2004) self-control scale for high school students: liking school, important to get good grades, trying hard in school, finishing your homework, caring what teachers think of you, mother knows where you are, share feelings with mother, would like to be the kind of person your mother is, and no friends picked up by police. Obviously, the original bonding items are now being defined as indicators of self-control. A major change from the early social control theory is that association with criminal others is now seen as very important. Now, not having criminal friends indicates that the anticriminal opinions of peers are likely to serve as inhibiting factors. Indeed self-control is measured as the number of inhibitors of criminal behavior.

But where is "a history of antisocial behavior"? By Hirschi's (2004:537) own bold statement, "the best predictor of crime is prior criminal behavior." Yet Hirschi (2004) continues to believe that "a history of antisocial behavior" should not be assigned a causal role in his "control" theory. As we have already seen in Chapter 2, there are many examples of predictive accuracy being increased by the inclusion of the history variable along with attitudes and associates and so on. Moreover, the causal significance of behavioral history will become much clearer as we allow motivational factors (rewards) to enhance the understanding of crime provided by the control perspectives (and their emphasis on costs). Briefly, for example, a long history of antisocial behavior promotes highly causal beliefs supportive of criminal behavior. Two key elements of self-efficacy are: (1) the belief that antisocial behavior will be rewarded, and (2) the belief that one can enact the behavior. Of course, a dense history of antisocial behavior supports both elements of self-efficacy (Bandura, 1989, 2001).

Finally, looking forward, Travis Hirschi (2004) continues to miss a key element of the Freudian and the Glueck and Glueck positions. Yes, weak self-control is crucial in the psychodynamic perspectives. But equally important is restlessly aggressive energy and the motivational elements of resentment and feeling mistreated. Recalling Chapter 2 and looking forward to Chapters 5 and 6, temperament and personality factors such as weak self-control do link with criminal behavior. Empirically, however, so does a relatively independent dimension of negative emotionality (feeling mistreated) and/or low agreeableness.

Summary of the Psychodynamic Perspective

The psychodynamic perspective has been promising for criminology from its beginnings in Freudian psychoanalytic theory. The underlying model of human nature fits well the task of explaining antisocial behavior. The classic research of Glueck and Glueck (1950) was our starting point for systematic empirical explorations of psychodynamic theory and subsequent refinements of psychodynamic conceptions of criminal conduct. The psychoanalytic perspective is so broad and diverse that it affords a large variety of reasonable routes to persistent criminal conduct. The most obvious routes are weak internal controls (in terms of ego and superego functioning), which in Freudian theory are directly linked to family process and parenting.

Sheldon Glueck and Eleanor Glueck attended to these concerns and conducted a comprehensive survey of additional variables suggested by the biological, human, and social sciences of their day. Their findings were strong and clear. The major correlates of persistent and serious delinquency were antisocial attitudes, antisocial associates, a complex set of indicators of an antisocial personality pattern (restless energy, aggressiveness, impulsivity, callousness), a set of problematic family conditions (psychologically disadvantaged parents, weak affection, poor parenting, structural instability), and problematic circumstances in school and the broader community. These variables functioned well relative to financial and scholastic worries, indicators of personal distress, and culture conflict or feelings of helplessness. They developed a tentative causal formula that was dismissed and/or denied by much of mainstream sociological criminology (see the account of this dismissal by Sampson and Laub, 1990), but was carefully read by Travis Hirschi.

Hirschi (1969) offered a milder, more "socialized" statement of the Glueck and Glueck theory by emphasizing ties to convention (that is, crime reflects weak attachment to conventional others, institutions, and pursuits). He maintained the causal status of "antisocial attitudes" but, just as Glueck and Glueck had done, he hesitated to offer causal status to "antisocial associates." Hirschi then moved (Gottfredson

& Hirschi, 1990) toward emphasizing the self-control element of Glueck and Glueck's complex of personality, downplaying what was the strongest correlate in his 1969 theory (belief in the validity of the law). Other researchers are retaining causal status for antisocial attitudes, the personality complex, the bonding set (family in particular), and antisocial associates. The importance of associates is examined in the next section, in which additional contributions of psychodynamic theory are found.

Toward Social Learning via Frustration-Aggression

From Freud to Social Learning: Frustration-Aggression

A recurring theme in the psychology of crime has been the frustration-aggression hypothesis. At first, Freud's hypothesis was integrated with radical behavior theory and the conditioning models of socialization. Subsequently, the principles of observational learning and the cognitive models of self-control were incorporated. In these later models, the frustration-aggression link is still evident but no longer dominant. What has emerged is a model of human behavior that appreciates human diversity and complexity and that includes an active, organizing individual.

The beginning of modern conceptions of aggression and criminality can be dated to 1939 at Yale with the publication of *Frustration and Aggression*, by Dollard, Doob, Miller, Mowrer, and Sears. This group of psychologists and sociologists linked Freudian concepts with the methods and concepts of an emerging behavioral perspective on human behavior:

1. Aggression is always a consequence of frustration. All aggression is preceded by frustration, and frustration is always followed by some form of aggression.
   Frustration is interference with a behavior sequence that has a valued goal-response.
   Aggression is an act that has the goal of injuring another person.

2. The strength of instigation to aggression (i.e., the amount of frustration) increases with:
   a) the strength of instigation to the frustrated response;
   b) the degree of interference with the frustrated response;
   c) the number of frustrations.

3. The strength of inhibition of any act of aggression increases with the amount of punishment anticipated as a consequence of that act.

4. The instigation to aggress is strongest against the agent perceived to be responsible for the frustration.

5. The greater the degree of inhibition specific to the frustrating agent, the more probable the occurrence of indirect aggression and/or displaced aggression.

6. The occurrence of an aggressive act is followed by a temporary reduction in the instigation to aggress (catharsis).

Dollard and his colleagues were well aware of the many problems associated with the state of knowledge in criminology in the 1930s. However, upon reviewing that knowledge base, they proposed that the frustration-aggression hypothesis could account for the majority of "facts" regarding criminal behavior. They viewed the correlates of criminality as indicators of frustration and/or as indicators of the inhibitors of criminal behavior. The frustration-aggression hypothesis also had a major influence in the development of social learning theory.

The Rise of Social Learning Theory

In 1962, Berkowitz published a major update and revision of the frustration-aggression hypothesis called *Aggression: A Social Psychological Analysis*. The work reflected the tremendous amount of research that had been conducted in the quarter century since the publication of the original Yale monograph. Most notable was the introduction of more sophisticated learning principles, the introduction of cognitive-emotional mediators, and the increased attention paid to the concept of aggressive personalities.

For Berkowitz (1962), and for Buss (1966), there is an important distinction between instrumental aggression and angry aggression. Instrumental aggression is aggression primarily oriented toward some goal other than doing injury (e.g., the acquisition of money as a goal of armed robbery). The learning of instrumental aggression follows the principles of operant conditioning. On the other hand, angry aggression is a response to a specific frustration, and the goal is injury.

A frustration creates a predisposition to aggression by arousing anger. Anger is a drive that leads to drive-specific behaviors (i.e., aggression) in the presence of appropriate cues or releasers. A person displays violence if anger is high and/or if violent behavior has been reinforced in the past. The aggressive person has learned to interpret a wide variety of persons and situations as threatening or frustrating and has learned habits of aggression to these cues.

The aggressive personality will differ from less aggressive people in the following ways:

1. The number and variety of events defined as a threat and that arouse anger.

2. The level of affective-physiological arousal, and the cognitions supportive or not supportive of violence.

3. The specific forms of aggressive behavior that have been reinforced in the past, and the availability of alternative nonaggressive responses.

This model, which we have only sketched here, is the basis for treatment programs that target the control of anger (e.g., Novaco, 1975, 2000).

Megargee's Algebra of Aggression

Megargee (1982) provided a framework that incorporates the vast majority of the elements of psychological research on aggression and criminality. The variables associated with criminal violence are represented within the following broad categories:

1. Instigation to aggression (A). The sum of all internal motivators. Some examples are personal gains such as money, anger in response to frustration, and jealousy.

2. Habit Strength (H). Behavioral preferences learned by rewarded experience and observation.

3. Inhibitions against aggression (I). The sum of all internal factors opposing an aggressive act, including conditioned fear of punishment, learned attitudes and values, and identification with the victim.

4. Stimulus factors in the immediate environment that may facilitate (S_a) or inhibit (S_i) violence.

5. Response competition. Other possible responses are subject to their own algebra and nonaggressive responses may have a more favorable cost-benefit ratio than the aggressive response.

The occurrence of an aggressive act, then, depends upon the following formula:

$$A + H + S_a > I + S_i$$

Stated differently, the motivational factors must outweigh the inhibitory factors.

We have traced the evolution of psychological thought through the development of the Freudian hypothesis of frustration-aggression. The links with Freud remained clear in the early behavioral reformulations. However, as general psychology was influenced by radical behaviorism and highly cognitive social learning theories, aggression and criminality were increasingly seen to be complex functions of facilitators, inhibitors, prior learning, and the immediate situation. This appreciation of human diversity and complexity contrasts dramatically with the class-based sociological theories of criminal conduct.

Class-Based Sociological Theory: Social Location, Social Reaction, and Inequality

The class-based sociological perspectives on delinquency and crime entail anomie/strain theory, subcultural theory, labeling theory, and conflict/Marxist theory. These theories, in their social psychological versions, each purport that social class of origin is a major source of variation in illegal conduct at the individual level. The research evidence (as reviewed in Chapters 2 and 5) has shown that such an assumption is empirically indefensible in that class of origin is at best a minor risk factor. None of the class-based sociological theories are capable of providing images of crime and offenders that can even begin to approach the predictive validity of the psychodynamic and general personality and cognitive social learning models.

Remaining open to new evidence, it must be stressed that several of the class-based theories are so poorly specified that ideological commitments are bound to remain powerful. For example, some statements of anomie/strain theory suggest simultaneously that: (a) too much conventional ambition causes crime, (b) too little conventional ambition causes crime, (c) frustrated conventional ambition causes crime, and (d) conventional success may produce uncontrolled conventional ambition and greed (which, in turn, will cause crime). In other words, there is no way that any finding regarding conventional ambition, conventional success, or conventional failure does not relate to crime in a way that may be supported by some anomie theorists.

Anomie/Strain Theory

According to Robert Merton (1938, 1957), social structures exert a pressure upon certain persons to engage in deviant behavior. This text includes examples of the fact that certain social structures are indeed criminogenic. The core assumption of Merton's theory, however, was that lower-class persons were more likely to engage in criminal behavior than middle- and upper-class persons. Thus, position in the socio-economic system (that is, social location) was said to account for a major portion of variability in criminal behavior. Social location could be assessed by parental education, occupation, and income, as well as by the socioeconomic characteristics of neighborhoods.

Deviant behavior is said to occur when conventional aspirations exceed the levels of achievement that are possible by way of legitimate behavior. In America, the dominant aspiration to which all people are socialized (or which people come to share) was said to be "success" (money, property, and prestige). Anyone can grow up to be President and the legitimate route to success is working hard in school and on the job. The power of this aspect of the theory is clear because it is nothing less than the "American dream." Counter to the dream, however, is the fact that access to the conventional routes to success is blocked for many members of the lower class. Thus, criminal behavior was conceptualized as an innovative route to the same rewards that conventional employment would bring if only legitimate channels were available.

Here is where Merton turned psychoanalytic images of crime and criminals upside down and provided sociology with a socialized theory of crime. Crime was not the unsocialized expression of unbridled sexual-aggressive energy but rather an expression of socialized conventional ambition. Offenders were not "deviants" but "innovators."

Interestingly, Merton suggested that there were different modes of adaptation to anomie and that innovation (i.e., crime) was only one such mode. Here too, Merton drew upon the frustration-aggression hypothesis. The other adaptations to limited opportunities were retreatism (mental disorder and substance abuse among the real "down and out" of society), rebellion (attempts to create a new social order on the part of the more able and intellectual within the lower class), and ritualism (the mindless grinding away of the working poor who have transferred the dream to that of their children "making it"). No matter how questionable the underlying psychology and no matter how potentially offensive the image of the poor (drunks, drug addicts, criminals, the mentally disordered, mindless ritualists), anomie theory is a politically powerful statement that has fascinated social scientists and the public for years.

The notions of anomie and strain enter as mediating variables between the disjunction of legitimate means and the pursuit of illegitimate means. Merton reformulated psychoanalytic thought in sociologically acceptable ways. We have already discussed the frustration-aggression hypothesis wherein anger is a primary psychological mediator between frustration and aggression. For traditional strain theorists, the psychological mediator is anomie (i.e., feelings of alienation). Thus, it is not anger, hate, resentment, defiance, the search for adventure, or even too much conventional ambition (greed) that causes criminal activity. Rather, criminal behavior reflects awareness of limited opportunity and feelings of alienation, isolation, powerlessness, normlessness, and personal distress. Empirically, these are all very weak predictors compared to the psychoanalytic factors.

In summary, anomie/strain theory attempted to rid criminal motivation and criminals of all that "rude psychoanalytic stuff." Psychologically, a social location translation of frustration-aggression theory homogenized the abilities and diversity of human beings and created a banal image of the person.

General Strain Theory. Robert Agnew (1992) severed the ties of anomie theory to the political and professional ideology surrounding social class; replaced the structural anomie-alienation-innovation path with the original psychodynamic, social-learning path of frustration-anger-aggression; and relabeled the now massive evidence regarding the link between crime and difficulties at home, school, and work as indicators of a strain-crime link. He appears to have adopted what we call a general personality and social psychological perspective that has virtually nothing to do with traditional strain/anomie theory. Agnew calls his perspective *general strain theory* (GST), and the sources of negative affect (that is, anger rather than alienation) extend well beyond an aspiration-achievement discrepancy in the arena of conventional success.

The work on GST by Robert Agnew and his colleagues and students brought a new energy to the annual meetings of the American Society of Criminology in the 1990s. For example, the multiple potential motives for crime were being explored (Agnew, 1994): (a) moral evaluations of crime (unconditional approval as in "theft is not that wrong," conditional approval as in "a hungry person has the right to steal," moral imperative as in "people who disrespect me must be hurt"); (b) systematic review of the multiple potential rewards and costs; and (c) negative affect (cognitive-emotional states with an emphasis on anger).

With GST, anomie theory is no longer anomie theory but a general social psychology of criminal behavior with a particular interest in negative emotionality (anger rather than anxiety, depression, and/or generalized feelings of hopelessness). The multiple findings from the general psychology of aggression were brought into mainstream criminology in a strong manner. In 2001, Robert Agnew also admitted personality into his general theory (Agnew et al., 2001). Some feminists are particularly attracted to general strain theory because they feel that victimization is a major cause of female crime (Holtfreter & Cupp, 2007). They don't seem to realize that they are adopting a GPCSL perspective because they continue to suggest weaknesses in social learning theory.

Studies of recidivism from correctional psychology (Brown, St. Amand & Zamble, 2009; Zamble & Quinsey, 1997), forensic mental health (Quinsey et al., 1997), and youth services (Rowe, 2008) are revealing that acute dynamic indicators of negative emotionality may enhance the predictability of criminal recidivism. Thus, the general personality and social learning perspective may gain empirical status and inform practical parole, probation, and relapse prevention programming.

Sociologists were aware of problems with anomie theory well before Agnew's (1992) return to a more informed social psychology. In the early years, the response was to embrace subcultural theory and the idea that criminal behavior was conformity to the norms and values in opposition to mainstream, middle-class society. Furthermore, these deviant norms and values were shared mainly by the disenfranchised segments of society. The subcultural theories are reviewed from the perspective of a social psychology and, from this position, we find a gold mine for the psychology of criminal conduct.

Subcultural Perspectives in the Bold Sociological Mode

Subcultural theorists spoke primarily of young, urban, lower-class men who conformed to the urban, lower-class culture in which they were located. This culture devalued conventional routes to success and valued hedonism and destruction. Merton's people were not allowed to be "deviant," but at least they were allowed to "innovate." Within subcultural theory, though, criminal behavior is conformity. Stealing was conforming with the criminal subculture, using drugs was conforming to the retreatist subculture, and fighting was conforming to the conflict subculture. The nonconformists in the deviant subculture (the nonoffenders) were the real deviants.

Matza (1964) was among those social scientists who became concerned that subcultural theories were: (1) overpredicting delinquency among the young lower-class males, and (2) not even attempting to account for the delinquency of occupants of other social positions. In addition, it was clear that the delinquent cultures were difficult to identify except by examining personal attitudes and personal behavior. One obvious solution to this problem was to give credit to personal attitudes and values. Instead, however, it was hypothesized that there was a "subculture of delinquency" not bound by the limits of geography, age, sex, race, or class. Therefore, we are all surrounded by a subculture of delinquency.

Why then are there individual differences in criminal behavior? Matza provided a vague answer. He refers to an "impetus" that realizes the criminal act. This impetus comes from being pushed around, which then leads to a mood of fatalism and a feeling of desperation. Not everyone is exposed to and affected by this impetus, but for those affected, engaging in delinquent behavior serves to overcome these feelings and provide a sense of control and power. Matza warns us, however, not to test his ideas because the subcultural delinquent is no different from other boys. Indeed, he says, the lack of a difference between delinquent and nondelinquent persons is "precisely the point" of his theory. (We thank Hirschi, 1969, for underscoring Matza's point—this theory actually makes its empirical untestability a point of pride.)

Uncovering Social Psychological Value in Sociological Criminology

Cloward and Ohlin (1960) increased the sophistication of Merton's class-based theory by recognizing that the values supportive of frequent, serious, and persistent criminal activity were not at all conventional. Indeed, these values were explicitly anticonventional and procriminal. Through direct links with differential association theory (to be reviewed later in this chapter), they suggested a number of variables that had not been developed in strain/anomie theory. These additions have proven to be more important within the social psychology of crime than the correlates suggested by strain/anomie theory.

A major contribution of subcultural theory was to suggest that there may be important individual differences in degree of access to illegitimate means. While Merton emphasized differentials in the availability of socially prescribed means, Cloward and Ohlin said that the criminally-prone have been exposed to and have internalized a different set of rules and beliefs. Cloward and Ohlin, similar to Merton, were not particularly interested in the possibility that personal factors might be responsible for the differentials in opportunity.

For purposes of a Psychology of Criminal Conduct (PCC), it is important that certain personal sentiments and behavioral preferences can be shown to relate to criminal behavior. A bonus would be to find that being a member of groups in which certain values were dominant actually impacted on criminal behavior in a manner independent of the values of the individual (recall this point from Chapter 1).

The Content of Criminal Subcultures

Initially, the content of the values and norms said to be dominant in deviant subcultures was examined. Cohen (1955) was explicit in suggesting that criminal subcultures shared procriminal sentiments in direct opposition to the middle-class values of reason and verbalization, delayed gratification, and respect for property. That is, the major values were hostility and aggression, immediate gratification and short-term hedonism, and destruction. Interestingly, just as Merton called upon Freud in his specification of reactions to frustration, so did Cohen call upon the Freudian mechanism of reaction formation to account for the development of oppositional values supportive of delinquency. Thus, dropping out of school and not working were acts of defiance toward middle-class values. Cohen can then account for the fact that some hostile and destructive acts often accompany break-and-enter offenses.

Miller (1958) was still more informative in his specification of the content of procriminal sentiments. We do not need to view the following "focal concerns" as peculiar to the lower classes in order to appreciate their potential role in criminal behavior: trouble (generalized difficulty), toughness (physical prowess, "masculinity," daring), smartness (out-smarting others, "con"), autonomy (independence, not being bossed), fatalism (luck), and excitement (thrills, danger).

Within the "gang," major concerns have to do with belonging and status; both are achieved through demonstrations of toughness, smartness, and the other focal concerns. With reference to status within a group of male adolescents, Miller was explicit on the point that early expressions of adulthood were highly valued (recall the Glueck and Glueck findings that delinquents would smoke, drink, and engage in sexual behavior at an earlier age). Finally, the establishment and maintenance of the reputation of the gang often provided the motivation for delinquent activities such as gang fights.

Here, antisocial or procriminal attitudes, values, and beliefs, which in psychodynamic theory are a primary (albeit not total) reflection of a lack of socialization, are being externalized as properties of cultures. In turn, then, these external "values" are internalized. In addition, something else is happening. What the subcultural theorists and researchers are doing is giving PCC a new, more extensive, more grounded, and more complete vocabulary to be included in any theoretical representations of the cognitive processes that lead to criminal activity. Sykes and Matza (1957) made an outstanding contribution to the analysis of the cognition of crime.

Sykes and Matza (1957) were less inclined than subcultural theorists to accept the image of the delinquent as one committed to criminal values. They suggested that relatively few people would endorse the position that it was "OK" to steal or to inflict pain upon another person deliberately. The important variable was not so much delinquent subcultures but a subculture of delinquency.

The subculture of delinquency is characterized by a set of verbalizations that function to say that, in particular situations, it is "OK" to violate the law. Further, in some situations, violating the law is the only appropriate action. These verbalizations have been referred to as "techniques of neutralization," "rationalizations for law violations," and "a vocabulary of motives for illegal action" (Hartung, 1965). Note that they may be used prior to action and are considered causal. Their use is not limited to deflecting blame or controlling guilt after an offense has occurred. In social learning/social cognition theory, these types of cognitions are called "exonerating mechanisms" or processes of "moral disengagement" (Bandura et al., 1996).

For Sykes and Matza, the verbalizations are not at all discontinuous with patterns of belief evident in everyday living—deviant as well as non-deviant. Many are extensions of the aggravating and mitigating factors that play a formal role in legal decisionmaking. In fact, most people use them to make behavioral choices in moral situations. The subcultural perspective suggests, however, that offenders may make more extensive use of them, and may apply them more widely. The techniques by which guilt is neutralized (or the rationalizations for law violations) include each of the following:

The denial of responsibility: "I couldn't help it," "The devil made me do it," "It's not my fault," "It was an accident." If delinquent acts are due to factors beyond the control of the individual, then the individual is guilt-free and also free to act. Many of these rationalizations have the apparent support of social science: living in a slum, coming from a broken home, having been the victim of abuse, bad companions, having an exceptionally strong sex drive, drinking too much, and so forth.

The denial of injury: "I didn't hurt anyone," "I borrowed the tape recorder," "We just took the car for a ride around town." In employing these rationalizations, the delinquent admits responsibility for the act but not for any serious injury.

The denial of the victim: In situations in which responsibility and/or injury are difficult to deny, one can deny a victim by reversing the offender and victim roles. The victim "had it coming to him" or "deserved what she got." Thus, homosexuals, disobedient wives, nasty kids, and unfair teachers are appropriate candidates for abuse and harassment. There is no end to the list of "offenders" whose "punishment" is justifiable in the eyes of some—from corrupt politicians to the "fat cats" in business.

Condemnation of the condemners: With this type of rationalization, those who would disapprove of the offender's actions are defined as immoral, hypocritical, or criminal themselves. Thus, one hears "lawyers are no good," "courts can be fixed," "the police are brutal," and "everyone has their own racket." Have sociologists not proven that criminal justice processing reflects not the criminality of the accused but the social power of the accusers? Did Marx not show that the major institutions of society function to serve the interests of the powerful, while keeping the oppressed down?

Appeal to higher loyalties: "I didn't do it for myself." Rather, one was being loyal to a brother or sister, to a friend, or to the gang. The demands of the larger society were sacrificed for the demands of more immediate loyalties. While not illustrated by Sykes and Matza (1957), presumably appeals also may be made to the longer-term good, such as burning a video shop in order to interfere with the distribution of por-nography or taking hostages in order to publicize a social wrong.

The pool of procriminal sentiments suggested by subcultural theo-rists has not been exhausted in our brief discussion. Nor have we been careful in making distinctions among attitudes, values, beliefs, norms, rationalizations, or neutralizations. This is saved for an examination of the specific psychological processes involved in the cognitive control of behavior. However, we are now in a position to summarize the potential predictors suggested by the social psychology of subcultural theory:

1. Personal association with delinquents or with groups within which procriminal sentiments are endorsed;

2. Personal endorsement of antisocial/procriminal sentiments;

3. Having acquired the skills necessary to conduct some criminal acts and/or having access to the necessary materials or resources such as a drug supplier, a "fence" for stolen goods, or access to weapons.

These three correlates of delinquency and crime are of unquestioned empirical significance (although the third has been less well-studied than the first two). They are in no way incompatible with psychodynamic or control theory.

From Differential Association to Social Learning

Admitting our bias from the start, we are favorably disposed to differential association (DA) theory (Andrews, 1980), just as we were favorably disposed to early psychodynamic thought (Andrews & Wormith, 1989). In our opinion, there is much of immediate value within DA theory, as there was in early psychodynamic theory. Our presentation of DA theory will not delve into some nagging irritants or ambiguities in the theory for the same reasons that we did not concentrate on the difficulties and flights of fancy within classic psychoanalytic thought. When a theory rings true and identifies powerful correlates of criminal conduct that are readily validated empirically, we believe it deserves serious attention. (Resource Note 3.1 outlines the principles of DA.)

Interest increases further when the theory has obvious practical value for purposes of prediction and prevention (Andrews, 1980). In addition, as we did in the case of Freud, we encourage readers to consult the original statements of DA theory by Edwin Sutherland (1939; Sutherland & Cressey, 1970). In the case of Sutherland, however, we alert readers to the fact that the man who produced one of the most powerful PCCs is the same man who helped make antipsychological bias part of the institution of mainstream sociological criminology (Andrews & Wormith, 1989; Gottfredson & Hirschi, 1990; Laub & Sampson, 1991).

An attractive aspect of DA theory is the inclusion of two of the best validated correlates of criminal conduct in the whole of PCC: antisocial

Resource Note 3.1

The Principles of Differential Association Theory
Edwin Sutherland (1939, 1947; Sutherland and Cressey, 1970)
[With Some Minor Modifications]

1. Criminal behavior is learned.

2. Criminal behavior is learned in interaction with other persons in a process of communication.

3. The principal part of the learning occurs within intimate personal groups.

4. The learning includes techniques of crime and the specific direction (procriminal vs. anticriminal) of motives, drives, rationalizations, and attitudes.

5. The process of learning by association with criminal and anticriminal patterns involves all of the mechanisms that are involved in any other learning.

6. A person becomes delinquent because of an excess of definitions favorable to violation of law over definitions unfavorable to violations of law.

7. Differential associations may vary in frequency, duration, priority, and intensity.

Behavioral Reformulations

Criminal behavior is learned according to the principles of operant conditioning.

Learning occurs both in nonsocial situations and social interaction.

attitudes and antisocial associates. This text has already shown that assessments of antisocial/procriminal attitudes have consistently proved to be meaningful correlates of a criminal past and predictors of a criminal future. We have even seen evidence that changes in procriminal sentiments are predictive of future criminal activity. This evidence is highly relevant to DA because a central causal assumption of DA is that criminal acts reflect cognitions favorable to criminal activity: A person becomes delinquent because of an excess of "definitions" favorable to violation of law over "definitions" unfavorable to violations of law (Sutherland, 1947). Remember also that every perspective on crime we have reviewed would give causal status to antisocial attitudes. Even Merton's original statements regarding structurally induced anomie were qualified by a footnote to the effect that alienation would not lead to criminal acts if there were internalized prohibitions against law violation.

Second, antisocial associates are a major correlate of antisocial behavior even though Glueck and Glueck (1950) and Hirschi (1969; Gottfredson & Hirschi, 1990) did not assign it the causal significance that the findings of their research would suggest was reasonable. From the earliest explorations of the empirical validity of antisocial associates (e.g., Short, 1957) through to the latest reviews of a now vast empirical literature (Resource Note 2.1), it is clear that assessments of antisocial associates are able to distinguish between offenders and nonoffenders with a level of accuracy rivaled only by assessments of antisocial personality and antisocial attitudes, or by a very broad sampling of risk factors in the home, school, work, and the broader community. Within DA, the importance of antisocial associates resides in a fundamental theoretical principle: Criminal behavior is learned by associations with criminal and anticriminal patterns, and the principal part of that learning occurs in interaction with other persons in a process of intimate communication (Sutherland, 1947).

Thus, the fundamental causal chain in classical DA theory is from antisocial associates to the acquisition of antisocial attitudes to antisocial behavior in particular situations. With the development of behavioral reformulations of DA theory (Andrews, 1980; Burgess & Akers, 1966) and the impressive background of empirical research, a more powerful causal model is one that allows antisocial associates some direct causal significance unmediated by antisocial attitudes. With this model, antisocial attitudes and antisocial associates not only influence each other but may each contribute to the definitions of particular situations that are favorable to criminal activity.

Another positive feature of DA theory, as in the case of early psychodynamic and behavioral/social learning theory, is that it actually reflects a psychology of action based on the person in immediate situations. Moreover, the immediate psychology of action underlying DA theory is not very different from the psychology underlying early psychodynamic perspectives—or for that matter the immediate psychology of Megargee's (1982) algebra of aggression noted earlier in this chapter. In psychodynamic theory, criminal behavior reflected the ego's resolution of the id, superego, and immediate situational variables in the interest of maximizing pleasure and minimizing pain. In radical behavioral terms, behavior in a particular situation is determined by the discriminative properties of the situation whereby the probability of a particular act is a function of the reinforcement history of the act in similar situations. Our understanding of symbolic interactionism, on which DA theory is based, suggests a similar psychology of action. People behave in accordance with their cognitive "definitions of situations." A particular behavior occurs in a particular situation when that behavior is defined as appropriate or "OK." That behavior will not occur when the definitions of the situation are unfavorable to engaging in that particular behavior.

This perspective on the immediate situation of action fits neatly with one of the best validated models of human behavior in the whole of social psychology. This well-validated model is Ajzen and Fishbein's (1980, 2005) theory of reasoned action. (We appreciate the irony that the psychodynamic/control theories of crime place such a heavy emphasis upon impulsive action, that is, unreasoned action and weak self-control.)

According to Ajzen and Fishbein, people behave in accordance with their intentions. The behavioral intentions reflect attitudes favorable to the act, perceived social support for the act, and perceived barriers to enactment. This model of the immediate situation of action also fits well with Albert Bandura's emphasis on the immediate causal significance of self-efficacy beliefs, according to which people engage in those behaviors that they believe will be rewarding and successfully enacted. This general model is developed further in Chapter 4.

Cross-sectional studies of DA variables have delivered an image of delinquency and criminality that is remarkably consistent from study to study, cross-culturally, and across a variety of measures of deviance. The latter point has been well demonstrated in the studies conducted by Jessor and Jessor (1977), by Ronald Akers (1985), and by Delbert Elliott and colleagues (Elliott, Huizinga & Ageton, 1985). Jessor and Jessor, as well as Akers, have consistently taken the position that the principles that yield high levels of differentiation between criminals and noncriminals may also yield high levels of differentiation between alcoholics and non-alcoholics, and between marijuana users and nonusers.

Ronald Akers and John Cochran (1985) reported on a direct comparison of the abilities of social learning, anomie, and social control theories to account for variability in the use of marijuana within a sample of students in midwestern United States schools, grades 7 through 12. They obtained self-report questionnaire responses from 67 percent ($N = 3,065$) of the target population. Several measures of anomie and alienation, based on Merton's theory, could account for only 3 percent of the variability in marijuana use. Measures derived from the social control theories (e.g., parental attachment, grade point average, commitment to school, and the valuing of education) accounted for no more than 30 percent of the variability in drug use.

However, measures derived from the behavioral reformulations of differential association theory (that is, the social learning variables) accounted for 68 percent of the variability in drug use. The most potent variables within the social learning set included the following: (1) personal attitudes favorable to the use of marijuana; (2) having close friends who use marijuana; and (3) having close friends who approve of one's use of marijuana.

The addition of the anomie and control variables to the prediction formula was unable to increase the R square significantly above the 68 percent level achieved by the social learning variables on their own. In brief, these results strongly support the position that, in cross-sectional studies, the most important variables are the personal endorsement of delinquent values in combination with close delinquent associates who approve of one's engaging in delinquency.

The body of theoretically relevant work completed by Ronald Akers (1994, 1999) and his colleagues is truly impressive. They have demonstrated the power of attitudes and associates across a wide rang of criterion variables, including general delinquency, general criminality, alcohol use, marijuana use, and violence against women. The wide applicability of Akers's version of social learning theory is evident in an analysis of computer crime among college students (Skinner & Fream, 1997). Computer crimes such as piracy of computer software and illegal access were clearly a reflection of personal cognitions favorable to such crime as well as associations with friends favorable to such crime. As will become apparent in the next chapter, we look forward to Ronald Akers taking an interest in intervention studies because the behavioral reformulation of DA theory not only suggests major predictors but directs attention to the powerful influence strategies of modeling and reinforcement in the context of prevention and treatment.

The social learning and general social psychological perspective will be developed further in Chapter 4. Resource Note 3.2 summarizes a series of experimental tests of behavioral reformulations of certain principles of differential association. The two key principles are the *relationship principle* and the *structuring (or contingency) principle*. In situations of interpersonal influence, the chances of influence increase with the quality of the interpersonal relationship. High-quality relationships tend to be characterized by mutual respect, caring, and mutual liking as opposed to being cold, uncaring, and disrespectful. The direction of the influence depends upon what attitudes and behavior are being modeled and reinforced. The direct prediction is that anticriminal learning depends upon the exposure of anticriminal patterns under high-quality relationship conditions.

Resource Note 3.2

Some Experimental Investigations of Principles of Differential Association (DA) Through Manipulation of the Social Structure of Miniature Social Systems (based on Andrews, 1980)

By the end of the 1970s, there was already near massive cross-sectional and longitudinal support for the predictive validity of assessments of one or both of antisocial attitudes and antisocial associates. Experimental evidence, however, was virtually zero. In two of the leading collections of the day (Cressey & Ward, 1969; Rubington & Weinberg, 1973), only one experimental study was found in a sample of more than 100 studies.

In 1955, Donald Cressey presented an interesting rationale for the application of the theory of differential association to "changing criminals," but it did not generate many controlled program evaluations. Guided group interaction (GGI) programs certainly emphasized using delinquent peers as change agents in a programmed manner. As noted in the treatment chapter, however, this self-described "clinical sociology" did not employ structured cognitive change or

Resource Note 3.2 *(continued)*

skill-building strategies and appeared to want the "group" to adopt anticriminal values on their own without staff prompting. Such passivity was apparent because attitudes were thought of as properties of groups and not really properties of individuals, and because active modeling on the part of staff might promote "rejection of the rejectors." For all of this, LaMar Empey (with Erickson, 1972; with Rabow, 1961) and Stephenson and Scarpitti (1974) were very important leaders in introducing approximations of experimental ideals into criminology and corrections. Briefly, GGI programs did no better than community-based probation supervision (although sometimes clearly better than incarceration).

During the 1970s, a research program involving Carleton University and the Ontario Ministry of Correctional Services explored the treatment implications of a behavioral reformulation of differential association. A behavioral/social learning approach not only helps make sense of the predictive validity of risk factors suggested by DA theory but prevents treatment programs from relying on passive and weakly supported influence strategies. Notably, behavioral and social learning theory provide the powerful influence strategies of modeling and reinforcement and also are specific about self-management processes.

Three key principles of DA were recast into two broad sets. One set has to do with the conditions that promote criminal learning, and the other with the conditions that promote the translation of criminal learning into criminal behavior. The principles relating to promotion of criminal learning are the contingency principle and the relationship principle. The contingency principle reflects the importance in DA of differentials in exposure to criminal and anticriminal patterns. Behaviorally, the contingency principle directs attention to what patterns are being modeled (or demonstrated)—if you want to get a behavior going, demonstrate that behavior. The contingency principle also directs attention

to the immediate consequences of criminal and anticriminal expressions—the immediate consequences of interest are reinforcing consequences and punishing consequences, the former increasing the chances of a behavior recurring, the latter decreasing the chances of a behavior recurring. The contingency principle is also called the normative principle and sometimes the structuring principle. The contingency principle influences the direction of learning or the direction of interpersonal influence. For anticriminal learning, look for vivid expressions of anticriminal alternatives to procriminal patterns of thinking, feeling, and acting; for differential reinforcement of anticriminal alternatives; and for differential disapproval of expressions of procriminal patterns.

The relationship principle reflects the importance in DA of differentials in exposure occurring within intimate personal groups. The principle may also be called the socioemotional principle or the control principle. It directs attention to what influences the amount of learning or the amount of interpersonal influence. A high density of powerful rewards and costs is found within "intimate" personal groups. We define "intimacy" in terms of open, warm, understanding, sensitive, caring, nonblaming, enthusiastic, respectful, and frequent communication. Under these conditions, attention and warmth are strong reinforcers, mutual liking and caring increases the chances of modeling, frequency increases the opportunity for reinforced practice, and settings within which such interactions are apparent are approachable environments rather than ones to be avoided. In addition, even cost contingencies such as disapproval are more powerful in a pleasing environment (behaviorists speak of the "4 to 1 rule," at least four rewards for every punishment delivered).

Potentially, these are powerful principles that may guide assessments of the primary prevention/rehabilitative potential of naturally occurring and/or deliberately designed treatment environments. They may also guide the selection, training, and supervision of correctional and clinical staff. But let us return to the research program.

The third principle is called the self-management principle. It reflects the DA position that criminal behavior occurs when there is an excess of favorable definitions. In social learning terms, attitudes translate into behavior through self-control. In brief, attitudes, values, beliefs, rationalizations, and cognitive emotional states such as anger and resentment provide the standards that influence self-management through comparisons of behavior with the standard. In addition, self-approval, self-disapproval, and self-instructions to proceed or cease a behavior sequence are emitted. In brief, people talk to themselves, and that talk (and imagining) may support or not support criminal behavior depending on antisocial attitudes and self-management skill.

The principles were explored in a series of studies in prison and probation settings. The first few studies focused on the criminal learning and the later ones on the self-management principle. Consistent with DA's applauded ability to serve at the structural and individual levels, the experimental manipulations of relationship and contingency dimensions of interpersonal influence were conducted at the structural level of miniature service systems. Structurally, we varied the composition of groups and the roles assigned to group participants.

Rideau Correctional Center was a medium-security custody setting established to contain short-term adult recidivists and, in a separate facility on the same grounds, young first-time incarcerates. It was a rural facility that actually operated a farming enterprise (and during some growing seasons, the crops were actually brought in without contracts being set with local farmers). A systematic offender-based need survey had established that there was a need for a variety of programs at Rideau. A host of short-term structured groups were introduced. Many programs were subjected to experimental

evaluations as student research and thesis projects. While controlled evaluations revealed effects on a variety of short-term outcomes, including internal rule violations, social skills, and knowledge of community post-release resources, one outcome was not achieved over and over again. Shifts in antisocial thinking were not being accomplished. It appeared that a way was required in which to introduce the exposure of real alternatives to antisocial styles of thinking, feeling, and acting.

The prison chaplain, Jerry Brown, had introduced an interesting program in which citizen volunteers (typically elderly and Christian) visited the prison one night a week and met with inmates in groups to discuss current affairs or whatever consensus suggested as the topic of the night. Discussions with Brown led to the introduction of "community groups," in which citizen volunteers and prisoners were co-participants in weekly discussion groups. The discussion groups were composed of eight to 14 participants that met one night a week for eight weeks. The leaders of the groups initially were clinical staff of the prison and then other staff such as shop instructors and ultimately nonoffender graduates of earlier groups. The leaders encouraged open, warm, honest, and enthusiastic talk, and structured that talk around issues of rules, rationalizations for law violations, and self-management processes. The community group became very attractive, the number running increased, and the citizen volunteer participants were supplemented by undergraduates from Carleton University.

Study One: The effects of participation in "community groups." Prisoner volunteers and citizen volunteers were assigned randomly to community groups or to a waiting list. Pre-group and post-group assessment were conducted on the same paper-and-pencil questionnaire measures of antisocial attitudes that had been unable to show change in earlier programs. [A little aside: Among sociological criminologists at Carleton University

Resource Note 3.2 (continued)

at the time, the "bet" was that citizen volunteers and prisoners would not differ in antisocial attitudes (remember, it was the 1970s).] In fact, compared to the citizen volunteers, at pretest, the prisoners presented with more negative attitudes toward the law, courts, and police, with higher levels of identification with criminal others, and with greater acceptance of rationalizations for law violations. At posttest, and for the first time in our research, and consistent with the contingency principle, prisoner participants showed reduced antisocial thinking compared to prisoner non-participants. Notably, and consistent with the contingency principle, but not anticipated, the participating citizen volunteers showed increased antisocial thinking. Pleased with evidence supporting the contingency principle, we introduced additional service programs for evaluation. Not so pleased with the effects on citizen volunteers, we enhanced the preservice training and the debriefing of citizen volunteers.

Study Two: The effects of participation in "community groups" versus "recreation groups." Recreation groups do not involve structured opportunities for exposure to the anticriminal patterns of citizen volunteers. Rather, citizens and prisoners play cards or other board games. In brief, reduced antisocial attitudes were found only in the community groups. It appeared that the effect was due to differentials in exposure to anticriminal patterns rather than simple exposure to anticriminal others. An unanticipated finding emerged in that inmates who were in the recreation condition showed increases in self-esteem while inmates in the community groups did not. Fortunately, we had a waiting-list control group, and they too showed increases in self-esteem. It began to appear that increases in self-esteem were a routine consequence of incarceration that was blocked by exposure to community groups.

Study Three: The effects of enhanced interpersonal relationships within "community groups." Prior to participation in community

groups, the interpersonal relationship skills of citizen volunteers were assessed. Community groups were then formed, with some groups including citizens who were above average in their relationship skills and other groups in which the citizen volunteers were below average in their interpersonal skills. Please note that as a group, citizen volunteers score well above average in their relationship skills as compared to nonvolunteers. Thus, even the low-relationship group included relatively high-functioning citizens. The actual results were not as clean as the findings we had begun to expect. It was only low-anxiety inmates who responded best to the high-functioning volunteers. It appeared that interpersonally anxious offenders did better with lower-intensity volunteers.

Study Four: The effects of discussion groups with and without citizen participants. This study was conducted with long-term incarcerates in the Canadian federal system. The findings depended on considering how inmate-rated relationship conditions were associated with reduced antisocial thinking. Within inmate-only groups, open communication was associated with increased antisocial attitudes. Within the community groups, open communication was associated with decreased antisocial attitudes. This pattern of findings supports the theoretical position that a high-quality relationship promotes influence and that the direction of that influence depends upon what is being modeled and reinforced.

Study Five: The relationship, contingency, and self-management principles in probation as explored in the Canadian Volunteers in Corrections study (CaVIC). In this study, 190 probationers were randomly assigned to professional probation officers or to citizen volunteers who were assistants to professional probation officers. The volunteer program was directed by Jerry Kiessling, a senior probation officer in Ottawa, Ontario. Jerry was so respected by his colleagues and citizen volunteers that the university-based researchers and students were allowed to conduct

Resource Note 3.2 *(continued)*

personality assessments of the probation officers and probationers and to ask both groups to report on their impressions of the supervision process and short-term outcomes. Additionally, some supervision sessions were audiotaped with the consent of both probation officers and probationers.

Many assessment instruments were administered, but the basic ones for our purposes were Empathy, Socialization, and Antisocial Attitudes. Officer Empathy scores were positively associated with probationer and officer ratings of the quality of the interpersonal relationship. Officer Socialization scores were positively associated with probationer and officer ratings of the help received. Officer Empathy scores were unrelated to tape-based assessments of modeling and reinforcement, but officer Socialization scores were positively correlated with anticriminal modeling and anticriminal reinforcement. In

brief, the officers were classified according to their scores on Empathy and Socialization, and the recidivism rates of their probationers were compared. Probationers assigned to officers who scored high on both the relationship indicator (Empathy) and the structuring indicator (Socialization) recidivated at lower rates than probationers assigned to other officers. The high-Empathy officers established quality interpersonal relationships with their probationers and they had a positive (anticriminal) message to deliver, and that combination resulted in reduced crime on the part of their probationers. The overall pattern of results led us to pursue a general personality and cognitive social learning model of criminal behavior. Now it appeared that both practical prediction and practical influence might be enhanced through the cognitive social learning approach (see Chapter 4).

In the next chapter we will see additional experimental evidence in support of behavioral reformulations of DA theory and find real value in a general personality and cognitive social learning approach that recognizes that the causes of criminal conduct are situational, circumstantial, personal, interpersonal, familial, and structural/cultural.

Worth Remembering

1. The structure of human personality provided by classical psychodynamic theory provided outlines of major risk/need factors that continue to resonate today. Of particular importance are ego skills and superego strength. They operate as internal sources of control over the expression of basic aggressive and sexual drives.

2. Now the psychodynamic, social bonding, differential association, and strain theoretical perspectives are converging on general personality and cognitive social learning perspectives. Psychodynamic theory led to early social learning theory via the frustration aggression route as early as the 1930s through the Yale school. Differential association theory was reformulated in behavioral

terms; in criminology, it is called social learning theory. Traditional strain theory has returned to its roots in frustration-aggression and thereby profited from the social learning and social cognition perspectives on anger and aggression. Social learning theory is now evident throughout criminology and PCC.

3. The research evidence is clear: personality factors such as weak self-control are best combined with assessments of attitudes and associates in order to enhance predictive accuracy.

Recommended Readings

This chapter traced the influence of psychodynamic theory on the major criminological theories and social learning perspectives of criminal conduct. Therefore, we would be remiss not to recommend Freud's (1953) *A General Introduction to Psychoanalysis*. Most of Freud's ideas are in this set of papers. For the reader wishing more of a summary than a detailed, firsthand account, Calvin Hall's (1954) *Primer of Freudian Psychology* is suggested.

The two other classics that we suggest to the reader are Sheldon Glueck and Eleanor Glueck's (1950) *Unraveling Juvenile Delinquency* and Dollard et al.'s (1939) *Frustration and Aggression*, a reformulation of Freud's frustration-aggression hypothesis into social learning terms.

A General Personality and Cognitive Social Learning Approach: The Personal, Interpersonal, and Community-Reinforcement (PIC-R) Perspective

This book opened with the objective of describing and assessing the empirical, theoretical, and practical status of the psychology of criminal conduct (PCC). Even without having yet detailed the evidence in regard to practical prediction (Chapter 10) and practical treatment (Chapters 11 and 12), Chapters 2 and 3 revealed a reasonably strong empirical base to PCC.

PCC has a highly meaningful criterion variable in that substantial individual differences are found in both initial criminal involvements and in repeat crime. This is true whether crime is defined by self-reports, victim reports, or official records, and when measured within any of the typical categories of social location defined by gender, race, and socio-economic disadvantage (Chapters 1, 2, and 10).

Knowledge of the correlates and predictors of individual criminal conduct is sufficiently strong to assert that the best-established risk factors for criminal conduct within almost any sample are *antisocial cognition, antisocial associates, a history of antisocial behavior*, and a complex of indicators of *antisocial personality pattern* (Chapter 2). These indicators of antisocial personality include elements of weak self-control such as being impulsive, lacking persistence, and being neither reflective nor planful. Additional indicators include elements of disagreeableness such as being spiteful, antagonistic, feeling mistreated, and being indifferent to others. In the middle range of predictive validity reside assessments of family and parenting, indicators of personal school/employment achievement, and leisure/recreation. Substance abuse also enters the middle set. In the lower range of predictive validity are lower-class origins and personal distress.

Accepting all of the above, empirical knowledge is still weak on some issues. First, the specific moderators of the covariates of criminal conduct (e.g., variation in the risk/need factors depending upon the stages of human development and/or with type of offense) remain an issue. Second, the impact of broader social arrangements on individual criminal conduct is poorly documented (Chapter 8 reveals that even the best of efforts to link ecology of neighborhoods to individual criminal conduct yield minor effects). Social science rhetoric aside, interesting and convincing demonstrations of the impact of broad structural/cultural factors on variation in individual criminal conduct are few. Third, limits placed upon the validity of particular constructs because of choice of research design or because of errors of measurement and/or conceptualization are known but not fully considered. Finally (and obviously), empirical knowledge can reflect only the findings of studies that have already been conducted and reported upon. Empirical knowledge is not only relative, political, and socially constructed, but it is also partial and incomplete.

Recognizing these problems, if a theory is to meet the criterion of empirical defensibility, it must deal with the empirical findings noted in the second paragraph of this chapter. For purposes of empirically derived theory, the obvious choice is to select the major causal variables from the list of the strongest correlates. We would choose antisocial attitudes, associates, behavioral history, and personality. We are unaware of any cross-sectional or longitudinal study in which at least one of the "Big Four" was not singled out from other potential predictors in the construction of an efficient and effective predictive model. Moreover, cross-sectional (e.g., Akers & Cochran, 1985; Johnson, 1979) and longitudinal (e.g., LeBlanc et al., 1988) research conducted as early as the 1950s through 1980s had already revealed that two or more of the four will be selected within the most potent and efficient prediction formula.

In the 1990s and up until today we have consistently found that the structured assessments of the Big Four risk/need factors account for the vast majority of valid predictions (Chapter 2; Chapter 10; Andrews, Bonta & Wormith, 2006). The meta-analytic work of Pratt and Cullen (2000) shows that assessment of weak self-control in combination with associates and attitudes yields higher correlations with crime than does either set alone. Our own work with adjudicated offenders convinced us years ago that the most empirically defensible theories will be those that assign causal significance to at least two of the four. Why we chose all four will become clear, but note now that the reasons are theoretical rather than "dustbowl empirical." The early statements of PIC-R preceded the explosion of meta-analytic evidence.

Building theories on the basis of existing data may be characterized as "dustbowl empiricism" at the extreme. Limitations admitted, the radical empirical approach to building theoretical understanding at least has the potential of organizing knowledge in a rational manner. Some criminologists complained that Glueck and Glueck's (1950) "tentative causal formula" was nothing but a list of admittedly powerful correlates of delinquency simply organized according to psychoanalytic principles. We remind such critics that the variables left out of the Glueck and Glueck causal formula included those empirically indefensible variables that class-based sociological theories continued to promote for decades. Given the choice of choosing causal variables through consideration of evidence as opposed to professional and ideological interests, rational empiricism within PCC prefers even a radical empiricism over theoreticism.

It is not enough, however, for radical empirical approaches to simply be better than theoreticism. Theories should also be fruitful. They should organize empirical knowledge in a rational and attractive manner and also assist in the search for new empirical understandings that lead to a deeper theoretical appreciation of criminal conduct. Moreover, we expect theories to be practically useful in decreasing the human and social costs of crime. A good theory also will be consistent with other strong theories in the broader domain of the biological, human, and social sciences.

The latter two concerns lead to the next steps in the empirically informed construction of a general personality and social psychology of criminal conduct. First, we seek an organizing set of assumptions that is consistent with the best-validated and most promising of psychological perspectives of human behavior. This means that we seek a general psychology that is empirically defensible and promising in terms of understanding variation in human behavior. Second, we seek an underlying theory of human behavior that is clinically relevant. No matter how professionally strong and moral our interests in aggregated crime rates, our interest in criminal justice processing, and/or our interest in political correctness, clinical relevance requires PCC to provide meaningful assistance in the design and delivery of direct services that reduce antisocial behavior and/or reduce costs of processing. If we find that prevention and rehabilitation through direct service are wasted efforts, so be it. The point is that a clinically irrelevant PCC is less valuable than a clinically relevant PCC.

Is there a human psychology that may serve the interests of PCC better than alternative psychologies of action? Our answer is that there are several such human psychologies, some clearly better than others. One of these promising psychologies was psychodynamic theory. The psychodynamic psychology of the person in immediate situations was outlined in Chapter 3, and the predictive validity of Glueck and Glueck's psychodynamic interpretation of risk factors has proved impressive on all counts except for their dismissal of antisocial associates as a major variable.

Glueck and Glueck were aware of the importance of the immediate environment in psychoanalytic theory but, for some reason, they failed to view antisocial associates as an indicator of facilitative versus inhibiting effects within many immediate situations of action. More generally, with the post-Freud and post-Glueck advances in human science, we can now do better than a psychology of action that depends on operationalizations of the very broad and relatively stable constructs of ego and superego. Such traits are required when the task is predicting behavior over the long term, but more acute characteristics are required for shorter-term prediction and for clinical relevance. In regard to clinical relevance, Glueck and Glueck themselves were not satisfied with psychoanalysis as a treatment model. Moreover, we find very few examples of successful psychodynamic treatment in corrections to this day.

Radical behaviorism offers a detailed and well-validated analysis of the determinants of action in particular situations. It is of demonstrated clinical value and has been integrated with psychodynamic theory (e.g., frustration-aggression theory). The result of the integration is most often called social learning or social cognition theory. These labels are also applied to that which emerged when behavioral principles were integrated with the symbolic interactionism underlying differential association (DA) theory.

Symbolic interactionism offered a potentially powerful psychology because of the emphasis on the cognitive control of behavior and the key causal significance assigned to attitudes, beliefs, and interpersonal interactions. Differential association theory, however, had little to say about the background predictors of how particular persons found themselves in particular situations. Clinically, symbolic interactionism fared poorly in directing clinical effort. Thus, once again, integration with behavior theory was indicated.

The Person in the Immediate Situation

Although the term "integration" is used loosely, rather than debate the issue, let us look at the immediate psychology of action in a General Personality and Cognitive Social Learning (GPCSL) perspective on criminal conduct. Figure 4.1 shows that immediate causal significance is assigned to constructs akin to definitions of situations favorable to criminal acts. Some theorists speak of "behavioral intentions," others of "self-efficacy beliefs," the "algebraic solution," or "personal choice"; some use phrases such as "the balance of rewards and costs." It remains to be seen whether operational distinctions among assessments of these variables may be differentiated in construct validity studies. We expect not; the main problem for the field may be to settle on a common vocabulary. So far, assessments of behavioral intentions and self-efficacy beliefs have impressive predictive validities in many different situations (Ajzen & Cote, 2008; Ajzen & Fishbein, 1980, 2005; Bandura, 1989, 2008; Bandura et al., 1996; Fishbein, 1997). There are now many specific models, but self-regulation is a dominant piece of personality and social psychology, cognitive psychology, and neuropsychology (see the wealth of partially overlapping models in Roy Baumeister and Kathleen Vohs's, 2004, edited collection). In the light of the explosion of research on

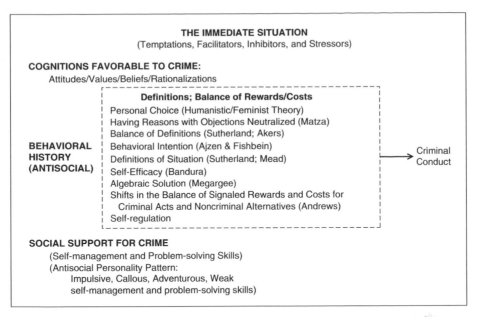

Figure 4.1
The Psychological Situation (or Psychological Moment) in a General Personality and Social Psychology of Criminal Conduct

self-regulation (automatic and effortful), Figure 4.1 now includes the generic causal variable of self-regulation.

An internal dialogue is often assumed here. Many acts of fraud and force do occur on the spur of the moment and are so "easy" (in the language of Gottfredson and Hirschi, 1990) that almost anyone could reach that stage of self-efficacy at which they believed that they were skilled enough to engage in the act. Not everyone, however, would assess the situation as one in which that behavior would be appropriate.

The major sources of variation in judgments of appropriateness are: (a) characteristics of the immediate environment, (b) the attitudes, values, and beliefs held by the person with regard to antisocial behavior, (c) social support for antisocial behavior, most often in the form of perceived support from others for that action but also including direct assistance, (d) a history of having engaged in antisocial behavior, (e) relatively stable personality characteristics conducive to antisocial conduct, (f) cognitive emotional states such as anger, and (g) self-management and problem-solving skills, including the use of rationalizations and justifications for law violations. Self-management and problem-solving skills are in parentheses in Figure 4.1 because they have contributed heavily to that particular person being in that particular situation; any additional contribution may only be in the form of moderator variables in interaction with attitudes or social support.

Psychodynamic theory and social learning theory suggest, however, that the psychological moment should incorporate some understanding of "ego skills" such as problem-solving and self-regulation. Here the emphasis is not on what we think (as in the case of antisocial attitudes) but on how we think. For some theorists, these skills and cognitive processes are accepted as given. For example, David Matza (1964) recognized that young people may engage in active rationalization wherein any anticipated guilt over rule violations is neutralized in advance by verbalizations such as "I couldn't help it" or "the 'victim' deserved it." At the same time, however, Matza was committed to the view that young offenders and nonoffenders could not be differentiated according to their propensity to or their ability to engage in these rationalizations. Today, cognitive skills are a major focus of research in developmental and cognitive psychology, and there is no question that there are major individual differences in both the "how" and "what" of thinking/interpreting/coping. Building on the work of Ross and Fabiano (1985), "cognitive" programming typically incorporates cognitive skill building in combination with a restructuring of the cognitive/affective content.

Consideration of cognitive skills may be of particular value in studies of young offenders because developmental delays in cognitive functioning may be of exceptional importance in the study of antisocial behavior (see Chapters 5, 6, and 7). In addition to self-regulation and problem-solving skills, there are several other candidates for inclusion in the psychological moment that are focused on in current research and theoretical debate. Intoxication through substance abuse is an obvious one in that it may disrupt normal controls. Similarly, particularly stressful circumstances and depressive or psychotic states may weaken normal controls. An ongoing concern is the extent to which combinations of variables are particularly crucial. For example, antisocial attitudes may translate into antisocial behavior most strongly in combination with antisocial associates. The interactionist models proposed by Mischel and Shoda (1998) and Fleeson (2001) appear promising in conceptualizing the interrelationships among multiple psychological and social processes.

The Cognitive-Affective Personality System (CAPS: Mischel & Shoda, 1998, 2006) is a particularly attractive model of self-regulation. The authors propose that there are mental representations (or cognitive-affective units) of the self, goals, expectations, beliefs, and affects. There are also mental representations of self-regulation competencies, plans, and strategies. The units are uniquely organized according to the biological and social learning history of the individual. Mischel and Ayduk (2002) describe how willpower operates to self-distance one from difficult or frustrating situations. Self-regulation involves balancing "hot" emotions and "cool" cognition (i.e., "chill").

Figure 4.2 provides a path-analytic summary of routes to the occurrence of particular people being in particular circumstances. It incorporates the more distal or background dispositional factors that shape both the person and the immediate context of action. Similar models have

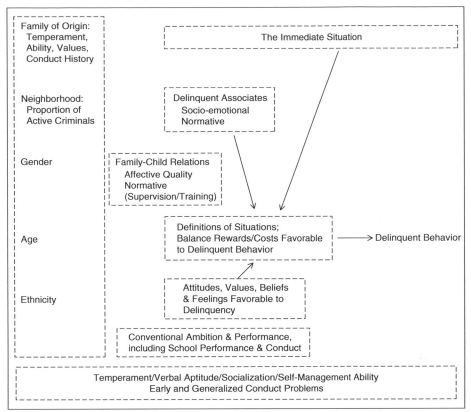

Figure 4.2
A General Personality and Social Psychological Perspective on Criminal Conduct

been presented by Jessor and Jessor (1977), Akers (1973, 1985, 2001), and many others, but we think that personality is best brought into the general cognitive social psychology of crime.

The model recognizes that there are multiple routes to involvement in illegal conduct, but suggests that antisocial attitudes and criminal associates are particularly strong risk factors. The model does not assume, for example, that all young offenders are temperamentally restless or aggressive, or that all young offenders are weakly tied to home and school. The chances of illegal conduct increase dramatically as the number and variety of the more proximal set of predispositional factors increase.

Where do political economy, social structure, and culture fit into this general personality and social psychology of crime? Because they are constants, they are distal background contextual conditions that cannot account for variation in individual conduct within particular social arrangements. Figure 4.3 shows the various classes of variables that may impact on individual behavior ordered from the broadest structural level down to the person in an immediate situation. Structure and culture have important roles to play in establishing the fundamental contingencies

THE BROAD CONTEXT: POLITICAL, ECONOMIC, CULTURAL, SOCIAL-STRUCTURAL

Dominant Values and Distribution of Wealth and Power
Legislation/Policy/Convention
Labor Market   Competitive Individualism

MORE IMMEDIATE SOCIAL STRUCTURAL AND CULTURAL FACTORS

Family of Origin, Membership   Neighborhood: Membership Composition
Composition: Personality,   (e.g., Proportion of Active Criminals)
Ability, Values, Mental Health,   and Roles and Statuses
Conduct History (Crime/Substance Abuse),
Educational, Occupational,
Parenting Skills and Resources

Community Settings:
School/Work/Recreational/Mental Health/Social Service Agencies
The Justice System: Police, Courts, Formal Agencies

THE INTERPERSONAL: PROCESS AND CONTENT OF INTERACTION

Family-Child Relations: Ties to Anticriminal Others
Affection/Supervision/
Neglect/Abuse
Interaction with Agencies   Ties to Criminal Others
(i.e., processing and service)

THE PERSONAL

Biological Given: Temperament/Aptitude/Verbal Intelligence
Age/Gender

Early Conduct Problems: Personality:
Lying, Stealing, Aggression   Socialization/Psychopathy in particular

(Self-regulation skills/problem-solving style)
(Internal/external monitoring for standards of conduct)

Conventional Ambition and Performance   School Performance and Conduct

Cognitions Favorable to Crime: Perceived Social Support for Crime
Attitudes, Values, Beliefs,
Rationalizations, Neutralizations,
and Feelings

History of Criminal Behavior

THE PERSON IN IMMEDIATE SITUATIONS

Immediate Situation: Signaled Outcomes
Facilitators, Inhibitors,   ⟶   Favorable to   ⟶   Criminal Acts
Stressors   Criminal Activity

Figure 4.3
A Personal, Interpersonal, and Community-Reinforcement Perspective on the Multiple Classes of Relevant Variables in the Analysis of Criminal Behavior

that are in effect within each particular social arrangement. A personal, interpersonal, and community-reinforcement perspective of deviant behavior attempts to account for this role within a model that seeks to explain individual differences in criminal conduct.

A Personal, Interpersonal, and Community-Reinforcement (PIC-R) Perspective on Criminal Conduct

One example of the general personality and cognitive social learning approach is the Personal, Interpersonal, and Community-Reinforcement (PIC-R) perspective on deviant behavior (Andrews, 1982a). The principles are outlined in Resource Note 4.1. Incidentally, the original outline of the principles of PIC-R was prepared in the decade before publication of the meta-analytic findings regarding the relative strength of different risk factors (for example: Chapter 2) and the characteristics of effective prevention (Chapters 2 and 11).

Resource Note 4.1

The Principles of PIC-R

1. Occurrences of deviant and nondeviant behavior are under antecedent and consequent control.

2. Inter- and intraindividual variations in the probability of occurrence of a given class of behavior (deviant or nondeviant) are due to variations in the signaled rewards and costs for that class of behavior.

3. The controlling properties of antecedents and consequences are acquired through the interaction of the person with the environment. The principles governing the acquisition, maintenance, and modification of the controlling properties of stimulus conditions include those of genetic and constitutional disposition and capability; biophysical functioning; cognitive functioning; human development; behavioral repertoire; state conditions; and respondent and operant conditioning, including observational learning, rule learning, symbolic control, and role enactment.

4. Antecedents and consequences are of two major types: additive events (stimuli are introduced, extended, or augmented) and subtractive events (stimuli are withdrawn, postponed, or diminished).

5. Variations in the probability of occurrence of a given class of behavior are a positive function of the signaled density of the rewards for that class of behavior and a negative function of the signaled density of the costs for that class of behavior.

6. Antecedents and consequences arise from three major sources: (1) the actor (personally mediated events), (2) other persons (interpersonally mediated events), and (3) the act itself (nonmediated or automatic and habitual events).

   a) The strength of personally mediated influence increases with a general predisposition toward high personal constraint, the availability of specific self-management elements such as problem solving and self-control skills, and when personal cognitions deviate from the neutral. The direction of the influence depends upon the procriminal versus anticriminal nature of the cognitions. In brief, the chances of criminal behavior increase when personal attitudes, values, beliefs, rationalizations, identities, and cognitive-emotional states are supportive of criminal behavior. The chances of criminal behavior decrease when

Resource Note 4.1 *(continued)*

cognitions are anti-criminal. Personally mediated control is weakened when cognitions are neutral.

b) The strength of interpersonally mediated influence increases with adherence to the relationship and structuring principles. If the other is respected, valued, and liked (and respectful and likeable), the effect of interpersonal influence is enhanced. The direction of the influence is determined by procriminal versus anticriminal nature of the other's cognitions, expectations, and behavior. A high-quality relationship with a person who is neutral toward crime will have an intermediate impact on criminal behavior.

c) Nonmediated influences are relatively automatic as a function of the act itself and primarily reflect a history of reinforcement for the target behavior. Through repeated associations of other stimulus events with reinforced behavior, the stimuli may also come to exert automatic control. Thus, for example, simply thinking of a significant other may influence the occurrence of behaviors preferred by the other. Movement from active and deliberate personally mediated control to automatic control will require careful and detailed plans of activity that are heavily rehearsed.

7. The magnitude of the effect of any one signaled reward for any class of behaviors depends upon the signaled density of other rewards for that class of behaviors. Generally, the magnitude of the effect of any one reward is greatest at some intermediate level of density, and the magnitude of the effect of any one reward is diminished at the lowest and highest levels of density. Similarly, the magnitude of the effect of any one cost for any class of behaviors is greatest at some intermediate level of density of costs.

8. Variations in the signaled rewards and costs for one class of behavior (deviant or nondeviant) may produce variations in the probability of occurrence in another class of behavior. The magnitude of the effect is a function of interconnecting contingencies and schedules for deviant and nondeviant behavior. The rewards for non-deviant behavior approach their maximum impact on the chances of deviant behavior under the following conditions:

a) when and where relatively noncostly and nondeviant behaviors produce a relatively high density of rewards, including rewards similar to those produced by deviant behavior;

b) when and where the costs for deviant behavior include a reduction, postponement, omission, or interruption in the delivery of those rewards produced by nondeviant behavior; and

c) when and where nondeviant behavior is incompatible with deviant behavior.

9. Variations in the probability of occurrence of any given behavior within each of the deviant and nondeviant classes of behavior may be understood or produced by the application of the preceding principles to that specific behavior.

10. Historical, geographic, and political-economic factors influence individual behavior primarily by way of the contingencies that they produce within settings and communities. For example, physical, environmental, and cultural variables, and the structure of social systems influence individual behavior through the reward-cost contingencies they maintain within the settings.

11. Two basic dimensions for the analysis of the effects of systems on the deviant and nondeviant behaviors of its members are

Resource Note 4.1 *(continued)*

the normative and the control dimensions. The normative dimension includes behavioral prescriptions and proscriptions and their distribution according to one's position within the system. The control dimension includes the visibility of normative and deviant behavior to persons who control resources (including potential rewards and costs); the quantity, variety, quality, and magnitude of potential rewards and costs; the immediacy, frequency, and regularity with which rewards and costs are delivered; and the maintenance of interconnecting contingencies for deviant and nondeviant behavior. In the context of

interpersonal interactions we are referring once again to the relationship and structuring dimensions of interaction.

12. The predictability of behavior and its amenability to influence increase with individualized assessment of the signaled reward/cost contingencies.

13. The human and social value of any perspective on human conduct is in some part a function of predictive efficiency and the ability to influence events. For the most part, its practical value is a function of ethical, legal, and humane applications.

As a broad cognitive social learning perspective on human conduct, PIC-R attempts to be both comprehensive and flexible. It considers factors that actively encourage or discourage deviant activity. In this sense, PIC-R incorporates elements of what sociological criminologists call motivational and control theories. It emphasizes both motivational and control elements, because of the nature of criminal activity and its consequences, rather than a priori theoretical preferences. Within general human psychology, it is well understood that both reinforcement and punishment operate to influence future behavior. It also recognizes that human motivation for crime extends well beyond strain. It recognizes social bonding but is explicit that the procriminal and anticriminal orientation of others is crucial in determining the influence of others. In addition, PIC-R explicitly recognizes factors at the personal, interpersonal, and community levels of analysis. PIC-R also stresses that the specific factors governing the conduct of persons are many, that they may be highly individualistic, and that their importance may vary over time and situations. Due to its comprehensive nature, PIC-R helps organize and locate what other less comprehensive theories attended to, as well as what they minimized.

PIC-R recognizes that an understanding of deviant behavior must draw upon knowledge from the biological, human, and social sciences in general, but emphasizes behavioral and cognitive social learning principles because of their demonstrated functional power in applied settings. The practical and clinical utility of PIC-R will reside in its ability to encourage comprehensive assessments and to assist in planning reasonable and effective interventions. Its contribution to the public good will depend on its ability to assist crime control policymakers to recognize that effective legislation must reach down and touch people in their immediate situations of action.

PIC-R draws upon radical behaviorism for its most fundamental principles in that the factors responsible for variation in human conduct are found in the immediate situation of action. Specifically, these include rewards and costs and those antecedents to behavior that signal the delivery of either rewarding or costly consequences for particular acts. These fundamental principles of behavioral analysis are summarized in Resource Note 4.2. The theoretical principle is that variation in the immediate contingencies of action is responsible for the acquisition, maintenance, and modification of human behavior. Behavioral principles are not limited to learning but are fundamental principles of performance.

Resource Note 4.2

Principles of Behavioral Analysis

The key concepts of the learning perspectives are summarized here.

- Classical (or respondent or Pavlovian) conditioning: The process by which a previously neutral stimuli comes to control a conditioned response through pairing with an unconditioned stimulus. The conditioned response is often some fraction or component of the unconditioned response to the unconditioned stimulus.

- Instrumental behaviors (or operants): Behaviors that operate upon the environment or that are instrumental in bringing about changes in the environment.

- The consequent control of operants: The changes in the chances of an act recurring that are due to the relatively immediate environmental consequences of an act.

- Rewards (or reinforcers): The immediate environmental changes produced by operants that are associated with an increased chance of the act recurring.

- Costs (or punishers): The immediate environmental changes produced by operants that are associated with a decreased chance of the act recurring.

- Modeling: Learning through observation and imitation (or, if the model: demonstrating a behavior).

- Antecedent control: Variations in the chances of an act occurring due to the immediately preceding stimulus conditions.

Some important antecedents include: other people as models; other people as potential sources of rewards or costs; self-talk; images and thoughts; affective states; the physical resources or aids necessary for the completion of an act; discriminative stimuli that, through experience, set the occasion for an act; unconditioned stimuli; conditioned stimuli, intentions or definitions of situations; beliefs regarding one's ability to perform; and the consequences of performance.

- An alternative act or an alternative response: In any situation, more than one act is under the influence of antecedent and consequent control. Those other acts are called alternatives.

Even what Gottfredson and Hirschi (1990) call the "easy and simple" criminal acts are under behavioral control within the PIC-R perspective.

Some contingencies may be or become relatively automatic, given the nature of some acts (theft produces property; ingestion of a drug produces sensory change) and/or given how often they occur together (habitual). Other contingencies are personally mediated (active self-management through self-instruction and self-reward), and still others are interpersonally mediated (e.g., other persons may explicitly approve or disapprove of one's actions). In addition, the political economy and social structure of both narrow and broader social systems will produce and maintain certain contingencies that may involve personal and/or interpersonal mediation. In clinical practice, without alteration of the personal, interpersonal, and community sources of rewards and costs, long-term behavior change is unlikely.

PIC-R draws upon the concepts of personality and the social sciences. While the immediate contingencies of action account for variation in human conduct, it is the personal, interpersonal, and community factors that are responsible for the development, maintenance, and modification of the contingencies themselves. Stable contingencies account for stability in behavior over time and across situations. Thus, for example, we will see how stability in personal attitudes and choice of associates, as well as personal temperament, may maintain relatively high chances of deviant conduct across a variety of situations. Indeed, apparently diverse situations may be psychologically equivalent in terms of the contingencies that they signal and the cognitions they elicit (Mischel & Shoda, 1995, 2006).

Finally, the contingencies in effect for nondeviant alternative behaviors are important in the analysis and practical modification of deviant behavior. When nondeviant alternative behaviors are highly rewarded, the motivation for some forms of deviance may be reduced. Thus, while there is some room for anomie theory, the psychological process is dramatically different from that proposed in the early sociological and psychological strain theories. The potential for reduced criminal behavior resides not so much in reduced motivation for crime but in the potential for dramatic increases in the costs of crime through increases in the subtractive costs of crime. As the rewards for "noncrime" increase, the individual has more to lose.

Antecedent and Consequent Control

Resource Note 4.1 provides a summary of the PIC-R principles. At this point, we will expand upon these principles and provide a fuller explanation. Principle 1 holds that occurrences of deviant and nondeviant behavior are under the control of antecedent and consequent events. Principle 2 holds that interindividual and intraindividual variations in the probability of occurrence of a given class of behavior (deviant or nondeviant) are due to variation in the signaled rewards and costs for that class of behavior.

Antecedent stimuli are stimulus events that precede and influence the behavior. They constitute the "A" in the A-B-C (antecedent-behavior-consequence) of behavioral analysis. Antecedents may be external or internal stimuli. Antecedent control implies that changes in stimulus conditions alter the probability of the behavior occurring. For example, the presence or absence of a police officer will affect the probability of jaywalking, and the thought that someone is out to kill you may affect the likelihood of an aggressive act of self-defense.

Antecedent stimuli gain control over behavior through the processes of classical conditioning, vicarious learning, and discrimination learning. When antecedent stimuli gain behavioral control through classical conditioning, there is almost an automatic quality to the stimulus-response relationship. Often the behavior is described as emotional behavior. For example, the sight of a syringe may elicit pleasurable emotions for a heroin addict. Modeling is a strong principle of antecedent control, whereby a demonstration of a behavior by one person increases the chances of the observer engaging in that behavior. When antecedent stimuli gain behavioral control via other learning processes, they function by providing information regarding the outcome of a particular behavior. That is, antecedent stimuli serve to signal the rewards and costs that will follow a given behavior. The strength of antecedent control increases with the repeated pairing of stimulus and behavioral consequences.

Consequent control (or outcome control) refers to the effect of the consequences of an act on the chances of a behavior recurring. Consequences that increase the probability of a behavior recurring are called reinforcers or rewarding consequences (i.e., rewards). The process is called reinforcement. Consequences that decrease the probability of a behavior recurring are called costs, and the process is called punishment. This time, the human tendency to seek pleasure and avoid pain is found at the heart of behavioral principles. This should warm the hearts of psychodynamic theorists and control theorists alike.

With regard to Principle 3, there are many "physical" and cognitive characteristics of the person that influence the capability to respond and learn. Sometimes these person factors are permanent (e.g., brain damage), sometimes they are transitory (e.g., developmental and maturational changes), and sometimes they are acute (e.g., intoxication; feeling mistreated in a particular moment in a particular situation).

Principle 3 emphasizes PIC-R's departure from radical behaviorism and invites knowledge from biological and cognitive psychology. In particular, this principle alerts us to the possibility that an individual's sources of control may vary with developmental changes (something that we will see in the next chapter).

Principle 4 holds that antecedents and consequences are of two major types: additive events (stimuli are introduced, extended, or augmented) and subtractive events (stimuli are withdrawn, postponed, or diminished).

Additive, or positive, rewards are consequences that add something pleasing to the environment (e.g., delivering praise to a child contingent upon a particular act). Subtractive, or negative, rewards are consequences that remove something unpleasant (e.g., the chances of an assault recurring will increase if the assault was successful in stopping someone from making derogatory comments). A clinical illustration is provided in Resource Note 4.3.

Resource Note 4.3

Case Study: The Simultaneous Operation of Additive and Subtractive Rewards

Julia was sentenced to 30 days in jail for prostitution and possession of drugs. She was 19 years old and this was her first time in jail. Upon entry to jail, Julia was processed like all the other offenders: fingerprints were taken, a medical checkup completed, and a brief social history recorded. Nothing out of the ordinary was noted.

On the first check of the nightly rounds, a correctional officer found Julia semi-conscious and bleeding from the forearms. Earlier that day she had asked for a razor to shave her legs. The razor was not collected, and she used it that night to cut her forearms. Julia was given prompt medical attention. Except for a few stitches, the physical harm Julia inflicted upon herself was minor.

The next day Julia was interviewed by the psychologist for a suicidal assessment. Julia was somewhat surprised that the staff thought she was suicidal and denied any intention of killing herself. "It was just one of those things," she said. That night, once again, she was found bleeding, having cut her arm with her eye-glasses (she took the glass out of the rim). Even though the cuts were superficial, staff members were alarmed. She was placed in the hospital ward under 24-hour nursing care.

Frequently, behavior such as Julia's is seen as a "call for help" or a "search for attention." Suicidal gestures often bring a great deal of attention from others and, for someone who is terribly lonely, the reinforcing properties can be powerful. When Julia was seen again by the psychologist, the working hypothesis was that the slashes to the forearm produced "interpersonal additive rewards."

What was surprising was that the behavior also brought subtractive rewards (i.e., the removal of unpleasant stimuli). On the second interview, Julia was more relaxed and open. She revealed a life of physical and sexual abuse, extreme poverty, and addiction to alcohol. She also reported that she had, in the past, cut her forearms when feeling particularly anxious. As painful as this was, it created a distraction from her problems. While watching the blood ooze out of her cut, for the moment her mind was not dwelling on her horrendous life. As the blood continued to flow, she felt a sense of relaxation and peacefulness (no doubt brought on by the gradual loss of blood). Finally, she could drift off to a sleep that would re-energize her to face a new day when she awoke.

Similarly, costs may be additive or subtractive. Thus, the principles of consequent control encompass both additive (positive) punishment and subtractive (negative) punishment. Admonishing a child's behavior is an example of additive punishment. Removing a positive aspect of a situation (e.g., withholding attention) is an example of subtractive punishment. The additive-subtractive distinction will be found to be very important in distinguishing among existing theories. Subtractive punishment in particular will be found to have value in the design of effective intervention programs (Hunt & Azrin, 1973; Meyers & Smith, 1995).

Thinking of Robert Agnew's general strain theory, three sources of strain are evident when antecedent events are conceptualized as additive and subtractive. The withdrawal of valued stimuli is strain-producing as is the delivery of aversive events or unpleasant conditions. Similarly, the nonappearance of expected pleasing consequences is frustrating. In behavioral terms; moving from reinforcement conditions to extinction conditions is frustrating.

Resource Note 4.4 (and Technical Note 4.1) illustrates how basic antecedent and consequent controls are related to effective cognitive behavioral therapy. Note in particular how behavioral functional analysis may individualize understanding of the controlling features of immediate situational variables.

Resource Note 4.4

Understanding Stimulus Control and Criminal Behavior: The ABCs of Cocaine Abuse (Carroll, 1998)

Functional Analysis

A functional analysis of a particular behavior (such as cocaine use) entails building a highly individualized understanding of the antecedents and consequences of cocaine use. The understanding is based on a review of the cocaine-dependent person's thoughts, feelings, and circumstances before and after cocaine use. The review of thoughts, feelings, and circumstances prior to an episode of cocaine use helps identify the antecedent determinants (or high-risk situations) for an individual's cocaine use. Functional analyses of many episodes of use will build a picture of what the "triggers" are for this particular person.

An understanding of the relatively immediate consequences of cocaine use suggest what the major reinforcements are for this individual's cocaine use. It may also alert one to what costs are apparently absent and may be introduced. Possible reinforcers are euphoria, relief of boredom, and a means of escaping interpersonal difficulties.

In cognitive behavioral therapy, the therapist and patient routinely complete functional analyses of behaviors of interest. They want to RECOGNIZE high-risk situations, AVOID those situations when appropriate, and COPE more effectively with the various antecedents associated with problem behavior. See Technical Note 4.1 for an expanded description of cognitive behavioral therapy.

With Principle 5, we see that variation in the probability of occurrence of a given class of behavior is a positive function of: (1) the signaled density of the rewards for that class of behavior, and (2) a negative function of the signaled density of the costs for that class of behavior.

Many forms of deviant behavior are multifunctional in that they produce multiple payoffs. Therefore, PIC-R stresses the density of the rewards and costs. "Density of reinforcement" refers to the number, variety, quality, and magnitude of rewards as well as the immediacy, frequency, and regularity with which they are delivered. The chances of an act occurring increase with the density of the rewards. The chances decrease with the density of the costs.

An appeal of the behavioral principles is that they focus directly upon the matter of interest, that is, variation in chances of a particular behavior occurring. Directly, the issue is what drives up and what drives down the chances of particular acts occurring. The concept of "density" is important because it encourages a comprehensive individualized assessment of current and potential rewards and costs, rather than a fixation upon limited types of rewards or costs. It also has tremendous implications for intervention programs aimed at altering the reward cost contingencies for crime and for noncriminal alternatives. The practical implications extend still further with attention to the sources of reward-cost contingencies (as in the next principle).

Principle 6 specifies the three major sources of antecedents and consequences and thereby identifies personal, interpersonal, and automatic controls over behavior. The supplementary principles of 6a, 6b, and 6c direct attention toward: (a) the importance at the personal level of both self-control skills and anticriminal versus procriminal cognition, (b) the importance of the mix of antisocial and prosocial associates in combination with concern for both relationship and structuring aspects of interpersonal influence, and (c) habitual and automatic behavioral control. These points will be developed below.

Principle 7 and Principle 8 suggest that the effects of rewards and costs may be interdependent and indeed interactive in their impact on behavior. Principle 7 reminds us that we should not expect massive behavior change with the introduction of a single or small incentive. For example, beginning to think that it might be interesting to try marijuana may not translate into smoking, but combine that personal interest with peer support for experimentation with drugs and the chances of drug use increase dramatically. Generally, Principle 7 suggests that the background density of rewards or costs is important in understanding the relative importance of any specific reward or cost. To illustrate, adding one specific reward to the situation of action may have little effect on behavior when the background density is very high or very low. However, that additional reward may have a great impact on behavior when the background density of rewards is at some intermediate level.

Principle 8 specifies how interconnecting reward/cost contingencies for criminal and noncriminal alternative behavior may impact on criminal behavior. In brief, build up rewards for noncriminal behaviors in a variety of settings so that the criminal source of rewards need not be explored *and* so that the subtractive costs of crime are enhanced. Briefly stated, but very powerful. Yes, low rates of rewards and satisfaction in conventional pursuits may motivate criminal behavior under a stress or strain interpretation, but the truly dramatic effect of low levels of rewards and satisfactions from conventional activity is the near total absence of subtractive punishment for criminal behavior. Once again, one is free to be criminal.

Principle 9 alerts readers to the fact that the preceding principles apply to any particular target behavior. For example, if you want to reduce antisocial attitudes, then arrange for a high density of rewards for prosocial expressions and reduced rewards for the expression of antisocial attitudes. If you want to encourage self-control, then increase the opportunity for the practice and reinforcement of self-control. This principle is crucial in suggesting how major causal variables may be altered in order to reduce criminal behavior.

Principle 10 and Principle 11 specify how to analyze social systems and cultures for their criminogenic potential. In brief, and by now, of course (what else): Analyze what is being modeled, what is reinforced, and what is punished.

Principle 12 is a simple reminder of the practical value of individualized understanding of the reward-cost contingencies in effect. Principle 13 is a reminder that research and practice proceed in a ethical, humane, and just manner.

A Closer Look at Sources of Control

Principle 6 holds that antecedents and consequences arise from three major sources: (1) the actor (personally mediated events), (2) other people in the situation of action (interpersonally mediated events), and (3) the act itself (nonmediated, automatic, habitual).

Consideration of the sources of the controlling stimuli expands the analytic and practical value of a behavioral perspective by turning PIC-R into a cognitive social learning perspective. We have located the source of these stimuli in the behavior itself (e.g., the pleasure that automatically derives from the injection of heroin) and in other people within the immediate environment (e.g., praise from a friend). PIC-R, however, adds another source of control: personally mediated control, that is, individuals have the potential to exercise active control over their own behavior. Here direct contact is made with symbolic interactionism and with the explosion of knowledge that began with Bandura's (1986) writings on social cognition theory and Meichenbaum's (1977) cognitive behaviorism. Radical behaviorism remains important because the analytic and technical power of the fundamental principles of behavior continue to serve well in applied settings, and the best of the cognitive approaches are antecedent and consequent-oriented approaches (see Chapters 11 and 12).

Albert Bandura (with colleagues such as Barbaranelli, Caprara, and Pastorelli, 1996) has made major contributions to understanding how personally mediated control operates. These authors describe in detail the mechanisms of moral disengagement through which self-punishment for immoral acts may not only be avoided but also diverted into expressions of self-reward. Similar to Sykes and Matza's techniques of neutralization (Chapters 3 and 7), these mechanisms of moral disengagement include all of the following:

1. Moral justification: "It is all right to fight/lie/steal in order to protect your friends/to take revenge for your family."

2. Euphemistic language: "It is all right to fight/steal/take drugs when you are just joking/giving someone a lesson/just borrowing property/doing it once in a while."

3. Advantageous comparison: "It is all right to fight/lie/steal when others are doing worse/other acts are worse."

4. Displacement of responsibility: "You can't blame me, if I live under bad conditions."

5. Diffusion of responsibility: "You can't blame me, when the whole gang was involved/friends asked me to do it."

6. Distorting consequences: "No one was really hurt."

7. Attribution of blame: "If I misbehave, it is the fault of my teachers/parents."

8. Dehumanization: "It is all right to hurt those who deserve it."

Carefully defined deficits in cognitive skills have been linked with criminal conduct, and many clinicians and researchers are pushing the cognitive skill approach to the limits (e.g., Friendship, Blud, Erikson, Travers & Thornton, 2003; Goldstein & Glick, 1994; Lowenkamp, Hubbard, Makasios & Latessa, 2009; Platt & Prout, 1987; Ross, 1995; Wilson, Bouffard & MacKenzie, 2005). Clinically, depending upon the criminogenic needs identified in particular individuals, a skill curriculum (Goldstein & Glick, 1994, 2001; Hatcher, Palmer, McGuire, Hounsome et al., 2008) might target interpersonal skills, including both the behavioral and cognitive elements of "starting a conversation," "apologizing," "expressing affection," "responding to failure," and "setting a goal." These skills range from basic interpersonal skills through the development of specific alternatives to aggression. Anger control management in the Goldstein and Glick system entails "identifying triggers," using self-statements and relaxation techniques to lower arousal, and using self-reinforcement to control anger. Other relevant need areas include problem-solving training and social perception training.

A particularly important aspect of the social learning concept of self-control is the ongoing specification and empirical validation of self-regulation processes. It is no longer necessary for self-control to be operationally defined by observations of its presumed effects (e.g., a history of impulsive acts, a history of pleasure-seeking, etc.). The more important point is the promise that these "skills" can be developed through direct training. This is something that parents of restlessly energetic children (and the children themselves) may find attractive. The processes of self-regulation may include, for example, the setting of standards of conduct, planning activities, choosing activities, self-monitoring, and even self-consequation in terms of delivering rewards and costs to oneself after self-evaluation of behavior. Here we are deliberately using a language consistent with radical behaviorism, but the process is pure social learning/social cognition.

The Baumiester and Vohs (2004) collection provides example after example of the way in which different researchers and practitioners are approaching self-regulation. One area of study is affect regulation (Laresen & Prizmic, 2004). Think about it. How do you gain control over your negative emotions? Distraction? Venting? Suppression? Cognitive reframe? Think of someone worse off than you? Think about the positive? Do something you really like doing? Seek out your friends? Withdraw? Hit someone?

The behavioral, cognitive behavioral, and social learning approaches have the overriding value of being active, experimental, and pro-intervention. The basics of skill training are well understood in terms of defining the skill, modeling the skill, and arranging plenty of opportunity for reinforced practice in the context of role playing. The review of the intervention literature later in the text indicates that society and PCC cannot afford not to take cognitive social learning theory seriously. Some alternative theories are able to account for the correlates and predictors of crime and to incorporate personality. None, however, have the demonstrated clinical applicability of cognitive social learning theory. An ultimate test of a theory is the ability to influence the phenomenon of interest. So far the cognitive social learning approach has virtually no competitors in that regard (as will be developed in the discussion of prevention and rehabilitation in Chapters 11 and 12). We recognize the irony associated with the fact that the theoretical perspective most notably linked to self-regulation is also the perspective least likely to recognize the amenability of criminal propensity to deliberate intervention (we are thinking of the Hirschi (1990, 2004) self-control perspective).

Relationship to Other Theories

Figure 4.4 provides a summary of principles through a cross-classification of types and sources of consequences. Behavior—both criminal and noncriminal—is under the control of antecedent and consequent events; in order to alter behavior, the antecedent and consequent conditions that govern the behavior must be altered. These controlling conditions can be additive or subtractive in nature, and they can be nonmediated, interpersonally mediated, and/or personally mediated. Many of the traditional theories of criminal behavior are limited in scope and weak in their underlying psychology of human behavior. A powerful theory will be open to the full diversity and complexity of human behavior.

Note how the major social psychological theories of deviance distribute themselves across Figure 4.4. The motivational theories fall in the first two columns (the rewards), while the control theories fall in the last two columns (the costs). Motivational theorists emphasize the potential rewards for deviant behavior, whereas control theorists emphasize the potential costs of—or the factors that deter—deviance. Anomie theory emphasizes the material rewards of money and property and makes some additional reference to enhanced power and prestige. While such outcomes may function as additive rewards, there is the distinct sense in Merton's writings that such events also serve as subtractive rewards. That is, they function to produce relief from a sense of frustration and alienation. The classic psychoanalytic and frustration-aggression theories (Berkowitz, 1962; Dollard et al., 1939) suggest that crime may serve an escape/avoidance function such as that proposed in the stress reduction model of alcoholism (Sobell & Sobell, 1972) and Lindesmith's (1947) perspective on opiate addiction.

Some valued end states may be more readily affected by deviant rather than nondeviant acts: for example, excitement and thrills (Akers, 2001; Miller, 1958; Quay, 1965), independence (Jessor, Jessor & Finney, 1973; Miller, 1958), or a demonstration of contempt for the existing social order or an affirmation of commitment to a new order (the conflict theorists). Depending upon the orientation of one's self and one's friends, deviant activity may also bring about the approval of the self and others.

Subcultural and labeling theorists emphasize some of the aforementioned personal values and social norms, though they tend to ignore the process by which norms guide behavior. In contrast, PIC-R shows the process and specifies that control will be evident at both the personal and interpersonal levels. As suggested by Burgess and Akers (1966) and Sykes and Matza (1957) years ago, and now endorsed by so many (e.g., Agnew, 1994), techniques of neutralization (i.e., rationalizations for deviance) are verbalizations that serve to avoid, escape, or deflect negative labeling

Sources of Consequences or Antecedents		Rewards		Costs	
		Additive	**Subtractive**	**Additive**	**Subtractive**
(Some typical descriptions of any concomitant emotional states.)		("Pleasure")	("Relief")	("Pain")	("Frustration"/ "Disappointment"/ "Grief")
A. Personal: Self-Mediated (Thoughts, images, self-talk, anticipation of the reactions of others.)	i) **Events:**	Positive self-labeling. Personal approval. Self-instructions to proceed.	Self-removal of negative labels. Avoiding or discounting negative labels.	Negative self-labeling. Personal disapproval. Self-instructions to cease.	Self-removal of positive labels. Recognition of potential losses.
(An "active," "conscious," "deliberate," "self-manag-ing" person is assumed.)	ii) **Examples:**	"This is great." "This is fun." "What a stone!" "I am at one with the universe." "I am free, independent, powerful." "That was one of the cleanest B & Es I have ever accomplished." "Wait until I tell Joe about this."	"I am not a wimp/coward." "This is relaxing." "This is exciting, it was so boring before." "Finally, some energy." "The drug laws are stupid anyway." "The SOB deserves it."	"I feel sick" "This is wrong, in my eyes, in the eyes of my mother, in the eyes of God." "This guy might fight back."	"Am I the type of person who would steal/hurt other people/leave my kids out in the rain while I buy a pack of cigarettes?" "If my mother says this...." "I am losing control."
Some general psychological perspectives on self-regulation: Bandura; Meichenbaum; Kanfer; Mahoney; Carver & Scheier.		Glaser Differential Identification	Lindesmith; Sykes & Matza	Reckless; Hirschi; Piliavin; Freud	
			Subcultural and labeling theorists with an emphasis on symbolic interaction	Control theorists with an emphasis on symbolic interaction	
			Differential Association Theory: with an emphasis on symbolic interaction		
B. Automatic: Nonmediated	i) Sensory/physiological effects and effective stimulation.	"Pleasure." The "stone," "rush," "high," "buzz." Arousal jag.	"Relief": from boredom; Quay frustration; Anomie: Frustration, Aggression anxiety/tension/guilt; Stress-reduction theories withdrawal distress; Lindesmith from a dry, scratchy throat.	"Pain" Nausea [Some interventions such as negative practice and "rapid smoking" exaggerate the naturally aversive consequences of specific behaviors.]	"Frustration" Loss of physical coordination. Removal of pleasant affective or sensory status.
	ii) Conditional emotional responses	"Hope"	"Relief"	"Fear"	"Frustration"
		The behavioral versions of Lindesmith	Eysenck; Hare; Lykken, Schachter & Latané		
	iii) External events tied in an intimate manner to specific types of acts such as theft and aggression.	Money, property. Sexual satisfaction. Signs of pain/submission.	Removal or destruction of a frustrating agent.	The possibility of retaliation; signs of conquest by another.	Interference with ongoing activities. Hunt & Azrin Loss of money (gambling).
C. Interpersonally Mediated	**Events:** i) Direct evaluation of expressions of others.	Approval, affection, attention.	Reduction of disapproval.	Disapproval.	Reduction of approval, attention.
	ii) Behavioral opportu-nities involving other person.	Opportunity to engage in "valued" activities. The approval of others and group membership brings the opportunity for a variety of social, recreational, and sexual activities.	Opportunity to escape/ avoid "disliked" activities (such as work and authori-ty; family responsibility; or being alone, bored, gener-ally frustrated.) Opportunity to engage in otherwise very costly behaviors (in the sense that intoxication may reduce the costs of aggres-sive/sexual displays).	Forced to engage in disliked activities (for example: hav-ing to listen to the same old stories told by drinking buddies; having to interact with disliked others).	Lost opportunity to engage in "valued" activities. Reduced approval, affection, and attention.
Some relevant general social-psychological perspectives on interpersonal influence: group dynamics theory; social learning theory; the relationship and contingency dimensions.		Subcultural and labeling theorists, with an emphasis on the inter-personal contingencies.		Control Theorists, with an emphasis on the interpersonal contingencies.	
		Matza ("Sounding")		Reckless; Hirschi; Piliavin; Hunt & Azrin	

Figure 4.4
A Cross-Classification of Type and Sources of Consequences

by oneself or by others. Gottfredson and Hirschi (1990) suggest that some behavioral reformulations of cultural deviance theories sound as if they are merely reformulations of the old notion of deviance as conformity. However, that is not what a broad social learning perspective purports. PIC-R incorporates the general rewards suggested by the narrower motivational theories of deviance, but it is not limited to them. Furthermore, PIC-R does not negate the possibility that for some individuals, under some circumstances, the motives for deviant behavior can be highly idiosyncratic (e.g., the pain of others, as in the case of sadism; or sexual attraction for children, as in the case of pedophilia). PIC-R also says that no matter what the rewards, the costs remain relevant.

Differential association theory (Sutherland & Cressey, 1970), one of the more conceptually and empirically satisfying of the general perspectives (Akers & Cochran, 1985; Andrews, 1980; Johnson, 1979) when not read as a cultural theory (Akers, 1996), appears sensitive to both rewards and costs. However, the original statement of differential association may have placed an overemphasis on the symbolic (or personal) level of control. The available empirical literature, with a few exceptions, suggests that peer support and personal sentiment measures make independent contributions to the predictability of indices of deviant behavior (Agnew, 2001; Andrews & Kandel, 1979; Andrews & Wormith, 1984; Jenson, 1972; Johnson, 1979). More will be said on this topic in Chapter 7, but for now, deviant associates increase the chances of deviant activity above and beyond the influence they have on personal beliefs regarding deviance. Social support involves interpersonally mediated approval as well as the possibility of increased resources for particular actions, such as access to a "fence" or to drugs.

Control theorists emphasize the costs of deviance but differ among themselves in terms of the types of costs given the most theoretical attention. Eysenck (1977) emphasized deficits in conditioned fear responses. Some researchers (cf., Hare & Neumann, 2008) have found specific correlates of psychopathy at the autonomic level and are exploring the neuropsychology of emotion. Others emphasize ties to conventional moral codes and affective ties to conventional others (Agnew, 2001; Hirschi, 1969, 2004; Reckless & Dinitz, 1972). When a person is strongly tied to convention, deviant activity occurs at the risk of personal and interpersonal disapproval as well as the loss of affection and esteem.

The personality correlates of criminality may also be located within PIC-R. Note that impulsivity and weak self-control are represented directly in personally mediated control (as discussed above). When high value is placed upon excitement and thrill-seeking, the probability of exploring crime increases. As noted, some valued consequences are simply more readily achieved through deviance. Egocentrism and disagreeableness suggest a reduction in the controlling potential of the reactions (anticipated or actual) of others to one's deviant acts.

Some relatively minor personal risk/need factors may also be operative within PIC-R. For example, even measures of psychological discomfort (such as anxiety, low self-esteem, and alienation) may be related to criminality under very particular circumstances. Certain forms of deviance may reduce psychological distress (a subtractive reward), and with a background of low levels of self-satisfaction, the personally mediated subtractive costs of deviance will be relatively low. Low scores on measures of social power and personal competence suggest that a person is unlikely to receive many rewards for nondeviant pursuits; hence, the subtractive costs of deviance may be slight and the motivation for crime increased. Low verbal IQ suggests interference with personally mediated control.

The construct of *antisocial attitudes* has a crucial role in PIC-R. It is these attitudes, values, and beliefs—i.e., procriminal versus anticriminal sentiments—that determine the direction of personally mediated control. They contribute to the standards of conduct that determine whether personally mediated control favors criminal over noncriminal choices. They also represent the pool of justifications and exonerating statements that the person has available in any particular situation.

The construct of *antisocial associates* is also very important. Antisocial associates (including parents, siblings, peers, and others in the immediate situation of action) influence the procriminal versus anticriminal nature of modeling in the situation of action as well as govern the rules by which rewards and costs are signaled and delivered. Antisocial significant others also impact on antisocial attitudes, which in turn may influence personally mediated control even in the absence of others.

The construct of a *history of antisocial behavior* is also theoretically relevant. It increases self-efficacy beliefs with regard to being able to complete the act successfully and serves as a measure of habit strength in the tradition of behaviorism. Empirically, rationally, and (as we shall see in Chapters 10, 11, and 12) practically, the Big Four factors are central to PIC-R and PCC in general.

The moderate factors in the list of the Central Eight risk/need factors also make some theoretical sense. Family, school/work, and leisure/recreation represent major behavioral settings, and the contingencies within those settings may have a great impact on the overall density of rewards and costs for criminal behavior. Developmentally, family origin, of course, is a major source of: (a) self-control skills, (b) attitudes, values, and beliefs, (c) associates, and (d) early behavioral history (see Chapters 5, 6, and 8). Marital arrangements too may impact dramatically on association patterns and on the patterns of behavior and thought that are signaled, reinforced, and punished. Rewards and satisfactions at school/work and leisure/recreation may favor or not favor the criminal alternative and yet again may impact on association patterns. Substance abuse can itself be against the law, and it can lead to criminal activity through a variety of routes including disruption of personally mediated control, both automatic and effortful (see Chapter 9).

Summary

The general personality and cognitive social psychological approach to building a predictive understanding of criminal conduct has made considerable progress. In order to move into the realm of demonstrated causal significance, PCC needs an approach that is linked with a general psychology of human behavior that has demonstrated functional value. We used general personality and cognitive social learning theory as the underlying psychology and presented the outline of PIC-R. PIC-R is a broad perspective that encompasses the contributions of many theories. Criminal behavior reflects not just particular motivations or particular constraints but the density of signaled rewards and costs. The implications of the perspective will be explored in the following chapters.

Worth Remembering

1. It make considerable sense to recognize that human behavior is outcome-oriented, and most behavior, including criminal behavior, is under antecedent and outcome control.

2. Variation in criminal behavior is profitably viewed as a reflection of the density of signaled rewards and costs for criminal and non-criminal alternative behaviors.

3. The sources of signaled rewards are personal, interpersonal, and automatic.

4. For prediction purposes, assessments of the Big Four reflect the extent to which outcome contingencies are favoring criminal activity.

5. A major feature of the general personality and cognitive social learning perspective is the strength of its implications for the design of prevention and rehabilitation programs.

Part 2

The Major Risk/Need Factors of
Criminal Conduct

Biological, Personal, and Social Origins of the Major Risk/Need Factors and Personal Strengths

To begin this chapter, it is instructive to quote, once again, Principle 3 from the Personal, Interpersonal, and Community-Reinforcement (PIC-R) perspective on criminal conduct (Resource Note 4.1):

> The controlling properties of antecedents and consequences are acquired through the interaction of the person with the environment. The principles governing the acquisition, maintenance, and modification of the controlling properties of stimulus conditions include those of genetic and constitutional disposition and capability; biophysical functioning; cognitive functioning; human development; behavioral repertoire; state conditions; and respondent and operant conditioning, including observational learning, rule learning, symbolic control, and role enactment.

The important point that arises from Principle 3 is that the influence of rewards and costs depends upon person factors. This is what is meant by the word *interaction*. Interactional effects are common in psychology, and they are what make people unique. One important set of factors that interacts with rewards and costs are biological and temperamental factors, which are the focus of this chapter. Another set of factors are personality-based (Chapter 6), and others are cognitive (Chapter 7). Interactions also explain why some person factors are risk/need factors and others may be strength factors. For example, opportunistic rewards for criminal behavior may be more appealing to the individual who is impulsive with low self-control (risk/need factors) whereas high self-control serves as a strength or protective factor against the very same opportunistic rewards for crime. Throughout this chapter and some of the following chapters, we will see how some biosocial, personal factors may be a source of risk/need while others are strengths.

Children begin life with certain inherent biological capabilities and predispositions that interact with specific familial, social, and cultural circumstances. Personal capabilities and predispositions affect how the environment influences the shaping of behavior and, reciprocally, the behavior can modify biological tendencies. For example, a child may be born with average intelligence, but a stimulating and enriching environment can lead to achievements beyond those possible in a deprived environment. In addition, these achievements may nourish further biological growth (e.g., increases in nerve connections, neurochemical changes, etc.; Beckman, 2004). This constantly changing nature of the interaction between biology and environment is one of the most exciting aspects of developmental criminology (Le Blanc & Loeber, 1998).

Biological factors lie at the base of criminal behavior. It is the foundation not only for personality development (Chapter 6) but also cognitive development (again, with more in Chapter 7). Some of the traits and styles of behaviors observed among youths and adults are often evident in infancy. We start with the relationship between heredity and crime followed with a summary of some of the other biological correlates of antisocial behavior. From there we continue the biological origins theme with our thoughts on a controversial area of investigation-evolutionary psychology/criminology. That is, does criminal behavior increase the chances of biological survival? Lastly, we touch upon the social origins of crime with a review of the role of social class in understanding criminal conduct. By the end of this chapter we hope that the reader will recognize the need to consider biological variables for our understanding of criminal behavior but also appreciate the limits to biological determinism and the effects of social class on crime.

Developmental criminology tries to understand how children and youths grow in and out of crime (Loeber & Stouthamer-Loeber, 1996). Most youths, especially males, engage in various antisocial acts as they grow into adulthood, but these youths follow different trajectories or criminal pathways. There is no consensus as to how many trajectories exist—three, four, five, or even six (Moffitt, 2007; Piquero, 2008), but it is safe to describe two general trajectories common across gender (Odgers, Moffitt, Broadbent, Dickson et al., 2008; Piquero, 2008) and race (Yessine & Bonta, 2009). Different labels have been used to describe these trajectories but we will adopt Terri Moffitt's lexicon. First, there is the "adolescent-limited" (Moffitt, 1993), which represents the majority of youths who will engage in delinquent activities at some point during adolescence. However, these youths will desist from criminal activity in early adulthood, as seen in the decreasing crime rates after the age of 18 or so. Then there are some youths who just continue along a criminal career trajectory (Blumstein et al., 1986; Moffitt, 1997). This trajectory is called the "life-course-persistent" (Moffitt, 2003). These are the offenders, and again most are males, who start behaving antisocially early and continue through to adulthood, often escalating in the seriousness of their acts. Life-course-persistent offenders represent the minority of delinquents (5–10 %) but commit most of the crimes (recall Technical Note 1.1). Most longitudinal studies of life-course-persistent offenders end by age 40, but there is some evidence that their criminal behavior, although less serious, continues to age 48 (Farrington, Coid, Harnett, Jolliffe et al., 2006; Farrington, Ttofi & Coid, 2009) and even past the age of 60 (Sampson & Laub, 2003). It seems that some offenders do not "burn out" of crime.

It is important to understand the factors that direct the development of life-course-persistent offenders because of the important implications for social policy and crime prevention. We will say more about the life-course-persistent offender in Chapter 7 and outline some of their psychosocial characteristics. For now, we will limit our attention to biological, temperamental, and social origins to crime.

The Biological Basis of Criminal Behavior

For more than a century, scientists have debated the relative influence of nature and environment on behavior. Most everyone agrees that both nature and nurture are important, but how much one or the other contributes to behavior will be argued for years to come. We certainly place our emphasis on the environment because the environment is the *immediate* source of control over behavior. Nevertheless, we need to examine the more distal factors that contribute to the development of criminal behavior for a fuller understanding of criminal conduct. Thus, we start with the role of heredity and then move to summaries of some specific biological factors associated with criminal behavior (for a more detailed description of the biochemical basis to heredity, see Technical Note 5.1).

Heredity and Crime

The idea that crime runs in families has been a high-consensus inference of casual observers for years. Almost anyone who has worked in a criminal justice setting can provide vivid examples of intergenerational criminality. A famous, early study of the heritability of criminal traits is Richard Dugdale's (1877/1970) analysis of the Juke family. Beginning with the children of Max Juke (circa 1750), Dugdale traced the Juke lineage to 1870. Of the 709 descendants, nearly 20 percent were criminals, and slightly more than 40 percent were dependent upon the state for financial support. Dugdale concluded that the high rate of criminality and "pauperism" was evidence for the heritability of criminality and poor social adjustment.

An example of intergenerational criminality comes from the Cambridge Study (see Technical Note 1.1 for a description). In this longitudinal study, the correlation between the fathers' criminality and the sons' criminality was quite high (r = .43; Rowe & Farrington, 1997). This intergenerational transmission of crime applies equally to boys and girls (Van De Rakt, Nieuwbeerta & De Graff, 2008), and it has been found across three generations (Smith & Farrington, 2004; Farrington, Coid & Murray, in press). However, these and other findings on intergenerational crime do not necessarily mean that there is genetic transmission of criminality. As we will see in Chapter 7, parental modeling, monitoring, and disciplining practices are extremely important. In addition, there is something called "assortative mating," by which individuals tend to mate with similar individuals, adding another environmental explanation to intergenerational crime (Krueger, Moffitt, Caspi, Bleske & Silva, 1998; Luo & Klohnen, 2005; Maes, Silberg, Neale & Eaves, 2007; Rhule-Louie & McMahon, 2007). In the Cambridge Study, 83 percent of the boys in the study grew up and married women who also had criminal records (Farrington, Barnes & Lambert, 1996). The likelihood that antisocial individuals tend to cohabit with antisocial partners or that antisocial children tend to be raised in dysfunctional, strife-ridden families all point to the influence of the environment rather than genes in the criminality of the children. In order to better separate the influences of heredity and the environment, investigators have turned to the study of twins and adopted children.

Twin Studies. Twin studies compare monozygotic (MZ) twins and dizygotic (DZ) twins. Zygote means egg. Thus, monozygotic twins, or "identical" twins, originate from one egg fertilized by one sperm. After fertilization, the egg splits into two, eventually producing two fetuses with identical genetic makeups. Dizygotic twins (DZ), or fraternal twins, originate from two separate fertilized eggs. Although the fetuses share the same placenta and are born often within minutes of each other, they are genetically as different as any brother and sister, or same-sex siblings, born years apart (when you see the "D" in DZ, think "different"). Identical twins are always of the same sex and are indistinguishable in appearance, while fraternal twins can be different genders and, even if they are the same gender, you can tell them apart. Now, if heredity has an influence, then the behaviors (and not just the physical appearance) of MZ twins should show more similarity or "concordance" than that found in the behaviors of DZ twins.

In the first study of twins and criminality, Lange (1929) identified 13 pairs of monozygotic (MZ) twins and 17 pairs of dizygotic (DZ) twins from birth registries in Germany. Criminality was defined as a history of imprisonment. Lange found that the similarity/concordance rate for MZ twins with respect to criminality was 77 percent and only 12 percent for DZ twins. That is, for 10 of the 13 pairs of MZ twins, both siblings had histories of incarceration, whereas only two pairs of the 17 DZ twins had joint histories of incarceration.

While the magnitude of the effect was impressive, Lange's study and those by others conducted during the same period were suspect for a number of reasons. For one thing, social scientists in Britain and North America were not about to be impressed by a report originating from Germany during the rise of Nazism (for a review of criminology in Nazi Germany and Fascist Italy, see Rafter, 2008). All of the early studies were also plagued by serious methodological problems. For example, Lange grouped the twins into MZ and DZ categories by looking at their pictures, knowing beforehand who had the history of imprisonment. This methodology makes it very tempting for an experimenter with a certain set of beliefs and expectations to place one set of twins that did not look quite identical into the MZ group.

Studies that were methodologically more refined became evident in the 1970s. For example, Christiansen (1977) drew upon the Copenhagen birth registry (see Technical Note 1.1) to locate a large sample of twins (3,586) that could be reliably identified as MZ or DZ. Criminal activity was defined according to official records. For MZ twins, the concordance rate was 35 percent; it was 12 percent for DZ twins. As twin studies became more sophisticated, the concordance rate for MZ twins decreased from the 77 percent reported by Lange to as low as 26 percent (Dalgaard & Kringlen, 1976). Except for a few exceptions that may be explained by methodological and sampling factors (Gurling, Oppenheim, & Murray, 1984; Rowe, 1983), general reviews and meta-analytic summaries of the twin literature find a moderate relationship between heredity and antisocial behavior (Carey & Goldman, 1997; Mason & Frick, 1994; Rhee & Waldman, 2002; Walters, 1992).

An important restraint on the interpretation of these twin studies is the fact that almost all of the studies used twins reared together. Identical twins may be treated more alike by their social environments (e.g., parents, friends, teachers, etc.), and they influence each other more than fraternal twins (Carey, 1992; Carey & Goldman, 1997). Thus, the similarities may be inflated by common environmental influences (Brennan & Mednick, 1993). The "ideal" twin study would involve MZ twins separated at birth and raised in different environments, but these studies are few. The largest study of MZ twins reared apart was conducted by William Grove and his colleagues (Grove et al., 1990). Thirty-two pairs of MZ twins who were separated before the age of five (one-half were separated within the first few months of birth) were followed into adulthood (median age of 43). The concordance rate for antisocial personality disorder was 29 percent, about the range found by most twin studies on crime. Thus, it appears that the shared environments of MZ twins reared together may not be as important as previously thought. To address some of the difficulties with the twin approach, researchers have conducted adoption studies that better separate the influence of environment and heredity.

Adoption Studies. Adoption studies use a method called the cross-fostering design. This design analyzes the behavior of children who are separated soon after birth from their biological parents and raised, or fostered, by nonrelatives. In adoption studies, the criminal futures of adopted children are analyzed in relation to: (a) criminal history of the biological parents, (b) criminal history of adoptive parents, and (c) particular combinations of criminality in the biological and adoptive parents. The assumption is that if the rate of criminality among adopted children is higher for those who have a biological parent with a criminal record than for the adoptees with a noncriminal biological parent, then heredity has an effect.

Mednick, Gabrielli, and Hutchings (1984) drew upon a databank that included social history information on more than 14,000 children who were adopted in Denmark between 1924 and 1947 (some of these findings were described in Chapter 1). The researchers tabulated the conviction rate of male adoptees in relation to the criminal convictions of their biological and adoptive parents. Inspection of Table 5.1 finds that the evidence is mildly consistent with a genetic effect ($r = .03$). Note in the bottom row of the table that adoptees raised by noncriminal parents but who had criminal biological parents were at a higher risk to be convicted than adoptees from criminal biological parents but raised by noncriminal foster parents (20% vs. 13.5%).

In a follow-up investigation, Mednick, Gabrielli, and Hutchings (1987) focused on what they called chronic (i.e., life-course-persistent) offenders. Chronic offenders were defined as having at least three prior convictions and represented 4 percent of the sample but were responsible for 69 percent of all the crimes. The biological parents were also categorized according to their convictions (from 0 to 3 or more). As the number of convictions for the biological parents increased, so did the number for the adoptees. These results, however, held for property offenses (e.g., break and enter, theft) only and not for violent offenses. Parental criminality by itself appeared insufficient to explaining violent crime in the offspring. One factor that may be relevant to understanding violence is the emotional stability of the parents. A number of investigators (Moffitt, 1987; Odgers, Milne, Caspi, Crump et al., 2007; Tehrani et al., 1998) have found that parental mental disorder was related to being life-course-persistent. However, the evidence is still unclear as to whether parental

Table 5.1
Cross-Fostering Analysis of Criminality in Male Adoptees by Criminality of Biological and Adoptive Parents

Criminal adoptive parents?	Criminal Biological Parents?	
	Yes	No
Yes	24.5% (of 143)	14.7% (of 204)
No	20.0% (of 1226)	13.5% (of 2492)

Adapted from Mednick, Gabrielli & Hutchings, 1984

emotional stability is specific to violent crime (Moffitt, 2003; Tehrani & Mednick, 2000).

Assembling the findings from studies of twins and adoptees, it is hard to ignore genetic factors in behavior. Carey and Goldman (1997) found that all six of the adoption studies in their review showed a genetic effect. In the meta-analyses by Walters (1992, 2006a) and Rhee and Waldman (2002), the concordance rate for the adoption studies decreased significantly from the rate found in the twin studies, but it was not zero. One important observation is that the severity of the problem behavior may have a higher heritability component. John Malouff, Sally Rooke, and Nicola Schutte (2008) examined eight meta-analyses of twin and adoption studies investigating a range of problems (e.g., intelligence, language ability, major depression, antisocial behavior). They found higher heritability was associated with the severity of the problem. Thus, severe language problems, drinking problems, and even smoking evidenced higher heritability than less severe problems. In the case of antisocial behavior, being female or having a diagnosis of a conduct disorder (a feature of the life-course-persistent offender) had higher heritability then being male or the absence of a conduct disorder. In other words, the more infrequent/severe type of offender (i.e., the female offender and the career criminal), the stronger the genetic influence.

The Search for a Crime Gene

Medicine has long recognized that there are some medical diseases (e.g., Huntington's disease, cystic fibrosis, muscular dystrophy) that are caused by abnormalities or mutations of a single gene. As described earlier, genes are the basic units of heredity that dictate the production of proteins and enzymes that, in turn, influence how we look and how we act (see Technical Note 5.1 for more detail). In 2003, the Human Genome Project identified the complete sequence of human DNA, the programming code for the organism that comprises each individual gene. While the exact function of each gene will require many more years of research, certain genes have been identified and their functions described (e.g., a mutation of an amino acid in chromosome 7 can lead to cystic fibrosis). These findings offer the promise of developing new medical treatments that alter the way our genes govern the biochemical processes and functions that lie at the heart of being human. This new knowledge may one day lead to the slowing of diseases and perhaps even eradicate some of them. Wouldn't it be nice if there was a single gene for crime that we could turn off with a flick of a switch?

Although there are some medical disorders that can be traced to a single gene, most (e.g., heart disease, schizophrenia) are influenced by many genes. Nevertheless, this has not stopped the search for a single "crime gene" (Tehrani & Mednick, 2000). After all, if evidence could be uncovered for a direct genetics-crime link, it would have enormous implications for theory development, prevention efforts, and even the determination of guilt (e.g., a genetic argument could be used as evidence for a "compulsion" to act and serve as a defense against punishment). Thus, let us tell you the story of the XYY chromosome abnormality.

Chromosomes are made up of DNA (the genetic programs), and humans have 46 chromosomes. Sometimes chromosomes can become damaged or fail to combine properly. Chromosomal alternations of the genetic sequence (mutations) can happen through unexplainable spontaneous means or through accident (e.g., X-ray exposure). These mutations may affect the location of the gene in the chromosome, result in the complete absence of a chromosome, or result in an extra chromosome. For example, Down syndrome is caused by the presence of an extra chromosome (chromosome 21). Another example is the XYY chromosomal aberration. It is the Y chromosome that carries the genes that determine male sexual features (e.g., genital development, hair distribution). In 1961, Sandberg, Koepf, Ishihara, and Hauschka described an individual with an extra Y chromosome. Although this individual was by no means a "super male" (he was a nonoffender with average intelligence), a subsequent study by Jacobs, Brunton, Melville, Brittain, and McClemont (1965) suggested a link between an extra Y chromosome and violent behavior. Enthusiasm over these findings spawned not only the expected court defense of the "gene made me do it" (e.g., Richard Speck, who strangled eight student nurses, tried unsuccessfully to use this defense) but also some drastic measures such as screening male infants and high school students for the extra Y chromosome (Katz & Chambliss, 1995). However, the early studies involved biased samples of institutionalized, often intellectually handicapped males (Jarvik, Klodin & Matsuyama, 1973).

The initial excitement quickly wore off when well-designed epidemiological studies found that having an extra Y chromosome was largely irrelevant. Witkin and colleagues (1976) found only 12 males with the XYY aberration in a sample of 4,558 Danish men, and Götz, Johnstone, and Ratcliffe (1999) found only 17 among a sample of 17,522 Scottish men. Upon follow-up, both studies found that XYY men had more criminal convictions than normals (XY men), but most of the offenses were for property crimes. Just to make sure that it was the extra Y chromosome and not just simply having any extra chromosome that accounted for differences in criminal conduct, the researchers compared the XYY men to men who had an additional X chromosome (a condition known as Klinefelter's syndrome, which is characterized by male genitals but often with sterility, breast enlargement, and intellectual retardation). Witkin et al. (1976) identified 16 XXY males, and Götz et al. (1999) found 17 XXY males in their sample (less than 1% of each sample).

There were no differences in violent offending between the men with an extra Y chromosome and the men with an extra X chromosome. Not only is an extra Y chromosome extremely rare, but it is also weakly associated with general criminal behavior and not at all with violence.

Lastly, in the only longitudinal study to our knowledge of XYY children (Geerts, Steyaert & Fryns, 2003), half of the 38 boys in the study evidenced psychosocial problems, but childhood autism was a more likely outcome than conduct disorder. Ike's (2000) review of the XYY literature found that most XYY carriers showed no behavioral problems, and the reports of antisocial behaviors may be the result of selective screening of individuals with the XYY syndrome. To conclude, the XYY abnormality, although an interesting story of genetic determinism, is largely irrelevant to a theoretical and empirical understanding of criminal conduct.

The failure to find a "crime gene" in the XYY anomaly does not mean that the search for specific genes should be abandoned. On the contrary, advances in genetic research have opened new opportunities for exploration of how genes may work together to influence criminal behavior. For example, dopamine is a neurotransmitter that has been associated with the regulation of emotions, attention deficit disorder, and cognitive ability (DeYoung, Petereson, Séguin, Mejie at al., 2006; Guo, Roettger & Shih, 2007). Guang Guo and his associates examined the genes that involve the transportation and reception of dopamine at the cellular level (DAT1 and DRD2). Based on a sample of 2,500 adolescents who participated in the National Longitudinal Study of Adolescent Health (Add Health), they found that variations within these two genes were associated with serious and violent delinquent trajectories. No doubt that the coming years will shed more light on the gene-crime relationship.

The Nature-Nurture Interaction

Moffitt (2005) estimated that there are more than 100 studies on the relationship between genetics and antisocial behavior. Recently, attention has focused on the interaction between biological predispositions and the environment on behavior (Rutter, Moffitt & Caspi, 2006; Tremblay, 2008). That is, under what environmental conditions do biological factors play a lesser or greater role? PIC-R Principle 3 highlights the importance of this interaction, and we have already seen, for example, that for females who engage in crime and offenders on a life-course-persistent trajectory, heritability plays a greater role. What other biological factors depend upon the environment for their behavioral expression?

Exploring the nature-nurture interaction can proceed on two levels. There is the molecular genetic level, and then there is research at the higher level of the behavioral markers representing the biological systems that underlie, in our case, criminal conduct. For example, negative emotionality reflects underlying biochemical processes that can be linked back to the operation of genes.

Interactions at the molecular genetic level are only now being reported (Caspi, McLay, Moffitt, Mill et al., 2002; DeYoung et al., 2006; Foley, Eaves, Wormley, Silberg et al., 2004; Haberstick, Lessem, Hopfer, Smokin et al., 2005). In a recent study, Guo, Roettger, and Cai (2008), using data from the Add Health longitudinal study (above), demonstrated that such simple routine activities as eating meals with parents mitigated the effects of the DRD2 gene (a dopamine receptor gene) on delinquency. They went further and also showed that school attachment and repeating a grade, both risk factors for delinquency, interacted with the MAOA gene (Monoamine Oxidase has been associated with aggression via serotonin and dopamine neurotransmission). This research at the genetic molecular level reinforces the view that the influence of heredity depends on the presence of certain environmental risk factors that, in a sense, release the power of the gene. For example, family dysfunction (Button, Scourfield, Martin, Purcell & McGuffin, 2005) and low socioeconomic status (Tuvblad, Grann & Lichtenstein, 2006) have been shown to increase the heritability of antisocial behavior.

Moffitt (2005:548) has listed a number of behavioral markers indicative of biological system processes that may interact with environmental factors. They include: sensation-seeking, overactivity, low self-control, emotionality, and callousness. Depending upon the environment, children with such characteristics differ in their antisocial outcomes. We will not review this literature here but we will make note of it in this chapter and Chapter 7. The general message is that the expression of genetic and biological factors is often dependent upon the right environmental conditions.

Neurological Defects, Faulty Wiring, and Crime

The brain as the center of thinking, emotion, and motivation is as undisputable as the fact that it is also the most complex of all human organs. How the processes in the brain influence antisocial and violent behavior has been a subject of study for many years. However, the findings from this area have often been ignored by criminological theory (Ellis, 2005). Note the almost complete absence of neurophysiological factors in theories of anomie and strain, differential association, and Hirschi and Gottfredson's self-control theory. Yet, biological factors in general, and neuropsychological factors specifically, can influence criminal conduct.

The complexity of the influence of neuropsychological variables can be told through the story of the search for the localization of aggression in the brain. The search started off simply enough but ended with a much more elaborate understanding of brain function and aggressivity. In 1970, Vernon Mark and Frank Ervin described a patient who would assault his wife and children during fits of uncontrollable rage. By surgically removing part of the brain (the right amygdala, to be precise), they were able to halt the violence. What is so special about the amygdala, and is this tiny structure the possible center of all that is evil and bad?

The amygdala is an almond-shaped structure found buried within the temporal lobe of the brain. Together with other nearby structures it forms a circuit called the limbic system. The limbic system is commonly referred to as the "old brain" because it looks like that found in lower-level animals and developed early in human evolution. In fact, in the human fetus, the limbic system develops first, and then the cerebral cortex (the soft convoluted tissue) grows over the area. The cortex mediates higher levels of thinking, and it is divided into four lobes—frontal, temporal (left and right side), parietal (top), and occipital (back).

The old brain (limbic system), having developed earlier, is thought to control the basic emotions (anger, fear) and motivations (hunger, thirst, sex). Thus, it became the natural target for localizing anger and aggression in the brain. Early studies would stimulate or remove parts of the limbic system, especially the amygdala, in order to observe the expression of anger and aggression (e.g., Kiloh, 1978). These studies also showed that the amygdala is not totally responsible for aggressivity and that other structures in the limbic system (e.g., hippocampus, thalamus, etc.) were involved along with the amygdala.

By the 1990s, it was clear that aggression does not depend upon what happens only in the limbic system (Golden et al., 1996). The brain is a network of interconnecting neurons that number in the billions. When some neurons do not function well, it is common to see other adjoining neurons assume the function of the damaged areas. This is referred to as "plasticity," and the human brain is much more plastic in youth than in adulthood. For example, a cerebral stroke may damage a portion of the brain affecting behavior, but the effect may be transitory as neighboring neurons take over the function of damaged neurons. This explains the difficulty in proving that one area of the brain, and one area only, mediates behaviors (we recognize that this is a general statement and that there are areas in the brain that have a very specific function and if damaged are irreparable).

Violent behavior appears to depend on a combination of processes within the limbic system and the prefrontal cortex (Barker, Séguin, White, Bates et al., 2007; Bufkin & Luttrell, 2005; Nelson & Trainor, 2007; Scarpa & Raine, 2007; Volavka, 2002). The frontal areas of the brain are associated with attention, planning, and the inhibition of behavior (Funahashi, 2001). In a way, the frontal lobes function like the psychological ego controlling the impulsive, instinctual id (i.e., the limbic system). For the non-Freudians and business students, you may think of the frontal lobes as the Chief Executive Officer of the brain. Although damage to the frontal lobes and the limbic system may result in violent behavior, there are not enough people with brain damage to these areas to explain the relatively high prevalence of violent behavior. Instead, it is likely that diffuse cerebral dysfunction affecting multiple sites of the brain plays the predominant role in aggressive behavior (Gontkovsky, 2005). Diffuse neurological dysfunction may have its onset early in development, perhaps neonatally, and long before the occurrence of a direct physical injury and trauma (Moffit, 1990). However, such a dysfunction often does not become apparent until later, when tests are able to measure verbal and memory deficits and intelligence.

The frontal lobes develop throughout adolescence, and the myelin around the nerves continues to develop to age 30 and perhaps beyond (Fields, 2005). Consequently, the frontal lobes are not fully developed until early adolescence. This delayed development may partially explain the impulsivity and poor attention span of young children. In addition, delays in neurophysiological development affect attention skills, verbal language development, and intelligence in general. Moffitt (2003) has argued that adolescence-limited delinquents may suffer from a "maturity gap" created by delayed neurophysiological development and the adolescent's desire to be treated like an adult. For the life-course-persistent offender, it may be more than slow neurological maturation but actual impairment to the frontal lobe and limbic systems (Nelson & Trainor, 2007; Raine, Moffitt, Caspi, Loeber et al., 2005). These findings have huge implications for the application of law with young offenders. If brain capacity and function is still developing, with the frontal lobes developing last, can we hold adolescents responsible for uninhibited, antisocial behavior (Steinberg & Scott, 2003)? State courts have considered this evidence and concluded that 16- and 17-year-olds cannot be held culpable for homicide. Thirty-one states have banned the death penalty for juveniles (the U.S. Supreme Court banned executions to youths under the age of 16 in 1988; Beckman, 2004). Finally, in March of 2005, the U.S. Supreme Court also decided that the death penalty was cruel and unusual punishment for youths between the ages of 16 to 18 (*Roper v. Simmons*, 2005).

In the Dunedin Multidisciplinary Health and Development Study (New Zealand), approximately 1,000 children born between 1972 and 1973 were tested on a range of factors every two years (Moffitt, Lynam & Silva, 1994). At age 13, they were administered neuropsychological and IQ tests; and at age 18, delinquency was assessed. Terri Moffitt and her colleagues found that many of the neuropsychological tests predicted delinquency at age 18. Tests that measured verbal abilities, as opposed to tests measuring visual-motor abilities, showed the highest correlations with future delinquency. The researchers found that poor performance on these tests was associated only with the life-course-persistent male delinquents. This was a very small group (12% of the sample), but its members accounted for 59 percent of all convictions. For those whose delinquency was adolescent-limited, neuropsychological test performance was not predictive of outcome. In general, these findings have now been extended to age 32 for both the men and women in the Dunedin sample (Odgers et al., 2008) and in other samples (Cauffman, Steinberg & Piquero, 2005; Piquero, 2001; Raine et al., 2005).

The findings that we just described speak to one of the major questions asked by developmental criminology: What are the factors that lead youths into chronic criminality? Moffitt and her colleagues (Moffitt, 2003; Moffitt, Lynam & Silva, 1994) have proposed a biosocial model of life-course-persistent offending that identifies neuropsychological factors, temperament (discussed in the next section), and socialization experiences (see also Dodge and Pettit, 2003, for a similar explanation of adolescent conduct problems). Thus, biological factors are one piece of the formula for the development of persistent, and often violent, criminal behavior. For many persisters, biological variables appear to increase the risk of offending, and the addition of psychosocial risk factors (recall the interaction effect) makes matters worse (Lynam, Caspi, Moffitt, Wikström, Loeber & Novak, 2000).

We wish to emphasize that the relationship between biology and crime is not direct and simple. The consistent findings are poor verbal/language skills, inhibitory deficits, and poor attention and planning abilities. Whether these deficits have direct effects or are mediated by other environmental factors (as they likely are) remains an unresolved question (Ellis, 2005; Moffitt, 2003). Generally, it appears that genetic and neurophysiological contributions to criminal conduct will be greatest when the social environment is least supportive of crime in general and serious crimes in particular (Cauffman, Steinberg & Piquero, 2005; Lynam et al., 2000; Malouff et al., 2008; Meier, Slutske, Arndt & Coderet, 2008; Rutter, Moffitt & Caspi, 2006; Scapra & Raine, 2007; Tibbetts & Piquero, 1999; Tuvblad et al., 2006).

Although we agree with those who argue that a comprehensive theory of criminal behavior must include biological and genetic factors (e.g., Ellis, 2005; Walsh, 2000), we must keep these factors in perspective. Walters's (1992) meta-analysis found that the strength of the gene-crime relationship varied with the type of study and the quality of the research design. Family pedigree studies (i.e., examining the criminal behavior of parents and relatives in relation to the child's criminal activity) showed the largest association (phi = .26), while the more sophisticated adoption studies showed the smallest association (phi = .07).

In closing this section, Plomin's (1989) comments on the heredity-behavior literature remain relevant today as they were 20 years ago:

> These same data (genetic research) provide the best available evidence of the importance of the environment . . . they also indicate that nongenetic factors are responsible for more than half of the variance for most complex behavior. (p. 108)

The Difficult, Impulsive, Sensation-Seeking Temperament

In general, personality refers to characteristic patterns of thinking, feeling, and acting. Temperament refers to inherent and stable characteristic tendencies of responding to our environment (Else-Quest et al., 2006). Temperament is usually thought to comprise a few dimensions of behavior describing how individuals react to the environment. For example, some babies always seem content and as they grow up they continue to adapt well to whatever challenges life presents. Other babies are quite fussy and squirmy and as they grow older they may be described as "high-strung." Certainly learning experiences can have a huge effect on how individuals behave in different situations, but underlying an individual's response is a general predisposition that is evident at birth. Temperament is the biological precursor to personality. We will see that temperamental characteristics have a significant genetic component (McCrae et al., 2000), are evident soon after birth (Saudino et al., 1995; Zukerman, 1993), and remain relatively stable throughout life (Saudino, 2005; Svrakic, Svrakic & Cloninger, 1996). Our more general discussion of personality and crime is saved for Chapter 6.

The origin for today's research on temperament can be traced to the work of Alexander Thomas, Stella Chess, and their colleagues. In the original study (Thomas, Chess, Birch, Hertzig & Korn, 1963), 133 newborn infants were assessed along nine characteristics that described how they typically responded to their environments. For example, a newborn's activity level can be categorized as low (lays still when being changed) or high (wriggles while being changed), the quality of mood as negative (fusses after nursing) or positive (smiles readily at parents), and distractibility as low (stops fussing when given a pacifier) or high (continues fussing when given a pacifier). The categories were further clustered into three types: "easy," "slow to warm," and "difficult." It is common for personality theorists to reduce specific descriptors to a few general, temperamental traits. We will use their terminology of "facets" and "traits." Traits are the big-picture descriptors of temperament (e.g., difficult temperament), and facets are more specific descriptors that make up a trait (e.g., activity level, negative mood, etc.).

Our interest is in what Chess and Thomas (1984) called the "difficult" child, a category that comprised 10 percent of the 133 children. The difficult child demonstrated the following facets:

1. intense reactions to stimuli

2. a generally negative mood

3. slow to adapt to change

4. irregular in sleep, hunger, and other bodily functions.

Following the difficult children into early adulthood (age 24), the researchers found that there was significant stability (Chess & Thomas, 1984). For example, at age 10, the difficult child had a varied sleep schedule, showed difficulties adjusting to school, threw tantrums when frustrated, and cried when he or she could not solve homework problems. In adolescence, 10 of 12 cases diagnosed with a behavior disorder were temperamentally difficult children.

Today, researchers have identified a number of temperamental traits, many of which are important to our understanding of delinquency, especially the life-course-persistent offender. Two temperamental traits appear to be particularly important. The first is a high stimulation-seeking level combined with low self-control. It is one thing to have a high activity level with an interest in the experiencing life to its fullest (a characteristic of many successful individuals), but if this energy level is not controlled then it can lead to problems. High stimulation-seeking that is well socialized is actually found predictive of high IQ scores (Raine, Reynolds, Venables & Mednick, 2002). However, unsocialized stimulation-seeking is quite another matter. This temperamental trait is commonly called impulsive/sensation-seeking and has been found associated with anti-social behavior (Baker & Yardley, 2002; Barnow, Lucht & Freyberger, 2005; Berkowitz, 2008; Glenn, Raine, Venables & Mednick, 2007; Séguin et al., 1999).

An impulsive/sensation-seeking temperament is expressed in the many general (Eysenck, 1977, 1998; Quay, 1965; Zukerman, 1993) and developmental theories of antisocial behavior (Farrington, 2005; Moffit, 2003). The writings of Gottfredson and Hirschi (1990) and Moffitt and her colleagues have had a particularly strong impact on the field. In Gottfredson and Hirschi's (1990) theory, criminality is reduced to one general deficit—the lack of self-control (i.e., impulsiveness). In Moffitt's three-factor model, one of the factors is called *constraint* (Moffitt, 2003). Offenders tend to score low on measures of constraint. The key descriptors of low constraint are impulsiveness and the need for excitement.

The second major temperamental characteristic related to criminal behavior is along a social-emotional dimension. A term that Moffitt uses, which we like, is *negative emotionality*. The facets of negative emotionality are *aggression* (causes discomfort for others), *alienation* (feels mistreated), and *stress reaction* (anger and irritability). Life-course-persistent offenders scored higher on negative emotionality than adolescent-limited offenders. Furthermore, a subset of life-course-persistent offenders (psychopaths) also showed a *callous-unemotional* quality to their social interactions (Frick & White, 2008). This temperamental characteristic is biologically-based (Viding, Jones, Frick, Moffitt & Plomin, 2008), and it is as relevant to girls as it is to boys (Hipwell, Pardini, Loeber, Sembower et al., 2007).

Regardless of the terminology used by researchers, some form of a "difficult" temperament is common to almost all classification schemes.

We will continue to use the term "difficult" because it conveys well the potential problems these children can create. A difficult temperament, as characterized by impulsive sensation-seeking and negative emotionality, would certainly tax many a parent. Although all children begin life with no self-control skills, most gradually do learn to control their impulses. Where self-control matters the most is in the inhibition of aggressive behavior, and learning to inhibit aggressive behavior takes time. As Richard Tremblay (2000, 2008) has noted that by the age of one year children are able to demonstrate physical aggression and that the highest rate of physically aggressive behavior is actually among three-year-olds and not older adolescents or young adults. In other words, research should attend not so much to how aggressive behavior is learned but more on how it is inhibited. Children with a difficult temperament, we expect, would have a more arduous time learning these skills.

A difficult temperament in infancy or early childhood has predicted aggressive behavior, adolescent delinquency, and psychopathy (see Chapter 6 for a discussion of psychopathy). Schwartz, Snidman, and Kagan (1996) followed young children assessed before the age of 31 months until the age of 13 years. Difficult ("uninhibited") temperament predicted delinquency and aggressiveness as reported by the parents. A Norwegian study of 759 twin pairs, age seven to 17, found "emotionality" associated with the Delinquent Behavior and Aggressive Behavior scales of Achenbach's Child Behavior Checklist (Gjone & Stevenson, 1997). The correlations ranged from .11 to .51, depending on the gender and outcome (girls tended to have lower correlations on the delinquent scale). Terri Moffitt and her colleagues found a difficult ("lack of control") temperament as early as age three to be predictive of self-reported and officially reported antisocial behavior at age 26 (Caspi, Harrington, Milne, Amell et al., 2003) whereas Glenn et al. (2007) found uninhibited sensation-seeking at age three to predict psychopathy at age 28.

If a child is born with a difficult temperament, how does this temperament promote the development of criminal behavior? As we have suggested, parenting such a child is demanding. A positive outcome for the child could result if the child has the "right" parent(s) (caring, patient, and flexible in adapting to the child's behavioral pattern). However, if there is a "poorness of fit" (Chess & Thomas, 1990) between parenting styles and the child's temperament, then there could be trouble. Parents who find it difficult to cope may distance themselves emotionally from the child (Larsson, Viding & Plomin, 2008; Pardini & Loeber, 2008; Shaw & Vondra, 1995) or may resort to inflexible and inappropriate disciplinary techniques (Hawes & Dadds, 2005). Gerald Patterson and his colleagues (Dishion & Patterson, 1997; Patterson, DeGarmo & Knutson, 2000), for example, hypothesized that hyperactivity is the first stage on the road to chronic delinquency. The child's hyperactivity interferes with effective discipline and consequently contributes to an early onset of delinquency. Matching a child with a difficult temperament with impatient, impulsive, and hostile parents (a likely scenario considering the intergenerational data) makes for unfortunate consequences (Jaffee, Belsky, Harrington, Caspi & Moffitt, 2006; Kimonis, Frick, Boris, Smyke et al., 2006).

In Moffitt's (2003) model, the major environmental risk factors are inappropriate parenting and poor parent-child relationships. Thus, the combination of a difficult temperament and the associated disruptive behavior of a child along with a high-risk family environment produce the perfect mix for the creation of the life-course-persistent offender. In Chapter 6 we will discuss the antisocial personality pattern found among some adult offenders who represent the highest risk for criminality and show the origins of an antisocial personality pattern are found in temperament and early socialization experiences.

In PCC, temperament is an ever-present characteristic of the individual. For the development of criminal behavior, a temperament characterized by impulsivity, high activity levels, and negative emotionality is very important. We portray temperament as a risk factor, but temperament also tells us something about how the individual tends to respond to the environment (e.g., with openness to new experiences? with anger? with trust?). Temperament is one of the biological foundations to the responsivity principle (recall Chapter 2). For example, socialization efforts and treatment effectiveness are enhanced when the socialization agent (parent or teacher) or service provider (clinician) is sensitive to the personality/temperamental style of the child. Patience, structure, and consistency can pay off with an individual who has a difficult temperament.

The concept of the energetic, impulsive, sensation-seeking temperament describes behavior. What causes this behavior? One important general factor is neurophysiological arousal (Raine, 1997). People differ in their general state of neurophysiological arousal or excitability. Some of these processes are obvious, such as heart and breathing rates, eye pupil dilation, and sweating, while others require special instruments to detect neurophysiological processes (e.g., the electrical activity of the brain). Some theories place neurophysiological underarousal as central to a predisposition to criminal behavior. Eysenck (1977; Eysenck & Gudjonsson, 1989) and Quay (1965) postulated that criminals are neurophysiologically underaroused. Think of all those neurons in your body operating like they were half asleep. In order to "wake up" and bring some balance to the neurophysiological system, you need to seek out stimulation and excitement. This behavior acts like a strong cup of coffee to the system. Pair this state of underarousal with impulsivity and poor self-control and it is little wonder that some find themselves in conflict with the law.

Another aspect of neurophysiological underarousal is how it affects learning self-control (or, as Eysenck writes, a "conscience"). In Sarnoff

Mednick's (1977) biosocial theory, self-control is learned through a combination of instructions, modeling, and the reinforcement of pro-social behaviors and the punishment of inappropriate behaviors. Normally, punishment elicits fear, which is a physiologically based emotion as indicated by increased heart rate, blood pressure, and sweating (these indicators can also describe excitement and anger—it all depends on how you cognitively label these feelings). Inhibiting the inappropriate behavior (i.e., self-control) avoids the unpleasant fear reaction.

Thus, critical inhibitory learning requires that: (1) antisocial behavior is punished, and (2) the child has the capacity to learn to inhibit anti-social behavior. The antisocial behavior of some people may be traced to the fact that they did not receive the appropriate socialization training. That is, they have normal neurophysiological arousal patterns, but either their parents did not monitor their behavior closely enough or the parents did not distinguish from immoral behavior and consequently failed to punish the antisocial behavior. The antisocial behavior of others may be traced to a breakdown in the biological ability to learn self-control (Beaver, Shutt, Boutwell, Ratchford et al., 2009).

The learning of inhibition (i.e., self-control) to avoid punishment involves "fear reduction"; it is called passive avoidance learning. Passive avoidance learning proceeds in this manner:

1. The child contemplates an aggressive act.

2. Previous punishment produces fear in the child (increased heart rate, blood pressure, sweating).

3. Fear, an unpleasant emotion, causes the child to inhibit the aggressive response in order to escape from feelings of fear.

4. The child no longer entertains the aggressive impulse, and the fear dissipates.

5. The immediate reduction of fear reinforces the inhibition of the antisocial act.

In addition to requiring a socialization agent to deliver the original lessons through punishment, the process requires an adequate fear response, the ability to acquire the fear response, and a rapid dissipation of fear in order to receive the natural reinforcement for inhibition (that sense of relief of avoiding punishment). Several studies have found that individuals with antisocial personalities show diminished fear responses to aversive stimuli, and once fear is aroused, the biological markers of fear (i.e., increased heart rate, high blood pressure, sweating) are slow to dissipate (Lorber, 2004; Raine et al., 2000). On the other hand, *faster* recovery from neurophysiological arousal is predictive of *desistence* from crime (Raine, Venables & Williams, 1996).

The extent to which neurophysiological underarousal is prevalent among general offender samples and children with difficult temperaments needs further exploration. The hypotheses and few studies that relate underarousal to impulsivity and poor self-control skills are enticing. A deficit in passive avoidance learning may, however, be caused by factors other than a fear deficit. For example, some psychopaths may have the potential to feel fear but simply do not attend to the stimuli that provoke fear (Hiatt & Newman, 2006).

Within the context of PCC, neurophysiological underarousal and the need for stimulation highlight the automatic, nonmediated reinforcement potential of criminal behavior. That is, some offenders may engage in criminal acts not so much because of peer approval or some type of self-reinforcement strategy but because the act itself feels good (here we are referring to nonsexual offenses). Compared to nonoffenders, criminals tend to score higher on measures of sensation-seeking (Gottfredson & Hirschi, 1990; Zuckerman, 1984) and will readily report a feeling of a "high or rush" when committing crimes (Wood et al., 1997). Thus, the neurophysiological arousal hypothesis provides a plausible explanation for antisocial behavior in the absence of interpersonal or personally mediated controls.

We gave a fair amount of attention to neurophysiological arousal because of its central role in a number of psychological theories of criminal behavior and poor self-control. However, arousal is not the only biological correlate of poor self-control. Some delinquents have normal arousal patterns but still demonstrate poor self-control. For example, Elizabeth Cauffman, Laurence Steinberg, and Alex Piquero (2005) found a connection between poor frontal lobe function (the area of the brain associated with planning, memory, and self-control) and serious delinquency. That is, there are multiple biological determinants to poor self-control as well as environmental determinants. However, we now leave the review of the proximal biological covariates of crime and turn to more distal biological factors, namely, evolution.

Evolutionary Musings

Darwin proposed the theory of evolution by natural selection in his book, *On the Origin of Species*, published in 1859. Most know Darwin's story. While visiting the Galapagos Islands he observed and categorized the flora and fauna living in very diverse environments. In particular, the Galapagos Islands had animals that existed nowhere else on earth, despite them being similar to species known elsewhere. He concluded that through gradual adaptations to the environment a species would evolve, over the course of time, into a new species quite different from its ancestor. The modifications made to a species' physical appearance and physiology are adaptive, and they are adaptive because they allow the organism to survive and reproduce (e.g., a swallow uses its wings to fly and catch aerial insects, while a penguin cannot fly but rather uses its wings to swim after fish; in both cases the wings assist the bird with obtaining food). From his observations, Darwin formulated his theory of evolution and natural selection. The two major tenets of the theory are: (1) today's species evolved from ancestral species, and (2) organisms that adapt to their environment are more likely to reproduce, thereby ensuring the continued viability of the species (organisms that fail to adapt are less likely to reproduce; these lineages die off, thus the "survival of the fittest").

At the time, Darwin did not understand how certain adaptations are passed from one generation to the next. Gregor Mendel, a contemporary of Darwin, was conducting his experiments on garden peas, which eventually pinpointed the gene as the mechanism for inheritance. Evolutionary theorists came to view the gene as the transmitter of various adaptations from one generation to the next. As we have already seen, genes hold the programs that influence biological, physiological, and (some argue) psychological processes. Congruent with the Darwinian perspective, genes are seen as trying to maximize their present and continued survival. The title of Richard Dawkins's (1989) book, *The Selfish Gene*, says it all. The sole purpose of genes is to "replicate" (using Dawkins's word), and genes use the body of the organism to get their way in a very competitive world (remember, there are other organisms out there with their own genes wanting the same thing).

Evolutionary criminologists and psychologists have proposed that some forms of criminal behavior can be understood as a product of evolution. The basic argument is that there is a genetic predisposition to criminal behavior that has origins going back thousands, if not millions, of years. Note the word "predisposition." Most evolutionary theorists today do not accept the concept of genetic *determinism* akin to the idea of instinct where the environment only functions to trigger the gene into action. Rather, predisposition opens the door to genes being influenced by the environment and changing themselves. When evolutionary theory is applied to criminal behavior, attention is given to temperaments, personality traits, and behaviors that maximize reproduction. Thus, risk-taking, aggression, and dishonesty may lead to consensual sex without birth control, nonconsensual sex (rape), and multiple sexual partners, thereby increasing the likelihood of offspring.

Evolutionary Missteps: The Caveman Awakened

Cesare Lombroso (1835–1909) is considered to be one of the founders of modern criminology. Trained as a physician with an interest in psychiatry (a "professor of mental disease"), he was particularly taken by the physical features of criminals. Lombroso measured and tabulated the size of the head, ears, and arms, and also noted unusual physical features such as eye defects and oddly shaped noses. Why this interest in physical characteristics, and what does it all mean? The answer to this question is best given in Lombroso's own words.

> I examined his skull . . . it presented an enormous occipital fossa in place of the occipital median spine . . . this is a characteristic wanting in superior apes and existing in all other vertebrates . . . I instantly perceived that the criminal must be a survivor of the primitive man and the carnivorous animals . . . I saw that the criminal was worse than savage, worse sometimes than the true carnivore (Lombroso, 1895/2004:65–66).

This observation was made while conducting an autopsy on a prison convict. The occipital part of the brain is at the back of the brain and is responsible for vision. Lombroso makes three important points. First, biologically the criminal has similarities more in common with lower-order animals than the rest of the human race. Second, because of this biological backwardness, the individual is likely to behave like an animal with few inhibitions. More to the point, the criminal is a biological throwback to an earlier evolutionary stage (Lombroso's theory of "atavism" means a reversion to the characteristics of some remote ancestor). Finally, *some* criminals are simply born bad.

For Lombroso, not all criminals are born bad and are "atavistic." Most criminals were the result of adverse environments and experiences. However, the minority of really unpleasant sorts (chronic, career criminals) suffered from a woefully inadequate biological makeup that prohibited successful coping in the modern world. If we review the physical characteristics of Lombroso's atavistic criminal (i.e., long arms, large jaw, ears standing out like a chimpanzee), then we get the picture of a Neanderthal. Can you imagine a cave man holding down a steady job and getting along with the likes of you and me?

Lombroso was greatly influenced by Darwin's theory of evolution through selective adaptation to the environment. For Lombroso, criminal man was a failure of successful adaptation and evolution to a higher level. The atavistic criminal had some success in reproducing because of aggressive sexual behavior (rape) and copulating with those who were similarly malformed (i.e., assortative mating). Lombroso did not limit his studies to males but also gathered morphological (physical) data on women (Lombroso & Ferrero, 1895/1980). Compared with normal women (a sample of "peasants"), criminal women (which included prostitutes) had shorter arms, smaller head size, and darker hair and eyes.

Lombroso's theory of the atavistic criminal and emphasis on biology were reflective of the times (the turn of the twentieth century). The validity of the theory depended partly on the demonstration that criminals do indeed show more physical anomalies than noncriminals. Lombroso's own work on this was limited to rather small samples (383 male criminals and 80 female criminals) with dubious comparison groups. Charles Goring (1913) put Lombroso's ideas to the test in a large-scale investigation of 3,000 English convicts who were compared on 37 physical characteristics to university students, hospital patients, and soldiers. He found no differences (though some commentators noted that Goring ignored differences that were found in an effort to disprove Lombroso).

In the United States, Hooten (1939) compared the physical characteristics of 14,000 inmates with 3,000 noncriminals. He found differences on 19 of the 33 physical characteristics, with criminals featuring low foreheads and protruding ears and being generally physically inferior to noncriminals. Hooten believed that physical inferiority was equated with mental inferiority and that this was all inherited. As if Hooten didn't stir the pot enough, he also believed that the way to deal with criminals was to make sure that they did not reproduce, either by enforcing segregation from the rest of the population or through eugenics (for a summary of Hooten's views on eugenics, see Rafter, 2004; also see Rafter, 2008, for the eugenics argument taken to the extreme in Nazi Germany.).

The academic community roundly criticized Hooten's work and his interpretation of the findings. Methodological faults were uncovered, and Hooten was challenged on his claim that physical inferiority was inherited (he never did provide any evidence for this claim, and nor could he without studying generations of criminals). Perhaps because of the rise of sociological explanations of crime advanced by Sutherland, Merton, and others, interest in biological explanations of criminal behavior waned. However, it did not disappear.

Glueck and Glueck's (1950) classic comparison of delinquents and nondelinquents was a social-psychological study of delinquency, but they also measured body type using William Sheldon's typology. Sheldon (1942) had developed a constitutional theory of personality based on three body types (ectomorph = skinny, endomorph = chubby, and mesomorph = muscular). Each body type was associated with different temperaments. For example, the mesomorph had a high activity level and was more aggressive. Of course, many individuals cannot be definitively classified into any one body type. To deal with this problem, Sheldon developed a rating scheme by which points were assigned for each body type (there was an atlas of more than 1,000 male college students, with 46,000 photographs to help assign ratings). In the Glueck and Glueck (1950) study, delinquents were more likely to fall in the mesomorph category. Although this body type pattern has been repeatedly found associated with criminal behavior (Ellis, 2000), we cannot conclude that this body type was predetermined by genes. The mesomorphic body type could just as well have been the result of a physical, adventuresome lifestyle.

Even today we see traces of Lombrosian-like explanations of criminal conduct. The most well-known and controversial views are those of Phillipe Rushton. Rushton, along with Arthur Jensen proposed that there are racial differences in intelligence, temperament, social organization (e.g., respect for the law, marital stability), and sexual restraint (Rushton, 1988; Rushton & Jensen, 2005, 2006, 2008). More to the point, they argue that Asians are the most advanced, followed by Caucasians, and then Blacks. Furthermore, these differences are explained by genetics and, by association, evolution. Thus, the higher crime rates observed among blacks may be traced to their lower intelligence, poorer sexual restraints, and social disorganization.

Rushton and Jensen draw on many different types of evidence, but in order to link our discussion of Lombroso and Hooten we point to their use of cranial measurement and brain weight as proxies for intelligence. The claim is that the differences in cranial capacities and brain weight, with Asians showing the largest values and Blacks the smallest values, reflect the corresponding differences found in IQ scores (Rushton & Ankney, 1996; Rushton & Jensen, 2005, 2006, 2008). We want to be clear, however, that Rushton's interpretation of morphological differences among races is not widely accepted (Cernovsky & Litman, 1993; Sternberg, 2005). We included a brief discussion of Rushton and Jensen's views only to show that Lombroso's work has had a long legacy.

Criminal Behavior as an Evolutionary Adaptation

In the previous section we described Lombroso's theory of atavism as a backdrop to modern evolutionary explanations of crime. Contrary to the opinion of many of today's evolutionary theorists, Lombroso took the position that criminal man and woman were defects of evolution—not at all a positive step in evolutionary development. Although modern evolutionary theorists stress the adaptive nature of the organism to the environment, i.e., the organism is the result of *successful* adaptation to the challenges of the environment, there are exceptions. For example, the HIV virus *kills* the host (the person). If the virus was truly adaptive, then it would keep the host alive to continue reproduction.

Lee Ellis and Anthony Walsh (1997) present the evolutionary perspective of criminal conduct nicely with their characterizations of *cads and dads*. Cads are men who reproduce with women in sneaky, aggressive, or cheating ways and then leave the women high and dry while they go looking for another reproducing partner (the term *cad* also applies to animal species; for example, male birds of paradise quickly fly off after copulation, leaving the female to sit on the eggs and raise the offspring). Dads, on the other hand, remain monogamous and participate in the raising of the young.

It doesn't take much to mold evolutionary theory to an explanation of the origins of criminal behavior. Simply think of the early sexual behavior of delinquents (Glueck & Glueck, 1950; Stouthamer-Loeber & Wei, 1998), the promiscuity and parasitic lifestyle of psychopaths (Hare, 1991), the behavior of the rapist (Lalumière & Quinsey, 1996), and the general dishonesty of criminals (Quinsey, Skilling, Lalumière & Craig, 2004). Evolutionary theory has also been used to explain domestic assault (the male controlling the women's chances of bearing someone else's child; Daly & Wilson, 1988) and child abuse and murder (nonrelated parents are more likely to neglect or abuse the child because there is no genetic investment; Daly & Wilson, 1994; Harris, Hilton, Rice & Eke, 2007).

Quinsey and his colleagues (Quinsey, 2002; Quinsey, Skilling, Lalumière & Craig, 2004) have suggested that there are actually two types of life-course-persistent offenders. The first is that described by Moffitt (1993) as the child with neuropsychological problems, a difficult temperament, and poor socialization experiences. The second is what Quinsey and colleagues (2004) call the psychopaths, who follow an evolutionary adaptive strategy throughout their lives. These individuals demonstrate few neuropsychological deficits, and their behavior reflects a genetically determined strategy to maximize mating success. It remains to be seen, however, whether future research will confirm these two types of chronic offenders.

Although we have been discussing the selfish behavior of the male, a woman's behavior with respect to reproduction also has adaptive significance. Women, according to evolutionary theory, would seek the "dad" who would commit to raising the child and ensure the continuity of the genetic pool. Child rearing by the single parent runs the risk of the offspring not reaching maturity and reproducing. Whether we are talking about birds, lizards, or humans, two parents are often in a better position to muster sufficient food and protection for the healthy development of the offspring than one parent. Therefore, it is in the mother's (gene's) best interest to pick a partner that she can count on for raising children. This does not discount the importance of physical attractiveness (Provost, Kormos, Kosakoski & Quinsey, 2006) but highlights the need for a long-time commitment to child rearing.

Ellis (2005) and Buss (2009) argue that mothers are also predisposed to pick "status-striving males," which puts evolutionary pressure on males to be highly competitive (and in the process of being competitive, people are also victimized—because of stepping on the little people to get ahead). Of course, the male is not entirely ignorant of the female's preferences, and men try to make themselves attractive and worth keeping (in many bird species, males have evolved colorful plumage; in humans, men buy fancy suits).

Alas, choosing a father that will remain loyal, considerate, and have the resources to care for the offspring is not easy. The high sexual and physical victimization rates of children attest to that. Nonetheless, we are not saying that choosing a "dad" and avoiding getting fooled by a "cad" is impossible. After all, we all know couples that have made good choices and remain committed to child rearing. We are also reminded by the possibility that the *control* of impulses, and not just uninhibited aggressive behavior, can be adaptive (Ferguson, 2008).

Looking closely at the mating behaviors of criminals, it is difficult to see that these behaviors are adaptive in the long run. Yes, delinquents and criminals do begin sexual intercourse earlier than noncriminals, have children earlier, and have more sexual partners. It seems that the male genes are winners. However, look at whom they pair with. Criminals tend to mate with partners who have similar temperaments, personalities, social backgrounds, and the problems associated with a criminal lifestyle, including poor health and early mortality (Farrington, Barnes & Lambert, 1996; Haynie et al., 2005; Jaffee, Belsky, Harrington, Caspi & Moffitt, 2006; Laub & Vaillant, 2000; Nieuwbeerta, 2008; Piquero, Daigle, Gibson et al., 2007; Tremblay & Paré, 2003). The male swindler fathering a child with a wealthy heiress or the female prostitute being swept off her feet by the dashing successful businessman is the stuff of movies. More likely is the situation of the male criminal mating with a woman who also has been in conflict with the law, has an erratic work history, and abuses alcohol and/or other drugs (e.g., Pogarsky, Lizotte & Thornberry, 2003). Finally, who are the products of these unions? It is much too often a child with a low birth weight, a difficult temperament, and neurological problems ranging from attention deficit and hyperactivity disorder to fetal alcohol syndrome. It is hard to see how this situation is in the best interest of the gene.

People also have readily available methods of birth control and, in many countries, access to abortion. These factors have the potential of altering the course of genetic reproduction. There is no firm evidence on the prevalence of birth control among offenders, although the criminal lifestyle of carelessness, substance abuse, and high rates of HIV suggests that offenders are less likely to use these methods (Sheeran, Abraham & Orbell, 1999). This may increase genetic reproduction, but the "quality" of the offspring may suffer. Donahue and Levitt (2001; Steven Levitt of *Freakonomics* fame) argued that the legalization of abortion following the U.S. Supreme court decision, *Roe v. Wade*, in 1973 would result in a drop in crime. The reasoning was that the availability of abortion to poor, young mothers would reduce the number of children who would grow up as criminals. Indeed, crime did drop in the early 1990s, but it was not due to teenaged, unmarried women resorting to abortion (Chamlin, Myer, Sanders & Cochran, 2008).

Evolutionary theory is changing. Although many evolutionary theorists deny adherence to genetic determinism, a close reading suggests otherwise (Lickliter & Honeycutt, 2003). Their views may be better called gene-based evolutionary theory. That is, the adaptations developed over generations, taking as little as a year (e.g., flu viruses) to thousands of generations, can be reduced to the actions of the gene. The way we look, feel, and act is because of our genes and not much else. Genes determine largely who we are, and the environment's role is often to trigger the gene to release its program. Gene-based evolution assumes a very deterministic function for the gene and that the behavioral expressions of genes are all adaptive (there are exceptions to the notion that everything that gene influences is adaptive; e.g., eye color has no adaptive function, Daly, 1996).

Many of the arguments for this one-sided view are based on studies of lower species and then extrapolated to human behavior (Dagg, 2005). However, humans are not guppies, and the more complex the organism, the greater the influence of extra-genetic factors. Even in lower-level species, environmental factors can profoundly alter genetic programs. For example, the sex (gene based) of turtles depends on the incubation temperature of the eggs. Gene-based evolutionary theory is morphing into a developmental biology–informed theory of evolution in which environmental influences are given equal billing to genetic influences (Lickliter & Honeycutt, 2003). There is still ample room, even in evolutionary theory, for the importance of the environment.

Social Origins of Crime

Social Class

No single variable has been more important in criminological theorizing than social class. According to most textbooks, no single fact was judged to be so well established than a negative association between social class and criminal behavior (i.e., the lower in social class, the higher the probability of criminal behavior). Many of the major sociological theories of crime and delinquency were theories of crime in the lower social classes. The social origins of crime were in being lower-class, deprived, poor, and frustrated in trying to acquire what the upper classes have.

Charles Tittle, Wayne Villimez, and Douglas Smith (1978) were the first to question the strength of the class-crime link through a meta-analysis of 35 studies that examined the class-crime link at the individual level, thus avoiding the ecological fallacy. Studies that characterized individuals in traditional measures (personal or familial, occupational, educational, and income) of socioeconomic status (SES), as well as the class structure of their areas of residence, were included. The important question is whether decreases in SES are associated with increases in the proportion of criminals. An effect size of zero would indicate that there is no relationship; a value of one would indicate a perfect 1:1 relationship. The sign of the effect size, minus or plus, indicates the type of relationship. Minus (–) signals an inverse association; plus (+) signals a positive association.

The 35 studies yielded 363 effect size estimates (gamma coefficients) for various combinations of sex, race, and other factors. The average effect size was –.09, a relatively modest relationship between class and crime. In addition, the mean effect sizes were in the same range for men (–.08) and women (–.11), and for whites (–.07) and nonwhites (–.01). Tittle and his associates recognized that some of the individual effect sizes were strong and negative, even though the average gammas were weak. Similarly, some effect size estimates were actually positive in sign, suggesting that under some circumstances, increases in SES were associated with higher, rather than lower, levels of criminality (a finding opposite to that predicted by class-based theories).

Further analyses found that the class-crime relationship did not depend on the type of offense (e.g., violent, nonviolent). However, the magnitude of the association did vary with how criminality was measured (self-report versus official records) and with the decade in which the study was completed. The mean effect size from the self-report studies was small (–.06) but larger (–0.25) for studies of official records. The relatively large effect size for official records was traced to studies conducted prior to the 1970s. Before 1950, the mean effect size was a whopping –.73 but then diminished. After 1970, the effect size dropped to +.04. On the other hand, the effect sizes based on self-reported criminality were relatively constant over time and trivial in magnitude (ranging from –.03 to –.11). This was interpreted to mean that in the 1970s there was essentially no relationship between class and criminality as evidenced by the marginal effect size estimates for both self-reported and official measures of crime. One may have existed prior to 1950, but may have reflected processing effects rather than criminality (thus explaining the large effect size in the early studies when official measures of crime were used).

Tittle at al.'s (1978) review cast serious doubt on the vitality of class-based explanations of criminal conduct. Their conclusions were not left without a fight (e.g., Braithwaite, 1981). After all, social class was central to most mainstream theories of crime. Some of the responses by defenders of the faith simply asserted that the relationship exists, period, without giving any evidence ("social inequality is the main cause of crime," DeKeseredy & Schwartz, 1996:463; "the linkage of poverty and crime is inexorable, despite the inability of researchers to establish it at the individual level", Short, 1991:501). However, reviews of the literature post-1978 (Gendreau at al., 1996; Loeber & Stouthamer-Loeber, 1987; Simourd & Andrews, 1994; Tittle & Meier, 1990, 1991) and more recent direct tests (Dunaway et al., 2000; Ring & Svensson, 2007) continued to find little evidence for a class-crime link. Recall Resource Note 2.1 from the second chapter in which class of origin produced a mean correlation .06, and compare these correlations to those found with antisocial personality pattern, antisocial attitudes, and antisocial associates (range .12 to .36). Overall, our conclusion is that the theoretical dominance of class of origin in mainstream sociological criminology from the 1960s forward was not based on evidence. When the social psychology of criminological knowledge is finally written, the theoreticism of mainstream sociological criminology in regard to social class may well become one of the intellectual scandals of science.

Attempts to rescue social class have continued. There are too many social scientists with too much invested in the concept for it simply to fade away. There will continue to be an interest in poverty, in crime in lower-class areas, and in redistributing societal wealth and power. Those interests, however, do not depend upon there being an inexorable link between class and crime. Recognizing a weak class-crime link does not dismiss the real problems of the poor, nor does it deny the existence of high-crime neighborhoods. What the recognition of a weak class-crime link does is to remind students, scholars, and policymakers that the socioeconomic context makes, at best, a minor contribution to variation in crime, relative to a host of other personal, interpersonal, familial, and structural/cultural variables, including the immediate situations of action.

There are other approaches to understanding the relationship, albeit weak, that does exist between crime and class. One approach is to specify the possible conditions under which a relationship may exist by focusing upon the levels of disposable income available to individuals at particular periods of time. What are the implications of having some loose change in your pocket or purse? Some American (e.g., Cullen, Larson & Mathers, 1985; Wright, Cullen & Williams, 2002) and British (e.g., West & Farrington, 1977) data suggest that relative wealth in the immediate sense is a correlate of juvenile delinquency. However, it is the delinquent kids who tend to have more money than nondelinquent kids. Having money may indeed give one power, including the power to remove oneself from parental control and to do what one wants to do, including acting in illegal ways (Hagan, 1989).

Another approach is to treat power as a "social fact" that may impact upon the behavior of individuals in social circumstances. For example, consider the Marxist concept of social power with respect to the "ruling class" versus the rest of society. Hagan, Gillis, and Simpson (1985) analyzed the self-reported delinquency of 485 high school students in which the head of household (gender not specified) was from the ruling class (i.e., owner of a business or a manager) or from the "suppressed class" (i.e., worker or unemployed). Conventional measures of social class (i.e., occupational prestige ratings) were unrelated to delinquency and, overall, there were no differences in the self-reported delinquency of the youths from the four Marxist categories. However, when the children of owners were compared with the other groups, a mild correlation emerged (r of approximately +.11). The children of the powerful were engaging in slightly *more* delinquency than the children of the less powerful. It was the offspring of the most powerful who were most free to be delinquent.

Society and Culture

Rewards and costs are the immediate sources of control over behavior. Furthermore, these rewards and costs can come from ourselves, from those around us (friends, parents, teachers, employers, etc.), or from the act itself (e.g., the high from taking cocaine). The availability of rewards and costs and the rules for delivering them vary from society to society and according to the economic-social-political conditions inherent in a particular society or culture. This is the essence of Principle 10 of PIC-R (Resource Note 4.1). For example, a society with high unemployment cannot provide sufficient rewards for prosocial behavior through jobs, thereby making alternative antisocial behaviors as a means to earn money more attractive. From a normative perspective, cultures will vary on what they expect from their members and what will be rewarded. Take, for example, drinking alcohol. The "rules" under which alcohol consumption is sanctioned can vary across cultures from drinking only under strict, ceremonial conditions to displays of public drunkenness.

The availability and distribution of rewards and costs can vary from a national level to subgroups within nations. Graeme Newman (1976) surveyed six nations and found general agreement on the acts viewed as criminal. However, there was variation. Incest was condemned (i.e., deserving of punishment) by 98 percent of pre-revolution Iranians and 71 percent by the Americans in the survey. The political structure of nations can also define what is, and is not criminalized. For example, a totalitarian government may not tolerate individuals who speak out against the government. Within many nations there are diverse groups in which certain behaviors are rewarded and others punished. These groups may vary by country of origin, race, and religion, and some have argued, by class (a "culture of poverty"). Much of mainstream criminology has struggled with understanding how culture and subcultures contribute to criminal behavior. From the PIC-R perspective, the contribution is through the norms held by the culture and the delivery of rewards and costs in adherence to these norms.

We strongly endorse the study of crime at all levels of class of origin, culture, and relationship to the means of production. Those interested in "social origins" would be well-advised to consult Glueck and Glueck's (1950) classic analysis of delinquent behavior. In addition to providing evidence regarding the predictive potential of various personal characteristics,

Glueck and Glueck also clearly suggested that "social origins" is a trivial variable compared to "the familial bio-social legacy." The major familial correlates of delinquency were not parental levels of education or occupation but parental attitudes toward employment; not having been on welfare but reliance upon welfare; not the socioeconomic circumstances of the family but intergenerational emotional, intellectual, and conduct problems that may impact upon parenting.

A Few Final Comments

Before closing this chapter we have a few comments relevant to a PCC. First, biological factors contribute to criminal behavior. It is not that biology determines crime but that the biological processes behind impulsiveness, sensation-seeking, negative emotionality, and the like increase the probability of antisocial behavior under the right environmental conditions. We may not be able to measure precisely the underlying biological processes but we certainly can differentiate individuals on the behaviors described. Furthermore, we can consider these behaviors as forming part of what we call *antisocial personality pattern*, representing one of the Big Four risk/need factors (Chapter 6 explores this concept more fully).

Second, biological factors appear to play a greater role with the life-course-persistent offenders. Although it is tempting to explain their behavior as a product of disadvantaged social environments, the evidence simply does not allow us to say this. Many children grow up in poverty and in homes with dysfunctional parenting, but not all of them follow a path of chronic and violent criminality. Why some children in these environments follow this path and others a less antisocial trajectory appears to reside in biological differences.

Third, we know that criminal behavior is likely when the density of rewards and costs are more favorable to criminal behavior than prosocial behavior. The ratio of rewards/costs favorable to criminal behavior will vary from one social context to another and according to person factors. Criminal history reflects the fact that early and frequent reinforcement of criminal behavior establishes a behavioral habit that is difficult to break. But, it also reflects the fact that some individuals with certain predispositions are more responsive to the quick and easy rewards for criminal behaviors than the rewards for prosocial behavior.

Worth Remembering

1. The environment controls how our biological predispositions are expressed in behavior.

There are many aspects to individuals that are biologically based—age, gender, race, and temperament. However, just because certain factors have a biological basis does not mean that behavior is predetermined. The path to crime or to good citizenship depends more on what happens as the individual grows up than on what capabilities the individual was born with.

2. Most crimes are committed by young males.

   The majority of youthful males will engage in crime during adolescence but then stop in early adulthood. Developmental criminologists refer to this trajectory as adolescence-limited. However, a small majority of youths will continue their criminal activity into adulthood. This trajectory is called that of chronic offenders or life-course-persistent.

3. There is a hereditary component in criminal behavior that interacts with the social environment.

   The findings from family lineage, twin, and adoption studies point to a genetic component to criminal conduct. It is not criminal behavior per se that is inherited but temperamental characteristics such as impulsivity, sensation-seeking, and a negative emotionality that are inherited. A "difficult" temperament may predispose some to an increase risk of crime, but it depends upon the environment whether the predisposition translates into criminal behavior (e.g., the influence of a dysfunctional family). Genes determine biochemical reactions, but it is the environment that determines what you think and feel and how you behave.

4. Other biological factors can play a role with some individuals, some of the time.

   A variety of biological factors (e.g., traumatic injuries to the brain) have been documented as risk factors in some individuals. These instances are relatively rare and one-of-a-kind. However, neuropsychological factors may be especially important with chronic and violent offenders.

5. Evolutionary explanations of criminal behavior have interesting implications, but the field remains highly controversial.

   The idea that criminal behavior has an adaptive function underlies evolutionary perspectives of crime. That is, the aggression and dishonesty of criminals have payoffs beyond immediate gratification. Such behaviors are indicative of a genetic predisposition that has been in the making for thousands of years. Developmental biologists question the evolutionary perspective that genes are all-important and try to keep things in perspective by reminding us of the tremendous importance of the environment.

6. Social class of origin is a minor correlate of crime.

Much of mainstream criminology has given a central role to social class as an explanation of criminal behavior. However, the evidence shows that social class is, at best, a modest correlate of crime. More important are personal characteristics such as a difficult temperament, parental monitoring and disciplining, social achievement, antisocial attitudes, and antisocial associates. Criminologists and psychologists may still ask the question why certain social classes have a greater distribution of individuals with the personal characteristics listed, but that question is different from the question of why individual X commits antisocial acts and individual Y does not.

Recommended Readings

For the reader interested in the work on developmental trajectories and the life-course-persistent offender, we recommend Terri Moffitt's (2007) chapter in *The Cambridge Handbook of Violent Behavior and Aggression*. Moffit reviews not only the findings from the Dunedin sample but also the other major longitudinal studies that have tracked the development of criminal behavior.

Genetics and Criminal Behavior (Wasserman & Wachbroit, 2001) is an excellent edited book that gives a detailed overview of topics on heredity and crime. Some readers will also be interested in the legal implications of genetic findings as they relate to crime. We refer these readers to the edited collection by Jeffrey Botkin and his colleagues, *Genetics and Criminality: The Potential Misuse of Scientific Information in Court* (Botkins, McMahon & Francis, 1999).

Jan Volavka's (2002) text, *Neurobiology of Violence*, serves as a comprehensive summary of the literature on the neurophysiological correlates of violent behavior. He covers a wide variety of possible risk factors from very rare and highly tenuous (e.g., murder while sleepwalking) to more plausible risk factors. Volavka accomplishes this thorough review with an eye always on the evidence.

A comprehensive description of gene-based evolutionary theory can be found in Richard Dawkins's (1989) highly readable book, *The Selfish Gene*. It is a nontechnical book with many examples of fascinating adaptations that animals (and plants) undergo in order to survive in their environments and reproduce. Those with a limited knowledge of biology and genetics are likely to be convinced of the merits of evolutionary theory. For this reason, we would suggest that the reader examine some of the limitations of gene-based evolutionary theory by reading Robert Lickliter and Hunter Honeycutt's (2003) article, "Developmental Dynamics: Toward a Biologically Plausible Evolutionary Psychology," in

Psychological Bulletin. The article may not be as easy to read as Dawkins's book, but it is shorter and not overly technical. At the very least, the article will make you think twice about all the popular articles on evolutionary theory.

For a general overview of the contributions of evolutionary theory to psychology the February 2009 special issue of *The American Psychologist* (Volume 62) is worth a review. For the application of evolutionary theory to criminal behavior, we would suggest beginning with the article by Lee Ellis and Anthony Walsh (1997). It presents an excellent summary of the literature. Also worth a read is the book by Vernon Quinsey and his colleagues, *Juvenile Delinquency: Understanding the Origins of Individual Differences* (2004). Chapters 1 and 2 of this book give a very good introduction to evolutionary psychology and genetics.

The article, "The Myth of Social Class and Criminality: An Empirical Assessment of the Empirical Evidence," by Tittle, Villemez, and Smith (1978), may be old, but it remains a classic. This was the first study that redefined social class as a major covariate of crime to the status of ideology. Furthermore, the authors accomplished this feat by applying meta-analytic techniques to the problem and giving us one of the earliest examples of meta-analysis in criminology.

Chapter 6

Antisocial Personality Pattern

Antisocial personality is one of the best predictors of criminal behavior. In fact, in Chapter 2 we placed it as one of the Big Four correlates of criminal conduct. The origins of antisocial personality were seen in what we called a difficult temperament (described in Chapter 5), and this personality constellation appears central in the makeup of life-course-persistent, high-risk offenders. This chapter explores the notion of antisocial personality in more depth, with discussions of different perspectives of antisocial personality.

We begin the chapter by first outlining current knowledge of personality in general. The study of personality is one of the branches of psychology, and the latest thinking about personality should inform our understanding of criminal conduct. Next we review criminology's position on personality vis-à-vis crime and trace the remarkable transition in criminology's respect for personality. Our third major section examines forensic/clinical psychology and psychiatry's preoccupation with mental disorder through the study of antisocial personality disorder and psychopathy. Finally, we end with a critique of forensic/mental health conceptualizations of antisocial personality and a call for a more general perspective of antisocial personality.

Psychology's View of Personality

Almost everyone has asked, at one time or another, "Who am I?" Usually the answer to the question involves evaluations of the self ("I am a good person"), motivations ("I am lazy"), intelligence ("I am smart"), emotionality ("I am nervous"), and relationships to others ("I am kind"). The answers to the question also imply relative stability. That is, if we say that we are nervous or kind to others, then we act this way most of the time and with most people. Personality reflects typical patterns of thinking, feeling, and acting.

Most personality researchers are interested in traits and understanding how individuals differ along these traits. Traits describe our general pattern of responding to different situations. Some examples of traits associated with criminal behavior are aggressivity, impulsiveness, risk-taking, dishonesty, and emotional negativity. Other traits, such as anxiety and shyness, may also be important, especially when we consider treatment interventions for offenders (to be discussed in Chapters 11 and 12). Sometimes when we look at the research on personality traits we are left feeling that it is a mess—there are so many different traits measured in so many different ways according to so many different theoretical perspectives. However, personality researchers and theorists have brought organization to the study of traits by developing descriptive systems of a few basic personality dimensions that encompass the multitude of traits.

Factor analysis is a statistical technique commonly used to group traits into a few broad categories. It involves the analysis of a large amount of data in the search for underlying common factors. Raymond Cattell (1957) pioneered research on personality using factor analytic techniques to reduce hundreds of descriptions of traits into 16 factors. He showed that trait descriptions such as tidy, fussy, overly precise, unable to relax, careless, and lazy could all be described by the dimension of "insistently orderly/relaxed." Note that the dimensions or factors are always bipolar (individuals can be placed from very low to very high on the dimension). However, 16 factors were too much for many personality researchers; further reductions were made. For example, Hans Eysenck (1977, 1998) formulated three dimensions, extroversion/introversion, neuroticism (emotionally unstable to stable), and psychoticism (aggressive, impulsive to friendly, and well controlled).

The Super Trait Perspectives of Personality

During the past decade there has been a remarkable convergence of opinion on a five-factor model of personality. That is, most personality traits can be described by five general dimensions or what is referred to as the Big Five (Digman, 1990). Not everyone agrees on the precise labels for the five super traits, but we will use the labels proposed by Paul Costa and Robert McCrae (1992; McCrae & Costa, 1999) and assessed by the NEO Personality Inventory (NEO originally referred to neuroticism, extraversion, and openness, but now is considered part of the name and not an acronym). The Big Five are comprised of subtraits or "facets." Here are the Big Five, along with examples of their corresponding facets:

1. *Neuroticism*—anxious, angry hostility, impulsive

2. *Extraversion*—positive emotions, excitement-seeking

3. *Openness to Experience*—creative, open-minded, intelligent

4. *Agreeableness*—trustworthy, altruistic, compliant

5. *Conscientiousness*—competent, orderly, self-disciplined.

Research on the Big Five suggests that these personality dimensions are found in both genders and across cultures and that there is a heritability component. For example, Schmitt and his colleagues (Schmitt, Realo, Voracek & Allik, 2008) found these five factors among men and women from 55 countries as diverse as the United States and Zimbabwe. The applicability across cultures suggests a biological basis to personality (Allik & McCrae, 2005). Further evidence for a biological basis to the Big Five comes from twin studies (Jang et al., 1998; McCrae et al., 2008).

Although the five-factor model is having a major influence on personality theory, it does not have a monopoly on the field. Some psychologists (e.g., Mayer, 2005) feel that the Big Five model fails to adequately capture some commonly studied traits such as locus of control and masculinity-femininity. Others have argued that we need to consider more factors, especially if we are to describe psychopathologies. For example, Christine Durrett and Timothy Trull (2005) add two dimensions, *Positive Valence* and *Negative Valence*, creating a Big Seven model. Positive Valence refers to evaluations of self that are flattering (e.g., "I am superior" vs. "I am ordinary"), while Negative Valence refers to evaluations of self that are unflattering (e.g., "I am a bad person" vs. "I am a decent person"). D and Trull (2005) argue that these two dimensions of personality are needed to explain personality disorders such as narcissism (an exaggerated sense of self-worth) and borderline personality disorder (a view of the self as bad or evil).

Much of the research on the Big Five has been conducted on normal samples, with a few forays into the area of deviance. When it comes to criminal or aggressive behavior, there are only a handful of studies with respect to the Big Five model. All of these studies used a cross-sectional methodology with extreme groups (e.g., college students vs. prisoners), thereby maximizing the chances of finding differences. What these studies find is that Agreeableness and Conscientiousness almost always differentiate antisocial individuals from prosocial individuals (Heaven, 1996; Miller, Lynam & Leukefeld, 2003; Samuels et al., 2004; van Dam, Janssens & De Bruyn, 2005; Wiebe, 2004). Most studies also find Neuroticism and Extraversion to be important (Wiebe, 2004, is an exception). Neuroticism and Extraversion have long been recognized as important personality variables playing central roles in Hans Eysenck's "Big Three" model of criminal behavior.

As we saw in the developmental chapter (Chapters 5), Moffitt and her colleagues formulated a three-factor model. We apologize to the reader for this array of theories of personality (Big Five, Big Seven, etc.) as well as our own Big Four and Central Eight but, we simply cannot think of a better way of summarizing all of these positions. I guess if we want the simplest model of personality and crime, we can add Gottfredson and Hirschi's (1990) theory of the Big One (i.e., criminals lack self-control). Moffitt's three-factor model consists of Constraint, Negative

Emotionality, and Positive Emotionality. However, it is the first two factors that are most strongly associated with criminality. They also correspond nicely to the Big Five factors of Conscientiousness and Neuroticism, although there is some overlap with the others (Extraversion and Agreeableness).

Caspi, Moffitt, Silva, Stouthamer-Loeber, Krueger, and Schmutte (1994) found Constraint and Negative Emotionality linked to crime across countries, gender, race, and methods. The facets of Constraint are traditionalism (endorses high moral standards), harm avoidance (avoids excitement and danger), and control (is reflective, planful). Offenders scored lower on Constraint than did nonoffenders. The facets of Negative Emotionality are aggression (causes discomfort for others), alienation (feels mistreated), and stress reaction (expresses anger and irritability). Offenders scored higher on Negative Emotionality than did nonoffenders. Offenders and nonoffenders did not differ on measures of Positive Emotionality (e.g., feelings of well-being and sociability).

Related to the above are the findings reported in a meta-analysis of the three factor models of Eysenck (1977) and Tellegen (1982). The two describe very similar factors that were labeled Extraversion/Sociability, Neuroticism/Emotionality (similar to Negative Emotionality in Moffitt's model), and Impulsivity/Disinhibition (similar to Constraint). In Cale's (2008) review, the best correlate of antisocial behavior was Impulsivity/disinhibition ($r = .37$, k = 96), followed by Neuroticism/Emotionality ($r = .18$, k = 90). Extraversion/Sociability evidenced the smallest effect size ($r = .10$, k = 94).

There is one important conclusion to be drawn from models of personality that either use the Big Five or some variation of it. That is, the Big Five (or Big Three, etc.) super traits are *normal* aspects of personality. They can describe all of us to some degree, and we all have more or less of these general dimensions of personality. We can use the super trait models to describe offenders without the need to invoke pathology and disease to explain their behavior, the usual approach taken by forensic psychiatry and psychology. Offenders fall on the wrong end of constraint (self-control, impulsive, low conscientiousness), emotionality (hostile, aggressive, callous disregard for others), and a general pattern of getting into trouble. This antisocial personality pattern reflects a constellation of personality dimensions that we all share, but where we are on these dimensions account for the differences between offenders and nonoffenders. Please keep this in mind. We will return to it at the end of the chapter.

Is Personality Just a Matter of Traits?

Up to this point we have been discussing personality from a trait perspective. The trait perspective emphasizes the stable, enduring features of personality. Certainly we have seen substantial evidence of the stability of traits. Simply review the evidence in Chapter 5 on temperament and the longitudinal studies of delinquency. However, we all know that sometimes we act differently than we usually do in certain situations. When faced with a crisis, the cautious individual may muster his or her courage to rise to the challenge, or the shy person will speak out when a loved one is criticized. So then, just how stable and consistent are personality traits?

Walter Mischel (1968) reviewed the stability of various personality traits and found that the average correlation between a particular trait and the expression of that trait in various situations was about .30. Mischel (1968) suggested that the view that personality traits are highly stable across situations has led us astray. He went on to say that we need to pay much more attention to how people interpret situations and the fact that these psychological processes are fundamental aspects of personality.

As a consequence to Mischel's (1968) review, the study of traits fell into disfavor until its re-emergence with the development of the Big Five model of personality. The study of psychological processes that tried to make sense of the immediate situations of action grew in favor. The goal was to specify under what situational conditions a trait was expressed. To attain this goal it was necessary to: (a) be very specific in describing the situation of action, and (b) understand how the individual personally interprets or encodes the situation. The encoding of information depended upon cognitive and social-emotional processes. Thus, if you wanted to predict whether an individual would behave aggressively, then you needed to know the specific situation (e.g., is a police officer present?) and how the individual interprets the situation (e.g., "the police officer may put me in jail" or "I hate cops").

Although the situation/psychological processing approach did yield improvements in the prediction of behavior, one could not escape the fact that, in general, people do have characteristic ways of responding to the environment. For 20 years following Mischel's (1968) seminal work, personality research consisted of two solitudes—a trait perspective and a situational/psychological-processing perspective. Recently, personality researchers have been trying to integrate the two perspectives, and some of this work is led by no other than Mischel (Mischel, 2004; Mischel & Shoda, 1998; Mischel, Shoda & Mendoza-Denton, 2002; Shoda & Mischel, 2006).

Mischel and Shoda (1998; Shoda & Mischel, 2006) describe their integrative theory as the Cognitive-Affective Personality System (CAPS). Cognitive-affective processing (i.e., encodings, affect, expectancies, self-regulatory plans) can be relatively stable mediators between personality traits and the situation. For example, the general belief that people are out to get you leads to many social situations being interpreted the same way, resulting in similar behavioral responses. Mayer (2005) has advanced a systems framework in which personality consists of motives and emotions (the bread and butter of trait theories) but also includes memory, intelligence, social attachments, and attitudes and expectations. The direction of today's personality theories is toward greater integrations of various psychological subsystems. Personality is no longer just the study of stable personality traits but also the study of the dynamic psychological processes that are the mediators between traits and the situation of action.

Criminology's View of Personality

In this section we summarize the remarkable shift in mainstream criminology's view of personality and crime. From the 1930s to about 1990, the importance of personality had been largely ignored. Early reviews tried hard to discredit the evidence on personality in order to maintain a central role for social class in criminological theory. Today, things are much different. Personality is seen as pivotal in many criminological theories, and researchers are almost tripping over themselves to study personality as it relates to crime. Here follows the story of this transition.

Then . . .

The first substantive review of the personality-crime link was by Schuessler and Cressey (1950). They reviewed 113 studies and found that 42 percent of those studies reported a difference in the personalities of offenders and nonoffenders. However, they concluded that personality and criminality were not linked. Granted, 42 percent is not 100 percent, but what about the hit rate for social class (about 20%)? Surely, we cannot ignore a 42 percent hit rate. Well, Schuessler and Cressey did, and so did other criminologists who followed.

Waldo and Dinitz (1967) reviewed 94 studies published after the Schuessler and Cressey (1950) review (i.e., 1950–1965). This review was more important than the previous one because the tests used to measure personality were more sophisticated and the studies better designed. A personality-crime association was found in 81 percent of the studies. However, Waldo and Dinitz also concluded that there was no real association between personality and criminal behavior.

Let us now jump to 1977. Tennenbaum (1977) located 44 studies of personality and crime published between 1966 and 1975. He noted that the methodological quality of the studies had improved and that a wider range of personality tests was being explored than in the earlier years. Eighty percent of the 44 studies reported a personality-crime association. Do we have to say it? Another negative conclusion.

One of the major findings in Tennenbaum's review, as well as the other two preceding reviews, was that assessments of antisocial personality consistently differentiated between offender and nonoffender samples. The concepts of antisocial personality and psychopathic personality will be developed later in this chapter, but for now the notions of a generalized disregard for conventional rules and procedures and a reckless, callous, egocentric, adventurous, and impulsive pleasure-seeking style captures the content of these measures.

Two widely used measures of antisocial personality are the Socialization (So) scale from the California Personality Inventory (CPI) and the Psychopathic Deviate (Pd) scale, as it was then called, from the Minnesota Multiphasic Personality Inventory (MMPI). These inventories are self-report, paper-and-pencil questionnaires. The scales are well-validated and have been the focus of volumes of research. Scores on So and Pd are known to correlate with familial and biological variables, measures of self-management skills and impulsivity, and measures of deviance that extend well beyond the issue of the legality of conduct. In addition to their known correlations with theoretically relevant constructs, the scale items were deliberately selected according to their documented criterion validity. In brief, during the construction of the Pd and So scales, items were deleted if they failed to distinguish between groups who differed in their levels of conduct problems. This empirical approach to scale construction is intended to ensure that the scale will indeed correlate with criterion variables of interest. In the preceding reviews, the Pd scale significantly distinguished between offender and nonoffender samples about 90 percent of the time, and the So scale had an interstudy hit rate of 86 percent.

How can one possibly conclude that there is no relationship between personality and crime when 42 to 81 percent of studies found a relationship? How can one possibly conclude that antisocial personality is irrelevant to the study of crime when 86 to 90 percent of studies showed it to be important? The answer is in the knowledge destruction techniques used by the reviewers to minimize the value of the evidence. Tennenbaum's (1977) paper serves to illustrate knowledge destruction in action. The process was as follows:

1. Tennenbaum first commented that he found it "disconcerting" that personality tests are no better predictors of criminality now than they were 10 years ago.
    Comment. He has told us that he is concerned, but about what? The interstudy hit rate was 42 percent in 1950, 81 percent in 1967, and 80 percent in his own review of 1977. Does he think an interstudy hit rate of 100 percent is required?
    Knowledge Destruction Technique #1. Plant a vague suspicion or sense of uneasiness in the minds of the readers.

2. Tennenbaum accepted the fact that assessments of antisocial personality have consistently demonstrated concurrent criterion validity. However, this achievement was then described as mere "surface validity." In Chapter 1 we discussed empirical understandings (e.g., functional or causal validity, predictive validity). What in the world is "surface validity"?

    Comment. Again, the reader is being emotionally prepared for an exercise in knowledge destruction. Initially we were alerted to a vague sense of negative concern. Now our uneasy feelings have been reinforced by the term "surface validity."

    Knowledge Destruction Technique #2. Raise suspicion by inventing scientific-sounding words. The term "validity" tends to work well.

3. When we arrive to how Tennenbaum tried to dismiss the evidence on the So and Pd scales, we really see knowledge destruction in full flight. Because the So and Pd were constructed so that they might successfully distinguish between offender and nonoffender samples, their success in actually doing so in one study after another is a hollow achievement. More specifically, Tennenbaum states that the measures of antisocial personality provide "no information not obtainable simply by procuring a list of offenders."

    Comment. What does Tennenbaum mean by this last statement? Is he bored by the finding that the So and Pd scales are related to criminal behavior? What about the huge literature showing that these scales are correlated with other relevant covariates of criminal behavior (e.g., family variables, self-management skills)?

    A few of the items from the Pd and So scales are direct indicators of criminal behavior. For example, the Pd scale has "I have never been in trouble with the law" and the So scale has "A lot of times it's fun to be in jail." Tennenbaum capitalized on this feature of the scales to conclude that there is no value added by the scales to a simple list of names of offenders. However, *most* of the items in the scales are not obvious measures of criminal conduct (e.g., "I am neither gaining or [sic] losing weight," from the Pd scale) and yet these items contribute to the differentiation of offenders and nonoffenders. Moreover, the scales have predicted future recidivism in samples in which everyone had a criminal record.

    Knowledge Destruction Technique #3. Minimize the importance of new knowledge by questioning the value added.

We outlined some of the knowledge destruction techniques used by Tennenbaum, but this does not exhaust the list of techniques that have been used to dismiss personality in the face of evidence. Here are a few more:

1. *Note that researchers and theorists with an interest in individual differences and the personal correlates of crime are not nice people.* Such interests perhaps indicate an "authoritarian personality" (as noted Matza, 1964:15). When really up against the wall, just say that such people are antisociological.

2. *Simply declare that prediction is impossible.* Matza (1964) knew that the risk factors suggested by diverse theories were "almost always" empirically undemonstrable. Taylor, Walton, and Young (1973:58) knew "the enterprise is doomed to failure: inconsistent results abound." Schur (1973:154) actually knew that "so-called delinquents" are not different from nondelinquents "except that they have been processed by the juvenile justice system."

3. *When it is obvious that prediction is possible, declare that it all "really" reflects social class.* Thus, for Taylor et al., (1973) "differential reinforcement histories" (p. 52), "personality" (p. 57), and "parenting" (p. 64) may be class-based value differences. For Gibbons (1986:510), the extraordinarily high rates of violence and crime in the United States were "clear indicators that the causes of crime lie not in biology or faulty socialization but in economic and social inequality, the lack of meaningful jobs . . . and other rents and tears in the social fabric of America."

And Now . . .

Well, the days of ignoring the evidence on personality are now gone. Today's criminology theories have incorporated personality as an important theoretical construct. There is considerable consensus regarding the aspects of personality that are most strongly associated with criminality. Most notably, assessments of antisocial personality pattern consistently differentiate between offender and nonoffender samples and predict criminal behavior. These findings have been replicated across gender, cultures, and race/ethnicity.

Gottfredson and Hirschi's (1990) *A General Theory of Crime* was, perhaps inadvertently, one of the most influential works to turn mainstream criminology to the study of personality. In their work, self-control is the cause of crime. Self-control is viewed as a personality construct by many psychologists and criminologists. However, Hirschi and Gottfredson (1993:49) strongly rejected the position that their notion of self-control is a personality trait, blaming "the logic of psychological positivism" for a misunderstanding of their theory (knowledge destruction again). For them, poor self-control is evident in the behavior itself, and there is no need to hypothesize a predisposition to crime. For example, reckless criminal behavior is an indicator of poor self-control, and poor self-control causes criminal behavior. As Ronald Akers points out in the following statement, Hirschi and Gottfredson's explanation is circular and not helpful at all:

> It would appear to be tautological to explain the propensity to commit crime by low self-control. They are one and the same . . . the assertion means that low self-control causes low self-control. Similarly, since no operational definition is given, we cannot know that a person has low self-control (stable propensity to commit crime) unless he or she commits crime . . . the statement that low self control is a cause of crime, then, is also tautological (Akers, 1991:204).

Putting aside Hirschi and Gottfredson's own views of self-control, their book did reintroduce personality to criminology. Tests of their hypothesis followed and with each new study suggestions for improving the theory were made (Burton, Cullen, Evans, Alarid & Dunaway, 1998; Grasmick, Tittle, Bursik & Arneklev, 1993; Longshore, Turner & Stein, 1996; Ratchford & Beaver, 2009). Twenty years after the publication of Hirschi and Gottfredson's thesis, self-control theory has continued to generate research and debate (Cretacci, 2008; Hirschi & Gottfredson, 2000; Pratt & Cullen, 2000; Rebellon, Straus & Medeiros, 2008).

From another perspective, the work of Terri Moffit and her colleagues, along with other developmental criminologists and psychologists such as Delbert Elliott, David Farrington, Rolph Loeber, Richard Tremblay, and Terence Thornberry, highlighted the importance of temperament, especially in the development of life-course-persistent offenders. A landmark study by Caspi and his colleagues (Caspi et al., 1994), which appeared in the influential journal, *Criminology*, firmly affirmed the study of personality in criminology. Drawing on their own New Zealand data and the Pittsburgh Youth Study, they convincingly showed that the personality characteristics of Negative Emotionality and poor Constraint were related to delinquency across culture, gender, and race. Miller and Lynam (2001) went further to show, through a meta-analytic review, how the five-factor model (Agreeableness and Conscientiousness) was related to antisocial behavior. The study of personality and crime was no longer limited to psychological and psychiatric journals.

One of the spin-offs from criminology's newfound interest in personality was a rediscovery of the importance of general psychology. Suddenly, we began to see articles in criminological journals that could have just as easily been published in psychological journals (we do recognize the heroic efforts of a few—e.g., Ronald Akers, Paul Gendreau—to make a dent in the criminological literature). For example, Peter Wood and his colleagues (Wood et al., 1997) wrote about how crime can be maintained by the act itself through nonmediated reinforcement (i.e., doing crime for the thrill of it). Personality has also found its way into mainstream criminological theories. We have already seen it in Hirschi and Gottfredson's extension of control theory via low self-control. We also see personality in strain theory (Agnew, 2006; Broidy, 2001) and anomie theory (Baumer, 2007; Konty, 2005). It appears that the personality is no longer shunned by mainstream criminology.

Antisocial Personality as Pathology

At the beginning of this chapter we noted that there are different meanings that can be assigned to the term "antisocial personality." The first meaning is simply the extremes of normal dimensions of personality that are common to all. The second meaning is rooted in psychopathology. A psychopathological perspective considers antisocial personality as a mental disorder, sees it as unhealthy and abnormal, as a disease. In medicine it is relatively easy to identify what is unhealthy and abnormal, but it is not so easy when it comes to psychological processes. How much hand washing is needed to cross the line between cleanliness and compulsiveness? How much lying and dishonesty is needed to call someone a psychopath? Much of psychiatry and clinical psychology deals with individuals who are seen as "crossing the line" into behavioral and thinking patterns that are considered abnormal, that is, considered to be a mental illness. Some of these mental illnesses show well-defined patterns that allow for reliable diagnosis and classification (e.g., schizophrenia, manic-depression). Other "mental illnesses" are not so clearly defined. Antisocial personality is one of them, and we will begin by describing two psychopathological perspectives of antisocial personality.

Psychiatry and Antisocial Personality Disorder

Psychiatry is the branch of medicine that studies mental disorders. In general, psychiatry views most psychological problems as having a biomedical basis, and practitioners will often prescribe medications, in addition to counseling, to treat individuals. Clinical psychologists, in most states, do not have prescription privileges. They specialize in psychological assessment and counseling services. What many in both professions have in common is a belief that psychological abnormalities can be classified into distinct groupings with their own etiologies, developmental course, treatment, and prognosis. Physical illnesses are diagnosed or categorized (e.g., a common cold) with a cause (e.g., viral infection), a natural course for the illness (e.g., develop a sore throat and runny nose), a treatment (e.g., drink your mother's chicken soup), and a prognosis (e.g., don't worry, you will be just fine in about 10 days). Mental illnesses can also be classified into diagnostic categories with an etiology, course of development, and so on.

One of the most influential taxonomies or classification systems for mental disorder is the *Diagnostic and Statistical Manual of Mental Disorders* or DSM-IV (American Psychiatric Association, 1994). DSM-IV describes behavioral patterns and psychological characteristics that are clustered into diagnostic categories. For example, someone with auditory hallucinations, bizarre delusions (e.g., a pet dog controlling the behavior of the person), and a history of these delusions and hallucinations lasting more than six months is likely to be diagnosed as schizophrenic. One general area covered by DSM-IV comprises personality disorders. The personality disorders include, for example, obsessive-compulsive personality, paranoid personality, narcissistic personality, and, of course, antisocial personality disorder (APD). Most of the personality disorders have an early onset, and APD is differentiated from the other personality disorders by a "pervasive pattern of disregard, and violation of, the rights of others" (p. 645). In children, the corresponding mental disorder is called *conduct disorder*. A summary of the diagnostic criteria for APD and conduct disorder is given in Table 6.1.

In the United States, APD is estimated to affect approximately 3.5 percent of all adults (Grant et al., 2004). Although APD has been associated with aggressive behavior (Crocker et al., 2005), the disorder is relatively common among nonagressive individuals who have broken no laws (e.g., alcoholics, compulsive gamblers). The disorder is seen as difficult to treat, and considerable research has focused on identifying the childhood predictors of APD in the hope that early intervention may be more successful (Lahey et al., 2005; Simonoff et al., 2004).

There are two points that we would like to make about APD before moving on to a discussion of psychopathy. First, the assessment of APD is usually conducted by an unstructured clinical interview. We will say more about unstructured clinical assessment in Chapter 10, but for now our point is that the diagnosis of APD in the real-world clinical practice tends to be quite unreliable. Researchers studying APD may use structured assessment tools, but they are not used often enough in daily clinical-forensic practice (Widiger & Samuel, 2005). Second, the criteria for APD in DSM-IV stress behavioral characteristics. As we will see shortly, the public and some researchers also view certain emotional characteristics as unique to some offenders. Think of the "cold-blooded killer." The DSM-IV criteria capture the aggressiveness and unremorsefulness but none of the emotional coldness of this individual.

Table 6.1
Psychiatric Disorders of Relevance to Antisocial Behavior

DSM-IV Criteria for Antisocial Personality Disorder

I.   Disregard for the rights of others. At least three of the following:
    a) behaves in a way that is grounds for arrest
    b) deceitful and manipulative
    c) impulsive
    d) aggressive
    e) irresponsible
    f) lack of remorse

II. Age 18 or more

III. A history of childhood conduct disorder

IV. Antisocial behavior not a product of a schizophrenic/manic episode.

DSM-IV Criteria for Conduct Disorder

I.   Disregard for the rights of others or violation of age-appropriate social norms. At least three of the following:
    a) bullies, threatens, or intimidates others
    b) initiates physical fights
    c) has used a weapon
    d) physically cruel to people
    e) physically cruel to animals
    f) has stolen while confronting a victim
    g) forced someone into sexual activity
    h) fire setting
    i) destroyed property
    j) broken into a house, building or car
    k) lies to obtain goods or favors
    l) steals
    m) stays out at night despite parental prohibitions beginning before age 13
    n) ran away from home at least twice
    o) truancy beginning before age 13

II. Childhood Onset Type: One criterion evident prior to age 10

III. Adolescent Onset Type: Absence of criteria prior to age 10

We now turn to a personality construct that: (a) is assessed in a highly structured manner, (b) captures not only behavioral but also personality characteristics, and (c) is strongly linked to criminal conduct. We are speaking of the psychopath.

Psychopathy

The term *psychopathy* is widely used by both professionals and the general public; it is firmly entrenched within our culture (see Resource Note 6.1 for a clinical illustration). The public's image of the psychopath is the smooth charmer who is also capable of violent and sadistic behavior. Variations of the concept have been within the professional domain for more than a century, from Pinel's "mania without frenzy" to Prichard's 1835 description of "moral insanity" (Pichot, 1978) to Freud's under-developed superego. However, it was Hervey Cleckley (1941, 1982) who presented the contemporary clinical description of the psychopath.

Resource Note 6.1

A Case Study of a Psychopath

Everybody called him "Red." He was 30 years old, tall and good looking, with red hair and a neatly trimmed red beard. Red came from a middle-class background. His father was a government civil servant, and his mother was a journalist for the city newspaper. When Red was four years old, his parents divorced and he went to live with his father until he was six years old. From age six on, he was sent to boarding school.

Boarding school was difficult for Red. He hated the school ("It was like the army"), the work, and the teachers. He ran away many times and, finally, at age 17, it was for good. Red ran to Florida, where he found his older sister. He told her that things were going so well in school and he was so advanced that the teachers said he could take a holiday and visit his sister. At his sister's house Red began to drink by sneaking liquor from the cabinet and replacing it with colored water. Three weeks later a telegram came to his sister. As she was not home, he opened the telegram and learned that their father died suddenly in a car accident.

Red returned to his home in New York state to claim his inheritance. He told authorities that his sister had committed suicide six months ago; he showed forged documents to support his claim. Red inherited everything. He lived in his father's house and began to party. Red's friends drank and took other drugs. Most had been in juvenile detention homes at some time in their lives or in jail. Red enjoyed his life: no school, no work, and lots of excitement.

The party ended quickly. One night he was drunk and assaulted his "best friend" with a baseball bat. Although the friend suffered a broken wrist, he refused to press charges. The police came, but there were no formal charges. For the next five years Red had numerous skirmishes with the law, was married one time, and became addicted to drugs.

At age 21 all the inheritance was spent. Red began moving from city to city. In each city he met a woman who worked at a low-paying job, and he moved in with her. Each woman learned after a few months that he brought trouble along with him. He continued to drink, injected cocaine, and committed "break and enters" and thefts to support his drug habit. Jail sentences rarely exceeded 60 days.

Then, at age 30, Red violently assaulted the woman with whom he was living. This time the judge gave him two years. The day after he was brought into custody, Red began phoning his common-law wife, pleading forgiveness. At first she would hang up, but this did not discourage Red. Within two weeks she was accepting his calls. Within the month, she was visiting him in jail; she continued to do so until his release. While Red was receiving visits from his common-law wife and accepting the money she brought, he was also busy with other plans. He was not only lining himself up with women introduced by his fellow inmates, but he was also phoning the "companions" advertisements in the newspaper.

At the time of his release, Red had offers from three women for a place to live. Tests completed in prison showed the following results:

Level of Service Inventory – Revised (LSI-R):	48 (maximum possible 54)
Psychopathy Checklist – Revised (PCL-R):	36 (maximum 40)
Gough's Socialization Scale:	8 (maximum 25) (low score indicates a disregard for rules)
Attitude toward the Law, Courts, Police:	14 percentile
Identification with Criminal Others:	92 percentile
IPAT Anxiety Scale:	4 (maximum is 10)
Bennett's Self-Esteem:	81 percentile

Resource Note 6.1 *(continued)*

The test results from the PCL-R indicate that Red meets the diagnosis of psychopathy (a score of 30 or more is needed), a diagnosis confirmed by Gough's Socialization Scale. Red is also at a high risk to reoffend, as measured by the LSI-R. Finally, we can say that Red is relatively free from debilitating anxiety (IPAT—Interpersonal Anxiety Test—results) and feels pretty good about himself as a criminal (a high score on Bennett's Self-Esteem measure and on the Identification with Criminal Others scale).

Drawing upon his many years of experience as a psychiatrist, Cleckley noted characteristic patterns shown by some of his patients. Our summary description of Cleckley's psychopath in Table 6.2 is intended to make three important points. First, psychopaths have all the outward appearances of normality. They do not hallucinate or have delusions, and they do not appear particularly encumbered by debilitating anxiety or guilt (Cleckley titled his book *The Mask of Sanity*). Second, psychopaths appear unresponsive to social control. For example, they continue to get into trouble despite punishment from society and those around them. Third, criminal behavior was not a necessary requirement for the diagnosis of psychopathy. In fact, Cleckley presented many examples of patients with no (known) criminal record.

Table 6.2
Cleckley's Checklist for Psychopathy

Key features
Manipulative
Superficial charm
Above-average intelligence
Absence of psychotic symptoms (delusions, hallucinations)
Absence of anxiety
Lack of remorse
Failure to learn from experience
Egocentric
Lacks emotional depth

Other characteristics
Trivial sex life
Unreliable
Failure to follow a life plan
Untruthful
Suicide attempts rarely genuine
Impulsive
Antisocial behavior

This last point is particularly important. If we accept the assumption that a psychopath is not necessarily a criminal, then a number of important corollaries follow:

1. Not all criminals are psychopathic.

2. An explanation of crime may not serve as an explanation of psychopathy, and vice-versa.

3. Following from Corollary 2, assessment and treatment methods for psychopaths and criminals should be substantially different.

The Assessment of Psychopathy: Hare's Psychopathy Checklist (PCL-R)

Robert Hare has taken the diagnostic criteria proposed by Cleckley and developed it into an objective assessment instrument based upon structured interviews and file reviews. Hare (1980) reduced more than 100 behaviors and characteristics listed by clinicians and researchers to 22 items, and then to 20 items (Hare, 1991), thought to represent the key indicators of psychopathy, with one important exception—he added three criminal behavior indicators. The result was the Psychopathy Checklist–Revised or PCL-R (Table 6.3), first published in 1990 and revised in 2003. Each item is scored on a three-point scale: "0" (zero) for not applicable, "1" for uncertain, and "2" for definitely present. The higher the score, the more likely the individual is a psychopath.

Table 6.3
The Psychopathy Checklist–Revised (PCL-R)

Glibness/superficial charm
Grandiose sense of self-worth
Need for stimulation/prone to boredom
Pathological lying
Conning/manipulative
Lack of remorse or guilt
Shallow affect
Callous/lack of empathy
Parasitic life style
Poor behavioral controls
Promiscuous sexual relations
Early behavior problems
Lack of realistic, long-term goals
Impulsivity
Irresponsibility
Failure to accept responsibility for own actions
Many short-term marital relationships
Juvenile delinquency
Revocation of conditional release
Criminal versatility

What is the difference between APD as defined in DSM-IV and psychopathy as measured by the PCL-R? When DSM-IV was being developed, the working group charged with overseeing the field trials for antisocial personality attempted to integrate the affective and interpersonal aspects of psychopathy (e.g., empathy, arrogant self-appraisal) into the diagnostic category (Hare, 1996). However, results from the field trials were mixed, and these characteristics did not find themselves into DSM-IV (Widiger et al., 1996). As a result, the essential difference between DSM-IV's APD and the PCL-R's psychopathy is on the emotional-interpersonal dimension (Hare, 1998).

This difference has a number of implications. First, DSM-IV's APD is not the same as psychopathy; two separate sets of criteria are used in making the diagnosis. Clinicians and researchers, however, often tend to use the two terms interchangeably. Second, the DSM-IV diagnosis, relying on behavioral antisocial history, may measure persistent criminality more than a personality characteristic. This limits the usefulness of the APD diagnosis in forensic and correctional settings. For example, in a survey of 12 countries and nearly 23,000 prisoners, 47 percent of male prisoners were diagnosed with APD (Fazel & Danesh, 2002; 21% of females were diagnosed with APD). In some correctional agencies, the rates are higher, falling in the 50 to 80 percent range (Ogloff, 2006). It is not surprising to find such a high base rate given the diagnostic criteria of age 18 and failure to conform to social norms with respect to lawful behavior. However, such high base rates are not very helpful in making decisions around treatment, security, and release. The problems with DSM-IV's APD (underinclusiveness and utility) have led many forensic and correctional researchers and clinicians to rely on the PCL-R for assessments of antisocial personality.

In earlier research, Hare and his colleagues (Hare et al., 1990; Harpur, Hakstian & Hare, 1988) reported that the PCL-R consisted of two factors. Factor 1, called Interpersonal/Affective, tapped the personality items (e.g., glibness, callous, conning/manipulative). Factor 2, called Social Deviance, consisted of behavioral indicators (e.g., need for stimulation, impulsivity, irresponsibility). More recently, Hare has adopted a four-factor model of the PCL-R (Hare, 2003; Hare & Neumann, 2006). Basically, the original two factors have been subdivided to yield Factor 1 (Interpersonal; e.g., glibness, pathological lying), Factor 2 (Affective; e.g., lack of remorse, callous), Factor 3 (Lifestyle; e.g., need for stimulation, impulsivity), and Factor 4 (Antisocial; e.g., juvenile delinquency, criminal versatility). We will return to this more recent development in the PCL-R at the end of this chapter, but for now note how psychopathy is being conceptualized into more discrete domains that could possibly serve as treatment targets (e.g., treatment to improve empathy, learn self-control).

An important question is whether psychopaths are qualitatively different from other criminals. In other words, is psychopathy a discrete personality construct, a taxon? Taxonomy is a branch of biology that is concerned with classifying diverse forms of life into separate categories; a taxon is a label for a specific category. A classification category (i.e., taxon) can be broad, for example, mammals are different from fish, or more specific (e.g., ducks are different from chickens, and mallards are different from wood ducks). The point is that a taxon defines a binomial category of yes (fits the category) or no (does not fit). It cannot be a bit of both.

Cleckley, followed by Hare and others (Harris, Rice & Quinsey, 1994; Skilling, Harris, Rice & Quinsey, 2002; Skilling, Quinsey & Craig, 2001), took the position that psychopathy is a distinct personality construct with a constellation of affective, cognitive, interpersonal, and behavioral characteristics not shared by other disorders. By using taxonomic analyses (statistical procedures intended to identify discrete entities) on PCL-R data from 653 mentally disordered offenders, Harris, Rice, and Quinsey (1994) found some evidence for the existence of a discrete personality construct that could be called psychopathy. However, the evidence for a taxon was mainly in favor of Factor 2 (impulsive antisociality) and not Factor 1 (the personality constellation of callousness, lack of remorse, etc.), which appeared more dimensional. Furthermore, most studies have found no support for a taxon among male offenders (Edens, Marcus, Lilienfeld & Poythress, 2006; Guay, Ruscio, Knight & Hare, 2007; Marcus et al., 2004) and female offenders (Guay, Ruscio, Knight & Hare, 2006).

An alternative to the taxon approach is the dimensional perspective. With this perspective, psychopathy is seen as a matter of degree and, therefore, all criminals are psychopaths to some extent—some more so than others. In his early writings, Hare clearly argued for psychopathy as a taxon (after all, his popular 1993 book, *Without Conscience*, was not titled "Without Some Conscience"). Since then he has tempered his position, talking of the "underlying dimensionality" of psychopathy (Hare & Neumann, 2006:73). The PCL-R has always presented a bit of a confusing picture regarding the question of psychopathy as a taxon. Scores on the PCL-R can fall between 0 and 40. At what point does one become a psychopath? Hare (1990; 2003) recommends a cut-off score of 30, but in practice, researchers have used scores varying from 25 (Harris, Rice & Cormier, 1989) to 32 (Serin, Peters & Barbaree, 1990). In terms of practice and recent research findings (Guay et al., 2007), the PCL-R appears to follow a dimensional model of psychopathy, and this may reflect a general trend to move away from considering personality disorders as diagnostic categories to dimensional classifications (Widiger & Trull, 2007).

PCL-R and the Prediction of Criminal Behavior. The PCL-R does a very good job of predicting both general recidivism and violent recidivism. A number of meta-analytic reviews on the topic have found almost identical average correlations between PCL-R scores and future general recidivism ($r = .27$, Salekin, Rogers & Sewell, 1996; $r = .28$, Gendreau, Little & Goggin, 1996). Using a broad definition of recidivism that included new charges and "institutional maladjustment," Leistico, Salekin, DeCoster, and Rogers (2008) found $r = .27$. Two meta-analysis of the PCL-R with violent recidivism reported an identical r of .27 (Campbell, French & Gendreau, 2009; Hemphill, Hare & Wong, 1998), whereas Salekin, Roger, and Sewell (1996) found an r of .32. Noteworthy about the Hemphill, Hare, and Wong (1998) meta-analysis was that the researchers then compared the PCL-R with other actuarial scales (e.g., SFS, SIR, and LSI-R). They found that the PCL-R correlated with general and violent recidivism as well as (and sometimes better than) the other scales and concluded that "the PCL-R should be considered a primary instrument for guiding clinical appraisals of criminal recidivism and dangerousness" (p. 160) and that it was the "*unparalleled*" (italics added) measure of risk.

However, further examination of the literature suggests that the PCL-R is not necessarily "unparalleled" when it comes to risk assessment. First, there is some evidence that the PCL-R may be improved upon by including additional risk factors. This is the approach adopted by Grant Harris and his colleagues at the Mental Health Centre in Penetanguishene, Ontario (Harris, Rice & Quinsey, 1993; Rice & Harris, 1997) in their development of the Violence Risk Appraisal Guide (VRAG). In addition to the PCL-R ($r = .34$), a number of other factors predicted violent recidivism. Examples were elementary school maladjustment, alcohol abuse, and separation from parents prior to the age of 16. Eleven additional predictors to the PCL-R were identified that, when combined to construct the VRAG, improved prediction beyond knowledge of only the PCL-R ($r = .44$).

More recently, the researchers at Penetanguishene have found that the PCL-R was not even necessary and could be replaced by a simple eight-item scale assessing childhood and adolescent problems (e.g., teenage alcohol problem, conduct disorder symptoms). This scale, called the Child and Adolescent Taxon Scale (CATS), removes the need for psychological/psychiatric professionals to make a diagnosis of psychopathy based on the PCL-R (Quinsey, Harris, Rice & Cormier, 2006). Using CATS as a replacement for the PCL-R has not affected the predictive validity of the VRAG (Quinsey, Book & Skilling, 2004; Quinsey, Harris, Rice & Cormier, 1998), nor of the SORAG, which is a VRAG-type scale for sex offenders (Bartosh, Garby, Lewis & Gray, 2003), and it has been demonstrated to predict general and violent recidivism among female offenders (Folsom & Atkinson, 2007).

Second, comparisons of the PCL-R do not always show the PCL-R to be a better predictor than other risk assessment instruments. In the Hemphill et al. (1998) meta-analysis, there was only one comparison of the LSI-R with the PCL-R, and this was a study of mentally disordered offenders in which a modified LSI-R was scored from files (the LSI-R is a general offender risk instrument to be described in more detail in Chapter 10). Meta-analytic reviews that included comparisons of the PCL-R with the LSI-R found comparable effect size estimates in predicting violent recidivism (Campbell et al., 2009; Gendreau, Goggin & Smith, 2002) and in the meta-analysis by Gendreau et al. (2002), the LSI-R actually performed better than the PCL-R when the outcome was general recidivism ($r = .39$ vs. $r = .25$). Walters (2003) compared the results from seven studies of the PCL-R and the Lifestyle Criminality Screening Form (LCSF), a 17-item risk instrument that can be scored simply from information available in files. Walters found nonsignificant differences in their average predictive validities (.26 for the PCL-R and .31 for the LCSF).

Third, we can ask ourselves what aspects of the PCL-R really do all the work in predicting criminal behavior? Earlier, we noted that the PCL-R consists of a number of factors. Recall that two of the factors deal with personality and the other two with antisocial lifestyle (e.g., early behavior problems, impulsiveness, thrill-seeking). Two meta-analyses have examined the relative contribution of the factors (Hemphill et al., 1998; Leistico et al. 2008). Both reviews found Factor 2 (antisocial lifestyle) a better predictor of general recidivism than Factor 1 (personality). These findings suggest that the personality features of psychopathy, as measured by the PCL-R, may have little to do with general criminality, although there is a possibility that the personality traits may be relevant to the prediction of violent recidivism.

The predictive validity of the PCL-R is impressive, and its core findings have been replicated across settings (prisons, psychiatric hospitals), gender, and race (Douglas, Vincent & Edens, 2006). Although the PCL-R predicts recidivism among different samples, it appears to predict significantly better with certain groups. Leistico and her colleagues (2008) found that the PCL-R had higher predictive validities among Caucasians, females, and psychiatric patients than with minority ethnic groups, males, and inmates. The PCL-R still predicted recidivism for the later groups but not as well as the former groups and therefore, caution was advised when applying the PCL-R for ethnic minorities, males, and prisoners.

However, we do have one important caution to give, and that is in regard to the use of the PCL-R and the very idea of psychopathy. In medico-legal-forensic settings, psychopathy is often equated with dangerousness and may provide grounds to subject psychopathic offenders to severe measures (Edens & Petrilla, 2006; Zinger & Forth, 1998). The popular media certainly paints such a picture, and it is hardly disputed by the clinical professionals. However, there is evidence that not all psychopaths are violent, nor are all violent offenders psychopaths. In fact, criminal behavior, some argue (Skeem & Cooke, in press), may not even be required for the construct of psychopathy (we will say more on this topic in the next section). Recall that Hare added a few criminal history items, which was a departure from Cleckley's original formulation. Based on the meta-analytic reviews, the average effect size between PCL-R scores and violent recidivism is not one, it is in the order of .30. Furthermore, Serin (1996) and Harris and colleagues (1991) found significant proportions of violent offenders who scored below 30 on the PCL-R. In a study of offenders declared by Canadian courts as "dangerous offenders," only 39.6 percent were assessed as psychopaths by the PCL-R (Bonta, Harris, Zinger & Carriere, 1996).

Are There Noncriminal Psychopaths?

Are there individuals with the personality characteristics of psychopathy whose behavior does *not* bring them into conflict with the law? Cleckley certainly thought so. Cathy Widom (1977) reasoned that it is possible that perhaps criminal psychopaths, the ones on which all the research is based, represent only the unsuccessful psychopaths (the ones that get caught). Perhaps, there are "successful" psychopaths who, though engaging in questionable behavior, elude the criminal justice system. The problem is: how do you identify these successful psychopaths?

Widom developed a procedure of recruiting psychopaths from the general population by placing advertisements in the newspaper searching for people who were "adventurous," "exciting," "impulsive," and "willing to do anything for a dare." In her first study (Widom, 1977), the majority reported no history of incarceration, but 32.1 percent of the sample (*n* = 28) had a history of incarceration as an adult. In the second study (Widom & Newman, 1985), although only 5.1 percent (*n* = 40) reported a history of incarceration, they had an arrest rate of 41 percent (the arrest rate for the first study was not reported). We can only suspect based on the incarceration rate that the arrest rate for the first study must have been as high and probably much higher.

Widom's research did not have the benefit of the PCL-R to make reliable assessments of psychopathy; more recent studies have used the PCL-R or variations of the PCL-R. Using Widom's method for recruiting subjects from the community, Belmore and Quinsey (1994) scored subjects on a 16-item scale, eight items of which were taken from the PCL-R. Their 15 highest-scoring subjects all had arrest histories. Similarly, DeMatteo, Heilbrun, and Marczyk (2005, 2006) found 41 percent of their sample of 54 males reported no history of arrest. However, not one of them scored above 30 on the PCL-R, the cut-off for a diagnosis of psychopathy (the highest score was 27). Furthermore, they reported that this group had a surprisingly high prevalence of violent behavior for which they were never arrested. Finally, in a survey of 638 individuals from households in the United Kingdom using the screening version of the PCL-R, less than 1 percent met the diagnostic criteria for psychopathy (Coid, Yang, Ullrich, Roberts & Hare, 2009). Although the rates of criminal convictions and incarcerations were not reported, scores on the instrument were strongly related to criminal behavior.

The issue of noncriminal psychopaths draws attention to Cleckley's original formulation of the psychopath. If the reader takes a moment and compares the features of psychopathy as described by Cleckley (Table 6.2) and Hare (Table 6.3) you will note that the major difference is the absence of criminal behavior in Cleckley's formulation. The PCL-R has three criminal history items and without them it would be extremely difficult to reach the cut-off score of 30 for a diagnosis of psychopathy (you would need to score "definitely present" for 15 of the 17 noncriminal items). Recently, Jennifer Skeem and David Cooke (in press) have argued for a return to Cleckley's description of the psychopath. In Cleckley's view, it was emotional detachment and fearlessness that were the main features and not criminal behavior. Furthermore, Skeem and Cooke (in press) warn of the reification of the PCL-R by equating a high score on the PCL-R to the construct of psychopathy. Hare and Neumann (2005), however, see criminal behavior as central to the construct.

Finally, we would like to comment on the idea of "successful" psychopaths. Almost everyone that we talk to has no trouble giving a name of a political or business leader, or even someone who they personally know, who they are convinced is a psychopath. These "psychopaths" are cunning, manipulative, and ruthless in their relationships with people—interested only in pursuing what is best for themselves. And, they are seen as "successful" in professional life although they may mess up in their personal life as a result of climbing to the top (Hall & Benning, 2006). One needs only to read Babiak and Hare's (2006) book, *Snakes in Suits: When Psychopaths Go to Work*, to get a flavor of who we are talking about.

Other than anecdotes of Enron officials and political leaders gone bad, what is the empirical evidence for a successful psychopath? Simone Ullrich and her colleagues (Ullrich, Farrington & Coid, 2008) scored 304 men from the Cambridge longitudinal study who were interviewed at age 48 on the 12-item screening version of the PCL-R. They also rated these men on 12 variables ranging from income to satisfaction with employment. Contrary to expectations, scores on the PCL-R (screening version) showed no association with indicators of life success (e.g., social status, wealth).

When we describe the successful psychopath, we are describing more of the personality features of psychopathy (the Affective and Interpersonal factors as described by Hare) and less of the deviant behavioral factors

(Lifestyle and Antisocial). That is, the noncriminal psychopath may be a different type of psychopath that has its own distinct etiology (Hall & Benning, 2006). Although we have described Hare's model of psychopathy because it is by far the most researched perspective, there are other views of psychopathy. These differing models describe different types of psychopaths (Blackburn, 2006). For example, Eysenck (1964) and Blackburn (1975) have long argued for a distinction between "primary" psychopaths (the classical version) and "secondary" psychopaths (those who feel some guilt but are able to "turn off" the guilt; Porter, 1996). Hicks and his colleagues (Hicks et al., 2004) describe "emotionally stable psychopaths" and "aggressive psychopaths." Thus, there is no 100 percent agreement as to what really constitutes psychopathy, thereby allowing for conceptualizations of noncriminal psychopaths.

The Treatment of Psychopaths

Clinicians, in general, have viewed psychopaths as incurable (Phillips & Gunderson, 1999; Reid & Gacono, 2000). Certainly, this has been Cleckley's view. Their intractability has been attributed to a biological deficit and/or early childhood experiences so severe that they are beyond hope. The notion that some psychopaths do not feel guilt and remorse hits at the core of treatability. Those with a capacity for emotionality and a "conscience" are more amenable to treatment (Blackburn, 1993; Eysenck, 1998). Treatment methods supposedly tailored for psychopaths, such as therapeutic communities (Blackburn, 1993; Hobson, Shine & Roberts, 2000), have shown that psychopaths are not very motivated for treatment (Ogloff, Wong & Greenwood, 1990). Unstructured treatment methods have actually shown increases in recidivism for psychopaths (Harris, Rice & Cormier, 1994). Despite the absence of evidence for unstructured, psychodynamic treatment, efforts continue to confront "psychopathic transference" and "paranoid regressions" (Kernberg, 1998) because it has "the ring of truth" (Cox, 1998).

Clinical anecdotes and a few published studies may fuel the belief that psychopaths are untreatable, but in our view, things may not be as dark as they seem. A number of reviews of the treatment literature have all come to the same conclusion: there is insufficient evidence to say whether treatment does or does not make a difference (D'Silva, Duggan & McCarthy, 2004; Harris & Rice, 2006; Lösel, 1995; Wong, 2000). Part of the problem is that almost all the treatment programs have been poorly conceived interventions and milieu therapies that permit psychopaths to fool staff into believing they are making progress (Hare et al., 2000; Hobson, Shine & Roberts, 2000). From what we know about effective correctional treatment, why would we expect such programs to be effective?

We have already seen some of the evidence that treatment with general offenders can be effective if certain principles are applied. That is, treatment will be more effective if: (a) intensive services are delivered to higher-risk offenders (risk principle), (b) treatment targets criminogenic needs (need principle), and (c) cognitive-behavioral interventions are used (responsivity principle). These principles have not been applied to psychopaths. There is hope on the horizon. Stephen Wong and Robert Hare (2005) have recently developed a treatment program for psychopaths that is heavily influenced by the principles for effective treatment outlined in Chapter 2. Until this program and others that adhere to the principles are evaluated, it is too early to accept the view that "psychopaths" are untreatable.

Can Children Be Psychopaths?

Psychopathy is usually seen as a stable personality pattern that changes little from year to year. Although the criminal activity of psychopaths decreases around the age of 40, it is unclear whether the reduction is due to avoiding apprehension or a real change in behavior. The stability of the psychopathic construct also suggests that the personality and behavioral traits must have started early in life. In Chapter 5, we saw that the origins of an antisocial personality pattern characterized by impulsiveness, sensation-seeking, restlessness, and a callous unemotionality could easily be identified in early childhood. Some researchers have taken a special interest in exploring the possibility of extending the notion of psychopathy to children or at least identifying the childhood precursors of adult psychopathy.

Adelle Forth and her colleagues (Forth, Hart & Hare, 1990; Forth, Kosson & Hare, 2003) modified the PCL-R for use with adolescent offenders (age 13 and up). The modifications involved deleting some items (e.g., "many short-term marital relationships") and altering the scoring criteria for some of the other items (e.g., "criminal versatility). Most of the research has demonstrated that the PCL:YV (Psychopathy Checklist: Youth Version) has good reliability, appears to measure what it is supposed to measure (i.e., construct validity), and produces scores that are correlated with past criminal behavior (Campbell, Porter & Santor, 2004; Salekin, 2006) and institutional misconduct (Edens & Campbell, 2007). With respect to the predictive validity of the PCL:YV, the evidence is mixed with some reporting positive results (Corrado et al., 2004; Gretton, Hare & Catchpole, 2004; Gretton et al., 2001; Vincent et al., 2003) and others finding little relationship with future recidivism (Douglas, Epstein & Poythress, 2008; Edens & Cahill, 2007). However, it performed no better than the youth version of the LSI-R, a general risk/need assessment instrument (Edens, Campbell & Weir, 2006).

Researchers such as Paul Frick (Frick, Barry & Bodin, 2000; Frick et al., 1994) have gone one step further and modified the PCL-R for use with children between the ages of six and 13 years. In the Antisocial Process Screening Device (APSD; Frick & Hare, 2001), the items are scored based on information provided by parents and teachers. Similarly, Donald Lynam (1997) began with the PCL-R as the model and then selected items from two other child maladaptive behavior tests to "translate" the PCL-R constructs into a 41-item Childhood Psychopathy Scale for use with children and adolescents (ages six to 17 years). The research with these scales has been limited to reliability and normative data, with some evaluations of their construct validity. Research on the factor structure of the children scales (including the PCL:YV) has generally found two factors: "callous-unemotional" and "conduct disorder" (Salekin et al., 2006, however, have reported a three- and four-factor model). Conduct disorder by itself is seen as a prognostic indicator of antisocial personality disorder, but when callous-unemotional traits are also present then it may be a sign of psychopathy and life-course-persistent offending (Dadds et al., 2005; Lynam, Loeber & Stouthamer-Loeber, 2008; Vincent et al., 2003).

Regardless of what the research will uncover in the coming years, we share the concerns of others about the utility of applying the construct of psychopathy to children and adolescents (Edens et al., 2001; Hoge, 2002). Basically, does it make sense to extend a personality construct that has always been limited to adults to children? Recall that the diagnostic criteria for antisocial personality disorder require a minimum age of 18.

John Edens and his colleagues (Edens et al., 2001; Edens & Vincent, 2008) provide a thoughtful analysis and critique of the assessment of "juvenile psychopathy." First, as we have already noted, the research on youth versions of the PCL-R and the other assessment instruments has included very little predictive validity data. Second, at times, the research has had serious methodological weaknesses. For example, the Frick et al. (1994) study was based on a small sample of 92 children, and Lynam (1997) was able to translate only 13 of the 20 PCL-R items for use with children. The most difficult problem, however, is that some of the items in the various youth versions may be normative or related to their development. What adult has not chuckled at the adolescent's "grandiose sense of self-worth" or "failure to accept responsibility"? Are impulsiveness, the need for stimulation, and lack of realistic, long-term goals reflective of normal adolescence? Edens suspects that modifications of the PCL-R may overestimate psychopathic features in adolescence. He and his colleagues conclude that "reliance on psychopathy measures to make decisions regarding long-term placements for juveniles is contraindicated at this time" (Edens et al., 2001:53).

A General Personality and Social Psychological Perspective: The Antisocial Personality Pattern

The DSM-IV, the PCL-R, and other clinical classification systems operate on the assumption that certain behavioral patterns "hang together" to create categories that can be reliably differentiated from other classifications and have their own etiologies and course of development. For example, someone who is diagnosed as schizophrenic has characteristics unlike a manic-depressive, with a different etiology and prognosis. The same can be said for antisocial personality disorder (APD) and psychopathy. One of the problems with APD and psychopathy is that there is no consensus as to their etiology and prognosis (Widiger, 2006).

Before outlining our position, we would like to reaffirm our admiration for the work of Robert Hare and his colleagues. The research surrounding the PCL-R has brought an empirical, actuarial perspective to the assessment of mental disorder and has saved forensic psychology from its dependence on professional judgment for decisionmaking. We also see the assessment of antisocial personality as critical for good offender assessment. After all, antisocial personality or our preferred antisocial personality pattern is one of the "Big Four" risk/need factors. However, we are not convinced by Hare's (1998:197) statement that "the personality and social-psychological factors that explain antisocial behavior in general . . . may not be applicable to psychopaths." We think that PCC has much to say about antisocial personality and psychopathy.

PCC's definition of antisocial personality pattern encompasses behavioral and personality characteristics that are relevant to the assessment and treatment of criminal behavior. We underscore the word "pattern" because it includes both the personality facets summarized in Chapter 2 (i.e., impulsiveness, sensation-seeking, fearlessness, egocentrism, hostile emotions, and attitudes) and a pattern of law-violating and problematic behaviors, often evidenced early in life. Note that there is no need to hypothesize the constructs of APD or psychopathy. We think that this more comprehensive definition adds significantly to our understanding of high-risk, high-need offenders. Furthermore, assessing antisocial personality pattern can be conducted by any reasonably trained correctional staff without the need for specialized credentials and training as with the PCL-R and DSM-IV.

Self-Control: A Facet of Antisocial Personality

Gottfredson and Hirschi (1990) argued that low self-control is sufficient to explain criminal conduct. Obviously, our General Personality and Cognitive Social Learning Perspective argues for many more variables to explain the frequency, severity, and variety of criminal acts we observe. The major factors are criminal history and antisocial attitudes and peers. We also have the moderate correlates of family/marital, school/work, leisure/recreation, and substance abuse (Chapters 8 and 9). Within the domain of antisocial personality, self-control is but one facet along with egocentrism and sensation-seeking, and we can even include poor social–emotional cognitive skills. Mindful of the preceding comment, a few words on the psychology of self-control are in order.

Self-control is a process through which an individual directs his or her behavior in the service of achieving a long-term goal. This process typically requires delaying immediate gratification. When we consider criminal behavior, it is often a choice between vice and the more long-term benefits of adherence to the social norms. Poor self-control is viewed by some as an overreliance on the present at the expense of long-term consequences. Criminal offenders, in this light, are too much focused on the concrete here-and-now and have difficulty with the more abstract future. Another model of self-control that has been growing in acceptance is the strength model of self-control first proposed by Baumeister and his colleagues (Baumeister, Heatherton & Tice, 1994).

The strength model views self-control as a limited energy resource and analogous to a muscle (Baumeister, Vohs & Tice, 2007). Like a muscle, self-control can be exercised to become stronger and more efficient, but it can also fatigue and not work as well. Laboratory studies show that when participants are first required to exercise self-control in a task (e.g., resist eating a chocolate and instead eat a radish for the long-term health benefits), they then do more poorly in the next self-control task. It is like the energy required to exercise self-control in the first task is sapped in the second task (Vohs, Baumeister, Schmeichel, Twenge et al., 2008).

This model has some interesting implications to our understanding of self-control among criminal offenders. Perhaps criminal offenders, on average, begin with lower levels of self-control (low constraint in Moffitt's model) and this baseline predisposes them to choosing the quick and easy over the slow and difficult. Furthermore, when they do exercise some self-control, their energy depletes more quickly, raising their vulnerability to giving in to crime. Baumeister et al. (2007) suggest that training in self-control may help, and other variables may delay the depletion of self-control strength. One variable with the potential to influence strength is antisocial attitudes. Kivetz and Zheng (2006) found that an attitude of entitlement can disengage self-control processes in favor of choosing immediate gratification (i.e., "I have worked hard and held off long enough that I deserve it."). In our view, self-control needs to be considered as part of a complex and interdependent variety of psychological processes.

Antisocial Personality Pattern: Risk and Treatment

By focusing on the characteristics that describe antisocial personality, we can avoid the pessimistic attitudes that the APD or psychopath is untreatable. In some jurisdictions, such a diagnosis and the associated "unable to learn from experience" is used to justify criminal justice sanctions (Bonta et al., 1996; Edens & Petrila, 2006; Wong, 2000; Zinger & Forth, 1998). As noted earlier, there is no evidence that psychopaths and APD offenders cannot learn from treatments that follow the principles of risk, need, and responsivity.

Psychopathy and APD are viewed as stable personality traits that change little with time. From a prediction perspective, they are static risk factors (Hare, 1998). However, viewing psychopathy/APD as a constellation of static risk factors may be a mistake. Examination of the items of the PCL-R finds that up to 14 of the 20 items are dynamic. There is no a priori reason to assume that readministration of the PCL-R following appropriate treatment would not show changes in scores. In addition, a number of studies have reported correlations in the range of .64 to .86 with the LSI-R, a static-dynamic assessment instrument (Simourd & Hoge, 2000; Stevenson & Wormith, 1987). Until recently, the assumption that antisocial personality is immutable has diverted researchers from studying the dynamic possibilities of the PCL-R. As we already observed, Wong and Hare's (2005) proposed treatment program for psychopaths draws heavily on criminogenic needs that are modifiable.

Gradually, the PCL-R (and the concept of psychopathy) is being considered in ways that are not bound to the psychopathological tradition. Earlier in this chapter we saw that the assessment of childhood and adolescent factors (i.e., CATS; Quinsey et al., 2006) can replace the PCL-R. Lynam and Derefinko (2006) have "translated" the PCL-R into the language of the Five Factor model, and Hare has also broken down the PCL-R into finer parts (from two factors to four factors, three of which are dynamic). In Table 6.4 we reconfigure the items of the PCL-R in accordance with a PCC (we take some liberty in categorizing the items). The PCL-R and the construct of psychopathy fit very nicely into the principles of risk, need, and responsivity. The predictive power of the PCL-R reported from around the world (Hare et al., 2000) may be traced to the static criminal history and dynamic/criminogenic risk factors. By conceptualizing psychopathy as a broad antisocial personality pattern within a PCC, we not only understand the basis for the predictive accuracy of the PCL-R but also are offered a positive, proactive agenda for treatment. Treatment targets are identified (criminogenic needs) and responsivity considerations outlined.

Such an application of PCC to the PCL-R has been reported by David Simourd and Robert Hoge (2000). The LSI-R and PCL-R were

Table 6.4
The PCL-R as Seen from a Psychology of Criminal Conduct

Static Criminal History
    Parasitic life style
    Early behavior problems
    Many short-term marital relationships
    Juvenile delinquency
    Revocation of conditional release
    Criminal versatility

Dynamic Criminogenic Needs
    Pathological lying
    Conning/manipulative
    Lack of remorse or guilt
    Poor behavioral controls
    Promiscuous sexual relations
    Lack of realistic, long-term goals
    Impulsivity
    Irresponsibility
    Failure to accept responsibility

Responsivity
    Glibness/superficial charm
    Grandiose sense of self-worth
    Need for stimulation/prone to boredom
    Shallow affect

administered to 321 inmates in a Canadian penitentiary. Approximately 11 percent scored 30 or above on the PCL-R. Comparing the psychopaths to the nonpsychopaths, the psychopaths scored higher on the LSI-R and on all of the dynamic subcomponents except for "financial." In other words, psychopaths are at high risk to reoffend, and their risk is partly accounted for by higher levels of criminogenic needs.

Perhaps psychopathic offenders are nothing more than high-risk, high-need offenders and if researchers selected the top tenth percentile of LSI-R scores or any other general offender risk scale, all the experiments conducted with the PCL-R would be replicated. At the risk of sounding like Tennenbaum, what is the added value of having a construct such as psychopathy or APD? With respect to the prediction of criminal behavior, we suspect none. However, the constructs may be relevant in how we approach psychopaths and persons with APD in treatment and case management. For example, a psychopathic cocaine addict may be placed into a treatment program targeting drug use, and this intervention could reduce future reoffending, but we would want to be careful of the addict's efforts to manipulate other group participants. Future research will undoubtedly clarify our understanding of this special subset of offenders. Until then, we at least offer hypotheses for testing and exploration.

Worth Remembering

1. General personality theory describes five basic personality dimensions.

   The Big Five model of personality reduces all the personality traits to five general dimensions. These personality dimensions are common to all and are seen as normal features of personality. Two of these "super traits," Weak Constraint and Negative Emotionality, are particularly relevant factors in our concept of antisocial personality pattern.

2. Personality encompasses traits and psychological processes that make sense of the situation of action.

   The expression of personal traits depends on the situations in which we find ourselves and the way we interpret or encode meaning from these situations. To understand behavior we need knowledge of the individual's personality traits, the situation, and the individual's characteristic way of encoding the situation.

3. Criminology has rediscovered the importance of personality in crime.

   For much of the twentieth century, mainstream criminology ignored the evidence linking personality, especially antisocial personality, with crime. Criminology's favorite explanatory variable, social class, had to be protected. Today, this is no longer the case.

4. Antisocial personality disorder (APD) and psychopathy view some criminals as psychopathological.

   Forensic mental health specialists see antisocial personality disorder (APD) and psychopathy as forming clearly defined diagnostic categories. However, there is some concern about the reliability of a diagnosis of APD. Both disorders are believed to be untreatable, although the evidence for this conclusion is very weak.

5. A general antisocial personality pattern may be more relevant than psychopathological models of antisocial personality.

   A major advantage of a general personality and cognitive social psychological perspective of antisocial personality over psychopathological models is that treatment becomes a possibility. The dynamic needs of highly antisocial personalities can serve as targets for planned interventions.

Recommended Readings

For a general introduction to the five-factor model of personality, we would highly recommend a chapter by McCrae and Costa in Pervin and John's (1999) *Handbook of Personality* (2nd ed.). The reader who wishes to pursue other personality perspectives may want to consult Mayer's article in the *American Psychologist* (2005) and some of the writings of Walter Mischel.

To fully appreciate the knowledge destruction techniques of the early criminologists, we would not hesitate to recommend Tennenbaum's (1977) review of the personality-crime link. After having read this chapter, the reader is well prepared to tackle this article with a critical eye.

We suspect that many readers are interested in the concept of psychopathy. As an introduction, take a look at Robert Hare's (1993) book, *Without Conscience: The Disturbing World of the Psychopaths Among Us*. This book is available in paperback and was written with the lay reader in mind. If you want depth and critical analysis of the concept of psychopathy, then consult Christopher Patrick's *Handbook of Psychopathy*.

The Role of Antisocial Associates and Attitudes in Criminal Conduct

Figure 7.1 is a simplified version of Figure 4.1, modified to reflect the content of this chapter. Here we see the Big Four operating on the decision to act within the context of the immediate situation. In the General Personality and Cognitive Social Learning (GPCSL) model, cognition (i.e., the decision of the self to act in a particular way) plays a central role. Ultimately, the cause of behavior resides in the cognitions of the individual. People make a choice, and they are responsible for their choices. Sometimes we may not be fully aware of our decision to act because of the automatic nature of some behaviors, or impulsive-emotional reactions, or the disruption of thinking processes due to alcohol or other drugs. However, even in these situations, we can trace back in the chain of behavioral events a point where an active choice was made that accounts for the present behavior. For example, an angry individual may choose to go to the bar and get drunk before ending up in a fight, or the drug addict chooses to leave his house to buy some drugs. Self-agency is a powerful construct.

The decision to act is influenced by the Big Four and, of course, the immediate situation. The presence of a police officer, a weapon, a car with the key in it, and so on are powerful inhibitors or facilitators of criminal conduct. Criminal history reflects a history of rewards for criminal behavior and the longer and more varied the history, the more "automatic" the behavior. At a certain point, there is almost a sense of

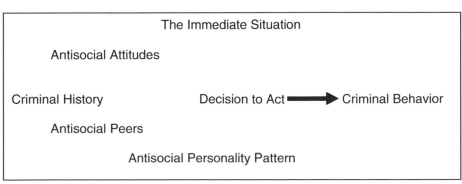

Figure 7.1
The Big Four and the Decision to Act in the Immediate Situation

criminal expertise that makes crime quick and efficient. A criminal history is also an indicator of a history of decisionmaking supportive of crime. An antisocial personality pattern (Chapter 6) of impulsivity, emotional callousness, sensation-seeking, and negative emotions also favors a decision to act in an antisocial manner. Finally, we have antisocial associates and antisocial attitudes completing our list of the major determinants of criminal behavior.

Each of the Big Four is predictive of criminal behavior with correlations in the lower .20 range (recall Resource Note 2.1). Although the Big Four (or, for that matter, the complete Central Eight) are intercorrelated, each factor has some additive value. Offender risk/needs assessment instruments that tap into the Big Four routinely exceed correlations of .30 with recidivism and sometimes go into the .40 range (Andrews, Bonta & Wormith, 2006). In this chapter, our focus is on two of the Big Four risk factors—antisocial associates and attitudes. We begin our discussion of antisocial associates by picking up from the developmental perspective in Chapter 5. From there we will examine how, specifically, associates may facilitate criminal acts. Then, we turn to antisocial attitudes. Many antisocial attitudes are learned and maintained in association with criminal others and exert a direct control over the decision to engage in antisocial conduct. Together they are powerful determinants and targets of change in understanding and changing criminal behavior.

When Parents Lose Control: The Path to Delinquent Associates

Adolescence is a period of profound biological, cognitive, and emotional maturation and a period when youths begin to define themselves as separate and independent from their parents. One potential path toward autonomy, suggested by Granic and Patterson (2006), is to engage in antisocial behavior. Delinquent behaviors represent more "adult-like behaviors" (at least in the mind of the youth), challenge the authority of the parents, and attract the attention of peers. Glueck and Glueck noted more than 50 years ago that adult-like behaviors (e.g., smoking, drinking, early sexual activity) differentiated delinquents from nondelinquents. We think that there is more to delinquent behavior than a need for autonomy. As we saw in the previous chapters, temperamental and personality factors play a role. For example, the desire for excitement and thrills among some youths can be fulfilled by engaging in behaviors frowned upon by many adults, and impulsiveness leads to the instant gratification afforded by some antisocial activities.

Poor parenting also has a profound impact on the development of antisocial behavior. A fuller discussion on family factors related to crime will be presented in Chapter 8 but, for now, there are four important points we wish to make. First, parents may actually model and reinforce antisocial behavior while discouraging prosocial behaviors and attitudes (Newcomb & Loeb, 1999). Recall in Chapter 5 our discussion of inter-generational crime and heredity. From Dugdale to the Cambridge longitudinal study, we see that crime runs in families and it is not simply all due to heredity. To illustrate the point of how parents can encourage (perhaps inadvertently) the wrong behaviors, we summarize some of the findings from the classic study by Glueck and Glueck in Table 7.1. Notice that for the delinquents the parents were more likely to be criminals themselves, fail to model prosocial behaviors (work), and supervise and discipline inappropriately.

Our second point is that in families with poor relationships and inade-quate monitoring and disciplining, aggressive and other antisocial behav-iors become established very early. This severely limits the type of peer social network that the child develops (Lacourse et al., 2006). Well-socialized children (and their parents) will not accept the friendship of antisocial chil-dren, and these children become socially excluded from their normative peers, putting them at risk to gravitate toward similarly deviant peers.

Thirdly, poor emotional attachments with the parent(s) may leave the child emotionally underdeveloped and lacking in self-esteem. The relationship between self-esteem and criminal behavior is complex (Baumeister, Campbell, Krueger & Vohs, 2003). With adults, self-esteem without attention to attitudes is a poor predictor of criminal behavior (Wormith, 1984). Baumeister and his colleagues (Baumeister, Bushman & Campbell, 2000) have argued that it is people with *high* self-esteem (i.e., narcissists) who are aggressive, while others think it is low self-esteem that is the culprit (Sprott & Doob, 2000). Analyzing data from the Dunedin longitudinal study, Moffitt and her colleagues found low

Table 7.1
Parents as Socialization Agents for Antisocial Behavior

Parenting Characteristic	Delinquent	Non-Delinquent
Criminal father	66.2	32.0
Criminal mother	44.8	15.0
Poor working habit (father)	25.7	5.7
Conduct standards poor (family)	90.4	54.0
Supervision by mother (unsuitable)	63.8	13.0
Hostile/indifferent affection by father	59.8	19.9
Mother discipline (lax/erratic)	91.4	32.8
Physical punishment (father)	55.6	34.6

Adapted from Glueck & Glueck, 1950

self-esteem, measured at age 11, predicted externalizing problems at age 13 (Donnellan, Trzesniewski, Robins, Moffitt & Caspi, 2005) and criminal behavior at age 26 (Trzesniewski, Donnellan, Moffitt et al., 2006). However, the relationship in both studies was described by the researchers as small and to be interpreted with caution. We raise the point of self-esteem because we will come back to it when we discuss theories of criminal subcultures.

Finally, as the child becomes older and spends more time outside of the home, opportunities to develop delinquent friends increase. If the parents do not know or do not care with whom the child associates, then involvement with delinquents and even joining a delinquent gang become more likely (Lahey et al., 1999; Osgood & Anderson, 2004; Rebellon, 2002; Tolan, Gorman-Smith & Henry, 2003; Warr, 2005). This differential association may be heightened among children with some of the risk markers for a life-course-persistent trajectory (e.g., callous-unemotional traits; Kimonis, Frick & Barry, 2004). In a study of 10- to 12-year-old "early starters" from 673 African-American families, Simons and his colleagues (Simons, Simons, Chen, Brody & Lin, 2007) found poor parental monitoring and discipline and parental hostility the best predictors of antisocial peer affiliation ($r = .12$ and $r = .19$, respectively).

Theoretical Perspectives on Delinquent Associates

Theoretical explanations of the influence of associates on antisocial activity have a long tradition in criminology (recall Chapter 3). Sutherland (1939) posited that criminal behavior is learned through differential associations with other criminals. However, the question of why criminals gravitate to each other did not become a major theoretical issue until the 1950s and 1960s. Subcultural theories were largely influenced by Merton's (1938) theory of limited opportunity. That is, those who are blocked from achieving societal goals (i.e., money and status) seek out others in the same boat to join forces and overcome the obstacles in front of them.

The two major subcultural theories at the time were those of Cloward and Ohlin (1960) and Cohen (1955). Both had as their starting point blocked opportunities but described slightly different responses to these obstacles. For Cohen (1955), it was to feel better because the others in the group give each other the social status that they cannot meet in normative society. For Cloward and Ohlin (1960), it was to adopt a set of attitudes, values, and beliefs in opposition to mainstream society that supported an aggressive approach to achieving social goods. We would draw to the reader's attention that both theories have at their root the idea of "us" versus "them."

From a psychology perspective, research on social exclusion can inform our understanding as to why delinquents seek out each other's company. Criminal behavior is non-normative behavior that is widely disapproved. Consequently, those who engage in crime will be excluded from the mainstream (the subcultural criminological theories also saw exclusion as a problem but exclusion was made on the basis of class and not crime). Developmental psychologists are well aware that exclusion from peers in young children leads to a host of problems. One problem in particular is the impact on self-esteem.

Mark Leary and his colleagues (Leary, Tambor, Terdal & Downs, 1995) found that the more participants (undergraduate students) in their experiments felt excluded from their peer group, the lower their self-esteem. On the other hand, the more that they felt included, the higher their self-esteem. The authors hypothesized that self-esteem is basically an internal measure of how socially appealing one is to his or her peers. It seems that decreases in self-esteem alert one to being potentially excluded from social groups and may motivate the individual to engage in efforts to increase social inclusion. For the criminal offender, joining antisocial groups promotes social inclusion and may increase self-esteem (à la Cohen). Of course, involvement in such groups also distances the offender from the influence of prosocial others.

Social exclusion has also been linked to aggressive behavior. In another series of laboratory studies, participants were told that others had rejected them, which resulted in aggressive responses from the misled subjects (Twenge, Baumeister, Tice & Stuke, 2001). The aggression, not surprisingly, was targeted at the people who told the subject that they were not picked to participate on a group task (i.e., excluded). What is interesting in the Twenge et al. (2001) study was that negative mood was unrelated to the aggressive behavior (delivering an aversive noise in the experiments). Furthermore, it appears that social exclusion leads to interpretations of neutral acts from others as hostile, and this interpretation of the situation triggers the aggression (DeWall, Twenge, Gitter & Baumeister, 2009).

Over the course of seven experiments, Twenge and her colleagues (Twenge, Baumeister, DeWall, Ciarocco & Bartels, 2007) went on to find that social exclusion also affects *prosocial* behavior. The students in the social exclusion condition demonstrated less charitable giving, were less helpful when an accident occurred to someone else, and generally were less cooperative. If we make the leap to antisocial groups, and granted it is a leap to jump from undergraduate students to criminal subcultures, then we cannot help but wonder how social exclusion may facilitate the formations of antisocial groups. Hopefully, the social exclusion research will extend beyond the university laboratories.

Delinquent Associates: Training in Antisocial Behavior

One of the consequences of associating with delinquents is the increased opportunity to learn a variety of criminal behaviors, particularly covert antisocial behaviors. Patterson and his colleagues (Granic & Patterson, 2006; Patterson & Yoerger, 1999) speak of "phase transitions" in describing the development of chronic offending as progressing from the overt, aggressive behavior evident at a young age to covert antisocial behaviors such as stealing and drug abuse in adolescence. Furthermore, antisocial peer groups contribute to this transition. Thus, the chronic offender becomes quite versatile, demonstrating both aggressive and nonaggressive antisocial behaviors. Although there is evidence that some forms of antisocial behavior (i.e., physical aggression) vary by gender and age (Broidy et al., 2003; Leschied et al., 2002; Tomada & Schneider, 1997), it appears that even the girls who follow a life-course-persistent trajectory show a versatility and level of aggressiveness similar to boys (Fontaine et al., 2008; Mazerolle et al., 2000).

Reviews of the literature consistently rank antisocial associates as one of the strongest correlates of criminal behavior (Gendreau et al., 1996). As expected, the influence of delinquents increases with age. In the meta-analysis by Lipsey and Derzon (1998), the average effect size for antisocial associates was .12 for children ages six to 11 years and .43 for children ages 12 to 14. The question that researchers have been grappling with is the interpretation of the relationship. Two hypotheses have been presented. The first, originally proposed by Glueck and Glueck (1950), is that the youths have already established antisocial behaviors and attitudes before joining delinquent social networks ("birds of a feather flock together" hypothesis). Similarly, Gottfredson and Hirschi's (1990) self-control theory also hypothesized that low-self-control individuals, already predisposed to delinquency, self-select others with low self-control. Thus, associating with other delinquents does not really increase the chances of criminal behavior; the youths would engage in crime regardless of with whom they associate.

The second hypothesis is that delinquent youths may be attracted to each other for the reasons noted above, but once they form association and friendship bonds, the interpersonal reinforcements for antisocial behavior would augment the risk for criminal behavior. That is, delinquent friends directly model and reward antisocial behavior and discourage prosocial behavior, thereby increasing the risk of criminal behavior (Matseuda & Anderson, 1998; Wright et al., 2001). Furthermore, the stronger the friendship bond, the more likely the youth will follow the lead of delinquent friends (Payne & Cornwell, 2007). Studies of the social interactions among delinquents clearly show antisocial peers encouraging antisocial attitudes and behaviors and punishing prosocial behavior

(Buehler, Patterson & Furniss, 1966; Dishion, Spracklen & Andrews, 1996; Shortt, Capaldi, Dishion, Bank & Owen, 2003).

The GPCSL perspective would suggest that there is truth to both hypotheses. An antisocial personality pattern characterized by poor self-control, callousness, hostile emotions, and egocentrism predisposes one to antisocial behavior regardless of antisocial peer networks. However, such a personality pattern increases the likelihood of joining deviant peer groups. An antisocial personality pattern would make it difficult to form relationships with well-controlled, emotionally stable individuals and to achieve success in school and work. Spending less time in school frees up time to spend with antisocial associates in aimless and deviant activity. Once antisocial peer attachments are formed, then modeling and learning processes take over. We know of only one study that considered simultaneously the impact of personality and peer associations on criminal behavior. McGloin and O'Neill Shermer (2009) found that self-control and antisocial peer associations were criminogenic in their own right and that a combination of poor self-control and associations with antisocial associates functioned as a unique contributory factor to crime—a path suggested by GPCSL.

Gangs. Over the past 20 years, the police, media, and the academic community have paid special attention to delinquent gangs. Gangs have always been an interest to the general public, but they tended to be romanticized (e.g., *West Side Story, Rebel Without a Cause*). They are no longer seen this way. Gangs operate at the street and prison levels, and many are extremely violent and, at least in prison settings, well organized (Decker, 2007). Criminologists have a long history of trying to understand the formation and maintenance of antisocial groups (e.g., Cloward & Ohlin, 1960; Cohen, 1955), and this interest has flourished in recent years.

The first challenge faced by researchers studying gangs is to answer the question: what makes a gang (Esbensen et al., 2001)? Do two delinquents regularly hanging around with each other count, or do you need more than two? Do members have to commit all their crimes together as though they were joined at the hip, or can they go off by themselves to commit crimes? Is actual participation in criminal activity required, or is simple association sufficient (the "gang wannabes")? Must there be some concrete symbol such as a colored kerchief indicating their affiliation? Is it necessary to have a high level of organization with leadership? Despite the complexity of defining a gang, the fact of the matter is that most studies simply ask: "Do you belong to a gang?" The approach seems to have worked well—individuals who say yes tend to be the same individuals that law enforcement officials use to ascertain gang membership (Curry, 2000).

It is estimated that there are more than 26,500 youth gangs in the United States, with 785,000 gang members (Egley & O'Donnell, 2008).

The question most often asked is whether gang membership increases the likelihood of criminal activity (Battin et al., 1998). The answer appears to be yes, with evidence coming from cross-sectional and longitudinal studies (Thornberry, Huizinga & Loeber, 2004; Thornberry et al., 2003). In a cross-sectional study, Ronald Huff (1998) interviewed 140 gang members and a group of 145 "at-risk" youths from four United States sites. Gang members were identified by a combination of self-reports and police and social service agency referrals. Gang members were significantly more likely than at-risk youths to be involved in assaults, drive-by shootings, and drug trafficking.

Two longitudinal studies found that while persons were in a gang, delinquent activity increased significantly (Gordon et al., 2004; Thornberry et al., 2003). The first study was drawn from the Pittsburgh Youth Study of 858 boys followed over a 10-year period as they joined and left gangs (Gordon et al., 2004), and the second study was based on 1,000 boys and girls from the Rochester Youth Study (Thornberry et al., 2003). Although gang members were already quite delinquent before joining, their delinquent activity increased more than expected when they joined a gang. For example, delinquents in the Rochester Youth Study who belong to a gang represented one-third of the sample but accounted for two-thirds of the crimes.

The longitudinal studies are also instructive in that membership in a gang is pretty fluid. Gordon and colleagues (2004) found that 85 percent of the boys who joined gangs had left the gangs within four years. In the Rochester sample, almost 93 percent of the boys and all of the girls had left the gangs (Thornberry et al., 2003). In addition, commitment to the gang varies widely. Some just like to "hang out" with the gang rather than directly engage in crime. Esbensen and colleagues (2001) describe "core members," and the data from longitudinal studies suggest that these core members represent no more than 15 percent of gang members.

There are remarkable similarities between delinquents who fully participate in gang activity and those who play a minimal role. The differences that do exist appear to be a matter of degree. For example, parental attachment, supervision, and monitoring are important for both groups but, in study of 940 gang members, the core members had much lower levels of parental monitoring than delinquents who were more casual in their commitment to the gang (Esbensen et al., 2001). On the whole, the risk factors for gang membership are similar to the risk factors for life-course-persistent delinquency. Coming from a disadvantaged neighborhood and being raised in a dysfunctional family (Esbensen et al., 2001; Hill et al., 1999; Lahey et al., 1999; Thornberry et al., 2003; Wyrick & Howell, 2004), as well as having antisocial attitudes and a broadly defined antisocial personality (aggressivity, emotionally callous, adventurous, and impulsive) have all been related to gang membership

(Hill et al., 1999; Le Blanc & Lanctôt, 1998). Moreover, the risk factors for girls appear to be no different than for boys (Hill et al., 1999; Thornberry et al., 2003).

Although an antisocial personality pattern has been indicative of gang membership, psychopathy per se does not appear to be a major element among gang members (despite mass media portrayals). Avelardo Valdez, Charles Kaplan, and Edward Codina (2000) administered the screening version of the PCL-R to 50 gang members and a matched sample of 25 non–gang members. They found that only 4 percent of gang members were psychopaths, while 24 percent of the non–gang members were diagnosed with psychopathy. The lower prevalence of psychopathy among gang members may indicate that these individuals have such low affectional bonds to others that they prefer to operate on their own rather than with others (or regular criminals with any amount of common sense want nothing to do with them).

Intervention efforts have focused on "get tough" approaches such as increased police patrols and aggressive prosecution. Not surprisingly, the "get tough" approach has not demonstrated much success (Decker, 2007; Wyrick & Howell, 2004). A more promising approach has been to try to prevent youths from joining gangs in the first place (there have been very few programs that have actually tried to disrupt antisocial peer groups). Gang Resistance Education and Training (GREAT) is a school-based prevention program that is used throughout the United States and internationally (Esbensen, 2004). Uniformed police officers speak to seventh-grade students about the negative aspects of gang membership and drugs, and conflict resolution techniques. The goal is to give youths the skills to resist peer pressure and the temptation to join a gang.

In a large-scale evaluation of the program, Esbensen and Osgood (1999) compared 2,629 students who completed the program to 3,207 students who did not complete it. GREAT completers reported lower rates of drug use, fewer delinquent friends, and more negative attitudes toward gangs. The researchers concluded that GREAT produced "modest short-term benefits," but the results were based on self-reports, and the participants were too young to allow researchers to conduct a follow-up about actual entry into gangs. The caution was well deserved. A longitudinal study of more than 3,000 children two years after completion of the program found no effect (Esbensen et al., 2002). The varied results question the effectiveness of GREAT in preventing gang membership, and as we will see when we describe the DARE evaluations, cast suspicion on the general use of education programs delivered by the police.

To our knowledge, there is only one treatment study that applied the risk-need-responsivity principles to gang members (Di Placido, Simon, Witte, Gu & Wong, 2006). A high-intensity cognitive behavioral treatment program was delivered to 40 gang members in a maximum-security forensic facility in central Canada. Most of the gang members came from Aboriginal gangs (61%), and the remainder came from various other gangs (e.g., Hells Angels, Bloods, Crips). Upon follow-up (average of 13.7 months post-release), 20 percent of the treated gang members recidivated violently compared to 35 percent for the untreated gang members.

Summary. One consequence of being in a family in which there are poor emotional bonds, monitoring, and disciplining practices is that the child is free to associate with other delinquent children. Social support for crime is theoretically and empirically one of the most important correlates of criminal behavior. From a preventive perspective, effectively intervening at the family level would not only benefit families directly but also impact on the associational patterns that the child develops. Another consequence of being raised within a dysfunctional family environment is the learning of antisocial attitudes, one of the other Big Four correlates of criminal conduct.

Cognitions Supportive of Crime: Antisocial Attitudes

Attitudes are evaluative cognitions and feelings that organize the actor's decision to act and behavior toward a person, thing, or action (recall Figure 7.1). One may view a teacher as knowledgeable, cars as polluters, and jogging as boring. These attitudes toward the teacher, cars, and jogging also imply a behavioral action. The teacher will be listened to attentively, a bus is taken rather than a car, or watching television becomes a major recreational activity. We do not really see "attitudes," but we infer them from the behavior of individuals. For many social psychologists, attitudes forms a major aspect of their work, and in the remainder of this chapter, we explore how certain attitudes influence criminal behavior.

The study of attitudes has a long history in both psychology and criminology. In psychology, the study of attitudes can be traced back to William James, the father of American psychology. However, the investigation of attitudes really came into its own with the experiments of Solomon Asch, Michael Argyle, Carl Hovland, and others in the 1950s. In criminology, Sutherland's "definitions" favorable, or unfavorable, to law remains the classic theoretical formulation of attitudes in relation to criminal behavior (Sutherland, 1947). Variations on the causal role of attitudes in criminal behavior are also evident in symbolic interactionist theories of crime (Rubington & Weinberg, 1968), Hirschi's (1969) control theory ("ties to convention") and subcultural theory ("identification with criminal others": Cohen, 1955; Glaser, 1956).

Generally speaking, antisocial attitudes are thoughts, feelings, and beliefs that are supportive of criminal conduct. If you think that there is nothing wrong with cheating on your income tax, or that a person deserves to be hit for insulting you, or because he is simply making you mad, then guess what is likely to happen? Notice the importance of making a favorable or unfavorable evaluation, considered by Ajzen and Fishbein (1980) to be a fundamental component of an attitude. Antisocial attitudes are all about when it is all right to break the law.

Development of Antisocial Attitudes

There are two ways we can look at the origins of attitudes relevant to criminal behavior. First, there are the perspectives that emphasize a *failure* in the development of a conscience or in moral reasoning. Second, there are the perspectives that highlight the social environment in shaping attitudes irrespective of a failure to understand what is right and what is wrong.

Freud's concept of lack of superego (or conscience) is the first perspective with a focus on personality as the foundation to attitudinal structure. As the child matures, the id (basic impulses) comes under the control of the ego (reality constraining id impulses) and eventually the superego (impulses under self-control). The development of the superego is dependent upon identification with the parents and the internalization of parental norms and values. As we noted earlier in the text, a weak superego, or conscience, can lead to antisocial behavior. Identification with a parental figure, or wanting to be liked by mommy and daddy, requires some affectional bond to the parent(s). Disruptions in caregiver attachment may interfere with the development of a conscience. Moreover, there is evidence that corporal punishment, which is relatively prevalent among delinquent families, can inhibit moral development (Gershoff, 2002).

Another example, but this time with a focus on cognitive development rather than personality development, is Kohlberg's theory of moral development (Kohlberg, 1958; Kohlberg & Candee, 1984). Kohlberg's theory is a product of the work of Jean Piaget who found that children do "the right thing" for different reasons depending upon their age. Kohlberg's three-level/six-stage model of moral reasoning is summarized in Table 7.2. Progress through the stages is orderly and dependent upon maturation and age (i.e., biologically-based). You cannot skip Stage 2 and go directly to Stage 3, although you can speed it up with some treatments (e.g., Moral Reconation Therapy; Little, 2005). In general, most offenders function at Stages 1 and 2 (Arbuthnot & Gordon, 1986; Craig & Truitt, 1996; Gibbs et al., 1984; Lee & Prentice, 1988; Palmer, 2003).

The second perspective on the origins of antisocial attitudes stresses the role of the social environment in shaping attitudes. Sociologists see the broad social groups that may vary along race, culture, religion, etc., as shapers of attitudes. The attitudes of interest are generally attitudes held by the group rather than individual specific attitudes. For example,

Table 7.2
Kohlberg's Theory of Moral Development

Level	Stage	Description
I Preconventional	1. Punishment and obedience 2. Instrumental hedonism	Egocentric (Obey the rules because it is a rule; What happens to me?)
II Conventional	3. Approval of others 4. Authority maintaining morality	Social expectations (What do others expect of me?)
III Principled law	5. Democratically accepted (What is best for all?) 6. Principles of conscience	Universality

Americans may have different attitudes toward work compared to Italians, attitudes regarding church attendance are different for Roman Catholics and Buddhists, and attitudes toward courtship are different for those from India and those from Canada.

In sociological criminology, smaller fragments of broader society (i.e., criminal subcultures) have their own normative attitudes, which are reinforced for their individual members. Thus, the lower classes have a general set of attitudes specific to that class. This is Miller's (1958) idea of "focal concerns." The upper classes do not share these focal concerns of toughness, fate, and so on—only the lower classes do so. Most people within the lower classes are thought to have these attitudes, and individuals are socialized into these beliefs. The same theme of adhering to shared group attitudes can be observed in the various subcultural theories.

Social learning also places the learning of antisocial attitudes within a social context but at the more immediate social contexts of family, associates, school, and work. However, there are two advantages to social learning theory. First, it specifies the mechanisms of learning (modeling and conditioning). This is important because it informs treatments designed to change antisocial attitudes. Second, it allows for inquiries into understanding of *individual* attitudes rather than just group-held attitudes. That is, people may hold attitudes very different from the larger group, and it is the understanding of attitudes at the individual level that helps in prediction and treatment.

The Attitude-Behavior Link

Studying antisocial attitudes is deemed important because it is assumed that there is a large correlation between attitudes and behavior. However, as Walter Mischel (1968) showed with personality and behavior (Chapter 6), the relationship between attitudes and behavior is far from perfect. Individual studies on the relationship between attitudes and behavior have ranged from the negative to the positive, with an average *r* of .40 (Kraus, 1995). What has become the focus of the psychological study of attitudes is to understand the conditions under which the degree consistency between the attitudes and the behaviour increases.

There are many factors that influence the attitude-behavior association (see Fishbein & Azjen, 1975, for a review). Recently, two important conditions have been subjected to meta-analysis. First, there is the issue of the social pressure to behave in accordance with an attitude. Obviously, this is highly relevant to individuals operating within an antisocial group such as a gang. In a review of nearly 800 studies on attitudes, Wallace, Paulson, Lord, and Bond (2005) found peer pressure to have an unexpected effect on behavior. The highest degree of consistency between attitudes and behavior was under moderate levels of peer pressure. Under high levels of peer pressure, the average correlation dropped from .41 to .30. Apparently, when the immediate situation requires a high degree of conformity to group norms, individually held attitudes have less of an influence. It is important to note, however, that the review did not include antisocial attitudes (examples of attitudes included were those toward smoking, donating blood, and drinking soft drinks). Studies specific to antisocial attitudes and peer affiliation are needed to expand upon the peer-pressure hypothesis.

A second general condition is the "accessibility" of the attitude. "Accessibility" means repetitive, easy to remember, and relevant to behavioral decisions. In other words, it is the saliency and personal meaningfulness of the attitude to the individual that increases behavioral adherence to the attitude. A review of 41 studies found an overall *r* of .50 under conditions of high accessibility, with some correlations from individual studies reaching the range of .70 (Glasman & Albarracín, 2006). Once again, the meta-analysis did not include antisocial attitudes, but we would suggest that accessibility would play a factor in interactions between the individual's antisocial attitudes and involvement in antisocial peer groups.

Classifying Antisocial Attitudes

There are many attitudes that support criminal behavior. Although there is no complete consensus on a grouping of these attitudes, it is helpful to have such a classification of antisocial attitudes. Partly based on theory and partly on research, we propose the following:

1. Techniques of Neutralization
2. Identification with Criminal Others
3. Rejection of Convention

Let us begin with the first categorization, *Techniques of Neutralization*. The label for this category of antisocial attitudes comes from Sykes and Matza (1957). We remind the reader of our earlier discussion of failure in the development of a conscience and moral reasoning. Sykes and Matza argued that most offenders have some belief in conventional values, and they *know* the difference between right and wrong. That is, they do not all have a deficit in conscience. Therefore, the important question to ask is: "Why do they continue to break the law when they know that it is 'wrong' and frowned upon by most people?"

For Sykes and Matza, the answer to the question is that offenders "neutralize" the potential punishment associated with criminal behavior. In Chapter 3 we summarized their five "techniques of neutralization." Variations on the theme of neutralization can also be found in the work of Hartung and Mills ("vocabulary of motives"; Hartung, 1965; Mills, 1940) and Bandura et al. ("exonerating mechanisms"; 1996). These techniques not only minimize punishment from interpersonal sources but also from personal sources. By providing a rationale for bad behavior, one not only minimizes negative repercussions from others (e.g., the joyrider saying that "I was going to return the car") but also may alleviate negative feelings and self-evaluations (e.g., "She wasn't hurt, it was only a little push"). Some techniques of neutralization (appeal to a higher loyalty) may even be considered a form of moral reasoning (perhaps Stage 4 from Table 7.2?) that can be used to justify bad behavior (Krebs & Denton, 2005).

Neutralizations, rationalizations, and excuses are but one general set of antisocial attitudes that essentially deal with how to avoid society's and the self's recriminations. In a sense, they allow the person to act outside of mainstream norms without giving up some belief in these norms. Another set of antisocial attitudes are cognitions that reflect a criminal identity. These attitudes assign favorable evaluations to criminal behavior and criminal others and become part of a criminal identity. That is, it does not matter that general society does not like the behavior; it is the approval of the self and antisocial associates that is important. Tony Soprano may have expressed many techniques of neutralization over the course of the popular television series, "The Sopranos," but he was also, quite literally, proud and satisfied with his criminal behavior (despite the scam that he pulled with his therapist). It was "the Family" and his own view as a competent criminal that was important to Tony, and he accepted no other normative value. Some delinquents may view the adoption of a criminal identity as simply a right of passage during adolescence (Hirschfield, 2008). We describe this set of antisocial attitudes as *Identification with Criminal Others* (IWCO).

Once again we find variations on the theme of IWCO in criminology. William Miller (1958) described the focal concerns of the lower classes, but one does not need to view these attitudes as tied only to the lower classes. Attitudes such as "I am tough", "I'm trouble," and "stuff happens" clearly signal an increased likelihood of law-breaking. The focal concern of a belief that what occurs in life depends more on fate than personal responsibility ("stuff happens") may justify disengaging personal self-control (Kivetz & Zheng, 2006). Albert Cohen (1955) described youths adopting a subcultural value system that rejected middle-class values (e.g., "spontaneous" vs. "rational"), and Daniel Glaser (1956) spoke of identification with a criminal reference group. Even a casual observation of organized crime syndicates and gangs quickly reveals patterns of thinking and values that are sources of pride in a violent image (e.g., the "code of the street"; Stewart, Schreck & Simons, 2006) and not efforts to make excuses and avoid negative consequences.

A third general set of antisocial attitudes can be labeled *Rejection of Convention*. Work and education are devalued, as are the institutions of law and order (e.g., police, the courts). Admittedly, negative attitudes toward work and school are not necessarily antisocial, but by minimizing their importance, crime becomes a more favorable alternative (we remind the reader of PIC-R Principle 8—if you do not have a job or you do not like school, you have less to lose by adopting a criminal lifestyle). From criminological theory, elements of rejection of convention are evident in the various subcultural and conflict theories.

To summarize, antisocial attitudes are central to most theories of criminal behavior and there has been considerable progress in describing the various types of antisocial attitudes. Some (Maruna & Copes, 2005; Ward, 2000) have complained that too much effort has been spent on developing lists of criminal attitudes and not enough on integrating them into more general theories of criminal behavior. We agree and see antisocial attitudes as integral to our GPCSL model of criminal conduct, representing one of the Big Four correlates of criminal conduct. Much more research is required to flesh out how antisocial attitudes specifically influence criminal behavior, its limits, and how they can be changed. However, this research is now under way.

Assessment of Antisocial Attitudes

We have already seen that antisocial attitudes are one of the best predictors of criminal behavior. In the meta-analytic reviews, the studies varied with regard to how antisocial attitudes were measured. Some studies used qualitative assessments (e.g., interviews to assess "thinking errors"; Yochelson & Samenow, 1976), and others used structured paper-and-pencil measures that were empirically validated. Here, we describe a few of the more structured assessment instruments and the major findings.

One of the earliest measures of neutralization is Ball's (1973) neutralization scale. The scale consisted of four scenarios (two assaults, an armed robbery, and shoplifting), followed by 10 neutralization statements for each scenario. Subjects are asked to rate each neutralization on a five-point scale from "strongly agree" to "strongly disagree." Cross-sectional research with Ball's scale and variations of it (e.g., Shields & Whitehall, 1994) found delinquents to endorse more neutralizations than did nondelinquents (Maruna & Copes, 2005). Longitudinal studies also showed neutralizations to predict antisocial behavior (Agnew, 1994; Minor, 1981; Shields & Whitehall, 1994).

A good example of a measure of Identification with Criminal Others (IWCO) is the Pride in Delinquency Scale (Shields & Whitehall, 1991). This is a very simple scale that lists 10 criminal behaviors, and each behavior is rated using a 20-point scale ranging from −10 (very ashamed) to +10 (very proud). The instrument has demonstrated acceptable psychometric properties (Simourd, 1997), and scores on the Pride in Delinquency Scale have been found to predict recidivism (Simourd & Van De Ven, 1999).

One widely researched measure of antisocial attitudes is the Criminal Sentiments Scale (CSS; Andrews & Wormith, 1984). What is interesting about the CSS is that it taps the three general categories of antisocial attitudes: Techniques of Neutralization, IWCO, and Rejection of Convention. Table 7.3 provides a few examples of the items, along with the categories they measure. There are a total of 41 items that are rated on a five-point scale, from "strongly agree" to "strongly disagree." Scores on the Criminal Sentiments Scale have predicted self-reported criminal behavior (Andrews & Wormith, 1984), officially measured recidivism (Simourd & Olver, 2002; Simourd & Van De Ven, 1999; Witte, Di Placido, Gu & Wong, 2006) and prison violence (Shields & Simourd, 1991).

Of course, there are many other measures of antisocial attitudes in addition to the ones described. Notable measures include the subscales from Glenn Walters's Psychological Inventory of Criminal Thinking Styles (Walters, 1996; for a summary of the evidence, see Walters, 2006b) and Measures of Criminal Attitudes and Associates (Mills, Anderson

Table 7.3
The Criminal Sentiments Scale

Item	Antisocial Subcomponent
A hungry person has a right to steal.	Neutralization
Most successful people used illegal means to become successful.	Neutralization
People who have been in trouble with the law have the same sort of ideas about life that I have.	IWCO
Police rarely try to help people.	Rejection of Convention
Laws are usually bad.	Rejection of Convention

& Kroner, 2004; Mills & Kroner, 2006; Mills, Kroner & Hemmati, 2005). In terms of structured interview-based assessments of antisocial attitudes, the most widely used is the Attitude/Orientation subcomponent of the Level of Service offender risk/need instruments (discussed in Chapter 10). For now, the basic message is that antisocial attitudes are important theoretically, they can be reliably measured, and they are predictive of criminal behavior. The next question is: does replacing antisocial attitudes with prosocial attitudes reduce criminal behavior?

Targeting Antisocial Attitudes in Treatment

Antisocial attitudes is a *dynamic* risk factor for criminal behavior. We know that changes in antisocial attitudes can result from something as simple as altering the associational patterns of participants. Recall in Resource Note 3.2 (Study One) that citizen volunteers participating in a prison recreation program showed increased scores on measures of antisocial attitudes after eight weeks of interactions with inmates (the prisoners showed decreases in antisocial attitudes). Stephen Wormith (1984) found that training the citizen volunteers described in Resource Note 3.1 to appropriately address the antisocial attitudes of the inmates not only led to decreases in antisocial attitudes among the inmates but also to reduced recidivism. Today, many cognitive-behavioral interventions with offenders include a component to address antisocial attitudes (e.g., Ashford, Wong & Sternbach, 2008; Lowenkamp, Hubbard, Makarios & Latessa, 2009; McGuire, Bilby, Hatcher, Hollin et al., 2008). Although there are many interventions that have demonstrated changes in attitudes (e.g., Hubbard & Pealer, 2009), relatively few have linked the changes directly to recidivism (e.g., Wormith, 1984).

To illustrate a group intervention program that focuses on antisocial attitudes, we present Counter-Point. Counter-Point was developed by a community agency (John Howard Society of Ottawa) in collaboration with the Correctional Service of Canada (Graham & Van Dieten, 1999). Over the course of 25 sessions the offenders learn to identify their antisocial attitudes and replace them with prosocial attitudes. The program is delivered in a group format. In an evaluation of the program (Yessine & Kroner, 2004), parolees who attended Counter-Point ($n = 332$) were compared to a group of parolees matched on risk level who received routine community supervision. Program participants were administered the measures of antisocial attitudes described earlier (i.e., CSS, Pride in Delinquency). For the program participants, not only were there reductions in scores on the antisocial attitudinal measures but also reductions in recidivism. The recidivism rate for the program participants, as measured by new offenses over a 1.4-year follow-up, was 33 percent; it was 45 percent for the comparison group.

Counter-Point is a group program. Treatment interventions delivered in a group format are efficient in that they can reach a large number of people, but there are also some disadvantages. What do you do with offenders from sparsely populated areas where there are insufficient numbers to warrant a group, or with an offender who has missed the start of a group and now must wait weeks or months for the next group? An alternative to group intervention is to deliver the treatment individually. Researchers from Public Safety Canada (Bonta, Bourgon, Rugge, Scott, and Yessine) have developed a program that trains probation officers to target antisocial attitudes and help offenders replace these attitudes with prosocial ones. The project is called Strategic Training Initiative in Community Supervision (STICS), and a description of the project is given in Resource Note 7.1.

Also noteworthy about STICS is that it is built entirely around the risk, need, and responsivity principles. Many group programs are built around these principles, but there have been no demonstrations of applying the principles to one-on-one community supervision. In an evaluation of STICS, probation officers were randomly assigned to either three days of training (described in Resource Note 7.1) or to a half-day information session on the principles of "what works." Recidivism outcomes will not be available until after publication of this text, but preliminary results are promising. Audiotaping of the interviews between the probation officers and their clients clearly showed that the STICS-trained probation officers, in contrast to the control group, spent more time on antisocial attitudes and teaching their clients to replace these attitudes with prosocial thinking, and also used more cognitive-behavioral skills. A six-month follow-up of the clients who were trained in STICS demonstrated fewer negative outcomes (i.e., new charges, failure to report, probation violations) compared to the probationers under routine supervision. We expect to see an explosion in programs specifically targeting antisocial attitudes in the coming years.

Resource Note 7.1

Strategic Training Initiative in Community Supervision (STICS)

Bonta and his colleagues (Bonta et al., 2008) audiotaped the supervision sessions that probation officers had with probationers. Their main interest was to ascertain how well the probation officers adhered to the principles of risk, need, and responsivity. Their conclusion was: not very well. Despite the fact that official policy directed staff to spend less effort on supervising low-risk offenders and more time with the high-risk clients, probation officers showed only modest adherence to the policy. With respect to criminogenic needs, probation officers showed good targeting of the criminogenic needs of family/marital and substance abuse but

Resource Note 7.1 (continued)

almost completely ignored antisocial attitudes. Finally, the application of cognitive-behavioral techniques (general responsivity) was infrequent. What was clear from the results was that probation officers needed training on spending effort on the higher-risk offender, targeting antisocial attitudes in their supervision, and making greater use of cognitive-behavioral intervention techniques.

The three-day STICS training program is based on our General Personality and Cognitive Social Learning (GPCSL) theoretical perspective. Thus, the first module of a total of 10 modules was a 90-minute didactic overview of GPCSL and the importance of adhering to the risk-need-responsivity principles. It was important that probation officers "buy in" to a theoretical view. The psychotherapy literature has long recognized the importance of an "explanation" for the problems of the patient and how these problems can be overcome (Wampold, 2007). In STICS, the first goal was to change the behavior of the probation officer, and the second was to have probation officers use the skills taught in training to change the behavior of their clients. Thus, probation officers needed an explanation as to why they should change their behaviors and how they can help their clients change.

The next module, which was very brief, was an overview of the risk principle. In the STICS evaluation, probation officers were asked to select only medium- and high-risk clients for the project. This structure ensured that minimal services were provided to low-risk probationers and more services directed to higher-risk clients.

The probation officers in the study used a validated risk/need assessment instrument (e.g., the LSI-R). This was important not only for assessing general risk but also for identifying the criminogenic needs to be targeted during supervision (e.g., procriminal attitudes, criminal associates, antisocial personality). Module 3 was on criminogenic needs, but Module 4 (antisocial attitudes) begins the core of the STICS protocol. Probation officers are taught to quickly recognize the expression of antisocial attitudes in their clients and how to help the probationers also recognize when they express antisocial thoughts. After all, you cannot change something if you do not recognize it as a problem. The first four modules of the training represented approximately three-fourths of the first day.

The responsivity modules had three components: (1) relationship building, (2) use of cognitive-behavioral techniques, and (3) attention to the particular learning style of the client. The power of rewards and punishments in situations of interpersonal influence resides in the relationship. A probation officer's ability to influence a client through the contingent delivery of a reward (e.g., words of praise, a smile) or a punishment (e.g., words of disapproval, a frown) depends upon the client having some respect and liking of the probation officer. To put it bluntly, if one does not care what the other thinks or feels, then one is free to act according to his or her own wishes. Relationship-building skills such as expressing warmth and respect and providing constructive feedback can be taught. Module 5 teaches the probation officers these skills, and they are practiced in exercises and role plays.

Having prepared the probation officers to recognize the importance of criminogenic needs, especially antisocial attitudes and the need to point this out to their clients within a respectful relationship, the next step is to exercise change in the appropriate direction. The structuring dimension of interpersonal influence begins on the second day of STICS training modules on the cognitive-behavioral model, cognitive restructuring, prosocial modeling, and the effective use of reinforcement

Resource Note 7.1 *(continued)*

and punishment. The challenge for the probation officers was that they were being asked to provide structured learning for their clients—to be interventionists in the positive sense. Many probation officers were much more comfortable with monitoring compliance to the probation conditions, advocating with social service agencies on their client's behalf and being supportive when clients were faced with distress and interpersonal problems.

On Days 2 and 3, probation officers were taught how to use cognitive-behavioral techniques with their clients one-on-one. What was critical in these modules was to teach the skills in a simple and concrete way so that the probation officers could, in turn, teach them to their clients. After all, probationers also need an "explanation" (i.e., a cognitive-behavioral theory) regarding what accounts for their problems and how they can use techniques derived from the model to change their own behavior.

Providing an "explanation" that is relevant to the probationers and persuading them that they need to change their procriminal attitudes was done in two steps. First, a simple cognitive-behavioral model, called the "Behavior Sequence," was taught. The Behavior Sequence model examines behavior as a function of antecedent stimuli, consequences, and attitudes, with an emphasis on how attitudes, or internal cognitive cues, are the root causes of behavior. Also demonstrated in the training were ways of teaching the Behavior Sequence model so that even a developmentally delayed client could understand how his or her thoughts lead to behavior. Second, probation officers were taught how to teach cognitive restructuring to their clients. Cognitive restructuring is a technique for replacing antisocial thoughts with prosocial thoughts. The theme throughout the cognitive-behavioral modules was to keep it concrete and make it relevant to

the wide range of clients (e.g., women, mentally disordered, racial minority) that are supervised by probation officers.

The three-day STICS training was delivered in a structured format (a training manual was used) with classroom exercises and role plays. Repetition is the hallmark of skill maintenance. However, practice during a three-day training program is not sufficient to maintain new behaviors over a period of weeks or months. One feature of STICS is that it included ongoing clinical supervision. After training, probation officers met in small groups on a monthly basis to discuss their use of STICS skills, and they teleconferenced with the trainers. Homework related to the skills taught in training was assigned to the groups and discussed in the meetings. During teleconferences, participants were given feedback on their homework, and clinical supervision was provided.

The overall purpose of STICS evaluation is to demonstrate that the key ingredients of the risk-need-responsivity (RNR) model can be successfully taught to probation officers and applied to their clients. Trotter (1996, 2006) showed that a few of the ingredients of the RNR model (i.e., prosocial modeling, collaborative goal-setting, and problem-solving) can be taught and applied with positive outcomes, but he did not train staff to target criminogenic needs nor was intervention aimed at medium- and high-risk offenders. Andrews and his colleagues (Andrews & Carvell, 1997; Dowden & Andrews, 2004) have described core correctional practices and, although training in these core correctional practices has been delivered, the training has not been formally evaluated. The evaluation of STICS fills these important gaps in research, and when the recidivism outcome findings become available they will shed further light on transferring "what works" into the real world.

Worth Remembering

1. Two factors that have a very strong influence on the decision to engage in criminal behavior are antisocial associates and attitudes.

   Antisocial associates provide opportunities to learn the techniques of crime and the learning of antisocial attitudes.

2. Poor parenting can lead the youth to antisocial associations and the learning of antisocial attitudes.

   Lack of parental monitoring and discipline allows the youth to associate with antisocial others without fear of censure from the parents. Poor emotional ties to the parents may further exacerbate the situation. Antisocial parents may also model and reinforce criminal behavior.

3. Gang membership enhances criminal behavior.

   Most individuals who join gangs already have a well-entrenched criminal propensity. However, being a gang member increases criminal behavior beyond what is expected from the individual.

4. Antisocial attitudes can be reliably measured and changed.

   Assessments of antisocial attitudes fall into three general categories: (1) Techniques of Neutralization, (2) Identification with Criminal Others, and (3) Rejection of Convention. A number of treatment programs have demonstrated that replacing antisocial attitudes with prosocial attitudes are associated with reduced recidivism.

Recommended Readings

Any of the classic writings on delinquent gangs is highly recommended. Sutherland (1939) may have been the first to highlight the importance of delinquent associations, but it was Cohen (1955) and Cloward and Ohlin (1960) who gave a face to it. Either book is easy to read—maybe short on empirical research but rich in narrative.

Shadd Maruna and Heith Copes's (2005) chapter in *The Crime and Justice* series gives a detailed and comprehensive review of Sykes and Matza's neutralization theory. They review the criminological roots of the theory and its present-day connection to cognitive psychology. In addition, they provide an excellent summary of the research and the issues that still need to be addressed.

Chapter 8

The Person in Social Context: Family, School, Work, Leisure/Recreation, Marital Attachments, and Neighborhood

The dominant and most theoretically relevant risk/need factors have been reviewed, and their causal significance in the PIC-R perspective has been surveyed. And, yes, we are once again going to review the causal process in cognitive social learning terms.

Antisocial attitudes, values, and beliefs suggest the standards that may be applied in personally mediated control. In assessing one's own behavior, the standards may be favorable to crime, unfavorable to crime, or neutral with reference to criminal activity. Antisocial cognition also includes negative cognitive-emotional states of resentment and feeling mistreated. These too may result in self-management that is favorable to crime. When antisocial cognitions are highly favorable or highly unfavorable to crime, their influence on behavior may even become relatively automatic and not require effortful self-regulation.

Antisocial associates suggest whether the reactions of others will tend to support noncriminal alternative behavior or to support criminal actions. Just thinking of the attitudinal position or even the person of another may automatically initiate mental processes supportive or not supportive of crime.

A history of antisocial behavior greatly increases the chances that self-efficacy beliefs will be highly favorable to crime and, of course, is a direct indicator of the habitual (automatic) strength of the criminal response. Antisocial personality pattern suggests a range of supports for criminal activity, including weak self-control generally and a tendency to feel mistreated by others. These traits may result in problematic circumstances in a variety of settings, including home, school, work, recreational facilities, and the other portions of the community. Problematic circumstances in such settings may greatly reduce the socialization value of those settings as well as the subtractive punishment of crime. If one is not regularly in receipt of a high density of rewards for noncriminal behavior in conventional settings, then the power of subtractive punishment of criminal behavior is greatly reduced. One is free to commit criminal acts: "Freedom is just another word for nothing left to lose" (Kristofferson, 1977).

In brief, the Big Four are the major causal factors. However, the contingencies in effect for criminal and noncriminal alternatives in the major behavioral settings of home and the broader community may greatly impact on the Big Four and have effects in interaction with the Big Four. In this chapter we explore family of origin, school/work, leisure/recreation, marital attachments, and neighborhoods as social setting variables. The research on family factors will be found to be the most highly developed, while that on marital circumstances and leisure/recreation is the least highly developed.

We will follow the PIC-R principles of relationship and structuring in the context of direct interpersonal influence. We will draw on the related principles of normative control and behavioral control in broader consideration of setting effects. Generally, what is the overall pattern of modeling and the reward and cost contingencies for criminal and noncriminal behavior within any setting? Are attitudes, association patterns, and behavior supportive of criminal behavior modeled, reinforced, punished, or ignored within the setting? Are real alternatives to antisocial styles of thinking, feeling, and acting modeled, reinforced, punished, or ignored? Have significant others entered into high-quality relationships with the person, and do the others have the structuring skills that are supportive of anticriminal learning? In any setting, what proportion of the "population" is involved in criminal activity?

Family of Origin

In Chapter 5 we described how biologically based factors may predispose one toward criminal behavior. Some people may be born with temperamental characteristics (e.g., impulsiveness, sensation-seeking, and negative emotionality) or neurological impairments that increase the risk for criminal behavior. This does not mean that these people are simply born bad. Perhaps the most important lesson from Chapter 5 is that the social environment can have an enormous effect on how our predispositions are expressed in behavior. The current chapter continues this lesson by exploring how the early socializing environment—the family—influences the development of criminal behavior.

We open our discussion with a review of social attachments, a concept that finds its beginnings in the caregiver-child relationship. There will be the distinct suggestion that the caregiver-child relationship may determine in part the quality of attachments formed in other social settings.

We then turn to a description of how family dynamics can profoundly influence the criminal trajectory of children. Parents can model and reinforce antisocial behaviors, sometimes inadvertently, and they can also model and reinforce prosocial behaviors. Parental affection, or the lack of it, can determine the child's motivation to please his or her parents. Finally, some of the more effective family interventions are described.

Learning to Care: The Parent-Child Relationship and the Development of Social Bonds

In Chapter 4 (covering the PIC-R perspective on criminal conduct), we explained that the probability of a behavior depends upon the number, variety, quality, and immediacy of rewards and costs for that behavior. In this section we will focus on the *quality* aspect of rewards and costs within the social context. That is, why are the rewards and costs delivered by some individuals so important to us? Why do we do things for only a smile or a word of praise? On the other hand, why do we inhibit some behavior in order to avoid a frown or a cold shoulder? The people around us can strongly influence our behavior, but it is clear that not everyone has the same level of influence over what we say and what we do.

The degree of interpersonal influence depends on the quality of the relationship between the giver and the receiver of rewards and costs. Travis Hirschi (1969) recognized the importance of this statement in his control theory (relationship bonds to the parents are central to his thesis). When the source of rewards and costs is a person who is highly valued, loved, and respected, then we attend to that person and care about that person's reactions to our behavior. Individuals who are poorly valued, unloved, and disrespected have little influence on our behavior. After all, why change for someone whom you do not like?

We all know adults who show great difficulty in establishing warm, friendly, enduring interpersonal relationships. They somehow lack the ability to form social attachments and are egocentric and uncaring individuals (Fonagy et al., 1997; van IJzendoorn, 1997). Certainly, some temperamental qualities (e.g., introversion, extreme cautiousness, callous-unemotional) may contribute to difficulties in forming positive social relationships, but social conditioning factors are also important. Most theorists and researchers look to the family context and attachment to parental figures as the prototype for all future social relationships.

Attachment theory has its roots in the work of John Bowlby (1971, 1988). Most children, beginning around 10 months of age and extending to 18 months or so, become emotionally distressed when separated from the parent. Bowlby saw this reaction (i.e., "separation anxiety") as an indication that the child had established an attachment to the parent. Originally, Bowlby thought that it was an attachment to the mother that was critical, but later (1988) he modified his view to include any consistent caregiver. In Bowlby's view, the critical function of attachment was that it provided the infant the security needed to explore the environment and develop independence. The mother/caregiver was the safe haven to return to when the world became frightening. Ideally, a healthy caregiver-child attachment needed to be established within the first two years of life in order to serve as a positive template for future social attachments.

With the parent-child bond as the building block for future inter-personal relationships, disruption of the bond was thought to herald difficulties in attachment to other adults, peers, and symbols of authority (teachers, employers, the social order, etc.). Thus, Bowlby's work focused upon analyzing what happened when a mother-child bond was disrupted, even briefly. One result is detachment (a lack of interest in the adult). Bowlby (1971) contended that lengthy and frequent disruptions would lead to a situation in which children "stop altogether attaching (them-selves) to anyone" (p. 50) and develop a "superficial sociability."

One way of examining the effects of disruptions of the parent-child bond is to study the impact of divorce on children. Studies of "broken homes" resulting from divorce (rather than parental death) show small to moderate relationships with future delinquency. Meta-analytic reviews have reported correlations between parental divorce and delinquency ranging from .12 to .23 (Amato, 2001; Leschied, Chiodo, Nowicki & Rodger, 2008; Wells & Rankin, 1991).

What are some of the factors that may mediate the relationship between broken homes and delinquency? A number of mediating mecha-nisms have been suggested. First, the antisocial behavior of children of divorce may be explained by inheritability of antisocial pathology of the parents. However, an analysis of 610 adoptive and biological children of divorce found no evidence for a genetic effect (Burt, Barnes, McGue & Iacono, 2008). Second, there may be differences in the children's behavior depending on whether there were "messy divorces" or "amicable separations." The available evidence suggests that the difficulties experienced by the children are more the result of the emotional conflicts within separating families than separation from a parent per se (Haas et al., 2004; Juby & Farrington, 2001). A third factor may be traced to the nature of the relationship with the parent following divorce. Whiteside and Becker's (2000) review of 12 studies on the effects of divorce for children under the age of five found that children who continued to have a positive relationship with their father were less likely to have "externalizing symptoms." In a study of more than 16,000 adolescents including nearly 7,000 youths from broken families, Demuth and Brown (2004) found the highest delinquency rates among youths who lived in single-father families. However, once the father-child relationship was taken into account, the high rates disappeared. That is, if the father maintained warm relations with the child, then the child was no more likely to be delinquent than a child from an intact family. On the other hand, an antisocial single father caring for the child creates a "double whammy" of genetic and environ-mental risk for future problems (Jaffee, Moffitt, Caspi & Taylor, 2003).

A positive parent-child relationship within a single-parent family can be a protective factor against delinquency, but it may not be as strong a protection as in a family in which there are two parents sharing a healthy relationship with the child. Hirschi (1969) suggested that a strong bond with at least one parent would protect the child from delinquency, but an analysis of the National Survey of Youth database by Joseph Rankin and Roger Kern (1994) found that a positive attachment to the caregiver in the single-parent family could not replace positive attachments to two parents in intact families. Others (Cookston, 1999; Demuth & Brown, 2004; Griffin et al., 2000) have reported similar results.

The importance of *when* the bond is disrupted was raised by Bowlby, who predicted that disruption of the parent-child bond at an early age would be more detrimental than at a later age. The evidence on this issue is mixed. Hirschi (1969) found that age at separation (before or after the age of five) was unrelated to delinquency. Mark Lipsey and James Derzon (1998) could not locate enough studies of children prior to age six to which they could apply meta-analytic techniques. They were able to compare studies of "broken homes" experienced between the ages of six and 11 to those of separations between the ages of 12 and 14. At the younger age, the average effect size for violent behavior was .06; it was .10 for the older children (the differences were not significant). However, Rebellon (2002) found that earlier parental divorce/separation was related to violent and nonviolent delinquency and offered an explanation for the relationship that is consistent with cognitive social learning theory. He used longitudinal data from the National Youth Survey (*n* = 1,725 adolescents). What is important about this data set is that it includes a variety of measures on family functioning, peer associations, and conventional beliefs. Rebellon's (2002) analyses suggested that early family disruption may provide earlier opportunities for the youth to associate with antisocial peers and learn antisocial attitudes.

Another potentially relevant variable is the *frequency* of disruptions between the child and the caregiver. Even a casual reading of crime stories in the local newspaper will reveal descriptions of offenders who went from foster home to foster home and institution to institution as they were growing up. Bowlby hypothesized that frequent disruptions will lead the child to avoid any attachment to adults and avoid "any risk of allowing our hearts to be broken again." It appears that when frequency of disruptions in child-caregiver attachments is added to the mix, we have the makings of the life-course-persistent offender so neatly described by Moffitt.

Drawing upon data from three longitudinal studies, Thornberry and his colleagues (Thornberry et al., 1999) found that 90 percent of youths who endured five or more disruptions engaged in criminal behavior. Rolf Loeber and his colleagues (Loeber et al., 2005) followed more than 1,500 boys from childhood into adulthood (30 years of age). Children who experienced two or more caregivers before the age of 10 were almost twice more likely to commit a violent offense than children without this experience. In an incarcerated sample, youths with a history of foster care were four times more likely to follow a life-course-persistent trajectory than youths without a history of foster care (Alltucker, Bullis, Close & Yovanoff, 2006). Interestingly, Ryan and Testa (2005) found in their sample of children removed from homes because of maltreatment that the frequency of disruptions was a risk factor for boys but not for girls. Boys with four or more home placements had a delinquency rate of 21 percent, compared to 12 percent for those with no change in placement. The comparable rates for girls were 7 percent and 6 percent.

A final comment concerns the association between parent-child attachment and later peer attachment. Recall that Bowlby saw the parent-child attachment as the prototype to future attachments with non-caregivers. In other words, if you mess up with your parents, you run the risk of messing up with your friends. In fact, there is some evidence that successful peer relations are related to positive attachments to the parent. For example, a meta-analysis of 63 studies found an average effect size of .20 between attachment to mother and successful peer relations (Schneider, Atkinson & Tardif, 2001). Fonagy and colleagues (1997) hypothesized that adolescence is a particularly important time, as there is a fundamental shift from the importance of the parent-child bond to more general adult and social bonds. There is a "moment of detachment when neither old [nor] new (attachment) patterns are fully active" (p. 241). This "moment of detachment" is a normal process, but it also represents a point when parental controls are loosened, possibly giving rise to adolescence-limited delinquency. Correspondingly, the hypothesis would suggest that a transition to new prosocial attachments is an important factor in desistance (Born, Chevalier & Humblet, 1997; Piquero, Brezina & Turner, 2005). Building social relationships and really caring about others may find its origins in the attachment patterns within the caregiver-child relationship, but the parents' role in producing delinquency goes beyond providing emotional warmth and security. Positive relationships between parents and their children are important, but so are parenting practices.

The Family and Delinquency

Few would dispute the statement that parents have an enormous influence on the child. As with any interpersonal source of influence described in PIC-R, parental influence also operates along the relationship and structuring dimensions. A negative parent-child relationship can arouse hostile emotions and lead to antisocial behavior (Dembo et al., 1998; Haapasalo & Pokela, 1999; Rohner, 2004; Smith & Thornberry, 1995; Widom & Maxfield, 2001). The parents also have a role to teach and instill prosocial norms, values, and beliefs, as well as the skills to succeed in society. Failure to model prosocial behavior, poor monitoring, and inconsistent discipline are critical in this regard.

The relationship and structuring dimensions are often difficult to separate in a particular study, which prevents us from assessing the relative importance of each. Our outline of the two dimensions is meant to organize the literature around the PIC-R perspective. Families that promote prosocial norms and are characterized by warm emotional attachments are predicted to have the lowest rates of delinquency. Families that fail to provide training in social conventions and are characterized by weak affective bonds would be expected to have the highest rates of delinquency. Finally, families may show other combinations of the structuring and affective dimensions (e.g., high prosocial norms and low attachment), with delinquency outcomes in the middle range.

Family Interventions and the Reduction of Delinquent Behavior

Every single longitudinal study of delinquency has found poor emotional relationships within the family and inconsistent monitoring and disciplining of the children predictive of antisocial behavior (e.g., Johnson et al., 2004; Leschied et al., 2008; Loeber et al., 2005). The reader has already seen much of the evidence in previous chapters. At this point, we jump directly to reviewing what can be done at the family level to prevent further crime.

In general, parental and family treatment programs have a positive impact on problem and delinquent behavior. Some programs focus on primary prevention. For example, an intervention aimed at high-risk seven-year-old boys from the Montreal Longitudinal Experimental Study found lower crime rates at age 24 (21.7%) for the treatment group compared to the control group (32.6%; Boisjoli, Vitaro, Lacourse, Barker & Tremblay, 2007). A meta-analytic review of 55 early interventions targeting children less than five years old reported a 22 percent reduction in antisocial behavior (Piquero, Farrington, Welsh, Tremblay & Jennings, 2009). Other meta-analytic reviews of the family intervention literature have found mean effect estimates ranging from an r of .15 (Latimer, 2001) to an r of .21 (Gordon et al., 1992) and r of .22 (Waldron & Turner, 2008). Furthermore, within these reviews, treatments that used behavioral methods yielded significantly greater reductions in recidivism than did less structured and less directive treatments of the psychodynamic or client-centered variety. Descriptions of the more effective family therapies follow.

Oregon Social Learning Center Program. Gerald Patterson and his colleagues in Oregon have focused on conduct-disordered and hyper-active children and their families. In their theoretical model, coercive family processes are central (Granic & Patterson, 2006; Patterson, 1982, 1997). Children learn at a very young age that behaving in an aversive and annoying manner results in reinforcement—for example, when the parent gives in to the child's temper tantrum. The parent not only rewards bad behavior but, by doing so ensures that the next time the child's inappropriate behavior will escalate. Thus, treatment focused on disrupting the coercive cycle by teaching parents to reinforce positive behavior and to ignore negative behavior.

The Oregon treatment program has been quite successful in changing family interactions and parental disciplining practices. Most of the studies have been with families of very young children, but there are a few that have targeted adolescents. A study by Bank, Marlowe, Reid, Patterson, and Weinrott (1991) randomly assigned delinquents (average age of 14) to the Oregon Social Learning Center (OSLC) treatment ($n = 28$) and to a community treatment program ($n = 27$). While in treatment, the OSLC group showed significantly less delinquent activity than the control subjects, but the differences disappeared over the course of a three-year post-program follow-up. The only enduring difference was that the OSLC treatment group spent fewer days incarcerated, producing an estimated cost savings of $100,000.

The failure of this structured behavioral program to decrease long-term recidivism is puzzling and not at all in line with the findings of other behavioral approaches. Patricia Chamberlain (2003) suggested that for extremely dysfunctional families with chronic delinquents, treatment might better be conducted in foster homes and residential settings. Consequently, researchers at the Oregon Social Learning Center began to develop a highly structured program for adolescents removed from their homes because of the delinquency. This program is called Multidimensional Treatment Foster Care (MTFC; Chamberlain, 2003).

MTFC provides family therapy and social skills training for the foster and biological parents, individual therapy for the children, and consultations with school teachers and probation and parole officers. This comprehensive approach to intervention is also characteristic of Multisystemic Therapy, which is to be discussed later. In a random assignment study of chronic male delinquents (average of 12.6 prior charges), the adolescents in the MTFC had fewer contacts with the criminal justice system one year later than the control group members who were placed in group homes (Chamberlain & Reid, 1998). A subsequent two-year follow-up found that only 5 percent of the MTFC participants had two or more criminal justice contacts compared to 24 percent of the control group participants (Eddy, Whaley & Chamberlain, 2004).

The effectiveness of MTFC has been replicated with female delinquents. Eighty-one adolescent girls with an average of nearly 12 prior criminal justice system contacts were randomly assigned to MTFC or regular group home placement (Leve, Chamberlain & Reid, 2005).

At one year after completion of the program, the MTFC participants had 42 percent fewer criminal justice contacts than the control group girls. This gain for the treatment group was maintained at the two-year follow-up (Chamberlain, Leve & DeGarmo, 2007). Interestingly, two evaluations of the MTFC program also found decreases in associations with delinquent and antisocial peers (DeGarmo & Forgatch, 2005; Leve & Chamberlain, 2005). That is, the MTFC may work not only by helping caregivers to reward and punish the child's behavior appropriately and to get out of the coercive cycle but also by altering peer associations.

Functional Family Therapy. The Oregon group's intervention program emphasizes the normative dimension (monitoring and disciplining). The approach adopted by James Alexander and his Utah colleagues is to target the relationship dimension as well. Functional Family Therapy (FFT; Barton & Alexander, 1980) tries to improve family relationships by changing family communication patterns. Their early work showed that delinquent families show a lot of "defensive communication" (i.e., harsh and angry communications, being highly critical, etc.) and little "supportive communications" (i.e., being empathic, providing helpful information, waiting until the other person is finished talking before interrupting). Hopefully, the reader sees that the communication patterns of reciprocal, supportive communications would facilitate warm emotional relationships among family members.

Based on these observations, the Utah group taught family members to use less defensive communication and more reciprocal supportive communication. Training in more effective communication was then integrated with training in parenting techniques similar to the approach used by the OSLC (i.e., rewarding positive behavior from the child and ignoring/discouraging negative behaviors). Evaluations of FFT with delinquents have been consistently positive.

In the first outcome study, families were randomly assigned to one of four groups (Alexander & Barton, 1976; Alexander & Parsons, 1973). All of the families had a child, ranging in age from 13 to 16 years, who was involved in relatively minor delinquent activity (e.g., runaway, truant, "ungovernable"). In addition to the FFT group, there were two other treatment groups (client-centered family therapy and psychodynamic-oriented family therapy) and a no-treatment control group. The client-centered program was nondirective and focused on family feelings. In psychodynamic family therapy, the goal of treatment was described as providing "insight."

By the end of treatment, the FFT group showed more supportive communications and less defensive communications. Parents also learned better behavioral techniques of reinforcing their child's behavior. As Table 8.1 shows, these intermediate targets translated to decreases in delinquent behavior. A second FFT group was later added, replicating the initial results (Alexander & Barton, 1976). The FFT group showed a

Table 8.1
Family Intervention and Recidivism

Group	N	% Recidivated
FFT: 1st group	46	26
2nd group	45	27
Client-centered	19	47
Psychodynamic	11	73
No Treatment	46	48

Adapted from Alexander & Parsons, 1973; Alexander & Barton, 1976

recidivism rate that was one-half the rate for those receiving no treatment. The client-centered treatment had no impact on future delinquent behavior, and the psychodynamic, insight approach actually increased the recidivism rate (73%).

FFT adheres to a family systems model. As a system, whatever happens to one family member also has an effect on other family members. (If mother is not happy, then no one is happy.) Herein is the strength of a system model of intervention. Changes in behavior can be seen not only in the child that first brought the family to the attention of the therapist but also in the siblings of the target children. Nanci Klein, James Alexander, and Bruce Parsons (1977) searched juvenile court records and found that for the no-treatment control group, 40 percent of the siblings had official court records. The recidivism rate for the siblings in the client-centered group was 59 percent; for the psychodynamic group it was 63 percent. The rate for the FFT group was 20 percent.

Finally, Barton, Alexander, Waldron, Turner, and Warburton (1985) provided FFT to 30 families of "hard-core" incarcerated delinquents (an average history of 22 offenses). For some families, the therapy started in the institution prior to the release of the youth to the family. This group was compared to 44 offenders from the same training school who attended various community treatment programs. The two groups were matched for age, educational level, ethnicity, and the severity and number of prior offenses. At a 15-month follow-up, 60 percent of the FFT group and 93 percent of the comparison group had received additional charges. Furthermore, for the recidivists, the number of new offenses was less for the FFT group (there was no difference in terms of severity).

Most of the early FFT evaluations were limited to Utah, where the majority of the subjects came from a middle-class community that is 70 percent Mormon. However, FFT has been shown to be effective elsewhere (Gordon, 1995; Gordon, Jurkovic & Arbuthnot, 1998). For example, FFT was provided to families of delinquents from a rural and depressed area of Ohio (Gordon et al., 1988). A 28-month follow-up found a recidivism rate of 11 percent for the treated delinquents and 67 percent for a nontreated probation sample. An extended three-year follow-up of these youths into adulthood yielded an 8.4 percent conviction rate for the treated sample and 40.9 percent for the control group (Gordon, Graves & Arbuthnot, 1995). In a review of FFT programs offered in the state of Washington, FFT delivered by competent therapists showed a 38 percent reduction in recidivism. However, FFT delivered by therapists judged to be incompetent showed a 17 percent increase in recidivism (Washington State Institute for Public Policy, 2004).

Recall that the client-centered and psychodynamic interventions were ineffective. We suspect it is because these therapeutic approaches rely too much on the client-therapist relationship and avoid direct training of prosocial skills. However, this does not mean that we ignore the relationship dimension and focus only on training parents in behavioral parenting techniques. Many parents of delinquents are often unhappy with their relationships, and this could interfere with effective monitoring and supervision of the children (e.g., Griffin et al., 2000). Therefore, both improving the marital relationship and teaching appropriate parenting skills are needed (Dadds, Schwartz & Sanders, 1987).

Multisystemic Therapy. Our final example of an effective family treatment program is Multisystemic Therapy (MST), developed by Scott Henggeler and his colleagues at the Medical University of South Carolina (Culpit, Henggeler, Tayor & Addison, 2005; Henggeler et al., 1998; Swenson, Henggeler & Schoenwald, 2001). MST was originally designed to deal with the more serious delinquent. At its core is a family therapy component ("family preservation") that teaches parents the skills needed to deal with adolescent problems (normative) and to reduce conflict within the family (relationship). Like the Multidimensional Treatment Foster Care program of the Oregon group, MST enlists the school, peers, and other key community agents in order to maintain the benefits of treatment (see Resource Note 8.1).

Resource Note 8.1

Theory and Application to Practice
Multisystemic Therapy
(Henggeler et al., 1998)

Multisystemic therapy (MST) has been widely disseminated and studied as an intervention for high-risk delinquents. Much of the success of MST in changing the behavior of difficult youths may be due to the comprehensive nature of the intervention. Scott Henggeler and his colleagues have drawn heavily on family systems and social ecolog-ical theories. The individual is part of a broad social context that includes family, peers, school, and community. This approach is consistent with the theoretical formulations of PIC-R. The effective interventions predicted from both models are similar. That is, high-risk individuals with many needs require multiple interventions that change the

Resource Note 8.1 *(continued)*

reward-cost contingencies associated with antisocial behavior.

MST attempts to promote positive changes in the family both through direct intervention and arranging community supports that help families maintain the benefits of family therapy. Youths are given assistance with school performance and social adjustment, including the development of prosocial friends. Finally, individual counseling is provided to meet the unique needs presented by the delinquent. All of these services are given in a highly professional context with extraordinary efforts to maintain treatment integrity.

At the family level, therapists work directly with families, observing their interactions. Strengths are noted and serve as building blocks to more effective family functioning. The family is viewed as a social system in which changes in one family member can alter the behavior of the other members. Family members are often asked to monitor their behaviors and the behaviors of other family members. After the initial assessment stage, parents are taught to change their discipline strategies and use rewards and punishments more effectively. MST therapists are also especially attentive to the personal problems that parent(s) may have. If a psychiatric disorder is evident, for

example, then the appropriate community treatment is secured. If the parent needs help in monitoring a child, then a neighbor may be enlisted to help. The value of community resources in helping families is taken very seriously by MST.

As the therapist works with the family, efforts are made to diminish associations with deviant peers. Therapists try to understand issues of prosocial peer rejection and teach parents to monitor their children's social interactions. Parents are taught to communicate more effectively to their children the harm that results from antisocial peer associations (e.g., they should not berate the child's delinquent peers, as it may only harden the child's resolve to associate with them). During individual counseling with the child, discussion of peers and the teaching of interpersonal skills are common.

The school is an important part of the social ecology of the high-risk delinquent. The youth is given assistance with academics, parents are supported in monitoring their children's school activities, and teachers are enlisted as agents of change. MST leaves no stone unturned in identifying the immediate social and community supports that can increase the rewards for prosocial behavior and interfere with the social forces that support antisocial activity.

In a carefully controlled evaluation, families with adolescents who had at least two prior arrests were randomly assigned to either MST or individual therapy (Borduin et al., 1995). The individual therapy was a mix of behavioral, client-centered, and psychodynamic therapies. The MST therapists had a minimum of two months training and received three hours of supervision per week, reflecting a high degree of program integrity. MST produced decreases in adolescent problem behavior and improved family relationships, whereas no such change was found for the individual therapy group. A four-year follow-up found recidivism rates of 26.1 percent for MST and 71.4 percent for individual therapy. A subsequent 13-year follow-up found that the treatment gains remained (Schaeffer & Borduin, 2005). The recidivism rate for the MST youths, who were now, on average, 28 years old, was 50 percent, and the recidivism rate for the individual therapy group was 81 percent.

MST has been applied to a variety of problems, including drug use (Borduin et al., 1995; Henggeler et al., 2002, 2006), violent and serious felonies (Henggeler, Melton & Smith, 1992; Henggeler et al., 1993), child abuse (Henggeler et al., 1998), and adolescent sex offenders (Borduin et al., 1990; Borduin, Schaeffer & Heiblum, 2009). A meta-analytic review of seven MST studies found a moderately large effect on delinquency reduction (Curtis, Ronan & Borduin, 2004). Most of the evaluations have been positive but not all. One evaluation of MST with high-risk youths in Canada showed no differences between the MST group and a group that received the usual services (Leschied & Cunningham, 2002). However, the problem may have been with difficulties implementing the program (Leschied, personal communication, January 31, 2006). Recall from the FFT discussion that poorly trained therapists were actually associated with increases in recidivism. In most evaluations of MST, the South Carolina group was directly involved in overseeing the programs and conducting the evaluations, thereby ensuring integrity of treatment delivery. In a review of MST in the state of Washington, implementation problems were so profound that no conclusions could be drawn. A test of MST in Sweden essentially failed because of problems in maintaining treatment fidelity (Sundell, Hansson, Löfholm, Olsson et al., 2008). Although further research is needed to understand whether MST can be properly implemented by program providers who are independent of the originators of MST, there are some promising developments. Timmons-Mitchell and her colleagues (Timmons-Mitchell, Bender, Kishna & Mitchell, 2006) randomly assigned juvenile offenders to MST or a treatment as usual condition. The MST was delivered by staff without oversight from the Scott Henggeler's group. An 18-month follow-up found a 67 percent rearrest rate for the MST group and 87 percent for the control group.

The RNR Model and Effective Family Therapy. The importance of the specific intermediate targets of change in the context of family counseling cannot be underestimated. The Carleton University meta-analytic databank was briefly described in Chapter 2 and will be reviewed in detail in Chapter 11. This databank examines the effect of treatment on recidivism in 374 tests, each involving a treatment group and a comparison group. Recall that the difference in the recidivism rates found in the two groups is a measure of effect size (often quantified as a Pearson correlation coefficient). In the total of 374 tests, the overall mean effect size was .08. Using the Binomial Effect Size Display, this translates to a 54 percent mean recidivism rate in the 374 control groups [(50 + 8)/2], compared to a 46 percent mean recidivism rate in the 374 treatment groups [(50 − 8)/2]—that is, a difference of eight percentage points (54 − 46 = 8).

Recall, that two major risk factors in the family sphere are poor parental relationship with offspring (e.g., nurturance/caring) and poor parental structuring skills (e.g., monitoring/supervision). Both are dynamic risk factors (or criminogenic needs) and hence are reasonable intermediate targets for change if reduced reoffending is an ultimate objective of programming.

Twenty-four of the 374 tests of treatment involved a family therapy program that targeted enhanced quality of relationship between parents and the child. The mean effect size in these 24 tests was .32 (95% CI = .24 to .40), reflecting, on average, a recidivism rate of 66 percent in the control group, compared to 34 percent in the treatment group—a 32 percentage point difference favoring treatments that targeted parent-child relationships. Seventeen tests involved family therapy programs that targeted enhanced monitoring and supervision of the young people. The mean effect size was an impressive .33 (95% CI = .30 to .49). The 11 tests that involved family therapy that targeted *both* affection and supervision yielded an extraordinary mean effect size of .42 (CI = .30 to .53).

Indeed, the mean effect size for 23 tests of family therapy that set intermediate targets of change other than parental relationship and/or structuring skills was .02 (95% CI = −.08 to .11). Other family variables that were targeted included anxiety, depression, low self-esteem, and/or other noncriminogenic factors. The value of .02 is no different from a zero effect (note that the confidence interval contains .00). The lesson is an important reminder of the need principle of effective correctional treatment: if an objective is reduced reoffending, then seriously consider targeting the major criminogenic need factors.

The need principle is only one of the three key principles of effective correctional treatment (as introduced in Chapter 2 and to be developed more fully in Chapters 10, 11, and 12). There are also the risk principle and the principle of general responsivity. Adherence to the risk principle (R) involves delivering services to higher rather than lower-risk cases. Adherence to the need principle (N) minimally requires that the number of criminogenic needs set as intermediate targets must exceed the number of noncriminogenic needs targeted. Adherence to general responsivity (R) requires that social learning and cognitive behavioral strategies be employed (that is, modeling reinforcement, role playing, skill building, etc.). The overall measure of adherence to RNR ranges from "0" to "3." A score of "0" indicates total nonadherence. A score of "1" indicates that the program is in adherence with at least one of RNR. A score of "3" indicates adherence to each of RNR.

Table 8.2 reveals how mean effect size varied with adherence to RNR for the family counseling programs. Inspection reveals that family counseling not in adherence with RNR does not work, but family programs in adherence with RNR reduced reoffending. We are unaware of any systematic evidence that the effect of family therapy that is in

Table 8.2
Mean Effect Size (*r*) by Level of RNR Adherence for Family, Academic and Vocational Programs (k = number of tests of treatment)

Level of RNR Adherence Program Type	0 (k) None	1 (k)	2 (k)	3 (k) Full ES	*r* with
Family Therapy	−.02 (6)	.06 (18)	.22 (17)	.40 (17)	.63
Academic	.03 (6)	.07 (20)	.20 (31)	.32 (15)	.47
Vocational	−.05 (5)	.05 (13)	.20 (16)	.38 (10)	.68

ES = Effect Size

adherence with RNR varies by gender, race/ethnicity, or socioeconomic circumstances of the families. Fortunately, for young people cut off from their biological parents, there is no reason to believe that comprehensive programs cannot be delivered with foster parents or other caregivers (see the economic benefits of Multidimensional Treatment Foster Care, as described by the Washington State Institute for Public Policy, Aos et al., 2001; this program was described above).

Summary. There are three important conclusions that we can draw from the family intervention studies. First, both the structuring and relationship dimensions are important.

Second, behavioral treatment approaches can change family interactions along the structuring and relationship dimensions, and these changes are associated with decreases in delinquent behavior. Improved family functioning and relationships through planned family interventions have also demonstrated decreased delinquent peer associations (DeGarmo & Forgatch, 2005; Huey et al., 2000; Leve & Chamberlain, 2005). There is absolutely no evidence that nondirective, insight-oriented, and cathartic interventions work with distressed families, any more than there is evidence that intrusive and insensitive introduction of behavioral technologies work. The effective family intervention programs all share a common, cognitive-behavioral, skills-oriented approach, and they are delivered by skilled therapists who establish high-quality relationships with family members.

Finally, the reasons for the success of family programs go beyond attention to relevant intermediate targets and the relationship and structuring dimensions of interpersonal influence. They each involve detailed attention to program integrity. The most effective programs have smaller samples where the intervention can be more easily implemented and monitored (Piquero et al., 2009). They are all closely tied to university-based training and research units that work from a relevant theoretical model and provide systematic training and supervision of therapists according to that model (Edwards et al., 2001; Huey et al., 2000). These programs take extraordinary steps to minimize treatment dropout rates by going to the home (Gordon, 1995), enlisting foster parents (Chamberlain, 2003), involving teachers and peers (Henggeler et al.,

1998), and forming strong relationships between the therapist and family members (Robbins et al., 2003). Program effectiveness depends upon appropriate and intensive strategies being carried out with integrity.

School

Relatively low levels of academic achievement are risk factors for criminal behavior, and their predictive validity persists into adulthood. But the predictive validity of indices of achievement pale in comparison to the predictive levels achieved by assessments of misconduct problems in school. The latter, for the most part, reflect the predispositions suggested by an early history of antisocial behavior, by antisocial personality pattern, and most likely by antisocial attitudes among older students. A well-established but relatively minor risk factor for criminal behavior is low verbal intelligence, and it is a stronger predictor of poor school performance than it is of antisocial behavior. Indeed, and let there be no doubt about it, a major predictor of poor academic and vocational achievement into late adolescence and adulthood is an early history of antisocial behavior. In an analysis of more than 8,000 youths, dropping out of school had no effect on delinquency after controlling for antisocial behavior and trouble in school (Sweeten, Bushway & Paternoster, 2009). In brief, early-onset antisocial behavior comes before poor academic performance.

It is somewhat sad that the work of Glueck and Glueck (1950), conducted in the 1940s, remains one of the most careful analyses of school-related issues and criminal behavior. Recall from Chapter 3 that their young delinquent males tended to achieve poor grades, were persistently truant, and were misbehaving from the early grades. Particularly interesting were the delinquent boys' reasons for disliking school. They reported resenting the restrictions and controls imposed at school and a distinct lack of interest in studying. It was the nondelinquent boys, not the delinquent boys, who disliked school because of reported learning difficulties or feelings of inferiority.

Robert Agnew (2001:158–161) provided a particularly valuable list of the characteristics of schools that link with the delinquency of their students. What are the correlates of school differences in delinquency? Rates of delinquency are higher in schools with higher percentages of students who are poor, male, and members of minority groups. Unfortunately, schools have not been characterized by student scores on assessments of the Central Eight because that would likely eliminate or greatly reduce the effects of demographic characteristics. Most interestingly, Agnew summarizes the school differences by reference to what we call the relationship and structuring principles. He calls the lower-delinquency schools "warm but firm" schools and thereby links effective schools with effective families:

> . . . the schools with the lowest rates of delinquency are firm on the one hand: they have clear rules that are uniformly enforced and they are academically demanding. On the other hand, they are "warm"; they treat students in a fair manner, teachers are interested in students, provide opportunities for success, and praise student accomplishments; and school staff attempt to create a pleasant environment for the students (Agnew, 2001:161).

Thinking in theoretical terms, Robert Agnew comments that such schools reduce strain for students (general strain theory), enhance social bonds (social control theory), and foster anticriminal reward and cost contingencies (social learning theory).

Can changes in school performance (academic achievement) and changes in attachment to school (to conventional activities and conventional others such as fellow students and teachers) influence criminal activity? Our theoretical answer is yes, if the school-based change actually produces changes in the actual density of rewards and costs relevant to criminal behavior. Recall that some early intervention programs with preschoolers that also paid appropriate attention to caregivers had effects on enhanced school performance in the future and on reduced future delinquency (Chapter 5).

Within juvenile and adult corrections, the evidence is promising regarding the value of educational programming with regard to effects on criminal behavior. Mark Lipsey and David Wilson (1998) described the effects of academic programs on young people as generally positive but small. Assuming a 50 percent recidivism rate in the comparison group, Adult Basic Education and General Equivalency Diploma participants had recidivism rates of 46 percent and 40 percent, respectively (Wilson, Gallagher, Coggeshall & MacKenzie, 1999). Participation in post-secondary education was associated with a recidivism rate of 36 percent, relative to 50 percent of the comparison offenders. In a recent meta-analysis of 20 correctional programs, Terri Simon and Stephan Wormith (2008) found a mean effect size of $r = .10$ (converted from their reported OR = .70). Although the reviews of educational programming have been positive, they are small in comparison to interventions that target more robust criminogenic needs (e.g., antisocial attitudes, drug abuse). What remains unclear is that the positive effect might well be based on lower-risk cases choosing to participate in advanced education programs.

School-based programs focusing on problematic/antisocial behavior in schools have reduced antisocial behavior among participants and particularly with higher-risk students (Wilson & Lipsey, 2007; Wilson,

Lipsey & Derzon, 2003). In an update of their earlier meta-analysis (Wilson et al., 2003), Sandra Jo Wilson and Mark Lipsey (2007) reviewed 399 school-based interventions on a variety of outcomes ranging from academic performance to aggressive and problematic behaviors. Interventions aimed at reducing problem behaviors such as fighting and rebelliousness were effective in reducing these outcomes particularly, and consistent with the risk principle of effective treatment, for higher-risk students. In addition, behavioral strategies were more effective than other treatment modalities (e.g., social problem solving, counseling).

A focus on school-related issues was associated with reduced offending within the Carleton University meta-analytic databank (recall the overview of treatment effectiveness in Chapter 2). In 72 tests, the mean effect size of programs that targeted the area of academics and school was .17 (CI = .13 to .22), which is clearly better than zero effect and indeed better than the overall average effect of .08 in the 374 total number of tests. The data do not allow us to explore actual effects on the academic and school-based targets of performance and bonding. However, we can explore how adherence to the principles of risk, need, and general responsivity impacted on mean effect size of school-related treatments. Inspection of Table 8.2 reveals that, just as in the case of family programming, the only academic/school programs that worked were those in adherence with RNR.

Once again, we are unaware of any evidence that school-related programs in adherence with RNR are differentially effective across considerations of age, gender, race/ethnicity, or social class (see also Wilson & Lipsey, 2007). However, certain social facts are so stunning that they must be noted. What we have in mind is the extraordinary incarceration rates of young black men who fail to complete high school in the United States (Pettit & Western, 2004). Among non-Hispanic American men born between 1965 and 1969, 3 percent of whites and 20 percent of blacks served penal time by their early thirties. Among high school dropouts, nearly 60 percent of the black men had been incarcerated by 1999. The corresponding figure for white male high school dropouts was 11 percent. Clearly, at the nexus of age, gender, and educational achievement, incarceration has become part of the life course for young poorly educated black men in America. In our opinion, variation on the Central Eight can account for a majority of the effects of age, gender, race, and class on crime. Statistics such as those noted immediately above, however, raise serious questions not only about the sources of variation in offending but also the impact of variation in the processing of crime and criminals.

Work

Work is part of being an adult for many people. Seeking work is also a reality for many unemployed adults. Not surprisingly most of this section deals with adults. However, work is also an issue for a large number of young people. Referring to U.S. data, Robert Agnew (2001) estimates that 90 percent of high school students work at some time, and 80 percent at some time work during the school year. It is his impression that the research evidence reveals a small criminogenic effect of work on the part of young people. The money and time away from home and the schoolyard are thought to support additional drug use and minor delinquency. The finding recalls that of Cullen and colleagues (Cullen, Larson & Mathers, 1985; Wright, Cullen & Williams, 1997) regarding the positive link between money-in-the-pocket and delinquency. That is, how much money do you have on your person at this moment? And does the probability of you engaging in antisocial behavior vary with the amount of money to which you have access?

Unlike class of origin, level of education, level of employment, and money earned (all combining to constitute socioeconomic class of achievement) are all mid-level risk factors for criminal behavior. Still, stability of employment is a stronger risk factor than is level of unemployment. In particular, criminal behavior increases with frequent unemployment and longer periods of unemployment. In Chapter 2, we very briefly described an offender risk instrument called the LSI-R and the LS/CMI. The instrument has an Education/Employment subcomponent that includes direct ratings of the rewards and satisfactions associated with employment and with relationships with fellow employees and the boss or supervisor. Based upon a number of studies, the mean predictive validity (mean r) between this subcomponent and reoffending was a substantial .28.

Vocational training and correctional industries are classic elements of correctional programming. In their review of such programs, Wilson, Gallagher et al. (2006) found a recidivism rate of 44 percent for work in correctional industries and a rate of 39 percent for vocational training (the rate was 50% in the comparison conditions). Again, however, the results are threatened by selection bias. In their meta-analytic study of programs for young offenders, Lipsey and Wilson (1998) found vocational programs to consistently show weak or null effects.

The Carleton University databank includes 44 tests of vocational programs. The mean effect size of these 44 tests was .18 (CI = .12 to .24). Inspection of Table 8.2 reveals, once again, that the mean effect of vocational programs increased directly with adherence to RNR. This pattern of results was evident with samples of young offenders and adult offenders. Additionally, we note that vocational programs that did not result in employment did not significantly reduce reoffending. Thirty-two tests of vocational programming *without* job placement yielded a mean effect size of .11 (.04 to .19). The corresponding value for programs *with* job placement was .32 (k = 12, CI = .25 to .48). Finally, we statistically controlled for methodological threats to the validity of the conclusions, and the conclusions did not change.

A discussion of employment cannot end without reference to the influential work of Robert Sampson and John Laub (1993). Following up the classic Glueck and Glueck (1950) sample (see Chapter 3), these researchers produced quantitative and qualitative evidence for the importance of obtaining meaningful long-term employment (and the love of a "good woman") as "turning points" in the life course of frequent and serious criminals. They argued against the position that early entry into criminal activity seals one's fate. They suggest that as unusual and unlikely it is that serious criminals would achieve a good job (or find a "good woman"), it does happen sometimes. And such unlikely events (as a result of chance or deliberate action) can result in cessation of criminal activity, over and above any of the standard stable predictors of crime. Of course, the authors of this text are attracted to a perspective that recognizes the dynamic nature of many of the predictors of criminal behavior. Sampson and Laub draw upon Hirschi's social control theory, but we do not doubt that employment (and marriage to a noncriminal other) can greatly redistribute the reward-cost contingencies in effect for criminal and noncriminal behavior.

The redistribution of rewards and costs associated with stable employment is illustrated in John Wright and Francis Cullen's (2004) analysis of the longitudinal National Youth Survey (NYS). The NYS study began in 1976 with interviews of a nationally representative sample of youths between the ages of 11 and 17. These youths have been reinterviewed at set time periods since 1976. Analyzing data from Waves 5 and 6, when the youths were between the ages of 15 and 24, they found that the number of hours worked per week and contact with prosocial coworkers were associated with reduced drug use and criminal offending. Additional analyses showed that contact with prosocial coworkers decreased associations with delinquents. That is, the influence of prosocial work colleagues on criminal behavior operates through its effect on antisocial supports for crime, one of the Big Four.

Not the least of the potential effects is to enhance the rewards and satisfactions for noncriminal behavior so that the potential subtractive costs of crime increase dramatically. The opportunity for a major shift in personally and interpersonally mediated influence may also be expected through reductions in antisocial associates and antisocial attitudes. Shadd Maruna (2001) in particular has suggested that turning away from a life of crime is dependent upon creating a new identity of being an ex-offender. The construct of identity change carries with it the notion of major cognitive change.

Leisure/Recreation

Frankly, our interest in leisure/recreation dates back to the creation of the two-item scale of the same name on the original LSI-R, and that scale continues to function well as a subcomponent of the new LS/CMI

General Risk/Need scale (Chapter 10). Data from our files finds a respectable mean predictive validity (r) of .21 on the Leisure/Recreation subcomponent. We consider the risk factors to be noninvolvement in conventional organized leisure-time activities and poor use of free time.

Unfortunately, the Carleton meta-analytic databank does not include a single experimental study of programs aimed at increasing involvement in anticriminal free-time activities. Forty-three tests involved programs that targeted increased physical activity and physical conditioning. The mean effect size was a nonsignificant .09 (CI = .02 to .15). This is consistent with our classification of physicality as a noncriminogenic need. It is also consistent with Lipsey and Wilson's (1998) description of wilderness and challenge programs having weak empirical support. Perhaps we have just missed the studies, but we could find few studies that explored leisure/recreation as an appropriate intermediate target of change in correctional treatment (Burton & Marshall, 2005).

Jones and Offord (1989) did develop and evaluate an after-school recreational program in a public housing project in our hometown of Ottawa, Ontario. They examined arrests in the project with the program and in a comparison project without a similar program. The findings were rather dramatic. Over a two-year pre-program period and a two-year program period, arrests in the comparison project increased, while arrests in the program project decreased by 75 percent. A replication of this study appears in order.

A review of comprehensive community and school-based interventions reminded us that many mentoring programs involve citizen and student volunteers spending time with persons, and often in recreational style activities (Catalano, Arthur, Hawkins, Bergland & Olson, 1998). You may recall from Resource Note 3.2 that recreational interactions with citizen volunteers had no impact on the antisocial attitudes of prisoners until the interactions were structured to deliberately increase anticriminal modeling and differential reinforcement. Indeed, citizen volunteer assistant probation officers with certain personality characteristics impacted not only on the attitudes of probationers but also lowered recidivism rates. The personality characteristics were relationship skills (above average on empathy) in combination with an anticriminal orientation (above average on a socialization measure). We agree with Catalano and colleagues: There is no reason to expect reduced antisocial behavior unless the learning opportunities are structured into the program.

Marital Attachments

There are a few evaluations of marital therapy in the correctional area, but all have reported on only immediate outcomes such as "marital closeness" (Carlson & Cervera, 1991) and facilitator's judgment of success (Accordino & Guerney, 1998). We can find no controlled evaluations with recidivism as the outcome criterion. There is some evidence that prison visits from a spouse or significant other are linked with reduced recidivism (Bales & Mears, 2008), and in our own prediction files, family/marital factors yielded a mean validity estimate of .18 (k = 8, CI = .11 to .24).

The "turning point" position of Laub and Sampson was noted in the discussion of work, and they have applied their position to marriage. Using a subsample (N = 52) drawn from the original 500 boys in the Glueck and Glueck classic study, Sampson, Laub, and Wimer (2006) examined the effects of marriage on criminal behavior. They found a 35 percent reduction in the odds of criminal behavior associated with being married. Further analysis indicated that being in a stable cohabitation relationship, although infrequent for this group, contributed to reduced crime after controlling for marriage. In another analysis of data (Waves 5 and 6) from the NYS study, Warr (1998) found that after marriage the amount of time spent with peers, prosocial or antisocial, decreased significantly. That is, as we found with work, marriage too may have its effect through altering the reward/cost distribution associated with one of the Big Four: antisocial supports for crime.

In an interesting New Zealand study of self-reported criminal activity at age 21, it was found that relative to single peers, those romantically involved with a deviant partner were at higher risk of offending (Woodward, Fergusson & Horwood, 2002). Those involved with a non-deviant partner were at lower risk of offending. These findings were apparent regardless of level of criminal involvement at age 18 and survived statistical controls for gender and antisocial associates. Romantic involvements within samples of both young offenders and adult offenders are an interesting area for future research. Examination of the criminal versus noncriminal partners is important to explore because generally there is a tendency for mating to occur among persons with similar backgrounds (recall the discussion of assortative mating in Chapter 5).

Neighborhood

Neighborhoods where families live can influence the behavior of parents and children. High-crime, disadvantaged neighborhoods can interfere with good parenting practices, stress parent-child bonds, expose youths to other criminals, and provide opportunities for crime. Recall from Chapter 3 that Glueck and Glueck (1950), the great psychodynamic researchers of the 1940s and 1950s, already knew that socially disadvantaged neighbourhoods could be criminogenic. In particular, they made reference to the many exciting opportunities supplied by the street in combination with a lack of controls. However, they proposed, not all children in disadvantaged neighborhoods are doomed to a life of crime. The relationship between neighborhood context and crime is not only complex but indeed minimal compared to the more immediate personal, interpersonal, and familial risk/need factors (Vazsonyi, Cleveland & Wiebe, 2006).

Some studies find that those at risk for delinquency do worse in highly disadvantaged neighborhoods. That is, there seems to be an additive effect between the family situation and the general neighborhood. In a study of African-American children, poor parental attachment and harsh and inconsistent parenting showed the worst outcomes for families living in the most disadvantaged neighborhoods (Brody, Ge, Kim et al., 2003). In another study by Donald Lynam and his colleagues (Lynam, Caspi, Moffitt, Wikström, Loeber & Novak, 2000), an interaction between impulsivity and neighborhood context was found. Analyzing data from the Pittsburgh Youth Study, impulsive children from the most impoverished neighborhoods were more likely to self-report delinquency than impulsive youths from better neighborhoods. Nonimpulsive youths from poor and well-off neighborhoods posed equal risk for delinquency. However, Vazsonyi et al. (2006) were unable to replicate the Lynam et al. (2000) finding in a large sample of 20,000 adolescents (differences in measures of impulsivity may account for the differences in the two studies).

Knowing that high-risk families may be worse off in poor neighborhoods has led to a few experiments in which families are moved into middle-class neighborhoods. These studies have shown to decrease delinquency, but the effects were small (Leventhal & Brooks-Gunn, 2000). Obviously, we cannot remove all disadvantaged families from their neighborhoods. One approach to protecting residents from crime is based on the "broken windows" hypothesis. The idea is that disorder in a neighborhood (e.g., graffiti, public drunkenness, litter in the streets) signals a social environment in which no one cares and, therefore, antisocial activity is unchecked. The typical ways of dealing with crime in these neighborhoods is by police crackdowns on minor crimes and trying to make neighborhoods more visually appealing. However, improving the look of the neighborhood and increasing police presence is not enough. What appears to be much more important is enhancing social control (Sampson & Raudenbush, 2001), which from our perspective means getting down to the major personal and interpersonal factors as risk/need and/or as strengths.

Many disadvantaged neighborhoods have characteristics (e.g., high concentrations of offenders) that increase the risk for crime (Tolan, Gorman-Smith & Henry, 2003), but within these neighborhoods there are some protective factors. There are residents with strong attachments to their neighborhood who respect the police (Silver & Miller, 2005), show confidence in their local schools (Eamon & Mulder, 2005), and demonstrate positive parenting practices (Chung, Hawkins et al., 2002;

Leventhal & Brooks-Gunn, 2000). Family and social support may be particularly important protective factors. Children with low levels of parental support living in neighborhoods with high levels of violence show a range of psychological problems, including difficulties in social cognition (Farver, Xu et al., 2005) and moral reasoning (Kuther & Wallace, 2003). Children with high levels of parental support in the same neighborhoods show much better adjustment. Parents who recognize the danger of the neighborhood ("be careful out there") and monitor closely their child's activities are also less likely to have delinquent children (Chung, Hawkins et al., 2002; Eamon & Mulder, 2005; Leventhal & Brooks-Gunn, 2000).

A number of studies have demonstrated that some children in high-risk neighborhoods avoid a delinquent trajectory. Chung and his colleagues (Chung, Hawkins et al., 2002) followed 423 poor children in Seattle from the age of 10 years to age 18. They found almost 19 percent reporting no delinquent activity. What made these nonoffenders so special were strong attachments to their parents and that the parents demonstrated good family management techniques. Emmy Werner (1987) studied children from impoverished backgrounds, and what interested her were the ones that did not become delinquent (the "invulnerable" children). Two sets of factors were important for this group. The first was temperament. Mothers of "invulnerable" children described them as being easy to love and nourish. They posed few caretaking difficulties and made reasonable and easy adjustments throughout life. The second set of factors dealt with the caretaking environment. The resilient children came from extended families that provided supervision, discipline, and emotional supports. That is, factors that other studies found absent among delinquents (warm parental bonds and supervision) also protected the children from future delinquency when risk factors were abundantly evident.

We remind readers yet again that the major characteristics of any setting (home, school, work, neighborhood) are membership composition (criminal versus noncriminal others), quality of the interpersonal relationships, and the criminal versus anticriminal nature of the cognitive and behavioral patterns modeled, reinforced, and punished. The work of Loeber, Stouthamer-Loeber, and their colleagues is highly relevant here. They have been carefully documenting the nature of disadvantaged neighborhoods as well as the contributions of disadvantaged neighborhoods to persistent and serious delinquency. We must note that a basic finding for them is that a disadvantaged environment has no impact on frequent and serious delinquency on the part of high-risk young people. Rather, they report that it is the low-risk young people who are influenced by "bad" neighborhoods. Their studies are characterized by an unusually broad definition of frequent and serious delinquency, and they employ a much more powerful assessment of risk/need and strengths than do the studies reporting that the disadvantaged area is particularly criminogenic for higher-risk kids. We expect from PIC-R (but we really don't know) that the criminal behavior of the highest-risk young people is so over-determined that an additional strong effect of area is unlikely.

Two of the findings of Loeber, Stouthamer-Loeber, and their colleagues are dramatic. First, one of the major characteristics of disadvantaged areas is a population of individuals and families characterized by high risk/need scores for offending and low strength scores. That is, there is a membership composition effect. Second, the correlation between assessments of risk, need, and strength with offending is large, while the correlation between the socially defined disadvantaged area and offending is real but relatively small in magnitude.

Again for interventions at the community level we strongly recommend the review by Catalano and colleagues (1998) and by Howell (1998). We also recommend our upcoming Chapter 11 review of classic community-oriented programs inspired by anomie, subcultural, and differential association theory (prior to its shift to social learning). These classic programs are primary examples of the failure to implement both of the relationship and structuring elements of effective prevention and treatment. Of course, we are in favor of enhancing conventional opportunity in school, work, and leisure settings. However, it is difficult for us to imagine effective neighborhood-level interventions that do not reach down and influence the relevant personal, interpersonal, and familial factors. In brief, adherence to RNR is strongly recommended.

Summary

This chapter has illustrated how the contributions of setting and social context may be approached from a general personality and cognitive social learning perspective. From a membership composition perspective on social structure, you want to get a handle on the proportion of criminals found in the settings of home, school, work, and leisure. You want an understanding of the rewards and satisfaction evident within the setting. You want to know where significant others such as parents and partners stand on the relationship and structuring/normative dimensions of interaction.

There are certainly dramatic differences in the state of knowledge in the various social contexts. In the domain of family of origin, the ability to predict and influence youthful offending is truly impressive. It is approaching causal or functional significance. Indeed, we saw dramatic gains in the achievement of reduced reoffending as both of the two major elements of parent-child relations were targeted and the family therapy was otherwise in full adherence with the principles of risk, need, and general responsivity. The level of knowledge in the domains of leisure/recreation and marital attachments is particularly weak when it comes to controlled efforts at influencing criminal activity.

The studies of school and work are at the intermediate level of knowledge development. The predictive validity of relevant assessments is reasonably well established in both domains. To date, however, the value of academic and vocational programming is most convincing only when those programs are also clearly adhering to the principles of RNR. We cannot expect much from programs that focus exclusively on school and work issues without attention to other aspects of RNR.

Worth Remembering

1. Forming social attachments is the basis to healthy relationships that could protect a child from a criminal trajectory.

   Children who become attached to a caregiver develop fewer psychological difficulties than young children who do not, and they grow up with healthier relationships with peers and adults. Problematic attachment patterns do not result simply from disruptions in the parent-child bond due to divorce. It is the nature and frequency of the disruption that is important. High-conflict families, parents who emotionally neglect their children or treat them harshly, and moving from one foster care home to another produce the most damage.

2. Families operate along two dimensions: the relationship and the structuring/normative dimensions.

   Children who are raised in families in which there is a poor parental relationship and the parents exercise poor parenting techniques are most at risk for delinquency. Furthermore, children in such families are more likely to associate with antisocial peers.

3. Family interventions can reduce delinquency.

   Treatment programs that address the relationship and normative dimensions of family functioning have demonstrated less delinquency in the problem child and even among siblings of the child. The effects also appear to be long-lasting, up to 13 years in one study.

4. The predictive validity of assessments in the domains of home, school, work, and leisure are impressive.

Meta-analytic findings from the family therapy literature show that targeting parent-child relationships and parental structuring skills are associated with positive effects. Although the literature on the predictive validity of assessments in the context of school, work, and leisure is not as large as in the home context, all indications are that they are in the expected direction and magnitude.

5. The ability of home-oriented intervention programs to influence offending is strong in the case of family-of-origin studies but basically unexplored in the case of romantic/marital attachments.

6. The impact of leisure/recreation programs has not been explored.

   Although leisure/recreation shows good predictive validity there have been no controlled studies of systematically altering the leisure activities and observing its impact on antisocial behavior.

7. Across all deliberate intervention programs explored in the broader social context, the influence piece that is unique to cognitive social learning perspectives (that is, the use of social learning/cognitive behavioral influence strategies) was crucial to reduced reoffending. Even when we turn to social context, the cognitive social learning elements of knowledge are important.

Recommended Readings

Any serious reading on attachment requires John Bowlby's two-volume work on *Attachment and Loss* (1971, 1973). If you do not have the time, try *Attachment and Psychopathology,* by L. Atkinson and K.J. Zucker (1997).

Multisystemic treatment is regarded as one of the more effective family intervention programs for delinquents and their families, and it is certainly, the most researched family intervention. The best description available of the program and the research can be found in the 2009 second edition of *Multisystemic Therapy for Antisocial Children and Adolescents* by Scott Henggeler and his colleagues.

Robert Sampson and John Laub's (1993), *Crime in the Making: Pathways and Turning Points Through Life*, a follow-up of Glueck and Glueck's (1950) study of 500 delinquents, makes for fascinating reading. It is one of the few studies that provides evidence for the importance of major adult life events (employment and marriage) on criminal conduct.

Chapter 9

Substance Abuse

Rounding off the Central Eight risk/need factors is substance abuse. Subsumed under substance abuse is alcohol misuse and the use of illegal drugs (we omit prescription drugs and tobacco). Our purpose in separating alcohol use from other drug use is twofold. First, the relationship between alcohol abuse and crime is generally weaker than the relationship between illegal drug abuse and crime. Second, the criminal justice system is far less tolerant of illegal drug abuse than alcohol abuse. For adults, purchasing alcohol is legal, and consuming alcohol is punished in only a few, specified situations (e.g., driving under the influence, public intoxication). Nonprescription drugs are illegal, and even small amounts of drug possession and use can result in severe criminal justice penalties.

Alcohol Abuse

Definition and Prevalence

The first task is to define what we mean by "alcohol abuse." At what point does drinking a legally available drug become an abuse? Is it a matter of quantity, and if so, how much? Is it a matter of age, and again, at what age? How about the situational context— driving a car, intoxicated in a public place? Finally, what about the interpersonal and personal context—marriage breakups, feelings of guilt and worthlessness due to drinking, etc.? Defining alcohol abuse has been a subject of controversy for a long time. The term "alcohol abuse" gained popularity when it became part of the disease nomenclature the second edition of *Diagnostic and Statistical Manual* (DSM) of the American Psychiatric Association. DSM is the major reference manual for classifying psychiatric disorders (more will be said about it in Chapter 14).

Unlike the "alcohol dependence" disorder in DSM, which requires at least three of nine criteria to be met, "alcohol abuse" is more narrowly defined (Hasin, 2003). In order to meet the diagnosis for alcohol abuse, the problem must have persisted for at least one month or it must be a repetitive pattern. Furthermore, meeting any *one* of the following criteria qualifies for the diagnosis:

1. Use in situations that are hazardous (e.g., driving while impaired)

2. Problems in the social, work, or psychological domains

3. Use leads to physical problems

The definition offered by DSM seems straightforward enough, except for one major problem. In surveys of alcohol abuse using the DSM criteria, as many as 70 percent of those meeting the diagnostic criteria are there because of the first criterion, hazardous use (Babor & Caetano, 2008; Harford, Grant, Yi & Chen, 2005). The problem with this criterion is that it is subject to changes in law. For example, at one time drinking and driving was not considered hazardous and subject to criminal justice sanctions. Moreover, Keyes and Hasin (2008) have suggested that since the hazardous-use criterion drives the diagnosis, there is an inherent class bias, with the upper classes having a higher alcohol abuse rate presumably because of greater access to cars.

Cognizant of the aforementioned problems, most epidemiological surveys use the DSM criteria for measuring the prevalence of alcohol abuse. In the 2001 National Household Survey on Drug Abuse, more than 55,000 adults from all 50 states were interviewed concerning their alcohol use over the previous year (Harford et al., 2005). The overall prevalence rate for alcohol abuse was 7.3 percent, with males having a rate twice that of women (10.4% vs. 4.4%). The U.S. prevalence rate for alcohol abuse is slightly higher than that found in other countries, but this may be due as much to differences in methodology as to culture (Somers, Goldner, Waraich & Hsu, 2004). It has also risen between 1991 and 2002 (Grant, Dawson, Stinson, Chou et al., 2006).

The Arrestee Drug Abuse Monitoring program interviews offenders and collects urinalysis within 48 hours of their arrest. In 2003, based on data from 39 sites and more than 180,000 male arrestees, 9.5 percent tested positive for alcohol, and 47.9 percent reported binge drinking within the past 30 days (Zhang, 2003). For females, an astounding 86.4 percent tested positive for alcohol and 34.9 percent reported binge drinking within the past month.

Another way of approaching the definition of alcohol abuse and its prevalence among offender populations is to use the results from risk/ need offender classification instruments. Risk/need instruments, to be discussed in more detail in the next chapter, sample a variety of criminogenic needs, including substance abuse. Although, the criteria for assessments of substance abuse in these risk/need scales are not as stringent as the DSM classifications and some other specialized assessment instruments, they have a number of advantages. First, risk/need instruments are routinely administered by correctional staff and thereby provide regular prevalence data without the need for expensive, specialized surveys. Second, the assessment of criminogenic needs by risk/need instruments drives the delivery of treatment services within a correctional system. Finally, we can investigate the predictive validity of the various crimino- genic needs. Predictive validity studies of DSM assessed substance abuse are relatively rare.

One family of risk/need instruments that assesses alcohol abuse is the Level of Service (LS) instruments. Chapter 10 will explore the research on the LS risk/need instruments in more detail. One of the areas covered is called Alcohol/Drug Problem. Table 9.1 shows this section. Two of the nine items are static risk factors (#37 and #38), and the remaining seven items are dynamic risk factors. Items #41 to #45 are scored only if there is a current problem with either alcohol or illegal drugs. An LS instru- ment is usually administered by trained staff to offenders in community and prison settings.

Table 9.2 presents some prevalence data based on assessments using an LS instrument. One advantage of using this data is that it permits us to separate alcohol abuse from illegal drug abuse. Many studies combine the two into a general substance abuse category. Among offenders, alcohol and illegal drug abuse often co-occur but not always. Some offenders misuse alcohol and avoid illegal drugs and vice-versa. As shown in Table 9.2, co-abuse is more frequent than alcohol abuse only. The LS permits further exploration into how illegal drug and alcohol abuse cause problems in the domains of law, family/marital, and school/work. For example, substance abuse and conflict with the law is by far the most prevalent problem for both men and women.

Alcohol Abuse and Crime

As we have just seen, the prevalence of alcohol abuse among offender samples is quite high, certainly much higher than that found in the gen- eral population. Offenders and victims also report a high incidence of drinking at the time of the offense (Greenfeld & Henneberg, 2001;

Table 9.1
Alcohol/Drug Problem Subcomponent of the LSI-R

Alcohol/Drug Problem

37	Alcohol problem, ever
38	Drug problem, ever
39	Alcohol problem, current
40	Drug problem, currently
41	Law violations
42	Marital/Family
43	School/Work
44	Medical
45	Other clinical indicators

From Andrews & Bonta, 1995. Reproduced with permission of Multi-Health Systems, Inc., 908 Niagara Falls Blvd., North Tonawanda, NY 14120-2060 (800/456-3003).

Table 9.2
Alcohol Abuse: Prevalence (%) with Drug Abuse and Alone

Sample (n)	Country	Co-Abuse	Alcohol Only
Male			
Prison (956)	Canada	47.2	42.3 (634)
Law violations		98.4	
Marital/family		48.8	
School/work		45.7	
Prison (16635)	U.S.	29.2	13.3 (9,344)
Law violations		90.4	
Marital/family		74.3	
School/work		61.6	
Community (664)	U.K.	30.9	27.6 (504)
Law violations		89.2	
Marital/family		70.4	
School/work		39.9	
Community (46417)	U.S.	35.5	19.9 (9,344)
Law violations		88.3	
Marital/family		73.5	
School/work		60.6	
Community (464)	Canada	15.3	13.3 (428)
Law violations		78.9	
Marital/family		46.5	
School/work		42.3	
Female			
Prison (647)	Canada	41.0	38.8 (312)
Law violations		92.8	
Marital/family		71.3	
School/work		47.5	
Prison (216)	Canada	33.8	39.8 (103)
Law violations		93.2	
Marital/family		76.7	
School/work		21.9	
Prison (1657)	U.S.	31.1	11.1 (614)
Law violations		65.7	
Marital/family		61.0	
School/work		52.3	
Community (2193)	Canada	24.0	21.1 (1,783)
Law violations		88.0	
Marital/family		63.1	
School/work		29.8	
Community (263)	Canada	20.9	19.7 (213)
Law violations		89.1	
Marital/family		70.9	
School/work		21.8	
Community (139)	U.K.	23.0	19.1 (89)
Law violations		71.9	
Marital/family		68.8	
School/work		34.4	
Community (10970)	U.S.	29.1	16.3 (4,471)
Law violations		87.7	
Marital/family		80.3	
School/work		65.0	

Kazemian & Le Blanc, 2004; Martin, Bryant & Fitzgerald, 2001). This is especially true in cases of homicide in which the relationship is likely mediated by the availability of guns (Phillips, Matusko & Tomasovic, 2007; Roberts, 2009). A meta-analysis by Lipsey et al. (Lipsey, Wilson, Cohen & Derzon, 1997) included correlational studies of alcohol abuse and violence. The average effect size (r) was .10 (k = 29) for their "criminal acute" (single incident of drinking) category and .15 for chronic alcohol abuse (k = 67). However, this does not mean that alcohol *causes* crime. To assess the possible causal relationship between alcohol and crime, a higher level of evidence is needed than a simple correlation (the reader is reminded the different types of covariates discussed in Chapter 1).

In Table 9.3 we once again draw upon various LS databases in which we can select only cases with a current alcohol abuse problem (in the past year) and that do not evidence a drug abuse problem. Referring to Table 9.3, we see that the predictive validity of alcohol abuse is modest (averaging an r of .09). This finding is slightly lower than that reported by Dowden and Brown (2002) in their meta-analysis (r = .12, k = 29).

Lipsey and his colleagues (1997), in addition to their meta-analysis of correlational studies, also reviewed *experimental* studies of the potential causal role of alcohol use to violence. In human experiments, alcohol was given to participants, and their aggressive behavior, usually electric shocks administered to another subject, was compared to that by participants in a no-alcohol condition. In these studies, the independent variable (alcohol) is manipulated by the experimenter, thus permitting evaluations of the effects of alcohol on aggressive behavior.

In comparing the alcohol versus the no-alcohol conditions in the laboratory experiments, the overall mean effect size (r) was 0.54 (k = 42). This finding was identical to an earlier meta-analysis of 49 experimental studies of alcohol consumption and aggression in laboratory settings (Ito, Miller & Pollock, 1996). However, both quantitative reviews found impor-

Table 9.3
Alcohol Abuse: Predictive Validity(r) with Recidivism (1 year)

Sample (n)	Source	Country	r
Male			
Prison (619)	Bonta	Canada	.06
Community (428)	Andrews	Canada	.03
Community (664)	Raynor (2007)	U.K.	.02
Female			
Prison (312)	Brews (2009)	Canada	.05
Prison (103)	Rettinger (1998)	Canada	.29
Community (1,783)	Brews (2009)	Canada	.07
Community (213)	Rettinger (1998)	Canada	.18
Community (139)	Raynor (2007)	U.K.	.01

tant variability in the findings, depending on experimental procedures and individual characteristics of the participants. In some circumstances, the results were in the opposite direction. As Lipsey et al. (1997:278) conclude: "While a causal influence of alcohol consumption on violence cannot be ruled out...it seems apparent that there is no broad, reliable, "main effect" of alcohol on violence."

Treating Alcohol Abuse

Treatments for alcohol abuse include a variety of interventions. We will not review all of them but select a few treatments that are widespread—pharmacological treatment and Alcoholics Anonymous. We will say more on cognitive-behavioral techniques when we discuss the treatment of drug abuse.

Pharmacological treatments include two classes of drugs. The most widely researched is disulfiram or Antabuse. Antabuse has been used for more than 60 years in the treatment of alcoholism (Fuller & Gordis, 2004). The mechanism of action is that when Antabuse interacts with alcohol (ethanol), it triggers a violent physiological reaction. The person becomes sick to the stomach and vomits, develops headaches, and feels highly anxious. It is presumed that this aversive conditioning to alcohol will deter the person from further drinking. As long as the person complies with taking the medication, Antabuse appears effective. However, the vast majority of patients do not comply (Buonopane & Petrakis, 2005; Garbutt, 2009). There have been efforts to ensure medication compliance by court-mandated treatment (Mustard, May & Phillips, 2006) and behavioral reinforcement of adherence (Azrin, Sisson, Meyers & Godley, 1982), but these efforts have had only modest success.

A new class of drugs has been introduced over the past 15 years that work by blocking the pleasurable effects of alcohol. Drugs such as naltrexone and acamprosate stop the "cravings." Given that these drugs have fewer of the ethical problems associated with Antabuse (i.e., purposely inducing harm) and higher compliance rates, they may soon replace Antabuse in the pharmacological treatment of alcohol abuse (Fuller & Gordis, 2004). With respect to treatment efficacy (usually measured by drinking frequency or abstinence), these drugs as the main treatment have also shown small effects. However, their effectiveness is enhanced when paired with behavioral counseling (Berglund, 2005; Buonopane & Petrakis, 2005; Mann, 2004; Weiss, O'Malley, Hosking, LoCastro & Swift, 2008).

Alcoholics Anonymous (AA) is a social support group for clients trying to quit drinking. Founded in 1935, AA has grown into an international organization operating in more than 40 countries. Participants must admit that they cannot stop drinking on their own and submit to a "higher power" (interpreted individually to mean a sponsor, or the group, or God). A sponsor, who has been abstinent for at least one year, acts as a 24-hour support and teacher for the newly initiated. Meetings are held regularly during which other members offer support as they follow the 12 steps to recovery (the twelfth step is a "spiritual awakening").

Evaluations of AA using stringent controls (e.g., random assignment) are difficult to conduct for a number of reasons. For example, records of membership are not kept, and not all AA meetings operate in the same manner (Krentzman, 2007). Reviews of the available literature, however, suggest that involvement in AA is associated with decreases in alcohol use. A meta-analysis of 74 studies of AA by Toniga, Toscova, and Miller (1996) found a mean r of .08 for the variable *affiliation* with AA (i.e., attending meetings), rising to .22 under conditions of AA *involvement* (e.g., leading a meeting, shares at meetings, etc.). Good outcomes through active involvement in AA as opposed to simply sitting in on the meetings have been a frequent observation (Tonigan, Connors & Miller, 1998; Vaillant, 2005).

So, why does AA work? There a number of plausible reasons for the efficacy of AA in reducing alcohol use (note that we are not talking about criminal recidivism). First, AA shares some of the therapeutic ingredients found in models of cognitive-behavioral therapy (Knack, 2009; Moos, 2008). For example, the sponsor functions like a therapist who has been trained in the AA model and instructs the newcomer to the approach. The sponsor models abstinence and reinforces it during interactions with the new member. Another important factor is the power of the group. The group not only motivates the individual to maintain abstinence but provides rewarding alternative activities to drinking and teaches coping skills to deal with the urge to drink. A review of 24 studies concluded that AA's greatest impact is on altering the social network of the recovering alcoholic (Groh, Jason & Keys, 2008).

Self-help groups provide a variety of supports to the individual. The group may support for example, general feelings of self-worth, or it can be specific to alcohol abstinence. There are groups that are highly structured and follow behavioral principles without reliance on AA. Perhaps, the earliest and best known example is Hunt and Azrin's (1973) Community Reinforcement approach (Resource Note 9.1). Most treatment programs, however, use AA as a means of altering the alcoholic's social network (Martin, Player & Liriano, 2003; McCrady, Epstein & Kahler, 2004; Witbrodt, Bond, Kaskutas, Weisner et al., 2007). For example, the Network Support Project actively encourages the client to attend AA meetings while giving up social interactions with drinking friends (Litt, Kadden, Kabela-Cormier & Petry, 2007). A two-year follow-up found that the alcohol-dependent participants assigned to the network support condition had 20 percent more days of abstinence than those in the alternative treatment conditions (Litt et al., 2009).

Resource Note 9.1

The Community Reinforcement Approach to Alcohol Abuse

In 1973, George Hunt and Nathan Azrin introduced an operant conditioning approach to the treatment of alcoholism. Eight men with serious alcohol abuse problems from a state hospital were selected to participate in a Community-Reinforcement (CR) program. The CR program enlisted the help of family, friends, and community groups to deliver rewards for nondrinking behaviors. The goal was to make life without alcohol more enjoyable and fulfilling. If more social reinforcement was provided for nondrinking behaviors, then reverting to drinking would result in a loss or time out from these reinforcements. The general approach involved rearranging the density of rewards and costs associated with drinking behavior.

Involving the family, usually the spouse of the alcoholic, is a major component of the program (Miller, Meyers & Tonigan, 1999). Beginning in the hospital, the husband and wife met to agree on a list of activities that would be mutually satisfying. In general, they would agree to make each other happy by addressing problem areas (e.g., finances, child responsibilities) and spending more time together in rewarding activities. For the alcoholic without a family, a "synthetic family" was created from relatives, an employer, or a church minister. The synthetic family would invite the alcoholic into their home for regular visits and meals. If the client was unemployed, they would join a "Job Club" that helped him search for a satisfying job and prepare a job interview. Because most alcoholics spend their time with other alcoholics, it was important to change the person's social network. One way that Hunt and Azrin achieved this change was to convert a former tavern into a social club that showed movies, provided dances, and ran bingo games.

Carefully and systematically the alcoholic's social environment was changed to redistribute rewards from drinking to nondrinking behaviors.

The eight men were matched to eight other alcoholics on age, employment history, marital status, and education. The control group went through the standard hospital program of 25 hours of didactic teaching on the effects of alcohol. A six-month follow-up showed dramatic improvements for the CR group. Not only did the CR group show a large decrease in the amount of time spent drinking (14% for the CR group and 79% for the control group), but the group was also less likely to be unemployed (5% vs. 62%). In terms of family life, prior to the program all five married men in the CR group were contemplating divorce. At follow-up, the five men remained married while two of the four couples in the control group had separated.

Since the 1973 demonstration study, the CR approach to alcohol abuse treatment has evolved. Its application has expanded from a hospital setting to include community settings and compliance with medication such as antabuse has become part of the approach (Sisson & Azrin, 1989). The CR approach has not only been used in the treatment of alcoholism but also in the treatment of drug abuse. Roozen and his colleagues (Roozen, Boulogne, van Tulder, van den Brink et al., 2004) reviewed 11 studies of the CR approach in the treatment of alcohol and other drug abuse. They found strong evidence that the CR approach resulted in fewer drinking days, although the evidence was mixed with respect to abstinence. With respect to drug abuse, two studies found the CR approach associated with abstinence from cocaine use.

Illegal Drug Abuse

Prevalence

In 2004, 7.9 percent of Americans over the age of 12 (approximately 19 million people) reported using an illicit drug in the past year (Substance Abuse and Mental Health Services Administration, 2005). Furthermore, it is estimated that approximately 1.8 to 3.6 percent of the population has a diagnosable drug abuse or dependency disorder (Baumeister & Hörter, 2007). Surveys of offender populations find much higher rates of substance abuse, ranging from 20 percent to as high as 79 percent (Fazel, Bains & Doll, 2006; Glaze & Palla, 2005; Karberg & James, 2005; Lurigio et al., 2003; Office of National Drug Control Policy, 2000; Pernanen et al., 2002). Among a sample of more than 180,000 arrestees (Zhang, 2003), the most frequently used drug was marijuana (44.1%), followed by cocaine (30.1). Drugs such as heroin (5.8%) and methamphetamines (4.7%) fell far behind. In some of our data sets (thankfully made available by our colleagues), the prevalence rates for illegal drug abuse, without alcohol abuse comorbidity, ranges from a low of 5.6 percent to a high of 56.1 percent (Table 9.4). As we noted in our discussion of alcohol abuse, the literature tends to combine alcohol and other drug abuse into a general category of substance abuse. At one level, this makes some sense, as the two are correlated. For example, in our large U.S. prison sample, $r = .39$ ($N = 18,313$), and for offenders supervised in the community, $r = .26$ ($N = 39,496$). However, the association is far from perfect, and we would encourage researchers to separate the two abuse disorders.

Unlike alcohol abuse, illegal drug abuse has a closer relationship to crime because of the illicit status of drugs such as marijuana, cocaine, and so on. Thus, an addiction to any of these drugs places one directly into contact with other criminals and, in many cases, may exert pressure to engage in other illegal activity in order to buy drugs. Furthermore, some drugs, in some people, may directly initiate thoughts that lead to antisocial behavior (e.g., cocaine use triggering paranoid ideations), or the intense cravings may lead to automatic behaviors that progress to drug abuse. Substance abuse, undifferentiated from alcohol misuse, is a commonly found risk factor for crime among adults (Cartier, Farabee & Prendergast, 2006; Gendreau et al., 1996) and young offenders (Cookson, 1992; Loeber et al., 2005). Two meta-analyses have found a significant relationship between drug use and recidivism.

Craig Dowden and Shelley Brown (2002) reviewed 45 studies, yielding 116 effect size estimates, where substance abuse was measured prior to the recidivistic event. Thirty-three estimates were solely on illegal drug abuse (the others included alcohol abuse). The average effect size between drug abuse and recidivism was .13. Trevor Bennett and his

Table 9.4
Illegal Drug Abuse: Prevalence (%) with Alcohol Abuse and Alone (LS data)

Sample (n)	Country	Co-Abuse	Drug Only
Male			
Prison (956)	Canada	33.7	27.4 (504)
Law violations		64.4	
Marital/family		29.1	
School/work		28.0	
Prison (16643)	U.S.	43.8	31.1 (11,773)
Law violations		49.6	
Marital/family		38.7	
School/work		32.8	
Community (663)	U.K.	24.0	20.5 (459)
Law violations		51.7	
Marital/family		19.9	
School/work		39.9	
Community (29779)	U.S.	52.9	41.6 (18,147)
Law violations		60.6	
Marital/family		48.2	
School/work		40.4	
Community (464)	Canada	7.8	5.6 (393)
Law violations		61.1	
Marital/family		33.3	
School/work		33.3	
Female			
Prison (647)	Canada	51.8	50.0 (382)
Law violations		89.9	
Marital/family		72.8	
School/work		56.1	
Prison (216)	Canada	52.3	56.6 (143)
Law violations		65.3	
Marital/family		55.6	
School/work		12.5	
Prison (1658)	U.S.	62.9	52.3 (1,659)
Law violations		65.7	
Marital/family		61.0	
School/work		52.3	
Community (2182)	Canada	18.3	15.3 (1,659)
Law violations		78.7	
Marital/family		57.1	
School/work		39.3	
Community (263)	Canada	19.0	17.8 (208)
Law violations		30.4	
Marital/family		25.9	
School/work		27.2	
Community (139)	U.K.	36.6	32.7 (107)
Law violations		43.2	
Marital/family		36.0	
School/work		20.1	
Community (9317)	U.S.	58.5	51.8 (6,628)
Law violations		60.9	
Marital/family		52.5	
School/work		41.2	

colleagues (Bennett, Holloway & Farrington, 2008) analyzed 30 studies that investigated the link between drug use and crime. On average, the odds of criminal behavior were 2.79 times greater for drug abusers than for non–drug users ($r = .27$). For crack users, the odds for crime were six times greater. In Table 9.5, the predictive validity of illegal drug abuse in our data sets, without the presence of alcohol abuse, is displayed. The most striking result was that drug abuse was more highly correlated with recidivism in all five female samples.

So what was to be done to cope with Elliott Currie's (1993) "American nightmare"? Initially, the answer was to declare "war" on drugs. However, as we know today, getting tough on offenders has not produced the desired effect. Instead of reducing drug crime, the results have been overworked police officers, clogged courts, and overcrowded prisons faced with the health problems (e.g., HIV, AIDS, hepatitis) that co-occur with intravenous drug use (Fagan, 1994; Webster et al., 2005; Worden, Bynum & Frank, 1994). Some have questioned whether the increased emphasis on punishment and control was merely a disguised effort to control the poor and the minorities in the inner cities of America (Byrne & Taxman, 1994; Currie, 1993; Daly & Tonry, 1997).

The general failure of the "war on drugs," and let us be clear that the "war" has not completely gone away, has brought renewed efforts to treat rather than punish substance-abusing offenders. In the 1980s there were increases in the number of drug treatment programs offered in prisons (Chaiken, 1989). These exploded in the 1990s and by the end of the twentieth century, approximately 40 percent of all correctional facilities in the United States offered substance abuse treatment programs (Welsh & Zajac, 2004). However, the demand far outstripped the supply. It is estimated that approximately 90 percent of adult state prisoners with a drug problem have not received treatment (Welsh & Zajac, 2004) and, in the state of Texas, 70 to 90 percent of youths with substance abuse problems go untreated (Kelly, Macy & Mears, 2005). In California,

Table 9.5
Drug Abuse Only (Without Alcohol): Predictive Validity (r) with Recidivism (1 year)

Sample (n)	Country	r
Male		
Prison (504)	Canada	.08
Community (393)	Canada	.03
Community (459)	U.K.	.17
Female		
Prison (382)	Canada	.19
Prison (208)	Canada	.26
Community (1,659)	Canada	.20
Community (143)	Canada	.42
Community (107)	U.K.	.24

only about 8,000 inmates in a population of more than 160,000 received drug treatment (Burdon, Messina & Prendergast, 2005).

Treating Drug Abuse

Evaluations of drug treatment programs indicate positive effects (Hepburn, 2005; Messina, Farabee & Rawson, 2003; Sims, 2005; Swartz, Lurigio & Slomka, 1996) and a high level of cost-effectiveness (Longshore et al., 2006). Two meta-analytic summaries of the research are available. The first review comes from the Correctional Drug Abuse Treatment Effectiveness project (CDATE; Pearson & Lipton, 1999; Pearson, Lipton & Cleland, 1996). The CDATE project conducted a comprehensive review of published and unpublished studies between 1968 and 1996 from around the world. Because they used a definition of treatment that was similar to the one used by Andrews et al. (1990a), we were able to compare the CDATE results with the Andrews et al. (1990a) meta-analysis, an analysis of the Carleton University databank specifically conducted for this text and also with respect to substance abuse programs only (see Table 9.6). The most important finding from the Pearson, Lipton, and Cleland (1996) meta-analysis is that treatment is more effective in reducing recidivism than sanctions or other unspecified forms of intervention.

The CDATE meta-analysis is consistent with a PCC. Treatment programs that are cognitive-behavioral and target criminogenic needs are effective in reducing the problem behavior.

The second meta-analysis is by Holloway, Bennett, and Farrington (2008). They reviewed 37 studies, which were broken down into types of treatment interventions used in the criminal justice system. They used Odds Ratio (OR) as their measure of effect size. An OR of 1.0 indicates no difference between the treatment and the control group. The overall OR for all treatments reviewed was 1.35 (r = .08), and the Confidence

Table 9.6
Effectiveness of Drug Abuse and Offender Treatment (phi)

| Study | Sanction | Adherence to RNR | | |
		No	Unclear	Yes
Andrews et al. (1990a)	−.02	−.03	.13	.30
Andrews & Bonta. (2006)	−.03	−.01	.12	.26
Carleton University (2006) (substance abuse programs only)	−.06	.07	.14	.30
Pearson at al. (1996)	.03	.06	.09	.22
Pearson & Lipton (1999)				
Boot camp	.05			
Unstructured group		.04		
Therapeutic community			.13	

Interval (CI) did not include 1.0 (CI = 1.22 to 1.50; note that with OR as the effect size, no effect is associated with an OR of 1.0 and not zero as with other measures of effect size). Table 9.7 summarizes Holloway et al.'s (2008) results, and also provides the *r* values converted from the OR estimates. Therapeutic communities showed a treatment effect whereas drug courts, methadone treatment for heroin users, and drug testing showed no significant effects (CIs included 1.0). The findings for therapeutic communities are larger than that found by Pearson and Lipton (*r* = .13; 1999).

Therapeutic communities are usually operated within prison settings where the inmates live together in segregated units helping each other toward abstinence and prosocial lifestyle change. Evaluations of therapeutic communities have been criticized on methodological grounds (e.g., subject selection bias, vague program description and implementation, etc.); however, they do appear to be associated with reductions in recidivism (Aos, Miller & Drake, 2006a; Holloway et al., 2008; Pearson & Lipton, 1999). Why they work remains unclear, with some researchers pointing to the aftercare component of therapeutic communities (Burdon, Messina & Prendergast, 2004; Prendergast, Hall, Wexler, Melnick & Cao, 2004) while others claim that aftercare is unnecessary (Welsh, 2007). There is also the aspect of a supportive social network similar to Alcoholics Anonymous and the Community Reinforcement approach to dealing with substance abuse that was discussed earlier. For example, a five-year follow-up of opiate-dependent persons found higher abstinence rates for those attending Narcotics Anonymous (NA) compared to those who did not participate in NA (Gossop, Stewart & Marsden, 2007).

Relapse Prevention

In 1980, Alan Marlatt and Judith Gordon wrote a paper that had a major influence in the treatment of addictions. They noted that behavior therapy was effective in producing change in behavior, but the maintenance of change was problematic. Reviewing the results of interventions with a variety of addictions (alcohol, cigarettes, and heroin), they observed that within a matter of months after completing treatment, most participants returned to their former addiction. Marlatt and

Table 9.7
Drug Abuse: Therapeutic Communities and Drug Courts (OR)

Treatment Type	k	OR	CI	r
Therapeutic Community	10	2.06	1.73 to 2.45	.20
Drug Courts	2	1.52	0.88 to 2.60	.11
Methadone	9	1.14	0.92 to 1.42	.03
Drug Testing	6	0.85	0.68 to 1.06	−.05

Gordon (1980) reasoned that the avoidance of relapse was not to be found in "bigger and better treatment packages" but rather in providing clients direct training in recognizing the situations that trigger relapse and teaching them how to cope with these situations.

Relapse prevention (RP) is a cognitive-behavioral intervention that promotes self-management skills in high-risk situations. It has been applied to a variety of addictions (smoking, alcohol, and illegal drugs), general criminal offending (Dowden & Andrews, 2007; Dowden, Antonowicz & Andrews, 2003), and even the treatment of sexual offenders (Yates & Ward, 2007). The first step is to recognize situations that elicit substance misuse. This may be done by a detailed review of situations in which the client misused a substance or with the aid of objective assessment measures such as the Inventory of Drinking Situations (Annis, 1982). The second step is to teach the client alternative responses to high-risk situations (e.g., refusing a drink, planning a different activity for Saturday night).

The RP model has considerable intuitive appeal, and research on its effectiveness has been promising. Most evaluations of RP use substance use and psycho-social adjustment as the outcome variables. A meta-analysis of 26 studies ($n = 9,504$) found RP generally effective for smoking, drug, and alcohol problems ($r = .14$; Irvin Bowers, Dunn & Wang, 1999). However, RP was significantly more effective for alcohol abuse ($r = .37$, $k = 10$) than for cocaine use ($r = -.03$, $k = 3$). For polysubstance use, the mean effect size was slightly lower than that found for alcohol abuse ($r = .27$, $k = 5$), but the difference was statistically non-significant. A meta-analysis of various interventions with drug abuse found polysubstance abuse yielding the poorest outcomes overall ($r = .12$, $k = 13$; Dutra, Stathopoulou, Basden et al., 2008). Moreover, RP interventions were equally effective compared with other interventions (i.e., cognitive behavior therapy, contingency management).

Summary. Our discussion of the addiction treatment field suggests that the effective ingredients are similar to those found in the general treatment of offenders. Programs that promote a positive therapist-client relationship but follow a structured format are associated with decreased relapse rates (Project MATCH Research Group, 1997). Moreover, cognitive-behavioral styles of interventions and intensive services appear to be more effective with higher-risk substance-abusing offenders. Community support and specific training on relapse prevention techniques may also enhance the long-term success of treatment. Many of the essential features of effective treatment with general offenders have made their way into programs specifically targeting offenders with substance abuse problems (Bourgon & Armstrong, 2005; Ramsay, 2003; Wanberg & Milkman, 1995).

From a theoretical perspective, offsetting the rewards associated with substance abuse involves altering many reinforcement contingencies.

Shifting the reward balance to favor nonabuse requires changes in the individual's attitudes, social community, and feelings of competency and self-control. Family members, employers, and friends can systematically learn to reinforce sobriety and express disapproval for substance abuse. Individuals can learn cognitive skills to cope with high-risk situations and stop themselves when they begin to rationalize their substance abuse or think in a way that supports substance abuse. The behavioral changes do not come easily. For many substance-abusing offenders, the behavior is frequent (often daily) and has a long history. The automatic, habitual nature of substance abuse presents a serious challenge. However, as the evidence suggests, there are interventions that can overcome these obstacles.

Dealing with Resistance to Treatment

Treatment programs for criminal offenders are faced with the challenge of getting offenders into treatment and keeping them there. High attrition rates from treatment are not only common for substance-abusing offenders but they are also a problem for offenders in other types of treatment (e.g., anger management). Attrition is particularly high among the offenders who need treatment the most (Wormith & Olver, 2002). Furthermore, those who need treatment the most have multiple criminogenic and noncriminogenic needs that compound the difficulties in delivering treatment. For example, the Criminal Justice Drug Abuse Treatment Studies encompasses 13 major studies. A description of the offenders served in treatment show a clientele with multiple drug dependencies, mental health problems, lengthy criminal histories, and high incidence of HIV (Fletcher, Lehman, Wexler & Melnick, 2007). Only 63 percent of the clients were self-referred to treatment.

Two general approaches have been used to direct substance-abusing offenders to treatment and keep them there. One approach relies upon psychological techniques to engage the client in treatment, while the other places a greater emphasis on the threat of negative consequences.

Motivational Interviewing

Motivational interviewing (MI) originated out of the need to deal with the client who by denying that he or she has an addiction is unmotivated to attend treatment. James Prochaska and Carlo DiClemente (1982, 1983) formulated a model that describes clients as being at different stages in their readiness to change. These stages range from just thinking about the possibility of having a problem to actually doing something about it. At the precontemplation and contemplation stages, the client does not see that he or she has a problem that requires a change. Behavior is rationalized or denied, or the client is "thinking about it." William Miller and Stephen Rollick (1991) developed motivational interviewing as a technique to move the client from "I am thinking about it" to "I am going to do something about it." Essentially, the therapist engages the client in a nonthreatening relationship, builds rapport, and gently and cautiously nudges the client in the direction of accepting that there is a problem that must be faced.

MI has its origins in Carl Rogers's (1961) client-centered therapy with its emphasis on building a relationship and Daryl Bem's (1967) theory of self-perception and how people deal with cognitive dissonance. However, there are elements of behavioral therapy with homework assignments often assigned (e.g., write in a log book what your family does and says after you have a drink) in order to direct the client toward problem identification. MI is often a preparatory first step to more formal, structured treatment and relapse prevention training. This technique recognizes that not all people referred to treatment are equally motivated. Considering that many offenders come to treatment because of external motives (e.g., mandated by court, applying for parole), motivational interviewing provides a way of enhancing motivation from within.

MI is a counseling technique that is congruent with the responsivity principle. The therapist's style of intervention is adjusted to the client's cognitive and affective characteristics at a particular point in time. At the precontemplative stage of therapy, a confrontative or highly structured intervention may have no impact (or a negative impact) on the client who does not think there is a problem or does not care about the impact of his or her behavior on others. Introducing such a client directly into a structured cognitive-behavioral program could invite dropout or failure. As the client becomes committed to a process of change and his or her cognitive-affective views change, then the therapist's style of interaction and the treatment modality is modified.

There have been at least four meta-analytic reviews of the MI literature, all targeting noncriminal populations. The outcomes in these reviews include adherence to medical advice (Rubak, Sanboek, Lauritzen & Christen, 2005), diet and exercise (Burke, Arkowitz & Menchola, 2003), gambling (Hettema, Steele & Miller, 2005), and, of course, addictions (Hettema et al., 2005; Vasilaki, Hosier & Cox, 2006). All reviews find MI to have a positive effect across the different outcomes (except for smoking cessation). With respect to alcohol and other drug abuse, the average effect size falls between $r = .13$ and $r = .25$, depending upon the length of follow-up.

Given the recalcitrant nature of most offenders, the positive findings from the general literature have led to an intense interest in the application of MI to offender populations. Many correctional agencies are training their staff in MI techniques, and it is promoted by the U.S. National Institute of Corrections as a useful approach to motivating offenders under community supervision (Walters, Clark, Gingerich & Meltzer, 2007). One point that we wish to make is that we cannot expect MI to have an impact on criminal recidivism. MI is basically a responsivity technique to increase motivation to attend and adhere to treatment. Hopefully, MI will get the offender to treatment, but if the treatment does not adhere to the risk-need-responsivity principles, then changes in criminal behavior are unlikely. Research with offender populations is in its early stages, but studies find that MI techniques are related to therapist's judgment of treatment progress (Farbring & Johnson, 2008; Ginsburg, Mann, Rotgers & Weekes, 2002), more positive attitudes toward dealing with problems (Harper & Hardy, 2000), and treatment retention (McMurran, 2009). There have been no offender studies that have substance abuse as an outcome, although a randomized trial is presently under way (Farbring & Johnson, 2008).

Mandated Treatment and Drug Courts

Not surprisingly, the criminal justice system is an area in which coercion is fairly commonplace. For example, courts routinely add treatment conditions to probation orders, and parole boards "expect" inmates to have taken advantage of prison treatment programs. Although such involuntary forms of treatment raise ethical concerns (Monahan, 1980; Shearer, 2003), the practice remains. Klag, O'Callaghan, and Creed (2005) view coercion as a complex construct and not a simple dichotomy of forced versus voluntary treatment. Within the criminal justice system, coercion is very much a continuous variable ranging from the compulsory to subtle pressures to participate in treatment. Recognizing the dimensional nature of coercion leads to a fuller understanding of ethical and motivational issues (e.g., if coercion to participate in treatment comes from family members rather than the courts, is it more ethically acceptable? Will the client be more motivated in treatment?).

There have been a number of narrative reviews of the coercion literature that concluded that offenders subjected to mandatory treatment do just as well as those who volunteer for treatment (Prendergast, Farabee, Cartier & Henkin, 2006; Stevens et al., 2005). However, a recent meta-analysis indicates that mandatory or coerced treatment is not equally effective with voluntary treatment. Karen Parhar and her colleagues (Parhar, Wormith, Derkzen & Beauregard, 2008) reviewed 139 studies of mandated and nonmandated treatment programs. Guided by Klag et al.'s (2005) recommendations, Parhar et al. coded treatment along a three-point scale from mandated (legal consequences for not participating in treatment), coerced (minor consequences for not attending treatment), and freely voluntary. Across all studies, treatment had a small effect on recidivism ($r = .06$, CI = .05 to .08, k = 129). However, when the results were broken down according to the three-point scale, an important difference emerged. Voluntary treatment displayed a larger effect than mandatory and coerced treatments ($r = .17$ vs. $r = .08$, respectively). At this point, we turn our attention to drug courts as an illustration of a widely used mandated treatment for substance-abusing offenders.

Drug courts began in the United States in 1989. By 2003 there were more than 1,000 drug courts, with drug courts in all 50 states. The popularity of drug courts has spread beyond the American border. Drug courts are now operating in Canada, Australia, and England (Weekes, Mugford, Bourgon & Price, 2007). The way they operate is that prior to sentencing, drug offenders are placed into community treatment, and the courts then monitor offenders' progress. Successful completion of treatment is usually rewarded by avoidance of a custodial sentence.

Do drug treatment courts help to reduce substance abuse and recidivism? Answering this question is difficult because many evaluations have been plagued by methodological problems. For example, the U.S. Government Accounting Office (1997) found that none of the 20 evaluations reviewed provided sufficient confidence in the evaluation methodology to say anything about these programs. Gutierrez (2008) could identify only one of 96 evaluations that was rated "high confidence" according to methodological standards. Although there are a few random assignment studies (Gottfredson & Exum, 2002), too many lack equivalent comparison groups and drug relapse data (Belenko, 2001). Despite the methodological weaknesses, meta-analytic reviews have found drug courts to be associated with reductions in recidivism (Aos, Miller, and Drake, 2006a; Latimer, Morton-Bourgon & Chrétien, 2006; Lowenkamp, Holsinger & Latessa, 2005; Wilson, Mitchell & MacKenzie, 2006). The average reduction in recidivism across all four meta-analyses is 12 percent (Gutierrez, 2008).

Many meta-analytic reviews of the drug treatment literature have focused on program and methodological factors that influence outcome. For example, Prendergast, Podus, and Chang (2000) found that the evaluator's involvement in delivering the program and how long the program has been in operation are associated with the mean effect size of treatment. We recognize that such factors are important in the treatment of offenders, and we will say more about them in Chapters 11 and 12. We also think that it is important to consider the nature of the treatment and especially, to ask whether the treatment adheres to the principles of risk, need, and responsivity?

A report by Douglas Marlowe and his colleagues (Marlowe et al., 2006) gives us an idea of how to maximize the effectiveness of drug courts. High-risk offenders (based on a diagnosis of antisocial personality disorder and drug abuse history) were assigned to either regular court reporting or a twice-per-week reporting schedule. High-risk offenders who had the biweekly reporting requirement attended more treatment sessions and had fewer positive drug tests than high-risk offenders with a monthly reporting schedule. Low-risk offenders showed no differences with respect to their reporting requirements. In other words, as the risk principle would predict, when high-risk offenders were matched with intensive service delivery, they did better.

Leticia Gutierrez and Guy Bourgon (2009) are conducting a meta-analysis of drug treatment courts that involves coding for the RNR principles. First of all, 71 of 96 studies were rejected as being too methodologically weak to be included in their meta-analysis. At this point, the results are preliminary but of the 25 remaining studies, 11 did not adhere to any of the RNR principles, 13 adhered to one principle, and only one drug treatment court study adhered to two principles. No drug treatment court adhered to all three principles. The coding of adherence to the criminogenic need principles required targeting a criminogenic need other than substance abuse, which was a given. The trend was supportive of the principles. The mean r (converted from their Odds Ratio) was .05 for no adherence, .11 for adherence to one principle, and .31 for adherence to two principles. We expect that future research on drug treatment courts, with an eye to RNR adherence, will strengthen the trend.

A Final Comment on Substance Abuse

Alcohol and illegal drug abuse by themselves have been inconsistently associated with criminal behavior. However, many offenders misuse both. When we consider offenders who abuse alcohol and other drugs, then the association crystallizes. Table 9.8 expands on the earlier Table 9.4 by considering the total score of the Alcohol/Drug

Table 9.8
Substance Abuse: Predictive Validity (r) with Recidivism (1 year)

Sample (n)	Country	r
Male		
Prison (923)	Canada	.17
Community (464)	Canada	.27
Community (666)	U.K.	.17
Female		
Prison (659)	Canada	.16
Prison (216)	Canada	.34
Community (2,193)	Canada	.23
Community (263)	Canada	.31
Community (138)	U.K.	.25

Problem subcomponent of the LSI-R. In this subcomponent, a more comprehensive survey of alcohol and other drug problems is available than what is usually provided in many studies. Items under the Alcohol/ Drug Problem domain include a prior history of illegal drug and alcohol abuse as well as items that examine how the problem interferes with many facets of functioning. This more detailed survey shows substance abuse as a risk/need factor among male and female offenders irrespective of the setting. Meta-analyses find substance abuse (i.e., alcohol and/or other drug abuse) to be a moderate predictor of recidivism. Gendreau et al. (1996) found an average effect size of .10, as did Dowden and Brown (2002). These findings are similar to that found among mentally disordered offenders (.11; Bonta et al., 1998) and sex offenders (.06; Hanson & Bussière, 1998). Substance abuse is not part of the Big Four, but it certainly earns a part of the Central Eight.

It is important to keep in mind that substance abuse among offenders is interrelated with other criminogenic needs. Illicit substance abuse draws one to antisocial others and exposure to antisocial attitudes. The presence of cognitions supportive of substance use is highly related to substance use behaviors ($r = .31$, $k = 89$; Rooke, Hine & Thorsteinsson, 2008). Chronic substance abuse interferes with stable marital and family relationships, hampers success at employment and school, and may lead to financial hardship. Too much of criminal justice policy has emphasized substance abuse as the root of crime. A more balanced approach that includes attention to the numerous needs presented by offenders offers a more evidence-based approach to the problem.

Worth Remembering

1. Alcohol and other drug abuse are quite prevalent among offender populations, but their relationship to crime is moderate.

    Meta-analytic findings of correlational studies of alcohol/drug use and crime show average effect sizes (r) in the range of .10. There is no conclusive evidence that alcohol use actually causes crime, although there is a more direct link with illicit drug use.

2. Treating substance abuse offenders has been more effective than the "war on drugs."

    Punishing drug offenders through the increased use of imprisonment has not reduced reoffending rates among this group of offenders. Treatment programs appear to be a more effective way of dealing with the substance abusing offender.

Recommended Readings

Elliott Currie's *Reckoning: Drugs, the Cities, and the American Future* (1993) is a terrific overview of the challenges brought on by the war on drugs. It is a very easy-to-read, nontechnical book that will give the reader the broader context to our section on the substance-abusing offender.

For an introduction to the treatment of substance abuse, we recommend *Rethinking Substance Abuse*, by William Miller and Kathleen Carroll (2006). In this text, Miller and Carroll provide a comprehensive, nonquantitative review of the science of treatment.

Part 3

Applications

Prediction of Criminal Behavior and Classification of Offenders

With Chapter 10 the text transitions to issues of the practical application of PCC. In this chapter, our interest is in the prediction and classification of risk. We ask the following three questions: (1) how well can criminal behavior be predicted? (2) what can we do with that knowledge in order to reduce the chances of criminal acts occurring? and (3) to what extent do the Central Eight risk/need factors apply to age, gender, race, and different offender samples?

The reader has already seen the broad outlines of the answers to these questions. As early as Chapter 1, with the brief introduction of theoretical perspectives provided in Resource Note 1.2, we began to note the applied potential of theories to inform the prediction and treatment of criminal behavior. This was augmented considerably in Chapters 3 and 4 on theoretical perspectives, with PIC-R as an example of a General Personality and Cognitive Social Learning (GPCSL) approach. That particular theoretical perspective is devoted to what drives increases and decreases in the chances of criminal behavior.

In Chapter 2, the expanded RNR model was introduced and provided some examples of how the principles of risk, need, and responsivity added value to the assessment and treatment of offenders. Furthermore, we provided brief summaries of the research evidence regarding the major predictor variables and the value of building composite risk/need assessment instruments, and even took a brief look at the LS/CMI General Risk/Need survey of the Central Eight factors. Indeed, in every chapter some reference was made to risk, need, and responsivity, typically with examples of predictive value and programming suggestions.

In Chapter 1 we outlined the three types of understandings that PCC attempts to address. Part 1 of the text dealt with theoretical understanding, and Part 2 expanded our empirical understanding of criminal conduct. In Part 3 we explore a practical understanding. We begin with a discussion of offender risk assessment and pragmatic approaches to the classification of offenders for purposes of effective correctional treatment.

The prediction of criminal behavior is perhaps one of the most central activities of the criminal justice system. From it stems community safety, prevention, treatment, ethics, and justice. Predicting who will reoffend guides police officers, judges, prison officials, and parole boards in their decisionmaking. Knowing that poor parenting practices lead to future delinquency directs community agencies in providing parenting programs to families. As we saw in Chapter 2, treatment programs may be most effective with moderate- to high-risk offenders. Ethically, being able or unable to predict an individual's future criminal behavior may weigh heavily upon the use of dispositions such as imprisonment and parole.

In prison, probation, and parole systems, one of the major purposes of offender risk assessment is the classification of offenders into similar subgroups in order to assign them to certain interventions. The most common type of classification is based upon risk level. For example, the risk for violence or escape forms part of the decision to classify inmates to maximum-security prisons or the risk of reoffending is critical in assigning the frequency of contact in parole supervision. How correctional systems reliably separate offenders into low-, medium-, and high-risk groups is part of the focus of this chapter. Of course, risk may be categorized in more than three groupings. We use the three grouping classification for illustration purposes because it is the most commonly used.

The various issues raised by prediction are relevant to the concerns of citizens as a whole because the human, social, and economic costs of prevention are not trivial, and because the power that criminal justice professionals have over people who are arrested, detained, convicted, probated, or incarcerated is extraordinary. The issues are of immediate interest to those who become entrapped in the process of criminal justice by way of being a victim, an offender, or a criminal justice professional. Whatever our current role might be—concerned citizen, offender, victim, or involved professional—we all share an interest in prediction. Thus, we all have a right to insist upon knowledge of the following aspects of prediction:

1. Demonstrations of the extent to which criminal behavior is predictable (the issue of predictive accuracy);

2. Clear statements regarding how the predictions are made so that the information used in making predictions may be evaluated on ethical, legal, sociopolitical, economic, and humanitarian criteria;

3. Demonstrations of the extent to which the ways of making predictions actually facilitate criminal justice objectives and practice;

On the assumption that general knowledge is enhanced through an integration of theory, research, and practice, a fourth issue is notable:

4. We may expect that predictions and the actions based on them are recorded, monitored, and explored empirically in a way that increases our understanding of crime and criminal justice.

We begin with a general discussion of what is meant by predictive accuracy and some of the challenges in its measurement. Although the focus is on the technical aspects of prediction, it is necessary because the discussion provides the backdrop for the topics that follow. Following the issue of predictive accuracy is a brief overview of how theory can inform the practice of risk prediction and the relevance of the principles of risk, need, and responsivity to the assessment of criminal offenders. We will showcase "fourth generation" assessments that integrate the assessment of risk, need, and responsivity with planned intervention and its wide applicability across age, race, and gender. Finally, we end the chapter with a summary of the obstacles to implementing the knowledge reviewed.

Assessing Predictive Accuracy

To this point, we have been content to limit the meaning of prediction to the magnitude of the association of variables measured at one point in time with an assessment of future criminal activity. Thus, the preceding chapters have made frequent references to statistically significant associations between predictors (information collected at Time 1) and the criterion (criminal behavior measured at Time 2). The phrase "statistically significant" refers to an observed level of association that exceeds chance or is significantly different from a correlation coefficient (r) of .00. For example, lower-class origins and criminal conduct are correlated with one another at the level of approximately .05. This level of correlation, when the sample size is large, may be statistically different from .00, but it represents a low level of association. Predictive correlations of antisocial personality and antisocial attitudes with criminal behavior have reached the level of .30 and greater. When the sample size is sufficiently large, an r of .30 is not only significantly greater than zero but is significantly different from an r of .05. On the basis of such findings, we may conclude that variables are (or are not) predictive of future criminal conduct, and that one variable is more predictive of a criminal behavior than another variable.

Correlation coefficients and similar statistical measures of association are valuable for research and theory. However, when it comes to everyday, practical situations, more meaningful measures of predictive accuracy are needed. Take, for example, the problem faced by a parole board that must decide whether to release an inmate. Many factors weigh on the minds of board members. Foremost is making a correct decision that encompasses both a safe release and the denial of parole for a highly dangerous individual. In addition, there is consideration of the costs of making a mistake, either by releasing someone who commits another crime or denying parole to someone who is unlikely to commit another crime. As we will soon show, prediction is never perfect, and the parole board members in our example must make decisions based on a reasonable balance between a correct choice and a mistake. To add to the difficulty in decisionmaking, the value placed on correct decisions and mistakes are usually socially defined. For example, for some, releasing someone who commits another crime is more serious then denying parole to an inmate who does not reoffend.

This very practical problem is illustrated by what researchers call the two-by-two (2 × 2) prediction accuracy table (see Part A of Table 10.1). Inserted in each cell is the language of prediction. There are four possible outcomes: (a) *True Positive*—"I am positive he will reoffend and it turns out to be true"; (b) *False Positive*—"I am positive he will reoffend but he doesn't" (prediction was false); (c) *False Negative*—"Negative, he will not reoffend, but he does" (prediction was false); and (d) *True Negative*—"He will not reoffend and he does not." Note that Cells (a) and (d) are correct predictions and Cells (b) and (c) are errors. Obviously, we want to maximize the numbers in (a) and (d) and minimize the numbers in (b) and (c).

In addition to the four outcomes that are generated from the 2 × 2 table, we can calculate the following indices of predictive accuracy:

1. the overall proportion of correct predictions (true positives plus true negatives divided by the total number of predictions): $(a + d)/(a + b + c + d)$;

2. the proportion of cases judged to be at risk that did recidivate: $a/(a + b)$;

3. the proportion of cases judged not to be at risk and that did not recidivate: $d/(c + d)$;

4. the proportion of recidivists correctly identified: $a/(a + c)$;

5. the proportion of nonrecidivists correctly identified: $d/(b + d)$;

Table 10.1
Two-by-Two Prediction Accuracy Tables

A: Two-by-Two Prediction Accuracy Table

Predict Recidivism?	Actually Recidivated?	
	Yes	No
Yes: High-Risk	(a) True Positive	(b) False Positive
No: Low-Risk	(c) False Negative	(d) True Negative

B: Two-by-Two Prediction Accuracy Table (Phi = .15)

Predict Recidivism?	Actually Recidivated?		N	Rate
	Yes	No		
Yes: High-Risk (male)	109	345	454	24.0%
No: Low-Risk (female)	3	59	62	4.8%
N	112	404	516	21.7%

Part B of Table 10.1 presents real data from our research files. The risk factor was being male, and the outcome measure was officially recorded reconvictions over a two-year period. The phi value, a statistic similar to r, was a moderate .15. What can be said about predictive accuracy in this case depends, in part, upon how we choose to report on the findings:

1. The recidivism rate of males (the "high-risk" cases) was five times that of females (24% vs. 4.8%);

2. Classifying males as high-risk identified 97.3 percent of the recidivists (109/112). A total of 112 offenders were reconvicted; of these, 109 were males predicted to recidivate;

3. The true negative rate was 95.2 percent (59/62) in that 59 of the 62 cases that we predicted would not recidivate did not recidivate (and thus, the false negative rate was only 4.8 percent (3/62);

4. However, the overall rate of correct predictions was only 32.6 percent: (109 + 59)/516;

5. The true positive rate was only 24 percent (109/454), and thus the false positive rate was 76 percent (345/454).

For assessing predictive accuracy, the lesson to be learned is that more information is required than any one of the above statements provides on its own. Imagine a parole board making decisions based on gender. In our example, many inmates would remain incarcerated unnecessarily and at great financial costs. For a more complete appreciation of predictive accuracy, one needs to be able to recreate the full 2 × 2 prediction table.

In Part B of Table 10.1, the outstanding accuracy achieved in capturing recidivists (97.3%) was due in large part to the fact that our risk assessment (gender) assigned a very large proportion of the cases to the category predicted to reoffend. That is, 88 percent of the cases were male (454/516). The proportion of cases assigned to the high-risk group (or to the category of people we predict will reoffend) is called the *selection ratio*. Because the selection ratio was high (88%), our hit rate for recidivists was high, but our hit rate for nonrecidivists was low (14.6% or 59/404). When the selection ratio is high, the false positive rate will also tend to be high—particularly when relatively few people actually do recidivate. The number of cases that actually do recidivate is called the *base rate*, which in our example was a fairly low 21.7 percent (112/516).

The rates of false positives, false negatives, true positives, and true negatives, as well as the magnitude of the association between the risk predictor and criminal behavior, are all influenced by base rates and selection ratios. In assessing the predictive accuracy of different approaches to risk assessment, examining the 2 × 2 tables they generate is the ideal. In practice, however, the risk assessment approach that yields the greatest number of overall correct predictions may not always be chosen. For example, one may be willing to tolerate a few more false positives in order to maximize the number of recidivists correctly identified; or there may be a situation in which it is judged more important to minimize false positives.

How many false positives and false negatives there are depends on: (1) the accuracy of the risk measure itself, (2) the selection ratio, and (3) the base rate. Most of this chapter deals with the accuracy of risk measures, but further comments on the effect of the selection ratio and base rate on errors is warranted. In our example of gender defining risk, the selection of high-risk cases is clear. If male, then high-risk; if female, then low-risk. Many offender risk scales, however, have more than one risk factor and produce a range of scores. For example, the Level of Service/Case Management Inventory, an offender risk scale that we will present in more detail later in the chapter, produces scores from 0 to 43. Thus, low risk can be defined as "0 to 7" or "0 to 14" or "0 to 30." Changing the "cutoff" score, or the selection ratio, will affect how many offenders are defined as low-risk or high-risk and, therefore, will influence the number of correctly identified recidivists and nonrecidivists and the proportion of errors.

One should also avoid getting caught in a situation in which prediction is no problem at all. These situations exist when the base rate for criminal behavior is either very low or very high. Take, for example, a situation in which the base rate of a certain type of criminal behavior, such as a sadistic sexual murder, is close to zero (e.g., 5%). Prediction is easy, and risk assessments are not needed because the best strategy is to predict that no one will recidivate; in this case you will be correct 95 percent of the time. Likewise, when the base rate is close to 100 percent (e.g., 96%), if you predict that everyone will recidivate, you will be correct 96 percent of the time. However, the base rates for most criminal behavior (e.g., property offenses, assaults, drug violations) fall in the 20 to 80 percent range. Thus, prediction through risk assessment can make a significant contribution.

We have been emphasizing the importance of considering the 2 × 2 tables for evaluating predictive accuracy. We have also observed that base rates and selection ratios can influence predictive accuracy as measured by statistics such as r and phi. There are, however, statistical measures of predictive accuracy that are hardly affected by base rates and selection ratios. One important measure is the *Receiver Operating Characteristic (ROC)*. A more detailed description of the ROC is given in Technical Note 10.1, but for now the key point to remember is that ROC analysis yields a measure called the *Area Under the Curve (AUC)*. If a risk instrument has an AUC of 1.0, then we have perfect prediction, and if the AUC equals .50, then the instrument performs no better than chance. The AUC can also be interpreted in the same way as the Common Language (CL) effect size. The CL gives the probability of a score drawn at random from one sample being higher than a score drawn at random from another sample. For example, let us suppose that we have a risk scale with an AUC of .75 and we have two groups of offenders. One group consists of recidivists and another consists of nonrecidivists. If we randomly selected an offender from the recidivist group, there is a 75 percent chance that his or her score will be higher then the score of a randomly selected nonrecidivist. By examining the AUCs we can compare the predictive accuracies of different offender risk scales after taking into account base rates and selection rates.

Although AUCs are now reported frequently, such was not always the case. Prior to 2000, most evaluations reported the accuracy of risk scales in terms of Pearson correlation coefficients (r) or some other statistical index. Fortunately, Marnie Rice and Grant Harris (2005) have provided a handy conversion table that allows one to convert various statistics to describe predictive accuracy to an AUC. A modified chart is provided below (Table 10.2) to allow the reader to interpret r values commonly reported as AUCs. Note that the values in the chart are approximations, as certain assumptions were made in the construction of the conversion chart (e.g., it assumes a 50 percent base rate). Formulas are provided by Rice and Harris (2005) to deal with different base rates, and the reader should consult these formulas for precise conversions.

Before proceeding, we wish to emphasize the unreasonableness of demanding perfect predictive accuracy from criminal justice and forensic professionals. Perfect prediction is impossible, and this is true in many fields, not just criminal justice. Take, for example, the risk factors for a heart attack that many readers probably know (e.g., high levels of bad cholesterol, smoking, and hypertension). These risk factors were identified in the Framingham study, which followed approximately

Table 10.2
Conversion Chart for Interpreting Predictive Validities of Risk Instruments

r	AUC
.00	.50
.05	.53
.10	.56
.15	.59
.20	.61
.25	.64
.30	.67
.35	.70
.40	.73
.45	.79

Adapted from Rice & Harris (2005)

5,000 people over a 12-year period. When the risk factors are combined, the AUC falls between .74 and .77 (Wilson et al., 1998). In this chapter we will see that offender risk measures also demonstrate similar values. In neither case is prediction perfect, but in both cases the knowledge of risk has practical value.

PCC and Prediction

In this section, we take a moment to explore how theories of criminal behavior can influence offender assessment. There are many theories or explanations of criminal conduct, but they can be grouped into the following three general categories: (1) sociological, (2) psychopathological, and (3) social learning (PIC-R). Sociological theories explain crime as a product of social-economic-political forces; psychopathological theories see a psychological-personal deficit as the culprit; and social-learning theories such as the PIC-R perspective ascribe criminal conduct to learning experiences in interaction with personal and situational factors.

As shown in Table 10.3, the three theoretical orientations posit assessment variables that differ in substance and usefulness. The risk factors derived from sociological theories tend to be static (e.g., SES, ethnicity), there are relatively few domains of interest, and they suggest that changing criminal behavior requires intervention at the broad social level. In contrast, the other two perspectives place great value on risk factors at the individual level, many of which are dynamic and, therefore, potentially useful with respect to offender rehabilitation.

Table 10.3
The Relationship Between Theory and Offender Assessment

Theoretical Perspective	Derived Risk Factor
Sociological	Social status (young, male)
	Race and ethnicity (member of a minority)
	Financial status (poverty)
Psychopathological	Emotional discomfort (anxiety, alienated)
	Self-esteem (low)
	Bizarre thoughts
PIC-R and the Central Eight	Criminal history
	Social support for criminal behavior
	Antisocial personality pattern
	Antisocial attitudes
	Employment and education problems
	Family and marital problems
	Lack of prosocial leisure pursuits
	Substance abuse
	Personal aptitudes (IQ, self-control skills)
	High-crime neighborhood

Adapted from Bonta, 2001

Which theoretical approach do we choose? The answer is that we choose the theoretical perspective that has the greatest support of evidence. As shown in Table 10.4 and throughout the text, the PIC-R perspective wins quite handily. The most striking finding from Table 10.4 is the agreement between the empirical evidence and the PIC-R perspective of criminal conduct. The best predictors match the Big Four theoretical factors: antisocial associates, attitudes, personality, and criminal history. Other relevant, mid-range predictors of recidivism were also those described by PCC theory as part of the Central Eight factors (e.g., family factors and social achievement indices such as education and employment). The poorest predictors were derived from the sociological and psychopathological theoretical perspectives. Thus, one important lesson to be learned is that good offender assessment instruments result from the use of theories that guide us in selecting *relevant* variables for assessment (Bonta, 2002).

The PIC-R perspective offers the following lessons for offender assessment:

1. *Sample multiple domains of criminal conduct.*
    We should not restrict our assessments to only a few domains. As we will soon show, some offender risk instruments have limited themselves to assessing one or two domains (e.g., criminal history and substance abuse). PIC-R posits that criminal behavior is a function of the number and variety of rewards and costs for both criminal and noncriminal behavior. These rewards and costs arise from multiple sources (e.g., family, friends, work). At a minimum we should be assessing the Central Eight risk factors.

Table 10.4
The Predictors of Recidivism

Predictor	*n*	k	*r*
Companions	11,962	27	.21
Antisocial cognitions	19,089	67	.18
Antisocial personality	13,469	63	.18
Race	56,727	21	.17
Criminal history	171,159	282	.16
Parenting practices	15,223	31	.14
Social achievement	92,662	168	.13
Interpersonal conflict	12,756	28	.12
Age	61,312	56	.11
Substance abuse	54,838	60	.10
Intelligence	21,369	32	.07
Personal distress	19,933	66	.05
Socioeconomic status	13,080	23	.05

n = sample size; k = number of studies
Adapted from Gendreau, Little & Goggin, 1996

2. *Assess the dynamic as well as the static covariates of criminal conduct.*

It is noteworthy that many of the predictors are dynamic or changeable. Social support for crime, procriminal attitudes, substance abuse, and so on are all amenable to change. Static factors such as a prior criminal record may predict but, once convicted, the record is a mark that stays. Dynamic predictors have the advantage of offering the correctional worker an idea of what needs to be changed in order to reduce the offender's risk to reoffend. For example, poor use of leisure time is a predictor of recidivism (Bonta & Motiuk, 1985; Raynor et al., 2000). It is also dynamic and subject to change (therefore, possibly causal). An individual with productive leisure pursuits receives rewards for prosocial behavior (from others or from the activity itself). A correctional worker faced with an offender without hobbies or involvement in organized prosocial activities may want to consider what can be done to promote prosocial leisure activities.

3. *Offender assessment can guide the intensity of treatment.*

A PIC-R perspective gives a major role to dynamic risk factors, the potential targets for intervention. However, the model also says that offender risk is directly proportional to the number of different risk factors present and the density of rewards and costs associated with antisocial and prosocial behavior. That is, a high-risk offender will have more risk factors (e.g., criminal friends, procriminal attitudes, substance abuse problems, unstable employment) than a low-risk offender who may simply have problems in only one or two domains of risk. In addition, the number and variety of risk factors reflect the density of rewards and costs for behavior. Consequently, knowledge of an offender's risk level tells us something about how much treatment is needed to reduce an offender's risk.

4. *Offender assessment can guide how we provide treatment.*

Recall also from PIC-R the principle that an individual's ability to learn from the environment is dependent upon a number of personal-cognitive-emotional factors. For example, an individual's responsiveness to advice from a therapist, correctional worker, or family member is dependent upon his or her cognitive ability. If the individual is of low intelligence, then providing the advice in a complex, abstract manner will be less effective then if the advice is given in a simple, concrete manner. Thus, one may choose to assess characteristics that may not be predictors of criminal behavior but are still relevant for the delivery of services.

Offender Assessment and the Principles of Risk, Need, and Responsivity

The assessment of offenders does not need to be limited to making judgments of the risk to reoffend. This is certainly important, but assessment can also be useful for guiding treatment. In Chapter 2, we presented the expanded RNR model. Here we revisit three principles that are fundamental, in our view, to offender risk assessment—the principles of risk, criminogenic need, and responsivity.

Risk Principle

The risk principle says to match the level of service to the level of risk. The principle tells us *who* to treat (i.e., the higher-risk offender). Recall from Chapter 2 in Andrews and Dowden's (2006) meta-analysis that appropriate treatment delivered to higher-risk offenders showed a modest correlation ($r = .17$) with reduced recidivism. Treatment delivered to low-risk offenders had hardly any effect (a mean effect size of .03). Therefore, if we are going to treat offenders effectively, then we must have a reliable way of assessing offender risk so that we can make sure it is the higher-risk rather than the lower-risk offender who receives most of the treatment services. A valid risk scale consisting of only static items can do the job of assigning offenders to treatment, but there is more to effective rehabilitation than adhering to the risk principle.

Criminogenic Need Principle

This principle makes a distinction between criminogenic needs (moderate to large dynamic risk factors) and noncriminogenic needs (weak dynamic risk factors). Furthermore, it is the criminogenic needs that should be targeted in treatment to reduce recidivism. The criminogenic need principle tells us *what* to treat. Thus, offender risk instruments should include assessments of criminogenic needs, and the Central Eight reflects seven of the most relevant criminogenic needs (remember that one of the Central Eight risk factors is criminal history, a static factor). Table 10.5 provides a summary of criminogenic and noncriminogenic needs drawn from Craig Dowden's (1998) review of 225 treatment studies.

Responsivity Principle

The responsivity principle tells us *how* to treat. First there is general responsivity that calls for the use of cognitive-behavioral techniques to

Table 10.5
Criminogenic and Noncriminogenic Needs

Criminogenic Need	Noncriminogenic Need
Antisocial Personality/Negative Emotionality	Vague Feelings of Personal Distress
Antisocial Attitudes and Cognitions	Poor Self-Esteem
Social Supports for Crime	Feelings of Alienation and Exclusion
Substance Abuse	Lack of Physical Activity
Inappropriate Parental Monitoring, and Disciplining	History of Victimization
Problems in the School/Work Context	Hallucinations, Anxiety, and Stress
Poor Self-Control	Disorganized Communities
Lack of Prosocial Activities	Lack of Ambition

influence change because they are the most effective techniques to help people learn new attitudes and behaviors. Specific responsivity calls for adapting our general cognitive-behavioral techniques to specific offender characteristics. These characteristics range from the biological (e.g., gender) to the social (e.g., culture) and the psychological (personality, emotions, and cognitive ability). It is under specific responsivity that issues concerning offender assessment arise. Traditional forensic assessment instruments that attend to cognitive and personality characteristics become important for identifying the factors that may serve as obstacles for addressing criminogenic needs. One cannot successfully deal with a substance addiction if the client is psychotic; one cannot deal with employment problems if the person is suicidal. Moreover the biological-social constructs of gender and race present their own unique considerations for assessment and treatment. In order to successfully address the criminogenic needs of women offenders, for example, parenting, victimization experiences, and issues of financial independence on a male partner may need to be integrated into assessment and treatment.

Approaches to the Assessment and Prediction of Criminal Behavior

We hope that at this point the reader has some appreciation that the assessment of offenders is not just a question of risk to reoffend but also of treatment. Here we continue with the story of how the assessment of offenders has changed over the past 30 years or so. This has been a remarkable period during which conceptualizations of how to assess offenders and our ability to predict recidivism has changed for the better. In 1996, Bonta reviewed the offender risk prediction literature and described "three generations" of risk assessment. Today, we have four generations (Andrews, Bonta & Wormith, 2006).

First-Generation Risk Assessment: Professional Judgment

> The more dangerous the behavior, the more difficult it is to predict. What the studies, taken in totality, actually show very clearly is the *you have to detain a much larger number of people than those who are actually dangerous in order to reach the dangerous* (Mathiesen, 1998:461) [emphasis in original].

> It is clear from the research literature that we cannot, and will never be able to, predict with reasonable medical certainty future violence (Meloy, 1992:949).

The two quotes above reflect the field's preoccupation with the prediction of violent behavior or dangerousness. The prediction of violence is important because of the seriousness of the harm caused to victims, but so too is the prediction of the more frequent, nonviolent criminal behavior. Our interest is in the prediction of both types of outcome, but we will describe first-generation risk assessment with an example of the prediction of dangerousness.

To understand the pessimistic assessments just quoted, one factor that we must consider is how the predictions are made (the predictors, models, and methods that are used). To explain what we mean, we examine the study reported by Steadman and Cocozza (1974). In the first study of its kind, 98 patients from a hospital for the criminally insane were released into the community upon a court order. Psychiatric staff had judged (predicted) these patients to be a danger to the community. The question was: were they? Upon follow-up, only 20 of 98 patients encountered an arrest, implying that in order to prevent one arrest we must imprison almost four people.

What this study showed, along with others during the time, was that professional judgments of risk by highly trained clinicians (i.e., first-generation assessment) were not very accurate. The reasons for such poor performance are twofold. First, there is the problem of using informal, nonobservable criteria for making decisions. Second, there is the problem of attending to offender characteristics that may not be empirically related to criminal behavior (e.g., psychopathological factors).

Here is what typically happens in a first-generation assessment. A professional, trained in the social sciences, interviews an offender in a relatively unstructured manner. The clinician may ask some basic questions of all offenders, but for the most part there is considerable flexibility in the questions asked of a particular offender. Sometimes psychological tests may be given; which ones are administered varies from one test administrator to another. Files may be reviewed, but what is attended to in these files is also at the discretion of the professional.

At the end of the process of information gathering, the staff member arrives at a judgment regarding the offender's risk to the community and his or her treatment needs. The key feature of the clinical approach is that the reasons for the decision are subjective, sometimes intuitive, and guided by "gut feelings"—they are not empirically validated.

Although it may be wonderfully flattering to clinical professionals to be viewed as having expertise in offender risk prediction, the evidence suggests that they are relatively poor prognosticians if they fail to attend to empirically validated risk factors in a structured way. Sometimes clinical judgments are structured in that they specify to the clinician what factors to consider, but they do not use an actuarial system to link the factors to the decision (i.e. "structured clinical judgment"). More preferable are the actuarial approaches to assessment.

Second-Generation Risk Assessment: Actuarial, Static Risk Scales

Such agreement does not happen often, but there is consensus on this point— actuarial assessments outperform clinical judgment (Ægisdóttier, White, Spengler, Maugherman, Anderson, Cook et al., 2006; Hanson, 2009; Hilton, Harris & Rice, 2006). One of the earliest examples of the actuarial method comes from Burgess (1928). Burgess examined more than 3,000 parolees and found 21 factors that differentiated parole successes from parole failures. Burgess then gave to every offender one point for each factor that was present. For the offenders scoring the maximum points, the recidivism rate was 76 percent; for those with the least points, the rate was 1.5 percent. The actuarial approach of summating items, perhaps because of its simplicity, has been the preferred choice in risk-assessment methodology. Sophisticated techniques (e.g., multiple regression, iterative classification) have been applied to the prediction problem, but these newer techniques have shown little improvement in predictive power (Jones, 1996; Silver, Smith & Banks, 2000).

Recent meta-analyses have confirmed the power of empirical, statistical approaches over clinical approaches. For example, William Grove and his colleagues (Grove et al., 2000) conducted a meta-analysis of 136 studies that compared actuarial approaches to risk prediction with clinical approaches. These studies were drawn from general clinical psychology and psychiatry. The results were that actuarial methods performed better than clinical procedures in 47 percent of the studies and equally as well in another 47 percent. In only 6 percent of studies did clinical judgment outperform actuarial prediction. A more focused examination of 67 studies relevant to counseling psychology found almost identical results, with 52 percent of the studies favoring actuarial methods and only 10 percent of the studies favoring the clinical method (Ægisdóttier et al., 2006).

Table 10.6 presents the AUC results from other meta-analyses, some dealing with specific offender groups (e.g., mentally disordered offenders; Bonta et al., 1998) and others with specific outcomes (violence).

Second-generation risk assessment instruments are evidence-based, but they have two major limitations. Nearly all second-generation risk assessments have no theoretical basis, and they consist almost entirely of static, historical items. In Table 10.7 we show three examples of second-generation risk assessment instruments—the Salient Factor Score (SFS) that was widely used in the United States in the 1980s and 1990s (Hoffman, 1994), the Statistical Information on Recidivism (SIR) scale used in Canada (Nuffield, 1982), and the Offender Group Reconviction Scale (OGRS) developed in the United Kingdom (Copas & Marshall, 1998). All three instruments have demonstrated satisfactory predictive accuracies, with AUCs ranging from .64 to .76 (Bonta et al, 1996; Hoffman, 1994; Hoffman & Beck, 1984).

Apparent in the risk scales is the neglect of many factors theoretically relevant to criminal conduct (e.g., antisocial peers and attitudes) and the predominance of items that are static or unchangeable. On this last point, look at the SFS scale—all but one item is static. An offender who was imprisoned at the age of 16 for an auto theft while high on heroin will fall into the "poor" category even if this occurred 20 years ago and he has been straight ever since. These scales give little credit to the offender who changes for the better. Nor do they inform the practitioner or supervising staff as to what needs to be done to reduce the offender's level of risk.

It seems clear to us that improvements to offender assessment can be made with a more comprehensive assessment of the factors—both static and dynamic—that are associated theoretically and empirically with criminal behavior. The single-minded focus on static variables (e.g., criminal history) without attention to other theoretically relevant variables places limits on the utility of risk assessment. Earlier we expressed the requirement that prediction should provide utility. The second-generation risk scales are useful for release decisions and security and supervision classification, but should we not demand more from prediction technology? The criminal justice system is also charged with

Table 10.6
The Superiority of Actuarial Risk Assessment: Meta-analytic Evidence (AUC)

Study	Criterion	Professional Judgment	Actuarial
Bonta, Law & Hanson (1998)	General Recidivism	.50	.73
	Violent Recidivism	.55	.67
Hanson & Bussière (1998)	Sexual Recidivism	.56	.74
Mossman (1994)	Violence	.67	.78
Andrews, Bonta & Wormith (2006)	General	.56	.75
	Violence	.57	.73

AUC derived from conversion chart of r to AUC by Rice & Harris, 2005

Table 10.7
Second-Generation Risk Scales

Item	SFS (U.S.)	SIR (Canada)	OGRS (U.K.)
Static:			
Type of offense	Yes	Yes	Yes
Prior criminal history	Yes (2 items)	Yes (5 items)	Yes (3 items)
Age	Yes	Yes (2 items)	Yes
Prior parole failure	Yes	Yes	No
Gender	No	No	Yes
Security classification	No	Yes	No
Sentence length	No	Yes	No
Risk interval	Yes	Yes	No
Drug abuse history	Yes	No	No
Dynamic:			
Unemployed	No	Yes	No
Marital status	No	Yes	No
Number of dependents	No	Yes	No
Total items	6	15	6

minimizing the offender's risk to the community and with reintegrating inmates into society. To reach these goals, a better theoretical understanding is needed and should be applied to offender assessment technology.

Third-Generation Assessment: Risk/Need Scales

Third-generation offender assessments distinguish themselves from second-generation assessments in that they measure offender needs. Two examples of risk/need instruments are the Wisconsin Risk and Needs assessment instrument (Baird, Heinz & Bemus, 1979) and the Level of Service Inventory–Revised (LSI-R; Andrews & Bonta, 1995). Although evidence of the predictive validity of the risk component of the Wisconsin system has been positive (Baird, 1981, 1991; Baird et al., 1979; Bonta et al., 1994), the predictive validity evidence for the need component has been problematic (Bonta, Parkinson & Barkwell, 1994; Bonta et al., 1994). Therefore, we will focus on the LSI-R because of the large literature on this instrument and because it is the precursor to fourth-generation assessment.

The Level of Service Inventory-Revised. The Level of Service Inventory-Revised or the LSI-R (Andrews & Bonta, 1995) is a theoretically based risk/need offender assessment. The LSI-R samples 54 risk and needs items, each scored in a zero-one format and distributed across 10 subcomponents (e.g., Criminal History, Education/Employment, Leisure, etc.). Most of the LSI-R items and subcomponents are represented in Section 1 of the Level of Service/Case Management Inventory (LS/CMI), which will be discussed under fourth-generation assessment (see Table 10.9 for the LS/CMI).

The items on the LSI-R are those that the research shows to be associated with criminal conduct and that are theoretically relevant. Thus, the Big Four are represented in the subcomponents of Criminal History, Companions, and Attitudes/Orientation and in some of the items from the Emotional/Personal subcomponent. Additionally, the other Central Eight risk/need factors, such as family, substance abuse, and social achievement, are represented. Theoretically speaking, almost all of the items from the LSI-R can be derived from PIC-R. For example, in the Companions subcomponent, information is gathered on: (a) criminal associates (i.e., sources of interpersonal rewards for deviant behavior and costs for prosocial behavior), and (b) prosocial associates (i.e., interpersonal sources of rewards for prosocial behavior and costs for criminal behavior). The distinction between "acquaintances" and "friends" taps the density (quality and frequency) of rewards and costs.

Since the first report on the predictive validity of the LSI-R (Andrews, 1982b), there have been more than 40 articles published on the LSI-R in professional journals and a score of others in government and agency reports and university theses (Vose, Cullen & Smith, 2008). The research has ranged from examination of the psychometric properties of the LSI-R, such as its reliability, convergent validity, and factor structure (e.g., Hollin, Palmer & Clark, 2003; Lowenkamp et al., 2004), to the predictive validity of the instrument (e.g., Kelly & Welsh, 2008; Raynor et al., 2000). The evidence on the predictive validity of the LSI-R has been summarized by Andrews et al. (2006). The mean AUC for the prediction of general recidivism was .71 ($r = .36$); for violent recidivism, it was .64 ($r = .25$; AUCs calculated using the conversion tables of Rice and Harris, 2005).

There have also been a number of comparisons of the LSI-R to other offender risk instruments. All of the comparisons have showed the LSI-R to predict as well or better than the other instruments (Campbell, French & Gendreau, 2009; Dahle, 2006; Kroner & Mills, 2001; Loza & Loza-Fanous, 2001; Motiuk, Bonta & Andrews, 1986; Raynor et al., 2000). In the meta-analysis by Gendreau and his colleagues (1996), the LSI-R was compared to the SFS and Wisconsin classification instruments. The fact that the LSI-R produced the higher correlation coefficients led Gendreau and colleagues (1996) to conclude that the LSI-R . . . is "the current measure of choice" (p. 590). A more recent meta-analysis by Gendreau, Goggin, and Smith (2002) compared the LSI-R with the Psychopathy Checklist-Revised (PCL-R; this instrument was described in Chapter 6). With respect to general recidivism, the average AUC was .73 ($r = .39$) for the LSI-R and .64 ($r = .25$) for the PCL-R.

The most important application of the LSI-R, however, is the delivery of supervision and services to the higher-risk offenders who are likely responsible for most of the criminal activity in the community. By attending to criminogenic needs as well as static risk, the overall risk level of some offenders may be decreased.

Criminogenic Needs and the Dynamic Validity of the LSI-R. The majority of the items that comprise the LSI-R are dynamic. Thus, we would expect that scores on the LSI-R would change with reassessments. The change could result from naturally occurring events (e.g., the offender finds a job) or as the result of treatment (e.g., stops drinking). This information could prove useful for monitoring improvement or deterioration in offenders if it could be shown that changes in LSI-R scores are related to recidivism (that is, the LSI-R measures criminogenic needs). Do changes in LSI-R scores empirically relate to recidivism? There have been five studies demonstrating the dynamic validity of the LSI-R (Andrews & Robinson, 1984; Arnold, 2007; Motiuk, Bonta & Andrews, 1990; Raynor, 2007; Raynor et al., 2000).

The major results from the studies on the dynamic validity of the LSI-R are shown in Table 10.8. The largest evaluations were conducted by Thomas Arnold (n = 1064; Arnold, 2007) and Peter Raynor (n = 203; Raynor, 2007). The remaining studies had smaller samples ranging from 55 (Motiuk et al., 1990) to 157 (Raynor et al., 2000). The test-retest intervals were 8.6 months in Arnold's study and averaged one year in the other studies. Note that low-risk offenders who became worse (had higher LSI-R

Table 10.8
The Dynamic Validity of the LSI-R (% recidivated)

Study/Intake	Re-assessment	
	Low Risk	High Risk
Andrews & Robinson (1984)		
Low Risk	4.2	28.6
High Risk	0.0	57.1
Arnold (2007)		
Low Risk	13.0	26.0
High Risk	32.0	54.0
Motiuk et al. (1990)		
Low Risk	0.0	33.3
High Risk	0.0	54.5
Raynor et al. (2000)		
Low Risk	26.2	54.8
High Risk	55.3	78.4
Raynor (2007)		
Low Risk	29.0	59.0
High Risk	54.0	76.0

scores on retest) showed higher recidivism rates, and high-risk offenders who showed decreased scores demonstrated lower recidivism rates.

Summary of the LSI-R. The LSI-R has been expanded into another third-generation assessment instrument called the Level of Service/Risk, Need, Responsivity (LS/RNR; Andrews, Bonta & Wormith, 2008a). The LS/RNR includes the Central Eight risk/need factors as measured by the LSI-R but adds a number of specific risk/need factors (e.g., sexual assault, weapon use, homelessness, victimization experiences) as well as responsivity considerations (e.g., cultural and ethnic issues). Both instruments are products of the available research and a social learning perspective of criminal behavior. The LSI-R has demonstrated considerable evidence as a predictor of criminal conduct (Andrews & Bonta, 1995; Andrews et al., 2006, 2009; Clements, 1996; Gendreau et al., 1996, 2002). Particularly important is that *changes* in LSI-R scores have predicted correctional outcomes. Together these findings suggest that when we consider some of the essential ingredients of effective prediction (variety, functional and historical characteristics, etc.) within a sound theoretical context—as the LSI-R attempts to do—we are able to predict a wide variety of rule-violating behavior among different offender samples.

Fourth-Generation Risk Assessment: The Integration of Case Management with Risk/Need Assessment

Having well-researched, evidence-based assessments and treatment interventions does not mean that they will be used in "the real world." The translation of knowledge to practice is a problem in the criminal justice system, just as it is in other fields (e.g., medicine). For example, even though the risk principle is widely known across the United States and Canada, a survey of 97 correctional programs in Ohio found only 20 percent adhered to the principle (Lowenkamp, Latessa & Holsinger, 2006). We will say more about obstacles to translating knowledge of risk assessment to practice at the end of this chapter, but here we begin with a description of a study pointing to the need for the development of fourth-generation risk assessment.

Third-generation risk/need instruments are intended to assist staff in allocating supervision resources appropriately (risk principle) and targeting intervention (need principle). In a study of probation in the province of Manitoba, Bonta and his colleagues (Bonta, Rugge, Scott, Bourgon & Yessine, 2008) reviewed the case management practices of 64 probation officers. Case files were reviewed and probation officers submitted audiotapes of their sessions with probationers. There were a couple of important findings relevant to the present discussion. First, and just as Lowenkamp et al. (2006) found, probation officers showed poor adherence to the risk principle (e.g., medium-risk offenders were being seen as frequently as low-risk offenders). Second, the analysis of the audiotapes indicated that probation officers were not focusing on the criminogenic needs identified by the risk/need assessment.

The Manitoba probation study confirmed the fear that although empirically based offender assessments were being *administered*, they were not being *used*. A more structured mechanism was clearly needed to ensure that probation officers do not lose sight of the assessment when dealing with offenders.

Fourth-generation instruments emphasize the link between assessment and case management. This means more than adhering to the risk principle and targeting criminogenic needs. It also acknowledges the role of personal strengths in building a prosocial orientation, the assessment of special responsivity factors to maximize the benefits from treatment, and the structured monitoring of the case from the beginning of supervision to the end. Building upon the LSI-R is the Level of Service/Case Management Inventory (LS/CMI; Andrews, Bonta & Wormith, 2004). There are other fourth-generation assessments (e.g., OASys; HM Prison Service and National Probation Directorate, 2002), but because the LS/CMI has such a well-developed theoretical base, our description of fourth-generation assessment will be limited to the LS/CMI.

A general outline of the structure and sampling of items of the LS/CMI is presented in Table 10.9. The 10 original LSI-R subcomponents have been reorganized to better reflect the Central Eight risk/need factors. Section 1 of the LS/CMI provides the overall offender risk score. As this section is based on the items of the LSI-R, scores on the LS/CMI have been found to predict both general and violent recidivism (Andrews et al., 2004, 2006, 2009; Bourgon & Armstrong, 2005; Campbell et al., 2009; Girard & Wormith, 2004; Rettinger, 1998).

In addition to the core risk/need assessment of Section 1, the LS/CMI, like the LS/RNR, measures specific risk and need factors (Section 2) and responsivity issues (Section 5). Section 2 recognizes the need to assess aspects of the offender and the offender's situation that may have criminogenic potential for that particular individual. For example, a sex offender would be asked questions about his relationship to the victim, and a male batterer would be queried about intimidating and stalking behavior.

In Section 5, attention is given to responsivity considerations that may influence how the correctional officer will relate to the offender and supervise the case. Thus, the LS/CMI covers the three major principles of effective intervention—risk, need, and responsivity. The assessment of responsivity factors is certainly not exhaustive in the LS/CMI, nor is it highly detailed. It covers only some of the major responsivity factors, and correctional staff are encouraged to explore other potential responsivity variables.

Table 10.9
Level of Service/Case Management Inventory (LS/CMI)

<hr>

Section 1.   General Risk/Need Factors

1.1   Criminal History
    1   Any prior youth dispositions or adult convictions
    4   Three or more present offenses
    5   Arrested or charged under age 16
    8   Charge laid, probation breached or parole suspended during prior community supervision

1.2   Education/Employment
    9   Currently unemployed
    13   Less than regular grade 12 or equivalent
    15   Participation/performance
    17   Authority interactions

1.3   Family/Marital
    18   Dissatisfaction with marital or equivalent situation
    19   Nonrewarding, parental
    21   Criminal—Family/spouse

1.4   Leisure/Recreation
    22   Absence of recent participation in an organized activity
    23   Could make better use of time

1.5   Companions
    25   Some criminal friends
    27   Few anticriminal friends

1.6   Alcohol/Drug Problem
    30   Alcohol problem, currently
    31   Drug problem, currently
    33   Marital/Family
    34   School/Work

1.7   Procriminal Attitude/Orientation
    36   Supportive of crime
    37   Unfavorable toward convention

1.8   Antisocial Pattern
    41   Early and diverse antisocial behavior
    42   Criminal attitude
    43   A pattern of generalized trouble (financial problems, unstable accommodations)

Section 2.   Specific Risk/Need Factors

B1.   Personal Problems with Criminogenic Potential
    (2)   Diagnosis of "psychopathy"
    (6)   Anger management deficits
    (9)   Poor social skills
    (12) Underachievement

B2.   History of Perpetration
    (2)   Sexual assault, extrafamilial, child/adolescent—female victim
    (8)   Physical assault (extrafamilial adult victim)
    (18) Gang participation

<hr>

Table 10.9 *(continued)*

Section 5.   Special Responsivity Considerations

1.   Motivation as a barrier
2.   Women, gender-specific
3.   Low intelligence
4.   Antisocial personality/psychopathy

Section 9.   Case Management Plan

Program Targets and Intervention Plan

Criminogenic Need	Goal	Intervention
1.		
2.		
3.		
4.		

Special Responsivity Considerations:

Responsivity Issue	Proposed Approach to Address Issue
1.	
2.	
3.	
4.	

Section 10.   Progress Record

Criminogenic Needs

Date	Criminogenic Need	Improvement	Deterioration	No Change

Finally, the most important feature of the LS/CMI is the integration of the assessment with case management. Referring back to Section 9 of Table 10.9, correctional staff must prioritize the criminogenic needs of the offender, engage the offender in setting concrete targets for change, and choose a means to reach these goals. Furthermore, each contact with the client (Section 10) requires a record of progress, or lack of progress, in reaching the goals. All of this information is in one booklet, ensuring that the staff remains focused on attending to an offender's risk and needs in a structured manner. In summary, fourth-generation offender assessment includes a comprehensive sampling of offender risk and needs, responsivity considerations, and the integration of this information with case management. The assessment of needs includes both criminogenic and noncriminogenic needs, as both types of needs influence the supervision plan. Figure 10.1 summarizes the four generations of risk assessment. Resource Note 10.1 gives a case example of a LS/CMI assessment.

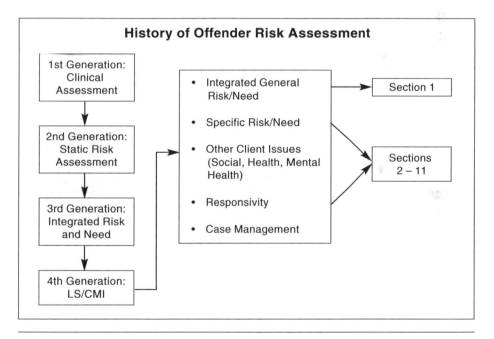

Figure 10.1
Generations of Offender Risk Assessment

Resource Note 10.1

An LS/CMI Offender Assessment

The LS/CMI can be used for a variety of purposes. The LS/CMI can be administered to assist probation officers in developing a case plan for community supervision, help parole boards in making release decisions and assigning conditions for release, and prison classification officers may administer the LS/CMI in order to make an appropriate security classification and program plan for the inmate. Sometimes a probation officer may administer the LS/CMI as part of his or her preparation of the Pre-Sentence Report (PSR). A PSR may be requested by a judge to assist the court in a sentencing decision. Administering the LS/CMI may not only help the court but also the probation officer when it comes to supervising the case as illustrated in the following case example.

In the following PSR report the bolded sections indicate information that is important for scoring the LS/CMI. The section in italics provides general comments on sections of the report.

Pre-Sentence Report
Name: Frank Brown
Date of Birth: February 14, 1984
Age: 23 years old
Date: April 13, 2006

Reason for Assessment

Her Honor, Judge Belinda McCormick, requested a pre-sentence report on Mr. Brown, who is awaiting sentencing on May 15, 2006. The court is considering the appropriateness of a community disposition and recommendations for treatment.

Sources of Information

The *Level of Service/Case Management Inventory* (LS/CMI) was administered to determine the degree of risk that the client presents to the community and the client characteristics that contribute to such risk, some of which may be addressed through various kinds of active intervention or treatment. The LS/CMI does not encompass traditional principles of sentencing—most notably, offense severity—and therefore should not be used to address sentencing in the absence of these other considerations.

Mr. Brown was interviewed on April 10. I was unable to contact his common-law wife to corroborate some of Mr. Brown's information, but I was able to speak to his mother, Mrs. Edna Brown, and one of his sisters (Mrs. West). Other sources of information included a previous PSR (March 25, 2000) and probation case notes pertaining to his previous supervision.

At this point, the PSR describes in a narrative from Section 1 (General Risk/Need Factors) of the LS/CMI. Section 1 of the LS/CMI covers the Central Eight risk/need factors and yields an overall risk/need score for the prediction of re-offending and identifies the important criminogenic needs associated with the case.

Criminal History

The scoring of criminal history information reflects the density of rewards associated with criminal behavior. A long and early onset history increases the likelihood of re-offending. In addition, this section of the LS/CMI taps into the individual's compliance with correctional supervision and seriousness of his or her offense pattern.

Mr. Brown was recently convicted of *three* property offenses (two counts of break and enter and one count of possession of stolen property). Mr. Brown completed a term of probation last year for a prior offense; he has *never been incarcerated*. Mr. Brown has *no* history as a juvenile delinquent. However, this is Mr. Brown's *second* set of convictions as an adult. Two years ago he received a sentence of one year of probation for possession of stolen property, which was *successfully completed* under my supervision.

Resource Note 10.1 *(continued)*

Education/Employment

The LS/CMI's Section 2 (*Specific Risk/Need Factors*) expands on the General Risk/Need Factors of Section 1 by including possible risk/need factors specific to certain kinds of offending (e.g., sexual offending, family violence). Reports based on the LS/CMI do not need to follow the order set out in the sections of the LS/CMI. In fact, if the report was written to exactly mirror the LS/CMI then it would be long and repetitive. During the course of an interview, the offender will give information that can be used to score different parts of the report. The reader can see in this section where such information is provided to inform different sections of the LS/CMI. The Education/Employment section is scored depending on whether the subject is a student or employed in the workforce. In the case of Mr. Brown, the scoring is based on the criminogenic need of employment and includes not only whether he is employed but also how rewarding employment is to Mr. Brown.

Mr. Brown *completed grade 12* and began working immediately in the automotive factory on the assembly line. Mr. Brown is trained to install windshields on cars and describes his work as "it's a job." He shows *very little enthusiasm for the work*, admitting that he is bored with the routine and would like to *find employment that is more challenging* (*Section 2.1, item "underachievement"*). Mr. Brown reported that he does *not get along with his foreman*, who he describes as narrow-minded and a "tyrant." His relationship with his *co-workers is satisfactory*. Mr. Brown eats lunch and spends coffee breaks with them. In sum, Mr, Brown presents as an individual who feels very unfulfilled in the workplace (*Once again, "underachievement" in Section 2.1*).

Family/Marital

In this section, the offender provides information that raises other client issues (*Section 4 of the LS/CMI*) that although not criminogenic needs are relevant to supervising this offender. Mr. Brown's victimiza-tion by his partner and father could create obstacles to making positive changes in his life and present an emotional stress that needs to be addressed. Also highlighted in this section is the antisocial support provided by his wife and the possibility that Mr. Brown's sisters may be helpful in his supervision.

The relationship between Mr. Brown and his common-law wife (Sherri) appears to be problematic. They have been living together for eight months and they have no children. Mr. Brown describes Sherri as a "bit wild." She would frequently leave the house unannounced and be absent for days. Mr. Brown suspects that she goes on drinking binges and *she has been arrested* a number of times. When at home, the couple drinks frequently, after which they often end up in an argument. Mr. Brown denies ever hitting his common-law wife. Quite the contrary, he reports that she has frequently struck him and often plays "mind games" with him by saying that she could go out with anyone she wants and that he is "nothing" (*Section 4, "victim of physical and emotional abuse"*). Mr. Brown becomes noticeably agitated when talking about his marital relationship and acknowledges that he does not know how to discuss these matters with his partner (*Section 2.1 "poor social skills"*). I was unable to confirm the above commentary from Sherri, but Mr. Brown's mother did agree with her son's description of his marital situation.

Mrs. Edna Brown reported that her son has had a difficult childhood. His father was an alcoholic and had been repeatedly abusive toward the children during his drinking. He took out his personal frustrations physically on Frank, as he was the only boy in the family (*Section 4, past physical abuse*). His *father died* in a car accident when Frank Brown was 16 years old. Mr. Brown only visits his mother at Christmas and on her birthday and acknowledges that he is *not able to discuss personal matters with his mother*.

There are two older sisters in the family living an hour away in Springfield. Nonetheless, Mr. Brown does manage to keep in touch with

Resource Note 10.1 *(continued)*

them on a regular basis on the phone and through e-mail. *Neither sister has had any difficulty with the law.* In my discussions with his married sister, Elizabeth West, it became apparent that both sisters are concerned about their brother and offer support in whatever way they can (*note, this may be a possible area of Strength*). She also noted that he often appears to be shy and withdrawn but becomes more relaxed and outgoing after a few drinks, suggesting that Mr. Brown uses alcohol as a disinhibiter.

Leisure/Recreation

This section shows both a positive side to Mr. Brown's leisure activities (i.e., his love of music) and the danger of too much unstructured time.

Mr. Brown is quite talented musically and he *devotes a considerable amount of time to practicing the guitar*, either on his own, or with a small group of fellow musicians. He and his colleagues, who Mr. Brown describes as older 'family' men, are asked to *play at various kinds of social events* about once a month, for which they are paid a modest fee. Mr. Brown finds this work *personally satisfying*, saying that he would love to make a career out music.

He *does not have any other personal interests or hobbies*. A typical day involves coming home, eating his dinner, and watching television or playing his guitar while he drinks beer with his common-law wife. On weekends, he and his wife usually sleep until midday, do the grocery shopping, and then go out to the pub in the evening with friends.

Companions

Companions form one of the Big Four correlates of criminal behavior and the LS/CMI gives special attention to this risk/need factor. No other offender risk instrument gives this kind of attention to social support for crime. Also note that at the end of this section, information is provided that will permit scoring items from the Procriminal Attitude/Orientation subcomponent of Section 1.

None of Mr. Brown's friends from work, as far as he knows, has a criminal record. Although Mr. Brown enjoys their company, he hardly sees them outside of the work environment. He claims that his current friends are limited to a couple of his fellow musicians, who he describes as being *very straight*. However, Mr. Brown has now been introduced to his common-law wife's large circle of friends and he has settled in with her crowd quite comfortably. All of these people drink, and some of them *abuse drugs* and have been *involved in crime*. When asked what he thought of these people, he replied that they "are a lot of fun" and "as long as they don't hurt anyone, who cares if they get a little high or get involved in petty crime?"

Alcohol/Drug Problems

In the Alcohol/Drug Problems area it is not simply a matter of whether the offender has a substance abuse problem but understanding how the problem contributes to criminal behavior. Thus, the interviewer collects information on how substance abuse interferes in the areas of work, family, and personal self-regulation. Notice again how Mr. Brown rationalizes his crimes by minimizing the harm to the victim. In addition, we see a responsivity issue be assessed when Mr. Brown indicates an unwillingness to participate in treatment.

Mr. Brown began to *drink regularly after his father's death*. He stopped drinking heavily after about a year and settled into work. Mr. Brown noticed that his drinking "picked up a little" after meeting his common-law wife. When I asked him to tell me how much he would drink on a daily basis, he estimated *5 or 6 beers during a weeknight and about 8 or 9 beers on the weekend*. The drinking would almost always be with his common-law wife, and they *often argued* about "stupid, little things." Mr. Brown's *mother reported that she has no interest in seeing her son* "until he breaks his father's habit" (referring to the alcoholism of Mr. Brown's father).

Resource Note 10.1 *(continued)*

As best as I can ascertain, Mr. Brown does not drink at work, but he has *missed work* on a number of occasions because of a hangover and was *reprimanded* on two occasions by his supervisor. In addition, the *present offenses were initiated after drinking* with his friends. Mr. Brown remembers little of that night but that *"not much damage had been done"* and the owners *"recouped the stolen property anyway."* In our discussions about possibly participating in a treatment program for his alcohol abuse, Mr. Brown quickly dismisses the suggestion, saying that he has curtailed his consumption in the past and will do so in the future, making any such treatment a waste of government money (*Section 5, Responsivity, "motivation as a barrier"*).

Mr. Brown asserts that he is *not currently using drugs* and has no interest in doing so. He acknowledges that he has tried marijuana on a few occasions with his friends, but that it just makes him sleepy.

Procriminal Attitude/Orientation

The assessment of procriminal attitudes, another of the Big Four, is usually conducted by listening carefully throughout the interview for expressions of attitudes toward criminal behavior and convention (work, authority, etc.).

Mr. Brown demonstrated his support for antisocial behaviours on a number of occasions during our meeting. He *minimized* his present involvement with crime by blaming it on the alcohol. Furthermore, Mr. Brown sees no problem with associating with his present friends and *values their friendship.* On a more positive note, Mr. Brown considers *working as an important activity* and feels that everyone should work for a living, "including those on welfare." Although he does not particularly like his present work and supervisor, he has no plans to quit and he wants to remain an active member of the workforce. Mr. Brown has been on probation supervision in the past and he always kept his appointments and *complied with the probation conditions.* In discussing his previous period of probation, it is clear that he had *established a positive working relationship with his probation officer.* Mr. Brown does, however, take exception to his current conviction. In spite of a finding of guilt, he thinks that the neighborhood shop owners should not have pressed charges because he was extremely *intoxicated.* When queried about the damage, he acknowledged responsibility and accepted the prospects of paying restitution, but added that he was certain the *businesses would have insurance.*

Antisocial Pattern

The Antisocial Pattern subcomponent assesses the general personality and behavioral patterns associated with criminal behavior. For the most part, Mr. Brown shows little of the instability often found among high-risk offenders with antisocial personality.

As an adult, Mr. Brown has had two run-ins with the law, both of which resulted in convictions. However, there is *no evidence of behavioral problems during his childhood* or delinquent behavior during his adolescence. He *does not have any history of perpetrating violent behavior*, either domestically or with others. Although somewhat self-centered, he *does not present as a particularly callous person.* Mr. Brown, on occasion, acts on impulse, particularly under the influence of alcohol.

There is *no history of mental health intervention* for Mr. Brown. Although currently anxious about his pending court disposition, there is *no evidence of depression* or suicidal ideation.

Mr. Brown *denied having any financial difficulties.* He has been renting an apartment and the car he owns has been completely paid for. Mr. Brown claims that he has no outstanding debts and is able to live within his means, but adds that he cannot afford many luxuries. Mr. Brown lives in a residential area of the city that is not noted for a high degree of criminal activity, and he has no intention of moving.

Resource Note 10.1 *(continued)*

Summary and Recommendations

Note in this section how the probation officer provides an estimate of Mr. Brown's risk to re-offend and outlines a plan that would allow the judge to consider a community placement as opposed to incarceration.

In reviewing Mr. Brown's personal history, the most noticeable change in his situation compared to his previous probation order is his return to drinking, precipitated by Mr. Brown's involvement with his common-law wife and her friends. The increased expression of attitudes and values supportive of criminal conduct may also reflect the influence of Mr. Brown's social circle.

When Mr. Brown was sentenced for his previous offense, he was assessed on the LS/CMI as falling into the low-risk/need category. Today, Mr. Brown's assessment places him in the moderate range for risk of re-offending. The increase in risk can be traced to his growing, but still limited, criminal history, his continued and more extensive alcohol abuse, his unstable marital situation, his increased exposure to and time spent with others who are involved in crime, and his growing dissatisfaction with his employment. Probationers within the medium-risk category have a 48 percent likelihood of re-offending within a two-year period. However, effective intervention may be expected to lower these probabilities to some extent.

The present assessment identifies a need for alcohol abuse counseling, in spite of the client's view that it is unnecessary, and a need to develop a more prosocial network of peers. Increasing ties to others who are not involved in criminal or drinking activity may lead to a more productive use of leisure time. His two older sisters have expressed positive sentiments toward their brother and can be helpful in providing encouragement to pursue prosocial activities (e.g., his interests in music).

In view of Mr. Brown's history of compliance while on probation, another probationary period with a condition to attend treatment may be advantageous in providing Mr. Brown the motivation and access to community resources to deal with his alcohol abuse. He already appears on the verge of severing ties with his common-law wife, which could assist in lowering his exposure to his current circle of antisocial associations, which in turn, may also contribute to reducing some of his procriminal attitudes. Furthermore, a community disposition would allow Mr. Brown to maintain employment and, with guidance from the supervisory probation officer, he may be able to build upon his workplace associations to expand his prosocial network.

J. Wordsmith
Senior Probation Officer

The General Applicability of Theory-Based Offender Assessment

The PIC-R perspective holds that variations in behavior are explained by the fundamental principles of cognitive social learning theory. The behavior of individuals is under the control of rewards and costs within the personal, interpersonal, and community situations of action. Reader, please note that we used the word "behavior" in the previous sentences without the qualifying adjective "criminal." We did this purposefully, because the general principles of learning (modeling, operant and classical conditioning, self-regulation in the service of the self) are applicable to all behaviors. For a psychology of criminal conduct, this means that assessment and treatment strategies that are derived from a general personality and cognitive social learning perspective would have wide applicability to different populations of offenders (e.g., women, minorities, mentally disordered) and different types of criminal behavior (e.g., violent, sexual). The Level of Service instruments (LSI-R, LS/CMI, etc.) were developed from such a perspective. In this section we turn to the applicability of the Level of Service (LS) instruments across offender samples and criminal outcomes.

LS Risk Assessment Across Different Populations

Within the criminal justice system there are many different offenders. There are young offenders and adult offenders, there are male and female offenders, there are the poor and rich, and there are offenders who suffer from mental illness. We can group offenders in many ways, and when we do so we will find variations in their criminal behavior. For example, men are more likely to engage in crime than women. However, does this mean that the risk factors differ substantially by group? We do not think so.

As an introduction to our discussion of the generality of risk/need factors, we present the association between three-year recidivism rates and LS/CMI overall risk/need scores for 561 Ontario probationers (Table 10.10). The recidivism rates are presented as proportions at each level of risk/need for the total sample and for each level of age (young offenders/adult offenders), gender (women/men), and poverty

Table 10.10
Recidivism Rates by LS/CMI Risk/Need Level (*N* = 561)

Group/Subgroup	Risk/Need Level				
	Very Low	Low	Medium	High	Very High
Total Sample	.09 (151)	.20 (169)	.48 (196)	.77 (43)	1.00 (2)
Young males relying on SA	.00 (1)	.00 (0)	.73 (11)	1.00 (3)	(0)
Young females relying on SA	.00 (1)	.00 (1)	.33 (3)	1.00 (2)	(0)
Adult males relying on SA	.17 (6)	.38 (13)	.46 (48)	.67 (15)	(0)
Adult females relying on SA	.00 (3)	.10 (10)	.30 (10)	1.00 (2)	(0)
Young males	.13 (23)	.34 (32)	.61 (33)	.88 (8)	1.00 (2)
Adult males	.09 (84)	.15 (97)	.44 (80)	.50 (8)	(0)
Young females	.00 (7)	.17 (6)	.25 (4)	.67 (3)	(0)
Adult females	.08 (26)	.10 (10)	.57 (7)	.50 (2)	(0)

Note: SA = Social Assistance

(reliance on social assistance/those who are less financially dependent on the state). Examining the first row, it is evident that 9 percent of the 151 probationers scoring as very low-risk recidivated, 20 percent of the 169 low-risk cases recidivated, through to 100 percent of the two very high–risk cases. The recidivism rate was clearly increasing with risk/need level, and the overall risk-recidivism correlation was .44. Now examine the remaining rows and you will see that in every subgroup recidivism increases as LS/CMI scores increase.

Age, gender, and poverty are risk factors on their own. Being young (under 18 years of age), being male, and being in a state of poverty (reliance on social welfare) are each risk factors, with predictive validity estimates (correlation coefficients) of .15, .09, and .16, respectively. However, once the total risk/need score was entered as a covariate, the contributions of gender and poverty were reduced to nonsignificant levels, and the r for age and reconviction was reduced to .11. On the other hand, controlling for age, gender, and poverty had little impact on the predictive validity of overall risk/need scores (the r dropped to .40 from .44). It appears that the contributions of age, gender, and poverty to criminal recidivism can be understood through their contributions to attitudes, associates, and so on. Let us now turn to a bit more detailed discussion of the Level of Service (LS) instruments with respect to age, gender, and race/ethnicity.

Age. The Youth Level of Service/Case Management Inventory (YLS/CMI; Hoge & Andrews, 2003) consists of 42 items organized around the Central Eight risk/need factors. There are also six parts to the instrument, which includes a general risk/need score based on the 42 items and a case management plan. Like the adult LS/CMI, the youth LS instrument is based upon theory and its relevance to youths (Hoge, 2009). Administration of the YLS/CMI is normally with youths between the ages of 12 and 17, although it has been used with youths as young as 10 years old. The psychometric properties of the instrument are summarized by Hoge (2009).

The YLS/CMI does not have as many studies on the predictive validity and generalizability of the instrument as the adult LS instruments, but this situation is rapidly changing. Mark Olver and his colleagues (Olver, Stockdale & Wormith, 2009) were able to conduct a meta-analysis of three risk instruments used with youths. They identified 44 studies for inclusion. Twenty-two studies were of the YLS/CMI (or slightly modified versions of it), 27 were youth versions of the Psychopathy Checklist (PCL), and there were nine studies of the SAVRY (Structured Assessment of Violence Risk in Youth). All three instruments predicted general and violent recidivism with no one scale outperforming the other. For the YLS/CMI, the average effect sizes (r) were .32 (k = 19) for general recidivism and .26 (k = .26) for violent recidivism.

The YLS/CMI does not make any special adjustments for gender or race and therefore, the validity of the instruments with these groups has come under intense scrutiny (Onifade, Davidson, Campbell, Turke et al.,

2008; we will say more about the gender and race issues in the following sections). Although considerably more studies are needed to form a clear conclusion, early indications are that the YLS/CMI applies to girls and some racial minorities. In a meta-analysis by Schwalbe (2008), the mean effect size (r) was .32 for young males (k = 4) and .40 for girls (k = 3). Note, however, the few number of studies that were available for analysis.

With respect to race, there are only a handful of predictive validity studies. Onifadde et al. (2008) followed 328 youths (ages 10 to 16 years) over a one-year follow-up. They found that the risk/need scores from the YLS/CMI predicted recidivism for whites but not for African Americans or Hispanics. However, in a much larger study of 4,482 youths by Bechtel, Lowenkamp, and Latessa (2007), the YLS/CMI predicted equally well for both white and nonwhite juveniles (scores also predicted equally well for males and females). Among the Canadian prairie provinces there are significant Native populations permitting evaluations of the YLS/CMI with Native youth offenders. In all of these evaluations, scores on the YLS/CMI have predicted recidivism (Gossner & Wormith, 2007; Luong, 2007).

Gender. Our position is that risk/need instruments based upon a General Personal and Cognitive Social Learning (GPCSL) theory, such as the LS instruments, would apply equally to men and women. We made this point earlier in Chapter 2 (see our discussion of Table 2.9), but some feminist scholars have been critical of the LSI-R for not giving sufficient attention to their favored gender-based variables. Some (e.g., Bloom & Covington, 2000) have emphasized the importance of emotional distress and low self-esteem. Neither is represented as a major risk factor in the LS instruments. And why should they be? Hubbard and Pratt's (2002) meta-analysis of risk factors for delinquency among girls found a mean effect size of .06.

In two studies by Holtfreter and her colleagues (Holtfreter, Reisig & Morash, 2004; Reisig, Holtfreter & Morash, 2006), the LSI-R was found to be a poor predictor of recidivism. However, the follow-up period was only six months in the first study. And in the second study, the average follow-up was still less than a year. Furthermore, they relied on self-reports of criminal behavior through interviews with the women. Curiously, those who were known to have officially recidivated or were unavailable for an interview were excluded from the analysis. Why ignore the women that you know committed another offense?

There will always be studies that report findings outside the norm. Findings from meta-analyses are so important because we can have a truer picture of what is the norm and what are the outliers. Recently, Paula Smith, Francis Cullen, and Edward Latessa (2009) conducted a meta-analysis of the LSI-R and recidivism for female offenders. In total, the studies reviewed involved 14,737 women. The average mean effect (r) was .35 (k = 27). Even Kristy Holtfreter in her own review of 11 studies (actually one study on the SIR risk scale was misidentified as an LSI study) concluded that "the LSI-R does indeed appear to 'work' fairly well for women" (Holtfreter & Cupp, 2007).

Despite the overwhelming evidence that the LSI-R is "gender-neutral," efforts are continuing to build "gender-informed" (GI) risk/need instruments. It is possible that GI factors may have some incremental validity. LS/CMI and LS/RNR instruments are examples of GI assessments. Other examples come from researchers at the University of Cincinnati. Patricia Van Voorhis and her colleagues, with the support of the U.S. National Institute of Corrections, have developed a "trailer" to be used for women in addition to the LSI-R (Van Voorhis, Salisbury, Wright & Bauman, 2008). The trailer consists of items thought to be particularly important for women (i.e., gender-informed or "gender-responsive," the term used by Van Voorhis et al.). Such items include adult victimization, parental stress, and self-esteem. Some of the GI items overlap with LSI-R items (e.g. family/marital and finance variables).

The approach is very interesting because it was not undertaken as a challenge to the notion of the gender-neutrality of the well-established risk/need factors assessed with instruments such as the LSI-R. Rather, it asks whether the addition of assessments of gender-informed risk/need factors may improve upon the predictive validity of LSI-R on their own. The validation of the "trailers" is only now being explored in cross-validation studies. Still, the findings to date are very interesting and informative.

Validation studies have been conducted in the states of Colorado, Hawaii, Minnesota, and Missouri. Colorado, Hawaii, and Minnesota use the LSI-R and, therefore, the predictive validity of the LSI-R may be compared with the validity of the GI trailer. The results distilled from the Van Voorhis et al. (2008) report are shown in Table 10.11. As shown in the table, the gender-responsive scale performed better than the LSI-R in two of the six comparisons (Colorado and Minnesota). In fact, in two of the six tests, the contributions of GI assessments were not even significantly greater than zero.

It is important to note that contrary to some interpretations of the Van Voorhis findings to date, the results do not speak at all to the issues of the gender-neutrality and gender-specificity of risk/need factors. As impor-

Table 10.11
Predictive Validity Estimates (r): LSI-R vs. Gender Informed (n)

Risk Assessment	Prison Sample		Probation Sample		Parole	Drug Court
	Colorado (156)	Minnesota (198)	Minnesota (233)	Hawaii (158)	Colorado (134)	Minnesota (150)
LSI-R	.16	.30	.31	.36	.21	.28
Gender-Informed	.27	.27	.34	.31	.00 (ns)	.00 (ns)

Note: ns = nonsignficant

Adapted from Van Voorhis et al. (2008; Table 3. Van Vooorhis et al. (2008) dropped the Drug Court sample from their Table 3 because the gender-informed assessment failed to yield any significant factors.

tant as the NIC-UC studies are, they studied female offenders exclusively and thus provide no direct information on gender similarities and gender differences in risk/need. Nowhere has this issue been rendered more important than in the Holtfreter and Cupp (2007) interpretation of the findings of "gendered" pathways to crime as reported by Reisig et al. (2006). There, as in the case of the LSI "trailer" studies, gender similarities and differences in risk/need factors are implied to exist when studies of males were not even conducted. As shown in Chapter 2, you cannot draw conclusions regarding "gender-informed," "gender-responsive," or "gendered" pathways without studying both males and females.

Please note that we are not trying to discount the contributions made by Daly (1992) through her suggestions regarding the differential pathways to crime followed by female offenders. We expect, however, that the pathways followed by female offenders are very similar to the pathways followed by male offenders. The limitation is the unexplored and nonvalidated emphasis placed on the phrase "gendered pathways." There is no evidence that male offenders do not follow very similar pathways to crime.

Essentially, the pathway approach centers on different routes or pathways to adult criminality (we see little difference between our own views of multiple routes to crime and the pathway model, although some feminist scholars would disagree with us). For example, abuse in the home may lead to running away, and in order to cope with life on the street, the young runaway may turn to prostitution, theft, and drug use and drug dealing. Likewise, early misconduct (including violence) may lead to early departure from the home and the increased likelihood of school dropouts, poor preparation for conventional work, and association with criminal others. You will note that the majority of indicators of "gendered" pathways are actually well-known risk/need factors. There is little in the Daly descriptions of "street women," "battered women," "drug connected," and "harmed and harming" that would not easily be found to be descriptive of male offenders.

Reisig et al. (2006) were very innovative in testing the validity of LSI-R with female offenders on "gendered" ($n = 155$), "nongendered" ($n = 30$), and "unclassifiable" ($n = 50$) subgroups. The LSI-R predicted recidivism for the nongendered and unclassified groups but not the gendered group. This finding appears to be an outlier. Otherwise, how would you reconcile the fact that the meta-analysis of more than 14,000 women offenders shows the LSI-R as predicting recidivism? The meta-analytic results suggest that the majority of women offenders are following a nongendered pathway, further diminishing the relevance of a "gendered" pathway.

Fortunately, the field has a more direct test of gender similarities and differences in the female and male criminal trajectories (albeit not with the LSI-R):

> Four antisocial behavior trajectory groups were identified among females and males. . . and included life-course persistent (LCP),

> adolescent-onset, childhood limited, and low trajectory groups... ...Although more males than females followed the LCP trajectory, findings support similarities across gender with respect to developmental trajectories of antisocial behavior and their associated childhood origins and adult consequences (Odgers, Moffitt, Broadbent, Dickson, et al., 2008:673).

The debate over the appropriate risk/need assessment of women continues (Hannah-Moffatt, 2009; Taylor & Blanchette, 2009). We do not see this debate being resolved in the near future, partly because the standards invoked by feminist scholars are becoming of a variety that are impossible to meet. Take, for example, the following quotes from Merry Morash's (2009) editorial introduction to a series of articles debating the appropriateness of the LSI-R with women offenders:

> The article and the responses to it put many other questions on the table. Is the LSI-R the *best* [italics original] predictor for women offenders? Are social learning theory and cognitive psychology (the theoretical rationale for the LSI-R) the *best* [italics added] theories to explain women's offending and desistence from offending? (p. 173)

> The particular theories *cannot* [italics added] be integrated in a clear and logical way (i.e., cognitive psychology and pathways explanations of girls' and women's lawbreaking) (p. 177).

How can the LSI-R meet such a standard of being the *best*? How can a General Personality and Cognitive Social Learning theory hope to explain female criminality when it is already proclaimed to be impossible?

Perhaps the need to enhance the LSI-R with gender-informed variables may be muted with the development of the gender-informed YLS/CMI, LS/CMI, and LS/RNR (Andrews, Bonta & Wormith, 2008b). Both of these instruments have added items that are gender-informed (e.g., history of victimization, parenting concerns). Although these additional items do not contribute to the total risk/need score, they open the opportunity to explore in a systematic way the factors that may provide incremental validity in the assessment of women offenders. Such research is under way, and it includes attention to female offenders and male offenders. Otherwise, conclusions regarding the gender-specificity and gender-neutrality of risk/need factors are in the world of speculation. We expect that the research and practice in regard to gender-responsiveness will shift to the domains of specific responsivity and the targeting of noncriminogenic needs in accord with the principles of the RNR Model of Correctional Assessment and Treatment (Chapter 2).

Race/Ethnicity. The number of studies on the LSI-R with respect to race and ethnicity pales compared to the female offender literature. At a general level, the predictive validity of the LSI-R has been demonstrated in countries outside of Canada, where the instrument was first developed. In addition to the United States, the validity of the LSI-R has been established in Singapore (Neo, Misir & Lee, 2006), the United Kingdom (Hollin & Palmer, 2006; Raynor, 2007; Raynor et al., 2000), Australia (Cumberland & Boyle, 1997), Portugal (Neves & Gonçalves, 2008), and Germany (Dahle, 2006).

Given the Canadian origins of the LS instruments, there has been some interest in the applicability of the instrument with North American Native offenders (Bonta, 1989; Gross & Srgoa, 2008). Stephen Wormith's lab at the University of Saskatchewan, with the collaboration of researchers in Ontario, has produced the largest study to date. Carrie Tanasichuk and Stephen Wormith (2009) examined the relationship between scores on the LS/CMI and recidivism for 3,960 Aboriginal offenders. Eighty percent of the sample was male, and the average follow-up time was slightly more than two years. Here is a summary of some of their major findings:

1. Total risk/need scores predicted general recidivism ($r = .37$) and violent recidivism ($r = .17$).

2. All of the Central Eight predicted both general and violent recidivism (correlations ranged from .06 for Leisure/Recreation and violence to .35 for Criminal History and general recidivism).

3. The predictive validity of the total risk/need score and the Central Eight subcomponents were similar for male and female Native offenders.

It appears that the LS instruments have validity among Canadian Native offenders, and there is also some evidence of its validity among American Native offenders (Holsinger, Lowenkamp & Latessa, 2006).

Whiteacre (2006) has warned of the need to evaluate an instrument thoroughly in order to ensure that the classification of risk levels based on instruments such as the LSI-R do not selectively bias against African Americans or Hispanics. Using cutoff scores first developed for Caucasians may lead to over- or under-classification of certain ethnic minorities. At this point, most of the research on other minorities is found in unpublished government reports and student dissertations (Arnold, 2007; Flores, Lowenkamp, Smith & Latessa, undated; Graves & Vellani, 2000; Washington State Institute for Public Policy, 2003), with only a few published studies (Fass, Heilbrun, Dematteo & Fretz, 2008; Lowenkamp & Bechtel, 2007; Schlager & Simourd, 2007). The findings have been mixed and contradictory. Most report supporting predictive validity for the LSI-R with African Americans, but two studies found no support with Hispanics (Fass et al., 2008; Schlager & Simourd, 2007). Further studies that can contribute to a meta-analysis are needed before reaching a more definitive conclusion.

Summary. In general, the Central Eight from the GPCSL, as measured by the LS instruments, apply across age, gender, and, for the most part, race and ethnicity. Primary studies continue to contribute to our understanding of the practical utility of a GPCSL perspective as represented in the LS instruments (Brews, 2009; Listwan, 2009; Manchak, Skeem, Douglas & Siranosian, 2009). The predictive validity of LS scores has also been demonstrated with mentally disordered offenders (Daffern, 2007; Ferguson, Ogloff & Thomson, 2009; Harris, Rice & Quinsey, 1993; Lovell, Gagliardi & Phipps, 2005; Thomas, Daffern, Martin, Ogloff et al., 2009), male batterers (Hanson & Wallace-Capretta, 2004; Hendricks, Werner, Shipway & Turinetti, 2006), sex offenders (Girard & Wormith, 2004; Vrana & Sroga, 2008; Washington State Institute for Public Policy, 2006), drug offenders (Kelly & Welsh, 2008), long-term offenders with sentences of more than 10 years (Manchak, Skeem & Douglas, 2008), and the frequently unemployed and those living in high-crime neighborhoods (Andrews, Dowden & Rettinger, 2001). What all of this means is that the risk factors identified by our theoretical perspective of criminal conduct are applicable to a wide range of offenders living in a variety of social conditions (e.g., poverty). This finding does not deflate the importance of gender, race, ethnicity, poverty, and so on. It just reveals the extent to which offending reflects the Central Eight risk factors in a variety of contexts and across samples.

LS Risk Across Different Outcomes

The Prediction of Violence. In the beginning of this chapter (predictive accuracy and the two-by-two table), we showed the difficulties in trying to predict low-base-rate behaviors. Compared to nonviolent offending, for which base rates often fall in the 40 to 60 percent range, violent offending is much lower (10 to 20% range), and certain forms of violence are lower still (e.g., sexual offending in the neighborhood of 5%). Despite the difficulties in predicting low-base-rate behaviors, the seriousness of the harm caused to victims demands special attention to the prediction of violent behavior.

The general approach for dealing with the assessment of risk for violent behavior is to develop specialized risk scales. Underlying this approach is the idea that those who commit violent acts are significantly different enough from the run-of-the-mill offender that we need a different set of predictors. Two risk instruments that are considered by many to be especially good at predicting violence are the PCL-R (Hare, 1991) and the Violence Risk Appraisal Guide (VRAG; Harris, Rice & Quinsey, 1993). Other "general violence" scales abound in the literature (Dolan & Fullam,

2007; Kroner & Mills, 2001; Loza, MacTavish & Loza-Fanous, 2007; Simourd & Mamuza, 2000; Ward & Dockerill, 1999; Wong & Gordon, 2006). The question that we ask is "Is an LS general risk assessment instrument, based on a PCC, useful in the prediction of violent behavior?"

One way to answer this question is to compare the array of instruments specifically designed to predict violent recidivism with the LS instruments. For example, in a direct comparison of the VRAG, PCL-R, and the LSI-R, Daryl Kroner and Jeremy Mills (2001) found the following correlations (AUC in parentheses) with violent recidivism: $r = .12$ (.56) for the PCL-R, $r = .15$ (.60) for the VRAG, and $r = .19$ (.68) for the LSI-R. More importantly, there are two meta-analytic summaries that found the LSI-R to predict violent recidivism as well as the PCL-R and other violence-specific risk scales (Campbell, French & Gendreau, 2009; Gendreau, Goggin & Smith, 2002). Table 10.12 summarizes these two meta-analyses. None of the violence-specific risk scales (PCL-R and VRAG) predicted better that the general LSI-R (the Confidence Intervals overlapped among the scales).

In general, research with the LSI-R suggests that a general, theory-based risk-assessment measure can predict violent behavior as well as the violence risk scales. As we have already noted, there is even some evidence that LSI-R scores predict some specific forms of violence such as sexual violence (Washington State Institute for Public Policy, 2006) and domestic violence (Hendricks et al., 2006). One advantage that the LSI-R has over the violence risk scales is that the LSI-R measures the dynamic risk factors that are so important for the management of high-risk violent offenders. Most of the violence risk scales are comprised of static items and have ignored dynamic risk factors (Douglas & Skeem, 2005). Can we improve on our prediction of violence? Of course we can. Research on violence-specific risk scales continues, and progress is being made. In the LS/CMI, the introduction of an antisocial personality pattern subcomponent and specific items that deal with violence is likely to bring improvements in predictive accuracy. Already we have seen promise in

Table 10.12
The LSI-R and Violent Recidivism

Study	k (N)	r	AUC
Campbell et al. (2009)			
LSI-R	19 (4361)	.28	.66
PCL-R	24 (4757)	.27	.65
VRAG	14 (2082)	.32	.68
Gendreau et al. (2002)			
LSI-R	9 (2777)	.29	.67
PCL-R	7 (1552)	.27	.65

Note: k = number of effect size, *N* = number of offenders. AUC conversion based on Rice and Harris (2005)

these changes in the LS/CMI. Lina Girard and Stephen Wormith (2004) found that a history of aggression together with the antisocial personality pattern yielded an r of .42 (AUC = .75).

Obstacles to Using Empirically Based Risk Prediction

We hope that the reader sees from this chapter the advantages to using evidence-based risk assessment with offenders. The evidence is strong, and there certainly is no shortage of instruments available to the interested practitioner. However, there remain disquieting indications that many practitioners and correctional systems are not enjoying the full benefits of the research findings. There are many possible reasons for this state of affairs; we will comment on only four of them.

1. *Adherence to psychopathological models of criminal behavior.* Jennifer Boothby and Carl Clements (2000) asked 830 correctional psychologists what tests they used in the assessment of offenders. More than one-half of the psychologists reported using tests (e.g., Rorschach, projective drawings) that are rooted in psychopathological perspectives of deviance and, as we would expect, have no evidence that they predict recidivism. Similarly, in a survey of 25 state correctional systems, projective tests were used in 10 states, and nearly all the states reported using the Minnesota Multiphasic Personality Inventory (MMPI), a general measure of personality maladjustment (Gallagher, Somwaru & Ben-Porath, 1999). At least among many psychologists, the use of test instruments to measure psychopathology suggests that there is still much work to do in making the PCC perspective as the model of choice.

2. *Reluctance to abandon clinical judgment.* Given that we are now on the cusp of fourth-generation assessments, why then, in our experience, do so many professionals still refuse to use empirical, actuarial methods for risk prediction and offender classification? The answer is complex and involves a number of factors. Resource Note 10.2 provides a listing of some of the possible "classification destruction techniques." We have heard many of these over the years, but the most important obstacle to actuarial, evidence-based prediction, in our view, is the training of professionals. How many criminal justice programs in North America educate graduate students in the psychometrics of risk prediction and methodologies to develop and evaluate risk scales? (And we mean more than a few introductory lectures.) In our experience, there are very few.

Also of concern is the emergence of structured clinical judgment (SCJ). These instruments structure what the professional should consider

Resource Note 10.2

Classification Destruction Techniques: Objections to Using Actuarial Risk Assessment

Objection	Reality
It is not "either/or"; I use both.	At the moment when a decision is made, if the two approaches do not agree, you have to use one or the other, you cannot use both.
The scale was developed on a different sample and does not apply to my sample.	There may be some slight statistical shrinkage on a new sample, but only when the sample is unique would this be an issue. Also, with the turnover of staff coming from different backgrounds, clinical predictions for the setting can also suffer. The relative advantage of actuarial prediction remains.
The research does not apply to me as the individual professional.	If there are more than 100 studies involving hundreds of professionals showing that they do not predict as well as actuarial instruments, then what makes you think you are so superior to others?
It is too expensive.	Possibly, but what of the time spent in team meetings, the cost of incarcerating someone needlessly, or placing the public at risk by not identifying the dangerous offender?
I want to change behavior, not just predict it.	If the goal is to change behavior, you need to know the probability of an outcome so you can judge whether your actions have an effect.
Predictions are based on group data; I deal with the unique individual.	Life is guided by probabilities. If the individual is similar to the reference group and there are no obvious differences, it would be foolish to ignore the data. If a doctor told you that surgery is successful in 90 percent of cases similar to yours, would you ignore it?
The important data is not measurable; people cannot be reduced to numbers.	Anything that is written can be coded. Further, rational and empirical does not mean being cold and unfeeling with clients.

Adapted from Grove & Meehl, 1996

in the assessment but do not yield a final "score" that categorizes the offender in terms of risk, leaving this decision to the professional. An example of an SCJ instrument is the HCR-20 (Webster et al., 1997). The HCR-20 is an 20-item instrument consisting of 10 historical items (e.g., previous violence), five clinical items (e.g., lack of insight), and five risk management items (e.g., plans lack feasibility). Although each item is scored (0, 1, or 2) and the scores are added up for a total score, there is no instruction as to what score corresponds to low, moderate, or high risk. The professional makes the final judgment. Although SCJ is an improvement over unstructured clinical judgment, its predictive accuracy lies somewhere between first- and second-generation assessments (Hanson & Morton-Bourgon, 2009).

We are not advocating the exclusive use of actuarial risk instruments. Professionals often, and should, exercise discretion in making decisions—it is an important part of a fair and just system. However, professionals must first attend to the results of actuarial risk assessments before invoking a professional override. In addition, we must be careful that professional overrides are not used in a haphazard and irrational manner and that they do not become the preferred choice for making predictions. Rather, we should look on overrides as an opportunity to improve our assessments. This can be done by systematically monitoring our use of overrides and, if patterns emerge, incorporating (or perhaps discovering) a new principle of assessment. Simply put, we should use science in a constructive manner.

3. *Organizational inattention to the integrity of assessment.* Rarely studied in the correctional assessment literature is whether the assessment instruments are used as they were designed to be used. That is, do classification and probation officers follow the instructions for completing the scales, and do they make use of the information?

Training is probably the single most important thing an agency can do to maximize success with a new offender assessment instrument. Implementing a new risk instrument requires time, money, and staff buy-in. Failure to devote sufficient resources to training can result in a number of problems. Staff are often reluctant to change what they have done for years and adopt a new assessment procedure (Haas & DeTardo-Bora, 2009; Lowenkamp, Latessa & Holsinger, 2004; Mair, Burke & Taylor, 2006; Maung & Hammond, 2000; Whiteacre, 2004). For example, according to Schneider, Ervin, and Snyder-Joy (1996), when staff were surveyed about their views of a newly introduced classification system, only 27 percent thought that the instrument was more accurate then their professional judgment. Not surprisingly, staff who are poorly trained or not convinced of the value of the new risk assessment tool will produce assessments with poor predictive accuracy (Flores, Lowenkamp, Holsinger & Latessa, 2006).

Second, even after careful training, steps must be taken to ensure that levels of competency are maintained. For example, soon after the introduction of the LSI-R in the state of Colorado, a review of LSI-R records found that 13 percent of 336 files had errors (Bonta et al., 2001).

Many of the errors were simple addition mistakes, but others dealt with misunderstandings of how some of the items were to be scored. To the credit of Colorado's correctional system, the administration of risk/need assessment was monitored and steps taken to improve the assessment process. Many jurisdictions fail to monitor and correct such an important process.

    4. *Socio/political/legal skepticism to risk assessment.* Skepticism to the application of offender risk instruments has come from feminist scholars (Hannah-Moffat & Shaw, 2001; Holtfreter et al., 2004), critical criminologists (Rigakos, 1999), and legal experts (Birgden, 2009; Cole, 2007; Cole & Angus, 2003), who are either trying to protect their favored variables (e.g., socioeconomic factors are more important than individualized risk factors, in the case of some criminologists) or are concerned about the application of fair justice (e.g., punishment administered because of the crime and not because of one's risk to reoffend). We welcome this skepticism; it is what drives new ideas and new research.

    However, we also have enormous respect for the evidence. If actuarial risk scales that provide a comprehensive survey of risk factors, including dynamic risk factors, predict recidivism, then how can we justify ignoring this information. As we said at the beginning of this chapter, are not all players in the criminal justice system concerned about making the best decisions about community safety, prevention, treatment, and the delivery of justice? As our colleague Ivan Zinger (2004:607) observed, "failure to conduct actuarial assessment or consider its results is irrational, unscientific, unethical, and unprofessional."

The Future of Offender Assessment

    There has been considerable progress in offender assessment over the past 20 years. The "professional judgment," first-generation approach to assessment is now hard to defend, but it is still used in some jurisdictions. Evidence-based, second-generation assessments are widely accepted, but many of them focus on static risk factors and thus limit their usefulness for offender risk management. The importance of the objective assessment of offender needs has been recognized for quite some time (Clements, 1986), but there was no appreciation of the distinction between criminogenic and noncriminogenic needs until recently. This is a distinction demanded by a general personality, cognitive social learning perspective of criminal conduct.

    Most second-generation assessments will likely remain for some time yet, as they are simple to use and quick to complete. Improvements will be made in their ability to predict criminal behavior, particularly violent behavior. However, the results may prove unsatisfactory because the static nature of these instruments fails to deliver what so many professionals want and need—help with intervening and reducing the risk posed by offenders.

Third-generation assessments will continue, but these will be gradually replaced by fourth-generation assessments. Evaluations of third- and fourth-generation assessments will be conducted with diverse samples and various outcomes, which will lead to new applications and improvements. This is already happening with the youth and adult versions of the LS/CMI and the LS/RNR.

One exciting development that we see on the horizon is growing interest in the assessment of what Karl Hanson and Andrew Harris (2000) call "acute" dynamic risk factors. These are risk factors that can change in a very short period of time (e.g., intoxication, loss of a job, collapse of social support system) and appear to be the proximal determinants of offending (Brown, St. Amand & Zamble, 2009; Quinsey et al., 2006; Rowe, 2008; Zamble & Quinsey, 1997). Indeed, the future looks promising, but we can only progress if we adhere to the present research findings. Therefore, we leave this chapter with a reminder of some general guidelines for the use of offender assessment instruments (see Resource Note 10.3).

Resource Note 10.3

Guidelines for Offender Assessment

The research on offender assessment has been impressive. Much has been learned, to the point where we can make specific suggestions as to what would formulate good practice when it comes to assessment. The following are our "top 10" considerations when the task is to assess offenders:

1. *Use actuarial measures of risk.*

   The evidence is unequivocal-actuarial assessments of risk are significantly superior to clinical assessments. This is true not only with general offenders but also for very specific offender groups such as the mentally disordered, sex offenders, and male batterers.

2. *Risk assessments should demonstrate predictive validity.*

   There are many assessment instruments available for use, but sometimes the research on them is limited to psychometric properties such as internal reliability, face validity, inter-rater reliability, and so on. Practitioners must ask about the predictive validity of the instruments they use because it is this type of validity that has the greatest utility in a correctional context.

3. *The assessment instruments should be directly relevant to the business of corrections.*

Resource Note 10.3 *(continued)*

When dealing with offenders, we have interest in two general classes of behaviors: (1) rule violation and (2) psychological instability. They are both important and sometimes interrelated (e.g., paranoid delusions and violent assaults), but not always (e.g., depression is unrelated to recidivism). What we need to be clear about is that emotional and psychological functioning is often unrelated to criminal behavior. Thus, assessment of psychological instability *for purposes of assessing risk for criminal behavior* is largely irrelevant. Test administrators should be aware of what the test does predict and understand that their assessments should be specific to the predicted outcome the situation demands.

4. *Use instruments derived from relevant theory.*

The correlates derived from traditional criminological and psychopathological theories of crime have proved to be minor. The social learning perspectives have the strongest empirical support. In these theories criminal behavior is seen as a product of the interaction between cognitive-emotional-personality-biological factors and environmental reward-cost contingencies. Offender assessment instruments that are based on a general personality and social learning theory of criminal conduct offer robustness in their predictive accuracy and generalizability to a range of settings and samples.

5. *Assess criminogenic needs.*

Criminogenic needs are the dynamic risk factors that are highly important for risk management. For correctional staff who are concerned about how to intervene and reduce the risk posed by offenders, knowledge of their criminogenic needs is vital. Assessing and reassessing criminogenic needs permits the evaluation of progress in treatment and changes in risk level during the course of normal supervision.

6. *Use general personality and cognitive tests for the assessment of responsivity*

The responsivity principle of offender classification states that the style and mode of treatment must be matched to the cognitive, personality, and sociocultural characteristics of the individual. There are a number of offender classification instruments and general personality measures that have utility for the assessment of personal characteristics that could affect the individual's responsiveness to treatment. Test administrators must be cognizant that many personality and cognitive tests have very little evidence regarding their ability to predict criminal behavior. However, they are excellent tools for assessing responsivity.

7. *Use multi-method assessment.*

No test measures a single domain perfectly, and each method has a weakness. An important way of dealing with the shortcomings associated with a specific assessment methods is to use multiple, diverse methods. In this way, the weakness of one assessment method is compensated by the strength of another method.

8. *Use multi-domain sampling.*

There are many factors or domains that contribute to criminal behavior (i.e., the Central Eight). Many of the tests used with offenders, however, measure relatively few domains. Therefore, offender assessment that incorporates multi-domain sampling should become a standard in offender risk assessments.

9. *Exercise professional and ethical responsibility.*

What is done with the results from assessments administered to offenders can have serious consequences. Therefore, those who conduct offender assessment have a responsibility to be well trained and knowledgeable of the strengths and weaknesses of the tests they use, and to apply the tests appropriately.

Adapted from Bonta, 2002

Worth Remembering

1. Criminal behavior is predictable.

   Predictions of criminal behavior exceed chance levels. However, these predictions are not perfect, and to expect perfection is unrealistic. Other fields (e.g., medicine) do not have perfect prediction, but their predictive accuracies are sufficient to have practical value. The same can be said for the criminal justice field.

2. Prediction is enhanced through knowledge of theory.

   We found that theory and research in PCC may be translated into valid, objective, and practical assessment instruments. The highlighting of the Central Eight and dynamic risk factors are desirable features to have in offender assessment.

3. The principles of risk, need, and responsivity can be reflected in offender assessment.

   The principles of effective intervention suggest who may profit from treatment services (the risk principle), what should be targeted (the need principle), and how treatment is delivered (the responsivity principle).

4. Fourth-generation assessments are integrated with the case management of offenders.

   First-generation assessments are unstructured, clinical judgments of risk, and they perform poorly in the prediction of criminal behavior. Second-generation assessments predict well but are comprised mostly of static risk factors. Third-generation risk/need instruments identify the criminogenic needs of offenders, while fourth-generation assessments (e.g., LS/CMI) guide the actual delivery of services targeting criminogenic needs.

5. Assessment based on PCC has wide applicability.

   The evidence suggests that the correlates of criminality are much the same across differing populations (e.g., gender). The evidence also suggests that many of the factors that predict general offending also predict violent offending.

6. Implementing the research knowledge remains a challenge.

   We have a great deal of research that speaks to the characteristics of efficient and accurate predictions of criminal conduct. However, ideological beliefs and organizational shortcomings can affect the integrity of offender assessment.

Recommended Readings

The Grove et al. (2000) and Ægisdóttier et al. (2006) meta-analyses are perhaps the definitive reviews comparing first-generation, unstructured professional judgments with actuarial assessments. These reviews are not specific to criminal justice but speak to the broader issues of prediction.

For those interested in the wide applicability of theory and research-based risk assessment, we would recommend the chapter by Andrews, Dowden, and Rettinger (2001) in J.A. Winterdyck's *Corrections in Canada: Social Reactions to Crime*. This chapter includes applications not covered in this chapter and reinforces our general position that a PCC can greatly expand the uses of risk assessment.

Finally, for a summary of the four generations of risk assessment, we would suggest the Andrews, Bonta, and Wormith (2006) article, "The Recent Past and Near Future of Risk and/or Needs Assessment" in *Crime & Delinquency*.

Chapter 11

Prevention and Rehabilitation

The first objective of this chapter is to tell the "what works" story. This chapter provides an overview of how mainstream criminology and criminal justice reached the conclusion that the literature on the effectiveness of prevention and correctional programming supported a "nothing works" position. The second aspect of the story describes recognition of the value of human service in justice contexts (that is, the debate moved toward a "what works" position). Another objective of this chapter is to consider "what works and what does not work" from the perspective of different theoretical accounts of criminal behavior. Any bets on whether personality cognitive social learning theory will look good on this issue? How do you think class-based theories will do?

Finally, this chapter summarizes the meta-analytic evidence in regard to the effectiveness of adherence with the risk-need-responsivity model (the model was described in Chapter 2). This includes adherence with the core clinical principles along with the organizational principles (settings, staffing, and management). Much of the quantitative detail—and there is plenty of it—will be located in resource notes. Program integrity— "making what works work"—will be developed in some detail in the next chapter of this book (that is, Chapter 12) in order to assist in building the future of PCC and its applications. That chapter goes well beyond the principles of effective prevention and treatment and describes the "what and how" of modeling, reinforcement, and skill building. These are often called the core practices in effective correctional treatment. There we spell out the relationship and structuring aspects of interpersonal influence in some detail, including a new program aimed at building the skill level of correctional professionals. Do you have the skills to be an effective human service worker in corrections?

The justice contexts in which treatment may be provided include community and institutional corrections as well as the young offender and adult systems. A detailed review of the effects of official punishment on reoffending is included in Chapter 13. The primary focus of the current chapter, however, is the effects of human service delivered within a justice context on reoffending. The justice context most often involves imposition of some type of judicial sanction. It is important to emphasize that the review in this chapter is speaking to human service programs often operating in a punishing justice context. Typically, our concern

345

here is called "rehabilitation," "reintegration," or "correctional treatment," and the objective is reduced recidivism. Other, and often overarching, purposes of judicial sanctioning include retribution and/or restoration.

Retributive justice is concerned with doing harm to offenders—harm was done to the victim (often defined abstractly as the "state") and justice entails harming the offender in turn. Just deserts theory adds that the severity of the penalty should be matched to the seriousness of the offense. Just deserts notions may place some upper limits on degree of harm, but it is difficult not to conclude that retribution and just deserts have played a major part in the explosion of punishment in the United States and an accompanying "mean spirit" (Cullen, 1995). Part of "being mean" includes not just more incarceration but a reduction of services and programs in prisons. Under retribution and just deserts, there is no expectation of reduced reoffending because holding the offender accountable is deemed sufficient. Thus, human service in the context of retributive service may be difficult, but many of the programs to be reviewed were offered under such conditions. Offering human services in the context of intensive supervision programs ("turning the heat up on offenders") provides a detailed discussion of how the promise resides not in the "heat" but in the human service (Gendreau, Cullen & Bonta, 1994).

Restorative approaches seek justice through efforts to repair harm done to the victim, to restore the community that may have been offended or disrupted by the criminal act, and to hold the offender accountable. Holding the offender accountable may involve, for example, requiring them to pay restitution or complete community service. The rhetoric of restorative justice is not always favorable to human service for the offender, but the restorative context may provide an easier setting for the delivery of human service. We will return to a more detailed discussion of restorative justice in Chapter 13.

An additional purpose of sanctioning is incapacitation. Here the primary concern is the control of reoffending during the period of imprisonment. The most obviously incapacitative type of sanctioning is a custodial sentence, although community sanctions involving intensive monitoring may also be considered to be in the interests of incapacitation. Sometimes, then, human service may be introduced under an incapacitation context with the hope that the control of recidivism may extend beyond expiration of the sentence. Sanctions based on general deterrence are intended to influence the criminal conduct of those nonoffenders (or offender "wannabees") who might be deterred by knowing that criminal activity has negative consequences. Once again, human service may be offered under conditions in which the primary purpose of sanctioning is general deterrence.

Specific deterrence, like rehabilitation, is intended to contribute to reduced recidivism. Specific deterrence, at the sanctioning stage, entails enhancing the offender's fear of official punishment. In criminal law, fear of official punishment is assumed to increase with the severity of the penalty imposed. Hence, reductions in reoffending are expected to increase with more severe penalties. It is possible that under conditions of a severe sentence handed down in order to reduce reoffending, human service may also be introduced with rehabilitation in mind.

As if the circumstances of rehabilitation were not complex enough to begin with, correctional agencies are subject to evaluation on a number of other considerations. Correctional agencies are asked to administer a sanction that may have been meted out for a variety of restorative, retributive, and other purposes. In addition, correctional agencies are asked to administer the sanction in ethical, legal, decent, humane, and cost-efficient ways. If the sanction involves restitution or community service, then agencies may additionally be evaluated in terms of restitution dollars paid and community service hours worked. Justice agencies within young offender systems additionally may be asked to keep child welfare concerns paramount and to attend to the special needs of the young person. In sum, correctional agencies are asked to do a lot of things. One of those things is to contribute to reduced reoffending, and that is to what we turn now.

From Idealism to "Nothing Works" and Back to Human Service: The How and Why of "Nothing Works"

The following is a critical summary of some of the most influential reviews of the correctional treatment literature (many of which were briefly introduced in Chapter 2). Kirby (1954) classified "treatments" as follows: probation and parole, institution-based, capital punishment, psychotherapy, and noninstitutional. These classes of "treatment" may make some sense to administrators, bureaucrats, and policymakers, but they are of little direct relevance to the analysis of behavioral influence processes. At best, they are broad descriptions of the structures within which services are delivered, as opposed to descriptions of the content and processes of direct service. Kirby thereby set the stage for a continuing problem in the literature on the effectiveness of correctional treatment, namely, the failure to make a clear distinction between structural/setting variables and the clinical aspects of service (i.e., the behavior influence processes) that occur within that structure or setting.

The important variables determining the effectiveness of counseling are to be found within the broad setting conditions established by a criminal sanction. Restated in practical rather than methodological terms, correctional counselors have little immediate influence over the boundaries set by a criminal sanction. What they do influence are discretionary aspects of the management of a sentence and the specifics of services delivered (recall the discussion of knowledge through practice in Chapter 2).

Up to the 1990s, to our knowledge, not a single review of controlled studies on the effects of the criminal penalty (diversion, probation, custody, restoration) found consistent evidence of reduced recidivism. From the earliest to the latest reviews of the research literature, only the studies on the delivery of direct human service have shown promise—promise evident across a variety of settings, including nonjustice settings, diversion programs, probation, and custody. The conclusion "nothing works" may well be drawn from studies of official punishment, but it never made sense in terms of the effects of prevention and rehabilitation services.

Not surprisingly, Kirby (1954) found that the literature available in the early 1950s was methodologically weak. However, at least four studies of *direct* service included comparison conditions and objective measures of outcome. The studies were relevant because the broad setting conditions were roughly controlled within each of the studies. Three of the four better-controlled studies yielded findings favorable to counseling; they were Fox's study of a new training institution with an organized counseling service, Shulman's study of a community-based activity group, and Levy's study of therapy. The fourth (and less favorable) study was the grand Cambridge-Somerville Youth Study. (The latter will resurface in our detailed analyses of counseling processes, but for now note that the findings of three of four reasonably well-controlled studies were supportive of counseling.)

Kirby's conclusion was noncontroversial: "Most treatment programs are based on hope and perhaps informed speculation rather than verified information." He also made a plea for university-agency cooperation in research. Research was obviously required if the "treatment" of criminals was to have a solid empirical base.

Walter Bailey (1966) found 100 studies of correctional effectiveness; 22 of the studies approximated the experimental ideal. This was a considerable improvement over the state of the literature in the early 1950s. Sixty percent of the *better-controlled* studies (n = 22) reported "marked improvement" or demonstrated statistically significant gains relative to the comparison conditions; 23 percent reported "harm" or "no change." Considering the total sample of 100 studies, approximately 50 studies reported "considerable improvement" in the treatment group.

Bailey's conclusions included a recognition that both the quality and quantity of studies had improved since the Kirby report. However, Bailey also stated that there had been no apparent progress in demonstrating the validity of correctional treatment. Bailey did not state the standard against which he assessed this lack of "progress." As Ted Palmer (1983) has noted, the standards set by the antitreatment forces were cloudy. By the mid-1960s, however, the proportion of well-controlled studies of correctional treatment that reported positive outcome was now 13 of 22, relative to Kirby's three of four. The proportion of "successes" had not increased, but the quantity of supportive studies certainly had.

Lest the reader begin to think positively in the glow of a "hit rate" of 50 to 60 percent, Bailey reminded his readers that it was the authors of the studies who wrote the reports. This gratuitous comment has since been enshrined in Michael Gottfredson's (1979) list of "treatment destruction techniques," and it is echoed in our sample of anti-rehabilitation themes (see Technical Note 2.3). In the same paragraph Bailey also stated that one could "substantially decrease the relative frequency of successful outcomes based upon reliably valid evidence" (p. 157).

What is "reliably valid evidence" (what standards are being set?), and why do these standards seem only to be applied to studies with findings favorable to counseling? Perhaps Bailey meant that if one chooses to consider all potential threats to validity (e.g., external, construct validity), one could indeed find that each study reporting positive findings was limited. It would be amazing indeed if such limits could not be found, as it is inconceivable that any piece of research could be free of all potential threats to validity.

However, should not these absolute standards also be applied to those studies that failed to establish treatment effects? After all, it is equally likely that the "null effect" studies probably also failed to provide "reliably valid evidence" for treatment *noneffectiveness*. Bailey chose to accept the studies that found unfavorable results for direct human services. He concluded that the "evidence supporting the efficacy of correctional treatment is slight, inconsistent, and of questionable reliability" (1966:157). To be true to the anti-empiricism inherent in his unspecified "reliably valid" criterion, he might better have concluded that empirical investigations of effectiveness will forever yield evidence that is of questionable validity by someone's standards—no matter the quantity and consistency of the evidence produced.

In his last paragraph, Bailey returned to the empirical issues by providing four possible explanations for what he considered to be an overall negative situation for correctional treatment: (1) treatment is really ineffectual, (2) the treatments are being ineffectually applied, (3) the wrong treatments are being applied, or (4) the effectiveness of treatment is being hidden by offender-by-treatment interactions. These four "explanations" are true to the spirit of systematic empirical approaches in that there is an invitation—indeed a challenge—to explore both service and client variables further.

"Knowledge destruction" proliferated in the 1970s. Charles H. Logan (1972) examined 100 studies and summarized their findings as follows: High Success ($n = 20$), Good Success (35), Fair Success (15), Failure (16), and Can't Say (14). The latter category included three studies in which the success varied with particular combinations of clients and treatment. Overall, 73 studies provided some evidence of success, 16 were clear failures, and 11 had unclassifiable outcomes.

Logan set seven methodological criteria that he described as the minimal requirements for an adequate study of effectiveness. In an important advance for meta-evaluation, Logan listed his criteria and showed in tabular form how he had evaluated each of the 100 studies. Some standards were now at least open to inspection.

It is valuable to examine Logan's findings in some detail. Eighteen studies of psychotherapy/counseling included a comparison condition based on random assignment and/or matching. We will accept Logan's judgment without arguing about the inappropriateness of registering the Cambridge-Somerville Youth Study twice in the "failure" category (two separate follow-ups of the same study found no evidence for the effectiveness of this program). Similarly, we will accept for now that the findings of the PICO project (Grant, 1965; see Table 2.4) were assigned to the "uncertain outcome" category when they could have been represented twice in the "positive outcome" category (the PICO project found that "amenable" inmates responded best to personal counseling, while "nonamenable" inmates responded best to routine casework services). The success rates, as defined by Logan himself, showed that, minimally, 50 percent (9/18) of the better-controlled studies reported positive effects of counseling. If offender-by-treatment interactions (which suggest that treatment works for certain types of offenders) are considered, the success rate jumps to 78 percent (14/18).

However, Logan's interpretation of the findings was negative. Applying his methodological standards to the 100 studies, he found that not a single study was adequate (i.e., met all the criteria). Thus, his conclusion (p. 381) regarding the effectiveness of correctional treatment was presented by means of a quotation from Schur's summary of a few years earlier:

> No research has been done to date that enables one to say that one treatment program is better than another or that enables us to examine a man and specify the treatment he needs. There is no evidence that probation is better than institutions, that institutions are better than probation, or that being given a parole is better than escaping … much of what is now being done about crime may be so wrong that the net effect of the actions is to increase rather than to decrease crime.

With Logan's review, the effectiveness debate broke with the discipline normally associated with scientific discourse. The most negative of the possibilities (i.e., human service does not work) is highlighted by a failure to differentiate between official punishment and treatment services. Yet, that most negative of possibilities in regard to effective human service is the one possibility least consistent with the evidence that he himself reviewed. It appears that any positive study that is limited (as all studies must be) may be dismissed.

Moreover, Logan goes a step beyond Bailey regarding the acceptance of the validity of the "null effect" studies. Bailey simply reminded us that the authors had themselves written the reports (i.e., "you can't trust those authors"). Logan implies that suspending the judgment that treatment had failed is a sign of character weakness: "[T]here is a strong current of optimism in these studies, with only a small minority (16%) *admitting* to failure" (p. 381; emphasis added). After describing all studies as inadequate according to "minimal" methodological criteria (and, hence, unworthy of serious consideration), Logan closed with a recommendation that experimental research be abandoned. The field was now ready for the next step in the destruction of correctional treatment: the recommendation that service efforts too should be abandoned.

The Martinson "Nothing Works" Debate

The reviews conducted by Martinson (1974) and his colleagues (Lipton, Martinson & Wilks, 1975) provided a summary of studies that was a major accomplishment. Two hundred and thirty-one controlled studies were reviewed, carefully described, and tabulated. Depending upon how the studies are classified, some 40 to 60 percent of the studies included reports of positive effects on at least some types of offenders. Although the review consisted of 231 studies, Cullen and Gendreau (2001) remind us that the outcome variables included measures such as institutional adjustment and substance abuse relapse. One hundred thirty-eight studies included measures of recidivism. Furthermore, if studies of probation, parole, and imprisonment are removed as "treatments," 83 studies are left (with 48% showing a reduction in recidivism).

The conclusions drawn by Martinson and his colleagues took various forms both in the original review articles and in subsequent commentaries, but the dominant message remained "nothing works." The Martinson review also served to demonstrate *knowledge destruction*:

1. Studies that reached negative conclusions regarding the effectiveness of treatment were accepted almost without question.

2. Studies that were supportive of treatment were subjected to intense criticism of a pseudoscientific variety that Gottfredson (1979) has called "treatment destruction" (see Technical Note 2.3). These techniques include "stressing the criterion problem," "contaminating the treatment," and "discounting the underlying theory" (see below for definitions of these techniques).

3. What was almost never considered in these reviews was the possibility that the reasons provided for discounting the positive findings are the very factors that may be responsible for hiding or underestimating the effects of treatment.

For example, unreliability in the measurement of outcome variables such as recidivism ("the criterion problem") should decrease, not increase, the chances of detecting the effects of treatment. Unreliability of measurement is a possible reason why effects are not found, and not a reason why effects are found.

Similarly, errors in the conceptualization of crime and treatment should have the effect of preventing positive outcomes, not of promoting them. If the psychological model of crime is wrong ("discounting the underlying theory"), we would not expect to find any effects when service is guided by that model.

A primary example of "contamination of treatment" is to suggest that the positive effects of counseling reflect nothing but the "natural interpersonal skills" of the counselor. If the findings are that counseling is effective when it is offered by interpersonally skilled therapists, so be it. Such a finding begins to say something about the conditions under which counseling is effective. It is not a reason for discounting treatment.

Stuart Adams (1975) and Ted Palmer (1975) reminded their readers of the nature of the evidence. Reports of success in the better-controlled studies (40% to 60%) compared favorably with research payoffs in medicine and industry. Moreover, as Bailey (1966) had suggested a decade earlier, there was now considerable evidence that the effectiveness of treatment may depend upon how the specifics of treatment are matched with the characteristics of offenders.

Ted Palmer's (1975) paper was a particularly strong document because his descriptions of effective programs were often direct quotes from the descriptions provided by Martinson and his colleagues. In response, Martinson (1976) made it clear that he was never really concerned about recidivism anyway. Rather, he said, there was no evidence that treatment programs influence aggregated crime rates. Although this was true, the issue of the impact of correctional intervention on aggregated crime rates was not being been explored by either Palmer or Martinson. Antipsychological criminologists often switch criterion variables from the psychological to the social.

Martinson went on to attack Palmer personally: "To review one of Palmer's research projects is ... something like translating the Moscow telephone book into Swahili." He attacked correctional treatment in general: "[it] is nine-tenths pageantry, rumination, and rubbish," and he revealed his position on the issue of type-of-offender-by-type-of-treatment interactions (matching): "a 'partly positive' result is probably akin to a partly pregnant girl friend." He summarized his evaluation of correctional research thus: "[with it] and thirty cents you can buy a cup of coffee in New York."

Depending upon where one stood on the correctional effectiveness issue, Martinson's (1976) response to Palmer (1975) marked either the ultimate end of the rehabilitative ideal or a source of embarrassment for those in the human and social sciences who maintained a respect for evidence. However, what remains unknown to many in both camps is that Martinson had the courage to recant and admit that while some programs did not work, others clearly did provide positive evidence of effectiveness ("I have often said that treatment...is "impotent"...the conclusion is not correct"; Martinson, 1979:254). He committed suicide shortly after the public recanting.

Martinson's turnabout on the effectiveness issue was largely ignored. The "nothing works" perspective appeared to better serve the interests of various groups. Mainstream criminologists seemed pleased with "nothing works" because that conclusion fit with their general antipsychological bias. Moreover, as we shall see later in this chapter, many sociologists who had earlier been pro-intervention had become anti-intervention because many of the sociological theories had been translated into programs that were nearly universally ineffective. Finally, the political left was becoming suspicious of state intervention in view of the events of the late 1960s and early 1970s. A conservative public seemed ready to promote the punishment of offenders, and scholars of the due process/just deserts schools could proceed with their agenda of "punishment with dignity" (as opposed to what they called the "tyranny of treatment"). The conservative political agenda was allowed to thrive because the left withdrew their support for rehabilitation.

As comfortable as "nothing works" was for many people, the fact remained that positive and promising evidence resided in the research literature. Indeed, positive evidence was growing at a fast rate. Paul Gendreau and Robert Ross prompted many people to look again at the evidence. Gendreau and Ross (1979; Ross & Gendreau, 1980) updated the reviews and directed attention to programs that did appear to "work." Their update was impressive: 95 experimental or quasi-experimental studies were published between 1973 and 1978; 86 percent of these reported positive outcomes. Not all of the 95 studies approximated the experimental ideal, but the evidence from studies published in the early 1970s was (like the earlier evidence) more supportive than nonsupportive of correctional counseling.

Gendreau and Ross provided a neat summary of the essential weakness of many of the "nothing works" arguments. They noted that rhetorical references to a "partly pregnant girl friend" could not dismiss the fact that type-of-offender-by-type-of-treatment interactions were frequently encountered in the research literature, and that the conclusions of studies that failed to uncover treatment effects were as subject to threats to validity as were the conclusions that treatment effects were found. Indeed, in science, acceptance of the null hypothesis is even more threatened than the rejection of the null hypothesis. They reminded readers that the effects of "treatment" were dependent upon the specifics, the "dosage," and the "integrity" of treatment. They concluded that the whole "nothing works" and antirehabilitation position implied that we were all too ready to escape some degree of responsibility for recidivistic crime.

The work of Francis Cullen and colleagues (Cullen & Gilbert, 1982; Travis & Cullen, 1984) was refreshing in that it asked whether the alternatives to rehabilitation are any more effective or humane than is rehabilitation. The answer was that without the rehabilitative ideal, one might expect increased use of incarcerative sentences for longer periods in less humane institutions, as well as increased recidivism (and as we will see in Chapter 13, the prophecy was realized). Cullen and his associates underscored the point that it was ludicrous to promote and justify theories of punishment over rehabilitation on the grounds that rehabilitation promoted punishment.

In the same time period, Ted Palmer (1983) provided a valuable update on the issue of the effectiveness of correctional rehabilitation. According to Palmer, some middle ground may eventually be found between the current camps of the "skeptics" and the "sanguines." Wherever that point may be located, Palmer perceived the current divisions to be less than those that separated the "nothing works" and "some things work" camps of the 1970s. Indeed, he anticipated that the justice system may soon reap benefits from the debate. He felt that points of agreement that had policy implications were appearing among the opposing camps. For example, effective programs must be appropriately intensive, multifocused when necessary, and matched to the needs and abilities of the clients.

Palmer postulated that the residual of the "nothing works" proponents was composed of two groups. The first group, Skeptics I, believed that the rehabilitation issue was settled. Sufficient research had been conducted to demonstrate that a few rehabilitation programs work, but they do not work very well. The other group, Skeptics II, felt that neither the research conducted to date nor the programs studied had been of sufficient quality to determine the degree to which rehabilitation has (or can) work. However, unlike the Skeptics I, they were open to (and encouraging of) the empirical exploration of well-implemented programs.

The Sanguine types believed that many programs and approaches have been shown to work for some types of offenders. Palmer noted that some believed that a proportion of offenders (the amenables) respond positively to a variety of approaches in a variety of settings. Others believed that success is a function of matching types of offenders with the appropriate approach. With an inappropriate match, neutral or even negative outcomes may be expected. Thus, some reasonable promise of rehabilitation resides in our ability to classify both clients and services, and to link those two sets of classes so that the chances of positive outcome are maximized. Palmer (1983) noted that the knowledge base for the Differential Intervention (DI) position is neither vast nor empirically flawless, and that the principles and processes of DI have not been systematically outlined.

In the mid-1980s, the authors of this text, and many of our colleagues and students, constituted a camp that we called "Sanguine Plus." We thought that the outcome literature was sufficiently strong to provide clinically workable hypotheses regarding the attributes of clients and services that are relevant to effective correctional counseling. Moreover, we thought that matching type-of-client-by-type-of-treatment interactions was an obvious consideration flowing easily from a broad social learning perspective on criminal conduct and on the situations of interpersonal influence (Andrews, 1980, 1983). Those early ideas were the beginnings of the risk-need-responsivity (RNR) model outlined in Chapter 2, which is to be tested in some detail in the present chapter.

Our conclusions in the early 1980s were more radical than Palmer's (1983) view that criminologists and correctional professionals would, through debate and research, eventually converge into one camp that would be located somewhere between the skeptical and the sanguine. Our conclusion was that correctional counselors might best debate the possibility of breaking away from the field of criminology. They would find a more professionally rewarding environment in psychology and social work than they could expect to find in criminology. Criminology seemed to be preoccupied with social location, power, punishment, and the promotion of sociology and, as honorable as such interests might be, these areas of interest would not provide useful guidelines for human service professionals. Indeed, our pessimism regarding criminology was reinforced by the fact that while the reviews of the research evidence clearly supported the delivery of direct service, those same reviewers of the literature were contributing to a climate in which treatment was losing ground to variations on themes of official punishment.

Thus, we decided that in every presentation on the psychology of crime in which we were involved (whether in classrooms, symposia, criminal justice and correctional settings, professional conferences, or published articles), the antipsychological and prosociological biases of mainstream criminology would be noted and the contempt for evidence demonstrated. It was unacceptable to us that an influential discipline with strong ties to government policy units would so systematically deny the importance of human diversity (individual differences) and human service, while contributing directly to the implementation of (sometimes ethically repugnant) variations on themes of official punishment.

Paul Gendreau and Robert Ross (1981, 1987) first underscored the theoretical and empirical weakness of official punishment. In 1987, they reported on studies of rehabilitation published between 1981 and 1987. The 1987 report revealed that findings favorable to rehabilitation were continuing to accrue, and findings for programs guided by labeling and deterrence theory yielded the least positive outcomes.

Andrews, Bonta, and Hoge (1990) restated the clinically relevant and psychologically informed principles of risk, need, responsivity, and professional discretion that had been in development at Carleton University for years. In addition to a restatement, their paper provided many examples of the validity of the principles. The Carleton University group then published their meta-analysis of the treatment literature (Andrews, Zinger et al., 1990a). The following section reports on that and more recent meta-analyses, but first we note how the criminal justice environment has changed since 1990.

In dramatic contrast to mainstream textbook criminology and criminal justice in the 1980s and early 1990s (which had changed almost not at all), the actual practice of corrections changed dramatically in many jurisdictions. Canadian correctional systems embarked upon major expansions of human service programs, with particular attention paid to the principles of risk, need, and responsivity. Similarly, a number of U.S. and international jurisdictions (e.g., Great Britain, Australia, New Zealand) introduced major reforms that took human service seriously. The dissemination of the evidence on treatment effectiveness became widespread, ranging from training seminars organized by the National Institute of Corrections (NIC), an arm of the U.S. Department of Justice, to "what works" conferences in Denmark, Finland, Iceland, The Netherlands, Norway, Portugal, Sweden, New Zealand, Australia, Scotland, and Wales.

The systematic quantitative reviews of the correctional treatment literature have contributed to the turnaround in the shift from "nothing works" to "what works." The major issues now have to do with making "what works" work. The issue of program implementation is no longer the "forgotten issue" but the major issue (Bernfeld, Farrington & Leschied, 2001; Gendreau, Goggin, French & Smith, 2006). Much more will be presented on the issue of integrity and program fidelity later in Chapter 12. Now, let us get back to the "what works" story and the rise of the systematic quantitative reviews of the literature (that is, the meta-analyses).

Meta-Analytic Reviews of Treatment Effectiveness

By 1990, the number of reports published in English on controlled evaluations of community and correctional interventions with offenders was fast approaching 500. Now it was clear that, on average, "treatment" reduced recidivism to at least a mild degree. Even some "skeptical" scholars agreed with this fact (e.g., Lab & Whitehead, 1990). As noted years before, even the most notorious of the critics of rehabilitation, Martinson (1979), acknowledged that some programs had positive effects, some had no effect, and some increased recidivism.

The Work of Mark Lipsey

The most comprehensive review completed by the early 1990s was that by Mark Lipsey (1989, 1992). His was the most comprehensive not only of the qualitative reviews of the literature but of the systematic, quantitative, meta-analytic reviews of correctional treatment effectiveness. Recall that meta-analysis involves the derivation of a common quantitative estimate of the degree of association between treatment and reduced recidivism based upon a number of different studies. The meta-analytic approach is not without its own particular limitations, but it does allow a synthesis of the findings of many studies with a decreased likelihood that reviewers of the literature are applying different criteria of effectiveness in the different studies (Gendreau, Smith & Goggin, 2001; Glass, McGraw & Smith, 1981).

Lipsey found that 64 percent of 443 effect sizes found differences in recidivism that favored treatment over comparison conditions. This value of 64 percent is consistent with our reading of the earlier reviews of the literature, which concluded that 40 to 80 percent of the surveyed studies reported reduced recidivism. On average, according to Lipsey's (1989) meta-analysis, the treatment effect was equivalent to a reduction in recidivism from 50 percent for the control group to 45 percent in the treatment group [a 10 percent (5/50) reduction]. Note that Lipsey was using neither the simple r nor the binomial effect size display outlined in Resource Note 1.1. Rather, Lipsey assumes a 50 percent recidivism rate in the control group and expresses the r in terms of how the recidivism rate of treatment groups deviates from that 50 percent value. This positive (but very modest) effect was an underestimate in view of the well-known unreliability in the assessment of official recidivism (i.e., the offenses of some who reoffend may go unnoticed). Correcting for this unreliability, Lipsey estimated that the average effect of treatment more accurately represented a reduction from 50 percent to 40 percent (a reduction of 10 percentage points, or a 20% reduction, in that 10/50 = .20).

Estimates of the overall average effect of treatment (whether or not corrected for unreliability), however, do not recognize that methodological and treatment variables may be contributing to variation around the mean effect. In other words, are some types of studies and some types of treatment associated with larger effects on recidivism?

Appropriately, Lipsey adopted a conservative approach to determining the effect of type of treatment on recidivism. He insisted that any contributions of treatment variables to reduced recidivism would be considered only if they were evident after controls were introduced for methodological variables. As many reviewers of the treatment literature had suspected (but had not been able to demonstrate in a convincing way), Lipsey (1989) showed that the contribution of methodological variables to the magnitude of the effect of treatment was substantial (an overall correlation of 0.50). To a considerable extent these methodological contributions reflected the following:

1. Small sample studies yielded larger effect size estimates;

2. Studies with the longest follow-up periods and with criterion variables of weak reliability and validity yielded the smaller estimates of effect size;

3. Less explicit reporting of methodological and statistical procedures was associated with higher estimates of effect size;

4. Initial nonequivalence of treatment and control groups was associated with larger or smaller effects depending upon the specifics of the nonequivalence;

5. Greater attrition from either the treatment or the control group was associated with smaller effect sizes;

6. Comparisons of treatment with "alternative treatment" yielded smaller estimates of effect size than did comparisons of treatment with "no treatment."

The last finding actually favors conclusions regarding the effectiveness of treatment, because, on average, it appears that even some form of "alternative" treatment (doing something) is better than no treatment (doing nothing). The first five methodological findings, however, demonstrate more clearly than ever that the characteristics of the research design and procedures do influence estimates of the effects of treatment independently of the variations in treatment being studied. This is the systematic empirical tradition of PCC at its best. After asserting and empirically demonstrating the effects of various sources of error on estimates of the effects of treatment, Lipsey moved forward in the process of *knowledge construction*.

Lipsey (1989) found that, with methodological concerns controlled statistically, type of treatment made substantial incremental contributions to variation in effect size estimates (47% of the total explained variance). The major treatment variables associated with reduced recidivism included:

1. Longer duration of treatment and more meaningful contact (except for the continuous contact provided by institutional care);

2. Services provided outside of formal correctional settings and institutions;

3. Services under the influence of the evaluator;

4. Behavior-oriented, skill-oriented, and multimodal treatment;

5. Service for higher-risk cases;

6. Treatment that attends to extrapersonal circumstances (e.g., family).

The best treatments were structured and focused and, according to Lipsey, those treatments reduced recidivism rates by about 30 percent on average. Lipsey (p. 39) concluded that the best treatments (with few exceptions) were those that had been defined independently as most "clinically relevant" by the Carleton University group (Andrews, Bonta & Hoge, 1990). As many authors have been suggesting over the years (e.g., Andrews, 1979, 1980; Andrews & Kiessling, 1980; Gendreau & Ross, 1979, 1987; Glaser, 1974; Palmer, 1974; Ross & Fabiano, 1985), it appears that some approaches to treatment clearly are better than others, and to some extent, the effectiveness of treatment depends upon type of client.

The Risk-Need-Responsivity Approach

Recall from Chapters 2 and Chapter 10 that the core clinical principles consistent with a psychology of crime are as follows (Andrews, Bonta & Hoge, 1990; Andrews, Zinger et al., 1990a):

1. Introduce human, social, or clinical services, and do not rely on official punishment

2. Treatment service is delivered to moderate and higher-risk cases (as opposed to lower-risk cases).

3. Criminogenic needs are targeted for change predominately (e.g., procriminal attitudes rather than self-esteem).

4. Styles and modes of treatment are employed that are capable of influencing criminogenic needs and are matched to the learning styles of offenders (i.e., cognitive behavioral and social learning approaches rather than nondirective, relationship-oriented counseling or psychodynamic, insight-oriented counseling; or specific matching according to the principle of specific responsivity). Several specific responsivity systems were described in Chapter 2 (Table 2.4).

5. The professional reviews risk, need, and responsivity considerations as they apply to a particular person, and makes those treatment decisions that are most appropriate according to legal, ethical, humanitarian, cost-efficiency, and clinical standards.

These principles of effective treatment were hypothesized to apply regardless of the setting within which treatment was delivered. The settings themselves were hypothesized to be of minimal significance in the control of recidivism. That is, variation in criminal processing *without* systematic variation in the delivery of correctional treatment service is minimally related to recidivism. This reflected the view that variations in the type and severity of justice processing would have no systematic and positive effects on criminogenic need areas (e.g., antisocial attitudes, delinquent companions, family processes, school success, skill deficits, etc.). Fundamentally, none of the theories of criminal justice processing (labeling, deterrence, just deserts, or restorative justice) represent or reflect a well-developed social psychology of delinquency or crime.

Following these hypotheses, Andrews, Zinger, and colleagues (1990a) undertook a meta-analysis of 154 treatment comparisons, 30 of which were assigned to the criminal sanction set. Criminal sanctions involved variations in the type or severity of judicial processing. These included: official processing versus police cautioning, probation versus informal adjustment, probation versus open custody, closed versus open custody, and probation versus closed custody. Two comparisons involved completors versus noncompletors of restitution programs. None of the comparisons involved variation in the duration of custody dispositions.

Analysis of the 30 comparisons revealed that not a single positive phi coefficient of .20 or greater was generated. Overall, the criminal sanction hypothesis was supported in that the mean phi coefficient was minimal: −.07. The fact that the phi coefficient was negative indicates that more, as opposed to less, criminal justice processing was associated with slightly increased recidivism rates. This finding was mildly consistent with labeling theory, and inconsistent with deterrence theory. In brief, if the type and severity of official punishment has any effect on recidivism, it appears to be that "less" is better than "more."

This negative effect of more severe judicial sanctions was maintained with statistical controls introduced for methodological variables and for particular treatment modalities. Additionally, Lipsey (1989) reported that nine specific tests of deterrence theory (shock incarceration and "Scared Straight") yielded the most negative effects of all the treatment modalities tested (an average increase of 24% in recidivism rates).

Thus, meta-analysis confirmed what the earlier narrative reviews of the literature had uncovered. The mean effect of correctional treatment service, averaged across a number of dispositions, was clearly greater and more positive than that of criminal sanctioning without the delivery of treatment services [mean phi coefficients of 0.15 ($N = 124$) and –.07 ($N = 30$) for treatment and sanctioning, respectively]. Now we turn to differentiations within the treatment studies.

The 124 tests of treatment services were assigned to the categories of "appropriate," "unspecified," or "inappropriate" treatment according to the principles of risk, need, and responsivity. In fact, few studies differentiated clients according to risk, and not many studies were clear on the criminogenic need areas that were being targeted in treatment. Moreover, many studies were quiet on the specifics of the style and mode of service employed. Thus, the major criterion governing assignment to "appropriate correctional treatment service" proved to be the simple designation of a program as "behavioral," and 70 percent (38/54) of the "appropriate" treatments were behavioral.

Additional treatments in the "appropriate" set were those clearly delivered to higher-risk cases, structured programs that were specific and appropriate regarding criminogenic need (e.g., targeting criminal thinking), and a small set of treatments involving appropriate matching according to responsivity systems such as interpersonal maturity level.

Thirty-eight treatments were coded "inappropriate" because they employed deterrence methods (e.g., "Scared Straight"), nondirective client-centered/psychodynamic approaches, nonbehavioral milieu approaches, intensive nonbehavioral group interaction, or mismatched cases with treatment. Thirty-two comparisons entailed the delivery of some treatment service, but it was unclear whether that treatment was appropriate or inappropriate according to the clinical principles of effective service. These 32 comparisons were coded as "unspecified."

The average effect of appropriate treatment service (phi = .30) was significantly greater than unspecified treatment (.13), inappropriate treatment (–.06), and criminal processing without treatment (–.07). The mean phi coefficient of .30 for appropriate treatment represents an average reduction in recidivism of a little more than 50 percent from that found in comparison conditions. Using the binomial effect size display (see Resource Note 1.1), an average correlation of 0.30 represents an average recidivism rate of 65 percent in the comparison condition, compared to 35 percent in the appropriate treatment group.

Even with the dimensions of risk and need ignored, behavioral and cognitive social learning treatment strategies had a substantially greater average effect on recidivism than did nonbehavioral treatments [.29 ($N = 41$) versus .04 ($N = 113$)]. However, the correlation between effect size estimates and the four-level type of treatment variable was much stronger than that between effect size and the simple behavioral/nonbehavioral variable. This suggests that the principles of risk and need were contributing to appropriate service. They will be reviewed in more detail.

The substantial correlation (which approached .70) between type of treatment and treatment effect size remained robust as controls were introduced for various methodological considerations. For example, consistent with Lipsey (1989), the evidence favorable to rehabilitation withstands controls for quality of the research design, sample size, length of follow-up, and ratings of therapeutic integrity. Indeed, Hill, Andrews, and Hoge (1991) reported that under higher-integrity conditions, the effects of inappropriate treatment tend to be particularly negative, while the effects of appropriate treatment are particularly positive. Small sample sizes as well as studies of treatments with evaluator involvement were associated with relatively large mean effect sizes. Even cynical interpretations of these findings (e.g., Lab & Whitehead, 1990) deserve serious attention, but it is important to note that the positive effects of appropriate treatment were also found in larger sample studies and in studies with less involved evaluators. At least in part, the amplification effect of small samples and involved evaluators may reflect therapeutic integrity. The robustness of the effect of appropriate treatment extends to tests conducted before and during the 1980s, to studies of young offenders and adult offenders, to samples varying in gender composition, and to programs offered in the community or in residential settings.

In regard to custody, there was a mild but detectable tendency for the effects of inappropriate service to be particularly negative in custody settings, and for the effects of clinically relevant service to be particularly positive in community settings. This finding, in combination with the mean negative effect of criminal sanctions, led Andrews and colleagues (Andrews, Zinger et al., 1990a) to conclude that they had initially underestimated the negative effect of custody. These research findings affirm a widely shared belief that custody is best viewed as the last resort. Moreover, it is important that the clinical appropriateness of service be attended to in residential settings.

Two additional aspects of custodial dispositions have not been addressed adequately in the correctional treatment literature. The first issue has to do with the possibility that failing to consider the incapacitation potential of custody has resulted in underestimates of the value of custody. The second issue has to do with the deliberate clinical use of custody.

First, the systematic research literature, including the reviews described above, does not deal with the issue of the control of recidivism through the incapacitation effects of custodial dispositions (Bonta & Gendreau, 1990, 1992). Our review of the treatment literature has not uncovered explorations of incapacitation effects sufficient to make strong statements on the relative in-program and postprogram effects on recidivism of custodial and noncustodial dispositions (for a discussion of this issue, see Andrews, 1983, and Chapter 13).

By way of illustration, Barton and Butts (1990) demonstrated that intensive supervision programs and custodial dispositions were statistically indistinguishable in their effects on recidivism over a two-year period. However, this was the dominant finding only when statistical adjustments of recidivism were made for the fact that the cases receiving the noncustodial dispositions were "at large" for significantly more time than the custody cases. When some unadjusted measures of recidivism (e.g., actual number of charges) were employed as the outcome measure, it was clear that over the two-year follow-up period the cases receiving a noncustodial disposition had significantly higher mean numbers of both status and criminal charges than the custody cases. The only finding that was clearly and unequivocally favorable to the noncustodial disposition was the fact that the mean seriousness of the recidivistic offenses of the custody cases was greater than that of the noncustodial cases.

Overall, determination of the relative value of noncustodial and custodial dispositions to the control of recidivism is a complex function of many considerations. Such considerations include in-program incapacitation effects and postprogram effects on recidivism; the quality of treatment services delivered within noncustodial and custodial settings; the seriousness of the offenses prevented through community-based treatment; and the human, social, and economic costs of official processing of less serious offenses. Interestingly, Barton and Butts (1990) concluded that, even considering the threat of net-widening (the application of sanctions to a wider group of offenders), the introduction of noncustodial alternatives was cost-efficient on a system-wide basis.

Second, the systematic research literature has not yet sufficiently explored the possibility that residential placements, based not on "just deserts" considerations but on the more immediate concern of the prevention of harm to self or others, may be just, ethical, decent, humane, and effective routes to reduced criminal recidivism. In our view, one of the outstanding contributions of the California research on the use of community versus residential placements is the evidence that correctional professionals may reduce recidivism through the exercise of discretionary short-term residential placements (Palmer, 1974). As much as we are ready to place severe restraints on the use of custody, many of us also feel that some young people may gain from the short-term protection, care, and service that a humane residential placement may provide.

Since the publication of the Mark Lipsey (1989) review, the Carleton University review (Andrews, Zinger et al., 1990a), and Whitehead and Lab's (1989) meta-analytic review, there has been a tremendous amount of activity. The earlier work of Carol J. Garrett (1985) and Leah Gensheimer, Jeffrey P. Mayer, Rand Gottschalk, and William S. Davidson (1986) has been rediscovered. Others contributing to the expanding knowledge base include Steve Aos and his fellow researchers at the Washington State Institute for Public Policy (Aos, Miller & Drake, 2006a); fellow Canadians Paula Smith and Paul Gendreau along with our

American colleagues (Lipsey, 2009; Lipsey & Cullen, 2007; Smith, Gendreau & Swartz, 2009); Friedrich Lösel (1995), from Germany; James McGuire (2002), from England; and Santiago Redondo and his colleagues, Vicente Garrido and J. Sanchez-Meca (1999), from Spain.

Douglas Lipton was the director of the Effective Correctional Treatment project in New York in the late 1960s, which led to the influential 1975 book by Lipton, Martinson, and Wilks (1975) on which the infamous Martinson (1974) paper was based. Douglas Lipton has re-entered the effectiveness debate as Principal Investigator on the huge CDATE project. CDATE, sponsored by the United States National Institute on Drug Abuse, has assembled, annotated, and subjected to meta-analytic review all treatment studies reported from 1968 to 1997. Douglas Lipton and colleagues Frank S. Pearson, Charles Cleland, and Dorline Yee (1997; Pearson & Lipton, 1999) detected trends more favorable to some types of treatment than to others (for example: cognitive behavioral/social learning strategies relative to deterrence-based programs). Mark Lipsey (1995, 1999) has continued to explore the effectiveness issue. His practical advice for practitioners continues to emphasize a focus on behavioral and skill issues in a structured manner, attention to integrity in implementation and delivery, and adequate dosage (100 or more contact hours, two or more contacts per week, over a period of 26 weeks or more; for high-risk offenders a minimum of 300 hours has been recommended; Bourgon & Armstrong, 2005).

Early Criticism of RNR-Related Approaches

All the activity has not been without criticism. Lab and Whitehead's (1990) response to the Carleton University meta-analysis continues to surface, most notably by persons committed to retributive or restorative justice. A few, but not many, continue to argue for models of justice that dismiss or discount the introduction of human service in a justice context. Andrews, Zinger, and colleagues (1990b) addressed the 1990 critique but did not cover everything. Charles Logan, along with colleagues from the U.S. Federal Bureau of Prisons (Logan et al., 1991; Logan & Gaes, 1993), reaffirmed allegiance to just deserts and their antirehabilitation stance but, in the process, discounted the meta-analytic evidence, deplored the "missionary zeal" of "believers," and made reference to "smoke and mirrors." Gerald Gaes has recently moderated his earlier antirehabilitation stance and now accepts the fact that some offender treatment programs are effective in reducing recidivism (Gaes, 1998; Gaes et al., 1999).

Lab and Whitehead (1990) found the findings were perhaps too conveniently consistent with our hypotheses in regard to risk, need, and responsivity, and where bias could not account for the findings, they noted that the explanation was probably due to a "tautology." The tautology, they suggested, reflected the fact that the principles themselves were derived from our pattern of findings in the particular group of studies reviewed (ignoring the fact that the principles were outlined prior to the meta-analysis). The fact remains, however, and as noted in our 1990 response to the critics, that some criticisms are simply beyond the realm of empirical exploration. For example, how do researchers respond to assertions that they are "wizards"?

The Carleton University databank now includes more than 374 tests of the effects of judicial and correctional interventions on recidivism (Andrews & Dowden, 1999; Andrews, Dowden & Gendreau, 1999; Dowden, 1998; Dowden & Andrews, 1999a, 1999b, 2000: see Resource Note 11.1 for a more detailed summary). The overall mean effect now is 0.08 (N = 374), which is close to the value revealed in Friederich Lösel's (1995) independent meta-analysis of the existing meta-analyses. That level of effect is mild, but clearly positive and utterly inconsistent with a blanket "nothing works" position. Using the binomial effect size display (recall Resource Note 1.1), an r of 0.08 reflects a difference of eight percentage points between the recidivism rates of the intervention and comparison groups: 46 percent reoffending in the intervention group compared with 54 percent reoffending in the comparison group.

Resource Note 11.1

Recent Findings from an Ongoing and Expanded Meta-Analysis of the Effects of Human Service in a Justice Context

The PCC perspective on effective correctional treatment is relatively straightforward. A general personality and social learning perspective on criminal behavior suggests that offenders may be differentiated according to their risk of reoffending; recognizes that the risk/need factors are personal, interpersonal, and tied to immediate situations in an array of behavioral settings such as home, work, school, and leisure; differentiates between major and minor risk factors; identifies the dynamic risk factors that may best be targeted if the objective is reduced reoffending;

and—more than *any* alternative perspective—is very clear regarding some fundamental and very practical processes of behavioral influence and behavior change.

Thus, we hypothesize that: (1) human service in a justice context will have greater impact on reduced recidivism than will variation in retributive and/or restorative aspects of sanctioning, and (2) the positive impact of human service will increase with adherence to the principles of risk, need, and general responsivity. Reflecting Lipsey (1990) and Andrews et al. (1990a; Andrews, 1996), we

Resource Note 11.1 *(continued)*

hypothesize further that: (3) the positive impact of clinically appropriate and PCC-relevant human service will be enhanced when offered in community-based nonresidential settings, (4) when staff make use of core correctional practices that constitute the relationship and structuring principles, and (5) when programs are delivered with integrity. Indicators of integrity include the selection, training, and clinical supervision of staff and the structuring of programming through manuals and monitoring of service delivery. Finally, we hypothesize that: (6) the crime reduction potential of clinically appropriate and PCC-relevant service will be evident across and within categories of control variables suggested by threats to internal, external, construct, and statistical conclusion validity.

Our extensions of the 1990 study (Andrews et al., 1990a) incorporate considerations of a variety of research design, case, study, and setting factors. In this resource note, however, we focus upon the issues of human service versus criminal sanctioning and, within human service, upon applications of the principles of risk, need, and general responsivity.

According to PCC as outlined in this text, deterrence, labeling, and other justice theories are so underdeveloped in psychological terms that any interventions based on those perspectives will have weak effects compared to the effects of human service interventions based on a general personality and social learning perspective. In an expanded set of 374 tests, this pattern of results continues. Inspection of Table 11.1.1 reveals that the mean effect size for criminal sanctions (−0.03) is lower than the mean effect size for human service (.12). Not presented in the table is the fact that human service in a restorative justice context was no more effective than human service in a nonrestorative justice context (a mean effect size of .17 in eight tests within a restorative context, compared with a mean effect of .12 in 265 tests within a nonrestorative context). To date, evaluated restorative justice programs have not been very concerned with the introduction of human service.

In this report, only the general responsivity principle was coded, and no attempt was made to code for the personality responsivity systems or any of the other specific

Table 11.1.1
Mean Effect Size by Adherence to Principles of Effective Correctional Treatment in 374 Tests and Correlation of Adherence with Effect Size

Principle	Adherence to Principle		Correlation with Effect Size (eta)
	No	Yes	
Human Service	−.03 (101)	.12 (146)	.35***
Risk: Services Delivered to Higher-Risk Cases	.03 (96)	.10 (278)	.17***
Criminogenic Needs: # of Criminogenic Needs Targeted Exceed Noncriminogenic	−.01 (205)	.19 (169)	.54***
General Responsivity: Social Learning/Cognitive Behavioral Strategies	.04 (297)	.23 (77)	.40***
Full Adherence: Clinically Appropriate Treatment (adheres to all of the above)	.05 (314)	.28 (60)	.42***
Community-Based Full Adherence: Clinically Appropriate Treatment	.06 (219)	.35 (30)	.49***
Residential-Based Full Adherence: Clinically Appropriate Treatment	.002 (95)	.17 (30)	.38***
k = number of tests of treatment			

*** p < .001

Resource Note 11.1 *(continued)*

responsivity considerations. Thus, the single coding requirement for conformity with the responsivity principle is the use of behavioral, social learning, and/or cognitive behavioral strategies. Adherence to the responsivity principle was associated with enhanced effect sizes. Similarly, Table 11.1.1 also shows the significant contribution of adherence to the criminogenic need principle and to the risk principle. Table 11.1.2 summarizes the mean effect sizes found when personal and interpersonal domains are targeted appropriately and when they are targeted inappropriately. Personal targets such as self-control deficits and antisocial cognition yielded relatively large effect sizes, while the targeting of personal distress and fear of official punishment yielded weak effects on reduced re-offending.

Clinically and Psychologically Appropriate Treatment. Clinically and psychologically appropriate treatment refers to

adherence to risk-need-responsivity. The variable Appropriate Treatment is a composite of Any Service, Risk, Need, and General Responsivity. The two levels of inappropriate service represented in Table 11.1.1 are "No" (criminal sanctions without human service, or human service that is not consistent with each of risk, need, and responsivity) and "Yes" (human service consistent with each of risk, need, and responsivity). Recall that the four-levels of RNR adherence are "0" (criminal sanctions without human service or human service inconsistent with each of risk, need, and responsivity) and "1," "2," and "3," representing human service consistent with one, two, or three of the human service principles. The corresponding mean effect sizes were −0.2 (k = 124), .02 (k = 106), .18 (k = 84), and .26 (k = 60) for the four levels of RNR adherence. You have seen this pattern of results at several points in the book to this point.

Table 11.1.2
Mean Effect Size and Correlation of Need Targeted with Effect Size (k)

Need Area Targeted	%	Mean Effect Size Not Targeted	Targeted	Correlation with Effect Size
CRIMINOGENIC NEEDS				
Personal Criminogenic Targets: Antisocial Cognition and Skill Deficits	26	.04 (277)	.21 (97)	.39***
Interpersonal Criminogenic Targets: Family and Peers	19	.05 (392)	.22 (72)	.37***
Individualized Matching with Need (specific needs not identified)	17	.06 (313)	.21 (61)	.30***
School/Work	24	.06 (286)	.15 (88)	.21***
Substance Abuse	10	.08 (338)	.11 (36)	.06 (ns)
NONCRIMINOGENIC NEEDS				
Personal Noncriminogenic Needs (personal distress, fear of official punishment)	46	.11 (203)	.04 (171)	−.18**
Interpersonal Noncriminogenic Needs (e.g., family processing other than nurturance, supervision)	12	.09 (329)	.01 (45)	−.13*

k = number of tests of treatment
%: percentage of tests with need targeted
* p < .05; ** p < .01; *** p < .001
ns = nonsignificant

Resource Note 11.1 *(continued)*

Community/Nonresidential Settings. The mean effects size increased with level of Appropriate Treatment both in community settings and institutional/residential settings. However, the positive effects of Appropriate Treatment were enhanced in community settings (mean effect size = +.35, k = 30), while the negative effects of inappropriate service were augmented in residential settings (mean effects size = –.10, k = 25).

Core Correctional Practices. Table 11.1.3 lists the basic elements of behavioral influence. We call them "core correctional practices" because they represent what we and others (e.g., Trotter, 1999) believe should be part of the essential skills and qualities for those who work with offenders. As shown in the table, indicators of a high-quality relationship and structuring are associated with enhanced effect sizes. The structuring indicators include modeling, reinforcement, problem-solving, structured learning, and others.

Exploration of a Variety of Study, Organizational, and Validity Considerations. Effect size increased to at least a mild degree with all indicators of program integrity presented in Table 11.1.4 except two.

Those two were Rated Dosage and Monitoring of Process. Other factors related to effect size but not shown in Table 10.1.4 were random assignment (eta = .10) and follow-up periods of less than two years (eta = –.12). Once again, statistical controls for these considerations did not erase the positive effects of RNR adherence. Similarly, considerations of age, gender, and ethnicity of cases did not influence the effects of Adherence.

In the end, however, four variables were linked with effect size in a positive manner once controls for RNR Adherence were introduced. They were Community-Based Programs, Involved Evaluator, Non-Justice Ownership of the Program, and Referral to Program by Justice Officials. As presented in the main body of Technical Note 11.1, the strength of RNR Adherence was evident even when offered under the conditions least favorable to large effect sizes. Overall, conditions that limit the magnitude of the mean effect size do not negate the evidence to date in favor of clinically relevant and psychologically informed human service in a variety of justice contexts.

Table 11.1.3
Mean Effect Size by Elements of Core Correctional Practice (CCP)

Element of CCP	Element Present (k) No	Yes	Correlation with Effect Size
Relationship Skills	.07 (361)	.34 (13)	.26***
Structuring Skills	.06 (330)	.27 (44)	.37***
Effective Reinforcement	.07 (359)	.31 (15)	.25***
Effective Modeling	.06 (337)	.28 (37)	.36***
Effective Disapproval	.08 (366)	.30 (8)	.18***
Structured Skill Learning	.06 (336)	.30 (38)	.39***
Problem Solving	.06 (329)	.25 (45)	.33***
Advocacy/Brokerage	.08 (321)	.11 (53)	.10*
Effective Authority	.07 (359)	.26 (15)	.19***

* p < .05; *** p < .001
k = number of tests of treatment

Resource Note 11.1 *(continued)*

Table 11.1.4
Mean Effect Size by Indicators of Integrity of Implementation and Service Delivery (k = 374)

Indicator	Indicator Present		Correlation with Effect Size
	No	Yes	
Staff Selected for Relationship Skills	.07 (361)	.34 (13)	.26**
Staff Trained	.04 (206)	.13 (168)	.26**
Clinical Supervision of Staff	.06 (305)	.16 (69)	.21**
Number of Hours of Service	(metric nonbinary variable; k = 84)		.20**
Rated Appropriate Dosage	.07 (221)	.09 (153)	.05 (ns)
Printed/Taped Manuals	.05 (303	.20 (71)	.30**
Monitor Process and/or Intermediate Change on Targets	.07 (227)	.10 (147)	.07 (ns)
Specific Model	.03 (173)	.12 (201)	.23***
New/Fresh Program	.05 (250)	.13 (124)	.20**
Small Sample (100<)	.04 (340)	.15 (134)	.28***
Involved Evaluator	.04 (296)	.23 (78)	.41***

k = number of tests of treatment
** p < .01; *** p < .001
ns = nonsignificant

The mean r of 0.08 is an average, and the 95 percent confidence interval of .06 to .10 does *not* contain .00. In other words, correctional interventions do have an effect on recidivism. There is, however, a tremendous amount of variability around that mean. The poorest outcome within all 374 estimates is in the area of −0.40, while the best single outcome is in the area of +0.80. Perhaps the really interesting question is what are the sources of this variation? Note that increases in severity of the penalty continue to yield mild negative effects (mean $r = -0.03$, k = 101), while variation in human service delivery continues to yield modestly positive effects (mean $r = +0.12$, k = 273).

The mildly negative effect of increases in the severity of the criminal sanction is now so well established that specific deterrence may be declared to be empirically indefensible as a rationale for increases in the severity of the penalty. In Chapter 13, we present Paul Gendreau and colleagues' meta-analytic review of the effects on reoffending of the whole range of "innovative" and "traditional" punishments that were experimented upon in the 1980s and 1990s. These variations on themes of punishment included "turning the heat up on probationers," "turning the heat up on parolees," "boot camps," "Scared Straight," "more prison," "mandatory arrest of male batterers," and so on. Recall Mark Lipsey's negative findings regarding programs based on deterrence theory.

Further, read Michael Tonry's (1994) commentary on the war on drugs in the United States. He reminds us that governments in Canada, Great Britain, and the United States, from the 1960s on, have repeatedly and consistently heard from blue-ribbon commissions and expert advisory bodies that harsher penalties will not significantly increase public safety.

On the other hand, the evidence favoring the delivery of human service in a justice context continues to grow and deepen, albeit with many questions unanswered. As in the original sample, a simple coding of human service as behavioral or nonbehavioral yields striking differences in mean effect size (0.04, k = 297, for nonbehavioral treatment compared with 0.23, k = 77, for behavioral treatment). The shorthand phrase "behavioral" may be better described as "behavioral/social learning/ cognitive behavioral." The coding of treatment programs was based on indication of the use of the following type of strategies: modeling (if you want to get a behavior going, demonstrate it), reinforcement (if you want to keep a behavior going, reward it), role-playing (set up opportunities for practice with corrective feedback), graduated practice (some behavior actually constitutes a complex skill that may best be broken down and practiced in smaller steps), extinction (assure that antisocial styles of thinking, feeling, and acting are not inadvertently rewarded), and cognitive restructuring (pay attention to the risky content of thought and assist in trying out less risky thoughts). To our knowledge, every meta-analysis that has been reported upon, with the exception of Whitehead and Lab's (1989), has found the pattern noted above. As noted in the chapter on a general personality perspective (Chapter 4), the social learning models of criminal behavior have virtually no serious competitors when attention turns away from simple prediction and toward actually influencing criminal behavior.

The overall pattern of results favoring "clinically appropriate" human service continues in the expanded sample of studies. With the coding of risk, need, and responsivity once again defining "appropriate" treatment, the mean correlation coefficients with reduced reoffending were as follows: Criminal Sanctions (−.03, k = 101); Human Service inconsistent with each of risk, need, and responsivity (−.01, k = 23); Human Service consistent with only one of risk, need, and responsivity (+.02, k = 106); Human Service consistent with two of the three principles (+.18, k = 84); and Appropriate Service (consistent with all three principles: +.26, k = 60). The counting of number of principles adhered to was made possible by certain important changes in coding in the latest Carleton sample.

In our work with the expanded sample of tests of effective treatment, a more careful examination is being made of each of the three principles. One such look was described immediately above in the report on the social learning/cognitive behavioral aspect of responsivity. Separate explorations also were introduced for the risk and need principles. This allowed the counting of adherence with principles evident in the paragraph above.

In the Andrews et al. (1990a) report, the risk principle was explored within those particular studies that allowed such an exploration. That is, within any particular study of a particular treatment program, if the effects of treatment were reported separately for lower- and higher-risk cases, the separate estimates were placed in our meta-analysis (the estimate for the higher-risk subgroup was placed in the appropriate treatment category and the estimate for the lower-risk group in the inap- propriate treatment category). The raw data in the appendix to the 1990 report reveals clear differences, with much larger effects found in the higher-risk subsamples relative to the lower-risk samples. Lab and Whitehead (1990) presented an intellectually serious criticism of our "within sample" approach; we agreed with some of their points. Overall, however, our "within sample" approach strongly supported the risk principle. We were more concerned with Mark Lipsey's finding that the risk principle indeed was supported but only to a minor degree. Lipsey (1989), unlike us, coded samples as a whole as either lower-risk or higher-risk. He used an aggregate approach wherein samples that included a predominant number of first offenders were coded as "lower-risk," while samples that included a predominant number of repeat offenders were coded as "higher-risk." We now employ the Lipsey approach when the more direct test of the risk principle is impossible because of insuffi- cient data. What is found is that the risk principle continues to be sup- ported for otherwise appropriate treatment, but the level of support is attenuated relative to the more direct "within sample" approach. Notably, Mark Lipsey and David Wilson (1998) endorsed the risk principle in their meta-analytic review of effective service for serious young offenders.

Lab and Whitehead (1990) were particularly negative about our tests of the need principle. Indeed, we did apply the need principle in a less-than-direct manner. Our applications of the need principle were basically reflected in the comments section of an appendix to the 1990 report. Then a graduate student at Carleton University, Craig Dowden, enthusiastically took on the task of systematically and objectively evalu- ating the validity of the need principle. Dowden (1998) took the original Table 15.3 from this text and applied it to the analysis of our expanded set of studies. Table 15.3 rewords the dynamic risk factors supported by PCC in terms of more promising and less promising intermediate targets of change within programs concerned with the more ultimate target of reduced recidivism. Table 15.3 dates back to the 1980s, and is not a summary of the findings of our earlier meta-analysis of correctional treatment.

Dowden counted the number of promising targets represented in treatment programs as well as the number of less promising targets rep- resented in treatment programs. His counts agreed with the counts of an independent reader in more than 90 percent of the codes. The findings were strong: across three samples of studies (Andrews et al. 1990a; Whitehead & Lab, 1989; new studies in Carleton University database), the mean effect size for studies of programs that targeted a greater number of the more promising targets than the less promising targets was +0.19 (k = 169), compared with a mean effect size of −.01 (k = 205) for studies of programs that emphasized less promising targets. The simple correlation between appropriate targeting and reduced recidivism was .47 in the Whitehead and Lab sample of studies (k = 87), .60 in the sample pulled together by Andrews, Zinger, and colleagues (1990a: k = 67), .50 in our 1998 additional sample of studies (k =140), and .57 in the most recent set of studies added by Dowden (k = 80). Cross-sample findings as robust as the criminogenic need findings are inconsistent with a tautology argument. The importance of the criminogenic need principle should not be underestimated. Programs that placed a greater emphasis on less promising intermediate targets tended to increase reoffending rates. Not one program that targeted noncriminogenic needs predominately was associated with reduced recidivism. The overall correlation between the number of criminogenic needs targeted and recidivism was .55.

This chapter has shown that the objective and quantitative findings of the existing literature on correctional effectiveness do not support a "nothing works" perspective. The "nothing works" perspective makes sense only if one limits one's view of the effects of treatment to that literature which deals with the effects of variations in the type and/or severity of official processing and sanctioning on recidivism. In dramatic contrast, the research literature on the effects of treatment service, offered under a variety of conditions of official processing, has revealed positive effects on average—and notably positive effects when the principles of risk, need, and responsivity have been applied.

These conclusions apply to the findings represented in the research literature. They do not apply to the vast majority of treatment programs that are being offered currently. Only a very small proportion of programs are evaluated, and few of these evaluations make their way into the published research literature. As noted elsewhere, over a recent 10-year period in which millions of young American and Canadian citizens came into contact with the justice system, the total number of published studies on what we have described as "appropriate" treatment was 21 (Andrews, Zinger et al., 1990a). We do not claim that this review provides a representative sample of current programming or that it speaks to the effectiveness of programs that have not been evaluated. Indeed, we are open to the possibility that the situation in juvenile justice is similar wherein lists of the most popular treatments and the best-validated treatments do not overlap at all. We are also open to the possibility that unvalidated but popular treatments may prove to be effective upon systematic exploration. The most important indication of this review is that there should be ongoing exploration and development of decent, humane, just, and effective means of introducing human service for purposes of reducing antisocial conduct.

In practical terms, what does clinically appropriate service look like? Summarizing the studies reviewed by Andrews and colleagues, the programs consistent with the principles of effective service were not at all mysterious. They included: (1) short-term behavioral/systems family counseling in which family process is targeted for change and/or in which relevant systems are expanded to include the school, peers, and other relevant settings in the community, (2) structured one-on-one paraprofessional programs in which the helpers were encouraged to be of active and direct assistance, (3) specialized academic/vocational programming, (4) intensive structured skill training, and (5) behaviorally-oriented individual counseling, group counseling, and structured milieu systems.

Most of the effective programs contained elements whose importance has been noted in this review. Additionally, Don Gordon, Don Andrews, James Hill, and Kevin Kurkowsky (1992) worked on an expanded and refined measure of therapeutic integrity in the delivery of family therapy. The measure of integrity reflects the specificity of the model that links intervention to outcome, the training and clinical supervision of direct service workers, adequate dosage, and monitoring of service process and intermediate gain. Their findings are so strong that they demand comment. The effects of therapeutic integrity may be incremental to the effects of appropriate treatment and to the methodological variables known to influence estimates of effect size. In brief, many of the programs that were found effective in our review are notable not only according to the principles of risk, need, and responsivity, but also according to their exceptional attention to the specifics of service delivery and to organizational issues. Of course, these facts are now represented in the organizational principles of the RNR model (as reviewed in Chapter 2).

Meta-Analytic Summaries of the Effects of RNR Programming

Resource Note 11.1 is a concise but comprehensive summary of the major RNR findings as briefly reviewed in Chapter 2 and just reviewed in a narrative fashion in this chapter. Technical Note 11.1 provides a systematic review of the applicability of elements of RNR in the total sample and with subgroups based on age, gender, and ethnicity. Both Notes draw upon the Dowden (1998) expansion of the data set that was originally reported upon by Andrews, Zinger et al. (1990). The wide applicability of the core clinical principles, the core correctional practices, and the elements of program integrity is quite striking. Of course, it was also expected because the theory of criminal conduct and the RNR model of rehabilitation were highly general by design.

The Carleton University analyses (Resource Note 11.1) also suggest that a host of indicators of integrity are linked with positive outcome when the conditions are favorable to clinically and psychologically appropriate treatment. The latter types of treatment are human service programs consistent with the principles of risk, need, and responsivity. A problem with the meta-analytic findings is that so few primary studies report in detail on the indicators of integrity.

In summary, evidence to date suggests that the delivery of clinically relevant treatment service is a promising route to reduced recidivism. Whatever the social role of punishment, there is no evidence that a reliance on just deserts or deterrence-based sanctioning is followed by meaningful reductions in recidivism (see Chapter 13 for further evidence on sanctioning). The possibility of large reductions in recidivism resides in delivering appropriate treatment services to people at risk and in need. Notably, however, the meta-analyses reviewed here suggest that the use of community alternatives to custodial sanctions will enhance the effectiveness of treatment services that are in adherence with the core clinical principles.

Recent Reviews by Mark Lipsey

Two decades ago, Lipsey (1989) and Andrews, Zinger et al. (1990) almost simultaneously began to explore the possibility of evidence-based general principles of effective correctional treatment. Both groups of researchers thought that the meta-analytic approach was a promising way of achieving such an understanding. Few, if any, other research teams were so committed to the development of general principles. We have already shown how closely their findings overlapped two decades ago. How do the findings of the two groups fit together today?

The current section of the current chapter updates the conclusions of the Lipsey and the Andrews groups. There are now many meta-analyses of the effectiveness of correctional treatment. McGuire (2004) identified more than 40 meta-analytic studies and by now the number is likely in the area of 60 or 70. Our readers must have noted that in this book we have already reported on the results documented in multiple investigations of the effectiveness of family programs, substance abuse programs, educational vocational programs, and many others. The vast majority of meta-analytic studies of correctional treatment tend to focus on particular programs or types of programs. Some types of programs are defined by the methods employed (e.g., cognitive-behavioral therapy), by structure (e.g., group counseling), by intermediate targets (e.g., substance abuse), by who is involved in treatment (e.g., family therapy), and/or by particular subtypes (e.g., MST in the family domain or FFT in the family domain).

Recently, Mark Lipsey (2009; Lipsey & Cullen, 2007) has returned to the issue of a broader and more general understanding of the principles of effective correctional treatment. He is referring to studies that collect and meta-analyze all the available research on the effects of intervention with offenders. As he did in the late 1980s, he wants to broaden the scope of interventions beyond types defined by particular programs or types of programs. As in Lipsey (1989, 1992), Lipsey (2009) limits his review to investigations of the effects of intervention on the recidivism of young offenders.

Lipsey (2009) argues that broadening the scope of interventions serves three major functions. First, less well-defined programs will be reviewed (e.g., brokering/referral programs) along with the more typical programs such as family therapy. Second, the broadening of scope encourages and allows exploration of the relative effectiveness of different approaches (e.g., family therapy versus personal skill building) with controls for types of designs (e.g., randomized versus nonrandomized) and risk levels of participating cases and such. Third, and most importantly, the broader approach entails testing or searching for the factors associated with effectiveness, that is, to answer the questions of: Generally, what are the principles of effective correctional intervention? Adherence with what principles will be associated with the reduction of criminal recidivism? In brief, what works?

Mark Lipsey (2009) identifies two groups of researchers who pursue general principles. One group is composed of the authors of the current book and their colleagues. The other group is composed of Lipsey and his colleagues. Readers are aware of our approach and its defining characteristics: The risk-need-responsivity approach is rooted in a theory of crime and reflecting a model of correctional assessment and rehabilitation. We like to think that we will travel wherever the evidence leads us, but our readers know that we begin by following maps that have been drawn by our theoretical understandings and by considerations of the values underlying our approach to the psychology of criminal conduct. If the evidence points to new rewarding routes, we will follow the new paths (even if we do so with some kicking and screaming).

The Lipsey approach has been quite different: the Lipsey approach is atheoretical and heavily descriptive. His analyses are not associated with theories of crime or even with theoretical positions in regard to the processes of behavioral influence and behavior change. He is also much more interested in the technicalities of measures of effect size than we have been. Basically he works with sets of potential moderators of effect size estimates, as described below:

Study methodology

- Type of measure of recidivism (e.g., conviction, incarceration, number of arrests, self-reported, follow-up period, etc.).

- Design issues (e.g., random assignment, matching, covariate adjustments, etc.).
- Attrition from intervention and control groups.

Publication bias

Journal article, book chapter, sample size, unpublished, etc.

Characteristics of the young offender samples

Mean age, gender mix, risk level, history of aggression, etc.

Supervision and control

None, diverted from justice system, probation/parole, incarceration.

Type of intervention

- Any particular intervention could be coded as falling in more than one of the seven categories. Various particular types may be nested within the following categories:
    — Surveillance (e.g., intensive supervision)
    — Deterrence (e.g., Scared Straight)
    — Discipline (e.g., Boot camp)
    — Restorative (e.g., restitution, mediation).
    — Counseling. Individual; mentoring; family; short-term family crisis; group; peer; mixed; mixed with referrals.
    — Skill-building. Behavioral contacting, token economies; cognitive-behavioral; social skills training; challenge; academic; vocational.
    — Multiple coordinated services. Case management; service brokerage.
- Amount and quality of service. Best assessed by the program evaluator having been involved in the design and the delivery of the service program.

The Findings of Lipsey (2009). The first three of the following factors clearly differentiated between less effective and more effective interventions with young offenders:

1. "Therapeutic" interventions (counseling and skills training) were significantly more effective than interventions based on control or coercion (surveillance, deterrence, and discipline);

2. Effectiveness increased with the risk level of young offenders;

3. Effectiveness increased with the quality of implementation (program integrity)

A few additional findings were equally interesting:

4. Intervention was equally effective for younger and older juveniles, for males and females, and for whites and nonwhites.

5. Cognitive-behavioral programs were more effective than all other programs with behavioral programs ranked second. Group

counseling programs and mentoring programs, however, were statistically indistinguishable from the behavior programs in their effects.

6. The effectiveness of counseling programs was reduced in samples of incarcerated young offenders.

7. The effectiveness of skill-building programs was enhanced when delivered in the community to young people not under correctional supervision.

Lipsey (2009) also stressed another finding in the abstract of his report:

8. Once statistical controls for other variables are introduced, relatively few differences were found in the effectiveness of different types of therapeutic interventions.

Comparing the RNR Findings with the Findings of Lipsey

The Lipsey findings regarding the effectiveness of therapeutic approaches relative to deterrence and control is highly consistent with our evidence in regard to the effectiveness of human service relative to reliance on the official punishment approach. Likewise, Lipsey's findings in regard to effectiveness across categories of age, gender, and ethnicity is consistent with: (a) our theoretical position regarding the general applicability of the theory and principles, and (b) our evidence in regard to the relative value of human and social services even in a judicial context. With regard to the importance of implementation integrity, both meta-analyses are in agreement, although Andrews and Dowden (2005) surveyed a greater number of indicators of integrity. Our indicators, however, were correlates of the Lipsey measure of the evaluators' direct involvement in the design and/or delivery of the service. Similarly, and despite the differences in measurement of adherence with the risk principle, the reviews by Lipsey and his colleague, Nana Landenberger (Landenberger & Lipsey, 2005; Lipsey, 2009), support the risk principle.

There is partial agreement in regard to the principle of general responsivity, but Lipsey appears not to have considered the coding of cognitive social learning strategies in programs described as counseling. You may recall from Chapter 8, in our analyses, family counseling, educational/vocational programming, and other types of service programs worked best when in adherence with the core clinical principles of RNR.

The RNR principles suggest that human service programs that are in adherence with the core clinical principles of RNR are effective in both community and residential or institutional settings but the effects are dampened within institutional settings. Lipsey's findings number 6 and 7, as described above, are somewhat consistent with our findings.

The criminogenic need principle was simply not tested by Lipsey (2009). We are sure a difficulty for the Lipsey coders would have been that not all programs are very explicit about the nature of their intermediate targets of change. It was a problem for us as well, but if the intermediate targets were not specified, we coded any criminogenic and noncriminogenic needs as "0" (that is, not present).

It is something of a problem that after 20 years of research on the RNR principles, the RNR team remains the only group of meta-analytic investigators attending to intermediate targets in a systematic manner. If we are off base in our coding, we would appreciate evidence regarding how the crucial issue of intermediate targets might be better explored. It is too important an issue for the primary investigators to not be specific about it and for meta-analysts to be paying so little attention to it.

Mark Lipsey and the RNR group share another key concern. Recall the opening paragraph of this chapter. Therein, the story of effective crime prevention in the context of corrections was described as a movement from "no serious consideration given," to "nothing works," through "what works," to "making 'what works' work."

It is now obvious that there at least two sets of studies in the controlled outcome literature. One set is composed of highly controlled demonstration projects in which often the evaluator of the program himself or herself was involved in the design and/or delivery of the program being evaluated. These studies tend to be relatively well-controlled studies involving small numbers of cases who receive services from trained and supervised service deliverers.

Another set of studies are often called investigations of "real world," "routine," or "regular" correctional programming. As you may expect, on average, the effectiveness of regular correctional programming is much lower than the effectiveness of demonstration programming. "Regular" correctional programs score lower on indicators of integrity and even on measures of adherence with the principles of RNR. This is perhaps the major challenge in applications of the psychology of criminal conduct. The challenge and implications are so great that in this edition of PCC "making 'what works' work" now has the status of requiring its own chapter. In the next chapter, Chapter 12, the challenge and responses to the challenge are outlined in some detail.

Here we turn directly to methodological threats to the validity of the conclusions derived regarding the positive impact of risk-need-responsivity (RNR) adherence on reduced recidivism.

Can the Contributions of Appropriate Treatment Survive Controls for Competing Variables?

We have noted how Mark Lipsey's (1989, 2009) meta-analyses provided estimates of the impact of methodological issues, threats to validity, and treatment variables on effect size. His analysis was important in dealing with the ongoing criticism that treatment effects can be explained away by nontreatment variables. If critics did not agree with the findings surrounding offender rehabilitation, then they claimed that the results were due to the quality of the design, the treatment was tried with a particular group of offenders and could not work with others, and the evaluation was flawed because the researchers who designed the program did the evaluation. Against this backdrop of knowledge destruction, Lipsey's analyses actually showed that treatment effects survived controls for the effects of the methodological variables that he measured and tested.

The findings from the Carleton University meta-analyses confirm what Lipsey and others have found. When methodological and implementation factors are considered, the effectiveness of appropriate treatment remains a viable, practical approach for dealing with criminal behavior. In the remaining sections of this text, the evidence for this conclusion is presented. We leave it to our readers to decide whether they are convinced by the analyses. As noted in Resource Note 11.1, we found that clinically and psychologically appropriate treatment (that is, RNR adherence) was the single strongest correlate of effect size (the correlation with effect size was .42, k = 374). The mean effect sizes at each level of the four-level appropriate treatment were –.02 (k = 124) for punishment only or human service inconsistent with each of risk, need, and responsivity); .02 (human service adhering with only one of risk, need, and responsivity); .18 (human service in adherence with two of risk, need, and responsivity); and .26 (human service consistent with each of risk, need, and responsivity).

With appropriate treatment controlled, and a host of competing variables considered, only four variables enhanced the prediction of effect size over and above appropriate treatment. The four were "an evaluator involved in the design and/or delivery of service," "community based setting," "nonjustice ownership of program," and "referral to program by a justice person." The question addressed here is how clinically relevant and psychologically appropriate treatment relates to outcome when the four most powerful control variables are considered. The first row in Table 11.1 gives the average effect size for the four levels of treatment (from least appropriate to most appropriate) while controlling for the effects of the four extra-treatment variables. The next three rows reveal the effect of treatment when conditions favor the enhancement of effect

Table 11.1
Mean Effect Size by RNR Adherence and the Major Control Variables
(k = number of tests of treatment)

	Level of RNR Adherence				Correlation with Effect Size
	Low: Inappropriate		High: Appropriate		
	0	1	2	3	

Mean Effect Size Adjusted for Involved Evaluator, Community Setting, Nonjustice Ownership, and Justice Referral

	−.02 (124)	.03 (106)	.17 (84)	.25 (60)	.53***
					(partial correlation)

Mean Effect Size by Number of Major Control Variables Favorable to Large Effect

	0	1	2	3	Corr
None/One	−.09 (27)	−.02 (28)	.07 (23)	.11 (13)	.48***
Two	−.01 (88)	.03 (55)	.17 (25)	.22 (21)	.56**
Three/Four	.04 (9)	.06 (23)	.25 (36)	.38 (26)	.60***

*** p < .001
k = number of tests of treatment

size. For example, appropriate treatment (coded 3) was positive and strongest when three or four of the control variables favoring a large effect size were present (mean effect size of .38). The average effect of most appropriate treatment was reduced when only two of the four control variables favored a large effect size (.22), but the mean effect of most appropriate treatment remained greater than the mean effect of less appropriate treatment (−.01). The mean effect of most appropriate treatment is very low when none or only one control variable favors a large effect size but, once again, even that low mean effect of treatment (.11) is much greater than the mean effect of the least appropriate treatment (mean effect size of −.09).

In summary, clinically and psychologically appropriate treatment—as specified by the RNR model and a general personality and social learning perspective—outperforms alternative treatments whether the background conditions are favorable or unfavorable to reduced reoffending. We expect there are conditions under which clinically relevant and psychologically informed human service will not prove superior to alternative interventions. We look forward to tests of those limits of human service in justice and primary prevention contexts. Now, the chapter closes with a discussion of "what works" and the linkages among the major theories of criminal conduct and the design and outcomes of correctional counseling programs.

Theory and Intervention

The Central Eight risk/need and strength factors are closely linked with the PIC-R model of criminal conduct. This is particularly true with the Big Four factors. The principles of reinforcement, behavioral punishment, antecedent control, and modeling are fundamental cognitive social learning processes. PIC-R also stressed two fundamental principles of behavioral influence that are judged important whether interpersonal influence is occurring in family, peer, work, school, leisure, or formal treatment settings (Andrews, 1980; Resource Note 3.2 of this book).

1. *The Relationship Principle*: Interpersonal influence by antecedent and consequent processes is greatest in situations characterized by open, warm, enthusiastic, and nonblaming communication, and by collaboration, mutual respect, liking, and interest.

2. *The Structuring Principle*: The procriminal versus anticriminal direction of interpersonal influence is determined by the procriminal/anticriminal content of the messages communicated or by the procriminal/anticriminal nature of the behavior patterns that are modeled, rehearsed, and subject to reinforcement and punishment contingencies. This principle is also known as the contingency principle. The structuring dimension reflects the use of effective authority practices, anticriminal modeling, differential approval and disapproval, problem-solving, skill building, advocacy, brokerage, the structuring aspects of motivational interviewing, and cognitive restructuring (Andrews, 1980; Andrews & Carvell, 1997; Andrews & Kiessling, 1980; see also Chapter 12 of this book).

These two fundamental dimensions of interpersonal exchanges have a long history in the general social psychology of interpersonal interaction (e.g., Bales, 1950), counseling theory (e.g., Rogers, 1961), and the social psychology of criminal conduct (e.g., Sutherland's theory of differential association). Indeed, we saw them in Chapter 3 in the discussion of Freudian models of parenting practices, in Chapter 4 in discussions of PIC-R, and in Chapters 7 and 8 in the discussions of family process and family therapy, peer influences, and relationships in the context of school, work, and marital and romantic.

The indicators of relationship and structuring are another way of describing general responsivity practices. The indicators of a positive relationship establish the conditions favorable to modeling effects, to effective interpersonal reinforcement and/or effective interpersonal disapproval, and to creating an attractive rather than aversive setting for intervention. We also use the core practices as factors on which the selection, training, and clinical supervision of staff can be designed.

The first set of conditions (relationship), if positive, tends to promote learning and enhance interpersonal influence. The second set (contingency) determines what is learned or the direction of influence. In correctional counseling, the structuring dimension is responsible for movement or changes that are favorable to criminal behavior or unfavorable to criminal behavior. If the content of interactions is irrelevant to criminal behavior, the effects on criminal conduct will be negligible.

Our overall model of programming (Figure 11.1) suggests that the design and operation of effective programs are contingent upon a number of sets of variables:

1. Selecting appropriate intermediate targets (focusing on attributes of people and their circumstances, which, if changed, are associated with shifts in the chances of criminal behavior);

2. Offering services that are able to produce the desired intermediate changes (the process and content of intervention on the relationship and contingency dimensions);

3. Building a program structure that will support effective process (for example, selecting and training counselors in ways compatible with desired process and outcome);

4. Matching cases and programs to clients according to risk, need, and responsivity;

5. Conducting programs with due concern for justice, ethicality, and cost-effectiveness.

We are ready to explore the relationship between intervention effectiveness and theories of criminal conduct. This discussion begins with psychodynamic theory and continues with the other theoretical perspectives of criminal conduct.

```
1) Surrounding Community and/or Agency Conditions

2) Preservice Client          3) Preservice Counselor
   Characteristics               Characteristics
(risk, need, responsivity)   (training, relationship skills)

        4) Program Characteristics
         (sociocultural, economic)

   5) Process and Content of Treatment Service
      (relationship, direct training, advocacy)

        6) Intermediate Treatment Goals
        (gains and losses on need factors)

            7) Ultimate Outcomes
(recidivism, other outcomes, consumer satisfaction)
```

Figure 11.1
Some Major Elements for Correctional Program Evaluation

Psychodynamic Theory and Psychotherapy

The broad outlines of psychoanalytic theory received strong support from cross-sectional and longitudinal studies. Recall that parent-child conflict, poor parenting skills, early involvement in antisocial behavior, and the various indicators of a weak superego (generalized misconduct, egocentricism) were all among the best validated correlates and predictors of criminal conduct. It is clear that psychodynamic theory suggests a number of important need factors (or intermediate targets for intervention).

Psychoanalysis, however, does not provide a powerful technology of behavioral influence for correctional purposes. Without question, orthodox psychoanalysis appears to be geared to "freeing" people from neurotic misery as opposed to inhibiting antisocial behavior. Psychoanalytic "talking therapy" focuses on the past and involves the search for unconscious motivators and "insight." A prerequisite for success is a reasonable level of verbal intelligence and relatively strong motivation to sit through weekly (or more frequent) sessions over periods of a year or longer. Traditionally, it is assumed that the "good" client for psychoanalysis is one experiencing some level of internally generated neurotic misery. However, according to psychoanalytic theory, the majority of persistent and serious offenders are not bothered by misery because they act out rather than internalize conflict.

We are unaware of any explicitly psychoanalytic programs that have impacted positively on delinquency prevention or corrections. As noted by Glueck and Glueck (1950), long-term psychoanalysis may be too expensive and inefficient for wide-scale use in prevention and corrections. However, other powerful elements of psychoanalysis (e.g., the importance of transference relationships and the possibility of identification with the therapist) are found in other approaches to counseling.

Evaluations of more or less psychodynamic, yet unstructured, approaches to therapy, counseling, and casework are more plentiful. By "unstructured" we mean that the counselors appeared not to make use of direct training procedures such as behavioral rehearsal, systematic conditioning (classical or operant), role-playing, or coaching. What we refer to here are approaches to counseling that rely heavily upon "talk," "psychological interpretation," "emotional expression and ventilation," "emotional support," and "therapist-client relationships" in group or individual therapy. The published studies tend to have explored eclectic programs that draw on many different models of therapy and counseling. Because so few studies have systematically monitored the ongoing process of treatment, our descriptions of process are based on the declared orientations of the counselors studied.

Our reading of this literature suggests that these "insight-oriented," "evocative," and "relationship-dependent" approaches to correctional counseling and casework were either ineffective or criminogenic in their effects. This trend is particularly evident when such unstructured programs are offered to high-risk and/or interpersonally immature cases (e.g., Craft, Stephenson & Granger, 1966; Goodman, 1972; Grant, 1965; Grant & Grant, 1959; Harris, Rice & Cormier, 1994; Kassenbaum, Ward & Wilner, 1971; Murphy, 1972; Truax, Wargo & Volksdorf, 1970).

In summary, these studies suggest that focusing exclusively on the relationship dimension without a focus on establishing anticriminal contingencies is ineffective or harmful. They also illustrate intervention programs that were not closely tied to theories of criminal conduct in terms of either the intermediate targets selected or the intervention procedures employed.

From the earliest days of the "talking cure," Freud (1953) warned psychodynamic therapists that their highly verbal, evocative, relationship-dependent, and insight-oriented therapy was inappropriate for cases with poor verbal ability and/or cases displaying narcissistic and/or psychotic disorders. He stressed that some degree of experienced discomfort and an ability to enter into an emotional relationship with the therapist were crucial to success. He added that without immediate social support for both treatment and personal change, the chances of successful treatment were minuscule. Freud went so far as to admit that once his therapeutic reputation was established, he accepted only cases that were personally and socially committed to service gains (Andrews, Bonta & Hoge, 1990:37–38).

The results of the above-noted programs contrast dramatically with the findings of studies that employed more structured approaches to counseling and focused upon influencing more theoretically relevant need factors (the "appropriate" set in Andrews, Zinger et al., 1990a).

Subcultural and Differential Association Theory

The subcultural, differential opportunity, and differential association perspectives led to a number of community-action interventions. The assumption was that the criminogenic subcultures (and/or isolation from legitimate opportunity) were a reflection of community disorganization, inadequate access to the services that make conformity possible, and gang membership. Thus, programs were initiated in various settings, including New York's Lower East Side (The Mobilization for Youth Project), Chicago (Chicago Area Project), and Boston (Midcity Youth Project).

These programs were reviewed in detail by Schur (1973) and by Klein (1971). Klein's book, *Street Gangs and Street Workers*, is particularly rich in the attention paid to the specific processes of intervention. The community-action components of the programs tended to focus not on individuals as the targets of service but on the development and strengthening of welfare agencies, neighborhood organizations, and inborn leadership. The focus on gang members was operationalized through the introduction of detached workers. These workers were to establish relationships with gang members and serve as advocates, brokers, sometime counselors, companions, and recreational agents.

The majority of the programs were not well evaluated. However, those that were explored systematically were found to have either no impact on delinquency or to *increase* delinquency. The latter finding deserves serious review. An increase in delinquent behavior as a consequence of intervention is not only practically significant but of tremendous theoretical interest. Such a finding suggests that the programs were impacting upon variables of true causal significance, albeit inadvertently.

According to Klein's and Schur's reviews, the community development aspects of some programs were successful in terms of creating improved neighborhood conditions, new welfare agencies, and recreational opportunities. However, this intermediate change appeared irrelevant to the ultimate goal of reducing delinquency.

In Klein's review of the evidence, the increased delinquency was linked to the detached worker programs. In particular, increased delinquency was found when workers "succeeded" in increasing the cohesiveness of delinquent groups. In other words, prior to the introduction of workers, the gangs were relatively weak groups—disorganized, often lacking in leadership, composed of relatively few hard-core members, and often characterized by infighting. With the introduction of a worker, the gangs became more organized and cohesive, and delinquency increased. Klein's work also demonstrated that the removal of the worker could be associated with reduced gang cohesiveness and reduced delinquency. Specifically, Klein argued that the intermediate goal of work with street gangs should be to weaken the groups, not strengthen them.

This pattern of findings underscores the need to consider both the relationship and contingency aspects of interpersonal functioning. Facilitating and encouraging interaction within delinquent groups, without simultaneously establishing anticriminal contingencies, will have the effect of increasing delinquency. This is a direct implication of behavioral reformulations of differential association theory. Why, then, would delinquency prevention programmers deliberately offer programs that are bound to be either ineffective or detrimental?

The answer is twofold. One reason is that subcultural theory carried a lot of excess baggage with it. As Chapter 3 showed, some sociologists were determined to respect "culture"—not to tamper with it directly, but rather to open up legitimate opportunities. Similarly, the disorganization of the gangs must have looked like just another part of the disorganized lower-class areas. Thus, to organize was considered "good" because community disorganization caused powerlessness, poverty, and crime.

The second part of the answer is that subcultural theory did not have a solid theory of human behavior at its base. (The idea was that people merely conform to their cultures, and thus the focus must be on the culture.) Therefore, according to Klein, the goals of the program often had little to do with either the prevention or control of delinquency. Instead, the projects were intent on doing good for the disadvantaged. This meant offering help and assistance regardless of the intermediate value of that assistance in the control of delinquency. Moreover, a focus on reducing delinquent associations or an attempt to reduce procriminal values would imply that "their" culture was somehow inferior to "our" culture. The negative contribution of the concept of culture deflected attention away from the "causal variables"—personal attitudes, values, and beliefs supportive of crime; personal problems in the area of self-management and cognitive control; antisocial associates; and distressed families with problems of cohesiveness and parenting practices.

The dual problem of not having a powerful model of human behavior to work from and not being willing to intervene actively at the level of associates, attitudes, and personal skills was evident in other major sociological intervention projects. Two examples follow. The first is Jim Hackler's (1966, 1978) Opportunities for Youth Program. The second involves tests of guided group interaction programs.

Hackler's program is one of the best formulated and best evaluated in the literature. Hackler carefully detailed the underlying model of human behavior, program structures, and outcomes. Well aware of the poverty of the personal psychology of labeling and subcultural theory, he attempted to formulate a psychological model that was compatible with sociological theory yet helpful in the design of intervention programs. Specifically, he (1978:35) postulated a complex causal chain in which being held in low esteem by others (and perhaps the self) leads to deviant behavior (see Figure 11.2).

This is a somewhat dramatic symbolic interactionist integration of anomie, labeling, and subcultural theories. The model suggests that it is not useful to attempt to change prodelinquent attitudes and values because it is not deviant norms that cause delinquent behavior but delinquent behavior that causes delinquent norms. Similarly, the low esteem with which the lower class is held by representatives of the dominant culture is outside the realm of reasonable short-term intervention. Thus, Hackler decided to focus upon Step 4, that is, a boy's perception that others perceive him as delinquency-prone.

How might a program be structured to bring about the desired perception on the part of the boy? Hackler opted for two approaches: a "work group" experience and a "teaching machine testing" experience. Approximately 240 young boys (13–14 years old) who lived in Seattle housing projects were randomly assigned to either a "work program," a

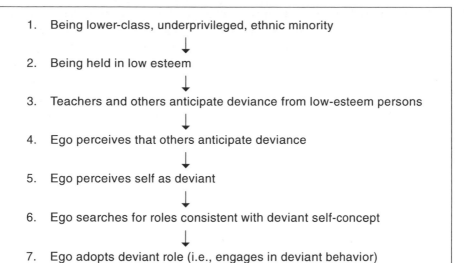

1. Being lower-class, underprivileged, ethnic minority

2. Being held in low esteem

3. Teachers and others anticipate deviance from low-esteem persons

4. Ego perceives that others anticipate deviance

5. Ego perceives self as deviant

6. Ego searches for roles consistent with deviant self-concept

7. Ego adopts deviant role (i.e., engages in deviant behavior)

8. Ego accepts deviant norms.

Figure 11.2
Hackler's Causal Chain

"teaching machine testing program," or no-treatment control groups. The experiences had no effects on attitudes as assessed by self-report questionnaires and no obvious effects on postprogram delinquency. Although the data are weak, the higher-risk cases ("bad" boys as rated by teachers, mothers, and peers) exposed to the work program performed more poorly postprogram than did the higher-risk controls.

What specifically were these programs? What were the details of the intervention processes that failed to influence intermediate attitudes and ultimate behavior? The teaching machine program was designed explicitly not to be a remedial education program. Rather, the boys were to test the machines and advise the teachers whether they found the machines interesting and/or useful and whether they discovered ways to cheat with the machines. The "teachers" were instructed *not* to reward the boys for good academic performance. The work program involved groups of boys engaging in community clean-up projects (e.g., in public parks) under the supervision of an adult leader. The leader was instructed *not* to reward the boys for good work performance, because direct reward contingencies would lead the boys to believe that the leader thought that they were irresponsible, lazy, or inadequate.

In all, it would be difficult to conceive of a less direct approach to behavioral influence than those employed in the Seattle Project. With hindsight, it is obvious that these programs were focusing on inappropriate intermediate targets in inadequate ways. Still, this project continues to be promoted as evidence that nothing works. Perhaps what it really shows is the poverty of anomie, labeling, and subcultural theory for designing effective intervention programs. We owe a great debt to Hackler for having the drive, tenacity, and respect for evidence to conduct and report on such a direct test of sociological notions of the 1960s.

The high levels of passivity of intervention in the Seattle Project are also evident in several evaluations of guided group interaction programs. Here the difficulty of sociologically based intervention programs is revealed in rather broad ways. LaMar Empey, like Hackler, rigorously outlined the rationale for what is known as the Provo Experiment (Empey & Erickson, 1972; Empey & Rabow, 1961). Stephenson and Scarpitti (1974) provide a useful review of a number of controlled-outcome evaluations of guided group interaction programs. As in the case of Hackler's work, these evaluation studies are classics in the psychology of crime. Stephenson and Scarpitti's conclusion was that the programs were not any more effective than regular probation.

Much can be learned from the evaluations of guided group interaction (though we wish there had been more attention to treatment process). We have no objection to group programs when their activities are structured so that real alternatives are provided to antisocial ways of thinking, feeling, and acting (Agee, 1986; Andrews, 1980; Bush, 1995; Bush & Bilodeau, 1993; Polaschek et al., 2005) and real opportunities are given for the acquisition of new cognitive and interpersonal skills, such as perspective-taking and self-regulation (Robinson & Porporino, 2001). However, at the heart of the clinical sociology version of guided group interaction was the belief that attitudes were not really properties of individuals but instead were properties of groups. There was also the notion that the "group" must adopt anticriminal values for the learning to transfer to the individual. Workers were encouraged to reinforce candor more than they did anticriminal expressions, and there was a fear that too much of an emphasis on the anticriminal would establish conditions of "rejection of the rejectors." We believe that to hope that collections of antisocial young people with some guidance will form anticriminal groups is hoping for too much. It is placing excessive reliance on the relationship principle and ignoring the contingency principle. Quite simply, it is not consistent with the psychology of human behavior.

Many programs are still operating on the basis of weakly formulated principles of group dynamics, often infused with a mishmash of Rogerian and existential notions of the underlying goodness of humankind (e.g., Burlingame, Fuhriman & Mosier, 2003; Cordess, 2001; Mobley, 1999), which would become evident if only the person or group could experience trust, openness, and noncontingent valuing. The work of Jack Bush (1995), along with his colleagues Brian Bilodeau and Mark Kornick, has made great strides in managing this problem. Candor must be encouraged when antisocial cognitions are being explored. In their

Cognitive Self Change program, absolute candor without judgment and without "counseling" or "correction" is the practice when a "thinking report" is being prepared. At the stage of trying out less risky cognitions, however, guidance through modeling and encouragement is the norm, and the principle of respectful and caring communication is not violated.

Programs that concentrate on the relationship principle without attention to contingencies are disturbing. Equally disturbing are programs that take the contingency principle to the extreme and focus on confrontation with name-calling, humiliation, and abuse. Yelling at and otherwise abusing people contingent upon expressions of procriminal sentiments or behavior is not consistent with the relationship or structuring principles of effective interaction. In human service, people should be treated with respect, concern, and care.

Finally, helping to change the circumstances of at-risk people and changing their personal, interpersonal, familial, and community characteristics is a real challenge when the reduction of criminal recidivism is the goal. It does not happen magically, nor through the incidental learning opportunities provided by not being arrested and/or not going to court (diversion), nor through the incidental learning opportunities that might be provided by paying restitution, completing a community service order, or by a trip to court or somewhere even further into the system ("accountability" through just processing, restoration, or punishment). It does not happen in groups that are relationship-oriented, evocative, sensitive, and supportive but too respectful of the "subculture" to offer alternatives to antisocial styles of thinking, feeling, and acting. Nor does it happen in groups that employ oppressive and abusive techniques. It does not happen when neighborhoods get a new park or a new human service agency. It happens when well-developed, well-validated services focusing on criminogenic factors are delivered to at-risk individuals and their families.

Paraphrasing Andrews and Kiessling (1980:462–463), effective rehabilitative efforts involve workers who are interpersonally warm, tolerant, and flexible, yet sensitive to conventional rules and procedures. These workers make use of the authority inherent in their position without engaging in interpersonal domination (i.e., they are "firm but fair"); they demonstrate in vivid ways their own anticriminal-prosocial attitudes, values, and beliefs; and they enthusiastically engage the offender in the process of increasing rewards for noncriminal activity. The worker exposes and makes attractive the alternatives to procriminal attitudes, styles of thinking, and ways of acting. The worker does not depend upon the presumed benefits of a warm relationship with the offender and does not assume that offenders will self-discover these alternatives. The alternatives are demonstrated through words and actions, and explorations of the alternatives are encouraged through modeling, reinforcement, and specific guidance (Andrews, Bonta & Hoge, 1990:36–37). We may be "pigheaded," but now at the end of the first decade of the new millennium, we would not change a word of the above. In fact, we are inclined to underline or **bold** the whole paragraph (but we exercise self-control and only underline "underline" and bold "bold").

Behavioral and Social Learning Approaches

As we outlined in Chapter 4 (PIC-R), and throughout this text, behavioral, cognitive-behavioral, and social learning approaches to treatment provide the greatest likelihood of success. This is not simply a technology of behavioral influence. It reflects an underlying psychology of human behavior that, in turn, offers an empirically defensible psychology of criminal conduct. Offenders, being human, seek pleasure and try to avoid pain. Their behavior is influenced by the immediate contingencies of action that are situationally induced and personally and interpersonally mediated. Stability in human behavior is evident because these contingencies are maintained by such personal variables as personality, attitudes, competencies, and incompetencies, and by important others such as parents and peers.

PIC-R suggests that if some of these contingencies can be changed, then the density of the incentives and disincentives for criminal acts and noncriminal acts may be shifted more in the favor of noncriminal alternatives. The research literature provides a number of reasonably well-validated program models for changing those contingencies so that the chances of criminal conduct are reduced.

Although there has been little rehabilitative work with a focus on antisocial attitudes, some direction is provided by Andrews (1980), Wormith (1984), and Bush (1995). Generally, well-trained and well-supervised paraprofessionals working within a well-formulated model of criminal conduct and service delivery can have demonstrably positive effects. The work of William S. Davidson and colleagues is outstanding in this regard (Davidson et al., 2001). They have produced detailed manuals for the training of paraprofessionals in one-on-one behavioral advocacy approaches and family system approaches. Similarly, Jack Bush's (1995) Cognitive Self Change program is supported by manuals and training opportunities along with research support (Henning & Frue, 1996).

Intensive, structured skill development programs with detailed models for service delivery and training of therapist/coaches are available (Bogue, Nandi & Jongsma, 2003; Goldstein & Glick, 1987; Hollin & Palmer, 2001; McGuire, 2000). Similarly, the relationship and structuring aspects of short-term behavioral family system approaches (such as functional family therapy) have been implemented in many settings outside of their Utah origins. Multisystemic family service also has moved well beyond its South Carolina origins (see Chapter 8).

Cognitive-behavioral programs have been employed with sex offenders (Hanson et al., 2002, in press; Lösel & Schmucker, 2005; Olver, Wong & Nicholaichuk, 2009), high-risk violent offenders (Polaschek et al., 2005; Serin, Gobeil & Preston, 2009), psychopaths (Olver & Wong, 2009; Wong & Hare, 2005), and men who physically abuse their female partners (Babcock, Green & Robie, 2004; Dobash et al., 2000). To date, the evidence is favorable to treatment. The latter area of work is producing detailed accounts of the specific antisocial attitudes, values, and beliefs that support the sexual and physical abuse of women and children. In the area of sex offenders, Hanson and Harris's (2000) ongoing work documenting, organizing, and assessing denial and minimization among offenders may provide a model for more general assessments of the "cognitive distortions" that support antisocial conduct and interfere with progress in treatment.

The sex offender literature, along with progress in the field of addictions (Dutra et al., 2008; Irvin et al., 1999), is also exploring the promise of relapse prevention approaches (Yates & Ward, 2007). The cognitive and situational focus of relapse is interesting from the perspective of social learning: high-risk situations are identified for particular cases, and detailed cognitive and behavioral strategies are developed for those situations. Evaluations on the effectiveness of relapse prevention with sexual and general offenders are being reported that suggest promise (Dowden et al., 2003; Hanson, 1996).

Indications are that we may be on the verge of an explosion of knowledge regarding the design and implementation of effective services of the cognitive-behavioral, social learning variety. Even within specialized school and vocational programs, it is the focused and structured programs that have been linked with reduced recidivism (e.g., Le Marquand & Tremblay, 2001). We expect that advances in prevention and rehabilitation will reflect developments of the cognitive-behavioral approaches.

We envision community-based human service agencies that are staffed by well-trained and well-supervised persons able to deliver effective programs in the context of both prevention and corrections. Such agencies may receive referrals from the police and the courts with due consideration of just deserts. The expansion of community corrections may well deliver on these promises, with plenty of false starts and rerouting to be expected.

Examples of effective programs have been distributed throughout the text. The structuring elements of effective programming are described in more detail in the next chapter. In Chapter 12, our particular interest is whether the positive effects of RNR adherence can be found in the "real world" of regular ongoing programming. As Mark Lipsey (1999) carefully showed in an analysis of 196 "practical" and "real world" programs in ordinary youth service or juvenile justice settings, programs can work out there in the "real world." Of course, the programs with the strongest effects tend to be small highly controlled demonstration projects with the evaluator of the program having been involved in the design and/or delivery of the service. We explore the issue in Chapter 12 with particular attention paid to the value of RNR adherence, including the selection, training, and clinical supervision of staff and others in relation to effect size.

Worth Remembering

1. From "nothing works" to "what works" is an astonishing story at the nexus of ideology, professional identity, science, and public policy.

   Literally, the evidence did not matter for many years. Now evidence does matter. and evidence-based practice is an ideal in a least some university departments and some justice, correctional, forensic, and community prevention agencies

2. The positive effects of adherence to RNR are very robust across different types of programs, persons, settings, and methodological conditions.

   The effectiveness of treatment has been attributed to a host of variables outside the RNR principles. However, even after accounting for these factors, the RNR principles continue to offer the major explanation for program effectiveness.

Recommended Readings

For reviews that take a broader community perspective than that emphasized here, read Chapters 10, 11, and 12 in Part Two of Loeber and Farrington's (1998) *Serious and Violent Juvenile Offenders: Risk Factors and Successful Interventions*.

In regard to ineffective corrections, read "Beyond Correctional Quackery" by Ed Latessa, Francis Cullen, and Paul Gendreau (2002). Quackery is based on theories of crime such as the need to get back to nature, the need to climb a mountain, the need for acupuncture, the need for a haircut, and, of course, the need to experience a military-style boot camp.

Generally, the web sites of Public Safety Canada (http://www.psepc-sppcc.gc.ca) and Correctional Service Canada (http://www.csc-scc.gc.ca) and their research reports are a good source of what is new and happening.

Chapter 12

Creating and Maintaining RNR Adherence: A Real-World Challenge

In evaluations of the effectiveness of interventions, "evaluator involvement in the design and/or delivery of service" is associated with enhanced effect sizes; that is, with greater reductions in reoffending. Readers saw this in Table 11.1. Readers also saw that the positive effect of RNR adherence remained in effect even with controls introduced for involved evaluators. Having an external evaluator did not eliminate the effect of appropriate treatment. Some have interpreted the finding that effect sizes are larger when a researcher is involved as evidence of an artificial inflation of the effectiveness of treatment. Because many "evaluator-involved" studies are one-shot, demonstration studies with extensive training and supervision of staff, the demonstration projects do not accurately represent what is really "out there." Programs may be efficacious in tightly controlled demonstration projects but less effective in routine ("regular" or "real-world") programming.

Careful training and supervision are indeed important factors—they speak to program integrity. Quay (1977) observed more than 30 years ago that the widely touted failure of Kassebaum et al.'s (1971) prison treatment program was likely due to the inadequate conceptualization of the program and the fact that staff were poorly trained and did not believe in the efficacy of the treatment. Program integrity (or "fidelity") refers to the extent to which treatment staff actually do what the program model says they should do. In order to ensure that the program is consistent with the therapeutic principles and techniques, we can ask the following types of questions:

1. Are staff selected to enhance the effectiveness of treatment?

2. Is there a clearly defined theoretical model underlying the program?

3. Is there written documentation that lays down what is to be done?

4. Are staff trained to follow the model?

5. Are staff clinically supervised and monitored during the delivery of the program?

6. Is the program delivered with appropriate intensity and in the manner it was designed to be delivered?

An examination of the Carleton University databank revealed that a variety of indicators of core correctional practice and of program integrity were related to outcome and they were related to outcome across a range of offender samples (see Tables TN 11.1–1 through TN 11.1–4 in Technical Note 11.1). Staff selection, training, and supervision; structured programming manuals; and a clearly specified model of behavioral influence were all related to effect size. The exception was the monitoring of change on the intermediate targets and hours of service with minorities. However, controlling for program integrity factors did not diminish the impact of clinically appropriate treatment.

Indeed, we now know meta-analytically that indicators of integrity are associated with enhanced reductions in recidivism only when the programs under consideration are in adherence with RNR. Figure 2.7 revealed that the correlation of the sum of integrity indicators with effect size was .29 (k = 230) when programs were in adherence with RNR (a score of at least "2" on the four-level RNR Adherence scale from "0" through "3"). The correlation of integrity items with effect size was only .06 (k = 144), with programs scoring "0" or "1" on RNR Adherence.

What does it mean? It means that "real-world" programs that are offering noncognitive behavioral and poorly targeted programs to low-risk cases will not be reducing recidivism no matter how much attention is paid to the integrity of the non-RNR programs. It means that "real-world" programs that adhere to RNR principles may enhance their positive impact still further through attention to staffing and program integrity.

Lipsey (1999) selected from his database of 400 juvenile treatment studies only those studies that were "initiated and supervised by personnel other than the researcher and implemented in ordinary youth service or juvenile justice settings." Lipsey's (1999) analysis of 196 "practical rehabilitative programs" led him to conclude that "rehabilitative programs of a practical 'real world' sort clearly can be effective" (p. 641).

Petrosino and Soydan (2005) reviewed 12 meta-analyses that explored the effects of program developer involvement in evaluations. Eleven of the 12 meta-analyses reported a positive correlation between involvement and effect size. Additionally, they conducted their own quantitative review of 300 randomized experimental evaluations. Averaged across 24 tests in which the evaluator was the program developer or creator, the rate of successful correctional outcomes was 61.75 percent in the experimental group, compared with to a success rate of 38.25 percent for the control group.

We define "real-world" programs somewhat differently than did Lipsey (1999). We define routine programs as ones dealing with large numbers of cases (i.e., their research sample included more than 100 cases) and in which the evaluator of the program was an external researcher (not part of the service design or service delivery team).

Inspection of Table 12.1 reveals that routine correctional programs are not at all like the small sample highly controlled demonstration project. Routine programs are less likely to introduce a human service element; they score much lower on the adherence with the clinical RNR principles; they target very few criminogenic needs; and they score much lower on the staffing, core correctional practice, and program integrity factors. Note that the mean effect sizes in the routine and demonstration projects are dramatically different.

Large differences were illustrated in Table 12.1, but let us go after the big issue: To what extent is RNR adherence associated with increased effectiveness in real-world/regular programming? Inspection of Table 12.2 reveals that RNR adherence was associated with enhanced recidivism reduction in the case of each of the three types of programs. With adherence, the mean effects of .09 and .15 for real-world programs are modest compared to the comparable mean effects reported for demonstration projects (.31 and .34). Yet, mean effects of .09 and .15 look very good compared to the increased crime associated with real-world programs that score low on RNR adherence (–.02 and .04). Moreover, there is the very real possibility that enhancements in program integrity might still boost the crime reduction yielded by those programs (recall Figure 2.7 in Chapter 2).

Table 12.1

Adherence with RNR Principles in Demonstration Projects and in Routine Corrections: The Principles of RNR Clinical Practice, Staffing and Management, Core Practices and Program Integrity

Indicators of RNR Adherence (k)	Type of Programming			Correlation with ES (374)
	Routine (209)	Mixed (118)	Demonstration (47)	
Any Human Service (Mean Score 0, 1)	.65	.77	.98	.24
RNR Clinical (Mean score 0 to 3)	.82	1.47	2.30	.48
Breadth (Mean Score –3 to +5)	.06	1.01	2.11	.39
Staff Selection, Training and Clinical Supervision (Mean Score 0 to 4)	.43	1.05	1.72	.46
Sum Core Correctional Practices (without Staff, Involved Evaluator, and Adjustment for Sample Size) (Mean Score 0 to7)	1.52	1.91	2.32	.20
Sum Integrity (without Staff) (Mean Score 0 to 5)	1.52	2.91	4.32	.45
Mean Effect Size (ES)	.03	.10	.29	.42

Notes: k = number of tests; Mixed = Small Sample or Involved Evaluator; Staff Selection based on relationship and structuring skills; ES = Effect Size.

Table 12.2
Mean Effect Size by Level of RNR Adherence and by Demonstration and Regular Programming (k = number of tests)

Program Type	Level of Adherence with the RNR Clinical Principles				
	0 (None)	1	2	3 (Full)	r with ES
Demonstration (47)	.01 (1)	.07 (7)	.31 (16)	.34 (23)	.44
Mixed (118)	−.03 (30)	−.02 (28)	.20 (34)	.24 (26)	.53
Real World/Regular (209)	−.02 (93)	.04 (71)	.09 (34)	.15 (11)	.41

Notes: Mixed = Small Sample or Involved Evaluator; ES = Effect Size.

Remember the trajectory is from "nothing works," through "what works," to "making 'what works' work." The latter is a crucial issue now. It is the classic issue of needing to bridge the gap between research and practice (Lipsey & Cullen, 2007). Before proceeding, however, what is the explanation for the "demonstration project" effect? The effect is well-known in the general psychotherapy literature, where it is often called the effect of researcher allegiance to the program under review. There are two obvious interpretations of the established fact of enhanced effects of interventions when the evaluator is involved in the design and/or delivery of the service under investigation (Lipsey, 1995; Petrosino & Soydan, 2005). The "cynical" interpretation is that involved researchers make decisions or take actions that improperly (if sometimes unknowingly) bias the findings in the direction favorable to the effectiveness of the program under investigation. The "high-fidelity" interpretation is that involved researchers take steps to enhance the integrity of service delivery in legitimate ways.

We add a third and fourth interpretation. Third, it is quite possible that evaluators who are involved with the programs they are evaluating are simply more knowledgeable of "what works" in corrections and their programs (and/or their evaluations of programs are more sophisticated than those of external evaluators). In the very direct words of Petrosino and Soydan (2005:445), involved researchers may be designing and testing "smarter interventions." They may know the offenders, correctional workers, and effective correctional programming much more so than external evaluators. A fourth interpretation is that the positive effects of involved researchers reflect some combination of the "bias," "high-fidelity," and "smart" interpretations.

In the absence of additional evidence, we tend to support the fourth interpretation. Reanalysis of the data in Table 12.2 reveals that 79 percent (37/47) of the demonstration projects were at level "2" or "3" of adherence with the clinical principles of RNR. The corresponding value for routine programming was only 22 percent (45/209). It borders on the astonishing: 78 percent (164/209) of the routine programs involved no human service at all or, at best, human service that was in adherence with only one of the principles of risk, need, and general responsivity. That is not "smart programming" to anyone who is familiar with the major risk/need factors and with the General Personality and Cognitive Social Learning (GPCSL) perspective on human behavior. In the "real world" of corrections, weak adherence with RNR is the rule rather than the exception.

The situation is worse than simple nonadherence with the core clinical principles of RNR. As demonstrated in Table 12.1, routine correctional programs also score low on staffing, core correctional practice, and indicators of program integrity. Routine programming is not very "smart," and it is weak on "fidelity."

Recall from the first row of Table 12.1 that the correlation between routine versus demonstration projects and effect size was .42. However, once we control for RNR adherence, breadth, staffing, and integrity, the correlation between routine and demonstration programming drops to .17. While greatly reduced from a correlation of .42, the latter correlation of .17 leaves some room for the as yet undemonstrated operation of the "cynical" or "bias" interpretation, along with the already demonstrated evidence in support of "smart" and "fidelity" interpretations.

Of course, we will be drawing further upon meta-analyses, but it is time to take a look at some very recent "failures" in the successful implementation of some "star" programs (Andrews, 2006). Some of these "star" programs came with the endorsement of meta-analysts (including endorsements by the authors of this text).

Brief Case Studies of Recent Failures in Correctional Treatment

Proposition 36 in California. The state of California sponsored a program of substance abuse treatment as an alternative to the incarceration of drug-involved offenders. To the dismay of the sponsors, the early evaluations revealed increased recidivism among the participants (Farabee et al., 2004). Having reached this point in your review of the psychology of criminal conduct, what questions would you raise in regard to "failure" of the program? You may well have questions regarding the risk level of those receiving treatment, their criminogenic needs, and whether the intensity of treatment and the intermediate targets of change were matched to risk and criminogenic needs. Were the therapists/counselors trained and supervised with regard to relationship and structuring skills? To what extent was the substance abuse treatment in adherence with the principles of RNR?

A quick hint on what was reported in the early report: the high-risk offenders were denied access to the most intensive substance abuse programs in California. Recall, you have already seen that substance abuse programs that are not in adherence with the core clinical principles of RNR are ineffective in reducing recidivism.

Multi-systemic Family Therapy (MST) in the State of Washington. The effect of MST was increased criminal recidivism relative to routine treatment controls. Apparently, the failure was due to a failure to implement with integrity (Barnoski, 2004). Note that unlike the difficulties with functional family therapy and aggression replacement therapy (described immediately below), the problems with integrity were not empirically documented independently of the measurement of the poor outcomes. According to a meta-analysis of the effects of MST, described by Petrosino and Soydan (2005), generally, the positive effects of MST are reduced dramatically when the developers of MST are not actively involved in the evaluation and the therapists are not Ph.D-level students. The latter is surprising in that professional credentials rarely are associated with effectiveness. Yet, the effect of developer involvement is well-established.

Functional Family Therapy (FFT) in the State of Washington. Overall, FFT had no effect. However, young offenders who were lucky enough to receive services from higher-functioning therapists showed reduced recidivism. Young offenders who were assigned to lower-functioning therapists showed increased crime. Putting the two groups together resulted in the overall finding of no effect (Barnoski, 2004). The positive effects achieved by high-functioning therapists were cancelled out by the negative effects of low-functioning therapists. The ability of the therapists was rated by the trainers of the therapists before treatment took place.

Aggression Replacement Therapy (ART) in the State of Washington. Overall, ART had no effect. The positive effects achieved in sites where fidelity was higher were cancelled out by the negative effects achieved in sites where fidelity was lower. As in the case of the evaluation of FFT, the quality of implementation was assessed in a manner distinct from the measure of outcome (Barnoski, 2004).

Halfway Houses in Ohio. On average, halfway house residents reoffended at higher rates than comparison offenders (Lowenkamp et al., 2006). Programming in the halfway houses was rated by independent raters on a variety of indicators of RNR adherence. The only halfway houses that reduced recidivism were the few houses that scored highest on RNR adherence.

Cognitive Skill Programs Offered in England and Wales. The early reports of system-wide failure were very disappointing for many correctional professionals and managers throughout the system of England and Wales (Raynor, 2008). Claire Goggin and Paul Gendreau (2006) provided an extraordinarily detailed autopsy of the "problems" within England and Wales' experience with large-scale implementation:

- Risk/need assessments were not available on a routine basis;
- "Therapists" reported being poorly trained and poorly supervised;

- Sessions were videotaped but apparently never employed as part of clinical supervision (the tapes were never looked at);

- Many staff were displeased with the introduction of the program (to state the situation in mild terms);

- The linkage between case management and programming was questionable;

- Very high dropout rates;

- Organizational upheaval (a county-based probation system became a national system during implementation).

Reasoning and Rehabilitation in New York (Project Greenlight). A shortened version of the Reasoning and Rehabilitation program (Ross & Fabiano, 1985) was delivered in the context of a prerelease (or "reentry") project. A substance abuse program was also delivered. The effect was a 10 percent increase in recidivism (Wilson & Davis, 2006). A few points are striking. The inmates, without discussion or consent, were taken abruptly from their prison and transferred to the program site. Many "clients" experienced program participation as the equivalent of being mistreated by the system. No reference is made to the employment of risk/need assessment instruments. Indeed, participation in the substance abuse program was mandatory, even for inmates who did not have a substance abuse problem. The selection of program staff explicitly did not follow the recommendations of the creators of the program. The negative outcomes associated with two of four workers totally accounted for the program failure.

The brief case studies of program failure described above strongly suggest that even programs that were designed with reference to "what works" are often not well implemented. The field is facing a major challenge. There are many ways of phrasing that challenge. If agencies and agents are serious about crime prevention, then routine programming has to:

1. become more like demonstration projects;

2. deliver smart programs with high levels of integrity;

3. strive for adherence with the clinical, staffing, managerial, and normative principles of the RNR model of correctional assessment and treatment.

Note, however, that implementation problems in the "real world" can be enormous. Looking back at Table 12.2, only 5 percent (11/209) of the real-world programs achieved a score of 3 on RNR Adherence. In the case of the demonstration projects, 49 percent (23/47) were in adherence with RNR principles. Equally low were mean scores on the staffing, core practice, and integrity scores as outlined in the routine column of Table 12.1.

Major Problems

A major issue here is whether the empirically validated principles of human service, RNR, and breadth can be implemented in the real world with sufficient levels of adherence so that reduced reoffending is actually achieved. It may appear straightforward but, in fact, it requires major policy and organizational changes and significant efforts on the part of managers and staff for adherence to be accomplished.

Think about it:

1. Many correctional agencies are viewed by their staff and managers as the administrators (or managers) of punishment. Under the justice models of retribution, just deserts, general deterrence, and/or specific deterrence, the police apprehend suspects, the courts establish just sanctions, and correctional or analogous agencies carry out and administer the sanction. With the addition of an expectation of crime prevention through rehabilitation, the role of correctional agencies and agents changes dramatically. Now they are being asked to come to see themselves as human service agencies, albeit in a justice context. What might the staff be thinking?

    "Our job is to administer the penalty in a just manner."

    "We are more like the police than social workers, and we like it that way."

    "Our job is not to reduce reoffending but to help offenders achieve the objectives that: (a) they value (reduced stress, greater personal freedom), and/or (b) what we value (helping them become more creative, more self-fulfilled), and/or (c) locking up the bad guys."

2. Even those agencies that do have mental health counselors on staff must bring their counseling staff to think in RNR terms. Yet, many mental health counselors have never heard of "RNR" or "breadth" and do not even think of reduced reoffending as a valued objective. A mental health agency itself may be threatened by the very presence of criminals. Over and over again we have heard counseling staff focus on reducing anxiety and increasing

self-esteem. Moreover, the thought of getting out of the office and actually working within the "real" settings of family, school/work, and leisure/recreation may be judged "unprofessional." What might the staff be thinking?

"The client comes to me, I don't go to her (I also do not seek out her family, peers, and teachers)."

"If he is not motivated enough to arrive on time for his appointments, I don't want to work with him."

"The little brat, he just does not appreciate what I am trying to do for him."

"S/he is lazy, irresponsible, uncaring . . . unworthy really of my professional attention."

3. Even if the setting buys into RNR, it may not know how to do it. Staff have to learn about RNR assessment and how to use specific instruments. They have to learn how to build a service plan consistent with RNR. They have to learn how to deliver that service. They may have to acquire the necessary relationship and structuring skills. They need feedback and reinforcement on how well they are doing so that their good work can continue and their poor work may get better. But who in the agency is functioning at a level at which they could supply value-added clinical supervision?

4. Even if the agency and agents have it all worked out, the broader system may begin to interfere. A local judge may begin to sentence low-risk cases to the program, or to send cases without a substance-abuse problem to a substance-abuse program, or to send psychopaths to a program built for moderate-risk cases. We have seen it again and again—inappropriate cases placed in a program because the available seats need to be filled.

5. Staff considerations are very important if RNR programs are going to succeed. If relationship and structuring skills are crucial to quality programming, there are three key management functions. One, select your staff on the basis of their possession of the relationship and structuring skills required in the program where they will be working. Two, provide preservice and in-service training in those skills. Three, provide high-quality clinical supervision to the workers. Staff needs to know how they are doing; they require ongoing reinforcement when they are doing well and immediate assistance when they are not performing at the highest levels.

6. A major issue is self-selection out of services by higher-risk cases. Higher-risk cases are less likely to voluntarily enter service programs and more likely to drop out (Wormith & Olver, 2002). In part, the self-selection factor is a specific responsivity factor (Andrews, 2006). Thereby, careful attention to several elements is called for, including all of the following: remove barriers to participation, build on strengths, and be responsive to motivational issues. Respect for personal autonomy and being collaborative in program planning are very important. Just as clinicians and correctional workers need to know how they are doing (as in Number 5 above), high-risk offenders may profit from information on the meaning of their, risk, need, and strengths scores and the consequences of program completion relative to the consequences of dropping out.

7. Some supervisors of direct service staff may not possess a deep understanding of the program for which they are responsible, and they may not possess or even be aware of the relationship and structuring skills that are basic to the high-quality selection, training, and clinical supervision of staff. In brief, we have here a recipe for disaster (if you consider criminogenic programming a disaster). According to our reviews, clinical supervision in the context of corrections is almost unheard of.

8. How many community colleges, undergraduate programs, or graduate programs in psychology, social work, criminology, criminal justice, and sociology are offering anything that might prepare potential correctional workers and professionals for a role in effective correctional treatment? As we are not aware of any recent relevant surveys on the matter, no answer will be given on these pages. Later in this chapter, a training program for probation officers will be described in which the fundamentals of modeling, reinforcement, and skill training are described, demonstrated, and role-played for officers-in-training. Are there any colleges or universities doing anything in the way of serious preparation for effective correctional practice? The University of Cincinnati is a dramatic example in the domain of criminology and criminal justice. We would like to think maybe Carleton University, the University of Saskatchewan, and the University of New Brunswick (Saint John campus), all in Canada, also provide such preparatory training.

9. There is still a need to promote broad and narrow political support for crime prevention through human service delivery. Frankly, however, in a liberal democracy, the people may decide they want a justice and correctional system that is first and

foremost about catching the "bad guys and gals" and second about having those people suffer according to just deserts. Apart from incapacitation, the crime prevention mumbo jumbo may be judged to be gibberish, and all of this psychological drivel only interferes with the honorable pursuit of justice.

10. This listing of points has barely scratched the surface of barriers to enhanced RNR adherence. We admit that. We ask that the reader think about it and let us know what we have missed.

Assessment Approaches to Enhancing Routine Programs

A major issue is the extent to which the community that surrounds correctional and other agencies places any positive value on crime prevention through the delivery of social, human, and clinical services. The retributive just deserts agenda in combination with the antipsychological/prosociological agenda of mainstream criminology and criminal justice became very strong in the United States in the 1960s and 1970s (see Chapters 3 and 13 for the evidence). Support for rehabilitation approaches collapsed. Now, with a more receptive environment, crime prevention programming is more of a possibility.

Systematic assessment is a promising route to enhancing routine programming. A focus on RNR-based assessment of offenders is one way of making progress. Another is to take a systematic approach to the assessment of ongoing programming.

Assessment of Offenders

On the issue of practical prediction, there is no question that change has been revolutionary over the last 30 years. Unstructured clinical judgment does so poorly relative to structured assessment approaches that the ethicality of unstructured risk assessment is now a serious professional issue. As reviewed in Chapter 10, several second-generation instruments are doing as well as third- and fourth-generation instruments in the simple prediction of recidivism. However, second-generation instruments that do not sample a variety of criminogenic needs cannot assist in the building of an individualized treatment plan that is in adherence with the need and/or breadth principles. Nor can their predictive validity be improved through reassessments on static variables.

The great promise of fourth-generation instruments is that they will enhance adherence with risk, need, breadth, general responsivity, and specific responsivity. Recall from Chapter 10 that fourth-generation instruments follow the case management process from initial assessment through case management planning, service delivery, reassessment, and case closure. Evidence is emerging that the use of such instrument in combination with RNR adherence is associated with reduced reoffending (Luong, 2008).

Assessment of Programs and Agencies

The Correctional Program Assessment Inventory (CPAI; Gendreau & Andrews, 2001) is a measure of RNR adherence, of adherence with the breadth principle, and of a number of indicators of therapeutic integrity. For years (forever it seems), the first author (DAA) and Paul Gendreau have been playing with the issues of effective consultation, dissemination, treatment, and program integrity. It is basic to the cognitive social learning perspective that human beings gain knowledge of the world and their place in it by paying attention to outcomes (that is, through the consequences of their actions and through feedback). The interests of Andrews and Gendreau have resulted in a series of versions of the CPAI. The latest version is called CPAI-2000 because it was introduced in the new millennium (it is not the two-thousandth version, only perhaps the sixth). The content is briefly reviewed in Table 12.3.

Feedback from CPAI users has often been positive because just going through the exercise is a tremendous learning experience for agencies.

Table 12.3
Scorable Content of the Correctional Program Assessment Inventory – 2000 (Gendreau & Andrews, 2001)

B.   Organizational Culture: A 10-item survey of clarity of goals, ethical standards, harmony, staff turnover, in-service training, self-evaluation, and agency outreach.

C.   Program Implementation/Maintenance: A 10-item survey of the context within which the program was initiated, of value congruence with stakeholders, piloting, maintenance of staffing and credentials, qualifications of managers and staff with specific attention to selection, training and clinical supervision with a focus on key skills and attitudes.

D.   Management/Staff Characteristics: A 17-item survey of management and staff experience, training, skill levels, and attitudes and beliefs regarding treatment services.

E.   Client Risk/Need Practices: A 12-item survey of adherence to the principles of risk, need, and responsivity assessment.

F.   Program Characteristics: A 22-item detailed survey of adherence to the RNR principles with an emphasis on breadth of targeting, general responsivity, and relapse prevention.

G.   Core Correctional Practice: A 45-item survey of observed elements of core correctional practice including relationship skills and the structuring skills of problem solving, modeling, reinforcement, and skill building.

H.   Inter-Agency Communication: A 7-item survey of brokerage, referral, advocacy, and coordination.

I.   Evaluation: An 18-item survey of in-program and post-program research and monitoring activity.

It asks them to consider what their program is about and why they do what they do. It asks them to link intermediate objectives to ultimate effects on criminal behavior (and some folks in some agencies have never thought about either type of objective, let alone why or how the intermediate and the ultimate may be associated).

Often, they do what they do because that is what they have always done, or because that was what they were told to do. It may have nothing to do with outcomes, and they may have no idea what outcomes are of interest anyway. "The agency gets funded and I get paid by doing what we have done in the past and what we continue to do." In other words, effectiveness with reference to criminal behavior is often irrelevant to an agency's day-to-day operations. The CPAI will be of interest to an agency (or the funders of the agency) if crime control is considered to be one of their objectives.

The CPAI is completed by on-site visitors who: (1) interview staff, managers, and clients, (2) review agency documents and case files, (3) complete casual observations of ongoing activity, and (4) conduct systematic observation of staff relationship and structuring skills in their interactions with clients (see Section G in Table 12.3). Alexsandra Nesovic (2003) completed the first full psychometric evaluation of the CPAI as part of her PhD research and studies. She found high levels of inter-rater agreement based on interview and paper-and-pencil questionnaire versions of the CPAI. The internal consistency of the scale was also impressive, meaning that the items formed a meaningfully interrelated set. She also found that professional and student raters were impressed with the relevance of the content surveyed by the CPAI. Most importantly, she found that the component and total scores of the CPAI were correlated with effect size (overall, the r was .50).

Indeed, the validity of the instrument was impressive across a variety of different types of correctional programs, correctional settings, and offender types. For example, RNR adherence and therapeutic integrity as assessed with the CPAI was correlated with effect size in family, substance abuse, academic/vocational, and even physical training programs. Validity was evident with female and male offenders, young and adult offenders, programs run by justice and nonjustice staff, and in community and residential correctional settings. Because the validity portion of the Nesovic study was based on meta-analyses, however, the author had to work with many missing data points. Studies conducted with ongoing programs will have more complete CPAIs with which to work.

Chris Lowenkamp (2004) surveyed 37 halfway houses in Ohio with the CPAI. Lowenkamp, along with Ed Latessa and others at the University of Cincinnati, also surveyed 16 community-based correctional facilities. All in all, with the data that they generously shared with us, they are working with a total of 13,221 offenders—the largest study of community correctional treatment facilities ever done. Figure 12.1 reveals the

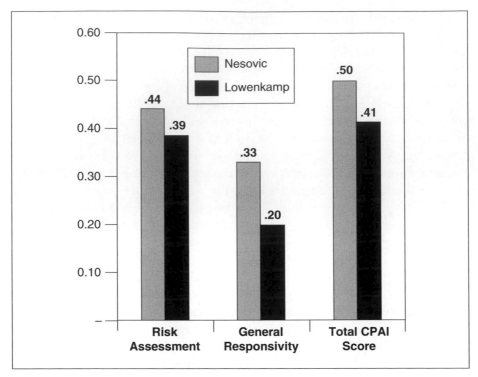

Figure 12.1
CPAI Correlations with Effect Size: CPAI Risk Assessment Items, CPAI General Responsivity Items, and CPAI Total Score

correlations with effect size reported in both the Nesovic and Lowenkamp studies. Overall, CPAI total scores were associated with greater reductions in recidivism. The same pattern of results was found for items sampling risk/need assessment and general responsivity (cognitive social learning strategies of influence). The risk/need assessment findings in particular begin to fill a gigantic gap in the correctional treatment literature. The predictive validity of risk/need assessments has been known for years. What we now are seeing is evidence that agencies that adopt risk/ need technology actually do enhance their contribution to public safety.

Training Approaches to Effective Correctional Supervision and Treatment

It is insufficient to describe the specifics of effective practice as adherence with the general responsivity principle of RNR. To simply say employ behavioral and cognitive social learning procedures does not provide sufficient guidance to program planners and program managers. That is why the subset of Organizational Principles is part of the RNR model (Chapter 2). Principle 14 specifies two crucial sets of skills and competencies. The skill sets of relationship factors and structuring factors are based on GPCSL theory, but they are very practical. It is possible for correctional workers and managers to come to recognize when the skills are being employed and when they are not. They are clear enough that with some rehearsal undergraduate students can observe an interaction between a correctional worker and an offender and "score" the interactions in terms of adherence with the principle of core correctional practice. The practices provide guidance for the crucial managerial tasks of the selection of staff and volunteers, the training of service delivery people, and the ongoing clinical supervision of those responsible for the delivery of services.

You have already seen that when programs are rated for adherence with the principles, less successful and more successful programs may be differentiated. Recall Resource Note 11.1 wherein the presence of elements of core practice was associated with reduced recidivism. Table 11.2.3 demonstrated that the positive contribution of adherence with the core practice principle was associated with success among younger and older offenders, female and male offenders, and whites and nonwhites. At the beginning of this chapter, you saw that adherence with core correctional practices differentiated between routine programming and demonstration projects.

Examples of effective programs have been distributed throughout the text. We close this portion of this chapter not with more data but with material intended to induce the look and feel of effective correctional counseling.

The Dimensions of Effective Correctional Counseling: The "What and How" of Effective Modeling and Reinforcement

An important role for the correctional worker is to serve as an anticriminal model for clients and as a source of reinforcement for their clients' anticriminal expressions and efforts. This is consistent with the relationship and structuring role of family therapists, the nurturance and training roles of parents, and the communication and instructional roles of teachers. We are not referring here to the application of any particular program or technique but to how probation and parole officers, case managers, youth workers, and staff in residential settings interact with antisocial individuals. The manual from which the following notes were drawn was prepared to assist in the training of citizen volunteers for direct-contact, one-to-one roles with young adult probationers (Andrews, 1979). The following notes are also consistent with Chris Trotter's (1999, 2006) guidelines for probation officers working with involuntary clients.

We are assuming that the agency (and its management and staff) value the objective of reduced recidivism. Thus, one task of agency staff and managers is to increase anticriminal expressions and decrease procriminal expressions of clients.

The first step is to ensure that managers and staff are able to recognize and distinguish between anticriminal and procriminal expressions. This knowledge and skill cannot be assumed to exist, just as parents of antisocial children cannot be assumed to be able to differentiate the deviant and nondeviant activities of their children (Patterson, 1997; Van Dieten, 1991). Similarly, in probation agencies there are individual differences in the level of socialization among probation staff and volunteers, and we have found that the anticriminal expressions of officers in interviews with their probationers link with the recidivism of their probationers (Andrews, 1980). Consultation and clinical experience also tell us that staff and managers are sometimes not attentive to their own expressions of antisocial attitudes. For example, some staff may develop a cynicism regarding the criminal justice system that is readily reinforced by clients. Some staff or volunteers may adopt "con talk" to show their clients how "down to earth" they can be and to gain their acceptance.

Procriminal expressions include the antisocial attitudes/procriminal sentiments to which we have repeatedly referred: the specific attitudes, values, beliefs, rationalizations, and techniques of neutralization that imply that criminal conduct is acceptable (recall Chapter 7). These include: (1) negative attitudes toward the law, courts, and police; (2) tolerance for rule violations in general and violations of the law in particular; (3) identification with offenders; and (4) endorsement of exonerating mechanisms. Anticriminal expressions include: (1) an emphasis on the negative consequences of law violations for the offender, the victim, and the community at large; (2) rejection of, or placing more realistic limits on, "rationalizations" or "justifications" for law violations; and (3) expressions of the risks involved in associating with criminal others or in accepting their belief systems. Some specific criminal acts, such as sex offenses, violent sex offenses, spouse abuse, and violence in general, have their own supporting cognitions and vocabulary to which workers must be sensitive.

Procriminal expression includes association with criminal others; anticriminal expression is reduced association with criminal others and increased association with anticriminal others. Procriminal expressions include continuing to seek out risky situations or circumstances (e.g., the same old bar scene) rather than avoiding them. The following examples of anticriminal expressions are based on the links between self-management and problem-solving skills in relation to criminal behavior: (1) probationers examining their own conduct, making a judgment about how well their behavior corresponds to their anticriminal values and beliefs or how well they are attaining their goals, and making self-evaluative comments "good"–"bad" depending upon how well the standards are being met; (2) thinking before acting, pausing to consider consequences of a given action; and (3) weighing the merits of alternative ways of behaving in a given situation. Procriminal expressions in this area include: (1) a lack of self-observation, self-evaluation, or self-monitoring; (2) evaluation against standards that are too severe, too lax, or frankly procriminal; (3) an insensitivity to or denial of significant problems; and/or (4) an inability to consider new ways of behaving in problem situations.

Attending sessions and doing the homework exercises following the treatment plan are also anticriminal expressions to be encouraged. One should watch out in particular for clients supporting the anticriminal efforts of other clients. When front-line staff support, rather than ignore or even ridicule, the anticriminal efforts of clients, this is an example of anticriminal modeling and reinforcement. When both staff and clients support expressions of anticriminal efforts, a therapeutic community of some criminological potency has been created. This element of correctional counseling speaks clearly to group and residential programming.

Two studies have assessed the procriminal/prosocial direction and reward-cost contingencies in the social interactions of delinquents and nondelinquents. Buehler, Patterson, and Furniss (1966) directly observed and behaviorally analyzed inmate-inmate and inmate-staff interactions in an institutional setting, while Dishion et al. (1996) videotaped the interactions of 186 boys ages 13 to 14 years. Both studies were powerful demonstrations that the contingencies of interaction within delinquent groups were procriminal. Rule-breaking talk was followed by reinforcement, and prosocial talk was punished by delinquent associates. A construct such as "subculture" is not needed to understand that when procriminal people are brought together in groups, what is created is differential modeling, reinforcement, and punishment that favors procriminal expressions. When volunteers, staff, and managers are selected, trained, supervised, and rewarded without reference to their value in the process of anticriminal modeling and reinforcement, we may expect that contingencies favoring procriminal expressions will be maintained. This is especially the case when the model of treatment explicitly demands that the volunteers, staff, and managers not attend to procriminal expressions. The way to create anticriminal groups and residences is to select, train, supervise, and reward the nonclients (volunteers, staff, and managers) according to their value in the modeling and differential reinforcement of anticriminal expressions.

In good correctional practice, procriminal and anticriminal expressions are determined not just by standardized risk, need, and responsivity assessments but through individualized assessments of the criminogenic factors and situations that apply to particular individuals. Many expressions that we may like or not like for various professional, political, and ideological reasons are not typically criminogenic. Correctional programs should not attempt to produce "perfect people" according to some standard of perfection.

Many expressions are neutral with regard to criminal activity. Criminally neutral expressions are often confused with procriminal expressions. They include thoughts, feelings, and actions that are not associated in any functional manner with future criminal conduct. Thus, in the absence of any evidence to the contrary, indicators of self-esteem, vague feelings of emotional distress, generalized anxiety, low self-confidence, little interest in interpersonal fun and games, or preferring to be alone at times should be considered to be such neutral expressions. A particular problem for residential programs is the tendency to focus on maintaining housekeeping duties and schedules. Thus, being neat, clean, quiet, willing to clean toilets, and/or willing to go along with a particular program's emphasis upon sports, religion, "12 steps," or whatever, may gain more attention than anticriminal expressions that actually transfer to the chances of criminal behavior in the community.

Effective Workers. Workers who are successful with their clients: (1) establish high-quality relationships with them, (2) demonstrate anticriminal expressions (modeling), (3) approve of the client's anticriminal expressions (reinforcement), and (4) disapprove of the client's procriminal expressions (punishment), while at the same time demonstrating alternatives.

High-Quality Relationship Conditions. A high-quality interpersonal relationship creates a setting in which modeling and reinforcement can more easily take place. Important to such a relationship is an open, flexible, and enthusiastic style wherein people feel free to express their opinions, feelings, and experiences. Also needed are mutual liking, respect, and caring. The expression of disapproval is meaningful against a background of attentiveness, expressions of understanding ("real," not "phony"), mutual enjoyment of recreational activities, pleasant discussion, use of humor, and frequent contact. Most high-quality relationships are characterized by a shared agreement on the limits of physical and emotional intimacy. Openness, warmth, and understanding are offered within those limits.

Effective Modeling. The effective model:

1. Demonstrates behavior in concrete and vivid ways;

2. Takes care to illustrate the behavior in some concrete detail when only a verbal description is being offered;

3. Is rewarded himself/herself for exhibiting the behavior and makes specific reference to the rewards if only a verbal illustration is offered;

4. Rewards the person for exhibiting the modeled behavior or some approximation of it;

5. Is generally a source of reinforcement rather than only of punishing or neutral events;

6. Makes evident the general similarities between himself/herself and the other person (e.g., "I had a similar problem at your age");

7. Recognizes that the other person may have good reason to fear or distrust the modeled behavior and hence will model a "coping" as opposed to a "master" style (Officer: "I too was afraid to approach the teacher about my grades but, scared as anything, I went up and asked her about it," versus "I just walked up to her and . . .").

Effective Reinforcement. With a behavioral approach, there is no reason to believe that any one set of events will always function as reinforcers for all persons at all times. Thus, it is important that one who is going to influence behavior through reinforcement has a wide variety of potential reinforcers at hand. The characteristics of a high-quality relationship constitute just such a collection of reinforcers. Sometimes simply eye contact and statements that show the person is listening will be sufficient; at other times, there must be emphatic expressions of support and agreement. Sometimes more concrete events (such as a shared movie or shopping trip) will be the reinforcers. Generally, what we have described as a high-quality relationship constitutes one of the most widely applicable and powerful sets of reinforcers.

High-level reinforcement in an interpersonal situation includes the following elements:

1. Strong, emphatic, and immediate statements of approval, support, and agreement with regard to what the probationer has said or done (nonverbal expression, eye contact, smiles, shared experiences);

2. Elaboration of the reason why agreement and approval are being offered (i.e., exactly what it is you agree with or approve of);

3. Expression of support should be sufficiently intense to distinguish it from the background levels of support, concern, and interest that you normally offer;

4. While less important than Items 1, 2, and 3, the worker's feedback should at least match the probationer's statement in emotional intensity (i.e., be empathic), and his or her elaboration of the reason for support should involve some self-disclosure (i.e., openness).

With high-level verbal and gestural approval and with elaboration on the reasons for approval, there is an opportunity to demonstrate anticriminal expressions while offering feedback. The officer's statement of approval may close with a gentle probe that encourages the probationer to explore further the issues involved in the anticriminal expression.

Effective Disapproval. Just as a high-quality relationship sets the occasion for effective modeling and reinforcement, so does it establish the conditions necessary for effective disapproval. Within the context of an open and warm relationship, disapproval may be delivered with less fear that the offender will try to avoid or escape future contact with the officer, and less chance of an aggressive response by the client. Within such a relationship, a simple reduction in the normal levels of expressed interest and concern may function as a punisher. Expressed disapproval is more punishing within an open and warm relationship than it would be in a relationship characterized by distrust and dislike. Finally, we have the "4-to-1" rule: give at least four positive supportive statements for every punishing one. Someone who is routinely austere, judgmental, and "proper" is likely to be avoided.

High-level disapproval in an interpersonal situation is characterized by:

1. Strong, emphatic, and immediate statements of disapproval, non-support, and disagreement with what the client has said or done (including the nonverbal: a frown, or even an increase in the physical distance between you and the client);

2. Elaboration of the reason why you disagree and disapprove (this is an opportunity to model an anticriminal alternative);

3. The expression of disapproval stands in stark contrast to the levels of interest, concern, and warmth previously offered the probationer;

4. The levels of disapproval should be immediately reduced and approval introduced when the probationer begins to express or approximate anticriminal behavior.

From the point of view of most correctional clients (and most volunteers and professionals), it would be silly to communicate a blind support for the criminal justice system in all of its day-to-day operations, to accept the notion that there are no situations under which criminal activity is reasonable, or to state that "crime never pays." At the same time, correctional workers who have direct contact with clients will be ineffective if they are explicitly nonsupportive of the system, enamored with the positive aspects of criminal activity, or accepting of the rationalizations for law violations. The effective correctional worker exposes the client to anticriminal alternatives, is able to distinguish between specific negative instances within the criminal justice system and its general ideals (e.g., between a particularly obnoxious policeman and the role of the police), and can explore with clients the limits of the common justifications for criminal activity.

Effective Use of Authority. Most workers in corrections are in a position of power and authority relative to the offender. Ineffective use of authority relies on monitoring for compliance with the rules and initiating negative sanctions when violations are detected. The effective style for authority figures is "firm but fair." Effective practices include monitoring but also entail respectful guidance toward compliance. We see this pattern as consistent with John Braithwaite's (1989) idea of "reintegrative shaming," but without the "shaming."

Skill Building Through Structured Learning. The important skills to be taught include problem-solving and other aspects of self-management including cognitive self-change (Bush, 1995). The elements of structured learning are those outlined by Arnold Goldstein (1986): (1) describe the components of the skill in detail; (2) model or demonstrate the skill components; (3) arrange for reinforced practice of the skill components through role-playing with corrective feedback; (4) extend learning opportunities through homework assignment; and (5) generally, provide opportunities to enhance the skill. In brief and boldly:

- Describe
- Model
- Role Play
- Reinforce
- Correct
- Reinforce
- Repeat

Motivational Interviewing (MI). The principles are well known and include all of the following: express empathy, develop discrepancy, roll with resistance, support self-efficacy, and communicate hope. The MI stories and evidence are becoming so strong that MI must be considered a core set of correctional skills.

Cognitive Self Change. Jack Bush's distillation of cognitive restructuring into four steps also appears to be a core set of skills. First, pay attention to your thoughts and feelings (facilitated by the completion of thinking reports in the antecedent-behavior-consequence chain). Second, recognize risky cognitions. Third, practice new, less risky cognition. Fourth, practice until you get really good at it.

When the pleasures of crime reside deep in the very act, one needs to work on changing the motivation and enhancing the costs of the activity. When a full analysis of the contingencies of action reveals a repeated history of disregard for the rights of others with resulting serious harm, and reveals no areas of intervention of reasonable promise, justice professionals should advise authorities (courts and parole boards) of the results of their comprehensive assessment and let justice be done in a pure just deserts, incapacitation, or restorative sense. Although rare, there may be some contexts in which human service will not contribute to reduced reoffending with high-risk cases.

Strategic Training Initiative in Community Supervision (STICS)

The second author of this text (JB), along with his colleagues from Public Safety Canada—Guy Bourgon, Tanya Rugge, Terri Scott, and Annie Yessine—developed a training program for probation officers that tried to maximize adherence to the RNR principles during community supervision. The reader has already been introduced to this project in Resource Note 7.1. Here, our interest is more on the implementation issues surrounding making "what works" work.

In a meta-analysis of 15 studies yielding 26 effect size estimates, Bonta and his colleagues (Bonta, Rugge, Scott, Bourgon & Yessine, 2008) found community supervision associated with only a 2 percent reduction in recidivism. In the same report, analysis of audiotaped interviews between probation officers and their clients from the Canadian province of Manitoba showed that probation officers engaged in relatively few practices based on the RNR model (e.g., spent too much time on low-risk cases, did not target criminogenic needs sufficiently, made inadequate use of cognitive-behavioral techniques of influence). The Bonta et al. (2008) findings set the stage for the STICS project. The goal of the project was to deliver and evaluate the efficacy of training in intervention practices that are consistent with the RNR model. In designing STICS, the overall challenge was to translate the RNR model into specific, concrete actions that would be useful for probation officers, train the officers in their application, and evaluate the training's impact on the behavior of the officers and the clients they supervise.

Training Issues

Whether it is a treatment program for offenders or, as in our case, a training program for probation officers, the issues are the same. The program must be guided by theory, be attentive to the general principles of risk-need-responsivity, and be concerned about the maintenance of skills.

The first task was to convey the message to probation officers that the antisocial behavior of their clients is under the control of the individual's cognitions and attitudes, with rewards and punishments playing a role in the maintenance of behaviors. If probation officers accepted this General Personality and Cognitive Social Learning (GPCSL) view, as opposed to a medical model (offenders are sick) or a sociological perspective (poverty causes crime), then they would be more amenable to the idea that offenders can learn prosocial behavior through the same processes that resulted in their criminal behavior.

The importance of having probation officers "buy in" to a theoretical view has been underestimated in many studies. The psychotherapy literature has long recognized the importance of an "explanation" for the problems of the patient and how these problems can be overcome (Wampold, 2007). Like the patient of the psychotherapist, probation officers also need an explanation as to why they should change their behaviors and those of their clients and how they can do it. Therefore, the training program included didactic presentations of the research in support of GPCSL along with exercises to demonstrate the power of cognitive restructuring, prosocial modeling, reinforcement, and punishment. Furthermore, probation officers were trained to teach their clients how cognitions control their behavior, how rewards and punishments influence future occurrences, and what they can do about it.

Eighty probation officers from three Canadian provinces (British Columbia, Saskatchewan, and Prince Edward Island) volunteered for the training and evaluation of that training. They were then randomly assigned to either a training or no-training condition. In order to enhance adherence with the risk principle, probation officers were asked to select only medium- and high-risk clients for the project. Although a few low-risk probationers were recruited to the study, there were very few of them. Approximately 95 percent of the clients were medium- and high-risk offenders.

All three sites used validated risk/need assessment instruments, and these assessments formed the basis for the identification of criminogenic needs that served as targets of intervention (e.g., antisocial attitudes, criminal associates, substance abuse, etc.). The training placed considerable emphasis on recognizing expressions of antisocial attitudes in the clients, and how to use cognitive-behavioral techniques to replace these cognitions and attitudes with prosocial ones. Much of the first day of the three days of training was devoted to the issues just discussed.

Adherence to the responsivity principle was supported through exercises and practice on establishing rapport and common goals with the clients of the probation officers and teaching cognitive-behavioral techniques such as cognitive restructuring, prosocial modeling, the effective use of reinforcement and disapproval, and various rehearsal strategies. Probation officers supervise male and female offenders and often have clients from many different cultures and backgrounds. In Canada, Native offenders are quite common in the provinces of Saskatchewan and rural British Columbia. Therefore, training attended not only to gender issues but also to race and culture (i.e., specific responsivity).

The core of STICS training, and the most difficult task for the officers, occurred on the second day, when the focus was on the cognitive-behavioral model and cognitive restructuring. It was a challenge for probation officers because they themselves had to learn the basics of the cognitive-behavioral model and because it required them to actually learn how to convey the model and teach cognitive restructuring skills to their clients (see Resource Note 7.1 for a description of the model and how it was taught). The emphasis was on making it concrete and understandable to the client (for example, "antisocial thoughts" were called "tapes," and "prosocial thoughts" were called "counters"). Except for a few probation officers who led group programs, participants felt uneasy with the role of a teacher. They were much more comfortable with monitoring compliance to the probation conditions, advocating with social service agencies on their client's behalf, and being supportive when clients were faced with distress and interpersonal problems.

It was also important to provide probation officers with a structure to their individual session (typically lasting about 25 minutes). Most probation departments have policies that are relatively silent on what the probation officer should do whenever he or she meets the client for supervision. The only exception is to ensure that the client is complying with the conditions of probation. As we noted earlier: "Our job is to administer the penalty in a just manner." Probation officers were asked to structure each and every individual session into four components. The first component was a brief "check-in" lasting no more than five minutes. The check-in involved spending time enhancing the working relationship with the client, checking for any new developments in the client's situation that may require immediate attention, and making sure that the probation conditions were being kept. The second component was a "review" of the last session, including the homework (see below). This review was designed to facilitate learning via discussions and/or rehearsal of previous material and linking one supervision session to the next. The third component was to actually conduct an intervention. This could be teaching the cognitive-behavioral model or doing a role-play exercise (about 15 minutes). Lastly, "homework" (e.g., something as simple as trying a behavior and reporting on it at the next supervision session) was assigned that reinforced the learning of new concepts, skills, or prosocial cognitions.

Finally, in order to maintain and further develop staff skills, clinical supervision was provided to the probation officers after training. Probation officers met once a month in small groups to discuss their use of STICS concepts and skills. The trainers assigned specific exercises to be completed and discussed at the monthly meetings. During the monthly meetings, the officers teleconferenced with the trainers and were given feedback on the exercises. In addition, approximately one year after the initial three-day training, the probation officers attended a one-day STICS refresher workshop facilitated by one of the trainers.

The Evaluation Methodology of STICS

There were three key issues regarding the evaluation of STICS: (1) choosing the research design, (2) the assessment of change in the behavior of the probation officers and their clients, and (3) maintaining participant motivation. Of particular importance was the effect of STICS training on the behavior of the probation officer, as it is the officer's behavior during supervision sessions that was hypothesized to influence change in the client's future criminal behavior.

Research Design. There are many different approaches to evaluating the effects of an intervention. The randomized experiment is often held to be the "gold standard." By randomly assigning cases to the experimental and control conditions, internal validity is maximized. Consequently, researchers are in a confident position to attribute causality to the independent variable (e.g., STICS training). In the evaluation of STICS, 80 probation officers who volunteered for the study were randomly assigned to either an experimental (i.e., training) or a control group. The selection of volunteers was not seen as problematic because random assignment would hold initial motivation constant. At this point in the evaluation of STICS, the interest was whether the training would have any impact on motivated probation officers. If successful, then training could be evaluated with unmotivated probation officers (we suppose that this would be a test of the RNR model in the "real, real world").

Attrition is a problem in almost all experiments in criminology, and this study was no different. Despite selecting volunteers, there were 28 probation officers (18 experimental, 10 control) who did not recruit any clients for the study post-training. This represents an attrition rate of 35 percent. A total of 15 probation officers (nine experimental, four control) did not participate for reasons related to the extra workload required by the project. An additional 13 officers were transferred into new job positions or withdrew from the project for personal reasons (e.g., maternity leave) before they could recruit clients. Staff turnover is a very real concern in any "real world" effort. In addition to the 28 officers who did not submit any post-training data, an additional seven officers submitted some post-training data but terminated their participation in the project early due to a new job or maternity leave. However, analyses of the personal-demographic characteristics of the staff who remained in the project and those who dropped out for various reasons showed no differences.

Looking at What Goes on Beyond Closed Doors

Evaluating the effects of the training consisted of measuring the behavior of probation officers and their clients through a combination of direct observation, self-report, and official records of criminal behavior.

In order to evaluate the behavior of probation officers, they were asked to audiotape their sessions with new clients at intake, after three months of supervision, and again after approximately six months of supervision. Teams of two trained raters assessed each audiotaped session following a detailed coding guide. Raters evaluated the frequency of specific behaviors (e.g., discussions of criminogenic needs identified on the initial risk assessment) as well as the quality of the specific skills and interventions of the officers (e.g., active listening skills and the use of cognitive restructuring interventions).

In addition to the audiotapes, other methods of evaluating how well the experimental group learned and applied the skills from the training program were used. For example, the STICS trainers rated the officers on their understanding, skills, and abilities to utilize STICS concepts and skills immediately following the three-day training and again one year later. Probation officers also completed paper-and-pencil questionnaires that tested their knowledge of the GPCSL perspective and RNR principles prior to training and again three months post-training. Approximately one year post-training, officers completed a consumer satisfaction questionnaire.

Project Commitment

Maintaining participation in a research project is challenging, particularly for a lengthy and demanding project such as STICS. One aspect of project commitment and program integrity is managerial support (see Principle 15 in Table 2.1). Therefore, all of the managers of the frontline officers who volunteered were required to attend the three days of training. It was made clear by the respective Directors of Probation that this was mandatory for the managers and that partial attendance was not an option. A third trainer also led the managers through the exercises and role plays in the training. The attendance of managers not only showed support to their staff during training but also yielded dividends when staff returned to the field to practice what was taught. The managers were more cognizant of the demands placed upon the officers by the research and often worked with staff to organize their workload to facilitate participation in the research.

Encouraging commitment to the project for the trained group came from frequent e-mails, telephone contacts, and monthly clinical supervision conducted by the evaluators. Encouraging commitment for those officers who were assigned to the control condition was more of a challenge. It was a clear possibility that the motivation to participate in the research could diminish significantly once some of the officers learned that they were assigned to the control condition. Therefore, three incentives to participate were introduced. First, all the control probation officers were brought together for a half-day special seminar. In this seminar, the probation officers were given an overview of the "what works" literature, the research requirements, and the importance of random assignment. By providing an overview of the offender rehabilitation literature, it addressed the possibility that probation officers may engage in certain core correctional practices if they were not doing them already. Second, the STICS research team held bimonthly teleconferences with the control group to answer their questions about the research and to reiterate their importance in the evaluation. Finally, the control group was promised the three-day training if the results turned out to be favorable.

Results to Date

At the time of this writing, the project is still ongoing. However, analyses of the audiotaped sessions indicate that STICS has had a significant impact on the behavior of probation officers. There are a total of 295 post-training audiotapes available for analysis. The majority of the post-training recordings were from the first supervision session ($n = 140$) followed by recordings at three months ($n = 93$) and six months ($n = 62$).

Intervention skill quality variables were calculated from ratings on individual audiotape-coded items that were grouped a priori into four broader constructs. These included the *Structuring Skills* (e.g., conducting a check-in, review of last session, etc.), *Relationship Building Skills* (e.g., establishing a collaborative working relationship), *Cognitive Techniques* (e.g., focus on procriminal attitudes, cognitive restructuring), and *General Behavioral Techniques* (e.g., problem-solving, rehearsal, use of reinforcement and disapproval, and modeling). On average, the supervision sessions between the officer and the client lasted about 25 minutes.

Significant differences were found on all the constructs except for General Behavioral Techniques (it is likely that most of the probation officers in this study were generally quite good at prosocial modeling and reinforcement without the need for any specific training). Officers in the STICS group, compared to the control group, demonstrated significantly greater use of Structuring Skills, Relationship Building Skills, and Cognitive Techniques. For example, 70 percent of the STICS probation officers used Cognitive Techniques compared to only 5 percent of the control group, and the STICS probation officers spent a greater proportion of their supervision sessions discussing identified criminogenic needs (61% vs. 45%). Furthermore, discussions around antisocial attitudes were more frequent in the sessions of the STICS probation officers than the for the non-STICS probation officers (45.2% vs. 17.9%).

Summary

In general, the research is unequivocal—correctional systems can reduce recidivism through rehabilitation, and the RNR principles can guide those seeking to design, implement, and evaluate effective correctional interventions. However, there are considerable challenges in translating these principles into everyday practice, maintaining the integrity of such services, and ensuring adherence to the principles. Some of these challenges were addressed in the design, implementation, and evaluation of STICS.

In developing a training program on what probation officers could do to facilitate client change and how they could do this, it was important to ensure that the services adhered to the RNR principles. Of particular importance was the criminogenic need principle. STICS training focused on targeting procriminal attitudes and cognitions and using specific skills and interventions to change these attitudes and thoughts. Moreover, the STICS model was sufficiently flexible to allow officers to address a wide spectrum of criminogenic and noncriminogenic needs with a variety of clients. Part of the training included presenting evidence to persuade the officer, and how in turn the officer could persuade the client, that a cognitive-behavioral model was relevant. All skills, concepts, and interventions were designed specifically to adhere to the responsivity principle by following a simple, concrete, and cognitive-behavioral approach. In addition, the training provided officers with a clear structure for supervision and for individual officer-client sessions.

Although designing a program is one challenge, implementing it into routine practice is another. Training staff to deliver the service as intended, ensuring the integrity of service delivery, and maintaining staff skills and commitment are critical. The STICS project ensured adherence to the RNR principles via the selection of high- and medium-risk clients based on validated risk/need assessment instruments and structuring officer-client interactions. Monthly clinical supervision meetings and refresher workshops facilitated maintenance of STICS skills and interventions. Audiotaped recordings of officer-client sessions provided a means to assess integrity by evaluating the behavior of the officers "behind closed doors."

Finally, there are a number of methodological challenges that are critical to evaluating recidivism reduction efforts. The type of research design employed, what factors are measured, how these factors are assessed, as well as the overall level of "contamination" (e.g., attrition, breakdown in randomization) will impact the study's internal and external validity. A significant focus of STICS was the behavior of probation officers during supervision sessions, which in turn was hypothesized to influence the client. Officers were randomly assigned to experimental or control conditions. Direct observation, official records, and self-report measures provided detailed pre- and post-training data on the officers and the clients. Commitment to the project was encouraged through early involvement of managers, regular contact with the officers throughout the project, and providing incentives to both officers and clients.

All told, STICS is a comprehensive package that attempts to translate "what works" knowledge into effective and sustainable everyday practice. The results pertaining to officer behavior during supervision sessions are encouraging. The data showed that STICS-trained officers, compared to controls, demonstrated significantly more and qualitatively better core correctional practices during their interactions with clients. Soon the researchers will be able to evaluate the impact of these changes in officer behavior on client attitudes, behaviors, and ultimately recidivism. Overall, it is hoped that the STICS project will provide insight into how to effectively transfer empirical knowledge into the real world of community corrections.

The Routine-Demonstration Distinction in the Validity of Risk/Need Assessment: Author Involvement in Validation Studies

Meta-analytic explorations of the predictive validity of particular assessment instruments reveal inter-study variation in the magnitude of the validity estimates. Of course, potential sources of variability include the usual set of "suspects." Those potential sources include characteristics of the offender such as age, gender, ethnicity, and socio-economic circumstances, as well as subgroup differentiation according to personality and pathways (life-course versus adolescent-limited). Other possibilities are the nature of antisocial conduct being predicted (institutional misconducts versus recidivism; general versus violent reoffending; less serious versus more serious misconducts). Even the particular measure of validity chosen may be important (e.g., AUC estimates are less sensitive to variation in base rates than are r estimates). Another potential factor is the length of the follow-up period. Very short follow-up periods may not give higher-risk cases sufficient time to reveal their potential. Very long follow-up studies may reduce the validity of dynamic risk factors because offenders may have changed on the dynamic factors. The "best" follow-up period may be a period of intermediate length.

A major factor is likely that of researcher allegiance or author involvement in the validation of the instrument. Just as in the case of effective programming, there are four possibilities. The "cynical" interpretation suggests experimenter bias ("unconscious" and/or "deliberate"). Two other interpretations would be described as "smarter instruments/smarter evaluations" and "fidelity" (higher integrity of implementation through assessor training and supervision, the introduction of quality assurance procedures, and such). In the treatment literature, Mark Lipsey tends to view researcher allegiance as a proxy for "integrity." Our research in the treatment area demonstrated that integrity considerations accounted for most of the contribution of allegiance, but some room was left for a minor contribution by the cynical interpretation. To our knowledge, the issues have not been explored as systematically in the domain of the validity of assessments.

Recently, we have explored the sources of variability in estimates of the predictive validity of LS risk/need assessments with female offenders. The meta-analytic data set included 41 validity estimates based on a total of 12,505 girls and women. The median r value was .35, and the mean r was .36 (CI = .31 to .41). The mean estimate is virtually identical to the Smith et al. (2009) estimate. The variability about the mean was large. The two largest estimates were .61 and .60. The weakest estimates were −.13 and .08. Neither the highest estimates nor the lowest estimates are the best representation of the validity of the instrument. What does account for the variability?

A small set of factors were unrelated to effect size estimates. Young offender status, being a prisoner (as opposed to being in community corrections), and seriousness of the new offense were factors not associated with the magnitude of the validity estimate. All of the following were significantly correlated with the magnitude of the validity estimate: allegiance (author involvement in the evaluation), follow-up years (mean of 2.21), and the fact that the instrument was LS/CMI (as opposed to the LSI-R). An overall proxy for integrity was allegiance combined with a follow-up period of longer than a year. The correlation with effect size was .56, $p < .001$. The apparent superiority of LS/CMI risk/need relative to the LSI-R was totally attributable the integrity measure. With integrity controlled, there was no significant difference in the mean validity estimates for the LSI-R and the LS/CMI.

The mean validity estimates increased directly with the proxy measure of integrity of the implementation of LS assessments. At the "0" level of integrity, the mean r was .23 (CI = .15 to .31, k = 12). At the level of "1," the mean validity estimate was .37 (CI = .30 to .44, k = 15). At the highest level of integrity, the mean validity estimate was .46 (CI = .38 to .54, k = 13). In step, predictive validity increased from a moderate level of validity to a strong level to a very strong level.

Beyond author involvement, direct tests are required of a full array of independent indicators of integrity in assessment and in the design and operation of the validation study. Just as we have a CPAI for the evaluation of program implementation, we need a systematic survey of the indicators of good assessment practices. Some of the particular factors that need to be explored in more detail are as follows:

1. the training and clinical supervision of assessors;

2. knowledge and skill level of assessors, supervisors, trainers, and researchers;

3. use of quality assurance tools by assessors, supervisors, and researchers;

4. follow-up periods of sufficient length;

5. reviews of internal consistency and inter-rater reliability;

6. assessors' access to multiple sources of information on risk/need factors;

7. self-reported recidivism supplemented by official records;

8. researchers' access to multiple sources of information on recidivism;

9. use of the results of the most recent assessment (because LSI-R and LS/CMI are known to possess dynamic predictive validity); and

10. inter-rater reliability checks on coding of data.

Additional factors of potential importance are as follows:

1. subgroup classifications that correlate strongly with base rates of recidivism and mean LSI-R and LS/CMI scores will dampen within subgroup validity estimates;

2. treatment that is in adherence with the principles of RNR will dampen the predictive validity of pretreatment LS assessments;

3. total predictive validity estimates may increase with supplementary assessments of non-LS factors (e.g., gender-informed assessments in combination with LS risk/need); and

4. assessments of acute dynamic representations of the major risk/ need factors may increase predictive validity (Rowe, 2007).

Cost-Benefit Evaluations

Our final focus here is cost-benefit studies of treatment rather than an assessment of cost-effectiveness. Cost-effectiveness may estimate the probability of an outcome, but it does not assign an estimate of the monetary value for the outcome. The simple question is: "How much does it cost to treat an offender who does not recidivate?" In a cost-benefit study, a monetary value is placed on the benefits of successfully treating an offender. For example, by successfully treating an offender rather than incarcerating him or her, we may avoid lost wages, welfare costs that may be needed to support the family of an incarcerated offender, and the "pain and suffering" of potential victims. Even such intangible costs such as "pain and suffering" can be estimated by reviewing recent jury settlements. For readers who wish to learn more about the techniques of cost-benefit analysis, we recommend an excellent "how to" book chapter by Mark Cohen (2001), along with Brandon Welsh and David Farrington's (2000a) comprehensive summary of the difficulties surrounding cost-benefit analysis.

Studies that have directly applied cost-benefit analyses to controlled evaluations of treatment programs are few. The number of studies falls between seven (Welsh & Farrington, 2000b) and nine (Farrington, Petrosino & Welsh, 2001). However, the following sampling of conclusions clearly demonstrates that offender rehabilitation programs have substantial cost-benefits:

- "the present value of saving a high-risk youth is estimated to be $2.6 to $5.3 million at age 18" (Cohen & Piquero, 2009:46).

- "if a 14 percentage point reduction in recidivism is achieved . . . this could result in an economic gain of $39,870 per prisoner, or $3.98 million for 100 treated prisoners" (Donato & Shanahan, 1999:1).

- "our lowest plausible estimate for the dollar benefits of avoided criminal activity . . . was $26.42 million, or $10,918 per treatment client" (based on an analysis of 2,242 drug abusers; Rajkimar & French, 1997:318).

The most important analysis, to date, on the cost-benefits of prevention and treatment is found in a report by Steve Aos, Polly Phipps, Robert Barnoski, and Roxanne Lieb (2001). Aos and his colleagues applied a cost-benefit analysis to 305 studies ranging from early childhood intervention programs to adult offender treatment studies. Their meta-analytic review provided both a positive conclusion—"(some) programs are good bets both to lower crime rates and to lower the net costs of crime to tax payers" (p. 5)—and also a wealth of cost-benefit data on individual programs. Table 12.4 gives a few examples of some of the treatment programs discussed.

This brief review suggests that effective treatments can be delivered in real-world settings. Appropriate treatments delivered with high levels of integrity can have significant impacts on recidivism and cost-benefits. Our knowledge of the principles of effective treatment and the program integrity/implementation factors has been valuable for the delivery and monitoring of offender program systems. We know a great deal about

Table 12.4
A Sampling of the Economic Benefits per Offender of Treatment Programs

Program	k	Average Benefit ($) per offender	Range ($)
Multi-Systemic Therapy	3	81,789	31,661 – 131,918
Functional Family Therapy	7	36,608	14,149 – 59,067
Aggression Replacement Training	4	20,715	8,287 – 33,143
Moral Reconation Therapy	8	5,134	2,471 – 7,797
Reasoning and Rehabilitation	6	4,653	2,202 – 7,104

k = number of studies

From Aos et al., 2001

the pitfalls in implementing treatment programs and a little bit about how to avoid at least some of them.

Worth Remembering

1. In the domains of both effective correctional treatment and valid assessment, having an evaluator who was involved in the design of the treatment (or the construction of the assessment intervention) was associated with an evaluation whose conclusions were favorable to the intervention (or to the validity of the instrument).

   There are four interpretations to this effect. They are: "cynical" (experimenter bias), "smart" (programs or instruments), "fidelity" (treatment and/or assessment implemented with integrity), and "combination of the first three." Meta-analyses in the treatment domain support the combination interpretation.

2. Consideration of the involved evaluator effect has led to the distinction between short-term tightly controlled demonstration projects and routine programming (sometimes called "regular" programming or "real-world" programming).

   A huge challenge is to help make routine programming more like demonstration projects on the dimensions of "smart" and "fidelity." Demanding exquisitely clear reporting on methodological and operational aspects of research may additionally reduce "bias."

3. Three concrete ways of improving routine programming are: (1) RNR-based structured assessments of offenders, (2) RNR-based structured assessments of ongoing programming, with feedback on level of RNR adherence, and (3) RNR-based training and supervision of service providers (and their managers).

Recommended Readings

For those wishing to read an excellent example of an after-the-fact "autopsy" of failed programming, we highly recommend Claire Goggin and Paul Gendreau's (2006) chapter "The Implementation and Maintenance of Quality Services in Offender Rehabilitation Programmes" in Clive Hollin and Emma Palmer's edited book, *Offending Behaviour Programmes: Development, Application and Controversies*. The other chapters in the book also provide commentaries on the range of issues surrounding implementation of best practices.

The paper by Christopher Lowenkamp, Edward Latessa, and Paula Smith (2006), "Does Correctional Quality Really Matter?" in *Criminology and Public Policy* is an excellent example of the emerging literature on the actual prediction of which programs will be effective and which will not. In this article, the authors employed the Correctional Program Assessment Inventory (CPAI) to help identify the most effective programs.

Chapter 13

Getting Mean, Getting Even, Getting Justice: Punishment and a Search for Alternatives

When someone is hurt or wronged, a common response is to strike back. It occurs at both the individual and societal levels. Hurts are to be punished, but not unduly so. Fairness and justice must also apply. In almost all societies, punishment is a consequence of breaking the law, and the application of punishment is highly regulated. There are many purposes for punishment within the criminal justice system. They include retribution, denunciation of the act, and deterrence. In this chapter, we touch upon these varying purposes, but our focus will be on the deterrent function of punishment.

Criminal Justice Sanctions and Just Deserts

Laws define unacceptable behaviors and set the penalties for engaging in those behaviors. For the sake of simplicity, we will use the term "sanction" to refer to the official application of punishment for breaking the law (more generally, sanctions can also refer to the approval of behavior). Sanctioning criminal behavior follows three simple ideas. First, there is the moral imperative that wrongs do not go unpunished (retribution). Second, the sanction must be proportional to the crime ("just deserts"). A punishment should not be overly harsh or too lenient; it must be fair and just. Finally, it is anticipated that sanctions will deter the individual (specific deterrence) and other members of society (general deterrence) from behaving illegally.

It seems that with each edition of this text, the U.S. incarceration news becomes bleaker. In the last edition we reported that the United States accounted for approximately one-quarter of the world's prison population. At the end of 2007, America accounted for nearly *one-half* of the world's incarcerated population (Walmsley, 2008), with an incarceration rate of 756 per 100,000. In 2006, approximately 7.2 million people—3.2 percent of the U.S. adult population—were either in custody or on probation or parole (Glaze & Bonczar, 2007; Pew, 2008). In California, the proposed 2009–10 corrections budget of $10.3 billion was only $2.5 billion less than the budget for higher education (California, 2009). Spending on corrections has outpaced all state budget categories except for Medicaid, rising 202 percent between 1985 and 2004 (Stemen, 2007) and costing states $48 billion (Pew, 2009). Not only is imprisonment a common (and expensive) penalty, but many jurisdictions have introduced measures to make prisons as unpleasant as possible. It is not enough to limit freedom and remove offenders from their families and communities; the "no frills" prisons in the United States have added the deprivation of television, cigarettes, library and exercise facilities, and other "perks."

With respect to the most severe penalty, capital punishment, there were 3,233 inmates on death row and 42 executions in 2007 (Snell, 2008). Almost 11 percent of those under a sentence of death were arrested under the age of 19. However, the U.S. Supreme Court banned the execution of youths under the age of 16 in 1988 (Beckman, 2004), and the ban was recently extend to youths between 16 and 18 years of age (*Roper v. Simmons*, 2005).

Even community sanctions have become "tougher." At one time, the range of sanctions available to the courts was relatively modest. Now there is an array of "intermediate sanctions." In addition to regular probation, there are intensive supervision programs that use urine testing for drugs or satellites to track the whereabouts of offenders. Sometimes offenders are required to spend a brief period in prison before beginning a probation sentence. As Erwin (1986:17) wrote, probation should be as "punishing" as prison.

It is unclear when exactly we started "getting tough" on crime. We have heard the "nothing works" story in the rehabilitation chapter, but the major points bear repeating. Most scholars place the beginnings at some time in the 1970s with the social-political conditions that laid the seeds to a toughening of attitudes toward crime (Clear, 1994; Cullen & Gilbert, 1982; Tonry, 2004). Add to the social-political events of the 1970s the proclamation that "nothing works" and academic criminology's anti-individual position, and we can understand the shift away from individualized rehabilitation programs to a reliance on punishment to deal with crime.

There was also a revival of classical criminology (Vold & Bernard, 1986). Classical criminology saw individuals as rational beings who calculated the benefits and risks for certain behaviors. Therefore, if crime pays, then the costs for crime must increase. This utilitarian model also hypothesized that reducing the rewards for crime (forget about increasing costs) should also alter the probability of crime. In fact, the utilitarian model is not entirely inconsistent with the multiple options offered by the PIC-R model of criminal behavior (see Table 13.1). Reducing criminal behavior can be achieved by shifting the rewards and costs for criminal and prosocial behavior. However, for many reasons, increasing punishment or the costs to crime (Cell B) was the preferred choice in U.S. criminal justice policy.

Table 13.1
Decreasing the Chances of Crime

Behavior		Rewards		Costs
Criminal	(A)	reduce	(B)	add
Prosocial	(C)	add	(D)	reduce

A report of the Committee for the Study of Incarceration authored by Andrew von Hirsch (1976) proved to be influential. The report questioned the effectiveness of rehabilitation, the ability to predict criminal behavior, and the whole idea of "individuation" within a criminal justice context. Consequently, incarceration, except for rare situations, should have nothing to do with the potential danger an offender might pose or the likelihood of rehabilitation. Parole and indeterminate sentences, which rested so much in the rehabilitation of offenders, were unnecessary. Furthermore, punishment is morally justified because people who do wrong *deserve* to be punished. The purpose of sanctions is to give the offender his or her "just deserts."

Sanctions that were tailored to fit the crime not only were to result in a fair and just criminal justice system but also were presumed to deter criminal behavior. The United States went on a spree of adding sanctions and increasing the severity of sanctions. Limits were placed on judicial discretion with the introduction of sentencing guidelines and minimum mandatory penalties (von Hirsch, 1987). The state of Washington introduced a "three strikes and you're out" law in 1993, making life imprisonment mandatory for a third felony conviction. Three-strikes laws followed in California and 24 other states (Turner et al., 1999). Some states (e.g., Georgia, Montana, South Carolina, Washington) went further and made two strikes sufficient to merit life in prison without parole (Austin et al., 1999; Boerner & Lieb, 2001). Discretion at the "back end" of the criminal justice system was also curtailed by the abolishment of parole boards and the introduction of "truth-in-sentencing" laws. A "penal harm movement" (Clear, 1994) emerged with little consideration as to whether the promise of safer communities and a fairer system was achieved.

The Effects of Imprisonment on Crime and the Community

The "get tough" approach to crime is reflected in laws with mandatory minimum penalties, longer prison sentences, and other efforts to make sanctions more unpleasant. Many jurisdictions have had mandatory minimum penalties, but the penalties were limited either to very serious crimes, such as an intentional act of murder, or to a few specific crimes (e.g., brief periods of incarceration for impaired driving). What changed was that the list of offenses for which mandatory penalties were prescribed increased dramatically, and the penalties became more severe.

Three-strikes laws and truth-in-sentencing legislation are the most common examples of the "get tough" legislation. Three-strikes laws basically require a judge to give a life prison term after the third offense. Truth-in-sentencing laws require offenders to serve a minimum amount of their sentence (approximately 85%) before release on parole or some other form of conditional release. Both types of legislation are usually intended to target violent offenders but, as we will soon see, this is not always the case.

The 1978 report of the National Academy of Sciences (Blumstein, Cohen & Nagin, 1978) questioned the value of indiscriminately imprisoning offenders. The value of incapacitation rested with selectively incapacitating the high-risk, high-frequency offender (i.e., "career criminal"), the 6 to 15 percent of offenders who commit 50 percent of all crimes. This small but highly active group of offenders was the group that required incapacitation.

The effectiveness of selective incapacitation depends on the ability to identify that small segment of offenders who commit the majority of crimes. Peter Greenwood (1982) constructed a seven-item prediction scale that, he claimed, would identify high-frequency robbers. Furthermore, imprisoning this select group of robbers for eight years was projected to reduce the number of robberies by nearly 20 percent and yield a 5 percent reduction in the prison population.

Greenwood's optimistic claims were soon deflated. Jan Chaiken and Marcia Chaiken (1982), fellow researchers at the RAND Corporation, reanalyzed Greenwood's data and concluded that neither robberies nor the prison population would be significantly affected. In a subsequent study, Visher (1986) reached a similar conclusion. Later, Greenwood himself tempered his estimates (Greenwood & Turner, 1987). However, it was too late. Many academics and the U.S. federal and state governments embraced the concept of selective incarceration.

The three-strikes laws are products of a belief in selective incapacitation. Putting aside the difficulty in identifying high-risk, high-rate offenders (Bushway & Smith, 2007), the results from three-strikes laws have been disappointing. First of all, the laws do not always target the high-risk violent offender. For example, in California, approximately 20 percent of third-strike offenses are drug-related (Meehan, 2000), and 60 percent are for a nonviolent offense (Austin et al., 1999). Second, the application of the law varies considerably across states. In California, 40,000 offenders have been given 25 years to life under three-strikes legislation while Florida has used similar legislation on 116 offenders (Turner et al., 1999). Chen's (2008) analysis of three-strikes laws across the United States found that California's small decline in some crimes could have been achieved with the less draconian laws found in some of the other states. Even within California, there are significant discrepancies in the application of the legislation across counties (Austin et al., 1999; Meehan, 2000), and the counties that most used three-strikes laws had higher crime rates than the counties that rarely used the legislation (Center on Juvenile and Criminal Justice, 2008).

Three arguments are usually given to support get-tough legislation. They are:

1. It takes bad people off the streets so they cannot commit crimes.

2. It restores faith in the criminal justice system.

3. It deters people from committing crime.

Let's take a look that these three arguments a bit more closely.

Incapacitation Effect: Taking the Bad Off the Streets

Without a doubt, if you remove someone from the community, then he or she cannot commit a crime in the community. Therefore, so the argument goes, the more criminals that are imprisoned, the lower the crime rate. When crime rates decreased in the United States during the 1990s, many were quick to point to the increased policing and stiffer sentences as the reasons for the reduction in crime rates. To their thinking, that meant that the skyrocketing prison populations were well worth it. The real questions here are: (a) does imprisonment reduce criminal behavior in our communities? and (b) at what cost?

Was increasing prison capacity partly responsible for decreased crime rates in the United States? The answer is a bit unclear, but it appears not. There are two reasons why we do not think that imprisonment explains the decrease in crime rates. First, the increase in imprisonment began in the early 1970s, while the decrease in crime rates did not appear until 20 years later. Second, states that showed the highest increase in the rate of incarceration showed smaller decreases in crime than the states with below-average imprisonment rates (King, Mauer & Young, 2005). We would have expected that the states that used imprisonment the most would have the higher rates of crime reduction.

Some researchers continue to advocate the notion that increasing prison capacity will prevent crime (Spelman, 2000; Weatherburn, Hua & Moffatt, 2006). Their arguments are usually based upon the application of mathematical formulae, with certain assumptions about the rate at which offenders commit crimes; the probability of getting caught, convicted, and sent to jail; the average time spent in jail; and the average time left in the offender's "career" when returned to the community (see Piquero and Blimstein, 2007, for a review of some of the issues). As the reader can see, we have to make a number of educated guesses about the variables that go into the equation to estimate the number of crimes avoided through incarceration.

William Spelman (2000) estimated that *doubling* the prison population could reduce crime rates by 20 to 40 percent. However, is doubling, or increasing significantly, the prison population cost-effective? In 1987, Edwin Zedlewski claimed that the $25,000 of prison costs associated with one year in prison would avoid a whopping $430,000 in social costs. Almost as soon as Zedlewski's claim was published, his analysis and conclusions were challenged (Zimring & Hawkins, 1988). Today, there is general agreement that the cost-benefit ratio is far smaller than what Zedlewski estimated. Bernard and Ritti (1991) estimated that if the incarceration rate was increased from two to six times for serious juvenile delinquents, the crime rate would decrease only by 6 percent. A number of other investigators also report that significant increases in imprisonment would produce only modest reductions in crime, with the associated costs exceeding the benefits (Blokland & Nieuwbeerta, 2007; Fass & Pi, 2002, Weatherburn et al., 2006).

Another reason why the cost-benefit ratio has changed since Zedlewski's original analysis is that the profile of who is in prison has changed significantly. It used to be that imprisonment was reserved for the more serious offender. The "war on drugs" changed all of that. More than one-half of the prisoners in the U.S. federal system are there for drug crimes, and they are mostly low-risk offenders (about 13% committed a violent crime). In addition, incarcerating drug offenders does little to alter the "replacement effect." That is, as soon as you put a drug offender into prison, another takes his or her place on the street (King et al., 2005).

Earlier analyses took a relatively narrow view of the costs and benefits of imprisonment. If we take a broader view, then we see the enormous social costs. It is not just the individual offenders who pay the price, but families and whole communities are destabilized at significant economic costs (Haney, 2006; Schirmer, Nellis & Mauer, 2009). Not only has the "war on drugs" resulted in joblessness for those captured in the net and economic hardship for the families of those captured but also the loss of basic rights in a democratic society. Although some states are now reversing their stance on disenfranchisement, in 1998 it was estimated that 13 percent of all black males in the United States had lost the right to vote (Jensen, Gerber & Mosher, 2004). Moreover, almost all inmates are released, returning to the neighborhoods from which they came. The result is a high concentration of individuals who have few job prospects and loose ties to the community. This high concentration of ex-inmates in areas referred to as "million dollar" blocks (because of the costs associated with incarcerating so many individuals) drives out small business and those law-abiding citizens who can afford to leave and contributes to neighborhood decay (Clear, 2008; Clear et al., 2003). In Brooklyn alone, it is estimated that there are 35 of these "million dollar" blocks (Gonnerman, 2004). Moreover, the fact of being imprisoned with other offenders for many years may actually be criminogenic (Vieraitis, Kovandzic & Marvell, 2007).

We have one more final comment before leaving the incapacitation effect. We need to consider if there are better and more cost-effective ways of reducing crime than through imprisonment. We believe that treatment is a more cost-effective alternative. For example, an evaluation of an intensive treatment program for violent delinquents produced a benefit-to-cost ratio of 7.4 to one and a savings to the taxpayer of $320,000 for every treated offender (Caldwell, Vitacco & Van Rybroek, 2006). Cohen and Piquero (2009) have estimated that "saving" a high-risk juvenile from a life of crime can produce savings of between $2.6 million to $5.3 million. In a cost-benefit analysis of providing a "moderate-to-aggressive" implementation policy of effective treatment programs, researchers at the Washington State Institute for Public Policy (Aos, Miller & Drake, 2006b; Drake, Aos & Miller, 2009) estimated that the State of Washington could avoid the need to build new prisons without any increase in crime rates and were successful in enhancing the budget for treatment programs. It appears that incapacitation is not as promising a crime reduction strategy as first thought.

Restoring Faith in the Criminal Justice System

Political leaders argue that the consequences for law violation must be quick and severe in order to ensure law and order. Furthermore, they say, this is what the public expects and wants. Whether the public really wants a "get tough" approach depends upon how the question is posed. Public opinion surveys that ask very general questions (e.g., "Do you favor tougher sentences for criminals?") do find the majority of respondents agreeing to a "get tough" approach. The public thinks poorly of parole, that courts are too lenient, and that prisons are "country clubs." However, when the public is given *choices* or more factual and detailed information, a less punitive attitude emerges (Cullen, Fisher & Applegate, 2000; Roberts, 2003).

A number of factors moderate what Cullen and colleagues (2000) call the "mushy" "get tough" attitudes of the public. First, when questions

434 The Psychology of Criminal Conduct

are posed that provide alternatives to the most serious penalty (e.g., death penalty versus life in prison), it is the minority who endorses the harshest alternative. If more detail is given about the crime (e.g., the robbery did not cause physical harm) or about the offender (juvenile or mentally disordered), then the public is more understanding and tolerant. When questioned specifically about three-strikes laws, only 17 percent of sampled residents in Ohio would give life sentences to all offenders after the third strike (Applegate et al., 1996). Nonetheless, "get tough" policies abound. It is understandable that the public cannot be informed on all facts related to public policy. However, it appears inexcusable to us that so many political leaders are neither well informed nor interested in educating their constituents. Perhaps, this reflects the new correctional politics (Zimring, 2001). As Tonry (2004:15) writes, "Political courage is required . . . a vote to repeal, narrow, or weaken a three-strikes law can be portrayed as being soft on crime. This makes elected officials risk averse."

Deterrence

There is little evidence that "get tough" interventions such as three-strikes and truth-in-sentencing laws deter crime (Tonry, 2008). What researchers typically find is that crime rates have not been affected very much. In one study, states were grouped into whether or not they had three-strikes and truth-in-sentencing laws. Contrary to expectations, the lowest general and violent crime rates were found in states that did not have either type of legislation (Turner et al., 1999). In analyses of the data from California, no decreases in crime, violent or petty, have been found (Auerhahn, 2003; Austin et al., 1999; Greenwood et al., 1998; Stolzenberg & D'Alessio, 1997).

When we consider the general literature on the impact of imprisonment on recidivism, we do not find a deterrent effect. Narrative reviews of the literature agree that the severity or length of the sentence is unrelated to crime (Doob & Webster, 2003; von Hirsch et al., 1999). Meta-analytic reviews also reach the same conclusion. In one review, Paula Smith, Claire Goggin, and Paul Gendreau (2002) found longer sentences associated with a 3 percent *increase* in the recidivism of offenders released from prison (see Resource Note 13.1). In another meta-analysis, "get tough" policies were associated with approximately a 5 percent increase in crime (Pratt & Cullen, 2005). Sure, prisons can impact on crime if we incarcerate for life everyone who commits a crime. However, even if we were willing to embark on such a questionable economic and social experiment, we would still have crime. There are always children who grow up delinquent and who can easily "replace" those whom we imprison.

Resource Note 13.1

The Effects of Prison Sentences on Recidivism
(Smith, Goggin & Gendreau, 2002)

As with all negative sanctions, the imprisonment of offenders is expected to deter offenders from further crime. Incarceration curtails personal liberty and deprives one from the pleasures normally enjoyed in daily life. These are thought to be punishing enough that when experienced, individuals would avoid the behavior that led to the punishment. If imprisonment does not deter, then perhaps the period of deprivation was simply not long enough to give the full impact of punishment. Penal policy over the past decade has clearly followed this argument. Society needs to increase the length of incarceration for various crimes in order to reduce recidivism. However, does increasing the time spent in prison really reduce recidivistic crime?

Paula Smith, Claire Goggin, and Paul Gendreau tried to answer this question through a meta-analytic review of the prison literature. Two types of studies were selected. There were 27 studies that compared community-based offenders (e.g., probationers) to inmates and 23 studies that compared prisoners serving longer sentences to inmates serving shorter sentences (e.g., inmates released on parole with inmates who were ineligible for parole). To be included in the review, there had to be a minimum of a six-month follow-up. Moreover, as with all meta-analytical reviews, the results had to be reported in a way that permitted the calculation of a common effect size.

Altogether, 57 studies representing more than 375,000 offenders were identified for analyses. Almost all the studies had methodological weaknesses. Only one study used random assignment. Despite the methodological problems with the studies analyzed, the general results confirmed the findings reported in the narrative literature review by von Hirsch et al. (1999).

Smith and her colleagues used the phi coefficient (ϕ) as their effect size indicator. Phi is a measure of association used with dichotomous data, and its interpretation is similar to the Pearson correlation coefficient. The 57 studies produced 337 effect sizes. A summary of the findings is presented in the following table.

Type of Comparison	Sample Size	ϕ
Prison vs. community	268,806	.07
Longer vs. shorter time in prison	107,165	.03
All combined	375,971	.03

Regardless of the type of comparison, imprisonment was not associated with any decreases in recidivism. In fact, the results were the contrary. Offenders who were imprisoned had recidivism rates approximately 7 percent (ϕ = .07) higher than community-based offenders, and inmates with longer sentences had a recidivism rate that was 3 percent (ϕ = .03) higher than inmates with shorter sentences. Considering all the studies together, imprisonment was associated with a 3 percent increase in recidivism.

Some penologists have suggested that prisons may be "schools for crime." Prisons bring offenders together where individuals are given opportunities to learn the techniques for crime and rationalizations for antisocial behavior. Low-risk offenders may be particularly vulnerable to an "indoctrination" into criminal patterns of thinking and behaving. High-risk offenders, on the other hand, do not need to learn any new tricks of the trade or receive further encouragement for their antisocial ideas. Smith and colleagues tried to code, as best as they could, the risk levels of the offender samples found in the studies. They found no differential association between type of sanction (prison or community) and offender risk level.

To be clear, neither the authors of the report nor we are saying that there should be

Resource Note 13.1 *(continued)*

no prisons. Our sense of justice requires imprisonment for serious violations against society. We believe that society needs to encourage a respect for law and demonstrate that some acts will not be tolerated. There are also some offenders who pose such an extremely high risk to reoffend violently that the only way to prevent harm is to incarcerate these offenders. However, those offenders requiring lengthy periods of confinement are a small proportion of the offender population. Advocates of imprisonment may argue that even if imprisonment does not deter, it at least takes offenders out of circulation and public safety is achieved. One area of research rarely considered is the antisocial behavior that goes on within prisons. Inmates and guards are assaulted, rapes occur, possessions stolen, contraband smuggled, and drugs abused. Crime on the street may be simply shifted to a different environment hidden from the public view.

Before moving on to evaluations of noncustodial deterrents, we would like to make a few comments on the deterrent value of the most severe form of punishment—the death penalty. A meta-analysis of 95 studies of executions found a small deterrent effect on homicides, but the effect was largely influenced by the study's methodology (Yang & Lester, 2008). Some studies have found no deterrent effect when homicide rates are compared before and after the introduction of the death penalty (e.g., Decker & Kohnfeld, 1984, 1987) or when neighboring states with and without the death penalty are compared (e.g., Sellin, 1980).

There is an unsettling finding first reported by John Cochran, Mitchell Chamlin, and Mark Seth (1994). They found that murders by strangers actually increased following the resumption of executions in Oklahoma after 25 years of no executions. Homicides involving acquaintances, friends, and family showed no change. Rather than deterring others from killing, "the reactivation of capital punishment produces an abrupt and permanent increase in the likelihood that citizens of Oklahoma will die at the hands of a stranger" (pp. 123–124).

Cochran and colleagues (1994) interpreted the increase of stranger murder as due to a "brutalization" effect—the execution of offenders by the state "brutalizes society by legitimating lethal violence" (p. 108). Consequently, a stranger who finds himself or herself in a volatile situation has fewer inhibitions to use lethal violence. Yang and Lester (2008) identified five studies that tested the brutalization effect. Two studies supported brutalization, another two found no effect, and the last study reported mixed support.

Evaluations of Intermediate Sanctions

Twenty-five years ago, judges had essentially three sentencing options: prison, probation, or a fine. However, in the 1980s, because of the pressure of overcrowded prisons, alternatives to the two extremes of the punishment continuum were sought. Sanctions were needed that were harsher than probation but not as severe or costly as prison. Alternative punishments were to give judges more choices in order to fit the crime properly to the punishment and achieve a "rational" sentencing system (Morris & Tonry, 1990; Tonry & Lynch, 1996).

The most well-known forms of intermediate sanctions are Intensive Supervision Programs (ISPs), shock incarceration (e.g., boot camps, Scared Straight), and electronic monitoring programs. Georgia was the first state to introduce an ISP (1982). At the time, Georgia had the highest incarceration rate in the United States. However, simple probation would not do. Instead what was needed were probation sentences "to increase the heat on probationers in order to satisfy the public demand for just punishment" (Erwin, 1986:17). The ISP in Georgia consisted of 25 offenders supervised by two officers—a probation officer who did the counseling and case management and a "surveillance" officer who checked curfews, conducted drug tests, and made unannounced home visits. Within a decade, almost every state had an ISP (Cullen, Wright & Applegate, 1996).

Shock incarceration programs expose offenders to the harshness of prison life with the hope that it will shock them away from a criminal lifestyle. The most popular form of shock incarceration is the military-style boot camp. Once again, Georgia holds the distinction of opening the first shock incarceration/boot camp in the United States (1983). Georgia's program involved military-style drills and long hours of physical labor each day. There was no treatment. Although other boot camps had a counseling/treatment component, it was the drills, exercise, and labor that consumed eight or more hours of the day (Parent, Chaiken & Logan, 1989). By 2000, there were 95 boot camps for adults and 56 boot camps for juveniles (Armstrong, 2004). Boot camps were also established (briefly) in the Canadian provinces of Manitoba and Ontario and in the United Kingdom (Farrington et al., 2000).

One variant of shock incarceration was New Jersey's Juvenile Awareness Project, more popularly known as "Scared Straight." Youths visited "lifers" in Rahway State Prison where the inmates described to their audience, in colorful detail, the horrors of prison life. This "shock confrontation" approach was intended to show the youths what would happen if they followed a life of crime. A television documentary popularized the program and led to similar projects in other parts of the United States, Canada, and Europe (Finckenauer et al., 1999).

Electronic monitoring programs have an interesting origin. Judge Jack Love of New Mexico was reading a *Spider-Man* comic book in which the villain attached an electronic monitoring device to track Spider-Man. This allowed the criminal to carry out his crimes when Spider-Man was not around. Why not, thought Love, turn the tables and put electronic bracelets on the criminals so that the authorities would know their whereabouts? Thus was born electronic monitoring (EM) for criminal offenders. Today, EM programs can be found throughout the United States, Canada, and Europe (Cotter, 2005; Mair, 2005; Whitefield, 1999). It has been estimated that there are about 100,000 offenders in the United States (Conway, 2003) and 65,000 in Europe under electronic monitoring (Toon, 2005).

None of these intermediate punishments have demonstrated reductions in recidivism. Furthermore, under certain conditions, these programs have made matters worse by increasing recidivism and correctional costs. A brief summary of the evaluation literature follows.

Early evaluations of ISP often used prisoners as the comparison group and showed ISP participants in a favorable light. However, when ISP offenders were compared to offenders under regular probation, the reconviction and rearrest rates were no different (Lane, Turner, Fain & Sehgal, 2005). For example, Joan Petersilia and Susan Turner (1993) conducted a large-scale evaluation of 14 ISP programs involving 2,000 adult offenders. Offenders were randomly assigned to an ISP, prison, or probation/parole group. A one-year follow-up found 37 percent of the ISP offenders rearrested, compared to 33 percent of the controls. Not surprisingly, given the close monitoring of ISP participants, the ISP offenders were more likely breached with technical violations (65% vs. 38%). Reductions in recidivism in the range of 10 to 20 percent were found, however, in ISPs that provided treatment to the offenders. Incidentally, they also found that ISPs cost more per offender than for the control group ($7,200 vs. $4,700 per year). Similarly, Mario Paparozzi and Paul Gendreau (2005) found a 10 to 30 percent reduction in recidivism for only those parolees under intensive supervision who also received treatment.

Evaluations of shock incarceration and boot camps have also found that treatment is required to reduce recidivism. Doris MacKenzie, Robert Brame, David McDowall, and Claire Souryal (1995) examined eight state boot camps. Although groups were not randomly assigned, statistical controls were introduced for factors that could have influenced recidivism. One-half of the programs evidenced lower rearrest rates than the controls, but reductions in recidivism were associated with the boot camps that had a treatment component. Their conclusion: "military drill and ceremony, hard labor, physical training, and strict rules and discipline . . . in and of themselves do not reduce recidivism" (p. 351). More recent evaluations of boot camps have not altered this conclusion (Bottcher & Ezell, 2005). Only when there is a treatment component do we find positive findings (Weis, Whitemarsh & Wilson, 2005), and the results can be quite dramatic if targeted to higher-risk offenders (a 71% reduction in recidivism was reported by Kempinen and Kurlychek, 2003).

The New Jersey Scared Straight program was evaluated by James Finckenauer and his colleagues in the late 1970s. Forty-six juveniles who visited lifers in prison were compared to 35 control subjects. A six-month follow-up (Finckenauer, 1979) found that the youths who attended the Rahway program had *higher* rearrest rates (41.3%) than the youths who were not exposed to the program (11.4%). Surprisingly, 19 of the 46 youths attending the program did not even have a prior criminal record, and their recidivism rate was 31.6 percent. Despite the contraindicative findings, Scared Straight programs continued to be adopted in other U.S. jurisdictions and in the United Kingdom, Australia, and Norway. Evaluations of many of these programs have shown that none of them reduced recidivism (Finckenauer et al., 1999; Petrosino, Turpin-Petrosino & Finckenauer, 2000). In a meta-analysis of nine randomized studies, Petrosino, Turpin-Petrosino, and Buehler (2003) found that participation in Scared Straight, on average, actually was more harmful to juveniles than simple cautioning.

Finally, there are the electronic monitoring (EM) programs (and we include here the more recent GPS systems used to track offenders). EM was supposed to be an "alternative" to imprisonment. Instead of a prison sentence, the offender was given a community sentence and required to stay at home ("house arrest"). An electronic signaling device, usually attached to the ankle, permitted monitoring of the offender's location. Leaving the home without permission would set off an alarm, and the authorities would seek the apprehension of the offender.

Research on EM has left us with three general conclusions. First, most EM programs do not offer an alternative to prison. Offenders in these programs are often low-risk offenders who would have received a community-based sanction anyway. That is, EM programs, like many intermediate sanctions, appear to widen the correctional net, applying more rather than less controls (Cullen, Wright & Applegate, 1996; Gable & Gable, 2005). Second, EM does not reduce recidivism (Renzema & Mayo-Wilson, 2005). For example, a quasi-experimental study of three Canadian EM programs by Bonta, Wallace-Capretta, and Rooney (2000b) found that it was offender risk factors that accounted for variations in recidivism; EM had no effect. Evaluations claiming to show that EM reduces recidivism have had major methodological problems. For example, a large evaluation of Florida's EM program involving more than 75,000 offenders did not have a no-EM comparison group (Padgett, Bales & Blomberg, 2006). Third, and consistent with the findings reported earlier, it is the addition of a treatment component to EM that results in reduced recidivism (Bonta, Wallace-Capretta & Rooney, 2000a; Nellis, 2006). All in all, there is little evidence that any of the intermediate sanctions popular today will reduce recidivism. Only treatment produces the desired effect.

The Unfulfilled Promise of Fairness

Andrew von Hirsch and others have argued that the predictability of mandatory sentencing policy would reduce reliance on incarceration and bring fairness into the criminal justice system. Judges would be required to operate within sentencing guidelines that matched the punishment to the crime and not the person. Thus, a similar act committed by different people would receive the same consequence. With respect to reducing imprisonment, the evidence is mixed. Some report no changes in the use of imprisonment (Frase, 2005; Merritt, Fain & Turner, 2006; Moody & Marvell, 1996; Sorensen & Stemen, 2002), while others have found dramatic increases (Nicholson-Crotty, 2004; Wood & Dunaway, 2003). The variation in findings may be explained by differences in adherence to guidelines (in some jurisdictions prosecutors, judges, and corrections officials have found ways of sidestepping guidelines). Where there is strict adherence to sentencing guidelines, there have been large increases in the state prison population (e.g., in 2001, Mississippi hit an incarceration rate of more than 700 per 100,000; Wood & Dunaway, 2003).

When it comes to achieving fairness, one does not have to search for long to find examples in which fairness was clearly not achieved. Austin and colleagues (1999) presented a few "typical" cases from interviews with 100 three-strikes offenders. One offender received 27 years for attempting to sell stolen property valued at $90; another received 25 years for reckless driving (a police car chase). Currie (1993) describes a first-time offender who received life without parole for possession of 5.5 ounces of crack cocaine. Tonry (2004) adds the example of an individual who received a 50-year sentence for the theft of $150 worth of videotapes.

Some may see these examples as nothing more than exceptions to the rule and believe that for most offenders, fairness operates. Analyses of the racial composition of arrestees and prisoners suggest otherwise. With America's "war on drugs" and the police's targeting of drug crimes, African Americans have been differentially affected (Tonry, 2008). General arrest rates are four times higher for African Americans than for whites, and the discrepancy widens for drug offenses (Daly & Tonry, 1997; Parker & Maggard, 2005). In addition to differential arrest practices, mandatory prison sentences for most drug offenses have also affected African Americans. In 2004, 41 percent of the U.S. prison population consisted of African Americans (Harrison & Beck, 2005). Although legal factors are the best predictors of sentencing, a number of studies also report that racial factors often play a role in the sentencing of offenders (Leiber & Fox, 2005; Mitchell, 2005; Pratt, 1998).

Racial bias has also been reported in the application of the death penalty. One-third of persons executed in 2004 and 42 percent of the inmates on death row were black (Bonczar & Snell, 2005). Aguirre and Baker's (1990) review found that black offenders, especially if their victim was white, were more likely to receive the death penalty, although some studies (e.g., Stauffer et al., 2006) fail to support this victim effect. As Charles Lanier and James Acker (2004) note, the death penalty moratorium movement owes much of its momentum to the charge of racial bias.

Finally, it appears that mandatory sentencing policies have affected female offenders. Historically, female offenders have enjoyed leniency from the courts. Daly and Bordt (1995) found 45 percent of the 50 court data sets that they reviewed favored women in sentencing. Sentencing guidelines, however, require that criminal acts are treated equally and render personal factors (e.g., gender) inconsequential. Daly and Tonry (1997) noted that when sentencing guidelines are introduced, there are three possible options. First, sentences can be reduced for men to bring them more in line with the sentences women receive. Second, sentences for men and women can converge to some midpoint. Third, sentences can increase for women. It appears that our appetite for punishment has led to the third option. Evaluations of Minnesota's sentencing guidelines found that the sentences for women increased under the guidelines (Frase, 2005), replicating a trend found with implementation of Oregon's sentencing guidelines (Bogan & Factor, 1995).

Summary

It is astonishing that in spite of the negative findings, criminal justice sanctions still remain wildly popular. Legislators continually try to come up with harsher penalties, criminologists continue to conduct studies hoping to find that deterrence will work, and programs are made more demeaning. There is no shortage of ideas. In New Jersey, offenders were made to dress in woman's clothes in order to tear down macho attitudes (Wilson, Goldiner & Mickle, 1993); Graeme Newman (1995) suggested replacing prisons with corporal punishment; and the Labour government in the United Kingdom has proposed that offenders on community supervision wear special jackets identifying them as lawbreakers (Wintour, 2008).

A number of factors operate to keep punishment entrenched in criminal justice policy. First, people *believe* in the effectiveness of punishment (Deater-Deckard et al., 2003). Second, politicians and legislators, rightly or wrongly, think that being "tough on crime" is what the public wants. Third, rehabilitation is seen as being soft on crime and not effective. Finally, and borrowing from a point made by Finckenauer et al. (1999), the lack of awareness about the research facilitates program inertia. In some areas, this situation may be changing. For example,

Francis Cullen and colleagues (Cullen et al., 2005) have found that the negative research on boot camps is finally diminishing the appeal of this form of intermediate sanction. However, once a politically popular program is up and running, it takes a great deal of effort to alter its course.

The "get tough" approach has failed to deliver on its promises of improved public safety, cost-efficiency, and social justice. We see a need for a Winston Churchill, the Prime Minister who led England through the Second World War. Churchill chastened judges for passing sentences that were too long, limited the use of solitary confinement, and ensured that prisoners were provided with entertainment, education, and meaningful work (Gardner, 2000). Without such leadership, it will indeed be difficult to diminish our dependence on get-tough policies.

Punishment

Why Doesn't Punishment Work?

The answer to the question posed above can be found in the hundreds of studies conducted by psychologists. We know a great deal about when punishment works (i.e., inhibits behavior) and when it does not work. This knowledge comes from both laboratory and applied studies with animals and humans that were conducted 30 and 40 years ago. Here, we purposely cite studies from the 1960s and 1970s to underscore the point that knowledge of the effectiveness of punishment has been well known in the psychology community for a long time. Unfortunately, as Huessman and Podolski (2003) pointed out, these studies are rarely cited in the criminological deterrence literature. If only the deterrence advocates would have read this literature, then we might not have embarked on such a frustrating course of criminal justice policy. To us, the ineffectiveness of "get tough" policies reveals the need for criminal justice policy to be informed by a psychology of criminal conduct.

In this section, we summarize what is known about the effectiveness of punishment. Punishment is defined as a consequence to a behavior that decreases the likelihood of the behavior from reoccurring. There is no mention of pain or suffering in the definition. Any consequence to a behavior, painful or not, that reduces the probability of the behavior is a punishment.

As we outlined in PIC-R (see Chapter 4), there are two types of consequences to behavior: rewards and costs. Furthermore, rewards and costs can be additive or subtractive. Additive costs are what come to mind when most people think about punishment. Adding a painful stimulus (e.g., spanking a child, yelling at an employee, delivering an electric shock to a rat) is expected to inhibit or reduce the probability of behavior. However, removing a reward or something valued (i.e., a subtractive cost) can also decrease the probability of behavior. Giving your partner "the cold shoulder" or sending a misbehaving child to his or her room ("time out") are examples of subtractive costs.

The literature on the effectiveness of punishment is rich, and the types of punishments studied are varied. The majority of experiments use electric shock because of the high degree of control over its intensity and duration. However, there are studies using unpleasant odors, submerging a hand in freezing water, puffs of air to the eye, loud noises, removing money, placing children in a room away from rewards, forcibly repeating certain physical movements (overcorrection), and having disgusting and unpleasant thoughts (Matson & Kazdin, 1981).

Conditions for Effective Punishment

Drawing on this literature, we present a brief summary of the important conditions for effective punishment, along with a commentary on the relevance of the research to the crime problem.

Condition 1: Maximum Intensity. It is unclear whether the intensity of punishment is the most important factor in suppressing behavior, but it certainly ranks, along with immediacy, as one of the more important (Van Houten, 1983). At first blush, this last statement seems to say that if we simply "turn up the heat," then we can stop criminal behavior. However, it is not simply turning up the intensity dial. Studies suggest that we have to turn the dial to full in order to stop the targeted behavior completely.

In general, low levels of punishment do show an immediate suppression of behavior; however, the effects are temporary (Azrin, 1956). The behavior not only returns to its original levels, but it may even result in higher rates of responding. After all, the behavior must have been rewarded at some point for it to occur and, therefore, trying again and harder to gain reward should be expected. With the behavior returning at a higher rate, further increases in the intensity of punishment are needed to suppress behavior even for a short time. In addition, a low level of punishment intensity runs the risk of the subject learning to tolerate punishment (Solomon, 1964). In most Western countries and for most offenders, sanctions are increased gradually. For example, the first-time offender who commits a minor nonviolent crime is likely to receive a minor sanction; only with return to the court for new crimes does the penalty increase.

Producing complete behavior suppression requires *immediate* delivery of *very intense* levels of punishment (Azrin, Holz & Hake, 1963; Johnston, 1972). Retributionists may propose to give offenders the maximum penalty right off the bat. As we have already seen, in some jurisdictions, we are close to doing just that (e.g., three-strikes and two-strikes laws). Even when the maximum punishment as prescribed by law (barring the death penalty) is administered, the offending behavior continues for many. In a study of offenders who had their driver's licenses suspended *for life*, only 17 percent gave up driving completely (Chang, Woo & Tseng, 2006).

The problem with a policy of maximum punishment for a crime is that it offends our sense of justice and fairness. Imagine if we administer life imprisonment for the rapist, bank robber, pickpocket, income tax cheater, and jaywalker. Would most of us consider this to be fair punishment? Formalized systems of criminal justice try to follow a principle of proportionality (matching level of punishment to the severity of the crime). The option of maximum punishment is unacceptable to most.

Condition 2: Immediacy. The sooner the punishment follows the behavior, the more likely that the behavior will be suppressed. Introducing a delay between the behavior and the punishment can significantly alter the effectiveness of the punishment (Deluty, 1978; Dinsmoor, 1998). Why is this? It is mainly because there are opportunities for the behavior to be reinforced prior to the delivery of punishment (Skinner, 1953). One has to think of behavior as a chain of responses. The last response in the chain may be punished, and this may have some effect on the preceding responses, but the suppression effect diminishes the further the response is from the punishment.

To illustrate what could happen, consider an offender who is caught breaking into a car (the behavior) and is arrested and placed in a police cell (the punishment). What has the offender learned? Perhaps he or she learned that it is not worth opening a car door with a crowbar. However, the punishment will unlikely affect the behaviors leading up to the crime (e.g., visiting criminal friends, smoking some drugs, and then going out for a little excitement). We can go one step further and imagine that the offender is released on bail. What happens then? While waiting for trial and sentencing, he or she may still associate with criminal others, abuse drugs, and may even have occasion to commit undetected crimes. The opportunity for reinforcement of criminal behavior abounds.

Condition 3: Certainty. Avoidance theory explains how punishment "works" (Dinsmoor, 1954, 1998). Simply stated, punishment elicits an undesirable emotional response (fear, anxiety) and by not engaging in the behavior that produces punishment, the organism avoids the unpleasant emotion. In Chapter 5, we saw Mednick (1977) use avoidance theory to describe how people learn to suppress aggressive behavior. Although behavior is inhibited because it avoids something unpleasant, the unpleasant feelings of anxiety and fear do not last forever. The physiological responses that we label as anxiety and fear (e.g., increased heart rate, sweating, etc.) dissipate. It is as though we forget how bad the punishment was; to be reminded, it is important that the undesirable behavior is punished every time it occurs.

Unlike rewards, with which infrequent or unpredictable reinforcement (referred to as variable ratio or interval schedules) lead to high-rate and stable behavior, allowing an undesirable behavior to go unpunished once in a while is counterproductive. People and animals *behave*; they rarely sit still. The criminal must be caught almost every time he or she commits a crime and not be allowed opportunities to engage in other unwanted behavior that may be rewarded.

Consistency is also important in discrimination learning. A stimulus that is associated with the presence or absence of a reward or a punishment provides informational value regarding the outcome for a particular behavior. It becomes a signaled reward or cost. When a student walks into a classroom, he or she knows that looking attentive, taking notes, and asking reasonable questions will produce reinforcement (e.g., praise from the teacher, good marks, respect from fellow students). The classroom situation is associated with rewards for certain behaviors. Engaging in other behaviors (e.g., sleeping, eating, talking) will probably be punished. Some offenders are poor at making these discriminations (e.g., dealing drugs while a police cruiser is driving by increases the probability of punishment). Both the classroom and the police cruiser function as discriminative stimuli and *signal* the types of outcomes that are likely to occur given certain behaviors.

Another factor that can influence perceived certainty of punishment is the peer group. Matthews and Agnew (2008) examined the interaction between perceived certainty of punishment and antisocial peer group among 1,625 high school students. Using self-reports of antisocial behavior and peer affiliation, they found that the perceived certainty of punishment (measured by a five-point scale of getting caught by the police for four different crimes) had no effect on antisocial behavior for the students with delinquent peers. The authors hypothesized that antisocial peers may reduce the possibility of a deterrent effect by minimizing the chances of detection and reinforcing criminal behavior. As we have already seen in Chapter 7, antisocial peers have an enormous influence on the criminal behavior of individuals.

Condition 4: No Escape or Reinforced Alternatives. When punished, an organism attempts to escape the situation. Escaping from an aversive situation can have two consequences: (1) the escape behavior is reinforced, or (2) the original behavior may continue because the organism now finds itself in a nonpunishing situation (Van Houten, 1983). The behavioral outcome may be desirable (e.g., a boy leaves a group of children who are teasing him). Alternatively, the outcome could be undesirable (e.g., an inmate escapes from custody to rob again). Thus, a situation associated with punishment may serve as a cue to engage in escape behavior. To deal with such a situation, all routes to escape must be blocked to ensure that escape behavior is unrewarded.

We made the point earlier that people are always behaving and that behavior consists of a multitude of specific responses to our environment. Individuals have behavioral repertoires. For example, an individual may have the skills to read, cook an omelet, and paint murals. The activation of a certain set of behaviors depends upon whether the behavior is likely to be reinforced. It is unlikely that most people will read aloud a book to an empty classroom, cook a meal on an autobus, or paint a mural on the side of a stranger's house. The behaviors would not be reinforced in these situations. People choose behaviors that they think will be rewarded; if one behavior is not rewarded, then they choose another from their behavioral repertoire.

In any particular situation, an individual makes choices regarding what behavior to use. A young man who is introduced to an attractive woman will choose from his behavioral repertoire the behavior that he thinks may gain her admiration. Should he smile, engage in polite conversation, or show her his tattoo of "Mom"? All of these behaviors may be in his repertoire, but they do not have equal chances of being met with positive attention. Psychologists talk of a hierarchy of behaviors. In any given situation, behaviors form an ordering of their likelihood of being rewarded and punished. The most likely behavior in a specific situation is one that has the longest history of reinforcement and shortest history of punishment in similar situations. The other behaviors follow according to their own individual reward/cost histories. The young man in our example may start with the behavior that was most successful for him in the past. However, if the behavior is met with a frown, then he resorts to another behavior that was perhaps not as successful in the past but may work this time. Thus, a punished response is not simply eliminated; it is displaced by another response (Dinsmoor, 1955).

Antisocial behavior consists of many different specific acts, and high-risk, chronic offenders exhibit a variety of undesirable behaviors (e.g., dishonesty, physical aggression, thievery, etc.). Punishing one behavior (e.g., the dishonesty associated with fraud) leaves many other behaviors that could be used to achieve personal and illegitimate goals. Unless alternative prosocial behaviors are rewarded, criminal behavior, in one form or another, will continue.

Condition 5: The Density of Punishment Must Outweigh the Density of Reinforcement. Any behavior has both rewards and costs associated with them. Going to work every day may produce money and workplace friendship, but it also involves getting up in the morning, fighting rush-hour traffic, and coping with other irritants. Azrin, Holz, and Hake (1963) observed that behaviors with a significant history of reinforcement are more resistant to the effects of punishment than behaviors with a limited history of reinforcement. This has been observed many times and is reflected in PIC-R. The greater the density of rewards associated with behavior in terms of intensity, immediacy, consistency, and variety, the greater the density of costs required to suppress behavior. High-risk offenders have high densities of rewards for criminal behavior and, thus, their behaviors are highly resistant to punishment.

Condition 6: The Effectiveness of Punishment Interacts with Person Variables. Principle 4 of PIC-R states that the effects of rewards and costs interact with a variety of person factors (e.g., biological, cognitive, state conditions). In other words, people react differently to punishment (inter-individual differences) and even from one moment to another (intra-individual differences). A few days in jail may present very different costs for the individual who lives on the street versus the white-collar criminal. A verbal reprimand would have different effects depending upon whether an individual is intoxicated. Threats of punishment would be relatively meaningless for the impulsive person.

What does this say about the effectiveness of punishment with offenders? Gottfredson and Hirshi (1990) argued that the impulsiveness of many offenders would work against the threat of punishment. However, a few studies have found just the opposite, and offenders with low self-control or a "propensity" to crime were more susceptible to punishment (Pogarsky, 2007; Wright, Caspi, Moffitt & Paternoster, 2004). We must keep in mind, however, that there are many other offender characteristics that come into play. Their thinking tends to be concrete and oriented to the present situation, they have a childhood history of erratic and frequent punishment that shapes a certain level of tolerance for punishment, and some have biological-temperamental traits that make them unresponsive to punishment. Theories of psychopathy and antisocial personality hypothesize deficits in the physiological mechanisms underlying fear and anxiety (Eysenck, 1998; Hiatt & Newman, 2006; Lykken, 1995).

Inhibiting behavior requires judgments of the likelihood of certain outcomes. To the dismay of economic and rational choice theories of crime, offenders do not mimic computers. They do not always weigh the pros and cons of behavior carefully and accurately before making their choice (Wilson & Abrahamse, 1992). Studies of offenders show that they tend to underestimate the chances of being punished and overestimate the rewards of crime (Montmarquette & Nerlove, 1985; Nagin & Pogarsky, 2004; Piliavin et al., 1986). Finally, when we consider some of the developmental experiences of many offenders—abuse and neglect—where is the logic that more of the same will suppress antisocial behavior? For punishment to be effective, one of the necessary conditions is that it must be matched to characteristics of the offender. In our criminal justice system, a matching that depends on personal factors would violate the principles of fairness.

The Side Effects of Punishment

Even if we could replicate the conditions for effective punishment in the real world, we are still faced with what Skinner (1953:190) referred to as the "unfortunate by-products of punishment." Punishment may suppress behavior, but it can also lead to unintended and undesirable behaviors. A brief review of the "side effects" of punishment (Newsom, Favell & Rincover, 1983) should give us further reasons to consider non-punishment alternatives to deal with antisocial behavior.

Punishment is painful either physically, emotionally, or psychologically. It is the avoidance of pain that explains why punishment suppresses behavior. A painful stimulus, however, may have consequences other than suppressing a certain behavior. First of all, a painful stimulus of sufficient intensity may interfere with other *desirable* behaviors. For example, a severe beating suffered by a woman at the hands of her partner may prevent her from socializing with friends, going to work, and enjoying recreational activities.

Second, if intense punishment is coupled with a situation in which there is no escape, then there is the risk of developing "learned helplessness" (Seligman, 1975). Martin Seligman (1975) exposed dogs to frequent shocks in a cage that provided no opportunity to escape. After a number of trials, the dogs in the experimental group were then placed into another cage where a partition was low enough to permit them to jump to the other side and avoid the shocks. The dogs in the control group (no experience of unavoidable shock) quickly learned to jump over the partition and avoid further shocks. The dogs in the experimental group, however, whined and laid down in a corner, making no attempts to escape. They learned that there was nothing they could do to avoid the shocks. Learned helplessness has been used to explain human depression (Joiner & Wagner, 1995; Rehm, Wagner & Ivens-Tyndal, 2001), poor coping with stress (Mikulincer, 1994), and why battered women do not leave their partners (LaViolette & Barnett, 2000; Palker-Corell & Marcus, 2004).

The concept of learned helplessness highlights the importance of self-efficacy beliefs and cognitive attributions. When people are punished, they make attributions as to why they were punished. In the learned helplessness paradigm, the individual learns that he or she has no control over the environment. Whatever happens is attributed to fate. Fifty years ago, Miller (1958) hypothesized a belief in fate as a "focal concern" for delinquents. By attributing consequences to fate, taking responsibility for behavior is minimized. There are other attributions that can be triggered by punishment. One is to view antisocial behavior as inappropriate and that the punishment was deserved. This attribution, however, is dependent upon a commitment to prosocial values and respect for the law, a problematic area for many offenders.

If punishment is viewed as unfair and undeserving, then anger and hate toward the punisher or feelings of rejection may be elicited. These negative emotions may facilitate undesirable behaviors such as reflexive aggression toward the punisher or ignoring attempts at influence by the other (Church, 1963; McCord, 1997). Children who judge the disciplining techniques of parents as harsh tend to avoid parental contact, which further interferes with socialization efforts (Deater-Deckard & Dodge, 1997).

Vicarious learning is a highly important process. Bandura and Walters (1959) demonstrated that children may imitate the aggressive practices displayed by their parents. Watching parents and other authority figures (e.g., teachers) use physical punishment that is rewarded may provide learning opportunities for young children. By watching such models, children learn that using aggression to deal with offensive behavior is acceptable.

We have already seen from meta-analytic reviews that sanctions or punishments are associated with a small increase in criminal behavior. Perhaps, some of this increase in the undesirable behavior can be explained by the individual's tolerance for punishment, perception of the unfairness of punishment, and witnessing antisocial behavior (Piquero & Pogarsky, 2002). Another explanation of this increase in criminal behavior following punishment relates to the gambler's fallacy. The gambler's fallacy is, the belief that a string of bad luck will be followed by good luck. For the offender, it is saying "Yes, I have been caught the last few times, but next time I will get away with it." In a study by Pogarsky and Piquero (2003), college students were asked to decide whether they would take the chance and drive home after drinking or to leave the car at the bar. Prior to making this decision, the students were asked to imagine what side of the coin would show after it was flipped four times and always showed heads (the chances are 50/50). Approximately, 20 percent of the students said tails, endorsing a gambler's fallacy type of thinking. Endorsement of the gambler's fallacy was associated with the decision to drive, and the likelihood of using the gambler's fallacy was greatest among the most impulsive students. Although this effect has not been studied with offenders, it does raise some interesting ideas of how the higher-risk, life-course-persistent offender may think about punishment.

Psychology's Shift Away from Punishment

After reflecting upon the psychology of punishment, it seems that punishment creates more problems then it solves. In the 1960s and 1970s, punishment was widely studied, and laboratory experiments with animals showed that punishment can work (Leitenberg, 1976). With humans there were behavior modification studies that employed electric shock, pugnacious odors, and other physically aversive procedures on a variety of behaviors. Bedwetting in children, self-injurious behaviors among autistic persons, and even homosexual orientation were targeted. Antisocial behaviors such a pedophilic interest, sexual exhibitionism, and drug abuse were shocked or paired with noxious stimuli. Covert sensitization was taught to offenders by which they *imagined* negative consequences to their behavior (Cautela, 1970; see Resource Note 13.2 for an example).

Resource Note 13.2

Self-Directed Imagined Punishment: Covert Sensitization of Alcohol Abuse

Joseph Cautela (1970) developed a cognitive-behavioral intervention by which the therapist guides the client through imaginary scenes of aversive control over behavior. A behavior that needs to be suppressed is paired with thoughts of negative consequences. Association of the behavior with visualized punishment "sensitizes" the client to the negative consequences. The procedure is called *covert sensitization*, and it has been applied to a variety of behaviors, most notably alcohol abuse (Rimmele, Howard & Hilfrink, 1995) and sexual deviance (Perkins, 1991, 1993). The following is an example of covert sensitization with an alcoholic:

Therapist: "You are walking into a bar. You decide to have a glass of beer. You are now walking toward the bar. As you are approaching the bar you have a funny feeling in the pit of your stomach. Your stomach feels all queasy and nauseous. Some liquid comes up your throat, and it is very sour. You try to swallow it back down, but as you do this, food particles start coming up your throat to your mouth. You are now reaching the bar and you order a beer. As the bartender is pouring the beer, puke comes into your mouth . . . As soon as your hand touches the glass, you can't hold it down any longer. You have to open your mouth and puke. It goes all over your hand; all over the glass and the beer. You can see it floating around in the beer . . ." (Cautela, 1970:37).

The therapist instructs the client to rehearse the covert sensitization scenes until the imagery is automatic. The client is then encouraged to use the procedure when tempted to drink. Today, covert desensitization is sometimes used in cognitive-behavioral therapies but is rarely used as the sole therapeutic technique.

It soon became apparent to psychologists that if punishment was to be used, it had to be used sparingly and always coupled with the reinforcement of prosocial behavior. In addition, consequences that are particularly effective with people tend to be interpersonal in nature. Hunt and Azrin (1973) provide an excellent illustration of combining interpersonal punishment (time out) with reinforcement (this study is described in more detail in Chapter 9). The families and employers of alcoholics, as well as other community agents, were taught to systematically reinforce behaviors incompatible with drinking and ignore or discourage behaviors associated with alcohol abuse. As a result the experimental group spent less time drinking (14%) than the comparison group (79%).

Experimental and applied studies over the years have shown a shift in emphasis from punishing undesirable behavior to reinforcing desirable behavior that is incompatible with the target behavior. Reinforcement, compared to punishment, has two important advantages. First, only reinforcement can shape new behaviors; punishment only suppresses existing behavior. For offender populations with limited prosocial skills, all the punishment in the world will not teach them new skills. Second, reinforcement procedures avoid the obvious ethical and professional dilemmas associated with purposefully inflicting pain. We have learned that there are better ways to change behavior than to use punishment.

Summary on Punishment

A general policy of punishment is wrought with difficulties. Yet, we find it difficult to abandon belief in the efficacy of punishment. We are taught from childhood that punishment works. Years of socialization and anecdotes of how fear of punishment has "turned people around" are difficult to ignore. Add to this the political currency of "get tough" rhetoric and it seems we have little option but to punish.

We are faced with a need to discourage inappropriate behaviors and express dissatisfaction with violation of law. Punishing to express disapproval of antisocial behavior is one thing; punishing to deter is another matter. Scholars aware of the psychology of punishment have noted that the necessary conditions for effective punishment are virtually impossible to meet for the criminal justice system (McCord, 1999; Moffitt, 1983; Wilson & Abrahamse, 1992). Police cannot be everywhere to ensure the certainty of detection, the courts cannot pass sentence quickly enough, and correctional officials have difficulties ensuring adequate supervision and monitoring.

What many criminal justice policies fail to consider is that there are other ways of eliminating antisocial behavior. Increasing the rewards associated with prosocial behavior would make the rewards associated with crime less attractive. Rewarding prosocial behavior would also increase the costs of criminal behavior because there would be more to lose. A multipronged attack involving a shifting of the rewards and costs for both criminal and prosocial behavior rather than a one-sided attack would be more effective. As we saw earlier, offender rehabilitation programs that teach and reward prosocial behaviors can achieve the desired effect.

An Alternative to Retribution: Restorative Justice

Not everyone has been pleased with the "get tough" movement. Rehabilitationists (like ourselves) have continued to research and build knowledge around the effectiveness of offender treatment. Others felt that the focus on offenders, whether to rehabilitate or punish, ignored a critical piece in the puzzle of crime: the victim. Victims were dissatisfied with the criminal justice system for many reasons. They felt insignificant in the criminal justice process (i.e., reduced mainly to providing witness testimony) and ignored in the delivery of services (i.e., offenders received treatment services while victims had to cope on their own). In the 1980s, victims became better organized and acquired a political voice. Small improvements were made in service delivery to victims (e.g., women's shelters, trauma counseling). Larger gains, however, were made in the political arena in terms of influencing legislative changes (e.g., more severe sentences, victim rights legislation).

The victim movement was influential in ensuring that offenders received their just deserts. This usually translated into "getting tough." The dominant position among many victim advocacy groups was that the criminal justice system was too soft on offenders and that harsher penalties were needed to deliver justice for the harm suffered by victims. However, others saw things differently. In contrast to the just deserts and punitive perspectives was the view that the hurts need to be healed. This healing process required a collaboration among offenders, victims, and the community to correct the wrongs committed by offenders. The concepts of healing, collaboration, and making amends are central to *restorative justice*. The introduction of restorative justice into the criminal justice system has been influenced by two traditions: (1) Judeo-Christian notions of justice (with an emphasis on understanding and forgiveness as opposed to the retributive "eye-for-an-eye") and (2) Aboriginal/Indian approaches to justice.

The first restorative justice program can be traced to the small town of Kitchener, Ontario. In 1974, a probation officer with strong ties to the Mennonite church asked a judge to delay the sentencing of two adolescents convicted of vandalism while he tried something different (Peachy, 1989). He proposed to the judge that he would take the teenagers to meet their victims and offer to make amends. The youths would benefit by understanding how their behavior affected the victims, and the victims would have the opportunity to say what they needed to make things right. Surprisingly, most of the victims asked for restitution and not incarceration or probation. As for the young offenders, they reported a better understanding of the harm that they caused. From this experiment grew what are called Victim-Offender Reconciliation Programs (VORPs).

Before we proceed further, we want to be clear that there is controversy over what exactly is restorative justice. Is it a program with a certain expected outcome or a process, is it punitive or an alternative to punishment, is it complimentary to the traditional criminal justice processing or a whole new paradigm of justice (Gavrielides, 2008)? Our interest in restorative justice is to examine how it contributes to our understanding of criminal behavior through planned intervention. Thus, we use the term "program" to connote our interest in reducing recidivism outcomes.

Restorative justice programs such as VORP have a number of characteristics. First of all, crime is seen as a violation of interpersonal relationships. Second, all who are harmed, offender included, must take responsibility for "making right the wrong." This requires a dialogue between offender and victim wherein they discuss how the crime has affected them, preferably through face-to-face meetings. The offender has the opportunity to make amends and offer an apology. The victim has the chance to tell the offender how he or she has been affected by the crime and what is needed to heal the pain. Perhaps the victim may even forgive the offender, although this is not a necessary component. Finally, the victim and offender, sometimes with the support of community members, discuss how each of them can contribute to alleviating the harm created from the crime.

The views of justice from indigenous peoples overlap considerably with the views of restorative justice advocates. Both groups see crime as a community problem with the responsibility for a solution resting within the community (Zion & Yazzie, 2006). Crime hurts many people, and punishing the offender does not make the hurt go away for the victim and others who have been affected by the crime. Rather, a healing and a restoration of relationships are needed. Family group conferences (FGCs) and sentencing/peacemaking circles are two examples of restorative justice practices that have been influenced by aboriginal ideas of justice. FGCs began in New Zealand (Maxwell, Morris & Hayes, 2006). In an FGC, juvenile offenders and their parent(s) meet their victim(s) and any other interested member(s) of the community. In the presence of a mediator they discuss how best to deal with the hurts caused by the crime and to reintegrate the offender in the community. Sentencing circles started in the Yukon Territory of Canada, a region where the majority of the population is aboriginal (Stuart, 1996; Stuart & Pranis, 2006). In the presence of a judge, everyone who is affected by the crime works together in developing an appropriate response to the offender's antisocial behavior. The recommendations that result from an FGC or a sentencing circle may include punishment, but the emphasis is on healing and encouraging everyone who is affected by the crime to create a "satisfying" justice.

Offender responsibility and victim participation in resolving conflict are core to restorative justice. This said, however, there is controversy about how much victim involvement is required in order for a program to be called a restorative justice program (Braithwaite, 1999; Daly, 2006a; McCold, 2000; Sullivan & Tifft, 2005). Programs such as VORP, family group counseling, and sentencing circles are unambiguous restorative justice practices. On the other hand, there are programs in which there is little, if any, direct contact between the victim and the offender and agreements are brokered through an intermediary (Zehr & Mika, 1998). In these cases, the victim may agree to an offer of restitution (either financial or through community service) or to a written apology. Should court-ordered restitution or community service be considered "restorative" for the offender even though the victim provided no input?

454 The Psychology of Criminal Conduct

These are but two debatable illustrations of what could be considered restorative justice practices.

Restorative justice programs and practices exist in North America, Australia, New Zealand, Europe, and parts of Asia and Africa (McCold, 2006). Restorative justice principles are also exerting an influence on legislative policy and the criminal justice system. In New Zealand, the Children, Young Persons, and Their Families Act prevents the court from making a decision until a family group conference is held. Governmental agencies in Canada and the United States have initiated a dialogue on how restorative justice principles can be introduced into criminal law (Kurki, 1999; Lightfoot & Umbreit, 2004; Llewellyn & Hawse, 1999). Finally, we have seen various Truth and Reconciliation Commissions being formed to deal with such issues as human rights abuses during a period of apartheid in South Africa (Villa-Valencia, 1999) and abuses in residential schools in Canada (Indian and Northern Affairs Canada, 2008).

Restorative justice programs have proliferated, but the research has not kept up with developments. Many of the evaluations have been methodologically weak, are largely descriptive of processes, and the outcomes measured tend to deal with the participants' satisfaction with the process. In general, victims and offenders report being pleased with the process and the resolution to the conflict (Sherman & Strang, 2007; Strang, Sherman, Angel, Woods et al., 2006; Umbreit, 1995). For example, in one study, 86 percent of the offenders and 88 percent of the parents of the offenders expressed satisfaction, whereas 51 percent of the victims who participated in a family group conference were satisfied with the results (Morris & Maxwell, 1998). In a meta-analysis of 13 studies, the average effect size for victim satisfaction was .19 and effect sizes ranged as high as .44 (Latimer, Dowden & Muise, 2005).

Interpreting the results from evaluation studies is difficult because of the significant attrition rates found in many restorative justice programs. Table 13.2 summarizes the participation rates in 14 studies that attempted to bring victims and offenders together for face-to-face meetings. It is clear from the table that not all victims want to meet their offender. Thus, the high levels of satisfaction could be due to a subject selection factor. Not shown in the table is the fact that the majority of offenders have committed nonviolent crimes (about 85%; Bonta, Jesseman, Rugge & Cormier, 2006). Most programs typically exclude sex offenders, domestic violence cases, and other serious crimes, although there are exceptions (Acker, 2006; Daly, 2006b; Rugge, Bonta & Wallace-Capretta, 2005; Wilson & Picheca, 2005). For example, Mark Umbreit and Betty Voss (2000) presented two case studies in which surviving family members met the offenders who killed one of their family members. The two offenders were on death row.

Restorative justice is not only about repairing the harm done to the victim. Helping the offender address the factors that led to the conflict in the first place can contribute to the offender's restoration. Although some may not agree that recidivism is an important outcome measure by which to judge the value of a restorative justice program (Robinson & Shapland, 2008), many see enhanced public safety as an important goal (Bazemore, 1996; Bonta et al., 2006; Zehr & Mika, 1998). Bringing offenders to accept responsibility for their actions and repairing the harm to the satisfaction of all parties are the major goals. In addition, community involvement in the restoration process facilitates the acceptance and reintegration of the offender into the community.

We adopt the position that if restorative justice is to play more than a marginal role in the current criminal justice system, then demonstrating an effect on recidivism is vital. Since the fourth edition of this book, there have been more evaluations of restorative justice programs, many of which have involved very large samples (mostly from Australia and the United Kingdom). Table 13.3 provides a further update of our meta-analytic summary of restorative justice evaluations. To be included in the meta-analysis, a study must include a comparison group and must measure recidivism upon post-program completion. The average r was .07, representing an overall reduction in recidivism of 7 percent. This general finding is almost identical to that found in an independent review by Jeff Latimer and his colleagues (Latimer, Dowden & Muise, 2005). In

Table 13.2
Participation in Victim-Offender Meetings

Study	Referred(n)	Meeting(%)	Sample
Bergseth & Bouffard (2007)	164	49	youth
Bonta et al. (1983)	139	4	adult
Bonta, Wallace-Capretta & Rooney (1998)	243	10	adult
Crime & Justice Research Centre (2005)	577	36	adult
Coates & Gehm (1988)	196	50	youth/adult
Gehm (1990)	535	47	youth/adult
Marshall & Merry (1990)			
a) police-based	211	47	youth
b) court-based	162	51	adult
Maxwell & Morris (1994)	200	46	youth
McCold & Wachtel (1998)	189	43	youth
Nuffield (1997)	228	35	adult
Nugent & Paddock (1995)	296	65	youth
Perry, Lajeunesse & Woods (1987)	1021	46	adult
Umbreit (1995)	4445	39	youth/adult
Umbreit & Coates (1992)	2799	40	youth
Umbreit (1988)	179	54	youth
Umbreit & Roberts (1996)			
a) Coventry	276	13	youth/adult
b) Leeds	535	8	youth/adult
Wilcox et al. (2004)	13980	14	youth/adult

addition, our findings with respect to youths specifically are smaller than that reported by Bradshaw and Roseborough (r = .13; 2005), but our review includes more comparisons (k = 55 vs. k = 19) with a much larger sample size (n = 39,707 vs. n = 11,950).

The confidence interval (CI) in Table 13.3 gives the range at which the true value may lie with 95 percent certainty (the effect size is an *estimate* of the true value). If the confidence interval includes zero, then there is a 95 percent chance that there is no association with recidivism. Given the large sample size, the CI is extremely narrow. The average effect size of .07 across studies is not a particularly impressive result, and it is slightly smaller than providing any type of human service (r = .10). Furthermore, the programs that had an undeniably restorative component to them (i.e., VORPs and FGCs) fared no better than programs that had the more mundane elements of restorative justice (restitution, community service), raising the question of what restorative component contributes to reduced recidivism.

Though it is not shown in the table, there is considerable variability in effect sizes among the individual studies, suggesting that under certain conditions restorative justice may be associated with significant reductions in recidivism. Bonta and his colleagues (Bonta, Wallace-Capretta, Rooney & McAnoy, 2002) suggested that offender treatment delivered within a restorative justice context may work especially well in reducing recidivism. They used a quasi-experimental research design to evaluate a restorative justice program intended to divert offenders from prison and into the community. Program staff contacted victims and encouraged them to meet the offenders in order to develop a restorative plan for the court. Although only 14 percent of the victims agreed to face-to-face meetings, many victims contributed to the plan through the intermediary efforts of the staff.

Staff also helped offenders to identify their needs and obtain treatment services. More than 90 percent of the offenders participated in a treatment

Table 13.3
Meta-Analytic Results from a Review of Restorative Justice Programs

Type of Program	n	k	r	CI
All programs	25,771	67	.07	.06 – .08
Juvenile	21,766	50	.06	.05 – .07
Adult	3,507	16	.09	.06 – .12
VORP	6,949	40	.08	.06 – .10
Restitution	23,934	55	.08	.07 – .09
Community Service	23,252	57	.07	.06 – .08
FGC	3,741	16	.09	.06 – .12

Notes: n = total sample size; k = number of effect sizes; CI = 95% confidence interval; VORP = victim-offender reconciliation program; FGC = family group conference.

program. The reconviction rate for the restorative justice offenders at one year was 15.3 percent, and the rate was 37.5 percent for a matched group of probationers ($r = .25$). As the follow-up period increased, the differences in recidivism rates between the two groups also increased. At three years, the restorative justice participants had a recidivism rate of 34.7 percent, while the probationers had a recidivism rate of 66.1 percent ($r = .31$).

Drawing on the Carleton University data set, Andrews and Dowden (2007) identified 22 restorative justice studies conducted prior to 1998 (you can see the dramatic increase in studies when one compares their analysis to the one reported in Table 13.3). Eight studies had a treatment element that could be coded according to adherence to the RNR principles. With zero adherence, the mean effect of restorative programming was .02 (k = 14). With adherence to one principle, the mean effect size rose to .14 (k = 4); with adherence to two principles, it was .16 (k =3); and finally, and there was only one study, the mean effect size was .35 with adherence to all of the RNR principles. In the Bonta et al. (2002) study, appropriate treatment (i.e., adherence to all three principles) combined with restorative justice was $r = .31$). This compares very favorably to inappropriate treatments in restorative justice programs (average $r = .01$ for six programs; Bonta et al., 2006).

Theoretically, why should we expect restorative justice by itself to impact on criminal behavior? Besides possibly providing appropriate treatment to address offender needs, there are a number of other possible mechanisms associated with restorative justice principles that have been suggested to impact on reoffending. Understanding the impact of a crime on a victim may challenge an offender's rationalizations for crime. The forgiving, nonpunitive context of the victim-offender encounter may nourish a more prosocial attitude. When community members participate in a restorative justice process, they may act as an informal support system providing concrete assistance in acquiring prosocial behaviors and thus motivate the offender to change (Bazemore, Nissen & Dooley, 2000; Day, Gerace, Wilson & Howells, 2008; de Beus & Rodriquez, 2007). Increased empathy for the victim may act to inhibit hurtful behaviors. Unfortunately, evaluators of restorative justice program have done little to examine the impact of restorative justice on these potential intermediary targets. In one of the few studies on this issue, Jackson (2009) found no changes on measures of guilt, shame, or empathy among offenders exposed to victims describing the impact of crime on their lives but did find increased acceptance of responsibility only for nonviolent female offenders—violent female offenders actually got worse after exposure to victims (Jackson, Lucas & Blackburn, 2009). At this point, however, the mechanisms described are hypotheses that still need to be tested.

Worth Remembering

1. "Getting tough" has failed miserably in achieving the goals of fairness, cost-effectiveness, and enhancing public safety.

   Mandatory sentences, three-strikes, and harsher sentences have affected minorities disproportionately and at enormous costs. The costs are measured not only in monetary terms but also in terms of social consequences. In terms of deterrence, "getting tough" does not explain the reduction in crime rates seen over the past decade, and it has had no impact on offender recidivism. Despite what politicians think the public wants, when given the complete picture, most public opinion surveys show people are open to less punitive interventions.

2. The psychology of punishment shows that punishment will only "work" under very specific conditions, conditions that the criminal justice system cannot replicate.

   Laboratory studies of punishment clearly show that for punishment to be effective it must follow the behavior with certainty and immediacy and at the right intensity. In the real world, laboratory conditions are impossible. Furthermore, punishment has many undesirable "side effects" that are counterproductive in the suppression of antisocial behavior.

3. Restorative justice, with the inclusion of appropriate treatment, may offer a viable alternative to "get tough" approaches in reducing crime.

   We are seeing a shift away from an obsession with punishing offenders to more humane approaches for dealing with offenders. The growing influence of restorative justice and renewed interest in treatment reflect a growing dissatisfaction with the adversarial, punitive, offender orientation of the present justice system. How far the influence of restorative justice will reach remains to be seen. Offender rehabilitation, however, already has made tremendous inroads and holds a promising future.

Recommended Readings

For a sobering and lively review of the "get tough" approach and its consequences, we recommend Michael Tonry's (2004) *Thinking about Crime: Sense and Sensibility in American Penal Culture*. This book is an easy read and requires little criminal justice background. Also highly recommended is Tonry's (2009) provocative review of America's punishment policy in *Punishment & Society*, in which he blames such factors as the "paranoid style" of American politics for the problem. For a more academic analysis, Todd Clear's (1994) *Harm in American Penology: Offenders, Victims and their Communities* is worth a read. More specific "get tough" approaches are nicely reviewed by Doris MacKenzie and Gaylene Armstrong's (2004) *Correctional Boot Camps: Military Basic Training or a Model for Corrections?* and Finckenauer and colleagues' (1999) *Scared Straight: The Panacea Phenomenon Revisited*.

Those interested in the psychology of punishment should access Azrin and Holz's chapter in W.K. Honig's 1966 classic text, *Operant Behavior: Areas of Research and Application*. More recent reviews can be found in most general introductory psychology textbooks.

The literature on restorative justice has exploded over the past few years. For an introduction intended for the general reader, see Dennis Sullivan and Larry Tifft's (2005) *Restorative Justice: Healing the Foundations of Our Everyday Lives*. For a more academic treatment and extensive review, we suggest the edited readings in *The Handbook of Restorative Justice* (2005) by Dennis Sullivan and Larry Tifft. *Restoring Justice: An Introduction to Restorative Justice* (2010), by Daniel W. Van Ness and Karen Heetderks Strong, offers a clear explanation of the restorative justice movement.

Chapter 14

Criminal Subtypes:
From the Common to the Exceptional

In this chapter, we look at different "types" of offenders. We use the word "type" with some hesitation because the word conveys the idea of clearly defined categories with little or no overlap. However, many offenders do not neatly fit into any one category. In fact, very few offenders specialize in only one type of crime. Sex offenders commit non-sexual crimes, and male batterers assault others who are unrelated to them. The versatility of criminal offenders is illustrated in a survey of more than 2,000 male inmates from Australian prisons. Makkai and Payne (2005) found only 26 percent of the offenders reporting having committed just one offense type. Nevertheless, many criminals do show a preference for certain antisocial acts that allow us to make rough categorizations. For example, a sex offender is more likely to recidivate with another sexual offense compared to a nonsexual offender. These preferences permit us to use word "subtypes" in the title of this chapter.

Sometimes scholars begin with dissecting the criterion behavior, or the criminal act, and developing theories to explain the offense. Thus, there are theories of white-collar crime, vandalism, and serial killers. Instead of emphasizing these "mini-theories," we take the stance that much can be learned from a more comprehensive theoretical base and that the correlates of general criminal behavior show remarkable similarities for specific forms of criminal deviance. We will move from the relatively common groups among offender populations (male batterers) to the more infrequent (sex offenders) and then to the rare (stalkers, serial killers). We call the latter group "exceptional" because they truly distinguish themselves from the mainstream by their bizarre and violent behavior. On the face of it, these criminal subtypes may appear to represent extreme groups with little in common. However, sometimes there are more similarities than there are differences.

Domestic Violence Against Women

Surveys in the United States and Canada reveal a disturbing picture of the prevalence and incidence of violence within families. In 2007, more than a half million American women reported being violently victimized by intimates (Rand, 2008). Victimization includes murders (1,202 murders were attributable to intimate partners; Fox & Zawitz, 2004), rape (43% of sexual assaults on women were committed by a present or former intimate; Tjaden & Thoennes, 2006), and physical assault (about 9% of violent victimization; Smith et al., 2002). In Canada, 15 percent of all violent crime reported to the police was for spousal violence, with 83 percent of the victims being women (Bressan, 2008). Although men are also physically assaulted by their female partners (Field & Caetano, 2005; Langhinrichsen-Rohling, 2005), men cause more serious injury (Archer, 2000; Dutton, Nicholls & Spidel, 2005; Kessler et al., 2001). Intimate violence is also prevalent among same-sex couples (McClennen, 2005), but because the vast majority of victims are women, our discussion will focus on male batterers.

Studying family violence is important for a number of reasons. First, we are interested in learning what we can do to decrease the victimization within these families. The woman who is abused by her partner is not only at risk for her own personal safety (Keller & Wagner-Steh, 2005) but also for the safety of her children. A number of studies indicate that someone who is violent toward a spouse is also likely to be violent toward children (Ehrensaft et al., 2003; Osofsky, 2003; Ross, 1996). Second, both the women and the children who witness the suffering are more likely to experience emotional, psychological, and behavioral problems (Kitzman et al., 2003; McCloskey, Figueredo & Koss, 1995; Smith Stover, 2005). Two meta-analytic reviews found that the average effect size for exposure to domestic violence and children's emotional and behavioral problems was in the neighborhood of $r = .25$ (Evans, Davies & DiLillio, 2008; Wolfe et al., 2003).

Third, we need to know who are the high-risk abusers. The accurate identification of violent men is needed to inform police and other social agents who are empowered to remove aggressors for the protection of other family members. Because the majority of women, for various reasons, find it difficult to leave abusive relationships (Zlotnick, Johnson & Kohn, 2006), they are at risk for revictimization. Social service providers also require knowledge of effective interventions for male batterers. Even when a woman leaves an abusive partner, the violence may continue with another woman as the victim. Depending upon the follow-up and the risk level of the offender, estimates of the domestic violence recidivism have ranged from 16 percent (Wooldredge & Thistlethwaite, 2005) to as high as 60 and 80 percent (Klein & Tobin, 2008; Smith Stover, 2005).

Finally, understanding family violence is important for the primary prevention of future violence. Although not conclusive, there is research suggesting that children who experienced and witnessed family violence have an increased risk of growing up to be violent in both intimate and general interpersonal relationships (Kruttschnitt & Dornfeld, 1993; Smith Stover, 2005; Straus & Kantor, 1994; Widom, 1989). Furthermore, childhood aggression may also be predictive of spousal violence. The most persuasive study in this regard comes from the Concordia Longitudinal Risk Project (Temcheff, Serbin, Martin-Storey, Stack et al., 2008). More than 1,700 inner-city children from Montreal, Canada, were followed over a 30-year span. The investigators found that aggressive behavior in childhood predicted self-reported spousal violence in adulthood ($r = .14$).

In this section, we pose the following questions derived from a PCC:

1. Are men who commit violence against their partners similar to general offenders?

2. What are the effective interventions for those who assault their spouses?

Men Who Batter: Are They Made from the Same Cloth as Regular Criminals?

Considering the prevalence of spousal violence, until very recently, it is surprising how little research has been devoted to identifying risk factors for spousal abuse. When we contrast this body of research to the hundreds of studies with general criminal offenders, it is truly astounding how little has been done. Yet, research into identifying the risk factors for re-abuse is important not only for guiding intervention but also for helping to answer the question of whether male batterers are all that different from general criminal offenders. The research on risk factors comes from three sources: (1) surveys of spousal violence, (2) specific studies of conflictual relationships, and (3) the development and validation of actuarial risk measures.

Risk Factors from Surveys. Some surveys ask men to report on their behavior in domestic situations; other surveys ask victims to describe the characteristics of their assailants. From these surveys, it is possible to construct a list of potential risk factors. We remind the reader that surveys use cross-sectional research designs (i.e., abusers are compared to nonabusers) and not longitudinal designs that speak to the predictive validity of certain variables. An example of this approach is found in the Canadian Violence Against Women Survey (Lenton, 1995). Patriarchal values (jealousy and control over the women) and witnessing the father abuse the mother were significantly correlated with intimate partner abuse, but employment, income level, and education bore no relationship with spousal violence.

Risk Factors from the Study of Conflictual Relationships. Pan, Neidig, and O'Leary (1994) studied the marital relationships among more than

14,000 army personnel from 38 bases across the United States. First of all, nearly 70 percent of the respondents reported no physical aggression against their spouse. For the remainder, 24.4 percent reported "mild" physical aggression (e.g., slapped or threw something), and 5.6 percent reported "severe" aggressive acts (e.g., choked or used a knife on the spouse). The following five risk factors were identified:

1. Marital distress
2. Alcohol/other drug abuse
3. Depressive symptomatology
4. Age (being younger)
5. Income (lower)

Note that four of the five factors are also risk factors for general criminal behavior. The exception is depression. However, depression as a risk factor for domestic violence is not always found (Cattaneo & Goodman, 2005). Furthermore, Pan and colleagues (1994) were able to rank order the risk factors, finding that marital distress and alcohol abuse were more important than income (a rank ordering consistent with the general offender risk literature). Not surprisingly, in a recent meta-analysis of studies on the relationship between marital distress and partner violence, marital distress evidenced a sizeable mean r of .27 (k = 37; Stith, Green, Smith & Ward, 2008).

Alcohol abuse appears to be a greater risk factor in partner abuse than in general offending (Finney, 2004; O'Leary, Malone & Tyree, 1994). In a carefully controlled longitudinal study, William Fals-Stewart (2003) asked male batterers and their partners to keep a diary of drinking and aggressive episodes over a period of 15 months. He found that on days when the men drank, the likelihood of partner assault was eight times greater than on days when there was no drinking. Furthermore, the probability of *severe* aggression was 11 times higher on drinking days. The effect of drinking on intimate partner violence was moderated by risk as assessed by the presence of antisocial personality disorder (APD; Fals-Stewart, Leonard & Birchler, 2005). Drinking increased the risk of severe aggression for all the men in the study, but the increase was *greater* for men with APD.

Continuing to build our case that male batterers are very similar to regular criminal offenders, we describe a study by Andrew Klein (1996). Klein reviewed domestic violence cases before a *civil* court, with 90 percent of the complaints coming from the victims (police intervention accounted for the rest). Yet, 80 percent of the men had a prior criminal record with, on average, six prior court appearances that included offenses as serious as murder. During a two-year follow-up, 56.4 percent of the men were rearrested for a nondomestic crime; the rearrest rate for spousal assault was 34 percent. Two offender characteristics predicted new abuse: age and prior criminal history. Klein's (1996) major conclusion was that male batterers "look like criminals, act like criminals, and re-abuse like criminals" (p. 207). In another study, Klein and Tobin (2008) followed 342 batterers over a nine-year period. The correlation between rearrest for a domestic and a nondomestic incident was .34 (Klein & Tobin, 2008). More importantly, *all* the criminal history factors that predicted nonabuse arrests also predicted arrests for spousal abuse. The gap between male batterers and general offenders appears relatively narrow (Dutton & Hart, 1992; Kessler et al., 2001; Ramirez, 2005).

A consistent finding is that some form of an antisocial personality pattern is common among male batterers (Dutton & Hart, 1992; Hanson et al., 1997; Hilton & Harris, 2005; Huss & Langhinrichsen-Rohling, 2000; Magdol et al., 1997). However, some researchers report that it is the disturbed affect of the antisocial personality pattern that may be particularly important for understanding the male batterer (Hotzworth-Munroe & Mehan, 2004). For example, Dutton (1995, 2008) has proposed a borderline or "abusive" personality described as impulsive, quick to anger, a lack of "emotional intelligence" (as a probation officer once described to one of us—a "clueless Romeo"), and with such an intense fear of being abandoned that he uses violence to maintain control over the relationship. Similarly, Swogger, Walsh, and Kosson (2007) also found affect disturbance along with impulsivity to distinguish the batterer from the nonabusive offender.

The role of attitudes toward women is salient in the literature on male batterers. Social surveys frequently identify patriarchal values as a risk factor (Gilchrest et al., 2003; Hanson et al., 1997; Holtzworth-Monroe & Stuart, 1994). However, Dutton (2008) questions the relevance of such values, noting that in a large survey of men only 2 percent endorsed the statement "It's O.K. to hit your wife to keep her in line." Whether other attitudes toward women and violence demonstrate a relationship remains to be seen. Minimizing the seriousness of an assault or outright denial is frequent among male batterers, but this has not shown predictive validity (Henning & Holdford, 2006). Clearly, further research is needed on the role of attitudes in domestic violence.

Lastly, there is a gradual recognition that social support is an important risk factor. As the reader may observe, we are covering the Big Four. In fact, a number of social learning models have been applied to understanding the male batterer. For example, Holtzworth-Munroe and Gregory Stuart's (1994) model describes "distal correlates" (genetics, childhood family, and peer experiences) and "proximal correlates" (attitudes, impulsivity, attachment to others). In a direct test of social learning theory, Deborah Reitzel-Jaffe and David Wolfe (2001) administered a battery of measures to 611 male university students. The two best predictors of partner abuse were negative attitudes toward women and association with peers who shared similar beliefs and who were abusive in their relationships.

Actuarial Risk Scales for Intimate Partner Abuse. Murray Straus (1996) was perhaps the first to present an objective type of "checklist" for identifying high-risk male batterers. The checklist included items that we know are reliable predictors of criminal behavior (e.g., drug abuse, history of violence, rationalizations for abuse). However, the checklist was silent on social supports for the behavior and only indirectly tapped personality factors ("extreme dominance," "extreme jealousy"). Other experts in the area have presented similar lists based upon their reviews of the literature (Dutton & Kropp, 2000; Saunders, 1995; Thompson, Saltzman & Johnson, 2001). However, it is only recently that these "lists" have been formalized into objective assessment instruments.

Over the past decade there has been a significant growth in the number of actuarial risk scales specifically developed to predict domestic violence (e.g., Danger Assessment Scale, DAS: Goodman, Dutton & Bennett, 2000; B-SAFER: Au, Cheung, Kropp et al., 2008; Spousal Assault Risk Assessment, SARA: Kropp et al., 1995). The Ontario Domestic Assault Risk Assessment (ODARA) appears promising. The ODARA is a 13-item scale sampling historical and dynamic items (Hilton et al., 2004). It is noteworthy that a number of items are indicators of general criminal behavior (e.g., "has a prior nondomestic assault" and "offender is violent outside of the home"). A study of two samples of men (total of 589) with a follow-up of more than four years found that scores on the ODARA predicted new assaults and the severity of new assaults. The AUC for the developmental sample was .77, and it was .72 for the cross-validation sample. However, a new study of the ODARA found that the predictive validity estimates had significantly decreased (AUCs of .65 to .67 in two samples). This led the researchers to add the PCL-R to the ODARA, producing the Domestic Violence Risk Appraisal Guide (DVRAG; Hilton et al., 2008), but this only led to a small increase in AUC (.70 and .71).

Finally, we offer a few comments on the use of actuarial risk instruments validated on general offenders and applied to male batterers. A number of researchers have taken general offender risk instruments and tested them in the prediction of partner abuse (e.g., Bourgon & Bonta, 2004; Hanson & Wallace-Capretta, 2000; Rooney & Hanson, 2001). In a meta-analysis of risk instruments for male batterers, there were no significant differences in the predictive validities of risk scales developed specifically for partner abuse and scales for general offending (Hanson, Helmus & Bourgon, 2007; average correlations of .20 and .26 with overlapping confidence intervals). The findings from the Hanson et al. (2007) meta-analysis further reinforce the similarities between male batterers and general offenders.

Risk assessment research in the area of spousal assault is still in its early stages (Kropp, 2004). We see progress in this area as important for laying the foundation for effective interventions and the protection of women. At different points in this text, we have argued that effective rehabilitation programs begin with reliable assessments of risk and criminogenic needs. Effective programs are those that follow the risk, need, and responsivity principles. Without risk/need assessments, the effectiveness of treatment becomes less likely. As we turn to the treatment literature on men who assault their partners, and knowing that the field lacks systematic risk/need assessment, we prepare ourselves to find relatively few demonstrations of effective interventions.

Treatment of Male Batterers

In 1984, Lawrence Sherman and Richard Berk conducted a study in which police who responded to calls of domestic disputes were randomly assigned to one of the following three conditions: (1) arrest the suspect, (2) remove the offender from the home for eight hours, or (3) advise the offender and victim to seek help. A six-month follow-up found a lower re-abuse rate for the arrest condition (13%, according to police data). The rate was 26 percent for the removal from the home condition and 18 percent for providing advice. Similar differences in favor of the arrest condition were found when victim reports of re-abuse were used. Within a few years, a number of states had passed mandatory arrest legislation in domestic violence incidents, and now approximately 76 percent of police forces in the United States have mandatory arrest policies (Eitle, 2005).

Sherman and Berk's (1984) findings run counter to our meta-analysis of the offender rehabilitation literature, in which we found that sanctions did not decrease recidivism but actually demonstrated small increases in recidivism. Could it be that "getting tough" for male batterers was the exception to the rule? The beauty of meta-analysis is that it reminds us that no one study can define or explain a phenomenon. Many studies are needed, and replication is key to good science. There have been five published replications of the Minneapolis Domestic Violence Experiment. All of the studies used randomized assignment, all had arrest as one of their conditions, and all had sample sizes large enough so that interaction effects could be evaluated (Maxwell, Garner & Fagan, 2001). The findings from the replications were mixed, leading Schmidt and Sherman (1996) to conclude that the results justified repealing mandatory arrest laws.

As we noted in Chapter 13, giving up on punishment does not come easily. Researchers searched for something in the mandatory arrest experiments to show that getting tough worked. Early reports were that arrest "worked" for employed male batterers. Apparently, employed assaulters have a "stake in conformity" and, therefore, have much to lose by being arrested (Thistlethwaite, Wooldredge & Gibbs, 1998). However, replications were spotty (Wooldredge & Thistlethwaite, 2005), perhaps due to the fact that high-risk offenders with a low "stake in conformity" tend to drop out of batterer treatment programs (Daly & Pelowski, 2000).

Male batterers may be arrested but not necessarily prosecuted. Consequently, a number of jurisdictions have introduced "no drop" prosecution policies. Evaluations of mandatory prosecution policies have reported a slight decrease in recidivism but at the cost of huge court backlogs and victim dissatisfaction with the process (Davis, Smith & Nickles, 1998). In situations in which there is no mandatory prosecution policy, more than one-half of all charges are dropped—usually because the victim fails to appear in court (Ventura & Davis, 2005; Wooldredge & Thistlethwaite, 2005). Comparisons of the outcomes for cases that are dismissed and cases resulting in a conviction find a small decrease in recidivism among those resulting in a conviction (Ventura & Davis, 2005). However, these results may be explained by the extreme group comparison design (conviction vs. dismissal) that maximizes the chances of finding differences. In Wooldredge and Thistlethwaite's (2005) study, a probation disposition was associated with reduced recidivism, but a jail sentence followed by probation led to increased recidivism.

For the most part, getting tough with male batterers may bring temporary relief and safety for the women, but it does not lead to long-term change in the offender (Hilton, Harris & Rice, 2007; Klein & Tobin, 2008). Neither specialized probation supervision (Klein & Crowe, 2008) nor specialized courts that deal with domestic violence cases have demonstrated increased victim safety (Rempel, Labriola & Davis, 2008; Visher, Harrell, Newmark & Yahner, 2008). This should not be surprising, given that criminal justice sanctions do not address the criminogenic needs of male batterers. Although mandatory arrest and similar policies remain widely used, many are recognizing that treatment must be part of the solution.

The earliest well-designed evaluation of a treatment intervention is by Donald Dutton (1986). Fifty men attending a four-month cognitive-behavioral program were compared to a matched group of 50 men who were not treated because their probation terminated before space was available in the program. Dutton (1986) found a re-abuse rate of 4 percent for the treated men and 16 percent for the untreated group at a six-month follow-up. At two and one-half years, the treated group maintained the benefits of the treatment while the recidivism rate for the untreated group increased to 40 percent.

Since the early Dutton study, few subsequent evaluations of treatment programs have found such clear-cut results. Part of the problem has been that many evaluations have been hampered by weak methodologies

(Saunders & Azar, 1989), including a failure to use an appropriate comparison group (Hamm & Kite, 1991; Jacobson et al., 1996; Quigley & Leonard, 1996). Some evaluations compared treatment completers with drop-outs. This introduces a selection bias (dropouts are usually the higher-risk offenders) and exaggerates the effectiveness of treatment (Dobash et al., 2000). Despite the methodological problems, most evaluations find modest effects due to treatment.

More recently, Julia Babcock, Charles Green, and Chet Robie (2004) conducted a meta-analysis of 22 studies of treatment interventions for male batterers. The overall result was that treatment was associated with a small reduction in re-abuse ($r = .09$; transformed from Cohen's $d = .18$). The association was the same, regardless of how recidivism was measured (police reports vs. partner reports). In addition, there were no differences in the effectiveness of the Duluth model of intervention (a feminist approach to changing men's attitudes over control) and more broad-based cognitive-behavioral treatments.

Reviews of the batterer treatment literature are not as informative as the reviews of the general offender rehabilitation literature. Often there is a lack of information as to what actually goes on in treatment (Mears, 2003). A treatment may be described as "cognitive-behavioral," but that only tells us how the treatment was delivered and not what was being treated. For example, Daniel Saunders (1996) analyzed audiotapes from a cognitive-behavioral intervention and found that a significant amount of time was spent on relaxation training (supposedly to learn to manage anger) and discussions of cultural norms supportive of male dominance. Role playing and modeling were frequently used. Furthermore, the targets for intervention may not have been the most appropriate (e.g., substance abuse was not targeted). The general offender rehabilitation literature is detailed enough to teach us the importance of focusing on criminogenic needs and adhering to the risk principle. The male batterer treatment literature tells us little about the needs targeted in treatment and the value of assigning men to the appropriate intensity of treatment based on their risk to re-abuse.

The outlook for the future, however, is promising. Progress is being made on introducing actuarial-based risk assessments (Campbell, 2005), but there is a need to benefit from the general offender literature. After all, without counting assaults on partners, 50 percent and more of the men in male batterer treatment programs have a criminal history (Bowen, Gilchrest & Beech, 2008; Cattaneo & Goodman, 2005; Labriola, Rempel & Davis, 2008). We also expect that structured, behavioral interventions will become the norm. Finally, we see treatment becoming more integrated with criminal justice controls. A comprehensive approach that involves the treatment providers and various aspects of the criminal justice system appears to be warranted (Gondolf, 2002). Dutton (1995) has commented that the use of arrest or the threat of criminal justice sanctions may serve as a temporary suppressor of abuse and a window of opportunity for the introduction of treatment. Even fairly mild interventions, such as a simple social work visit following a police call, appear to have positive effects (Davis & Taylor, 1997). Hopefully, continued research will guide the development of an equitable balance between criminal justice controls and offender treatment.

The Mentally Disordered Offender (MDO)

When many people first hear the phrase "mentally disordered offender," the names that jump to mind are Charles Manson, David Berkowitz (Son of Sam), Albert de Salvo (the Boston Strangler), and Jeffrey Dahmer. Images of senseless, grotesque, and extremely violent behavior flood the mind. Lesser known but almost equally bizarre offenders are publicized daily in the news media, and even fictional television characters with mental illnesses are portrayed as highly violent (Diefenbach, 1997). To the average citizen, the prevalence of mentally ill offenders appears high. Moreover, their behavior seems incomprehensible and almost always violent. Determining whether these views correspond to the facts is one of the purposes of this section.

Estimating the incidence of mental disorder among criminal offenders requires a clear definition of the "mentally disordered offender" (MDO). Unfortunately, a widely accepted definition is virtually nonexistent. Part of the problem is that the two major social systems responsible for the MDO, the legal and the mental health systems, have differing interpretations of mental disorder. Furthermore, even within each system there is disagreement on the meaning of such terms as "insanity" and "mental illness."

One of the most influential taxonomies or classification systems for mental disorder today is the *Diagnostic and Statistical Manual of Mental Disorders* or DSM-IV (American Psychiatric Association, 1994). DSM-IV describes behavioral patterns and psychological characteristics that are clustered into diagnostic categories. For example, someone with auditory hallucinations, bizarre delusions (e.g., a pet dog controlling the behavior of the person), and a history of these delusions and hallucinations lasting more than six months is likely to be diagnosed as schizophrenic.

DSM-IV covers a wide range of disorders. For our purposes, we will focus on disorders classified as Axis I and Axis II disorders. Axis I disorders are what most would consider the truly clinical syndromes (i.e., schizophrenia, manic-depression, and major depression). Axis I disorders often form the basis for assessments of fitness to stand trial and pleas of not guilty by reason of insanity (NGRI). Axis II describes many of the disorders closely related to the study of criminal behavior. It is here that we find the personality disorders and, in particular, antisocial personality disorder (APD). As we described in Chapter 6, the criteria for diagnosis of APD include: minimum age of 18, history of a conduct disorder (e.g., truant and uncontrollable at home), dishonesty, irresponsibility in work and social settings, lawbreaking, and lack of remorse.

Estimating the Prevalence of Mental Disorders

Table 14.1 presents a sampling of studies on the incidence of mental disorders among criminal populations. Three important findings emerge from the table. First, hardly anyone escapes a diagnosis of a mental disorder (80 to 90 percent of offenders were diagnosed as having a mental disorder). Second, the major Axis I disorders were relatively infrequent. Only in the pretrial settings, where there are issues of fitness to stand for trial and NGRI decisions, are the rates high (Inada et al., 1995; Webster et al., 1982). Finally, the most frequent diagnosis was APD, an Axis II disorder. In the general population, the estimate of the prevalence of APD is 3.6 percent (Grant et al., 2004), much lower than what is found in Table 14.1. We would also like to note, and this is not reflected in the table, that the prevalence of a mental disorder is usually higher among women (Sirdifield, Gojkovic, Brooker & Ferriter, 2009).

Dangerousness and the MDO

The MDO has often been at the center of the debate surrounding dangerousness. Various criminal and civil commitment laws are used to

Table 14.1
The Prevalence of Mental Disorder (%)

Assessment Method/Study	Schizo	Manic-dep	Dep	APD	Alcohol	Drug	Any
Structured Interview Hodgins & Cote (1990) 495 inmates (Canada)	6.3	1.6	8.1	46.6	33.1	18.6	96.3
Teplin & Swartz (1989) 728 inmates (U.S.)	3.3	3.3	4.9				
1,149 inmates (U.S.)	1.4	1.5	4.9				
Daniel et al. (1988) 100 female inmates (U.S.)	7.0	2.0	17.0	29.0	10.0		90.0
Brink, Doherty & Boer (2001) 202 inmates (Canada)	3.5	0.5	4.5		3.5	2.4	
Webster et al. (1982) 248 pretrial (Canada)	39.4			27.0	13.7		96.0
Inada et al. (1995) 1,396 pretrial (Japan)	28.9	2.9	—	3.1	16.4	12.3	80.7

Schizo: Schizophrenia   Dep: Major depression
Manic-dep: Manic-depression   APD: Antisocial personality

confine MDOs for periods longer than the typical sentence given to non-MDOs for the same offense. The argument is that these offenders pose a risk for further violent behavior and that preventive confinement is needed until they are no longer "dangerous." One of the difficulties in making decisions about the individual's dangerousness is the lack of knowledge about the base rates of violent behavior for MDOs. Only a few studies provide such information.

One of the first studies was Henry Steadman and Joseph Cocozza's (1974) evaluation of the "Baxstrom patients." The story begins when inmate Johnnie Baxstrom took his case before the U.S. Supreme Court. Baxstrom was transferred from a prison to a hospital for the criminally insane because he was diagnosed as mentally disordered. Consequently, he was institutionalized beyond the end of his sentence. Baxstrom's lawyers argued that, without evidence of dangerousness, he must be released. The court agreed, and not only was Baxstrom transferred from the hospital for the criminally insane to a regular psychiatric hospital, but so too were 976 other offenders who had been housed in similar hospitals. Presumably, the most dangerous offenders in New York State were transferred to regular psychiatric facilities, and some were duly released at the completion of their sentence. (Baxstrom was released after a new trial in which the jury decided that he was not mentally ill; he died two weeks later from an epileptic seizure.)

The Baxstrom patients were assessed as "dangerous mental patients"; thus, their transfer to a regular hospital and their eventual release provided an estimate of the base rate of violent behavior among this group of MDOs. Steadman and Cocozza (1974) traced 98 of these offenders who were released over an average period of two and one-half years. Twenty (20.4%) were rearrested, 11 (11.2%) were reconvicted, and only two of the 98 offenders committed a violent offense (an assault and a robbery). Because patients released from psychiatric hospitals may be rehospitalized instead of arrested for a criminal offense, rehospitalizations were also examined (this would increase the base rate of the behavior). With the hospital and community information combined, the base rate of violent behavior was 14.3 percent. Steadman and Cocozza (1974:152) concluded: "The Baxstrom patients were not very dangerous. Only 14 of 98 releases ever displayed behavior that could be classified as dangerous." In another similar study, Thornberry and Jacoby (1979) found that of 432 mentally disordered offenders released into the community, only 14.5 percent committed another violent offense (again, average follow-up period of two and one-half years).

Before concluding that the Baxstrom patients and those from the Thornberry and Jacoby (1979) study were not dangerous, we must be reminded that all of these patients had already committed a violent offense that led to their hospitalization. Additionally, we must ask: Not dangerous compared to whom?

In general, psychiatric patients have higher arrest rates than nonpatients (Brennan, Mednick & Hodgins, 2000; Harris & Lurigio, 2007; Mullen, 2006). In a carefully controlled study, Bruce Link, Howard Andrews, and Francis Cullen (1992) compared various groups of mentally ill patients with a randomly selected sample of adults without any mental disorder. Table 14.2 summarizes the major criminal/violent behavior differences between the chronically disturbed patients and the nondisturbed adults. Whether the behavior was based upon official records or self-reports, the findings of the study were consistent. Chronically disturbed patients (having received treatment for at least one year) were more likely to be arrested and to have committed violent acts. Results such as these have suggested to some (e.g., Teplin, 1984) that the police have a bias in arresting those who appear to be a nuisance. However, a large-scale study involving five metropolitan police departments found no evidence for an arresting bias (Engel & Silver, 2001).

Mental illness is often viewed as a risk factor in combination with substance abuse (Mullen, 2006). However, a recent epidemiologic survey better situates the role of substance abuse in comparison to other risk factors for violence. Researchers under the direction of Eric Elbogen and Sally Johnson (2009) conducted structured mental health interviews with 34,653 persons between 2002 and 2003 and three years later asked them about their experiences during the prior three years (e.g., "Ever hit someone so hard that you injured them or they had to see a doctor?"). First of all, the base rate for violence was .029, and approximately 3,000 individuals had an Axis I mental disorder. Second, the rate for violence among those with an Axis I disorder was about *half* of the general base rate. Finally, Elbogen and Johnson identified the 10 best predictors of violence and rank ordered them. Mental illness came in at number nine but only when combined with substance abuse. Ahead of the list were the usual suspects (history of violence, history of juvenile detention, parental criminal history, etc.). Mental illness by itself pales in comparison to other risk factors for violence.

Beyond comparisons of mental disorder and nondisorder within the general population, how do mentally disordered *offenders* compare to the run-of-the-mill, non–mentally disordered criminals? The evidence shows that MDOs actually show *lower* rates of violent and nonviolent

Table 14.2
Criminal and Violent Behavior among Psychiatric and Nonpsychiatric Patients (%)

Group	OFFICIAL		SELF-REPORTED		
	All Arrests	Violent	Arrests	Weapon	Fighting
Patients	12.1	5.8	22.5	12.9	28.6
Nonpatients	6.7	1.0	9.9	2.7	15.1

Note: *N*s vary for patients (93–173) and nonpatients (185–386).
Adapted from Link, Andrews & Cullen, 1992

criminal behavior (Bonta, Law & Hanson, 1998). Thus, MDOs, with respect to the danger they pose to the public, lie somewhere between the common citizen and the common criminal. The interesting question now is: What are the risk factors for those offenders with a mental disorder?

The Prediction of Criminal Behavior Among MDOs

Psychopathological models of deviance have dominated research on the prediction of criminal behavior among MDOs. That is, the variables studied tended to be factors such as anxiety, feelings of depression, delusions, and so on—factors that are poorly related to criminal offending among non–mentally disordered offenders. However, we have been following a false trail.

Threat/Control-Override Symptomatology. In 1994, Link and Steuve proposed that delusions of "threat/control-override" (TCO) are closely linked to violence. That is, thoughts that people are trying to harm you or that your mind is being controlled by others increase the likelihood of responding violently to these perceived threats. They found that TCO delusions were associated with violence in both a patient and a nonpatient population. From a PCC perspective, cognitions supportive of antisocial behavior were key predictors of violence.

Link and Steuve's results were subsequently replicated in a large study of more than 10,000 adults who were interviewed as part of the Epidemiological Catchment Area survey. Swanson and his colleagues (1996) examined three groups of respondents: (1) those with no major psychiatric disorder; (2) those with a major, Axis I disorder; and (3) those with a major disorder with substance abuse. They also examined the presence of TCO symptoms and non-TCO symptoms (hallucinations, feelings of grandeur). Each respondent was asked about the commission of violent acts since the age of 18. A number of conclusions were drawn from their results (Table 14.3). First, TCO symptoms increased the likelihood of violence for mentally disordered and nondisordered individuals. Second, substance abuse greatly increased the chances of violence. Third, psychotic and non-TCO symptoms were still presented as risk factors, although modest in comparison to substance abuse and TCO symptoms.

Although most studies have reported the TCO-violence relationship (Hodgins, Hiscoke & Freese, 2003; Link, Steuve & Phelan, 1998; Stomp & Ortwein-Swoboda, 2004), there was one important exception. In the MacArthur Violence Risk Assessment Study, a prospective study of more than 1,100 acute psychiatric patients, initially a TCO-violence relationship was not found (Appelbaum, Robbins & Monahan, 2000). However, when the data was reanalyzed using the same retrospective methodology used in the earlier studies, a TCO-violence association was observed. In

Table 14.3
Threat/Control-Override (TCO) Symptoms as a Risk Factor for Violence
(Probability of self-reported violent acts since age 18)

	Axis I Disorder		
Symptom	No Disorder	Axis I Only	Substance Abuse
None	.17	.26	.70
Non-TCO	.27	.39	.75
TCO	.40	.63	.86

From Swanson et al., 1996

addition, the specificity of the TCO delusions was important. Most of the questions for TCO delusions tapped paranoid cognitions ("Have you believed people were spying on you?") and not specifically cognitions supportive of violent behavior. However, when the researchers asked a specific question about violent behavior ("Do you sometimes think about hurting people?"), the patients who responded positively to the question were significantly more likely to be violent than patients who denied such a thought.

In summary, the existence of a mental disorder appears to be a minor risk factor. Psychotic delusions, for the most past, also appear to have a minor relationship with criminal behavior. Rather, it is the risk factors found among general offenders (e.g., substance abuse, antisocial personality, cognitions supportive of violent behavior) that are relevant. This evidence is reviewed in the following section.

Risk Factors for MDOs. Concerned about the relevance of various theoretical models to explain the behavior of MDOs, Bonta, Law, and Hanson (1998) conducted a meta-analysis of 64 studies of the predictors of general and violent recidivism. They asked whether factors considered important by psychopathological and clinical perspectives would predict recidivism and how these factors compared to predictors drawn from a general PCC.

Table 14.4 presents the results for general recidivism (the pattern was similar for violent recidivism). Also shown in the table are the results from the meta-analyses by Gendreau, Little, and Goggin (1996) on general offenders and the results from various summaries of the risk for sexual recidivism (Hanson, in press; Hanson & Bussière, 1998; Hanson & Morton-Bourgon, 2004, 2005). What is striking is that the predictors of recidivism for MDOs follow a pattern similar to that for general and sexual offenders. Criminal history and antisocial personality, two of the Big Four, were among the best predictors of recidivism, whether violent or not. The other predictors—and their effect sizes—showed almost parallel results across the three samples.

In the MDO meta-analysis, there were too few studies measuring antisocial supports and antisocial cognitions. This gap in the research can be traced, in our opinion, to the dominating influence of

Table 14.4
Predictors of Recidivism by Sample (r)

Risk Factor	MDO	Sample General	Sex
Antisocial Support	nr	.21	nr
Antisocial Personality	.18	.18	.10
Antisocial Cognitions	nr	.18	.10
Criminal History	.22	.16	.15
Social Achievement	.04	.13	.10
Family Factors	.10	.10	.05
Substance Abuse	.11	.10	.06
Intelligence	.01	.07	.01
Lower-Class Origins	.00	.05	.00
Personal Distress	−.04	.05	.01

Notes: General (Gendreau, Little & Goggin, 1996); MDO (Bonta, Law & Hanson, 1998); Sex (Hanson & Bussière, 1998; Hanson & Morton-Bourgon, 2004, 2005). nr = not reported

psychopathological models to explain MDOs. The training of clinical psychologists and psychiatrists predisposes them to seek explanation in factors such as psychosis and other measures of psychological disturbance. However, the results from the Bonta et al. (1998) meta-analysis found these factors to be poor predictors of recidivism. In fact, a diagnosis of a major psychiatric disorder (e.g., schizophrenia) was *negatively* related to general ($r = -.05$) and violent ($r = -.04$) recidivism. Just as the clinical models contributed little to the prediction of criminal behavior, so did variables drawn from sociological criminology. Lower social class and race did not predict general recidivism (race was a moderate predictor of violent recidivism; $r = .09$).

Two other important findings from the Bonta et al. (1998) review deserve comment. First, actuarial assessments of risk once again proved themselves superior to clinical judgments of risk. For general recidivism, the average r was .39 for actuarial assessments and only .03 for clinical judgments; for the prediction of violent recidivism, the corresponding rs were .30 and .09. Second, studies that compared the recidivism of MDOs with nondisordered offenders showed that those with a mental illness were *less* likely to reoffend with any offense ($r = -.19$) or a violent offense ($r = -.10$), confirming the earlier conclusion that the MDO's risk for crime lies somewhere between the average citizen and the average criminal.

Since the Bonta et al. (1998) meta-analysis, there have been further confirmations that the major risk factors for MDOs are the same as those for general criminal offenders (Gray et al., 2004; Phillips et al., 2005; Skeem, Manchak & Peterson, in press). In summary, clinical psychopathology is important for the humane treatment of individuals and management of disturbing symptoms, but its presence does not appear to be a significant predictor of criminal behavior for most MDOs. What we find instead is that the variables identified by a PCC are far more important. Unfortunately, it is the psychopathological perspective and not PCC that has dominated the treatment of MDOs.

Treatment of the MDO

Clinical treatment of the MDO usually involves treating psychological complaints or the behaviors that are disruptive to the functioning of the institution (Harris & Rice, 1997; Müller-Isberner & Hodgins, 2000; Skeem et al., in press). Thus, a depressed offender may follow a cognitive-behavioral program for self-defeating thoughts or receive antidepressant medication; a manic-depressive is likely to be prescribed Lithium; and a schizophrenic is likely to receive a major tranquilizer. Upon elimination of the symptoms (or, at the very least, management of the symptoms), the patient is considered "cured" and no further treatment follows. In other words, most treatment programs with MDOs are no different than those provided for nonoffending, psychiatric patients. The evidence for these types of treatments has been disappointing. For example, Jennifer Skeem and her colleagues (in press) summarized 14 programs intended to reduce recidivism among MDOs and found that most were ineffective, and the worst were those interventions that focused on symptomatology.

The ineffectiveness of treatment programs to reduce recidivism among MDOs, in our view, can be traced to a neglect of the RNR principles. It is almost nonexistent to find the MDO undergoing treatment that targets, for example, criminal attitudes and associates. Robert Morgan and his colleagues (2007) could identify only six mental health studies from more than 12,000 documents that targeted criminogenic needs. However, the situation appears to be changing.

There have been two promising developments in the treatment of MDOs. First, there is a recognition that treatment should attend to the general offender rehabilitation literature (Blackburn, 2004; Greeven & Ruiter, 2004; Harris & Rice, 1997; Mullen, 2006; Müller-Isberner & Hodgins, 2000; Skeem et al., in press). Perhaps the time is near when psychiatric staff will treat higher-risk clients and target criminogenic needs using cognitive-behavioral techniques. A recent report by Ashford, Wong, and Sternbach (2008) is quite encouraging in this regard. They found that MDOs who participated in a cognitive-behavioral intervention targeting antisocial attitudes had fewer arrests for violent crimes compared to MDOs receiving standard services. Second, providing treatment and support post-hospitalization is being given more attention. Specialized aftercare programs and parole supervision practices have been developed for MDOs released on parole in a number of states, with promising results (Bloom & Williams, 1994; Swanson et al., 2001; Skeem et al., in press; Wiederanders, Bromley & Choate, 1997). We hope that these trends continue.

The Sex Offender

Along with mentally disordered offenders, sex offenders elicit a great deal of public apprehension and fear. According to the U.S. National Crime Victimization Survey, there was a 25 percent increase in sexual assaults between 2005 and 2006, with a rape incidence rate of 1.0 per 1,000 for victims over the age of 12 years (Rand, 2008). The rate for child sexual abuse has been estimated at 82 per 1,000 children (Finkelhor, Ormrod, Turner & Hamby, 2005). The fact that these criminal acts involve victims who are, for the most part, women and children, requires sustained attention from researchers, policymakers, and the general public.

How Unique are Sex Offenders?

Are sex offenders so different from nonsexual offenders that a fundamentally different approach to theory, assessment, and treatment is required? For example, besides the offense, how do sex offenders differ from other offenders in their behavioral histories, personalities, cognitions, and attitudes? Are their criminogenic needs limited to their sexual behavior, or are the criminogenic needs identified for the nonsexual criminal population (e.g., antisocial personality, drug addiction) just as relevant?

A commonly held view is that sex offenders are "specialists" (Lussier, 2005). That is, their crimes are almost exclusively sex crimes. If this is true, then treatment need only focus on factors directly associated with sexual behavior. For example, treatment should target sexual arousal, attitudes tolerant of sexual assault, inadequate intimate relationships, and so forth. These dynamic risk factors are important, but there is also evidence to suggest that *non*sexual criminogenic variables require attention.

Both retrospective (Maletzky, 1991; Weinrott & Saylor, 1991) and longitudinal (Bench, Kramer & Erickson, 1997; Lussier, Proulx & LeBlanc, 2005; Waite et al., 2005) studies show that sex offenders also commit nonsexual crimes. In a meta-analysis of sexual offenders by Hanson and Morton-Bourgon (2009), the sexual recidivism rate was 11.5 percent, and the violent recidivism rate (including sexual and nonsexual violent crimes) was 19.5 percent. In an earlier meta-analysis, Hanson and Bussière (1998) reported a nonsexual, violent recidivism rate of 9.9 percent for child molesters and a rate of 22.1 percent for rapists.

These studies suggest that there are important similarities between sex offenders and non–sex offenders. One example of the similarities is the role of antisocial supports. Many clinicians see sexual offenders as social isolates, awkward in social interactions, and introverted. This may be true for some, but not for all. Reports of sexual abuse by multiple offenders in daycare clinics (Finkelhor, Williams & Burns, 1988), the growth of organizations promoting "man/boy" love relations (Thorstad, 1991), and the use of the Internet for deviant sexual purposes (Alexy, Burgess & Baker, 2005) or to overcome social isolation via chat rooms (Tremblay, 2006) have painted a portrait of an underworld of child pornography and sex rings. As Richard Tremblay (2002) observed, sex offenders can find many ways to overcome any social isolation that may result because their behaviors are highly disapproved of by the general public.

We could find only find a few studies that speak to the role of social supports in sex offending. In a study of date rape, Kanin (1967) found that male perpetrators often told their friends about their sexual acts, even if it was coerced, with the expectation that their friends would approve. Alder (1985) also found a strong association ($r = .58$) between men admitting to sexually assaulting women and reporting that their friends also committed rape. In a study of convicted sex offenders, Karl Hanson and Heather Scott (1996) asked 126 sex offenders, 57 non–sex offenders, and 119 nonoffenders questions about their associations with others. Child molesters reported knowing other child molesters, and rapists reported knowing other rapists. Nonoffenders typically reported having no sex offenders in their social networks. Finally, Underwood and his colleagues (Underwood et al., 1999) asked 113 child molesters to report whether they had molested a child in the presence of another adult (they were not asked if the other adult was a convicted sex offender). Thirty-eight percent reported that another adult was present during the commission of the offense.

This is not to say that sex offenders are no different from non–sex offenders. One consistent finding is that a sex offender is more likely to recidivate with a sexual crime than a non–sex offender (Bonta & Hanson, 1995; Hanson, Scott & Steffy, 1995; Soothill et al., 2000). In a meta-analysis of 89 studies, Daniel Whitaker and colleagues (Whitaker, Le, Hanson, Baker et al., 2008) found sex offenders to differ significantly in terms of their attitudes. Sex offenders were more likely to minimize their responsibility in offending (with an r of about .27) and were more tolerant of adult-child sex (with an r of about .25). However, these findings are quite consistent from a General Personality and Cognitive Social Learning perspective. Attitudes are important and if the attitudes are more specific to the behavior, then, of course, the association strengthens.

Risk Factors for Sexual Offending

The first point that we would like to make is that not all sex offenders are equally likely to reoffend. Often, the public views anyone who commits a sexual offense as a high-risk offender. However, some offenders have a very low risk to reoffend sexually, while others pose a much higher risk. The simplest risk classification is to go by the offense type. For example, incest offenders have lower recidivism rates than nonfamilial child molesters (Hanson, Morton & Harris, 2003). Nevertheless, we can do much better in risk differentiation than using the type of offense and victim.

Much of the early research, driven by a psychopathological model of sexual deviance, focused on general personality characteristics and indices of personal distress. However, these clinical assessments appear to have had little success in outlining the important personal factors associated with sexual deviant behavior (e.g., Murphy & Peters, 1992). Many researchers have now come to the conclusion that it is more important to examine factors such as antisocial personality, drug abuse, unstable employment, and the other correlates of an antisocial lifestyle (Hanson & Morton-Bourgon, 2005; Marshall, 1996).

Deviant sexual fantasies are viewed as an important correlate of sexual offending (Howitt, 2004). They are often targeted in treatment, and they play a role in theoretical models of sexual offending (e.g., Ward & Beech, 2006). Although such fantasies may be correlated with sexual deviance, their role in *causing* sexual offending is less clear. A study by Langevin, Lang, and Curnoe (1998) illustrates the point. A sexual fantasy scale was administered to 129 sex offenders and 77 controls (22 nonoffenders and 50 non–sex offenders). They found that the overall reported rate of deviant fantasies for the sex offenders was relatively low (33.3%), although it was higher than for the controls (11%). (These rates of deviant fantasies are probably an underestimate, as people tend to hide shameful behavior). Furthermore, more of the controls reported some type of fantasy (deviant or not) than did the sex offenders (90.9% vs. 62.5%). The researchers interpreted the low rates of deviant fantasies and the finding that many of the sex offenders reported normal sexual fantasies to mean that fantasies are unlikely to have etiological significance.

Sexual fantasies are an indicator of sexual preoccupation, which is a risk factor for sexual offending. Another indicator of sexual preoccupation is the use of pornography. Pornography may serve to stimulate deviant fantasies, but here too the evidence suggests that it does not appear to have a causal role in sexual aggression (Seto, Maric & Barbaree, 2001). For example, a study of 561 sex offenders found that 19 percent used pornography at the time of their offense; the majority did not (Langevin & Curnoe, 2004). Among the child molesters, the rate was higher (55%) but consisted mainly of showing pornography to the victims rather than to arouse the offender directly.

One promising approach to understanding sexual deviance is the assessment of the cognitions that support sexual deviance. As noted earlier, sex offenders are more tolerant of sex with children and minimize their behavior (Whitaker et al., 2008). In particular, sex offenders make extensive use of cognitive distortions (Egan, Kavanagh & Blair, 2005; Tierney & McCabe, 2001). Cognitive distortions are similar to the neutralizations and rationalizations described in Chapter 7 (e.g., "Sometimes having sex with a child can be a way of showing love for the child"). The importance of these cognitions and attitudes is that they represent dynamic risk factors or the criminogenic needs that are important for the supervision and treatment of offenders.

The literature on the risk factors of sexual recidivism has been summarized in a number of meta-analyses by Karl Hanson and his associates (Hanson & Bussière, 1998; Hanson & Morton-Bourgon, 2005; Whitaker et al., 2008). Referring back to Table 14.4, we have a ranking of risk predictors for sex offenders, general offenders, and MDOs. Note the consistency in the ordering of predictors across all three groups of offenders. For sex offenders, as with MDOs and general offenders, criminal history was one of the best predictors, along with antisocial personality, antisocial cognitions, and social support for crime (for MDOs, there were insufficient studies to estimate the effect size for social support). Measures of personal distress and social class fell at the bottom of the list.

Although there are many similarities in the risk factors for sexual and nonsexual recidivism, there are some factors specific to sexual deviance, most notably, deviant sexual interests (i.e., sexual interest in children). In addition, some researchers consider a history of victimization to be an antecedent to sexual violence as an adult. A history of sexual abuse does differentiate sex offenders from nonsexual offenders (Whitaker et al., 2008), but prospective studies find a history of childhood sexual abuse unrelated to sexual recidivism (Hanson & Morton-Bourgon, 2005). Furthermore, Hanson and Morton-Bourgon (2005) found little evidence for other commonly held risk factors such as loneliness, motivation for treatment, and progress while in treatment. In summary, we quote one of their main conclusions:

> The substantial overlap in the characteristics of persistent sexual and persistent nonsexual offenders suggests that those concerned with the assessment and management of sexual offenders could profit from the substantial literature on the assessment and treatment of general criminal offenders (p. 1159).

One of the practical applications that arises from meta-analytic reviews of risk factors is that it facilitates the development of evidence-based actuarial risk scales. Hanson and Morton-Bourgon (2005) drew two important conclusions relevant to risk scales for sexual offenders. First, the individual risk factors showed only modest effect sizes. This suggests a need to combine the risk factors to increase predictive accuracy. Second, many risk factors (e.g., sexual preoccupations) were dynamic and could guide treatment because they represent potential criminogenic needs for offenders. If we combine both of these conclusions, then we may also suggest that future risk assessment with sexual offenders may move toward risk/need assessments similar to the LSI-R and LS/CMI (Chapter 10).

Hanson and his colleagues have been at the forefront of the development of actuarial risk scales for sexual offenders. Their early work focused on simple-to-use risk scales such as STATIC-99 (Hanson & Thornton, 2000), the updated STATIC-2002 (Hanson & Thornton, 2003), and the Rapid Risk Assessment for Sexual Offence Recidivism (RRASOR; Hanson, 1997a). These scales have shown satisfactory predictive accuracy, with AUCs in the .70 range (Hanson, 1997a; Hanson, Helmus & Thornton, 2009; Hanson & Thornton, 2000; Sjöstedt & Långström, 2002; Stadtland et al., 2005). Their disadvantage, however, is that they measure mainly static risk. Recently, however, there has been a notable shift in attention to dynamic risk factors in the assessment of sexual offenders (Craig et al., 2005; Hanson, 2006).

In the Dynamic Supervision Project (Hanson, Harris, Scott & Helmus, 2007), 997 sex offenders under community supervision were administered three types of risk scales—static, stable, and acute. Stable risk factors are dynamic risk factors that, although changeable, take longer to change (e.g., intimacy deficits, deviant sexual interests, sexual self-regulation). Acute risk factors can change very quickly (e.g., intoxication, sudden access to a victim, collapse of social supports). Static risk scales were administered at the start of community supervision; stable risk assessment was conducted every six months; and acute risk assessment was conducted at each supervision session. Over a 41-month follow-up period, Hanson et al. (2007) were able to validate two new dynamic risk scales for sex offenders, called STABLE-2007 and ACUTE-2007 (AUCs of .67 and .74, respectively). The two new risk assessment measures are now used throughout the world.

The Treatment of Sex Offenders

One approach to managing sexual recidivism involves decreasing deviant sexual arousal. Because high levels of the male hormone testosterone are assumed to be associated with high levels of sexual arousal (Hucker & Bain, 1990; Studer, Aylwin & Reddon, 2005), reducing testosterone levels has been targeted in biologically based treatments. There are two ways of doing this—through physical castration or through so-called "chemical castrations."

Studies of physical castration have shown low rates of recidivism, many in the 2 to 4 percent range (Bradford, 1997). However, most evaluations have not used comparison groups and further, castration does not guarantee a loss of sexual functioning (approximately 10% of castrated males continue to have erections; Brown & Courtis, 1977). Needless to say, this procedure involves serious ethical dilemmas as well as physical and psychological side effects. As a result, physical castrations are not widely performed except in a few isolated jurisdictions (the Czech Republic surgically castrated 94 prisoners during a 10-year period since 1999; Bilefsky, 2009). Instead, drugs that either block the release of the hormones (androgens) that stimulate testosterone secretion or compete with other hormones for the neurophysiological sites that release testosterone are used. Drugs such as cyproterone acetate (CPA, Androcur) and medroxyprogesterone (MPA, Provera) have been hailed as the new treatments for sexual offenders.

Reductions in general libido have followed with the administration of these drugs. However, although sexual drive may decrease, the drugs may have little effect on other behavioral correlates of sexual behavior (e.g., deviant sexual thoughts, Marshall et al., 1991). While many sex offenders show reduced recidivism rates while under medication (Bradford, 1997; Maletzky, Tolan & McFarland, 2006; Walker et al., 1984), there has been no experimental demonstration that recidivism is reduced solely as a result of these drugs and not due to the counseling/treatment programs that almost all offenders receive while on medication (Barbaree & Marshall, 1998). In essence, medication may provide early and immediate stabilization of the problem behavior, but psychologically based intervention is still needed.

In 1989, Lita Furby, Mark Weinrott, and Lyn Blackshaw reviewed 42 treatment studies of sex offenders. They concluded that "there is as yet no evidence that clinical treatment reduces rates of sex reoffenses" (p. 27). This review and their conclusion, like Martinson's, did not go unchallenged (Becker & Hunter, 1992; Marshall & Barbaree, 1990; Marshall et al., 1991). A major criticism was that the review failed to describe what actually comprised treatment. Our own meta-analyses of the general offender treatment literature show that treatments are not equally effective. It is possible that the failure of the treatment programs in Furby et al.'s (1989) review was the result of inappropriate treatments.

Subsequent to Furby et al.'s (1989) review, there have been many reports showing that the treatment of sex offenders can work (Barbaree & Marshall, 1998; Bilby, Brooks-Gordon & Wells, 2006; Looman, Abracen & Nicholaichuk, 2000; Maletzky, 1991; Worling & Curwen, 2000). However, there were also studies showing that treatment does not work (Hanson, Broom & Stephenson, 2004; Marques et al., 2005). As we have emphasized many times, the results from individual studies only tell part of the tale. Meta-analyses of the treatment literature with sex offenders provide us with a better answer. All the meta-analytic reviews agree that psychological treatment for sex offenders reduces recidivism, although the range in reduction is quite large, from 12 percent (Hanson et al., 2002) to as high as 37 percent (Lösel & Schmucker, 2005).

In 2002, Hanson et al. noted that the knowledge that has accumulated from the general offender treatment literature had not yet been fully applied to the treatment of sex offenders. Recently, there has been movement in this direction, with investigations of the risk, need, and responsivity principles in the treatment of sex offenders (Abracen et al., 2005; Looman, Dickie & Abracen, 2005; Mailloux et al., 2003; Olver & Wong, 2009; Olver, Wong & Nicholaichuk, 2009). For example, Lovins, Lowenkamp, and Latessa (in press) found that low-risk sex offenders undergoing intensive treatment showed no improvements compared to untreated sex offenders while the high-risk sex offenders showed reduced recidivism (unfortunately, they measured general recidivism and not sexual recidivism specifically). A meta-analysis by Hanson, Bourgon, Helmus, and Hodgson (2009) found strong support for the principles in the treatment of sex offenders. A review of 23 studies showed that treated sex offenders, compared to untreated sex offenders, had lower general recidivism rates (31.8% vs. 48.3%) and sexual recidivism rates (10.9% vs. 19.2%). The weakest effects were with studies that did not adhere to any of the principles, and the effectiveness of the treatments increased with adherence to RNR. Adherence to all three principles was very infrequent (k =3), but these treatments showed the largest decreases in recidivism.

Human Hunters and Predators

Sex offenders, in order to carry out their acts, must select, follow, and "capture" their victims. Certainly, some offenders may take advantage of unexpected opportunities, but for the most part, there is a certain amount of planning required to complete the act. This aspect of violent criminal behavior—the following, watching, and waiting—is one of the most fearful aspects of criminal behavior. When the goal is to commit the most violent and gruesome acts, fear and concern is intensified. Serial murderers, sex offenders (who are in effect, serial sex offenders), and ex-partners who stalk their lovers appear to form a class of offenders unlike most criminals. We have already seen that MDOs and sex offenders have some unique characteristics but also that they share commonalities with non–sex offenders. In the remainder of this chapter, we summarize the emerging literature on stalkers and serial murderers.

Stalkers

In 1989, Rebecca Shaeffer, a television actress, was shot and killed on her doorstep; her murderer was a fan who had a two-year history of following her, writing letters, and trying to meet her. The murder resulted in the first of the anti-stalking laws in California (1991), laws that are now found in all of the American states, Canada, Australia, and most Western countries (McEwan, Mullen & MacKenzie, 2007; Purcell, Pathé & Mullen, 2004). It also drew public attention to a behavior that had largely gone unnoticed. At first, the attention was directed to the stalking of celebrities and political figures, but later it broadened to include the far more prevalent stalking of a partner in a love relationship that had soured. Legal definitions of stalking have two components: (1) attempts to gain physical proximity to the victim, and (2) the intent to cause fear (Dennison & Thomson, 2005).

Interest in stalking was evident long before the introduction of anti-stalking laws. In 1942, the French psychiatrist de Clérambault described a syndrome characterized by the delusional belief that another higher-status and unsuspecting person was in love with the patient. This belief then served as the unrelenting motive for following and attempting to communicate with the victim. De Clérambault's syndrome eventually became a delusional disorder, erotomanic type, in DSM-IV. Many of the early studies were approached from the premise that stalking behavior was motivated by an obsessive love of the victim and a delusion that the victim loved the stalker.

Subsequent to de Clérambault's analysis, investigators began to differentiate types of stalkers (Mullen & Pathé, 2002). Some typologies were categorized according to the presence or absence of delusions, relationship to the victim, and the stalker's motivation. Mullen (2009) suggests five types of stalkers based on motivation. These types are presented in Table 14.5 along with the average time spent on stalking. A famous example of the Intimacy-seeker type is John Hinckley Jr., who shot President Ronald Reagan to demonstrate to actress Jodie Foster the depth of his love, hoping that she would reciprocate (Perez, 1993).

Sometimes stalking is associated with the delusion that the victim, who may be a complete stranger, loves the stalker (Kienlen, 1995). Other times stalkers are nondelusional but highly obsessive (Zona, Sharma & Lane, 1993). Regardless of the presence of delusions or the typology, "stalkers are rarely, if ever, drawn from the psychologically adequate or socially able world (Mullen, 2009:23).

Many descriptions of stalkers are based upon highly selective samples of celebrity and political stalkers who exhibit psychotic symptoms (James, Mullen, Meloy, Pathé et al., 2007; James, Mullen, Pathé, Meloy et al., 2008; Mullen, James, Meloy et al., 2008). We must note from the outset that these clinical cases are quite rare. Although millions may have

Table 14.5
A Typology of Stalkers

Type	Motive	Mean Duration (weeks)
Rejected	Express anger or to reconcile after a relationship falls apart	42.9
Intimacy-seeker	Gain the love of an acquaintance or stranger	178.8
Incompetent	Sex	11.5
Resentful	Revenge for real or imagined grievances	77.7
Predatory	Excitement from watching and rehearsing fantasies of a sexual and violent nature	16.6

Adapted from MacKenzie et al., 2008; Mullen, 2009

adoration for movie stars, sports figures, royalty, and political leaders, very few give up their everyday lives to pursue relentlessly a certain celebrity. We also wish to affirm that we are not talking about the political assassin (most are quite rational and their motives understandable (Fein & Vossekuil, 1999)).

When dealing with the delusional celebrity stalker, a question often asked is how likely it is that a stalker will actually cause physical harm. For the delusional stalker, it seems not very likely. Park Dietz and his colleagues (Dietz, Matthews, Van Duyne et al., 1991) analyzed 1,800 "nut mail" letters written to Hollywood celebrities by 214 subjects. They found that only 17.3 percent of the individuals who wrote to celebrities actually attempted to make physical contact with them. Furthermore, they found no relationship between writing threats and the act of actually approaching the celebrities. In a similar study, but looking at those targeting members of the U.S. Congress, those who threatened government leaders were less likely to approach the politician (Dietz, Matthews, Martell et al., 1991).

Unlike celebrity and political stalkers, most stalkers are rational and know their victims personally. How dangerous are they? Perhaps the best estimate of the danger is gleaned from Barry Rosenfeld's (2004) meta-analysis of 13 studies of stalking and obsessional harassment. He found a violence rate (broadly defined to include threats) of 38.7 percent. Unfortunately, he did not report his findings in terms of contact and non-contact violence. The nature of the threat and the target appear quite important. For example, Warren and his colleagues (Warren, Mullen, Thomas, Ogloff & Burgess, 2008) conducted a 10-year follow-up of 565 men and 48 women convicted of a threat to kill. Threats to kill a public figure or a stranger in the sample were relatively rare (0.2% and 5.9%). The majority of the threats were to family members (38.2%) and acquaintances or co-workers (36.4%). Over the course of the follow-up, 44.4 percent were convicted of another violent offense (3% actually killed someone). In another investigation of stalkers by Paul Mullen's research team, making threats was the single best predictor of assault (Thomas, Purcell, Pathé & Mullen, 2008).

In general, stalkers cause considerable emotional upset, but it is the minority that physically harm or kill the individuals they are following (we will discuss the extreme cases in our section on serial killers). In a community sample of 3,700 men and women, 432 reported being stalked. Of those stalked, 17.4 percent were physically attacked, with one-half of those attacked sustaining physical harm. Why is there not more physical violence? The answer is a reflection of the major risk factors of criminal behavior. In many stalking cases, the common pattern is a history of *non-violent* "following behavior." It is when the behavioral history is of a violent nature that stalking may lead to violence (Rosenfeld, 2004; Scalora et al., 2002). Regarding social supports for the behavior, stalkers tend to operate alone—informing others of their behavior is likely met with efforts to discourage the behavior. Finally, Meloy (1996) found that erotomanic stalkers were *underrepresented* by antisocial personality disorder (APD), presumably because APD individuals cannot feel love and attachment to the victim. All this said, there remain two types of stalkers that pose considerable risk to the victim: domestic stalkers and serial murderers.

Domestic Stalkers

Compared to men, women are eight times more likely to be stalked by their partner (Tjaden & Thoennes, 2006). Being stalked by a "rejected" ex-intimate represents at least 25 percent of all stalkers (Douglas & Dutton, 2001; MacKenzie et al., 2008; Mullen & Pathé, 2002), and the research suggests that the domestic stalker poses the greatest danger to the victim. Estimates of violence in these cases fall in the 35 to 80 percent range (Mullen, 2009; Mullen & Pathé, 2002; Palarea et al., 1999; Roberts, 2005). A number of risk factors have been identified for this type of stalker. First, women who experienced physical and verbal abuse during the relationship are more likely to suffer assault from the stalker after the relationship ends (Coleman, 1997; Mullen, Mackenzie et al., 2006; Roberts, 2005; Wright et al., 1996). Thus, a history of conflict during the relationship can carry beyond the end of a relationship. In an in-depth study of the problem, Russell Palarea and his colleagues (Palarea et al., 1999) compared the Los Angeles police files of 223 intimate (married, cohabiting, dating) and 88 nonintimate stalking cases. Intimate stalkers were more likely to carry out threats of physical violence (80.6%) than nonintimate stalkers (19.4%). Further analysis showed that a general history of violence was the best predictor of assault to the victim ($r = .43$).

In addition to behavioral history, certain personality traits come into play. At this point, considerable attention is being paid to an obsessive attachment disorder marked by a high need to control the behavior of the partner (Abrams & Robinson, 1998). Examples of controlling behavior are limiting contact with family members and insisting on knowing the whereabouts of the partner at all times. Excessive and obsessive control over the partner has been hypothesized as an important precursor to spousal murder (Wilson & Daly, 1992). With respect to antisocial personality disorder per se, the evidence is mixed (McEwan et al., 2007; Mullen & Pathé, 2002). Douglas and Dutton (2001) have suggested that the APD stalker may be relatively uncommon, although McEwan, Mullen, and MacKenzie (2009) found that a "resentful motivation" (i.e., hostile, irritable personality) coupled with intimacy-seeking was associated with high-risk cases of stalking.

Theoretical explanations of stalking are highly speculative because of the limited research on the topic. Research on stalking has only come into its own in the 1990s (Meloy, 1998). Explanations have centered on disrupted childhood attachments (Kienlen, 1998; MacKenzie et al., 2008) and sociocultural values that support male dominance through aggression (White et al., 2000). However, our theoretical perspective of crime suggests some plausible factors that are consistent with research on related topics such as family violence. This theoretical perspective becomes relevant when we specify the Big Four in relation to stalking behavior. A history of interpersonal conflict within an intimate relationship, an obsessive and hostile personality, and delusions/cognitions supportive of following behavior would suggest to us to be important for study. Antisocial supports for the behavior may not play as important a role because of the overall strength of the other Big Four factors and the cumulative effects of other variables such as alcohol abuse and employment stress.

Serial Killers

When it comes to a discussion of serial killers, we are forced to rely more on educated guesses than hard facts. Serial murderers are usually defined as murderers who have at least three victims over an extended period of time. This definition differentiates the serial murderer from the mass murderer, who kills many people in a brief period of time. Examples of mass murderers are Marc Lépine, who entered a classroom in Montreal and opened fire, killing 14 women; Thomas Hamilton, responsible for shooting and killing 16 school children and their teacher in Dunblane, Scotland; Eric Harris and Dylan Klebold, who killed 12 students and a teacher at Columbine High School in Colorado; and Nidal Malik Hasan, who allegedly killed 13 people at Fort Hood in Texas on November 5, 2009.

Both serial killers and mass murderers, to use Elliott Leyton's (1986:25) description, "appear to kill *for its own sake* [emphasis in original]." There are no other obvious goals, as with the professional killer or the revenge-seeking individual. However, because very little is known about the psychology of mass murderers, we will limit our presentation to serial killers.

Serial murderers have been with us for a long time (e.g., "Jack the Ripper"), but the tremendous media interest has created such a huge consumer interest that an industry popularizing serial killers has developed (Jarvis, 2007, calls it "Monsters Inc."). There are no reliable measures of the prevalence of serial killers, but estimates have ranged from 35 to 500 serial killers in the United States, with as many as 6,000 victims (Holmes & Holmes, 1998; Kiger, 1990). Quinet (2007) argues that the number of victims is an underestimate. When considering missing persons, there may be as many as 1,832 additional victims. Comparing these figures to homicide statistics, serial murders are extremely rare, representing less than 1 percent of all homicides in the United States (Fox & Levin, 1998).

There is an emerging literature on the characteristics of serial killers (Fox & Levin, 1998; Gresswell & Hollin, 1994; Hickey, 2006). First of all, serial killers are usually white males (approximately 15 to 22% are African Americans; Jenkins, 1998; Walsh, 2005). Female serial killers do exist but tend to be relatively rational and instrumental in their actions (Holmes, Hickey & Holmes, 1998). Keeney and Heide (1994) reviewed 14 female serial-killing cases (62 victims) and found that the most frequent motive was money and that the victims were well known to them (e.g., 37% of the victims were family members, and another 43% were "under care" from the murderer). In addition, unlike with the male serial killer, there was no sexual assault, stalking, torture, or "overkill" of the victims.

The male serial killer tends to stalk and seek out the victim, who is often a stranger. David Berkowitz ("Son of Sam") cruised the streets of New York and shot into cars occupied by unsuspecting women or couples. There was no sexual assault—only six people dead. Some male serial killers move in large geographical areas. For example, Ted Bundy began his string of 22 murders in the state of Washington, moved to Utah, then Colorado, and finally was apprehended permanently in Florida (Bundy had been arrested earlier but escaped from a Colorado jail).

The most frightening aspect of some serial killers is the sexual and sadistic form of their murders. This type of killer is definitely the minority among serial killers (Fox & Levin, 1999). These "lust murderers" are noted for their violent fantasies (Gray, Watt, Hassan & MacCulloch, 2003; Holmes, 1989; Holmes & Holmes, 1998). Prentky, Burgess, Rokous, Lee, Hartman, and Ressler (1989) found that 86 percent of 25 serial sexual murderers reported sadistic fantasies prior to the crime. The rate for nonserial sexual murderers was 23 percent. The frequently observed sadistic fantasies of the serial sexual murderer led Holmes (1989) to hypothesize that the fantasies serve as a cognitive rehearsal for the act.

Sex offenders have been thought to lack empathy for their victims. If they had empathy, then the suffering of the victim would inhibit their behavior. In a study of rapists, Rice, Chaplin, Harris, and Coutts (1994) found that rapists showed the greatest sexual arousal to stimuli in which the victim was raped as opposed to consenting to sex. A subsequent study with child molesters (Chaplin, Rice & Harris, 1995) found them to prefer depictions of sexual interactions in which the child suffered and was brutalized. The authors interpreted these findings as attributable to a lack of empathy. However, it is unlikely that sex offenders completely lack empathy. The exceptions may be the delusional, schizophrenic sex offender who commits extreme violence with little awareness of the consequences of his actions. Most sex offenders have some empathic capacity—they do not score zero on the paper-and-pencil measures of empathy. Two possibilities exist. The sex offender may engage in some form of cognitive "neutralization" technique to distance himself psychologically from the victim (e.g., "she deserves it," "she likes it"). The other possibility is that victim suffering is a goal of the assault. That is, the attacker is quite aware of the suffering experienced by the victim, and that is exactly what reinforces the behavior (Hanson, 1997b; Hanson & Scott, 1995). For the serial killer who is also a sexual sadist, sexual pleasure and victim suffering can be powerful nonmediated rewards.

Although not a study of sexual serial killers, a report by Dietz, Hazelwood, and Warren (1990) illustrates the power of cognitions supportive of deviant behavior. They described 30 cases from the FBI that involved sexual torture. Although more than one-half of the cases had no prior criminal record, nearly all of them had histories of deviant sexual behavior, and all had grandiose, narcissistic personalities, with 40 percent having antisocial personality features. The maintenance of deviant sexual cognitions was evident in that most of the sexual sadists either saved something from the women (e.g., clothing, hair) or recorded their crimes in some manner (e.g., diaries, pictures).

The sexual sadist is often portrayed as a social isolate (Martens & Palermo, 2005). However, Hucker (1997) found that there was an accomplice in one-third of the cases studied, a finding noted in other studies of nonsexual serial killers (Walsh, 2005). In the United States, five members of the "Death Angels" (the extremist sect of the Nation of Islam who committed the San Francisco "zebra killings") were convicted of 23 murders but suspected in 60 additional killings. In Canada, there was the notorious case of Karla Homolka, who assisted Paul Bernardo in the abduction, torture, and rape of young girls (allegedly including Homolka's own sister). These are but a few illustrations of social support for even the most heinous crimes.

Sexual serial killers also vary as to their psychological stability. Granted, killing someone for no other reason than to kill them or for sexual gratification can hardly be accepted as psychologically normal. What we mean is that some sexual serial killers are clearly delusional and psychotic while others are more "in control." Ted Bundy showed sufficient charm and skill to lure women to his car and eventually to their rape and death. Others engage in definitely bizarre and grotesque acts, ranging from collecting "trophies" (Edmund Kemper decapitated and kept the heads of his victims) to cannibalism (Jeffrey Dahmer) to sexual desecration after the death of the victim.

So, what can explain repetitive and sadistic murder? The explanations are many, including an XYY genotype in one case (Kraus, 1995); the obvious sexual gratification in sexual serial killers (or they kill to eliminate witnesses); neurological impairment (Langevin, 2003); dissociative, "out-of-body" experiences (Moskowitz, 2004); sexual abuse as a child (Hickey, 2006; Ressler et al., 1986); need for social contact to overcome feelings of loneliness (Martens & Palermo, 2005); need for power and control (Canter & Wentink, 2004); and, of course, the layperson's pronouncement that they are "crazy." Leyton (2005) attributes it to a social class tension, with the serial killer from the working class and the victim from the middle or upper classes.

In our opinion, Leyton (2005) is mistaken in his view that there is some sort of unconscious rebellion against the upper classes. However, he has a point regarding the lack of social controls over the serial killer. Almost all serial killers have had horrendous backgrounds marked by parental abuse and neglect and social isolation. Even the smooth-talking Ted Bundy was an outcast in high school and had only one date. Contrary to popular lore, most serial killers are not specialists, and their criminal versatility is little different from the person who commits only one murder (Wright, Pratt & DeLisi, 2008). Finally, many serial killers, and especially the sadistic sexual killer, experience delusional worlds that further distance them from social controls. The lack of interpersonal and personal controls "frees" the person to act according to idiosyncratic and bizarre fantasies. Coupled with a violent behavioral history, poor coping skills, and sadistic fantasies beginning in childhood, the results are not at all surprising.

Worth Remembering

1. There is more in common between male batterers and general offenders than there are differences.

    Contrary to some feminist theories, there are aspects to domestic violence that extend beyond patriarchal values. Male batterers appear very much like other criminals in their behavioral histories, personality, attitudes, and social support for intimate partner violence.

2. The risk factors for mentally disordered and sex offenders are similar to the risk factors for general offenders.

    Meta-analytic findings indicate that the best predictors of criminal behavior among MDOs and sex offenders are the same as those identified among general offenders (i.e., past history and antisocial personality). Thus, a general theory of criminal conduct can apply to these subtypes of offenders.

3. Knowledge of the varieties of criminal behavior can be forwarded by applying a psychology of criminal conduct (PCC) to the analysis.

    One of the themes in this text is that our knowledge of criminal behavior can be advanced by applying PCC to the analysis. The GPCSL approach to understanding criminal behavior does not rely on psychopathological models of behavior. Understanding of some of the offenders discussed in this chapter—the MDOs, sex offenders, and other human predators—is almost entirely founded upon the wholesale application of clinical models. The results have been unsatisfactory.

Recommended Readings

In the area of domestic violence, we recommend two readings. For those readers who would like a detailed and comprehensive review, we suggest Gondolf's book, *Batterer Intervention Systems: Issues, Outcomes, Recommendations* (2002). A much shorter summary of the subject can be found in Smith Stover's article (2005), "Domestic Violence Research: What Have We Learned and Where Do We Go from Here?" in the *Journal of Interpersonal Violence*.

Two meta-analytic review articles are highly recommended for those with an interest in the mentally disordered offender (Bonta, Law & Hanson, 1998) and the sex offender (Hanson & Morton-Bourgon,

2009). Both reviews show the importance of considering the general offender literature to understanding two groups of offenders. For the reader who would like a broad overview of the sex offender research, there is *Theories of Sexual Offending* (2006), by Tony Ward and his colleagues. This book consists of 20 chapters covering different theoretical and research perspectives of criminal behavior, from evolutionary theory to our own risk/need model.

Finally, for those interested in the more extreme cases of criminal behavior, see Mullen's chapter on stalking in *The New Oxford Textbook of Psychiatry* (pp. 22–28). Then there is Newton's (2000) *The Encyclopedia of Serial Killers*, which brings together the case histories of more than 1,500 serial killers from around the world. This is definitely not a coffee-table book, but for the student with a scholarly interest in the subject, it is a valuable compilation of information.

Part 4

Summary and Conclusions

Chapter 15

A General Personality and Social Psychology of Criminal Conduct: Summary and Conclusions

Welcome to the final chapter. We will review what we think is known and where we see serious gaps in knowledge. We begin with the three types of understanding we set for PCC: That is, an empirical understanding, a theoretical understanding, and an understanding of practical value. All in all, this chapter should provide a concise summary and evaluation of the key elements of PCC.

A distinct preference for general understandings was stated within each of the domains of research, theory, and applications. Important differences between girls and boys, women and men, the young and the older, and the rich and the poor are so easily visible and so readily established that it would be nothing short of silly to rule out important differences in the domains of risk, need, and responsivity. Likewise, the differences among and within community corrections, halfway houses, jails, and prisons are so obvious and so great that serious understandings of assessment and intervention must make some setting-specific accommodations. In addition to the obvious differences, there are host of nuanced differences. Gains from consideration of specificity are ruled out and to some extent are expected. Specificity is not denied by a preference for general understandings.

At the same time, similarities and differences are not simply assumed to exist or asserted to exist but are empirically explored. The empirical explorations strive to respect general theoretical positions along with gender-informed, racially informed, and/or other specific considerations. Likewise, theoretical considerations in regard to settings are open for investigation.

Empirical Understanding

The rational-empirical roots of the psychology of crime induce a healthy skepticism when summarizing research findings. They also feed a respect for evidence. The public that supports the development of a PCC has a right to hear what has been learned, and the people in positions to influence the revitalization of human service should know why they should support direct treatment services.

Incidence and Prevalence of Criminal Activity

Substantial Variation in the Criminal Behavior of Individuals. That there are substantial individual differences in criminal conduct is now well established within PCC. People differ in their frequency of criminal activity and in the number, type, and variety of criminal acts in which they engage. In addition, while accounting for a disproportionate amount of the total criminal activity, the more criminally active offenders tend not to be specialists. These findings are apparent across methods of measurement and particular types of offense, and they are found within the typical indicators of social location such as geography, age, race/ethnicity, gender, and social class. Over the life span, however, gender differences in bullying and relational aggression may make it difficult to build comparable measures of overall antisocial conduct (Odgers et al., 2008).

Early and Late Starters. The developmental criminologists have shown that there is considerable value in recognizing two major sets of offenders: the early starters, who tend to persist in their criminal activity, and late starters, who tend to desist. Of course, the "life-course-persistent" and the "adolescent-limited" typologies hide the fact that many within either group will show different patterns of being in and out of crime at different times.

Chronic and Serious Violent Offenders. As dramatic as is the image of life-course-persistent delinquency, remember that it is a tiny minority of juvenile offenders who are repeat violent offenders. In and around Phoenix, Arizona, only 1 percent of a cohort of 151,209 young persons were charged with two or more violent offenses over their youthful criminal career (Snyder, 1998).

Generality and Specificity. In regard to criminal pathways, and not surprisingly so in view of the well-established gender differences in the base rate of offending, males are overrepresented on the life-course–persistent pathway relative to females. However, the long-term consequences of being on the early and persistent pathway are characterized by gender similarities in terms of adult violence, poor health, poor mental health, and poor socioeconomic circumstances (Odgers et al., 2008).

The Correlates of Criminal Activity

A number of conclusions may be drawn in regard to the correlates of crime. You know that we find it useful to identify the major risk/need factors as the Central Eight, with particular emphasis placed on the

Big Four. Recall that the major risk/need factors may be conceptualized in other ways. For example, components of antisocial personality pattern and a history of antisocial behavior may be pulled together within the label "psychopathy" (as Robert Hare has done with the PCL-R). Travis Hirschi's latest definition of "weak self-control" could incorporate the total of the Central Eight. Others, taking an atheoretical position, will let a statistical procedure such as multiple regression determine what specific indicators within and across categories are selected to create an efficient prediction formula (recall the VRAG assessment approach, and many of the second-generation instruments described in Chapter 10). Another approach would be to sum assessments across the Central Eight and call the resulting score an assessment of general propensity for rule violations (as in the case of the LS/CMI General Risk/Need score).

For our purposes, we like the theoretical relevance of the Big Four in the General Personality and Cognitive Social Learning (GPCSL) perspective. We are also attracted to school/work, family/marital, and leisure/recreation as analytically distinct behavioral settings within which attitudes, behavioral history, and associates may be influenced.

The Central Eight

The Central Eight are outlined (yet again) in Table 15.1 (this is an abbreviated version of Table 2.5). The first four (the Big Four) typically yield predictive validity estimates in the area of .26 (95% CI = .22 – .30, k = 24). The remaining four yield validity estimates in the area of .17 (CI = .13 – .20, k = 23). Overall we estimate the simple predictive criterion validity of a pooling of the Central Eight (through LS/CMI General Risk/Need) to be in the area of .41 (CI = .32 – .50). These predictive values are clearly greater than zero and clearly greater than that achieved by risk/need factors in the minor set (such as lower-class origins and personal internal emotional distress). With reassessments of the dynamic risk factors, we expect predictive validity to nearly double. In brief, we expect that mean *r* of .41 to move up to a mean in the .50s-to-.60s range. This is particularly so when a multidomain sampling of predictors is supplemented by multi-method assessment and when temporal changes on the more dynamic risk factors are included in the prediction formula. Of course, you will also remember that validity estimates increase with attention to follow-up periods and when the assessors are trained professionals.

Wide Applicability

The same sets of risk factors appear to be involved within categories of geography, class, age, gender, and ethnicity. Furthermore, the correlations

Table 15.1
Major Risk/Need Factors and Promising Intermediate Targets for Reduced Recidivism

---

History of antisocial behavior. Early and continuing involvement in the number and variety of antisocial acts in a variety of settings.

    Dynamic need: build up noncriminal alternative behavior in risky situations.

Antisocial personality pattern. Adventurous pleasure-seeking, weak self-control, restlessly aggressive.

    Dynamic need: build problem-solving skills, self-management skills, anger management, and coping skills.

Antisocial cognition. Attitudes, values, beliefs, and rationalizations supportive of crime and cognitive emotional states of anger, resentment, and defiance. Criminal/reformed criminal/anti-criminal identity.

    Dynamic need: reduce antisocial cognition, recognize risky thinking and feeling, build up alternative less risky thinking and feeling, adopt reform/anticriminal identity.

Antisocial associates. Close association with criminal others and relative isolation from anti-criminal others, immediate social support for crime.

    Dynamic need: reduce association with criminal others, enhance association with anti-criminal others.

Family/Marital. Two key elements are nurturance/caring and monitoring/supervision.

    Dynamic need: reduce conflict, build positive relationships, and enhance monitoring and supervision.

School/Work. Low levels of performance and satisfactions in school and/or work.

    Dynamic need: Enhance performance, rewards, and satisfactions.

Leisure/Recreation. Low levels of involvement and satisfactions in anticriminal leisure pursuits.

    Dynamic need: Enhance involvement, rewards, and satisfactions.

Substance Abuse. Abuse of alcohol and/or other drugs.

    Dynamic need: reduce substance abuse, reduce the personal and interpersonal supports for substance-oriented behavior, enhance alternatives to drug abuse.

Note: The minor risk/need factors (and less promising intermediate targets for reduced recidivism) include the following: personal/emotional distress, major mental disorder, physical health issues, fear of official punishment, physical conditioning, low IQ, social class of origin, seriousness of current offense, other factors unrelated to offending.

---

with crime of these biological and social location variables is reduced, if not eliminated, when controls are introduced for the stronger of the personal, interpersonal, and familial risk factors. Remaining to be documented is whether the correlation between gender/ethnicity/race/class and crime that remains after controlling for the major personal and interpersonal factors is actually a result of the processing effects suggested by the social inequality versions of social location theories. PCC does not deny inequality and does not deny bias in both official and unofficial responses to rule violation.

    The same risk factors apply across different types of criminal behavior, although crime-specific indicators of antisocial attitudes, associates, and behavioral history may be most useful when the focus is on violence or sex offenses. For example, laboratory assessments of deviant sexual arousal may enhance predictive validity when working with pedophiles. Similarly, assessments of a history of violence will enhance the prediction of violent offenses.

The Ability to Influence Crime

Meta-analyses of deliberate intervention programs have convinced most readers of the PCC literature that tapping into theoretically based and empirically informed knowledge of risk/need factors will reduce reoffending to a statistically significant and practically significant degree. Two sets of reviews have been particularly influential: the statistically sophisticated reviews of Mark Lipsey and colleagues and the theoretically relevant analyses out of Carleton University with your authors and many others, including Craig Dowden.

The latter reviews have drawn on three aspects of the GPCSL perspective on crime to provide clear guidance on the delivery of effective correctional treatment. In brief, and first, assign service that is in adherence with the principles of *risk, need,* and general *responsivity* (RNR). Second, assign and deliver treatment that adheres to RNR. Third, act in adherence with. . . . Has the point been made?

Once again, first and foremost, all our evidence suggests that nonadherence with the principles of RNR has either null effects on crime or increases crime. Other variables and considerations do influence the overall level of crime reduction achieved through RNR adherence (for example, greater effects from demonstration projects than from "real world" programming), but no other considerations yet explored promote reduced crime in the absence of RNR adherence. The reviews by Lipsey and colleagues consistently support adherence with the human service, risk, and general responsivity principles, but to our knowledge the Lipsey group of researchers has not tested the need principle.

Table 15.2
Mean Effect Size by Targeting of the Central Eight and by Targeting of Noncriminogenic Needs

Need Area	Mean Effect	Size (k)
Criminogenic Needs As Intermediate Targets of Change (Mean ES = .20, CI = .15 — .25)		
Antisocial Attitudes	.21	(78)
Antisocial Associates	.22	(51)
Personality: Weak self-control	.22	(59)
Non-Criminal Alternative Behavior in High Risk Situations	.22	(18)
Parenting: Nurturance/caring and/or Monitoring/supervision	.29	(30)
School/Work	.15	(88)
Substance Abuse	.11 ns	(36)
Leisure/Recreation	not tested	
Noncriminogenic Needs as Intermediate Targets of Change (Mean ES = .05, CI = −.03 − .11)		
Fear of Official Punishment	−.05	(43)
Personal Distress	.08 ns	(101)
Physical Activity	.08 ns	(43)
Conventional Ambition	.08 ns	(29)
Family, other than relationship and Structuring	.01 ns	(45)

Our understanding of the importance of setting criminogenic needs as intermediate targets of change was greatly expanded with the completion of Craig Dowden's master's thesis. Meta-analytic evidence of the value of the targeting of criminogenic needs has been distributed through out the text. The top panel of Table 15.2 summarizes the findings with reference to targeting the dynamic aspects of seven of the Central Eight risk factors (we have no tests of enhanced functioning in the domain of leisure/recreation). The mean effect size associated with the targeting of the "central seven" was .20 (CI = .15 − .25). The mean effect size for the targeting of noncriminogenic needs was .05 (CI = −.03 − .11), as presented in the bottom panel of Table 15.2 on the previous page. The latter mean value is not significantly different than zero and is significantly lower than the corresponding value for the targeting of criminogenic needs.

Table 15.3 presents a more comprehensive description of criminogenic and noncriminogenic needs as promising and less promising intermediate targets of change. This table overlaps considerably with 15.1 and 15.2, but it has a special purpose. Table 15.3 (found on page 504) is based on our theoretically-based predictions, prior to completion of the meta-analyses.

Indeed, using the language of Ted Palmer (1992), Figure 15.1 illustrates how *breadth of criminogenic targeting* is linked with mean reductions in offending. The predictor variable represents the "number of criminogenic needs targeted" minus "the number of noncriminogenic needs targeted." Negative values on breadth indicate that noncriminogenic needs are predominately targeted. Positive values indicate that criminogenic needs are predominately targeted. Mean effect sizes (that is, the amount of reduced reoffending) increase directly with the breadth of the targeting of criminogenic needs. Once again, note that nonadherence is associated with increased crime.

Figure 15.1 is a repeat of Figure 2.3. We repeat in order to stress the importance of other researchers attending to the testing of the principle of criminogenic need. It is disturbing that other meta-analysts have ignored the major issue of the selection of intermediate targets of change. Thankfully, the principles of other key principles have been replicated by other researchers. These other principles include those of human service versus sanctioning, the risk principle, and the general responsivity principle.

When we are involved in training workers and managers we like to show Figure 15.1 (the effect of breadth) along with Figure 15.2 (the effect of adherence to RNR). We ask "where would you like your agency to be located on these graphs?" "You have some choice in your programming—you can be in adherence with RNR and breadth, or you can be part of a criminogenic agency." Now, please, don't forget the relationship principle during training. You must have established a decent relationship with the trainees at this point so that they do not interpret the figures as part of an attack on them and their agency. What you want to do is open up a discussion of the implications of the research findings for them and their agency.

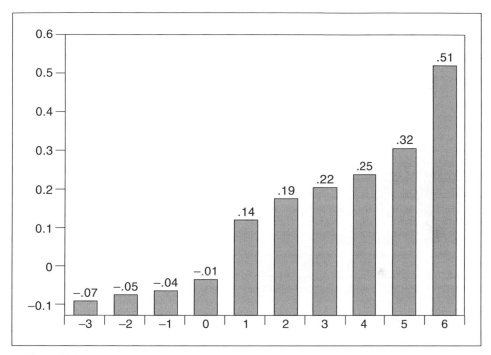

Figure 15.1
Mean Effect Size by Breadth of Targeting Criminogenic Needs (# of Criminogenic Needs minus the # of Noncriminogenic Needs)

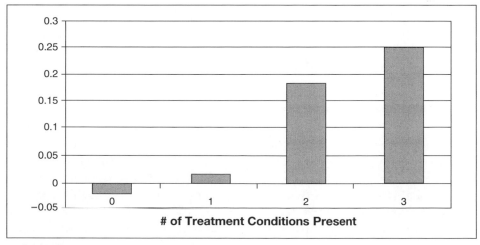

Figure 15.2
Mean Effect Size by Adherence to RNR

Table 15.3
Promising and Less Promising Intermediate Targets in Prevention and Rehabilitation from Andrews, 1989; Andrews, Bonta & Hoge, 1990; Andrews, Leschied & Hoge, 1992

Promising Targets for Change
- Changing antisocial attitudes
- Changing antisocial feelings
- Reducing antisocial peer associations
- Promoting familial affection/communication
- Promoting familial monitoring and supervision
- Promoting child protection (preventing neglect/abuse)
- Promoting identification/association with anticriminal role models
- Increasing self-control, self-management, and problem-solving skills
- Replacing the skills of lying, stealing, and aggression with more prosocial alternatives
- Reducing chemical dependencies
- Shifting the density of the personal, interpersonal, and other rewards and costs for criminal and noncriminal activities in familial, academic, vocational, recreational, and other behavioral settings so that the noncriminal alternatives are favored
- Providing the chronically psychiatrically troubled with low-pressure, sheltered living arrangements
- Ensuring that the client is able to recognize risky situations and has a concrete and well-rehearsed plan for dealing with those situations
- Confronting the personal and circumstantial barriers to service (client motivation; background stressors with which clients may be preoccupied)
- Changing other attributes of clients and their circumstances that, through individualized assessments of risk and need, have been linked reasonably with criminal conduct

Less Promising Targets
- Increasing self-esteem (without simultaneous reductions in antisocial thinking, feeling, and peer associations)
- Focusing on vague emotional/personal complaints that have not been linked with criminal conduct
- Increasing the cohesiveness of antisocial peer groups
- Improving neighborhood-wide living conditions without touching the criminogenic needs of higher-risk individuals and families
- Showing respect for antisocial thinking on the grounds that the values of one culture are as equally valid as the values of another culture
- Increasing conventional ambition in the areas of school and work without concrete assistance in realizing these ambitions
- Attempting to turn the client into a "better person," when the standards for being a "better person" do not link with recidivism

An Understanding of Practical Value

Prediction Instruments

On the issue of practical prediction, there is no question that change has been revolutionary over the last 30 years. Unstructured clinical judgment does so poorly relative to structured assessment approaches that the ethicality of unstructured risk assessment is now a serious professional issue. As reviewed in Chapter 10, several second-generation instruments are doing as well as third- and fourth-generation instruments in the simple prediction of reoffending. However, second-generation instruments that do not sample a variety of criminogenic needs cannot assist in the building of an individualized treatment plan that is in adherence with the need and/or breadth principles. Nor can their predictive validity be improved through reassessments on static variables.

The great promise of fourth-generation instruments is that they will enhance adherence with risk, need, breadth, general responsivity, and specific responsivity. Recall that fourth-generation instruments follow the case management process from initial assessment, case management planning, service delivery, reassessment, and case closure. Table 15.4 provides a summary of mean predictive criterion validities for a number of well known risk/need assessment instruments.

Effective Prevention and Treatment

The principles were summarized in Table 2.1. A major issue here is whether the empirically validated principles of human service, RNR, and breadth can be implemented in the real world with sufficient levels of adherence that reduced reoffending is actually achieved. It may appear straightforward but, in fact, it requires major policy and organizational changes and major efforts on the part of managers and staff for adherence to be accomplished

The issue is so important that this text now includes a separate chapter on the challenges faced by treatment in the real world (Chapter 12). The International Community Corrections Association (ICCA) was one of the professional associations that most strongly promoted RNR from

Table 15.4
Mean Predictive Criterion Validity Estimates (r) from Meta-analytic Studies by Generation: Based on Andrews, Bonta & Wormith (2006: Table 2)

Measure	Recidivism		
	General	Violence	
First Generation (Clinical Judgment)			
	.10	.13	
Second Generation (Actuarial / Mechanical with emphasis on historical)			
General criminality scales	.42	.39	Sex/MDO
SFS	.26		
Wisconsin	.31		
SIR	.36		
PCL-R	.27	.27	
VRAG		.39	
Third Generation (Mechanical with attention to dynamic risk factors)			
LSI-R	.36	.25	
Fourth Generation (Mechanical with structured case planning and follow-up)			
LS/CMI General Risk/Need	.41	.29	

MDO = Mentally disordered offenders

the early 1990s. Their 2005 conference (in Atlantic City, NJ) very aptly focused on making "what works" work.

As outlined in Chapter 12, many agencies are struggling with the implementation of RNR and need help now or the movement is going to suffer and the community will be exposed to more crime. Quite frankly, for some of us, it is difficult to bear the thought of prevention and corrections returning to that "nothing works—we can't predict—we can't influence" position of anticipatory failure. Never again do we want perspectives on offenders that negate human diversity, dismiss human agency, and indeed destroy hope.

Beyond incapacitation, we know that increases in the severity of judicial sanctions will only increase recidivism. As positive as we are toward restorative justice, we are sure that any justice models that do not introduce human service programs will have minimal impact on reduced victimization (Chapter 13).

A Theoretical Understanding

It is difficult to imagine any new or current perspective that would not recognize the importance of the Big Four and the Central Eight. However, the theories may differ considerably in the underlying model of human behavior. For us, a GPCSL perspective works as well or better than any alternative. The PIC-R perspective has served our interests in the domains of prediction, influence, and explanation. Cognitive research and service developments in the domains of both personally mediated control and automatic control promise even more powerful prediction and clinical interventions. And this promise for the future exists when the cognitive social learning interventions (when also in adherence with RNR and breadth) already have basically no serious competitors. Perhaps, however, we could make the PIC-R statement a little more attractive. In the early days, Walter Friesen, then an undergraduate student at Carleton and now an independent PhD psychologist, had a poetic comment:

> There once was a theory called PIC-R
> That suggested what makes offenders tinker
> Critics sputtered with rage
> As the prose kept getting thick-r and thick-r.

Make your choice among the theories. We have nothing left to say about it.

Some Big and Some Small Issues

There are a few additional issues and challenges that we would like you to consider.

Specific Responsivity

You may have noted that we have not developed the principle of specific responsivity to any serious degree. We have not done so because it remains underexplored. Indeed, we now find some of the old personality-based classification systems quite quaint and old-fashioned. Certainly, these differential treatment personality systems existed before we introduced the concept of specific responsivity. Readers familiar with earlier editions of this text will know that we have actually dropped that whole section from this edition. Patricia Van Voorhis (1994) has convinced us that those old systems basically come down to three or four personality subtypes. One very antisocial group sounds somewhat like a psychopath, while another very antisocial group appears more emotionally disturbed and perhaps with neuropsychological impairment. Another subtype is less antisocial and appears prone to worrying and anxiety. Another subtype is basically not antisocial at all by the usual personality and attitudinal indicators but is a low-risk, situational offender.

The major dimensions of psychopathy, immaturity, and emotional distress are represented in Table 15.5 where we summarize how we view current thinking on specific responsivity. Our cognitive/interpersonal skill level factor combines empathy, interpersonal maturity, self-regulation skills, and verbal intelligence. The treatment recommendation here is that styles of service that are verbally and interpersonally demanding and depend upon cognitive skills and interpersonal sensitivity be avoided with all offenders but the very high functioning ones. If you are in doubt about this factor, then use structured cognitive social learning strategies. Don't take a chance on inadvertently increasing crime through low structuring. In the main, always adhere to the principle of general responsivity but when working with high-functioning persons you may somewhat reduce the structure and build on their exceptional talents.

The remainder of the specific responsivity factors are fairly straightforward. Gender responsivity and motivational level are particularly interesting. A very lively literature has evolved in regard to woman-specific treatment recommendations (see Table 15.6). Entered in the table are the promising intermediate areas of change suggested by Bloom and her colleagues (Bloom & Covington, 2001; Bloom, Owen & Covington, 2003; Covington and Bloom, 1999) in work with women. Specific responsivity recommendations are also listed. We have noted those factors that are compatible with RNR and those that are less so. There are high levels of compatibility except in regard to these particular feminists' insistence on focusing on self-esteem, sexuality, and spirituality issues. We simply doubt that those foci are relevant to reduced reoffending. They may be very important targets for women but not, we expect, in relation to their antisocial behavior. Of course, RNR principles apply to correctional treatment programs and not necessarily to personal

Table 15.5
Principles of Specific Responsivity

Cognitive/interpersonal skill level (combination of empathy, interpersonal maturity, self-regulation skills, verbal intelligence). Styles and modes of service that are verbally and interpersonally demanding and depend upon self-regulation, self-reflection, and interpersonal sensitivity should be used only with very high-functioning persons.

Interpersonal anxiety. Avoid both interpersonal confrontation and very intense interpersonal exchanges.

Antisocial personality pattern (APP). In total, and in isolation, the personality elements of APP suggest not only risk (intensive supervision and service), criminogenic needs (multiple) but also specific responsivity issues.

   Low anxiety, low empathy, shallow emotion, manipulative: high structure including monitoring and supervision and wide-open communication among involved service and control staff Sensation-seeking: program novel and exciting opportunities and events.

   "Acting out" is reliably rewarded/low motivation for change: treatment is readily accessible, outreach, and part of the total environmental surround.

Weak social support for change. Neutralize antisocial associates, structure active exposure to others who model and reinforce real alternatives to antisocial styles of thinking, feeling, and acting.

Gender. Provide gender-responsive services.

Age. Developmentally appropriate services.

Ethnicity/cultural considerations.

Mental disorder Address needs specific to disorder.

Case Management Classification. The Wisconsin "responsivity" classification system.

* **Motivation**. Match services according to stages of change.

* **Strengths**. Build on the strengths of the person.

---

* Additions to the Andrews, Bonta & Hoge (1990) list

---

fulfillment programming. How do we express this clearly and yet with respect? How about this: where is the evidence that spirituality is associated with peace and security? It is not evident in the personality literature, and it is certainly not evident in the daily news reports from areas around the world.

For purposes of clarity, in the expanded RNR model (Table 2.1), the normative and specific responsivity principles are very important. Noncriminogenic needs may be set as intermediate targets for humanitarian and entitlement reasons in accordance with the normative principle. Additionally, collaborative treatment planning may establish the motivational value of targeting selected noncriminogenic needs for particular offenders. The earliest statements of RNR were not sufficiently clear on these points.

Motivational interviewing (MI) is creating a buzz in the fields of addiction and corrections. The promise of major behavior change through miniscule interventions is too attractive to ignore. MI was mentioned in our discussion of substance abuse in Chapter 9. In Table 15.7, we have tried to capture the spirit of MI while also drawing attention to how

Table 15.6
Woman-Specific Treatment Recommendations Assigned to Need and Responsivity Considerations (based on Recommendations of Bloom, 1999; Bloom & Covington, 2001; Covington, 2000; Covington & Bloom, 1999)

NEED: Promising intermediate areas of change

Expansion and Growth of Self: knowledge of sources of self-esteem; knowledge of the effects of sexism, racism, and stigma on sense of self; develop own sense of self; substance abuse as a "self-disorder";˙ address roles of mother, professional, wife, partner, daughter, offender; understand poor self-image and history of trauma and abuse; integrate outer selves (roles) with inner selves (feelings, thoughts, attitudes).

Relationships: explore roles in family of origin; myths of motherhood; relationships with mother; relationship histories including possible violence; ˙decisions re building healthy support systems; understand substance abuse as maintaining relationships with a drug-abusing partner or managing pain of abuse;˙ recognize unhealthy, illusory or unequal relationships with partners, friends and family.

Sexuality: explore sexuality, body image, sexual identity, sexual abuse, and fear of sex when clean and sober; dealing with sexual dysfunction, shame, fear and/or trauma; substance abuse as pain management.

Spirituality: introduce concepts of spirituality, prayer and meditation and how they relate to healing and recovery; in relation to transformation, connection, meaning, and wholeness.

*Decisionmaking: Objective observation to establish facts; Reflective emotional reactions; Interpretive assessment of meaning and impact; Decisive identification of actions or decisions.

*Express and contain negative emotions appropriately.

*Empowerment through skill building.

*Substance abuse: ˙enhance quality of relationships at home, school, work, leisure.

*Question unhealthy relationships.

Disability-related issues.

Appearance and overall health and hygiene.

*Life plan development.

RESPONSIVITY: Mode, style, influence strategies, service practices

*Women-only groups and individual sessions with female helper.

*Staff model healthy relationships.

*Create a community with a sense of connection.

*Not the clinical model.

*Emphasis on safety.

*Emphasis on connecting: mutual respect.

*Build on strengths.

Twelve-step programs.

*Some psycho-educational methods.

*Emphasis on raising and exploring issues.

*Least restrictive environment .

* Compatible with RNR

Table 15.7
Specific Responsivity: Stages of Change and Motivational Interviewing

Stages of Change	Motivational Interviewing Focus
Precontemplation	
Reluctance	Use reflective listening, summarizing, affirmation to explore situation
Rebellion	Roll with resistance, don't argue; Agree that change can't be forced upon one; encourage menu of options
Resignation	Instill hope, explore barriers, encourage small steps, build self-efficacy
Rationalization	Empathy and reflective listening; encourage mapping of pros and cons; don't argue
Contemplation	Accurate information on the risky behavior; Mapping of pros and cons; summarize; Affirmation; increasing self-efficacy
Preparation: Developing an acceptable plan	Listening, reflecting, pros and cons and realistic plan
Action: Implementing the Plan	Listening and affirming
Maintenance: Relapse	A "slip" is not failure. Return to earlier stages

The Spirit of MI: collaboration, evocation, autonomy. General Principles: Express empathy (acceptance, reflective listening, ambivalence is normal); Develop discrepancy (client presents arguments for change; discrepancy between behavior and important personal goals/values); Roll with resistance (avoid arguing for change; resistance is not directly opposed; new perspectives invited not imposed); Support self-efficacy (support belief in the possibility of change: "I know what to do, and I know how to do it"; Counselor's belief in clients ability to change is important).

Note: This table provides a very brief summary of key ideas from Miller & Rollnick (2002) and DiClemente & Velasquez (2002).

stages of change are differentially linked to MI interventions. This is a fascinating area with terrific energy and impressive research unfolding.

Some Feminist, Critical Criminological, and Clinical Psychological Challenges

Table 15.8 outlines ever so briefly the major challenges that have been thrown at PCC and RNR. We feel justified in reducing these challenges to one-line comments because, in fact, we have been addressing the majority of them throughout the text. Let us go through the challenges roughly in order of their presentation in Table 15.8.

In regard to point 1, of course, we all should be critical about the ability to predict or influence events. PCC and RNR attempt to be true to a rational empirical approach throughout. Unsparing criticism in combination with respect for evidence is the rule of the game. We have

Table 15.8
Some Feminist and Critical Criminological Criticisms of RNR

1. Skepticism regarding the ability to predict recidivism.

2. PCC and RNR do not care enough about poverty, gender, and race/ethnicity (favored variables of critical criminology).

3. "Risk" reflects a white, middle-class male norm.

4. "Risk" really reflects age, race, class, and gender.

5. RNR-based classification is immoral, inefficient, subjective, and discriminatory (as opposed to classification based on age, race, class, and gender; or to professional judgment; or to what?).

6. RNR-based treatment does not work with girls and women (or with blacks, or with the poor, or with the emotionally distressed, or with. ...: "Nothing works").

7. RNR-based classification and/or treatment is not as valid or as powerful as the alternative (what alternative?).

8. Victimization causes crime.

9. Offenders should be offered healing rather than correctional treatment.

10. It is more important to meet the noncriminogenic needs of women than it is to focus on criminogenic needs.

---

tried throughout to provide the reader with quantitative estimates of the magnitude of variation and covariation. Whenever a correlation coefficient or an AUC estimate was presented, the error was almost always specified. Additionally, we distinguished among research designs and hence placed highest value upon prospective longitudinal and experimental studies.

In regard to point 2, we could have done more about poverty, gender, and ethnicity, but we did what we were able to do while reporting upon existing systematic empirical investigations *and* keeping our focus on our major task of understanding variation in the criminal behavior of individuals. We know there are thousands of stories out there about the nexus of age, race, class, and gender, but that is a different playing field than the one we are on.

The rules of play on the field of rational empiricism are clearly different from the rules in effect on other fields. Smith, Cullen, and Latessa (2009) reviewed 27 tests of the validity of LSI-R general risk/need involving a total of 14,737 women. The mean r was .35 (CI = .34 − .36). What were the responses in the same edition of *Criminology and Public Policy*? Much of the rhetoric is just more of the same through repetitive appeals to the unique gendered context of crime—the importance of "gendered, racialized, and stratified" understandings. The use of quantitative approaches is discounted by declarations of its inattention to the "unique." However, there seems to be no hesitation in drawing upon quantitative studies that fail to support the LS approach. For example, Reisig, Holtfreter, and Morash (2006) reported one of the lowest validity estimates ever reported for LS risk/need. The findings of total outliers are accepted if not celebrated, while the overall results of 27 tests are discounted. Tests of "gender responsiveness" are cited in positive ways when only one of four tests of gender responsive assessments revealed significant incremental validity over LS risk/need in the prediction of recidivism. Such selectivity in criticism is of questionable value. The responses to Smith et al. (2009) did include a stunning advance that will be noted below.

In regard to points 3, 4, and 5, a major function of standardized risk/ need assessment has been to make the basis of judgments and decisions highly visible and subject to normative review. Do these critics really believe that unstructured judgment is automatically more moral and less discriminatory than open and visible decisionmaking? Do these critics truly believe that consideration of age, race, gender, and class of origin will predict better than RNR-based risk/need? Do they really believe that consideration of the social location variables is somehow more moral and less discriminatory? Who has done more for the reduction of discrimination in decisionmaking than the structured risk/need assessment folks (Gottfredson & Snyder, 2004)?

Challenges 6 through 9 are relatively straightforward empirical issues. Does RNR-based prediction and programming work for women and other demographic-based subtypes? We have explored this issue throughout the text. We have not found any evidence that personality, attitudes, associates, or behavioral history are unimportant for any demographically defined subgroup. Nor have we found that the impact of RNR adherence and breadth on future offending varies with age, race, or gender. A history of being victimized may well contribute to crime but, in terms of the research reviewed in this text, it does so through the Big Four. The experience of abuse may well activate feelings of being mistreated, and such feelings do link with criminal behavior. However, if one is predisposed to internalization of personal misery, there is little reason to predict a criminal response.

We all value healing, and we all believe that the noncriminogenic needs of men and women and of boys and girls are worthy of attention. The fact that personal fulfillment and spirituality do not link with criminal activity does not negate their importance in human and/or social terms. We are not convinced, however, that a focus on noncriminogenic needs will contribute to reduced offending no matter how impassioned the appeal of enhancing personal well-being and personal accomplishment (Ward, Melzer & Yates, 2007; Ward & Stewart, 2003). We do like the idea that PIC-R and RNR be integrated with a powerful model of human motivation. It is the case that our use of the term "need" is in the correctional tradition and suggests "problematic conditions." We wish Tony Ward and his associates all the best as they conduct research on their "good lives model" with due consideration of human motivation.

Allow us to once again express a value-based opinion. We would rather see faith-based, mental health, social service, human service, academic/vocational, and psycho-recreational dollars delivered to their respective agencies than to justice and corrections. We do not need to see any more precious resources irrelevant to crime diverted to justice and corrections. To the contrary, we would like to see some justice/correctional dollars diverted to family, social, health, and other services for the delivery of RNR programs that focus on reduced antisocial behavior. We should not ask justice and corrections to do all of the work required to enhance public safety.

More plainly: clinicians, please bring your considerable skills to the task of reduced victimization. The normative and specific responsivity principles of RNR stress the value of a concern with noncriminogenic needs for humanitarian and motivational purposes. Still, remembering the criminogenic need principle, it is best if the intermediate targets of change are predominately criminogenic needs. The task is to enhance the rewards associated with alternatives to criminal activity.

Inspection of Table 15.9 reveals the meta-analytic evidence on the effects of the targeting of noncriminogenic needs on the relationship between RNR adherence and reduced recidivism. Clearly, the simple targeting of noncriminogenic needs does not negate the crime prevention effects of RNR adherence. The picture changes dramatically when noncriminogenic needs are targeted predominately. Under those conditions, only two of 116 programs (less than 2%) were in adherence with even two of the core clinical principles of risk, need, and general responsivity. In the language introduced in our discussion of "routine" correctional programming, those programmers who are committed to working on noncriminogenic needs are not offering "smart" programs. Indeed, when noncriminogenic needs were targeted predominately, only 53 percent (61/116) were human service programs that were in adherence with one or more of the core clinical principles of RNR.

The programmers who focus on more noncriminogenic needs than criminogenic needs apparently believe that it is proper to practice in a

Table 15.9
Mean Effect Size (*r*) by Level of RNR Adherence and the Targeting of Noncriminogenic Needs (Based on Dowden & Andrews, 2004, databank; k = number of tests of treatment)

	Level of RNR Adherence				
	0 (k) None	1 (k) Low	2 (k) Moderate	3 (k) High	*r* with ES
1. Full Sample	−.02 (124)	.02 (106)	.18 (84)	.26 (60)	.56
2. Some Noncriminogenic Needs Targeted	−.03 (62)	.01 (81)	.23 (26)	.24 (11)	.51
3. Noncriminogenic Needs Targeted Predominately	−.03 (55)	−.00 (59)	.16 (2)	— (0)	.16 ns

ns: statistically nonsignificant (*p* > .05)

matter that ignores the key knowledge associated with GPCSL perspectives on human behavior. They possess a "special" knowledge (a unique understanding of crime and criminals) that allows them to deliver services that increase crime or have no effects. With all due respect, it is time for those who feel they are entitled to offer programs inconsistent with the GPCSL and RNR perspectives to show some social responsibility. They must begin to program and evaluate in a "smarter" manner. To our knowledge, the evidence base in support of their approaches flirts with nil.

In regard to point 10 in Table 15.8, what are the alternatives to RNR-based approaches? Return to unstructured professional judgment? Apply the totally unique "gendered, racialized, stratified" model? Concentrate on noncriminogenic needs? Assume that the promotion of personal well-being will automatically reduce criminogenic needs? None of this sounds very "smart."

One very recent answer, from a very surprising source, is as follows:

> The absence of empirical evidence to support the effectiveness of alternative feminist approaches to risk assessment, treatment, and programming places managerially minded correctional agencies in a quandary as to how gender 'ought to matter.' . . . research that is explicitly attentive to the literatures on gender (and race) as well as the expansive research literature on risk and correctional treatment can meaningfully advance theory, research and policy (Hannah-Moffat, 2009:216).

Hannah-Moffat (2009) now endorses an approach that was introduced in the province of Ontario in the mid-1990s. Back in the 1990s, Ontario introduced gender-informed, racially informed, and setting-informed RNR-based assessment approaches. Those instruments are now available worldwide as the YLS/CMI and LS/CMI.

The Hannah-Moffat statement suggests that significant movement has occurred. Frankly, her recognition of the "expansive research literature on risk and correctional treatment" comes as a total surprise to your authors. It appears that the Smith et al. (2009) meta-analysis has contributed to a major shift in the opinions of a prominent critical feminist who has been a persistent critic of GPCSL and RNR.

Giving Credit

We completed a paper for the ICCA conference in 2005 wherein we wanted to identify the many researchers and thinkers who have influenced PCC and RNR. Without comment, and at the risk of forgetting some, they are listed in Table 15.10.

Table 15.10
Contributions to a General Personality and Social Learning/Cognitive Perspective on Crime (see Andrews & Bonta, 2006: Chapters 3 and 4)

Freud: The structure of personality (id, ego, superego); Psychological maturity as strong self-control, stable familial affection, and social productivity.

The Yale school: The birth of social learning theory through (a) the integration of psychoanalysis, behaviorism, and sociology/anthropology, and (b) the specification of frustration aggression (Dollard, Doob, Miller, Mowrer, Sears).

Glueck and Glueck (1950): Identified the major risk/need factors recognized today while placing lower-class origins, personal distress, and psychopathology in the weak risk category.

Sociologists who recognized the importance of human diversity relative to social location: Robert Agnew, Francis Cullen, Michael Hindelang, Travis Hirschi, Walter Reckless, Edwin Sutherland & Donald Cressey, Gresham Sykes & David Matza.

Some behavioral, social learning, and social cognitive psychologists: Icek Ajzen & Martin Fishbein, Neil Azrin, Albert Bandura & Richard Walters, Roy Baumeister, Leonard Berkowitz, Charles Carver & Michael Scheier, Donald Meichenbaum, Walter Mischel, Gerald Patterson, B.F. Skinner, Michael Rutter.

Meta-analytic contributions to prediction and/or treatment: Don Andrews, James Bonta, Craig Dowden, Paul Gendreau, Claire Goggin, Karl Hanson, Mark Lipsey, Fredrich Lösel, Doris MacKenzie, Santiago Redondo.

Developmental criminologists: David Farrington, Alan Leschied, Rolf Loeber, Terri Moffitt, Richard Tremblay.

Practical assessment instruments: The Wisconsin group (Baird, Bemus, Heinz), the LSI group (Andrews, Bonta, Hoge, Wormith), the Penetanguishene group (Quinsey, Rice, Harris, Cormier), Danny Clark, Don Gottfredson, Robert Hare, Peter Hoffman, Wagdy Loza, Larry Motiuk, Joan Nuffield, Leslie Wilkins.

Some GPSL perspectives: Robert Agnew et al. (2002); Don Andrews & James Bonta (1994, 2003, 2006); Robert Burgess & Ronald Akers (1966); Curt Bartol (1998); Albert Bandura (1977, 1997, 2001); Ronald Blackburn (1993); Hans Eysenck (1964, 1977); Scott Henggeler & associates (1998); Richard Jessor & Shirley Jessor (1977); Walter Mischel & Yuichi Shoda (1995); Gerry Patterson (1993).

Great Disseminators and Trainers: Brad Bogue, Bob Cormier, David Dillingham, Liz Fabiano, Alex Holsinger, Ed Latessa, Chris Lowenkamp, David Perry, Frank Porporino, Bob Ross, Patricia Van Voorhis.

Responsibility for Programs

Some readers may have noted in this chapter that on several other occasions we began to flirt with the issue of who should own, run, and deliver human service programs in the justice and correctional context. We flirt with the idea and then always run away from it (weak coping with stress, perhaps). We are quite dismayed by the low level of RNR and breadth adherence we find in "real world" corrections. For example, when Anthony Flores and his colleagues (Flores, Russell, Latessa & Travis, 2005) asked 171 correctional practitioners to identify three of the Big Four criminogenic needs, none could. As obvious as RNR is to us, adherence is a problem in the field. William R. Miller and Kathleen M. Carroll (2006), two of our favorite people in the addiction area, have provided a nonquantitative review of the literature on what works in the field of substance abuse. The findings are highly compatible with what was reviewed here. In their last chapter, however, they say:

> Intervention is not a specialist problem but a broad social responsibility that should be shared by many public and private sectors (p. 302).
>
> The major modifiable risk and protective factors are not specific to drug problems, but influence a broad range of personal and social ills (p. 303).
>
> Successful interventions are not those that make a person's life more miserable, but rather those that offer a more rewarding alternative (p. 308).

They are arguing that substance abuse problems should be merged into mainstream health and social services. We think antisocial behavior is too serious an issue to be left in the hands of justice and correctional agencies. Mainstream health and social service agencies and agents may consider contributing by offering programs that build rewarding alternatives to crime for moderate- and higher-risk cases.

Conclusion

There now is a human science of criminal conduct. There are empirically defensible theories of criminal conduct that may be helpful in designing and delivering effective service. The literature is reasonably strong and supports vigorous pursuit of ethical, decent, humane, and cost-efficient approaches to prevention and rehabilitative programming for moderate- and higher-risk cases under a variety of conditions of just sanctioning—and under primary prevention conditions. The active and effective human service agency may contribute to a still more powerful knowledge base by building assessment, reassessment, and research into the agency.

In the few years between the fourth and firth editions of this text, considerable evidence has accrued that PCC and RNR-based understandings are coming into close contact with other approaches to understanding criminal activity. Some of those approaches had been quite distanced from RNR and PCC. This chapter has revealed the very recent appreciation of RNR and feminist approaches for each other. That movement is described best by Blanchette and Brown (2006). Another recent area of interaction, if not integration, is between PCC/RNR and assessment and treatment in the forensic mental health tradition. Advances are promised for PCC and perhaps for the feminist and forensic areas.

From the first edition of this book we stated that a major issue, one on which work was only beginning, entailed dissemination and implementation: How to make use of what works. The implementation issues remain huge.

Recommended Readings

James R.P. Ogloff and Michael R. Davis (2004) have completed an interesting assessment of the contributions of the RNR approach. You will appreciate their thoughtful analysis of the "good lives model" from clinical psychology and their attention to specific responsivity.

Kelley Blanchette and Shelley Brown have done an admirable job of trying to reconcile feminist perspectives with the RNR model in their book, *The Assessment and Treatment of Women Offenders*. The reader is exposed to the major arguments for a women-specific theory of crime and learns that many of these arguments dissipate when the RNR model is given fuller consideration.

Technical Notes

Technical Note 1.1

Exploring Variability in Criminal Behavior

A few illustrations of the facts regarding variability in the criminal activity of individuals follow. The examples illustrate the extent and magnitude of the variation. We will also see that variability is found within most samples of individuals, be they male or female, black or white, young or old, upper-class or lower-class. In these examples, it will also be apparent that age (being young), gender (being male), and several other variables are major correlates and predictors of criminal behavior. Understanding these correlations—their magnitude and their causal and practical significance—is part of the focus of later chapters.

Inferring Individual Differences from Aggregated Crime Rates

The quality of centralized records of officially processed criminal activity may be questioned in many ways. However, national criminal justice statistics do provide a meaningful glimpse of the variation in types and frequency of criminal acts.

- The number of officially recorded murders was 594 for Canada in 2007 (Dauvergne, 2008). This represents a rate of 1.8 based on 100,000 population. Unless we assume that a vast proportion of the Canadian population were accomplices to the murders, it appears that in 2007 the act of murder was engaged in by relatively few Canadians.

- In 2007, there were 29,600 robberies recorded in Canada, yielding a rate of 90 per 100,000.

- In the same year there were 1,094,703 property crimes reported to the police, a rate of 3,320 per 100,000

- Overall, 2,300,000 Canadian criminal code violations were recorded for a crime rate

of 6,9884 for 100,000 of the population in 2007.

- In sum, according to the national data banks that draw upon official records, relatively few Canadians were engaging in criminal activity in 2007. Certainly, in terms of having committed acts that contributed to the official counts for 2007, the vast majority of Canadians, but not all Canadians, would receive a criminal behavior score of zero.

Although the rates are higher in the United States, we still reach the same general conclusion: the vast majority of Americans, but not all Americans, commit few criminal acts. The rates per 100,000 persons as reported by the Federal Bureau of Investigation for various violent crimes in the United States in 2007 were as follows:

- 5.9 for homicide

- 155.7 for robbery

- 3,337 for property crimes

It is well known that official records provide underestimates of the overall level of criminal activity in the community. Thus, surveys of self-reported victimization are gaining some importance in criminology. Michael Hindelang (1981) studied the incidence of crime in the United States with data provided by the National Crime Survey. This survey involved interviewing all persons 12 years of age or older in a national sample of approximately 65,000 American households twice a year from 1973 to 1977. Interviewers asked questions regarding types of victimization in the last six months and inquired about the age, sex, and race of the offender in cases in which the offender had been seen by the victim. Hindelang's (1981) report, although not the most recent, is interesting because he employed

Technical Note 1.1 *(continued)*

several weighing strategies in order to generate national crime rate estimates for various combinations of offender age, sex, and race. Personal crimes were defined as rape, robbery, assault, and theft from the person. The annual rates reflect the number of personal offenses occurring for every 100,000 potential offenders within 12 categories of age, sex, and race. A sample of the findings is reproduced in Table TN 1.1–1. ("Total" refers to the total number of personal crimes, not only to the numbers of rape and robbery).

Table TN 1.1–1 not only reveals substantial evidence of individual differences in criminal behavior but also shows that age, sex, and race are correlates of criminality in the United States. Taking all three risk factors into account, the rates reached levels of more than 84,000 offenses per 100,000 young black males between the ages of 18 to 20. On the other extreme, with the three risk factors absent, the rates for white women over 20 years of age were less than 300 per 100,000 such women.

Inferring Individual Differences from Surveys of a Criminal Past

The field of criminology can now draw upon a vast number of self-report surveys of a criminal past. We have chosen the Travis Hirschi (1969) survey because of its immense importance to the development of PCC and criminology in general. Hirschi drew a stratified random sample of 5,545 students in 11 junior and senior high schools in Contra Costa County (California) in

1964. For 4,077 of the students, he was able to obtain both official (police files) and self-reported measures (questionnaires) of delinquency. For various reasons, Hirschi (1969) reported only on subsamples of this set of students. Thus, there are fluctuations in the composition of the samples referred to in the examples presented below. However, within each subsample there was evidence of the individual differences that constitute our main concern in this text.

- Within the subsample of 2,126 white boys: 68 percent had no police record, 8 percent had a record but no offenses had been recorded in the previous two years, 11 percent had one recorded offense in the last two years, 5 percent had two recorded offenses, and 8 percent had three or more recorded offenses.

- Within the subsample of 1,479 black boys: 43 percent had no police record, 12 percent had a record but no offenses had been recorded in the previous two years, 18 percent had one recorded offense in the last two years, 9 percent had two recorded offenses, and 18 percent had three or more recorded offenses.

Rick Linden and Kathy Fillmore (1981) compared the self-report data collected by Hirschi with the self-reported delinquent activity of young men and women who attended schools in Edmonton, Alberta. Their results are shown in Table TN 1.1–2. They reported extensive evidence of substantial individual differences in delinquent behavior.

Table TN 1.1–1
Estimated Annual Rates of Offending per 100,000 Potential Offenders

| | | MALES | | | | | |
| | | White | | | Black | | |
	Age	12–17	18–20	21+	12–17	18–20	21+
Rape		77	291	152	403	1,624	735
Robbery		1,203	2,245	463	16,663	35,030	7,000
Total		7,974	15,054	3,786	43,158	84,504	18,031

| | | FEMALES | | | | | |
| | | White | | | Black | | |
	Age	12–17	18–20	21+	12–17	18–20	21+
Rape		5	0	0	92	39	7
Robbery		212	71	33	1,307	703	164
Total		2,124	1,138	264	8,639	4,468	1,428

Adapted from Hindelang, 1981

Technical Note 1.1 *(continued)*

- Fifty-three percent of the 1,264 California boys and 60 percent of the 571 Alberta boys admitted to theft of property worth less than $2.00. Seven percent of the California boys and 2 percent of the Alberta boys admitted to theft of property worth $50.00 or more. Forty-two percent of the boys in the California sample and 41 percent of the boys in the western Canadian sample admitted to having assaulted someone. Almost 24 percent (23.7%) of the California boys and 23.0 percent of the Canadian boys reported having committed three or more delinquent acts.

- The corresponding data for the 563 young California women and the 583 young Canadian women are presented in Table TN 1.1–2, along with the data for the boys. The tabled values refer to the percentage of cases admitting particular offenses.

Inferring Individual Differences from Prospective Longitudinal Studies

The extent of individual differences in criminal behavior is now well established through a number of longitudinal studies in various countries and circumstances. These studies are so important to the development of the psychology of criminal behavior that several will be described in some detail here and will be referred to again throughout the text. A feature of some of these studies is that both incidence and prevalence were examined. That is, several of these longitudinal studies are able to report on both the number of offenders and the number of crimes committed by offenders.

The majority of the examples have been drawn from Katherine Van Dusen and Sarnoff Mednick's (1983) edited collection, *Prospective*

Studies of Crime and Delinquency. That classic collection is recommended to all students of the social psychology of criminal behavior. Our sampling of findings will confirm that the social psychology of criminal conduct has much to explain. James McGuire (2004) identified more than 20 longitudinal studies dating from 1974.

The Philadelphia Birth Cohorts. Marvin Wolfgang (1983) and his colleagues have been reporting on two major samples of Philadelphia youths. The 1945 birth cohort includes 9,945 males born in 1945 who lived in Philadelphia from at least their tenth to their eighteenth birthdays. A 10 percent random sample ($N = 975$) of these boys was drawn and 567 of them were found and interviewed around the time of their twenty-fifth birthday. Not one of the men located refused to participate in the interview. The interview sampled various indicators of personal and social history, including self-reports of criminal behavior for which the boys were not arrested. Police records were subsequently reviewed up to age 30. The 1958 birth cohort includes 28,338 people, 13,811 males and 14,527 females, whose official records have been reviewed up to age 18.

- A total of 459 (47.3%) of the 1945 cohort had an officially recorded arrest by age 30. Approximately 31 percent of the offenders had records of at least five offenses by age 30 ($N = 144$). These 144 "chronic offenders" had accumulated 1,683 offenses. Thus, approximately 15 percent of the individuals were responsible for 53 percent of all crime committed by the 1945 cohort.

- The official arrest records from age 10 to age 18 of the 1958 birth cohort revealed the following:

Table TN 1.1–2
Percent of Young People Self-Reporting Criminal Activity in California and Alberta by Gender

		MALES		FEMALES	
		California	Alberta	California	Alberta
	N	1,264	571	563	583
Theft under $2		52.7%	60.1%	30.5%	33.3%
Theft $50 +		6.6%	2.4%	2.0%	0.2%
Auto theft		10.8%	5.9%	3.6%	0.7%
Damaged property		25.5%	40.3%	8.6%	16.0%
Assault		41.7%	40.9%	15.6%	8.1%
Three or more		23.7%	23.0%	5.1%	5.0%

Table 1, p. 346, from R. Linden & C. Fillmore (1981). "A Comparative Study of Delinquency Involvement." *Canadian Review of Sociology and Anthropology*, 18, 343–361. Reprinted with permission.

Technical Note 1.1 *(continued)*

1. Twenty-three percent of the 6,587 white males accounted for a total of 4,306 offenses. Among these offenses were four homicides, nine rapes, 103 robberies, 117 aggravated assaults, 217 other assaults, 454 break and enters, and 263 narcotic offenses. Slightly more than one-half of the offenses (50.9%) were committed by 499 "chronic delinquents" (those who had records of arrest for five or more offenses). Thus, 7.6 percent (499) of the sample of white males accounted for more than one-half of the total amount of recorded criminal activity by white males.

2. Forty-one percent of the 7,224 non-white males accounted for a total of 11,713 offenses. Among those offenses were 52 homicides, 96 rapes, 1,223 robberies, 459 aggravated assaults, 1,342 break and enters, and 474 narcotic offenses. Almost 65 percent (64.7%) of the offenses were committed by chronic delinquents who represented 17 percent of the total sample of non-white males.

3. Similar trends were also found for the young women from the 1958 birth cohort. Overall, the repeat offenders (12.1% of 28,338) accounted for the vast amount of official delinquency (84.5% of 20,089 offenses) in the 1958 Philadelphia cohort.

The Psykologisk Institut (Copenhagen) Adoption Files. Sarnoff Mednick, William Gabrielli, and Barry Hutchings (1983) have described an analysis of the official records of all 14,427 nonfamilial adoptions in Denmark from 1924 to 1947. Court convictions for offenses committed by persons over 15 years of age were tabulated for male adoptees, female adoptees, and their biological and adoptive parents. Information was unattainable for some persons, but the Danish files provided a wealth of information on individual differences in officially recorded criminal activity. It was found that:

• 15.9 percent of 6,129 male adoptees had at least one criminal conviction and 6.9 percent had two or more;

• 2.8 percent of 7,065 female adoptees had at least one criminal conviction and less than 1 percent (0.8%) had two or more;

• 28.6 percent of 10,604 biological fathers had at least one conviction and 15.8 percent had two or more;

• 8.9 percent of 12,300 biological mothers had at least one conviction and 2.5 percent had two or more;

• 6.2 percent of 13,918 adoptive fathers had at least one criminal conviction and 1.6 percent had two or more; and

• 1.9 percent of 14,267 adoptive mothers had at least one criminal conviction and less than 1 percent (0.4%) had two or more.

The great value of this study resides in the possibility to examine the criminality of adoptees as a function of the criminality of biological and adoptive parents. The now famous Danish "cross-fostering" analysis found that criminality in the biological parents was associated with male adoptee criminality whether the adoptive parents were criminal (14.7% vs. 24.5%) or not criminal (13.5% vs. 20.0%).

The Psykologisk Institut (Copenhagen) 1944–1947 Birth Cohort. This cohort consists of all males born between 1944 and 1947 to mothers who were residents of Copenhagen and for whom criminal records were available (N = 28,879). Patricia Guttridge, William Gabrielli, Sarnoff Mednick, and Katherine Van Dusen (1983) reported upon the officially recorded criminal violence within this cohort up to the year 1974. Criminal violence included offenses of murder, rape, bodily injury, threats of violence, and robbery with violence. They found:

• 37.8 percent of the men had at least one arrest;

• 2.5 percent of the men were charged with at least one violent offense;

• 0.6 percent were charged with two or more violent offenses;

• the repeat violent offender accounted for 431 of the 993 violent offenses (i.e., 0.6% of the men accounted for 43.4 percent of the violent offenses that were recorded against the men); and

• the peak age for offenses in general was 17 years, while the peak age for violent offenses was 20 years of age.

Technical Note 1.1 *(continued)*

CONCLUSION

This survey of the findings of many research studies has established a few of the basic facts regarding the criminal behavior of official offenders—facts that have been established in many areas of the world. Students need not feel that they need to know the specific results of each of these studies. What they might find interesting is that individual differences in criminal behavior are substantial. Here are some basic facts:

1. Individual differences in criminal activity are apparent in many ways. They may be inferred from knowledge of aggregated crime rates based on both official records of crime and surveys of victims. They are discovered more directly by systematic surveys of criminal histories (officially defined or self-reported) and by systematic studies of criminal futures (officially defined or self-reported).

2. Individual differences in criminal activity are apparent within samples of people differentiated by country of origin, gender, age, race, and social class.

3. Repeat offenders, a small subset of all offenders, account for a disproportionate amount of total criminal activity. Careful study of career criminals reveals, however, that the nexus of frequent, serious, and violent offending contains a small number of cases.

PCC has much to explain.

Technical Note 1.2

Some Definitional Issues When No Act is Intrinsically Criminal

The anti-psychological rhetoric in criminology was loud and intrusive in the 1960s and 1970s. Brian MacLean's (1986) edited collection on the political economy of crime provides some near definitive illustrations of these themes.

There is no question that criminals are seen as heroes by some people. People may view some criminals as heroes because they view some criminal acts as heroic acts. Indeed, sometimes the status of hero is totally dependent upon the commission of criminal acts. Would Bonnie Parker and Clyde Barrow be folk heroes if they had not robbed banks? We doubt it. Does their heroic status reflect a belief that it is "OK" to rob banks? We also doubt that. One may enjoy the stories of Bonnie and Clyde's bank robberies without believing that bank robbery should be legalized. Similarly, one may believe that banks are the products of an evil social system and should be abolished without believing that theft, robbery, and the killing of bank employees should be decriminalized.

Brian MacLean (1986) explains how traditional criminologists are mistaken in viewing crime as an event that constitutes the breaking of a rule, be it a rule of law or a rule of morality. "In actuality," proclaims MacLean (p.4), "crime is not an event" but a "social process."

Because the study of individual differences is said to place the whole field at risk of degeneration, the student of PCC had better read further on this "disease of correctionalism" (which was never defined). Turning to Taylor, Walton, and Young (1973:281–282), we learn that catching this disease is inevitable unless the scientist is committed "to the abolition of inequalities in wealth and power, and in particular of inequalities in property and life-chances."

The disease, as they see it, is clear: By studying individual differences in criminal behavior, we will fail to advance the redistribution of wealth and power that will, in turn, create a society in which human diversity (i.e., individual differences) is not subject to punishment by the state. The major point here is that critical Marxists are not interested in understanding individual differences in criminal behavior.

Let us take a look at those aspects of human behavior that are subject to the power to criminalize under various social arrangements. What organic, personal, or social aspects of human diversity, left undefined by Taylor et al. (1973), are subject to punishment over social space? What "notions" of the "moral entrepreneurs" lead to the punishment of what aspects of human diversity? This question has been a focus of cross-cultural research and the answer need not be simply a matter of ideology, polemics, or political slogans.

As early as the mid-1970s, Wellford (1975) showed that cultural relativism, the possibility that crime is defined differently from one culture to the next, was not a threat to the study of individual criminal conduct. Anthropological inquiry suggests that some ethical principles are universal and that the cross-cultural differences are relatively trivial. Accepting the fact of cultural relativism at the levels of customs and traditions, Wellford concluded that universal condemnation was characteristic of those acts that have been the prime concern of criminology. These universally condemned acts were ones that involved violations of the physical integrity of the human organism; violations of property rights; violations of trust; murder, assault, and other acts of violence; rape and other forms of sexual assault; incest; robbery; theft; and destruction of property. These acts represent points of convergence or areas of overlap among the domains of illegal, immoral, unconventional, and antisocial behavior. In other words, the criminal acts that rate a high consensus of disapproval tend also to be immoral, unconventional, and antisocial. The relative insignificance of cultural relativism when defining "core behavior patterns" that are deemed criminal remains true today (Ellis & Walsh, 1997).

The near universality of condemnation of "criminal behavior" was demonstrated by Graeme Newman (1976) in a sophisticated survey of opinion in seven nations. Newman did not suggest that he had drawn representative samples of the populations of these nations. For example, the United States respondents were all New Yorkers, and the Italians were all Sardinians. New Yorkers are generally thought to represent a rather "liberal" lot, and Sardinians are thought to represent the notion of a subculture of crime and violence. The Iranian sample

Technical Note 1.2 *(continued)*

was drawn before the revolution. The other nations sampled were Indonesia, India, and Yugoslavia.

Newman's study is rich and detailed. It is a significant contribution in many ways. It demonstrates the sophistication and potential of serious explorations of the dimensions of cultural relativism and provides a convincing legitimization of the focus of PCC. A sample of the questions posed and the answers given follows:

1. "Do you think this act should be prohibited by the law?"
   - Robbery (a person forcefully takes $50 from another person who, as a result, is injured and has to be hospitalized): 100 percent of the Sardinians and American respondents said yes. The lowest rate of condemnation was found in India, where 97.3 percent answered yes.
   - Appropriation (a person puts government funds to his or her own use): The condemnation rates varied from 100 percent (Sardinia) to 92.3 percent (USA).
   - Incest (a man has sexual relations with his adult daughter): The condemnation rates varied from 98.1 percent (Iran) to 71 percent (USA).
   - Factory pollution (a factory director continues to permit his factory to release poisonous gases into the air): The range of variability was 98.8 percent (India) to 92.8 percent (Yugoslavia).
   - Taking drugs (a person takes drugs; "heroin" in the United States, "soft" in Sardinia, "opium" in Iran, "gange" in India and Indonesia): The condemnation rates varied from 93.3 percent in Indonesia to 74.9 percent in India.
   - Much greater variability was evident within and across nations in terms of the prohibition by law of abortion, homosexuality, public protest, and not going to the assistance of someone in danger.

2. Respondents were asked to rate the seriousness of each act on a 12-point scale from 0 (not serious) to 11 (very serious). The acts were ranked in order of seriousness within each country and the rankings were compared among countries.
   - There was a high rate of agreement among nations concerning the relative seriousness of the acts. The highest correlation was .99 (India-Iran) and the lowest was .59 (Sardinia-USA).
   - The acts judged most serious were robbery, appropriation, incest, drug-taking, and factory pollution.
   - Within countries, the deviations from mean ratings tended to be lowest for the acts of robbery, incest, and appropriation.
   - We leave it to the reader to ponder some of the "deviant" responses of the New Yorkers. The New Yorkers questioned apparently consider drug-taking to be more serious than incest, robbery, or appropriation. (We suspect that New Yorkers may know that heroin use is a major predictor of frequent and serious criminal activity in their neighborhoods.)

In summary, it appears that the aspects of human diversity subject to criminalization are such acts as assault, robbery, and theft. That many of these criminal acts are "high-consensus" ones, cross-culturally and subculturally, is also apparent. In brief, the psychology of criminal conduct has a criterion variable of generally recognized importance. Moreover, the fact is that psychology will continue to study antisocial behavior as it has from the beginning—whether the behaviors are high-consensus crimes or not. (It is comforting, however, to learn that many people from diverse social locations are not favorably disposed to sexual assault, robbery, and theft.)

What is also evident is that some social scientists, with an understandable and appreciated interest in social inequality and social control, have failed to make a major distinction between predictor variables and criterion variables. Human diversity is evident in behavior and in a variety of other organic, personal, and social variables. In the study of criminal behavior, the diversity evident in patterns of theft, assault, and pollution is the criterion variable.

Diversity in other areas that are not subject to the power to criminalize represents a host of potential predictor variables that may help explain the variability in criminal behavior. That is, the behavioral facts of human diversity that are judged criminal may well covary with other personal, organic, and social facts of human diversity. Understanding those correlations is a focus of the psychology of criminal behavior.

Aggregated Crime Rates and the Ecological Fallacy

Enthusiasts of the social science approach sometimes assume that the regional or aggregated correlates of aggregated crime rates have something to say about the correlates of individual behavior. The ecological fallacy is the assumption that the aggregated correlates of aggregated crime rates imply knowledge of the correlates of individual behavior. The ecological fallacy is a particular threat when the aggregated correlate is a measure of the membership composition of the area: for example, areas may be differentiated according to some indicator of average income, average educational level, proportion of population unemployed, and so on. This discussion of the ecological fallacy does not suggest that social structural effects are unimportant. Rather, the point is that the effects of social structure on individual behavior are best established through studies of individuals in different social contexts. Otherwise, the ecological fallacy is a real threat.

Consider the issue of the relationship between income and crime. What we are calling a sociological investigation would involve an exploration of how mean income levels and crime rates might covary across neighborhoods of a city. For example, a widely accepted sociological "truth" is that crime rates are higher in low-income neighborhoods than they are in higher-income areas of a city.

Without debating the truth value of that "finding," the sociological investigation of an income-crime link may be compared with a psychological analysis of that link. A psychological investigation of an income-crime link would: (1) examine the criminal behavior of individuals, and (2) examine the criminal behavior of these individuals as a function of personal income and the average income level in the person's neighborhood. Psychologically, personal income and average income of the neighborhood are two distinct variables. Of the two variables, only the latter qualifies as a "social structural" variable or as a "social fact." A "social fact" is a measured property of a social system. Whether social facts actually impact on individual criminal behavior may be established only through psychological analyses wherein one disentangles the effects of personal facts (e.g., personal income) and social facts (e.g., neighborhood attributes) on individual behavior. To illustrate this point we draw upon

Mayer's (1972) rational analysis of structural versus personal variables in relation to criterion variables. The illustrations contrast the interpretability of studies that focus on aggregate versus individual data.

Two quite different psychological findings are shown in Figures TN 1.3–1 and TN 1.3–2, yet both of the psychological findings are consistent with the hypothetical sociological finding that low-income neighborhoods have higher crime rates than do high-income neighborhoods.

In Figure TN 1.3–1, both lower-income and higher-income individuals tend to commit more crime when they live in lower-income areas. Here, with a focus on individuals, the psychological investigation was able to demonstrate that the "aggregate social fact" of below-average neighborhood income was impacting on both lower-income and higher-income individuals. The "social fact," a characteristic of the social environment, was a correlate of individual criminal conduct.

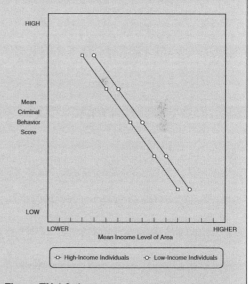

Figure TN 1.3–1
Criminal Behavior by Personal Income and Income Level of Neighborhoods: A Hypothetical Illustration

In Figure TN 1.3–2, only the lower-income individuals who live in low-income areas show high levels of criminality. Here, the psychological

Technical Note 1.3 *(continued)*

investigation reveals that personal income is the important variable, but it is important only in low-income neighborhoods. In this illustration, the "social fact" was moderating the association between personal income and criminal conduct. That is, personal income was only important in neighborhoods that had low average incomes.

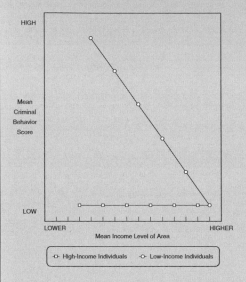

Figure TN 1.3–2
Criminal Behavior by Personal Income and Income Level of Neighborhoods: A Hypothetical Illustration

Not represented in either figure is the possibility that the high-income individuals in low-income areas were responsible for most of the criminal activity. This psychological finding too would be consistent with the hypothetical sociological finding that low-income areas have relatively high crime rates.

Finally, consider the possibility that neither the low-income residents nor the high-income residents were responsible for the high crime rates in low-income areas. This would be the case if nonresident offenders were attracted to low-income areas as the scene for their crimes.

The major conclusion is a simple one. If you are interested in the criminality of individuals, you must study individuals. To do otherwise is to risk committing the ecological fallacy (Mayer, 1972). The ecological fallacy assumes that the aggregated correlates of aggregated crime rates imply knowledge of the correlates of individual

behavior. An ecological linkage between income and crime is logically compatible with a number of possibilities at the individual level of analysis. In brief, ecological studies of aggregates are simply unable to establish the "facts" desired within PCC, whether those facts are personal or social.

We chose to illustrate the ecological fallacy with the income example because social-class explanations of criminal behavior are so widely assumed and because the data in support of a class-crime link are primarily of the aggregated variety. However, the "social facts" regarding the membership characteristics of social groups extend well beyond the issue of average income levels. For example, it is one thing to personally possess attitudes that are favorable to crime, and it is another to be a member of a group in which the dominant attitudes among group members are favorable to crime. Thus, both personal attitudes and the social facts regarding the dominant attitudes in groups are highly relevant variables in a psychology of crime. They, like income, must be independently assessed if their contributions to criminal behavior are to be understood.

There has been a strong tendency in sociology and social psychology to assign causal significance to group norms and group values. In the 1960s, much of criminology was dominated by subcultural theories of crime. According to this view, criminal behavior represented conformity to group norms that were antisocial. These norms were assumed to exist outside of and independently of the individual. Yet, in most studies, the existence of the norms was inferred from studies of the attitudes, values, and beliefs of individuals. Personal sentiment, like personal income, is not a proxy for a "social fact." The effect of the social fact can be established only by observing how variations at the group level are associated with the criminal behavior of individuals.

Consider how personal attitudes and social norms may relate to something like personal drug use. Using personal interviews or self-report, paper-and-pencil questionnaires, researchers are able to assess high school students according to whether the personal attitudes of the students are relatively favorable or unfavorable to the use of marijuana. If they have sampled widely enough, researchers also may be able to categorize schools according to

Technical Note 1.3 *(continued)*

the proportion of students with attitudes favorable to use of marijuana. Thus, schools too may be differentiated according to norms more or less favorable to use of marijuana.

Just as in the case of the income example, variations in personal use of marijuana may then be examined as a function of: (1) personal attitudes, (2) the normative context of the school that students attend, and (3) particular combinations of personal and contextual variables. A hypothetical finding is illustrated in Figure TN 1.3–3 The overall pattern of this hypothetical result will be evident in a number of studies reviewed in this text. That is, personal attitudes are more likely to be translated into personal action when the social context is favorable to that action (e.g., Andrews & Kandel, 1979).

A psychology of criminal conduct looks to social facts as well as other personal attributes and personal circumstances in the search for the sources of variability in individual criminal behavior. In developing a psychology of crime, we will not hesitate to draw upon the biological, social, and historical sciences when to do so truly informs the behavioral science of criminal conduct. As stated earlier, and as we shall see in later chapters, some of the best recent work on the psychology of criminal behavior has been completed by sociologists who conducted their work at the individual rather than the aggregate level of analysis.

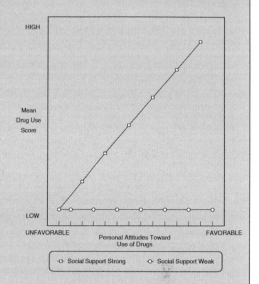

Figure TN 1.3–3
Drug Use by Personal and Social Support for Drug Use: A Hypothetical Illustration

In brief, knowledge of the correlates of aggregated crime rates tells us little regarding the sources of variability in the behavior of the individuals. However, a sociology of crime rates and a psychology of criminal conduct will hopefully share the same theoretical models. An integrative perspective may be possible through a powerful social psychology of criminal behavior.

Technical Note 1.4

Objections to the Goals of PCC

Some Marxist/critical criminologists, including even some "left realists," continue to assert that inequality in the distribution of social wealth and power is the major cause of crime. For example:

> After all, the United States is a nation characterized by gross economic inequality. . . . The high rates of violent crime are major symptoms of these problems, and these crimes are committed mainly by . . . [the] underclass . . . In fact, social and economic inequality—not personality or biological factors—are the most powerful predictors of predatory violent crime (DeKeseredy & Schwartz, 1996:190).

This quotation provides an example of the problems within left-wing sociological criminology once the process of discounting PCC began. Briefly stated, the fact that nations differ according to their crime rates says nothing whatsoever about the causal roles of biology and/or personality. Within PCC, statements regarding the causal significance of any variables (be they biological, familial, or social) would be based on observations relevant to those variables. Within this critical/radical (albeit new left realism) criminology, however, evidence of international variations in crime rates may be asserted to signify the irrelevance of psychobiology and socialization experiences and to show clearly the importance of social inequality in the generation of crime. The evidence that predatory violent crimes are best predicted by social and economic inequality is reviewed in this text.

Notable in the quotation is the very restricted range of variables considered to be of interest. The two sets of variables are "social and economic inequality" and "personality and biological factors." This reflects a narrow vision of human behavior. Any student of introductory psychology and anyone with a personal awareness of their contacts with other human beings would know that the classes of variables associated with human behavior extend well beyond "inequality" and "personality/biology." Most of us have a sense that individual human beings—whatever their social/economic status and their personal/biological predispositions—may still be more interestingly differentiated according to their thoughts and emotions, their associates, their behavioral histories, and their satisfactions and dissatisfactions in major settings such as home, work, school, and neighborhood. Note also that PCC's agreed-upon openness to biology and socialization does not imply that "rents and tears" in the social fabric are unimportant in the analysis of crime.

The authors of this text and our students and colleagues cannot help but be amused when we are told by so many criminological scholars that they personally were never anti-prediction, anti-treatment, ideological, or blindly sociological ("not me"). The personal exoneration is often paired with the idea that perhaps Andrews et al., Ellis, Gottfredson, Hindelang, Hirschi, Hoffmann, Jeffery, Osgoode, Rowe, Wormith—and many other critics of sociological criminology not quoted several paragraphs above—were exaggerating the anti-psychological bias within criminology. Indeed, those who argue for PCC are sometimes accused of being "zealots," of making use of "smoke and mirrors," or of being "cult" members. There is a long history of negative labeling when criminologists are confronted with evidence overwhelmingly favorable to PCC (witness Sutherland's attacks on Glueck and Glueck; see Laub & Sampson, 1991).

Some critical post-modern feminist scholars go further and suggest that applications of PCC do not care enough about gender, race, ethnicity, and inequality (Bloom & Covington, 1998; Hannah-Moffat, 1999). Moreover, the construction of risk "evokes a white, middle-class male norm" and risk is "gendered and racialized." Moreover, it has been said that "nothing is a risk in itself: there is no risk in reality" and yet "anything can be a risk; it all depends on how one analyses the danger, considers the event." Moreover, "risk and the enterprise of risk management appears on the surface to be moral, efficient, objective, and non-discriminatory, but they are not" (Hannah-Moffat & Shaw, 2001:12). (Racist, sexist, unreal, immoral, inefficient, and discriminatory! Dear reader, do you dare to proceed any further in this text?)

Following the leadership of Hirschi and Hindelang (1977), this text suggests four major sources of the anti-psychological themes once so prominent in criminology and now virtually confined to a few groups. These groups include

Technical Note 1.4 (continued)

critical/Marxist theorists, some feminist and racial scholars, and some justice scholars preoccupied with the decency of punishment and the tyranny of correctional treatment (discussed in the punishment and treatment chapters). The four roots are historical/professional roots, moral roots, political roots, and the decline of positivism and emergence of theoreticism.

1. **Historical/professional.** The historical and professional roots of mainstream "social" criminology have been described by many observers, such as those cited above. The interdisciplinary field of criminology became a subfield of sociology in many North American universities in the 1920s and was firmly established as such in most universities by the 1940s. Robert Merton, one of the most important sociologists of all time, clearly rejected the psychology of the first 50 years of the century and proclaimed the understanding of crime to be essentially sociological. Edwin Sutherland, another one of the most important sociological criminologists of all time, led this promotion of sociology through his now-discredited attacks on the work of Sheldon Glueck and Eleanor Glueck. These attacks were well-documented by John Laub and Robert J. Sampson (1991). Subsequent to the Sutherland attacks on PCC, individual differences research was considered antisociological (Hirschi & Hindelang, 1977). Moreover, avoiding the label of "being antisociological" obviously came to be judged more important than being defensible on rational and empirical grounds.

2. **Moral.** The denial of individual differences was motivated in part to protect the "deviant" from charges of "being different." Being found different, it was thought, might be used as an excuse for abuse. We do not doubt that being different may be used to excuse abuse, but it is a strange social science that attempts to protect individuals by denying human diversity and overemphasizing social location (i.e., where people are situated in the social hierarchy). We think that respect for human diversity protects individuals, while fixations with social locators such as geography, race, and class promote genocide (Andrews & Wormith, 1989).

3. **The political crisis of the 1960s and 1970s.** The political context of the "disorder" or the "awakening" of the 1960s and 1970s is described elsewhere (Andrews, Zinger et al., 1990b; Cullen & Gendreau, 1989). A brief 10-year period saw the rise of conservative politics (and a focus on law and order), the decline of liberalism (and a disenchantment with the benevolence of the state), and the move of left-wing social science to the self-consciously "social" in the extreme (as it became enchanted with labeling and critical/Marxist perspectives of deviance). During this period, left-leaning social science withdrew active support for human science and human service delivery. The collapse of support for the ideal of rehabilitation cannot be attributed to the political "right"—they always supported punishment. It was due to the left adopting perspectives such as due process and critical/Marxist perspectives. To this day, left/feminist/sociological/radicals are confused because PCC links reduced recidivism to enhanced human service in the form of structured rehabilitation efforts with moderate and higher risk cases. The risk principle of RNR does not promote enhanced punishment, it promotes enhanced service under the conditions of a just sanction.

4. **The death of positivism and the rise of theoreticism.** The 1960s saw increased appreciation of certain intellectual truths. These may not be summarized easily but certain slogans from post-modern scholarship assist in making our points. Each of these slogans contained valuable truths. They suggested that all knowledge is partial (no single theory or single research study accounts for everything). Moreover, all knowledge is relative (no theory/research finding exists independent of time and social context) and all knowledge is socially constructed (theory and research reflect socially situated human imagination). Finally, all knowledge is political (any theory or finding may serve the interests of one social group more than it serves another social group). These truths led rational empiricists to even more careful research and theory construction. However, these truths led major portions of criminology further away from a rational and empirical focus on crime and criminal justice, and toward the promotion of sociology, political-economy, and the political

Technical Note 1.4 *(continued)*

and personal interests of ideologues of the left and the right. In other words, large portions of criminology consciously adopted theoreticism as the sole method of seeking understanding. The search for these non-rational and non-empirical paths to knowledge is evident currently in some feminist approaches, in some transformative movements, in some aboriginal studies, in some restorative justice scholarship, and in some mainstream psychological studies of crime.

The essence of theoreticism, which is the alternative to a rational empiricism, is to adopt and discard knowledge insofar as it is personally or politically rewarding to do so, and to do so without regard for evidence (Crews, 1986). The theoreticists who were so dominant in mainstream textbook criminology of the 1960s, 1970s, and 1980s felt that they were the fortunate ones to whom "truth" had been revealed. Their visions were evident in three main ways:

1. Findings of systematic empirical investigations supporting their a priori positions were readily accepted and widely disseminated without critical review and qualification.

2. Research findings that were inconsistent with their a priori positions were ignored or discounted by essentially irrational appeals to what, when properly applied, are highly reasonable and well-known threats to the validity of the conclusions of systematic research.

3. The lack of research on many issues was treated not as a reason for caution but as a stimulus for the conversion of others to the revealed truths of a "superior" vision.

We have considered many ways of dealing with the anti-PCC and anti-empirical elements of criminology briefly summarized in the above quotations and comments. We considered simply presenting the research and theory, assuming that students would reject the anti-PCC biases within criminology on their own. As sensible as this approach seemed, our years of research, teaching, and practice in criminal justice convinced us that it would be inappropriate simply to ignore the anti-PCC themes. These themes have been so prominent within criminology over the years that they must be addressed more directly. As implied in some of the quotations earlier, criminological audiences were more likely to applaud anti-PCC expressions than they were to display respect for evidence. As a result, we think it is important that the anti-PCC themes be faced directly in this text.

This text does two things. Most important, students are exposed to the reasonably solid theorizing, research, and applications that are highly relevant to PCC. In the process, students will also become aware of some glaring theoretical, empirical, and practical deficits within PCC. Thus, throughout, we will stress the knowledge construction aspects of rational empirical investigation. This involves an appreciation for the methods of research and for the many threats to valid conclusions that systematic research renders open to assessment. Additionally, when the correlates of crime are identified, we will attempt to provide concrete estimates of the magnitude of those correlations so that readers may assess the strength of associations with one set of covariates relative to some other set of covariates.

Second, students are asked to examine directly those elements of criminology and criminal justice that are actively hostile to a serious exploration of individual differences in criminal conduct.

Technical Note 2.1
Summary of Meta-Analytic Explorations of Gender-Informed Factors and the Prediction of Criminal Recidivism by Gender: Mean *r* (k = number of primary estimates)

Meta-Analytic Report	Being Male	Being Younger		Being Non-White		Lower Class Origins		Emotional Distress		Abuse History		Poverty		Housing	
		F	M	F	M	F	M	F	M	F	M	F	M	F	M
1) Gendreau et al. (1996)	.06 (17)		.11 (56)	.17 (4)		.05 (23)			.05 (66)						
2) Lipsey & Derzon (1998)	.17 (5)			.04 (5)		.09 (7)					.06 (4)				
3) Cottle et al. (2001)	.11 (4)			.07 (6)		.07 (3)			.07 (2)		.11 (5)				
									.30 (7)						
4) Hubbard & Pratt (2002)		.09 (4)				.03 (10)			.06 (5)		.21 (3)				
5) Green & Campbell (2006)						.10 (2)	.09 (4)	.10 (21)	.11 (61)	.16 (7)	.02 (10)				
6) Van Voorhis et al. (2008)								Anxiety .13 (4); Psychosis .21 (3); LowSelf-Esteem .07 (8)	Child .10 (8); Adult .10 (8); Adult .14 (6); Child .09 (4)			Income .02 (5); Assistance .04 (3)		.11 (4)	
7) Andrews, Bonta, Wormith, Guzzo, Brews, Rettinger & Rowe (2008)	.13 (8)	.04 (9)	.20 (9)	.07 (5)	−.04 (5)			.07 (8)	.04 (8)	.11 (6)	.07 (2)	.19 (9)	.16 (8)	.20 (8)	.16 (8)
8) Simple Unadjusted Mean Estimates	.12	.06	.15	.07	.06	.06	.07	.11	.12	.13	.06	.19	.16	.16	.16

Notes: (1) In Cottle, Lee & Heilbrun (2001) .07 is the estimate for "severe pathology" (psychosis,). The estimate was .30 (7) for "non-severe pathology" ("anxiety and depression" were used as illustrations of the construct but there is the possibility that externalizing disorders may have been coded "non-severe").

(2) Nonsignificant estimates entered as .00 in the Van Voorhis at al. (2008) estimates. GI factors that failed to show any significant validity were not reported (Table 2, p. 11–13). A review of the final reports that reported on all nine research sites, averaged across all sites and measures, only 36% (40/111) of all of the tests with the gender-responsive scales yielded a significant predictive validity coefficient.

(3) The Van Voorhis et al. (2008) estimates for their GI scoring of income (reversed scored) and public assistance were not entered into the computation of the overall mean for poverty. It was obvious that their GI measures of poverty performed very poorly relative to LSI-R Financial (as reported in Van Voorhis et al., 2008, and in Andrews et al., 2008). In fact, the Van Voorhis et al. mean estimate for housing was also very mild relative to the Andrews et al. estimates based primarily on LSI-R Accommodation or the relevant items from LS/CMI Social, Health, and Mental Health.

A Sample of Some Anti-Rehabilitation Themes: How to Destroy Evidence of the Effectiveness of Correctional Treatment

1. Enthusiastically endorse the findings of studies that fail to uncover treatment effects, and promote those findings as scientifically sound evidence that rehabilitation does not work. Do not cast a critical eye on this set of studies.

2. Note that crime is socially functional in that it helps define the boundaries of acceptable conduct for society as a whole, and hence the pursuit of effective rehabilitation programs threatens the very existence of society.

3. Assert that rehabilitation, even when it works, is inherently evil and ideologically incorrect, and that it promotes both severe sentences and unwarranted sentencing disparity (relative to the dignity of just desert and radical nonintervention).

4. Discount rehabilitation because it involves, by definition, more social control than does absolute freedom.

5. Discount rehabilitation because it involves, by definition, less social control than does absolute social control.

6. Discount rehabilitation because any program, upon close inspection, may be found to include elements of sexism, racism, elitism, and/or homophobia.

7. Discount rehabilitation programs because they are not primary prevention programs (or some other personally favored program).

8. Discount evidence of reduced recidivism because it is not evidence of improvement in the bigger picture of criminal justice, or the even bigger picture of social justice, or a cure for cancer.

9. Discount evidence of reduced recidivism because it is not evidence of effects on community-wide (aggregated) crime rates.

10. Discount evidence of effects on officially recorded crime because it is not evidence of effects on self-reported crime.

11. Discount evidence of effects on self-reported crime because it is not evidence of effects on officially recorded crime.

12. Discount evidence of effects on any measure of recidivism by asserting that the program failed to increase self-esteem or to make the offender a better person in some other way.

13. Discount the positive evidence by asserting that rehabilitation is nothing but a state-sponsored attempt to make lower-class persons more acceptable to higher-class persons.

14. Discount positive evidence because criminals were being judged by middle-class morality.

15. Discount positive evidence by noting that it is a shame that offenders get access to quality programs (they deserve just punishment).

16. Discount reduced recidivism over a one year follow-up period because it is not evidence of effects over a two-year follow-up; discount reduced recidivism over a two-year follow-up period because it is not evidence of effects over a three-year follow-up; discount. . . .

17. Assert that rehabilitation can't possibly work because criminology has proven that the human science of criminal conduct is nonsense.

18. Assert that we all know, from prior experience, that rehabilitation does not work.

19. Regardless of the quality of the design or the magnitude of the treatment effect, suggest some ambiguity regarding what really caused the effect, and then note the absurdity of claiming effectiveness when the true cause of reduced recidivism remains unknown.

20. Regardless of the quality of the study, note that experimental designs are the patriarchal tools of criminology's male-dominated, paternalistic, and positivistic past, and the mere playthings of ritualistic positivists (we don't know what this means, but arguments like this are readily found in some sections of criminology).

21. Reject positive findings because it is immoral that the comparison clients did not have access to it.

Technical Note 2.2 *(continued)*

22. Reject a treatment program that has been found to be effective with some types of offenders under specific circumstances because it doesn't work for everyone under all circumstances. (A complex and differentiated world is inconsistent with the universally applicable and morally superior visions of truth to which theoreticists have been privileged.)

23. No matter what number and types of offenders were studied, note that the study failed to work with a sample of all types of offenders that one could possibly imagine. (That's fine, but what about the special contextual uniqueness at the nexus of age, gender, poverty, race, ethnicity, sexual orientation, personal history, and physical ability.)

24. Question the motives and objectivity of scholars and practitioners who speak in favor of human service in a justice context.

For example, assert that "they have an agenda," "they make use of smoke and mirrors," "they are liars and cheats," they are "social workers, psychiatrists and psychologists."

25. Be very bored with the whole issue. "Who cares? "Testing. Testing. Research. Research. All those research assistants running around." I am interested in the big picture of what the whole world would be like if only my vision was shared."

26. THE ULTIMATE KNOWLEDGE TECHNIQUE: Remind readers that studies that report positively on treatment "are based upon the conclusions of the authors of the reports themselves." Because all studies have authors, nothing is safe from being discredited. This is the ultimate way of destroying anything you don't agree with because all reports have authors.

Adapted from Andrews, 1989; Gottfredson, 1979

Cognitive-Behavioral Therapy: An Overview

Cognitive-behavioral therapy is highly structured, hands-on, concrete, and practical. Behaviors are learned by watching respected models demonstrate the behaviors and through the systematic application of rewards and costs. Behaviors to be learned are broken down into small, manageable steps that are practiced, rehearsed and role played. Cognitive-behavioral therapies match the learning style of the majority of the clients of the criminal justice system who learn through doing better rather than through didactic teaching. It is little wonder that cognitive-behavioral interventions are more effective with this clientele than other intervention techniques (Figure TN 4.1–1).

The Difference Between Cognitive-Behavioral Intervention and General Behavioral Intervention

Many programs say that they use cognitive-behavioral programming but on closer examination they are more "behavioral" with very little of the "cognitive" elements. General behavioral approaches are commonly found in skills training programs (e.g., job-related skills, assertiveness training, problem-solving skills). The analysis of behavior in general behavioral interventions involves the identification of antecedents of behavior or "outside cues" and the external consequences of the behavior. Thus, changing the behavior requires changing the outside cues (e.g., avoiding friends who drink) or the external consequences to behavior (e.g., friends expressing disapproval for drinking). Cognitive-behavioral therapies place greater emphasis on antecedents to behavior that come from within the person ("inside cues") and external consequences delivered by the self (i.e., personally mediated rewards and costs).

To illustrate the difference between the two approaches, a simple exercise is conducted as part of the training of probation officers in the Strategic Training Initiative in Community Supervision (see Chapter 12 for more details on this project). The exercise starts with the trainer asking the participants to "stand up." Invariably, almost everyone does stand up (a few rascals do remain seated). The trainer then asks each participant to explain to the group why they stood up or why they remained seated. The first explanation typically given is that "you told me to stand up." However, this explanation is insuf-

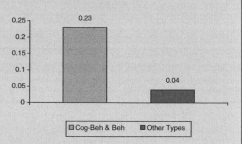

Figure TN 4.1–1
Effectiveness of Cognitive Behavioral Therapy

ficient given that some participants heard the same instruction but remained seated. With further discussion the group learns that each had a different thought running through his or her head that directly led to the behavior. A strictly behavioral explanation is all about the outside cues or antecedent stimuli and external consequences. A cognitive-behavioral explanation *requires* knowing the outside cues but also the inside cues or thought processes that directly led to the behavior and that follow the behavior.

Just as antecedents can be both external and internal, so are the consequences to behavior. As outlined in PIC-R (Resource Note 4.1), consequences can be personally mediated. The actor can deliver his or her own rewards or punishments, and they may function independently from any external consequences. In the example of the "stand up" exercise, the person who stands up may say to himself or herself, "by standing up I showed the group leader that I can be counted on," thereby delivering his or her own reward. The group leader may also praise those who stood up and increase the density of rewards, but it may not be necessary to ensure future compliance to the request to stand up. On the other hand, all the praise in the world from the group leader may have little effect on the person who remained seated and who says, "I showed him that no one orders me around!" Using the example of the "stand up" exercise, the differences between a strictly behavioral and cognitive-behavioral understanding of behavior are outlined in the Table TN 4.1–1 below.

The Steps in Cognitive-Behavioral Treatment

The cognitive-behavioral approach to understanding behavior requires examining cognitive

Technical Note 4.1 *(continued)*

antecedents and consequences. Cognitive-behavioral interventions require changing the cognitive antecedents and consequences. Antisocial attitudes, one of the Big Four, are clearly cognitive antecedents to criminal behavior and a target for change. If you can replace antisocial thoughts with prosocial thoughts, then the likelihood of criminal behavior is diminished. When working with offenders, this requires the following steps:

1. The offender must understand and buy into the idea that his or her thinking directly leads to behavior. Many offenders blame external events for their misbehavior and fail to see that there are intervening cognitions between the external events and their behavior. Therefore, they need to be taught that their inside cues (attitudes and cognitions) cause their behavior. Once they recognize this, then it also becomes apparent that only they can change their thoughts and control their behavior. The cognitive-behavioral model is self-empowering.

2. Teach the offender how to identify his or her personal thinking patterns related to the problem behaviors. Oftentimes, offenders (and sometimes ourselves) do not recognize when rationalizations and excuses are made for antisocial behavior.

3. After the offender understands the importance of cognitions in explaining behavior (steps 1 and 2) then teach the offender to replace

antisocial cognitions with alternative, prosocial cognitions. In the psychotherapy literature, this is referred to as *cognitive restructuring*.

The learning and maintenance of new behaviors is a gradual process that involves interpersonally mediated and nonmediated rewards and costs. In cognitive-behavioral interventions, personally mediated rewards and costs play a central role. The last step in cognitive-behavioral treatment is the following:

4. Facilitate the practice and generalization of the new cognitive and behavioral skills both in and outside of supervision sessions. This may involve modeling, role playing, graduated practice, and the assignment of "homework" (e.g., "try practicing this new thought the next time you get angry and tell me how it went at our next meeting"). At this point, not only is there abundant use of rewards from the therapist and others, but the client is also encouraged to deliver personally mediated rewards.

Cognitive-behavioral treatment is an effective approach to helping offenders become more prosocial. It acknowledges the powerful influence of rewards and costs on behavior and pays particular attention to personal sources of antecedent and consequent control. The cognitive-behavioral approach also highlights the importance of personal agency in human behavior.

Adapted from Bonta, Bourgon, Rugge, Scott & Yessine, 2009

Table TN4.1-1

Behavioral Explanation			
Outside Cue	*Inside Cue*	*Behavior*	*Consequence*
"STAND UP"		Stands up	Praise from trainer
Cognitive-Behavioral Explanation			
"STAND UP"	I should do what I am told!	Stands up	Outside consequence: Praise from trainer
	He's the trainer!		Inside consequence: "I can be counted on"
	Ok sure!	Stay seated	Outside consequence: Frown from trainer
	I don't take orders from anyone!		Inside consequence: "I showed him!"

Technical Note 5.1

Genetics and Heredity

When viewed under the microscope, each human cell has the same general structure, a round ball that is filled with various particles (called organelles) and a smaller ball, somewhere in the middle, called the nucleus. The nucleus houses all of the "programming code" for the organism. The code for our observable characteristics (phenotype) such as hair and eye color, foot size, etc., is crammed into the nucleus. This code is called DNA (deoxyribonucleic acid).

An organism's basic complement of DNA is called its genome. DNA is essentially a long chain of molecules (nucleotide base pairs, the so-called building blocks) that is wound into a double helix. Clusters of base pairs are known as genes, and genes code for a specific function (e.g., the protein that regulates hair color). There exist thousands of discrete genes within the millions of base pairs of DNA. And how does all this DNA fit into the nucleus? It does so by dividing itself from one long strand of DNA into 23 pieces of DNA that are coiled up into chromosomes. Thus, genes are simply the functional regions of chromosomal DNA.

Identifying and locating each of these genes is the grand goal of the Human Genome Project. While researchers have discovered the sequence of base pairs that make up human DNA, they are nowhere near finished identifying each discrete gene, and they are further still from understanding the role of each individual gene.

As mentioned, all of our programming code (DNA) exists as 23 chromosomes. However, within the nucleus we find 46 chromosomes. These 46 chromosomes exist as pairs, with each pair containing the same sequence of DNA. Each pair of chromosomes contains one derived from the mother and the other from the father. Thus, for example, the gene coding for skin color (melanin content) will code for darker skin from a mother of African descent and lighter skin from a father of European descent, with the result being a child whose skin color lies in between.

Of course, this genetic material must be transmitted to the offspring in order for inheritance to work. This pathway is through the combination of the sex or reproductive cells (i.e., the ovum or unfertilized egg and the sperm cell). The sex cells are different from the rest of the human cells in that each has only 23 chromosomes. It is the contribution of each parent to the genetic make up of the offspring that brings our total to 46 chromosomes. If a parent were able to pass on all of its genes, then the offspring would be a clone of the parent. Because some of a parent's genetic make up may be detrimental (e.g., one parent may lack the gene to enable color vision), it is more advantageous to have a mix of both parents' genes. In sexual reproduction, when a sperm fertilizes an egg, a cellular process termed *meiosis* takes place. It is during this event that each parent's contribution of 23 chromosomes undergoes a complex process of division and replication, with the end result being a single cell with 46 chromosomes that contains genetic material (DNA) from each parent. This one cell is the offspring of the two parents and rapidly undergoes division to become the embryo, fetus, and child of the two parents. This represents the chemical basis for heredity.

Of the 46 chromosomes (23 pairs) typically found in the human cell, one is referred to as the sex chromosome (the rest are referred to as autosomes and are numbered 1 through 22). As previously noted, the sex cell has only a single set of the 46 chromosomes that are found paired in other cells; 22 autosomes, and one sex chromosome, yielding a total of 23. The pairing of this lone sex chromosome determines sex, with males having an X chromosome paired with a Y chromosome (XY) and females having two X chromosomes (XX). It is the Y chromosome that carries the genes associated with male features (e.g., height, male genitalia development, hair distribution mediated through the production of testosterone; Chan & Rennert, 2002). The fact that males are over-represented in crime statistics and crimes of a sexual nature makes the Y chromosome of particular interest in some theories of criminal behavior.

Technical Note 10.1

The Receiver Operating Characteristic (ROC)

The Receiver Operating Characteristic (ROC) was first developed as an index of discrimination capacity when faced with confusing data. Within the context of signal-detection theory, the "detector" must make a decision of whether a signal did occur. For example, an air traffic controller must decide whether the blip on the radar screen is an airplane or a flock of birds, and a radiologist must decide whether the dark spot on an X-ray film is a mass of cancer cells or simply a muscle mass. In both of these examples, the detector must discriminate what is a real concern and what can be ignored. Similarly, in the prediction of criminal behavior, we would like to know whether an individual is a concern to the public.

How well we can discriminate the recidivist from the nonrecidivist can be measured in different ways (e.g., the Pearson correlation coefficient). Many of these measures are influenced by the base rate and selection ratio. The ROC is largely unaffected by base rates and selection ratios. The ROC is usually presented in the form of a curve (an example is given in Figure TN 10.1–1). Along the vertical axis, we

have the proportion of true positives or "hits" (also sometimes called sensitivity). Along the horizontal axis we have the proportion of false positives. The diagonal line going from the bottom left to the top right represents chance level, where the true positives equal the false positives. Most quantitative offender risk instruments have a range of scores and therefore we can plot for each score the proportion of hits and the proportion of false positives.

In Figure TN 10.1–1 we plotted an imaginary four-item risk scale on which each item can be scored 0 or 1. For example, one item could be gender, and we would assign females a score of 0 and males a score of 1. As a result, our four-item risk scale will have scores ranging from 0 to 4 and, assuming that we did a follow-up of a group of offenders, we can calculate the proportion of true positives and false positives associated with each score and draw a (rough) curve through the data points. From this ROC curve we can make two statements. First, we can evaluate whether our risk scale is better than chance. In Figure TN 10.1–1, the curve is above the diagonal, indicating

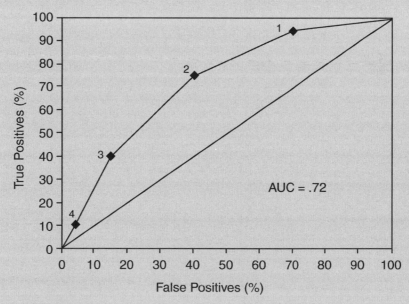

Figure TN 10.1–1
An ROC Curve for a Risk Scale

Technical Note 10.1 *(continued)*

that the scale predicts better than chance. Second, we can calculate the "area under the curve" (AUC). The AUC gives the overall discriminating power of the test. An AUC of 1.0 would represent perfect prediction; all recidivists would have scores higher than the highest score of the nonrecidivists. An AUC of .50 (the diagonal line) is chance, i.e., the scores of the recidivists and the nonrecidivists completely overlap.

In our example, the AUC has a value of .72. An easy way of interpreting this value is to say that there is a 72 percent chance that a randomly selected recidivist would have a higher score on our fictitious risk scale than a randomly selected nonrecidivist. The larger the area, the better the overall predictive accuracy of the scale (more hits and fewer false positives). Calculating the AUC for different risk scales would allow us to compare the predictive accuracy of the various scales, controlling for the effects of base rates and selection ratios.

Technical Note 11.1

How Applicable Are the Findings Regarding Appropriate Treatment with Different Types of Cases?

There is no limit to the setting, case-based, and other conditions that may be found to raise questions about conclusions regarding appropriate treatment. For example, with reference to the Carleton University databank, there is not a single experimental study that speaks to the effects of treatment on the violent reoffending of older female sex offenders who have spent 20 years in a maximum-security prison. There are not even many studies that have examined outcome with female offenders of any age. To date, however, the robustness of the findings regarding the effectiveness of human service is impressive across reviewers, settings, and types of cases.

Tables TN 11.1–1 through TN 11.1–5 provide a modest look at the applicability of the principles of effective service in the total Carleton sample and in subsamples defined by age (younger), gender (women), and ethnicity (minority group member, nonwhite). It is obvious that rates of adherence with principles of effective treatment were robust, as were the

correlation coefficients of adherence with effect size (Table TN 11.1–1).

The importance of school/work, personal distress, and noncriminogenic interpersonal targets (see Table TN 11.1–2) remains unclear with women and minorities. This we will be watching very carefully as new research comes in. In exploration of elements of core correctional practice (Table TN 11.1–3), the only evidence of weak general applicability was with the weakest of the correlates (advocacy/brokerage and effective authority) and with the smallest subsamples (women and ethnic minorities). These findings suggest that statistical power issues must be explored in view of the combination of small sample sizes and weak estimated effect sizes. It is too early to conclude that advocacy/brokerage and authority are unimportant with women and minorities.

In our view, the overall dominant finding is the robustness of the major correlates of positive program outcomes.

Table TN 11.1–1
Rate of Adherence with Principle and Correlation of Adherence to Principle with Effect Size (ES) by Subpopulation

Principle	Total sample (k = 374)	Young (k = 193)	Female (k = 45)	Minority (k = 106)
Human Service				
% Adherence	73	76	78	63
Correlation with ES	.35	.31	.31	.29
Risk: Services Delivered to Higher-Risk Cases				
% Adherence	74	74	80	80
Correlation with ES	.17	.20	.40	.18
Criminogenic Needs: # of Criminogenic Needs Targeted Exceed Noncriminogenic				
% Adherence	45	29	47	41
Correlation with ES	.54	.52	.49	.41
General Responsivity: Social Learning/Cognitive Behavioral Strategies				
% Adherence	21	29	33	22
Correlation with ES	.40	.43	.38	.43
Clinically Appropriate Treatment (adheres to all four of the above)				
% Adherence	16	21	27	17
Correlation with ES	.55	.46	.56	.46

k = number of tests of treatment

Technical Note 11.1 *(continued)*

Table TN 11.1–2
Percentage of Tests with Need Areas Targeted and Correlation with Effect Size by Subpopulation

Need Area	Total Sample	Young	Female	Minority
Criminogenic Needs Targeted				
Personal Criminogenic Targets: Antisocial Cognition and Skill Deficits				
% Adherence	26	33	18	29
Correlation with ES	.39	.39	.32	.33
Interpersonal Criminogenic Targets: Family and Associates				
% Adherence	19	23	31	15
Correlation with ES	.37	.33	.45	.34
Individualized Matching with Need (specific criminogenic needs not identified)				
% Adherence	17	19	07	12
Correlation with ES	.30	.30	.26	.28
School/Work				
% Adherence	24	26	16	21
Correlation with ES	.21	.23	−.08 (ns)	.10 (ns)
Substance Abuse				
% Adherence	10	03	11	08
Correlation with ES	.06 (ns)	.04 (ns)	−.01 (ns)	−.02 (ns)
Noncriminogenic Needs Targeted				
Personal Noncriminogenic Targets (personal distress, physical activity)				
% Adherence	46	45	24	40
Correlation with ES	−.18	−.20	−.03 (ns)	−.18
Interpersonal Noncriminogenic Targets (family process, not affection/supervision)				
% Adherence	12	17	13	13
Correlation with ES	−.25	−.20	−.23	−.16 (ns)

s = nonsignificant

Table TN 11.1–3
Elements of Core Correctional Practice (CCP): Percent of Tests with CCP Element Present and Correlation of CCP Presence with Effect Size

CCP	Total Sample (k = 374)	Young (k = 193)	Female (k = 45)	Minority (k = 108)
Relationship Skills of Staff				
% of tests	03	03	02	02
Correlation with ES	.26	.31	.32	.27
Structuring Skills of Staff				
% of tests	12	12	16	08
Correlation with ES	.37	.34	.56	.36
Effective Reinforcement				
% of tests	04	04	02	06
Correlation with ES	.25	.22	.45	.40
Effective Modeling				
% of tests	10	12	11	11
Correlation with ES	.36	.35	.29	.23

Technical Note 11.1 *(continued)*

Table TN 11.1–3 *(continued)*

Effective Disapproval				
% of tests	02	03	02	03
Correlation with ES	.18	.19	.32	.17
Structured Skill Learning				
% of tests	10	11	16	08
Correlation with ES	.31	.37	.56	.38
Problem-Solving				
% of tests	12	12	11	11
Correlation with ES	.33	.29	.29	.23
Advocacy/Brokerage				
% of tests	14	19	04	12
Correlation with ES	.10	.16	.14 (ns)	.26
Effective Authority				
% of tests	04	02	04	03
Correlation with ES	.19	.13	.24 (ns)	.08 (ns)

ns = nonsignificant

Table TN 11.1–4
Mean Effect Size by Indicators of Integrity of Imprementation and Service Delivery for Total Sample, Young Offenders, Female Offenders, and Minorities

Integrity	Total Sample (k = 374)	Young (k = 193)	Female (k = 45)	Minority (k = 105)
Staff Selected for Relationship Skills				
% of tests	03	03	02	02
Correlation with ES	.26	.31	.32 (ns)	.27
Staff Trained				
% of tests	45	54	44	35
Correlation with ES	.26	.32	.33	.34
Clinical Supervision of Staff				
% of tests	19	21	29	12
Correlation with ES	.21	.22	.51	.28
Number of Hours of Service				
% of tests	(reduced samples because of missing values)			
Correlaton with ES	.20	.41	.45	−.08
Rated Appropriate Dosage				
% of tests	41	40	40	32
Correlation with ES	.05 (ns)	.11 (ns)	.28	.22
Printed/Taped Manuals				
% of tests	19	24	16	17
Correlation with ES	.30	.32	.26	.22
Monitor Process and/or Intermediate Change on Targets				
% of tests	39	48	44	30
Correlation with ES	.07 (ns)	.07 (ns)	.22 (ns)	.12 (ns)

Technical Note 11.1 *(continued)*

Table TN 11.1–4 *(continued)*

Integrity	Total Sample (k = 374)	Young (k = 193)	Female (k = 45)	Minority (k = 105)
Specific Model				
% of tests	54	59	56	45
Correlation with ES	.23	.27	.36	.18
New/Fresh Program				
% of tests	33	40	38	28
Correlation with ES	.20	.19	.26	.33
Small Program/Sample				
% of tests	36	45	58	38
Correlation with ES	.28	.19	.26	.22
Involved Evaluator				
% of tests	21	26	18	21
Correlation with ES	.41	.42	.62	.53

k = number of tests
ns = nonsignificant

References

Abracen, J., J. Looman, D. Mailloux, R. Serin & B. Malcolm (2005). "Clarification Regarding Marshall and Yates's Critique of 'Dosage of Treatment to Sexual Offenders: Are We Overprescribing?'" *International Journal of Offender Therapy and Comparative Criminology*, 49, 225–230.

Abrams, K.M. & G.E. Robinson (1998). "Stalking Part I: An Overview of the Problem." *Canadian Journal of Psychiatry*, 43, 473–476.

Accordino, M.P. & B. Guerney Jr. (1998). "An Evaluation of the Relationship Enhancement Program with Prisoners and Their Wives." *International Journal of Offender Therapy and Comparative Criminology*, 42, 5–15.

Acker, J.R. (2006). "Hearing the Victim's Voice Amidst the Cry for Capital Punishment." In D. Sullivan & L. Tifft (eds.), *Handbook of Restorative Justice* (pp. 246–260). New York: Routledge.

Adams, S. (1975). "Evaluation: A Way Out of the Rhetoric." Paper presented at the Evaluation Research Conference, Seattle, Washington.

Ægisdóttier, S., M.J. White, P.M. Spengler, A.S. Maugherman, L.A. Anderson, R.S. Cook, C.N. Nichols, G.K. Lampropoulos, B.S. Walker, G Cohen & J.D. Rush (2006). "The Meta-Analysis of Clinical Judgment Project: Fifty-six Years of Accumulated Research on Clinical Versus Statistical Prediction." *Counseling Psychologist*, 34, 341–382.

Agee, V.L. (1979). *Treatment of the Violent Incorrigible Adolescent*. Lexington, MA: Lexington Books.

Agnew, R. (1992). "Foundation for a General Strain Theory of Crime and Delinquency." *Criminology*, 30, 47–87.

Agnew, R. (1994). "The Techniques of Neutralization and Violence." *Criminology*, 32, 555–580.

Agnew, R. (2001). *Juvenile Delinquency: Causes and Control*. Los Angeles: Roxbury.

Agnew, R. (2006). *Pressured into Crime: An Overview of General Strain Theory*. Los Angeles: Roxbury.

Aguirre, A. & D.V. Baker (1990). "Empirical Research on Racial Discrimination in the Imposition of the Death Penalty." *Criminal Justice Abstracts*, March.

Ajzen, I. (1996). "The Directive Influence of Attitudes on Behavior." In P.M. Gollwitzer & J.A. Bargh (eds.), *The Psychology of Action: Linking Cognition and Motivation to Behavior* (pp. 385–403). New York: Guilford.

Ajzen, I. & N.G. Cote (2008). "Attitudes and the Prediction of Behavior." In C.D. Crano & R. Radmila (eds.), *Attitudes and Attitude Change* (pp. 289–311). Mahwah, NJ: Lawrence Erlbaum Associates.

Ajzen, I. & M. Fishbein (1980). *Understanding Attitudes and Predicting Social Behavior*. Englewood Cliffs, NJ: Prentice Hall.

Ajzen, I. & M. Fishbein (2005). "The Influence of Attitudes on Behaviour." In D. Albarracin, B.T. Johnson & M.P. Zanna (eds.), *The Handbook of Attitudes* (pp. 173–221). Mahwah, NJ: Lawrence Erlbaum Associates.

Akers, R.L. (1973). *Deviant Behavior: A Social Learning Approach.* Belmont, CA: Wadsworth.

Akers, R.L. (1985). *Deviant Behavior: A Social Learning Approach*, 3rd ed. Belmont, CA: Wadsworth.

Akers, R.L. (1991). "Self-Control as a General Theory of Crime." *Journal of Quantitative Criminology*, 7, 201–211.

Akers, R.L. (1996). "Is Differential Association/Social Learning Cultural Deviance Theory?" *Criminology*, 34, 229–248.

Akers, R.L. (1999). "Social Learning and Social Structure: Reply to Sampson, Morash, and Krohn." *Theoretical Criminology*, 3, 477–493.

Akers, R.L. (2001). "Social Learning Theory." In R. Paternoster & R. Bachman (eds.), *Explaining Criminals and Crime* (pp. 192–210). Los Angeles: Roxbury.

Akers, R.L. & J.K. Cochran (1985). "Adolescent Marijuana Use: A Test of Three Theories of Deviant Behavior." *Deviant Behavior*, 6, 323–346.

Allik, J. & R.R. McCrae (2004). "Escapable Conclusions: Toomela (2003) and the Universality of Trait Structure." *Journal of Personality and Social Psychology*, 87, 261–265.

Alexander, J.F. & C. Barton (1976). "Behavioral Systems Therapy for Families." In D.H.L. Olson (ed.), *Treating Relationships* (pp.167–188). Lake Mills, IA: Graphic.

Alder, C. (1985). "Exploration of Self-reported Sexually Aggressive Behavior." *Crime & Delinquency*, 31, 306–331.

Alltucker, K.W., M. Bullis, D. Close & P. Yovanoff (2006). "Different Pathways to Juvenile Delinquency: Characteristics of Early and Late Starters in a Sample of Previously Incarcerated Youth." *Journal of Child and Family Studies*, 15, 479–492.

Alexy, E.M., A.W. Burgess & T. Baker (2005). "Internet Offenders: Traders, Travelers, and Combination Trader-Travelers." *Journal of Interpersonal Violence*, 20, 804–812.

Amato, P.R. (2001). "Children of Divorce in the 1990s: An Update of the Amato and Keith (1991) Meta-analysis." *Journal of Family Psychology*, 3, 355–370.

American Psychiatric Association (1994). *Diagnostic and Statistical Manual of Mental Disorders—DSM IV.* Washington, DC: The American Psychiatric Association.

Andrews, D.A. (1979). *The Dimensions of Correctional Counseling and Supervision Process in Probation and Parole.* Toronto: Ontario Ministry of Correctional Services.

Andrews, D.A. (1980). "Some Experimental Investigations of the Principles of Differential Association through Deliberate Manipulations of the Structure of Service Systems." *American Sociological Review*, 45, 448–462.

Andrews, D.A. (1982a). *A Personal, Interpersonal and Community-Reinforcement Perspective on Deviant Behaviour (PIC-R).* Toronto: Ontario Ministry of Correctional Services.

Andrews, D.A. (1982b). *The Level of Supervision Inventory (LSI): The First Follow-up.* Toronto: Ontario Ministry of Correctional Services.

Andrews, D.A. (1983). "The Assessment of Outcome in Correctional Samples." In M.L. Lambert, E.R. Christensen & S.S. DeJulio (eds.), *The Measurement of Psychotherapy Outcome in Research and Evaluation* (pp. 160–201). New York: Wiley and Sons.

Andrews, D.A. (1989). "Recidivism is Predictable and Can Be Influenced: Using Risk Assessments to Reduce Recidivism." *Forum on Corrections Research*, 1, 11–18.

Andrews, D.A. (2001). "Principles of Effective Correctional Programming." In L.L. Motiuk & R.C. Serin (eds.), *Compendium 2000 on Effective Correctional Programming* (pp. 9–17). Ottawa: Correctional Services of Canada.

Andrews, D.A. (2006). "Enhancing Adherence to Risk-Need Responsivity: Making Quality a Matter of Policy." *Criminology & Public Policy*, 5, 595–602.

Andrews, D.A. (2008). "Extensions of the Risk-Need-Responsivity (RNR) Model of Assessment and Correctional Treatment." In G. Bourgon, R.K. Hanson, J.D. Pozzulo, K.E. Morton Bourgon & C.L. Tanasichuk (eds.), *The Proceedings of the 2007 North American Correctional & Criminal Justice Psychology Conference* (pp. 7–11). Ottawa: Public Safety Canada.

Andrews, D.A. & J. Bonta (1994). *The Psychology of Criminal Conduct*. Cincinnati: Anderson.

Andrews, D.A. & J. Bonta (1995). *The Level of Service Inventory – Revised*. Toronto: Multi-Health Systems.

Andrews, D.A. & J. Bonta (2006). The *Psychology of Criminal Conduct*, 4th ed. Newark, NJ: LexisNexis Matthew Bender.

Andrews, D.A., J. Bonta & R.D. Hoge (1990). "Classification for Effective Rehabilitation: Rediscovering Psychology." *Criminal Justice and Behavior*, 17, 19–52.

Andrews, D.A., J. Bonta & S.J. Wormith (2004). *The Level of Service/Case Management Inventory (LS/CMI): User's Manual*. Toronto: Multi-Health Systems.

Andrews, D.A., J. Bonta & S.J. Wormith (2006). "The Recent Past and Near Future of Risk and/or Need Assessment." *Crime & Delinquency*, 52, 7–27.

Andrews, D.A., J. Bonta & S.J. Wormith (2008a). *The Level of Service/Risk, Need, Responsivity (LS/RNR): User's Manual*. Toronto: Multi-Health Systems.

Andrews, D.A., J. Bonta & S.J. Wormith (2008b). *Level of Service/Case Management Inventory (LS/CMI) Supplement: A Gender-Informed Risk/Need/Responsivity Assessment*. Toronto: Multi-Health Systems.

Andrews, D.A., J. Bonta & S.J. Wormith (2009). "The Level of Service (LS) Assessment of Adults and Older Adolescents." In R.K. Otto and K. Douglas (eds.), *Handbook of Violence Risk Assessment Tools* (pp. 199–225). New York: Routledge.

Andrews, D.A., J. Bonta, S.J. Wormith, L. Guzzo, A. Brews, J. Rettinger & R. Rowe (2008). Unpublished collaborative LS data analysis.

Andrews, D.A. & C. Carvell (1997). *Core Correctional Treatment—Core Correctional Supervision and Counseling: Theory, Research, Assessment and Practice*. Ottawa: Carleton University.

Andrews, D.A. & C. Dowden (1999). "A Meta-analytic Investigation into Effective Correctional Intervention for Female Offenders." *Forum on Corrections Research*, 11(3), 18–21.

Andrews, D.A. & C. Dowden (2005). "Managing Correctional Treatment for Reduced Recidivism: A Meta-analytic Review of Program Integrity." *Legal and Criminological Psychology*, 10, 173–187.

Andrews, D.A. & G. Dowden (2006). "Risk Principle of Case Classification in Correctional Treatment." *International Journal of Offender Therapy and Comparative Criminology*, 50, 88–100.

Andrews, D.A. & C. Dowden (2007). "The Risk-Need-Responsivity Model of Assessment and Human Service in Prevention and Corrections: Crime-Prevention Jurisprudence." *Canadian Journal of Criminology and Criminal Justice*, 49, 439–464.

Andrews, D.A., C. Dowden & P. Gendreau (1999). *Clinically Relevant and Psychologically Informed Approaches to Reduced Re-offending: A Meta-analytic Study of Human Service, Risk, Need, Responsivity and Other Concerns in Justice Contexts*. Ottawa: Carleton University.

Andrews, D.A., C. Dowden & J.L. Rettinger (2001). "Special Populations within Canada." In J.A. Winterdyck (ed.), *Corrections in Canada: Social Reactions to Crime* (pp. 170–212). Toronto: Prentice Hall.

Andrews, D.A. & J.J. Kiessling (1980). "Program Structure and Effective Correctional Practices: A Summary of the CaVIC Research." In R.R. Ross & P. Gendreau (eds.), *Effective Correctional Treatment* (pp. 439–463). Toronto: Butterworth.

Andrews, D.A. & D. Robinson (1984). *The Level of Supervision Inventory: Second Report*. Report to Research Services (Toronto) of the Ontario Ministry of Correctional Services.

Andrews, D.A. & J.S. Wormith (1984). *Criminal Sentiments and Criminal Behaviour*. Programs Branch User Report. Ottawa: Solicitor General Canada.

Andrews, D.A. & J.S. Wormith (1989). "Personality and Crime: Knowledge Destruction and Construction in Criminology." *Justice Quarterly*, 6, 289–309.

Andrews, D.A., J.S. Wormith & J.J. Kiessling (1985). *Self-reported Criminal Propensity and Criminal Behavior: Threats to the Validity of Assessment and Personality*. Programs Branch User Report. Ottawa: Solicitor General Canada.

Andrews, D.A., I. Zinger, R.D. Hoge, J. Bonta, P. Gendreau & F.T. Cullen (1990a). "Does Correctional Treatment Work? A Psychologically Informed Meta-analysis." *Criminology*, 28, 369–404.

Andrews, D.A., I. Zinger, R.D. Hoge, J. Bonta, P. Gendreau & F.T. Cullen (1990b). "A Human Science Approach or More Punishment and Pessimism—Rejoinder." *Criminology*, 28, 419–429.

Andrews, K.H. & D.B. Kandel (1979). "Attitude and Behavior: A Specification of the Contingent Consistency Hypothesis." *American Sociological Review*, 44, 298–310.

Annis, H.M. (1982). *Inventory of Drinking Situations (IDS-100)*. Toronto: Addiction Research Foundation.

Aos, S., M. Miller & E. Drake (2006a). *Evidence-based Adult Corrections Programs: What Works and What Does Not*. Olympia, WA: Washington State Institute for Public Policy.

Aos, S., M. Miller & E. Drake (2006b). *Evidence-based Policy Options to Reduce Future Prison Construction, Criminal Justice Costs, and Crime Rates*. Olympia, WA: Washington State Institute for Public Policy.

Aos, S., P. Phipps, R. Barnoski & R. Lieb (2001). "The Comparative Costs and Benefits of Programs to Reduce Crime." Olympia, WA: Washington State Institute for Public Policy. See http://www.wa.gov/wsipp.

Appelbaum, P.S., P.C. Robbins & J. Monahan (2000). "Violence and Delusions: Data from the MacArthur Violence Risk Assessment Study." *American Journal of Psychiatry*, 157, 556–572.

Arbuthnot, J. & D.A. Gordon (1986). "Behavioral and Cognitive Effects of a Moral Reasoning Development Intervention for High-Risk, Behavior-Disordered Adolescents." *Journal of Consulting and Clinical Psychology*, 54, 208–216.

Archer, J. (2000). "Sex Differences in Aggression between Heterosexual Partners: A Meta-analytic Review." *Psychological Bulletin*, 126, 651–680.

Armstrong, G.S. (2004). "Boot Camps as a Correctional Option." In D.L. MacKenzie & G.S. Armstrong (eds.), *Correctional Boot Camps: Military Basic Training or a Model for Corrections?* (pp. 7–15). Thousand Oaks, CA: Sage.

Arnold, T. (2007). *Dynamic Changes in the Level of Service Inventory-Revised (LSI-R) Scores and the Effects on Prediction Accuracy.* Unpublished Master's Dissertation, St. Cloud University, St. Cloud, MN.

Ashford, J.B., K.W. Wong & K.O. Sternbach (2008). "Generic Correctional Programming for Mentally Ill Offenders: A Pilot Study." *Criminal Justice and Behavior*, 35, 457–473.

Atkinson, L. & K.J. Zucker (eds.) (1997). *Attachment and Psychopathology.* New York: Guilford.

Au, A., G. Cheung, R. Kropp, C. Yuk-chung, G.L.T. Lam & P. Sung (2008). "A Preliminary Validation of the Brief Spousal Assault Form for the Evaluation of Risk (B-Safer) in Hong Kong." *Journal of Family Violence*, 23, 727–735.

Auerhahn, K. (2003). *Selective Incapacitation and Public Policy: California's Imprisonment Crisis.* Albany, NY: SUNY Press.

Austin, J., J. Clark, P. Hardyman & A.D. Henry (1999). "The Impact of 'Three Strikes and You're Out.'" *Punishment and Society*, 1, 131–162.

Azrin, N.H. (1956). "Some Effects of Two Intermittent Schedules of Immediate and Non-immediate Punishment." *Journal of Psychology*, 42, 3–21.

Azrin, N.H. & W.C. Holz (1966). "Punishment." In W.K. Honig (ed.), *Operant Behavior: Areas of Research and Application* (pp. 380–447). New York: Appleton-Century-Crofts.

Azrin, N.H., W.C. Holz & D. Hake (1963). "Fixed-ratio Punishment." *Journal of the Experimental Analysis of Behavior*, 6, 141–148.

Azrin, N.H., R.W. Sisson, R. Meyers & M. Godley (1982). "Alcoholism Treatment by Disulfiram and Community Reinforcement Therapy." *Journal of Behavior Therapy and Experimental Psychiatry*, 13, 105–112.

Babcock, J.C., C.E. Green & C. Robie (2004). "Does Batterers' Treatment Work? A Meta-analytic Review of Domestic Violence Treatment." *Clinical Psychology Review*, 23, 1023–1053.

Babiak, P. & R.D. Hare (2006). *Snakes in Suits: When Psychopaths Go to Work.* New York: Regan Books.

Babor, T.F. & R. Caetano (2008). "The Trouble with Alcohol Abuse: What Are We Trying to Measure, Diagnose, Count and Prevent?" *Addiction*, 103, 1057–1059.

Bailey, W.C. (1966). "Correctional Outcome: An Evaluation of 100 Reports." *Journal of Criminal Law, Criminology and Police Science*, 57, 153–160.

Bailey, W.C. (1998). "Deterrence, Brutalization, and the Death Penalty: Another Examination of Oklahoma's Return to Capital Punishment." *Criminology*, 36, 711–733.

Baird, C. (1981). "Probation and Parole Classification: The Wisconsin Model." *Corrections Today*, 43, 36–41.

Baird, C. (1991). *Validating Risk Assessment Instruments Used in Community Corrections.* Madison, WI: National Council on Crime and Delinquency.

Baird, S.C., R.C. Heinz & B.J. Bemus (1979). *Project Report #14: A Two-year Follow-up.* Madison, WI: Department of Health and Social Services, Case Classification/Staff Deployment Project, Bureau of Community Corrections.

Baker, J.R. & J.K. Yardley (2002). "Moderating Effect of Gender on the Relationship between Sensation Seeking-Impulsivity and Substance Abuse in Adolescents." *Journal of Child and Adolescent Substance Abuse*, 12, 27–43.

Bales, R.F. (1950). *Interaction Process Analysis.* Reading, MA: Addison-Wesley.

Bales, W.D. & D.P. Mears (2008). "Inmate Social Ties and the Transition to Society." *Journal of Research in Crime and Delinquency*, 45, 287–321.

Ball, R.A. (1973). "Ball's Neutralization Scale." In W.C. Reckless (ed.), *American Criminology: New Directions* (pp. 26–36). New York: Appleton-Century-Crofts.

Bandura, A. (1977). *Social Learning Theory.* New York: General Learning Press.

Bandura, A. (1986). The Explanatory and Predictive Scope of Self-efficacy Theory. *Journal of Social and Clinical Psychology*, 4, 359–373.

Bandura, A. (1989). "Human Agency in Social Cognitive Theory." *American Psychologist*, 44, 1175–1184.

Bandura, A. (2001). "Social Cognitive Theory: An Agentic Perspective." *Annual Review of Psychology*, 52, 1–16.

Bandura, A. (2008). "An Agentic Perspective on Positive Psychology." In S.J. Lopez (ed.), *Positive Psychology: Exploring the Best in People* (pp. 167–196). Westport, CT: Praeger.

Bandura, A., C. Barbaranelli, G.V. Caprara & C. Pastorelli (1996). "Mechanisms of Moral Disengagement in the Exercise of Moral Agency." *Journal of Personality and Social Psychology*, 71, 364–374.

Bandura, A. & R.H. Walters (1959). *Adolescent Aggression.* New York: Ronald.

Bank, L., J.H. Marlowe, J.B., Reid, G.R. Patterson & M.R. Weinrott (1991). "A Comparative Evaluation of Parent-training Interventions for Families of Chronic Delinquents." *Journal of Abnormal Child Psychology*, 19, 15–33.

Barbaree, H.E. & W.L. Marshall (1998). "Treatment of the Sexual Offender." In R.M. Wettstein (ed.), *Treatment of Offenders with Mental Disorders.* New York: Guilford.

Barker, E.D., J.R. Séguin, H.R. White, M.E. Bates, E. LaCourse, R. Carbonneau & R.E. Tremblay (2007). "Developmental Trajectories of Male Physical Violence and Theft." *Archives of General Psychiatry*, 64, 592–599.

Barnoski, R. (2004). *Outcome Evaluation of Washington State's Research-Based Programs for Juvenile Offenders.* Olympia, WA: Washington State Institute for Public Policy.

Barnow, S., M. Lucht & H.-J. Freyberger (2005). "Correlates of Aggressive and Delinquent Conduct Problems in Adolescence." *Aggressive Behavior*, 31, 24–39.

Barton, C. & J.F. Alexander (1980). "Functional Family Therapy." In A.S. Gurnam & D.P. Kniskern (eds.), *Handbook of Family Therapy* (pp. 403–443). New York: Brunner/Mazel.

Barton, C., J.F. Alexander, H. Waldron, C.W. Turner & J. Warburton (1985). "Generalizing Treatment Effects of Functional Family Therapy: Three Replications." *American Journal of Family Therapy*, 13, 16–26.

Barton, W.H. & J.A. Butts (1990). "Viable Options: Intensive Supervision Programs for Juvenile Delinquents." *Crime & Delinquency*, 36, 238–256.

Bartosh, D.L., T. Garby, D. Lewis & S. Gray (2003). "Differences in the Predictive Validity of Actuarial Risk Assessments in Relation to Sex Offender Type." *International Journal of Offender Therapy and Comparative Criminology*, 47, 422–438.

Battin, S.R., K.G. Hill, R.D. Abbott, R.F. Catalano & J.D. Hawkins (1998). "The Contribution of Gang Membership to Delinquency beyond Delinquent Friends. *Criminology*, 36, 93–115.

Baumer, E.P. (2007). "Untangling Research Puzzles in Merton's Multilevel Anomie Theory." *Theoretical Criminology*, 11, 63–93.

Baumeister, H. & M. Hörter (2007). "Prevalence of Mental Disorder Based on General Population Surveys?" *Social Psychiatry & Psychiatric Epidemiology*, 42, 537–546.

Baumeister, R.F., B.J. Bushman & W.K. Campbell (2000). "Self-Esteem, Narcissism, and Aggression: Does Violence Result from Low Self-Esteem or From Threatened Egotism?" *Current Directions in Psychological Science*, 9, 26–29.

Baumeister, R.F., J.D. Campbell, J.I. Krueger & K.D. Vohs (2003). "Does High Self-Esteem Cause Better Performance, Interpersonal Success, Happiness, or Healthier Lifestyles?" *Psychological Science in the Public Interest*, 4, 1–44.

Baumeister, R.F., T.F. Heatherton & D.M. Tice (1994). *Losing Control: How and Why People Fail at Self-Regulation*. San Diego, CA: Academic Press.

Baumeister, R.F. & K.D. Vohs (eds.) (2004). *Handbook of Self-regulation: Theory, Research, and Applications*. New York: Guilford.

Baumeister, R.F., K.D. Vohs & D.M. Tice (2007). "The Strength Model of Self-Control." *Current Directions in Psychological Science*, 16, 351–355.

Bazemore, G. (1996). "Three Paradigms for Juvenile Justice." In B. Galaway & J. Hudson (eds.), *Restorative Justice: International Perspectives* (pp. 37–67). Monsey, NY: Criminal Justice Press.

Bazemore, G., L.B. Nissen & M. Dooley (2000). "Mobilizing Social Support and Building Relationships: Broadening Correctional and Rehabilitative Agendas." *Corrections Management Quarterly*, 4, 10–21.

Beaver, K.M., J.E. Shutt, B.B. Boutwell, M. Ratchford, K. Roberts & J.C. Barnes (2009). "Genetic and Environmental Influences on Levels of Self-Control and Delinquent Peer Affiliation." *Criminal Justice and Behavior*, 36, 41–60.

Bechtel, K., C.T. Lowenkamp & E. Latessa (2007). "Assessing the Risk of Re-Offending for Juvenile Offenders Using the Youth Level of Service/Case Management Inventory." *Journal of Offender Rehabilitation*, 45, 85–108.

Becker, H.S. (1963). *Outsiders: Studies in the Sociology of Deviance*. New York: Free Press.

Becker, J.V. & J.A. Hunter Jr. (1992). "Evaluation of Treatment Outcome for Adult Perpetrators of Child Sexual Abuse." *Criminal Justice and Behavior*, 19, 74–92.

Beckman, M. (2004). "Crime, Culpability, and the Adolescent Brain." *Science*, 305, 596–599.

Bedau, H.A. (2004). *Killing as Punishment: Reflections on the Death Penalty in America.* Boston: Northeastern University Press.

Belenko, S. (2001). *Research on Drug Courts: A Critical Review 2001 Update.* See http://www.DrugPolicy.org/docUploads/2001DrugCourts.pdf.

Belmore, M.F. & V.L. Quinsey (1994). "Correlates of Psychopathy in a Noninstitutional Sample." *Journal of Interpersonal Violence*, 9, 339–349.

Bem, D.J. (1967). "Self-Perception: An Alternative Interpretation of Cognitive Dissonance Phenomena." *Psychological Review*, 74, 183–200.

Bench, L.L., S.P. Kramer & S. Erickson (1997). "A Discriminant Analysis of Predictive Factors in Sex Offender Recidivism." In B.K. Schwartz & H.R. Cellini (eds.), *The Sex Offender: New Insights, Treatment Innovations and Legal Developments* (pp. 15.1–15.15). Kingston, NJ: Civic Research Institute.

Bennett, T., K. Holloway & D. Farrington (2008). "The Statistical Association Between Drug Misuse and Crime: A Meta-Analysis." *Aggression and Violent Behavior*, 13, 107–118.

Berglund, M. (2005). "A Better Widget? Three Lessons for Improving Addiction Treatment from a Meta-Analytic Study." *Addiction*, 100, 742–750.

Bergseth, K.J. & J.A. Bouffard (2007). "The Long-Term Impact of Restorative Justice Programming for Juvenile Offenders." *Journal of Criminal Justice*, 35, 433–451.

Berkowitz, L. (1962). *Aggression: A Social Psychological Analysis.* New York: McGraw-Hill.

Berkowitz, L. (2008). "On the Consideration of Automatic as Well as Controlled Psychological Process in Aggression." *Aggressive Behavior*, 34, 117–129.

Bernard, T.J. & R.R. Ritti (1991). "The Philadelphia Birth Cohort and Selective Incapacitation." *Journal of Research in Crime and Delinquency*, 28, 33–54.

Bernfeld, G.A., D.P. Farrington & A.W. Leschied (eds.) (2001). *Offender Rehabilitation in Practice: Implementing and Evaluating Effective Programs.* Chichester, UK: Wiley.

Bilby, C., B. Brooks-Gordon & H. Wells (2006). "A Systematic Review of Psychological Interventions for Sexual Offenders II: Quasi-Experimental and Qualitative Data." *Journal of Forensic Psychiatry & Psychology*, 17, 467–484.

Bilefsky, D. (2009). "Europeans Debate Castration of Sex Offenders." *The New York Times*, March 11.

Birgden, A. (2004). "Therapeutic Jurisprudence and Responsivity: Finding the Will and the Way in Offender Rehabilitation." *Psychology, Crime and Law*, 10, 283–295.

Birgden, A. (2009). "Crime Prevention Jurisprudence? A Response to Andrews and Dowden." *Canadian Journal of Criminology and Criminal Justice*, 51, 93–117.

Blackburn, R. (1975). "An Empirical Classification of Psychopathic Personality." *British Journal of Psychiatry*, 127, 456–460.

Blackburn, R. (1993). "Clinical Programs with Psychopaths." In K. Howells & C.R. Hollin (eds.), *Clinical Approaches to the Mentally Disordered Offender* (pp. 179–208). West Sussex, UK: John Wiley and Sons.

Blackburn, R. (2004). "'What Works' with Mentally Disordered Offenders." *Psychology, Crime and Law*, 10, 297–308.

Blackburn, R. (2006). "Other Theoretical Models of Psychopathy." In C.J. Patrick (ed.), *Handbook of Psychopathy* (pp. 35–57). New York: Guilford.

Blanchette, K., & S.L. Brown. (2006). *The Assessment and Treatment of Women Offenders.* Chichester, UK: John Wiley & Sons.

Blokland, A.A.J. & P. Nieuwbeerta (2007). "Selectively Incapacitating Frequent Offenders: Costs and Benefits of Various Penal Scenarios." *Journal of Quantitative Criminology*, 23, 327–353.

Bloom, B. (1999). "Gender-Responsive Programming for Women Offenders: Guiding Principles and Practices." *Forum on Corrections Research*, 11, 22–27.

Bloom, B. & S. Covington (1998). "Gender Specific Programming for Female Offenders: What is Important and Why it is Important." Paper presented at the Annual Meeting of the American Society of Criminology, Washington, DC, November.

Bloom, B.E. & S.S. Covington (2001). "Effective Gender-responsive Interventions in Juvenile Justice: Addressing the Lives of Delinquent Girls." Paper presented at the Annual Meeting of the American Criminology Association, Atlanta, Georgia, November.

Bloom, B., B. Owen & S. Covington (2003). *Gender Responsive Strategies: Research, Practice and Guiding Principles for Women Offenders.* Washington, DC: National Institute of Corrections.

Bloom, J.D. & W.H. Williams (1994). *Management and Treatment of Insanity Acquittees: A Model for the 1990s.* Washington, DC: American Psychiatric Press.

Blumstein, A., J. Cohen & D. Nagin (1978). *Deterrence and Incapacitation: Estimating the Effects of Criminal Sanctions on Crime Rates.* Washington, DC: National Research Council.

Blumstein, A., J. Cohen, J.A. Roth & C.A. Visher (1986). *Criminal Careers and "Career Criminals."* Washington, DC: National Academy of Sciences.

Boerner, D. & R. Lieb (2001). "Sentencing Reform in the Other Washington." In M. Tonry (ed.), *Crime and Justice: A Review of Research*, Vol. 28. Chicago: University of Chicago Press.

Bogan, K. & D. Factor (1995). "Oregon Guidelines 1989–1994." *Overcrowded Times*, 6, 1, 13–15.

Bogue, B.M., A. Nandi & A.E. Jongsma Jr. (eds.) (2003). *The Probation and Parole Treatment Planner.* Hoboken, NJ: John Wiley & Sons.

Boisjoli, R., F. Vitaro, E. Lacourse, E.D. Barker & R.E. Tremblay (2007). "Impact and Clinical Significance of a Preventative Intervention for Disruptive Boys." *British Journal of Psychiatry*, 191, 415–419.

Bonta, J. (1989). "Native Inmates: Institutional Response, Risk and Needs." *Canadian Journal of Criminology*, 31, 49–62.

Bonta, J. (1995). "The Responsivity Principle and Offender Rehabilitation." *Forum on Corrections Research*, 7, 34–37.

Bonta, J. (1996). "Risk-Needs Assessment and Treatment." In A.T. Harland (ed.), *Choosing Correctional Options that Work: Defining the Demand and Evaluating the Supply* (pp. 18–32). Thousand Oaks, CA: Sage.

Bonta, J. (2002). "Offender Risk Assessment: Guidelines for Selection and Use." *Criminal Justice and Behavior*, 29, 355–379.

Bonta, J. & D.A. Andrews (2007). *Risk-Need-Responsivity Model for Offender Assessment and Treatment* (User Report 2007-06). Ottawa: Public Safety Canada.

Bonta, J., B. Bogue, M. Crowley & L. Motiuk (2001). "Implementing Offender Classification Systems: Lessons Learned." In G.A. Bernfeld, D.P. Farrington & A.W. Leschied (eds.), *Offender Rehabilitation in Practice: Implementing and Evaluating Effective Programs* (pp. 227–245). Chichester, UK: Wiley.

Bonta, J., G. Bourgon, T. Rugge, T. Scott & A. Yessine (2009). *Strategic Training Initiative in Community Supervision (STICS Project) 3-Day Training*. Ottawa: Public Safety Canada.

Bonta, J. & P. Gendreau (1990). "Reexamining the Cruel and Unusual Punishment of Prison Life." *Law and Human Behavior*, 14, 347–372.

Bonta, J. & P. Gendreau (1992). "Coping with Prison." In P. Suedfeld & P.E. Tetlock (eds.), *Psychology and Social Policy* (pp. 343–354). New York: Hemisphere.

Bonta, J., A. Harris, I. Zinger & D. Carriere (1996). *The Crown Files Research Project: A Study of Dangerous Offenders*. Ottawa: Solicitor General Canada.

Bonta, J., R. Jesseman, T. Rugge & R. Cormier (2006). "Restorative Justice and Recidivism: Promises Made, Promises Kept?" In D. Sullivan & L. Tifft (eds.), *Handbook of Restorative Justice* (pp. 151–160). New York: Routledge.

Bonta, J., M. Law & R.K. Hanson (1998). "The Prediction of Criminal and Violent Recidivism among Mentally Disordered Offenders: A Meta-analysis." *Psychological Bulletin*, 123, 123–142.

Bonta, J. & L.L. Motiuk (1985). "Utilization of an Interview-based Classification Instrument: A Study of Correctional Halfway Houses." *Criminal Justice and Behavior*, 12, 333–352.

Bonta, J., R. Parkinson & L. Barkwell (1994). "Revising the Wisconsin Classification System." Paper presented at the Annual Meeting of the American Society of Criminology, Miami, Florida, November.

Bonta, J., R. Parkinson, B. Pang, L. Barkwell & S. Wallace-Capretta (1994). *The Revised Manitoba Classification System for Probationers*. Ottawa: Public Safety Canada.

Bonta, J., T. Rugge, T-L. Scott, G. Bourgon & A. Yessine (2008). "Exploring the Black Box of Community Supervision." *Journal of Offender Rehabilitation*, 47, 248–270.

Bonta, J., S. Wallace-Capretta & J. Rooney (2000a). "A Quasi-experimental Evaluation of an Intensive Rehabilitation Supervision Program." *Criminal Justice and Behavior*, 27, 312–329.

Bonta, J., S. Wallace-Capretta & J. Rooney (2000b). "Can Electronic Monitoring make a Difference? An Evaluation of Three Canadian Programs." *Crime & Delinquency*, 46, 61–75.

Bonta, J., S. Wallace-Capretta, J. Rooney & K. McAnoy (2002). "An Outcome Evaluation of a Restorative Justice Alternative to Incarceration." *Contemporary Justice Review*, 5, 319–338.

Bonta, J. & S.J. Wormith (2007). "Risk and Need Assessment." In G. McIvor & P. Raynor, *Developments in Social Work with Offenders*. Philadelphia: Jessica Kingsley.

Boothby, J.L. & C.B. Clements (2000). "A National Survey of Correctional Psychologists." *Criminal Justice and Behavior*, 27, 716–732.

Bordnick, P.S., R.L. Elkins, T.E. Orr, P. Walters & B.A. Thyer (2004). "Evaluating the Relative Effectiveness of Three Aversion Therapies Designed to Reduce Craving Among Cocaine Abusers." *Behavioral Interventions*, 19, 1–24.

Borduin, C.M., S.W. Henggeler, D.M. Blaske & R. Stein (1990). "Multisystemic Treatment of Adolescent Sex Offenders." *International Journal of Offender Therapy and Comparative Criminology*, 34, 105–113.

Borduin, C.M, B.J. Mann, L.T. Cone, S.W. Henggeler, B.R. Fucci, D.M. Blaske & R.A. Williams (1995). "Multisystemic Treatment of Serious Juvenile Offenders: Long-term Prevention of Criminality and Violence." *Journal of Consulting and Clinical Psychology*, 63, 569–578.

Borduin, C.M., C.M. Schaeffer & N. Heiblum (2009). "A Randomized Clinical Trial of Multisystemic Therapy with Juvenile Sexual Offenders: Effects on Youth Social Ecology and Criminal Activity." *Journal of Consulting and Clinical Psychology*, 77, 26–37.

Born, M., V. Chevalier & I. Humblet (1997). "Resilience, Desistance and Delinquent Career of Adolescent Offenders." *Journal of Adolescence*, 20, 679–694.

Botkins, J.R., W.M. McMahon & L.P. Francis (1999). *Genetics and Criminality: The Potential Misuse of Scientific Information in Court*. Washington, DC: American Psychological Association.

Bottcher, J. & M.E. Ezell (2005). "Examining the Effectiveness of Boot Camps: A Randomized Experiment with a Long-term Follow-up." *Journal of Research in Crime and Delinquency*, 42, 309–332.

Bourgon, G. & B. Armstrong (2005). "Transferring the Principles of Effective Treatment into a "Real World" Prison Setting." *Criminal Justice and Behavior*, 32, 3–25.

Bourgon, G. & J. Bonta (2004). *Risk Assessment for General Assault and Partner Abusers* (User Report 2004-04). Ottawa: Public Safety and Emergency Preparedness Canada.

Bowen, E., E. Gilchrist & A.R. Beech (2008). "Change in Treatment Has No Relationship With Subsequent Re-Offending in U.K. Domestic Violence Sample: A Preliminary Study." *International Journal of Offender Therapy and Comparative Criminology*, 52, 598–614.

Bowlby, J. (1971). *Attachment and Loss, Vol. 1: Attachment*. Harmondsworth, UK: Penguin Books.

Bowlby, J. (1973). *Attachment and Loss, Vol. 2. Separation: Anxiety and Anger*. Harmondsworth, UK: Penguin.

Bowlby, J. (1988). *A Secure Base: Clinical Implications of Attachment Theory*. London: Routledge & Kegan Paul.

Bradford, J.M.W. (1997). "Medical Interventions in Sexual Deviance." In D.R. Laws & W. O'Donohue (eds.), *Sexual Deviance: Theory, Assessment, and Treatment* (pp. 449–464). New York: Guilford.

Bradshaw, W. & D. Roseborough (2005). "Restorative Justice Dialogue: The Impact of Mediation and Conferencing on Juvenile Recidivism." *Federal Probation*, 69, 15–21.

Braithwaite, J. (1981). "The Myth of Social Class and Criminality Reconsidered." *American Sociological Review*, 46, 36–47.

Braithwaite, J. (1989). *Crime, Shame and Reintegration*. Cambridge, UK: Cambridge University Press.

Braithwaite, J. (1999). "Restorative Justice: Assessing Optimistic and Pessimistic Accounts." In M. Tonry (ed.), *Crime and Justice: A Review of Research*, Vol. 25 (pp. 1–127). Chicago: University of Chicago Press.

Brennan, P.A. & S.A. Mednick (1993). "Genetic Perspectives on Crime." *Acta Psychiatrica Scandinavica*, 87 (Suppl. 370), 19–26.

Brennan, P.A., S.A. Mednick & S. Hodgins (2000). "Major Mental Disorders and Criminal Violence in a Danish Birth Cohort." *Archives of General Psychiatry*, 56, 215–219.

Bressan, A. (2008). *Family Violence in Canada: A Statistical Profile 2008*. Ottawa: Canadian Centre for Justice Statistics.

Brews, A., J.S. Wormith & L. Guzzo (2009). "An Examination of the LSI-OR and Its Supplementary Scales with Female Offenders." Paper presented at the Annual Meeting of the Canadian Psychological Association, Montreal, Quebec.

Brink, J.H., D. Doherty & A. Boer (2001). "Mental Disorder in Federal Offenders: A Canadian Prevalence Study." *International Journal of Law and Psychiatry*, 24, 339–356.

Brody, G.H., X. Ge, S.Y. Kim, V.M Murry, R.L. Simons, F.X. Gibbons, M. Gerrard & R.D. Conger (2003). "Neighborhood Disadvantage Moderates Associations of Parenting and Older Sibling Problem Attitudes and Behavior with Conduct Disorders in African American Children." *Journal of Consulting and Clinical Psychology*, 71, 211–222.

Broidy, L.M. (2001). "A Test of General Strain Theory." *Criminology*, 39, 9–33.

Brown, R.S. & R.W. Courtis (1977). "The Castration Alternative." *Canadian Journal of Criminology and Corrections*, 19, 196–205.

Brown, S.L., M.D. St. Amand & E. Zamble (2009). "The Dynamic Prediction of Criminal Recidivism: A Three-Wave Prospective Study." *Law and Human Behavior*, 33, 25–45.

Buehler, R.E., G.R. Patterson & J.M. Furniss (1966). "The Reinforcement of Behavior in Institutional Settings." *Behavioral Research and Therapy*, 4, 157–167.

Buffkin, J.L. & V.R. Luttrell (2005). "Neuroimaging Studies of Aggressive and Violent Behavior: Current Findings and Implications for Criminology and Criminal Justice." *Trauma, Violence, and Abuse*, 6, 176–191.

Buonopane, A. & I.L. Petrakis (2005). "Pharmacotherapy of Alcohol Use Disorders." *Substance Use & Misuse*, 40, 2001–2020.

Burdon, W.M., N.P. Messina & M.L. Prendergast (2004). "The California Experiment Expansion Initiative: Aftercare Participation, Recidivism, and Predictors of Outcomes." *The Prison Journal*, 84, 61–80.

Burgess, E.W. (1928). "Factors Determining Success or Failure on Parole." In A.A. Bruce, A.J. Harno, E.W. Burgess & J. Landesco (eds.), *The Workings of the Indeterminate-sentence Law and the Parole System in Illinois* (pp. 221–234). Springfield, IL: State Board of Parole.

Burgess, R.L. & R.L. Akers (1966). "A Differential Association-Reinforcement Theory of Criminal Behavior." *Social Problems*, 14, 128–147.

Burke, B.L., H. Arkowitz & M. Menchola (2003). "The Efficacy of Motivational Interviewing: A Meta-analysis of Controlled Clinical Trials." *Journal of Consulting and Clinical Psychology*, 71, 843–861.

Burlingame, G.M., A. Fuhriman & J. Mosier (2003). "The Differential Effectiveness of Group Psychotherapy: A Meta-analytic Perspective." *Group Dynamics: Theory, Research, and Practice*, 7, 3–12.

Burt, S.A., A.R. Barnes, M. McGue & W.G. Iacono (2008). "Parental Divorce and Adolescent Delinquency: Ruling Out the Impact of Common Genes." *Developmental Psychology*, 44, 1668–1677.

Burton, J.M. & L.A. Marshall (2005). "Protective Factors for Youth Considered at Risk of Criminal Behaviour: Does Participation in Extracurricular Activities Help?" *Criminal Behaviour and Mental Health*, 15, 46–64.

Burton, V.S., Jr., F.T. Cullen, T.D. Evans, L.F. Alarid & R.G. Dunaway (1998). "Gender, Self-Control, and Crime." *Journal of Research in Personality and Crime*, 35, 123–147.

Bush, J. (1995). "Teaching Self-Risk Management to Violent Offenders." In J. McGuire (ed.), *What Works: Effective Methods to Reduce Re-offending* (pp. 139–154). Sussex, UK: Wiley.

Bush, J. & B. Bilodeau (1993). *Options: A Cognitive Change Program*. Longmont, CO: National Institute of Corrections.

Bush, J., B. Bilodeau & Kornick (1995). *Options: A Cognitive Change Program*. Longmont, CO: National Institute of Corrections.

Bushway, S. & J. Smith (2007). "Sentencing Using Statistical Treatment Rules: What We Don't Know Can Hurt Us." *Journal of Quantitative Criminology*, 23, 377–387.

Buss, A.H. (1966). *Psychopathology*. New York: Wiley.

Button, T. M. M., J. Scourfield, N. Martin, S. Purcell & P. McGuffin (2005). "Family Dysfunction Interacts with Genes in the Causation of Antisocial Symptoms." *Behavior Genetics*, 35, 115–120.

Byrne, J.M. & F.S. Taxman (1994). "Crime Control Policy and Community Corrections Practice: Assessing the Impact of Gender, Race, and Class." *Evaluation and Program Planning*, 17, 227–233.

Caldwell, M.F., M. Vitacco & G.J. Van Rybroek (2006). "Are Violent Delinquents Worth Treating? A Cost-Benefit Analysis." *Journal of Research in Crime and Delinquency*, 43, 148–168.

Cale, E.M. (2006). "A Quantitative Review of the Relations Between the 'Big 3' Higher Order Personality Dimensions and Antisocial Behavior." *Journal of Research in Personality*, 40, 250–284.

California Office of the Governor (2009). "Governor's Budget Summary 2009–10. Downloaded February 15, 2009, from http://www.ebudget,ca,gov/pdf/BudgetSummary.

Campbell, D.T. & J.C. Stanley (1963). *Experimental and Quasi-experimental Designs for Research*. Chicago: Rand McNally.

Campbell, F.A., C.T. Ramey, E. Pungello, J. Sparling & S. Miller-Johnson (2002). "Early Childhood Education: Young Adult Outcomes From the Abecedarian Project." *Applied Developmental Science*, 6, 42–57.

Campbell, J.C. (2005). "Assessing Dangerousness in Domestic Violence Cases: History, Challenges, and Opportunities." *Criminology and Public Policy*, 4, 653–671.

Campbell, M.A., S. French & P. Gendreau (2009). "The Prediction of Violence in Adult Offenders: A Meta-Analytic Comparison of Instruments and Methods of Assessment." *Criminal Justice and Behavior*, 36, 567–590.

Campbell, M.A., S. Porter & D. Santor (2004). "Psychopathic Traits in Adolescent Offenders. A Evaluation of Criminal History, Clinical, and Psychosocial Correlates." *Behavioral Sciences and the Law*, 22, 23–47.

Canadian Sentencing Commission (1987). "Community Punishments as Sanctions in Their Own Right." In *Canadian Sentencing Commission, Sentencing Reform: A Canadian Approach* (pp. 338–343). Ottawa: Canadian Government Publishing Centre.

Canter, D.V. & N. Wentink (2004). "An Empirical Test of Holmes and Holmes's Serial Murder Typology." *Criminal Justice and Behavior*, 31, 489–515.

Carey, G. (1992). "Twin Imitation for Antisocial Behavior: Implications for Genetic and Family Environment Research." *Journal of Abnormal Psychology*, 101, 18–25.

Carey, G. & D. Goldman (1997). "The Genetics of Antisocial Behavior." In D.M. Stuff, J. Breiling & J.D. Maser (eds.), *Handbook of Antisocial Behavior* (pp. 243–254). New York: Wiley.

Carlson, B.E. & N. Cervera (1991). "Inmates and Their Families: Conjugal Visits, Family Contact, and Family Functioning." *Criminal Justice and Behavior*, 18, 318–331.

Carroll, K.M. (1998). *A Cognitive-Behavioral Approach: Treating Cocaine Addiction*. Rockville, MD: National Institute on Drug Abuse.

Cartier, J., D. Farabee & M.L. Prendergast (2006). "Methamphetamine Use, Self-reported Violent Crime, and Recidivism among Offenders in California who Abuse Substances." *Journal of Interpersonal Violence*, 21, 435–445.

Caspi, A., H. Harrington, B. Milne, J.W. Amell, R.F. Theodore & T.E. Moffitt (2003). "Children's Behavioral Styles at Age 3 Are Linked to Their Adult Personality Traits at Age 26." *Journal of Personality*, 71, 495–513.

Caspi, A., J. McClay, T.E. Moffitt, J. Mill, J. Martin, I.W. Craig, A. Taylor & R. Poulton (2002). "Role of Genotype in the Cycle of Violence in Maltreated Children." *Science*, 297, 851–854.

Caspi, A., T.E. Moffitt, P.A. Silva, M. Stouthamer-Loeber, R.F. Krueger & P.S. Schmutte (1994). "Are Some People Crime-prone? Replications of the Personality-Crime Relationship across Countries, Genders, Races, and Methods." *Criminology*, 32, 163–195.

Catalano, R.F., M.W. Arthur, J.D. Hawkins, L. Bergland & J.J. Olson (1998). In R. Loeber & D.P. Farrington (eds.). *Serious and Violent Juvenile Offenders: Risk Factors and Successful Interventions* (pp. 248–283). Thousand Oaks, CA: Sage.

Cattaneo, L.B. & L.A. Goodman (2005). "Risk Factors for Reabuse in Intimate Partner Violence: A Cross-disciplinary Critical Review." *Trauma, Violence, and Abuse*, 6, 141–175.

Cattell, R.B. (1957). *Personality and Motivation, Structure and Measurement*. Yonkers-on-Hudson, NY: World Book.

Cauffman, E., L. Steinberg & A. Piquero (2005). Psychological, Neuropsychological and Physiological Correlates of Serious Antisocial Behavior in Adolescence: The Role of Self Control." *Criminology*, 43–175.

Cautela, J.R. (1970). "The Treatment of Alcoholism by Covert Sensitization." *Psychotherapy: Theory, Research and Practice*, 7, 83–90.

Center on Juvenile and Criminal Justice (2008). *Research Update: Does More Imprisonment Lead to Less Crime?* See http://www.cjcj.org.

Cernovsky, Z.Z. & L.C. Litman (1993). "Re-analysis of J.P. Rushton's Crime Data." *Canadian Journal of Criminology*, 35, 31–36.

Chaiken, J.M. & M.R. Chaiken (1982). *Varieties of Criminal Behavior: Summary and Policy Implications*. Santa Monica, CA: RAND.

Chaiken, M.R. (1989). *Prison Programs for Drug-involved Offenders*. Washington, DC: National Institute of Justice.

Chamberlain, P. (2003). *Treating Chronic Juvenile Offenders: Advances Made through the Oregon Multidimensional Treatment Foster Care Model*. Washington, DC: American Psychological Association.

Chamberlain, P., L.D. Leve & D.S. DeGarmo (2007). "Multidimensional Treatment Foster Care for Girls in the Juvenile Justice System: 2-Year Follow-Up of a Randomized Clinical Trial." *Journal of Consulting and Clinical Psychology*, 75, 187–193.

Chamberlain, P. & J.B. Reid (1998). "Comparison of Two Community Alternatives to Incarceration for Chronic Juvenile Offenders." *Journal of Consulting and Clinical Psychology*, 66, 624–633.

Chamlin, M.B., A.J. Myer, B.A. Sanders & J.K. Cochran (2008). "Abortion as Crime Control: A Cautionary Tale." *Criminal Justice Policy Review*, 19, 135–152.

Chan, W-Y. & O.M. Rennert (2002). "Molecular Aspects of Sex Differentiation." *Current Molecular Medicine*, 2, 25–37.

Chandler, M. (1973). "Egocentrism and Antisocial Behavior: The Assessment and Training of Social Perspective-taking Skills." *Developmental Psychology*, 44, 326–333.

Chang, H.-L., H.T. Woo & C.-H. Tseng (2006). "Is Rigorous Punishment Effective? A Case Study of Lifetime License Revocation in Taiwan." *Accident Analysis and Prevention*, 38, 269–276.

Chaplin, T.C., M.E. Rice & G.T. Harris (1995). "Salient Victim Suffering and the Sexual Responses of Child Molesters." *Journal of Consulting and Clinical Psychology*, 63, 249–255.

Chen, E.Y. (2008). "Impacts of 'Three Strikes and You're Out' on Crime Trends in California and Throughout the United States." *Journal of Contemporary Criminal Justice*, 24, 345–370.

Chesney-Lind, M. (1989). "Girls' Crime and Women's Place: Toward a Feminist Model of Female Delinquency." *Crime & Delinquency*, 35, 5–29.

Chess, S. & A. Thomas (1984). *Origins and Evolution of Behavior Disorders: From Infancy to Early Adult Life*. New York: Brunner/Mazel.

Chess, S. & A. Thomas (1990). "The New York Longitudinal Study (NYLS): The Young Adult Periods." *Canadian Journal of Psychiatry*, 35, 557–561.

Christiansen, K.O. (1977). "A Preliminary Study of Criminality among Twins." In S.A. Mednick & K.O. Christiansen (eds.), *Biosocial Basis of Criminal Behavior* (pp. 89–108). New York: Gardner Press.

Chung, I.-J., K.G. Hill, J.D. Hawkins, L.D. Gilchrist & D.S. Nagin (2002). "Childhood Predictors of Offense Trajectories." *Journal of Research in Crime and Delinquency*, 39, 60–90.

Church, R.M. (1963). "The Varied Effects of Punishment on Behavior." *Psychological Review*, 70, 369–402.

Clear, T. (1994). *Harm in American Penology: Offenders, Victims and Their Communities*. Albany, NY: SUNY Press.

Clear, T. (2008). "The Effects of High Imprisonment Rates on Communities." In M. Tonry (ed.), *Crime and Justice: A Review of Research*, Vol. 37 (pp. 97–132). Chicago: Chicago University Press.

Clear, T.R., D. R. Rose, E. Waring & K. Scully (2003). "Coercive Mobility and Crime: A Preliminary Examination of Concentrated Incarceration and Social Disorganization." *Justice Quarterly*, 20, 33–64.

Cleckley, H. (1941). *The Mask of Sanity: An Attempt to Reinterpret the So-Called Psychopathic Personality*. St. Louis: Mosby.

Cleckley, H. (1982). *The Mask of Sanity*, 4th ed. St. Louis: Mosby.

Clements, C.B. (1996). "Offender Classification: Two Decades of Progress." *Criminal Justice and Behavior*, 23, 121–143.

Cloninger, C.R., D.M. Svrakic & T.R. Prsybeck (1993). "A Psychobiological Model of Temperament and Character." *Archives of General Psychiatry*, 50, 975–990.

Cloward, R.A. & L.E. Ohlin (1960). *Delinquency and Opportunity: A Theory of Delinquent Gangs*. New York: Free Press.

Coates, R.B. & J. Gehm (1988). "An Empirical Assessment." In M. Wright & B. Galaway (eds.), *Mediation and Criminal Justice: Victims, Offenders and Community* (pp. 251–263). Newbury Park, CA: Sage.

Cochran, J.K. & M.B. Chamlin (2000). "Deterrence and Brutalization: The Dual Effects of Executions." *Justice Quarterly*, 17, 685–706.

Cochran, J.K., M.B. Chamlin & M. Seth (1994). "Deterrence or Brutalization? An Impact Assessment of Oklahoma's Return to Capital Punishment." *Criminology*, 32, 107–134.

Cohen, A.K. (1955). *Delinquent Boys: The Culture of the Gang*. Glencoe, IL: Free Press.

Cohen, M. (2001). "To Treat or Not to Treat? A Financial Perspective." In C.R. Hollin (ed.), *Handbook of Offender Assessment and Treatment* (pp. 35–49). Chichester, UK: John Wiley & Sons.

Cohen, M.A. & A.R. Piquero (2009). "New Evidence on the Monetary Value of Saving a High Risk Youth." *Journal of Quantitative Criminology*, 25, 25–49.

Coid, J., M. Yang, S. Ullrich, A. Roberts & R.D. Hare (2009). "Prevalence and Correlates of Psychopathic Traits in the Household Population of Great Britain." *International Journal of Law and Psychiatry*, 32, 65–73.

Cole, D.P. (2007). "The Umpires Strike Back: Canadian Judicial Experience with Risk Assessment Instruments." *Canadian Journal of Criminology and Criminal Justice*, 49, 493–517.

Cole, D.P. & G. Angus (2003). "Using Pre-sentence Reports to Evaluate and Respond to Risk." *Criminal Law Quarterly*, 47, 302–364.

Coleman, F.L. (1997). "Stalking Behavior and the Cycle of Domestic Violence." *Journal of Interpersonal Violence*, 12, 420–432.

Conway, P. (2003). "Survey of Agencies Using Electronic Monitoring Reveals a Promising Future." *The Journal of Offender Monitoring*, 16, 5, 18–23.

Cookson, H.M. (1992). "Alcohol Use and Offence Type in Young Offenders." *British Journal of Criminology*, 32, 352–360.

Cookston, J.T. (1999). "Parental Supervision and Family Structure: Effects on Adolescent Problem Behaviors." *Journal of Divorce and Remarriage*, 32, 107–122.

Copas, J. & P. Marshall (1998). "The Offender Reconviction Scale: A Statistical Reconviction Score for Use by Probation Officers." *Journal of the Royal Statistical Society*, 47, 159–171.

Cordess, C. (2001). "Forensic Psychotherapy." In C.R. Hollin (ed.), *Handbook of Offender Assessment and Treatment* (pp. 309–329). Chichester, UK: John Wiley & Sons.

Corrado, R.R., G.M. Vincent, S.D. Hart & I.M. Cohen (2004). "Predictive Validity of the Psychopathy Checklist: Youth Version for General and Violent Recidivism." *Behavioral Sciences and the Law*, 22, 5–22.

Costa, P.T., Jr. & R.R. McCrae (1992). *Revised NEO Personality Inventory (NEO-PI-R) and NEO Five-Factor Inventory (NEO-FFI) Professional Manual*. Odessa, FL: Psychological Assessment Resources.

Cotter, R. (2005). "Implementing GPS Electronic Monitoring: A Survey of GPS Offender Tracking Programs in the U.S." *The Journal of Offender Monitoring*, 18, 12–13.

Cottle, C., R.J. Lee & K. Heilbrun (2001). "The Prediction of Criminal Recidivism in Juveniles: A Meta-Analysis." *Criminal Justice and Behavior*, 28, 367–394.

Covington, S.S. (2000). "Helping Women Recover: Creating Gender-specific Treatment for Substance-abusing Women and Girls in Community Corrections." In M. McMahon (ed.), *Assessment to Assistance: Programs for Women in Community Corrections* (pp. 171–233). Latham, MD: American Correctional Association.

Covington, S.S. & B. Bloom (1999). "Gender-responsive Programming and Evaluation for Women in the Criminal Justice System: A Shift from 'What Works?' to 'What is the Work?'" Paper presented at the 51st Annual Meeting of the American Society of Criminology, Toronto, Canada, November.

Cox, M. (1998). "A Group-analytic Approach to Psychopaths: 'The Ring of Truth.'" In T. Millon, E. Simonsen, M. Birket-Smith & R.D. Davis (eds.), *Psychopathy: Antisocial, Criminal, and Violent Behavior* (pp. 393–406). New York: Guilford.

Craft, M., G. Stephenson & C. Granger (1966). "A Controlled Trial of Authoritarian and Self-governing Regimes with Adolescent Psychopaths." *American Journal of Orthopsychiatry*, 34, 543–554.

Craig, L.A., K.D. Browne, I. Stringer & A. Beech (2005). "Sexual Recidivism: A Review of Static, Dynamic and Actuarial Predictors." *Journal of Sexual Aggression*, 11, 65–84.

Craig, R.D. & K. Truitt (1996). "Moral Problem Solving among Inmates in a Maximum-Security Correctional Institution." *International Journal of Offender Therapy and Comparative Criminology*, 40, 243–252.

Cressey, D.R. (1955). "Changing Criminals: The Application of the Theory of Differential Association." *American Journal of Sociology*, 61, 116–120.

Cressey, D.R. & D.A. Ward (1969). *Delinquency, Crime, and Social Control*. New York: Harper and Row.

Cretacci, M.A. (2008). "A General Test of Self-control Theory." *International Journal of Offender Therapy and Comparative Criminology*, 52, 538–533.

Crime and Justice Research Centre (2005). *Evaluation of the Court-Referred Restorative Justice Pilot: Technical Report*. Wellington, NZ: Ministry of Justice.

Crews, F. (1986). "In the Big House of Theory." *The New York Review of Books*, 29 (May), 36, 41.

Crocker, A.G., K.T. Mueser, R.E. Drake, R.E. Clark, G.J. Mchugo, T.H. Ackerson & A.I. Alterman (2005). "Antisocial Personality, Psychopathy, and Violence in Persons with Dual Disorders: A Longitudinal Analysis." *Criminal Justice and Behavior*, 32, 452–476.

Cullen, F.T. (1995). "Assessing the Penal Harm Movement." *Journal of Research in Crime and Delinquency*, 32, 338–358.

Cullen, F.T., K.R. Blevins, J.S. Trager & P. Gendreau (2005). "The Rise and Fall of Boot Camps: A Case Study in Common-sense Corrections." *Journal of Offender Rehabilitation*, 40, 53–70.

Cullen, F.T., B.S. Fisher & B.K. Applegate (2000). "Public Opinion about Punishment and Corrections." In M. Tonry (ed.), *Crime and Justice: A Review of Research*, Vol. 27 (pp. 1–79). Chicago: University of Chicago Press.

Cullen, F.T. & P. Gendreau (1989). "The Effectiveness of Correctional Rehabilitation." In L. Goodstein & D.L. MacKenzie (eds.), *The American Prison: Issues in Research Policy* (pp. 23–24). New York: Plenum.

Cullen, F.T. & P. Gendreau (2001). "From Nothing Works to What Works: Changing Professional Ideology in the 21st Century." *The Prison Journal*, 81, 313–338.

Cullen, F.T., P. Gendreau, G.R. Jarjoura & J.P. Wright (1997). "Crime and the Bell Curve: Lessons from Intelligent Criminology." *Crime & Delinquency*, 43, 387–411.

Cullen, F.T. & K.E. Gilbert (1982). *Reaffirming Rehabilitation*. Cincinnati: Anderson.

Cullen, F.T., M.T. Larson & R.A. Mathers (1985). "Having Money and Delinquent Involvement: The Neglect of Power in Delinquency Theory." *Criminal Justice and Behavior*, 12, 171–192.

Cullen, F.T., J.P. Wright & B.K. Applegate (1996). "Control in the Community: The Limits of Reform?" In A.T. Harland (ed.), *Choosing Correctional Options That Work: Defining the Demand and Evaluating the Supply* (pp. 69–116). Thousand Oaks, CA: Sage.

Culpit, C., S.W. Henggeler, I.S. Taylor & O.W. Addison (2005). *Multisystemic Therapy and Neighborhood Partnerships: Reducing Adolescent Violence and Substance Use*. New York: Guilford.

Cumberland, A.K. & G.J. Boyle (1997). "Psychometric Prediction of Recidivism: Utility of the Risk Needs Inventory. *Australian and New Zealand Journal of Criminology*, 30, 72–86.

Currie, E. (1993). *Reckoning: Drugs, the Cities, and the American Future*. New York: Hill and Wang.

Curry, G.D. (2000). Self-reported Gang Involvement and Officially Recorded Delinquency. *Criminology*, 38, 1253–1274.

Curtis, N.M., K.R. Ronan & C.M. Borduin (2004). "Multisystemic Treatment: A Meta-analysis of Outcome Studies." *Journal of Family Psychology*, 18, 411–419.

Dadds, M.R., J. Fraser, A. Frost & D.J. Hawes (2005). "Disentangling the Underlying Dimensions of Psychopathy and Conduct Problems in Childhood: A Community Study." *Journal of Consulting and Clinical Psychology*, 73, 400–410.

Dadds, M.R., S. Schwartz & M. Sanders (1987). "Marital Discord and Treatment Outcome in Behavioral Treatment of Child Conduct Disorders." *Journal of Consulting and Clinical Psychology*, 55, 396–403.

Daffern, M. (2007). "The Predictive Validity and Practical Utility of Structured Schemes Used to Assess Risk for Aggression in Psychiatric Inpatient Settings." *Aggression and Violent Behavior*, 12, 116–130.

Dagg, A.I. (2005). *"Love of Shopping" is Not a Gene: Problems with Darwinian Psychology*. Tonawanda, NY: Black Rose Books.

Dahle, K-P. (2006). "Strengths and Limitations of Actuarial Prediction of Criminal Reoffence in a German Prison Sample: A Comparative Study of LSI-R, HCR-20 and PCL-R." *International Journal of Law and Psychiatry*, 29, 431–442.

Dalgaard, O.S. & E. Kringlen (1976). "A Norwegian Twin Study of Criminality." *British Journal of Criminology*, 16, 213–233.

Daly, J.E. & S. Pelowski (2000). "Predictors of Dropout among Men Who Batter: A Review of Studies with Implications for Research and Practice." *Violence and Victims*, 15, 137–160.

Daly, K. (2006a). "The Limits of Restorative Justice." In D. Sullivan & L. Tifft (eds.), *Handbook of Restorative Justice* (pp. 134–145). New York: Routledge.

Daly, K. (2006b). "Restorative Justice and Sexual Assault." *British Journal of Criminology*, 46, 334–356.

Daly, K. & R.L. Bordt (1995). "Sex Effects and Sentencing: An Analysis of the Statistical Literature." *Justice Quarterly*, 12, 141–175.

Daly, K. & M. Tonry (1997). "Gender, Race, and Sentencing." In M. Tonry (ed.), *Crime and Justice: A Review of Research* (pp. 201–252). Chicago: University of Chicago Press.

Daly, M. (1996). "Evolutionary Adaptationism: Another Biological Approach to Criminal and Antisocial Behaviour." *Genetics of Criminal and Antisocial Behavior* (pp. 183–195). Wiley, Chichester (Ciba Foundation Symposium 194).

Daly, M. & M. Wilson (1988). *Homicide*. New York: Aldine de Gruyter.

Daly, M. & M. Wilson (1994). "Some Differential Attributes of Lethal Assaults on Small Children by Stepfathers versus Genetic Fathers." *Ethology and Sociobiology*, 15, 207–217.

Daniel, A.E., A.J. Robins, J.C. Reid & D.E. Wifley (1988). "Lifetime and Six Month Prevalence of Psychiatric Disorders among Sentenced Female Offenders." *Bulletin of the American Academy of Psychiatry and the Law*, 16, 333–342.

Darwin, C.R. (1859). *On the Origin of Species*. London: John Murray.

Dauvergne, M. (2008). *Crime Statistics in Canada, 2007*. Ottawa: Canadian Centre for Justice Statistics.

Davidson, W.S., S.D. Jefferson, A. Legaspi, J. Lujan & A.M. Wolf (2001). "Alternative Interventions for Juvenile Offenders: History of the Adolescent Diversion Project." In C.R. Hollin (ed.), *Handbook of Offender Assessment* (pp. 221–236). Chichester, UK: John Wiley & Sons.

Davis, R.C., B.E. Smith & L.B. Nickles (1998). "The Deterrent Effect of Prosecuting Domestic Violence Misdemeanors." *Crime & Delinquency*, 44, 434–444.

Davis, R.C. & B.G. Taylor (1997). "A Proactive Response to Family Violence: The Results of a Randomized Experiment." *Criminology*, 35, 307–333.

Dawkins, R. (1989). *The Selfish Gene*. New York: Oxford University Press.

Day, A., A. Gerace, C. Wilson & K. Howells (2008). "Promoting Forgiveness in Violent Offenders: A More Positive Approach to Offender Rehabilitation?" *Aggression and Violent Behavior*, 13, 195–200.

Deater-Deckard & K.A. Dodge (1997). "Spare the Rod, Spoil the Authors: Emerging Themes in Research on Parenting and Child Development." *Psychological Inquiry*, 8, 230–235.

Deater-Deckard, K., J.E. Lansford, K.A. Dodge, G.S. Pettit & J.E. Bates (2003). "The Development of Attitudes about Physical Punishment: An 8-year Longitudinal Study." *Journal of Family Psychology*, 17, 351–360.

de Beus, K. & N. Rodriquez (2007). "Restorative Justice Practice: An Examination of Program Completion and Recidivism." *Journal of Criminal Justice*, 35, 337–347.

Decker, S.H. (2007). "Youth Gangs and Violent Behavior." In D.J. Flannery, A.T. Vazsonyi & I.D. Waldman (eds.), *The Cambridge Handbook of Violent Behavior and Aggression* (pp. 388–402). Cambridge, UK: Cambridge University Press.

Decker, S.H. & C.W. Kohfeld (1984). "A Deterrence Study of the Death Penalty in Illinois, 1933–1980." *Journal of Criminal Justice*, 12, 367–377.

Decker, S.H. & C.W. Kohfeld (1987). "An Empirical Analysis of the Effect of the Death Penalty in Missouri." *Journal of Crime and Justice*, 10, 23–46.

DeGarmo, D.S. & M. S. Forgatch (2005). "Early Development of Delinquency Within Divorced Families: Evaluating a Randomized Preventive Intervention Trial." *Developmental Science*, 8, 229–239.

DeKeseredy, W.S. & M.D. Schwartz (1996). *Contemporary Criminology*. Belmont, CA: Wadsworth.

Deluty, M.Z. (1978). "Self-Control and Impulsiveness Involving Aversive Events." *Journal of Experimental Psychology: Animal Processes*, 4, 250–266.

DeMatteo, D., K. Heilbrun & G. Marczyk (2005). "Psychopathy, Risk of Violence, and Protective Factors in a Noninstitutionalized and Noncriminal Sample." *International Journal of Forensic Mental Health*, 4, 147–157.

DeMatteo, D., K. Heilbrun & G. Marczyk (2006). "An Empirical Investigation of Psychopathy in a Noninstitutionalized and Noncriminal Sample." *Behavioral Sciences and the Law*, 24, 133–146.

Dembo, R., J. Schmeidler, B. Nini-Gough, C.C. Sue, P. Borden & D. Manning (1998). "Predictors of Recidivism to a Juvenile Assessment Center: A Three-year Study." *Journal of Child and Adolescent Substance Abuse*, 7. 57–77.

Demuth, S. & S.L. Brown (2004). "Family Structure, Family Processes, and Adolescent Delinquency: The Significance of Parental Absence versus Parental Gender." *Journal of Research in Crime and Delinquency*, 41, 58–81.

Dennison, S.M. & D.M. Thomson (2005). "Criticisms or Plaudits for Stalking Laws? What Psycholegal Research Tells Us about Proscribing Stalking." *Psychology, Public Policy, and Law*, 11, 384–406.

Denno, D.W. (1990). *Biology and Violence: From Birth to Adulthood*. Cambridge, UK: Cambridge University Press.

DeWall, C.N., J.M. Twenge, S.A. Gitter & R.F. Baumeister (2009). "It's the Thought That Counts: The Role of Hostile Cognition in Shaping Aggressive Responses to Social Exclusion." *Journal Personality and Social Psychology*, 95, 45–59.

DeYoung, C.G., J.B. Peterson, J.R. Séguin, J.M. Mejia, R.O. Pihl, J.H. Beitchman, U. Jain, R.E. Tremblay, J.L. Kennedy & R.M. Palmour (2006). (2006). "The Dopamine D4 Receptor Gene and Moderation of the Association Between Externalizing Behavior and IQ." *Archives of General Psychiatry*, 63, 1410–1416.

DiClemente, C.C. & M.M. Velasquez (2002). "Motivational Interviewing and the Stages of Change." In W.R. Miller & S. Rollnick, *Motivational Interviewing: Preparing People for Change*, 2nd ed. (pp. 201–216). New York: Guilford.

Diefenbach, D.L. (1997). "The Portrayal of Mental Illness on Prime-time Television." *Journal of Community Psychology*, 25, 289–302.

Dietz, P.E., R.R. Hazelwood & J. Warren (1990). "The Sexually Sadistic Criminal and His Offenses." *Bulletin of the American Academy of Psychiatry and the Law*, 18, 163–178.

Dietz, P.E., D.B. Matthews, D. Martell, T. Stewart, D. Hrouda & J. Warren (1991). "Threatening and Otherwise Inappropriate Letters to Members of the United States Congress." *Journal of Forensic Sciences*, 36, 1445–1468.

Dietz, P.E., D.B. Matthews, C. Van Duyne, D.A. Martell, C.D.H. Parry, T. Stewart, J. Warren & J.D. Crowder (1991). "Threatening and Otherwise Inappropriate Letters to Hollywood Celebrities." *Journal of Forensic Sciences*, 36, 185–209.

Digman, J.M. (1990). "Personality Structure: Emergence of the Five Factor Model." *Annual Review of Psychology*, 41, 417–440.

Dinsmoor, J.A. (1955). "Punishment: II. An Interpretation of Empirical Findings." *Psychological Review*, 62, 96–105.

Dinsmoor, J.A. (1998). "Punishment." In W. O'Donohue (ed.), *Learning and Behavior Therapy* (pp. 188–204). New York: Allyn & Bacon.

Di Placido, C., T.L. Simon, T.D. Witte, D. Gu & S.C.P. Wong (2006). "Treatment of Gang Members Can Reduce Recidivism and Institutional Misconduct." *Law and Human Behavior*, 30, 93–114.

Dishion, T.J. & G.R. Patterson (1997). "The Timing and Severity of Antisocial Behavior: Three Hypotheses within an Ecological Framework." In D.M. Stoff, J. Breiling & J.D. Maser (eds.), *Handbook of Antisocial Behavior* (pp. 205–217). New York: Wiley.

Dishion, T.J., K.M. Spracklen & D.W. Andrews (1996). "Deviancy Training in Male Adolescent Friendships." *Behavior Therapy*, 27, 373–390.

Dobash, R.E., R.P. Dobash, K. Cavanagh & R. Lewis (2000). *Changing Violent Men*. Thousand Oaks, CA: Sage.

Dodge, K.A. & G.S. Petit (2003). "A Biopsychosocial Model of the Development of Chronic Conduct Problems in Adolescence." *Developmental Psychology*, 39, 349–371.

Dolan, M. & R. Fullam (2007). "The Validity of the Violence Risk Scale Second Edition (VRS-2) in a British Forensic Inpatient Sample." *The Journal of Forensic Psychiatry & Psychology*, 18, 381–393.

Dollard, J., L. Doob, N. Miller, O. Mowrer & R. Sears (1939). *Frustration and Aggression*. New Haven, CT: Yale University Press.

Donahue, J.J. & S.D. Levitt (2001). "The Impact of Legalized Abortion on Crime." *Quarterly Review of Economics*, 116, 379–420.

Donato, R. & M. Shanahan (1999). "The Economics of Implementing Intensive In-prison Sex Offender Treatment Programs." In *Trends and Issues in Crime and Criminal Justice*, No. 134. Canberra: Australian Institute of Criminology.

Donnellan, M.B., K.H. Trzesniewski, R.W. Robins, T.E. Moffitt & A. Caspi (2005). "Low Self-Esteem Is Related to Aggression, Antisocial Behavior, and Delinquency." *Psychological Science*, 16, 328–335.

Doob, A.N. & C.M. Webster (2003). "Sentence Severity and Crime: Accepting the Null Hypothesis." In M. Tonry (ed.), *Crime and Justice: A Review of Research*, Vol. 30 (pp. 143–195). Chicago: University of Chicago Press.

Douglas, K.S. & D.G. Dutton (2001). "Assessing the Link between Stalking and Domestic Violence." *Aggression and Violent Behavior*, 6, 519–546.

Douglas, K.S., M.E. Epstein & N.G. Poythress (2008). "Criminal Recidivism Among Juvenile Offenders: Testing the Incremental and Predictive Validity of Three Measures of Psychopathic Features." *Law and Behavior*, 32, 423–438.

Douglas, K.S. & J.L. Skeem (2005). "Violence Risk Assessment: Getting Specific about Being Dynamic." *Psychology, Public Policy, and Law*, 11, 347–383.

Douglas, K.S., G.M. Vincent & J.F. Edens (2006). "Risk for Criminal Recidivism: The Role of Psychopathy." In C.J. Patrick (ed.), *Handbook of Psychopathy* (pp. 533–554). New York: Guilford.

Dowden, C. (1998). "A Meta-analytic Examination of the Risk, Need and Responsivity Principles and their Importance within the Rehabilitation Debate." Unpublished master's thesis, Psychology Department, Carleton University, Ottawa.

Dowden, C. & D A. Andrews (1999a). "What Works for Female Offenders: A Meta-analytic Review." *Crime & Delinquency*, 45, 438–452.

Dowden, C. & D.A. Andrews (1999b). "What Works in Young Offender Treatment: A Meta-analysis." *Forum on Corrections Research*, 11, 21–24.

Dowden, C. & D.A. Andrews (2000). "Effective Correctional Treatment and Violent Reoffending." *Canadian Journal of Criminology*, 42, 449–467.

Dowden, C. & D.A. Andrews (2003). "Does Family Intervention Work for Delinquents? Results of a Meta-analysis." *Canadian Journal of Criminology and Criminal Justice*, 45, 327–342.

Dowden, C., D. Antonowicz & D.A. Andrews (2003). "The Effectiveness of Relapse Prevention with Offenders: A Meta-analysis." *International Journal of Offender Therapy and Comparative Criminology*, 47, 516–528.

Dowden, C.D. & S.L. Brown (2002). "The Role of Substance Abuse Factors in Predicting Recidivism: A Meta-analysis." *Psychology, Crime and Law*, 8, 243–264.

Drake, E.K., S. Aos & M.G. Miller (2009). "Evidence-Based Public Policy Options to Reduce Crime and Criminal Justice Costs: Implications in Washington State." *Victims & Offenders*, 4, 170–196.

D'Silva, K., C. Duggan & L. McCarthy (2004). "Does Treatment Really Make Psychopaths Worse? A Review of the Evidence." *Journal of Personality Disorders*, 18, 163–177.

Dugdale, R.L. (1877/1970). *The Jukes: A Study of Crime, Pauperism, Disease, and Heredity*. New York: Arno Press (originally published by G.P. Putnam).

Dunaway, R.G., F.T. Cullen, V.S. Burton, Jr. & T.D. Evans (2000). "The Myth of Social Class and Crime Revisited: An Examination of Class and Adult Criminality." *Criminology*, 38, 589–632.

Durrett, C. & T.J. Trull (2005). "An Evaluation of Evaluative Personality Terms: A Comparison of the Big Seven and Five-Factor Model in Predicting Psychopathology." *Psychological Assessment*, 17, 359–368.

Dutra, L., G. Stathopoulou, S.L. Basden, T.M. Leyro, M.B. Powers & M.W. Otto (2008). "A Meta-Analytic Review of Psychosocial Interventions for Substance Use Disorders." *American Journal of Psychiatry*, 165, 179–187.

Dutton, D.G. (1986). "The Outcome of Court-mandated Treatment for Wife-Assault: A Quasi-experimental Evaluation." *Violence and Victims*, 1, 163–175.

Dutton, D.G. (1995). *The Domestic Assault of Women: Psychological and Criminal Justice Perspectives*, 2nd ed. Boston: Allyn & Bacon.

Dutton, D.G. (2008). "My Back Pages: Reflections on Thirty Years of Domestic Violence Research." *Trauma, Violence, & Abuse*, 9, 131–143.

Dutton, D.G. & S.D. Hart (1992). "Risk Markers for Family Violence in a Federally Incarcerated Population." *International Journal of Law and Psychiatry*, 15, 101–112.

Dutton, D.G. & P.R. Kropp (2000). "A Review of Domestic Violence Risk Instruments." *Trauma, Violence, and Abuse*, 1, 171–181.

Dutton, D.G., T.L. Nicholls & A. Spidel (2005). "Female Perpetrators of Intimate Abuse." *Journal of Offender Rehabilitation*, 41, 1–31.

Eamon, M.K. & C. Mulder (2005). "Predicting Antisocial Behavior among Latino Young Adolescents: An Ecological Systems Analysis." *American Journal of Orthopsychiatry*, 75, 117–127.

Eddy, M.J., R.B. Whaley & P. Chamberlain (2004). "The Prevention of Violent Behavior by Chronic and Serious Male Juvenile Offenders: A 2-year Follow-up of a Randomized Clinical Trial." *Journal of Emotional and Behavioral Disorders*, 12, 2–8.

Edens, J.F. & M.A. Cahill (2007). "Psychopathy in Adolescence and Criminal Recidivism in Young Adulthood: Longitudinal Results From a Multiethnic Sample of Youthful Offenders." *Assessment*, 14, 57–64.

Edens, J.F. & J.S. Campbell (2007). "Identifying Youth at Risk for Institutional Misconduct: A Meta-analytic Investigation of the Psychopathy Checklist Measures." *Psychological Services*, 4, 13–27.

Edens, J.F., J.S. Campbell & J.M. Weir (2007). "Youth Psychopathy and Criminal Recidivism: A Meta-Analysis of the Psychopathy Checklist Measures." *Law and Human Behavior*, 31, 53–75.

Edens, J.F., D.K. Marcus, S.O. Lilienfeld & N.G. Poythress Jr. (2006). "Psychopathic, Not Psychopath: Taxometric Evidence for the Dimensional Structure of Psychopathy." *Journal of Abnormal Psychology*, 115, 131–144.

Edens, J.F. & J. Petrila (2006). "Legal and Ethical Issues in the Assessment and Treatment of Psychopathy." In C.J. Patrick (ed.), *Handbook of Psychopathy* (pp. 573–588). New York: Guilford.

Edens, J.F., J.L. Skeem, K.R. Cruise & E. Cauffman (2001). "Assessment of 'Juvenile Psychopathy' and its Association with Violence: A Critical Review." *Behavioral Sciences and the Law*, 19, 53–80.

Edens, J.F. & G.M. Vincent (2008). "Juvenile Psychopathy: A Clinical Construct in Need of Restraint?" *Journal of Forensic Psychology Practice*, 8, 186–197.

Edwards, D.L., S.K. Schoenwald, S.W. Henggeler & K.B. Strother (2001). "A Multilevel Perspective on the Implementation of Multisystemic Therapy (MST): Attempting Dissemination with Fidelity." In G.A. Bernfeld, D.P. Farrington & A.W. Leschied (eds.), *Offender Rehabilitation in Practice* (pp. 97–120). Chichester, UK: Wiley.

Egan, V., B. Kavanagh & M. Blair (2005). "Sexual Offenders against Children: The Influence of Personality and Obsessionality on Cognitive Distortions." *Sexual Abuse: A Journal of Research and Treatment*, 17, 223–240.

Egley, A., Jr. & C.E. O'Donnell (2008). *Highlights of the 2006 National Youth Gang Survey*. Washington, DC: Office of Juvenile Justice and Delinquency Prevention.

Ehrensaft, M.K., P. Cohen, J. Brown, E. Smailes, H. Chen & J.G. Johnson (2003). "Intergenerational Transmission of Partner Violence: A 20-year Prospective Study." *Journal of Consulting and Clinical Psychology*, 71, 741–753.

Eitle, D. (2005). "The Influence of Mandatory Arrest Policies, Police Organizational Characteristics, and Situational Variables on the Probability of Arrest in Domestic Violence Cases." *Crime & Delinquency*, 51, 573–597.

Elbogen, E.B. & S.C. Johnson (2009). "The Intricate Link Between Violence and Mental Disorder: Results From the National Epidemiologic Survey on Alcohol and Related Conditions." *Archives of General Psychiatry*, 66, 152–161.

Elliott, D.S., D. Huizinga & S.S. Ageton (1985). *Explaining Delinquency and Drug Use*. Beverly Hills, CA: Sage.

Ellis, L. (2000). *Criminology: A Global Perspective: Supplemental Tables, and References*. Minot, ND: Pyramid Press. See htpp://www.abacon.com/ellis/.

Ellis, L. (2005). "A Theory Explaining Biological Correlates of Criminality." *European Journal of Criminology*, 2, 287–315.

Ellis, L. & H. Hoffman (1990). "Views of Contemporary Criminologists on Causes and Theories of Crime." In L. Ellis & H. Hoffman (eds.), *Crime in Biological, Social, and Moral Contexts* (pp. 50–58). New York: Praeger.

Ellis, L. & A. Walsh (1997). "Gene-based Evolutionary Theories in Criminology." *Criminology*, 35, 229–276.

Else-Quest, N.M., J. Shibley Hyde, H. Hill Goldsmith & C.A. Van Hulle (2006). "Gender Differences in Temperament: A Meta-analysis." *Psychological Bulletin*, 132, 33–72.

Empey, L.T. & M.L. Erickson (1972). *The Provo Experiment: Evaluating Community Control of Delinquency*. Lexington, MA: D.C. Heath.

Empey, L.T. & J. Rabow (1961). "The Provo Experiment in Delinquency Rehabilitation." *American Sociological Review*, 26, 679–695.

Engel, R.S. & E. Silver (2001). "Policing Mentally Disordered Suspects: A Reexamination of the Criminalization Hypothesis." *Criminology*, 39, 225–252.

Erwin, B.S. (1986). "Turning Up the Heat on Probationers in Georgia." *Federal Probation*, 50, 17–24.

Esbensen, F.-A. (2004). *Evaluating G.R.E.A.T.: A School-Based Gang Prevention Program*. Washington, DC: National Institute of Justice.

Esbensen, F-A. & D.W. Osgood (1999). "Gang Resistance Education and Training (GREAT): Results from a National Evaluation." *Journal of Research in Crime and Delinquency*, 36, 194–225.

Esbensen, F-A., L.T. Winfree, N. He & T.J. Taylor (2001). "Youth Gangs and Definitional Issues: When is a Gang a Gang, and Why Does it Matter?" *Crime & Delinquency*, 47, 105–130.

Evans, S.E., C. Davies & D. DiLillo (2008). "Exposure to Domestic Violence: A Meta-Analysis of Child and Adolescent Outcomes." *Aggression and Violent Behavior*, 13, 131–140.

Eysenck, H.J. (1964). *Crime and Personality*. London: Routledge and Kegan Paul.

Eysenck, H.J. (1977). *Crime and Personality*, 2nd ed. London: Routledge and Kegan Paul.

Eysenck, H.J. (1998). "Personality and Crime." In T. Millon, E. Simonsen, M. Birket-Smith & R.D. Davis (eds.), *Psychopathy: Antisocial, Criminal, and Violent Behavior* (pp. 40–49). New York: Guilford.

Eysenck, H.J. & G.H. Gudjonsson (1989). *Causes and Cures of Criminality*. New York: Plenum.

Fagan, J.A. (1994). "Do Criminal Sanctions Deter Drug Crimes?" In D.L. Mackenzie & C.D. Uchida (eds.), *Drugs and Crime: Evaluating Pubic Policy Initiatives* (pp. 188–214). Thousand Oaks, CA: Sage.

Fals-Stewart, W. (2003). "The Occurrence of Partner Physical Aggression on Days of Alcohol Consumption: A Longitudinal Diary Study." *Journal of Consulting and Clinical Psychology*, 71, 41–52.

Fals-Stewart, W., K.E. Leonard & G.R. Birchler (2005). "The Occurrence of Male-to-Female Intimate Partner Violence on Days of Men's Drinking: The Moderating Effects of Antisocial Personality Disorder." *Journal of Consulting and Clinical Psychology*, 73, 239–248.

Farabee, D., Y.-I. Hser, M.D. Anglin & D. Huang (2004). "Recidivism Among an Early Cohort of California's Proposition 36 Offenders." *Criminology & Public Policy*, 3, 563–584.

Farbring, C.A. & W.R. Johnson (2008). "Motivational Interviewing in the Correctional System." In H. Arkowitz, H.A. Westra, W.R. Miller & S. Roonick (eds.), *Motivational Interviewing in the Treatment of Psychological Problems* (pp. 304–323). New York: Guilford.

Farrington, D.P. (1997). "Early Prediction of Violent and Non-violent Youthful Offending." *European Journal on Criminal Policy and Research*, 5, 51–66.

Farrington, D.P. (2005). "The Integrated Cognitive Antisocial Potential (ICAP) Theory." In D.P. Farrington (ed.), *Integrated Developmental and Life-course Theories of Offending* (pp. 73–92). New Brunswick, NJ: Transaction.

Farrington, D.P., G.C. Barnes & S. Lambert (1996). "The Concentration of Offending in Families." *Legal and Criminological Psychology*, 1, 47–63.

Farrington, D.P., J.W. Coid, L. Harnett, D. Jollife, N. Soteriou, R. Turner & D.J. West (2006). *Criminal Careers up to Age 50 and Life Success up to Age 48: New Findings from the Cambridge Study in Delinquent Development*. Home Office Research Study 299. London, England.

Farrington, D.P., J.W. Coid & J. Murray (2009). "Family Factors in the Intergenerational Transmission of Offending." *Criminal Behavior and Mental Health*, 19, 109–124.

Farrington, D.P., G. Hancock, M. Livingston, K.A. Painter & G.J. Towl (2000). *Evaluation of Intensive Regimes for Young Offenders*. Research Findings No. 121. London: Home Office Research, Development and Statistics Directorate.

Farrington, D.P., A. Petrosino & C.C. Welsh (2001). "Systematic Reviews and Cost-benefit Analyses of Correctional Interventions." *The Prison Journal*, 81, 339–359.

Farrington, D.P., M.M. Ttofi & J.W. Coid (1999). "Development of Adolescence-Limited, and Persistent Offenders from Age 8 to Age 48." *Aggressive Behavior*, 35, 150–163.

Farrington, D.P. & D.J. West (1995). "Effects of Marriage, Separation, and Children on Offending by Adult Males." In J. Hagan (ed.), *Current Perspectives on Aging and the Life Cycle, Vol. 4: Delinquency and Disrepute in the Life Course* (pp. 249–281). Greenwich, CT: JAI Press

Farver, J.A.M., Y. Xu, S. Eppe, A. Fernandez & D. Schwartz (2005). "Community Violence, Family Conflict, and Preschoolers' Socioemotional Functioning." *Developmental Psychology*, 41, 160–170.

Fass, S.M. & C.-R. Pi (2002). "Getting Tough on Juvenile Crime: An Analysis of Costs and Benefits." *Journal of Research in Crime & Delinquency*, 39, 363–399.

Fass, T.L., K. Heilbrun, D. Dematteo & R. Fretz (2008). "The LSI-R and the COMPAS: Validation Data on Two Risk-Needs Tools." *Criminal Justice and Behavior*, 35, 1095–1108.

Fazel, S., P. Bains & H. Doll (2006). "Substance Abuse and Dependence in Prisoners: A Systematic Review." *Addiction*, 101, 181–191.

Fazel, S. & J. Danesh (2002). "Serious Mental Disorder in 23,000 Prisoners: A Systematic Review of 62 Surveys." *Lancet*, 359, 545–550.

Federal Bureau of Investigation (2007). *Crime in the United States 2007. Uniform Crime Reports*. Washington, DC: U.S. Government Printing Office.

Fein, R.A. & B. Vossekuil (1999). "Assassination in the United States: An Operational Study of Recent Assassins, Attackers, and Near-lethal Approachers." *Journal of Forensic Sciences*, 36, 185–209.

Ferguson, A.M., J.R.P. Ogloff & L. Thomson (2009). "Predicting Recidivism by Mentally disordered Offenders Using the LSI-R:SV." *Criminal Justice and Behavior*, 36, 5–20.

Ferguson, C.J. (2008). "An Evolutionary Approach to Understanding Violent Antisocial Behavior: Diagnostic Implications for a Dual-Process Etiology." *Journal of Forensic Psychology Practice*, 8, 321–343.

Field, C.A. & R. Caetano (2005). "Intimate Partner Violence in the U.S. General Population: Progress and Future Directions." *Journal of Interpersonal Violence*, 20, 463–469.

Fields, R.D. (2005). "Myelination: An Overlooked Mechanism of Synaptic Plasticity?" *The Neuroscientist*, 11, 528–531.

Finckenauer, J.O. (1979). *Juvenile Awareness Project: Evaluation Report No. 2*. School of Criminal Justice, Rutgers University, Newark, NJ.

Finckenauer, J.O., P.W. Gavin, A. Hovland & E. Storvoll (1999). *Scared Straight: The Panacea Phenomenon Revisited*. Prospect Heights, IL: Waveland.

Finkelhor, D., R. Ormrod, H. Turner & S. Hamby (2005). "The Victimization of Children and Youth: A Comprehensive, National Survey." *Child Maltreatment*, 10, 5–25.

Finkelhor, D., L.M. Williams & N. Burns (1988). *Nursery Crimes: Sexual Abuse in Day Care*. Newbury Park, CA: Sage.

Finney, A. (2004). *Alcohol and Intimate Partner Violence: Key Findings from the Research*. London: Home Office, Communications Development Unit.

Fishbein, M. (1997). "Predicting, Understanding, and Changing Socially Relevant Behaviors: Lessons Learned." In C. McGarty & S.A. Haslam (eds.), *The Message of Social Psychology: Perspectives on Mind in Society* (pp. 77–91). Oxford, UK: Blackwell.

Fishbein, M. & I. Azjen (1975). *Belief, Attitude, Intention, and Behavior: An Introduction to Theory and Research.* Reading: MA: Addison-Wesley.

Fleeson, W. (2001). "Toward a Structure- and Process-integrated View of Personality: Traits as Density Distributions of States." *Journal of Personality and Social Psychology*, 80, 1011–1027.

Fletcher, B.W., W.E.K. Lehman, H.K. Wexler & G. Melnick (2007). "Who Participates in the Criminal Justice Drug Abuse Treatment Studies (CJ-DATS)?" *The Prison Journal*, 87, 25–57.

Flores, A.W., C.T. Lowenkamp, A.M. Holsinger & E.J. Latessa (2006). "Predicting Outcome with the Level of Service Inventory–Revised: The Importance of Implementation Integrity." *Journal of Criminal Justice*, 34, 523–529.

Flores, A.W., C.T. Lowenkamp, P. Smith & E.J. Latessa (undated). "Validating the Level of Service Inventory–Revised on a Sample of Federal Probationers." Unpublished manuscript. California State University at Bakersfield, California.

Flores, A.W., A.L. Russell, E.J. Latessa & L.F. Travis (2005). "Evidence of Professionalism or Quackery: Measuring Practitioner Awareness of Risk/Need Factors and Effective Treatment Strategies." *Federal Probation*, 69, 9–14.

Foley, D.L., L.J. Eaves, B. Wormley, J.L. Silberg, H.H. Maes, J. Kuhn & B. Riley (2004). "Childhood Adversity, Monoamine Oxidase a Genotype, and Risk for Conduct Disorder." *Archives of General Psychiatry*, 61, 1–7.

Folsom, J. & J.L. Atkinson (2007). "The Generalizability of the LSI-R and the CAT to the Prediction of Recidivism in female Offenders." *Criminal Justice and Behavior*, 34, 1044–1056.

Fonagy, P., M. Target, M., Steele, H. Steele, T. Leigh, A. Levinson & R. Kennedy (1997). "Morality, Disruptive Behavior, Borderline Personality Disorder, Crime, and Their Relationships to Security Attachment." In L. Atkinson & K.J. Zucker (eds.), *Attachment and Psychopathology* (pp. 223–274). New York: Guilford.

Fontaine, N., R. Carbonneau, E.D. Barker, F. Vitaro, M. Hébert, S.M. Côté, D.S. Nagin, M. Zoccolillo & R.E. Tremblay (2008). "Girls' Hyperactivity and Physical Aggression During childhood and Adjustment Problems in Early Adulthood." *Archives of General Psychiatry*, 65, 320–328.

Forth, A.E., S.D. Hart & R.D. Hare (1990). "Assessment of Psychopathy in Male Young Offenders." *Psychological Assessment: A Journal of Consulting and Clinical Psychology*, 2, 342–344.

Forth, A.E., D.S. Kosson & R.D. Hare (2003). *Hare Psychopathy Checklist: Youth Version (PCL:YV).* Toronto: Multi-Health Systems.

Fox, A.F. & M.W. Zawitz (2004). *Homicide Trends in the United States.* Washington, DC: Bureau of Justice Statistics.

Fox, J.A. & J. Levin (1998). "Multiple Homicide: Patterns of Serial and Mass Murder." In M. Tonry (ed.), *Crime and Justice: A Review of Research*, Vol. 23 (pp. 407–455). Chicago: University of Chicago Press.

Fox, J.A. & J. Levin (1999). "Serial Murder: Myths and Realities." In M.D. Smith & M.A. Zahn (eds.), *Studying and Preventing Homicide: Issues and Challenges.* Thousand Oaks, CA: Sage.

Frase, R.S. (2005). "Sentencing Guidelines in Minnesota, 1978–2003." In M. Tonry (ed.), *Crime and Justice: A Review of Research*, Vol. 32 (pp. 131–219). Chicago: University of Chicago Press.

Freud, S. (1953). *A General Introduction to Psychoanalysis*. New York: Permabooks.

Frick, P.J., C.T. Barry & D.S. Bodin (2000). "Applying the Concept of Psychopathy to Children: Implications for the Assessment of Antisocial Youth." In C.B. Gacono (ed.), *The Clinical and Forensic Assessment of Psychopathy: A Practitioner's Guide* (pp. 3–24). Mahwah, NJ: Lawrence Erlbaum Associates.

Frick, P.J. & R.D. Hare (2001). *Antisocial Process Screening Device*. Toronto: Multi-Health Systems.

Frick, P.J., B.S. O'Brien, J.M. Wootton & K. McBurnett (1994). "Psychopathy and Conduct Problems in Children." *Journal of Abnormal Psychology*, 103, 700–707.

Frick, P.J. & S.F. White (2008). "Research Review: The Importance of Callous-Unemotional Traits for Developmental Models of Aggressive and Antisocial Behavior." *Journal of Child Psychology and Psychiatry*, 49, 359–375.

Friendship, C., L. Blud, M. Erikson, R. Travers & D. Thornton (2003). "Cognitive-Behavioural Treatment for Imprisoned Offenders: An Evaluation of HM Prison Service's Cognitive Skills Program." Legal and *Criminological Psychology*, 8, 103–114.

Fuller, R.K. & E. Gordis (2004). "Does Disulfiram Have a Role in Alcoholism Treatment Today?" *Addiction*, 99, 21–24.

Funahashi, S. (2001). "Neuronal Mechanisms of Executive Control by the Prefrontal Cortex." *Neuroscience Research*, 39, 147–165.

Furby, L., M. Weinrott & L. Blackshaw (1989). "Sex Offender Recidivism: A Review." *Psychological Bulletin*, 105, 3–30.

Gable, R.K. & R.S. Gable (2005). "Electronic Monitoring: Positive Intervention Strategies." *Federal Probation*, 69, 21–25.

Gaes, G. (1998). "Correctional Treatment." In M. Tonry (ed.), *The Handbook of Crime and Punishment* (pp. 712–738). New York: Oxford University Press.

Gaes, G., T.J. Flanagan, L.L. Motiuk & L. Stewart (1999). "Adult Correctional Treatment." In M. Tonry & J. Petersilia (eds.), *Prisons. Crime and Justice: A Review*, Vol. 26 (pp. 361–426). Chicago: University of Chicago Press.

Gallagher, R.W., D.P. Somwaru & Y.S. Ben-Porath (1999). "Current Usage of Psychological Tests in State Correctional Settings." *Corrections Compendium*, 24, 1–3, 20.

Ganem, N.M. & R. Agnew (2007). "Parenthood and Adult Criminal Offending: The Importance of Relationship Quality." *Corrections Management Quarterly*, 3, 19–29.

Garbutt, J.C. (2009). "The state of Pharmacotherapy for the Treatment of Alcohol Dependence." *Journal of Substance Abuse Treatment*, 36, S15–S23.

Gardner, D. (2000). "Managing Crime and Punishment." *The Ottawa Citizen*, November 17.

Garret, C.J. (1985). "Effects of Residential Treatment of Adjudicated Delinquents: A Meta-analysis." *Journal of Research in Crime and Delinquency*, 22, 287–308.

Gavrielides, T. (2008). "Restorative Justice—The Perplexing Concept: Fault Lines and Power Battles with the Restorative Justice Movement." *Criminology & Criminal Justice*, 8, 165–183.

Geerts, M., J. Steyaert & J.P. Fryns (2003). "The XYY Syndrome: A Follow-up Study on 38 Boys." *Genetic Counseling*, 14, 267–279.

Gehm, J. (1990). "Mediated Victim-Offender Agreements: An Exploratory Analysis of Factors Related to Victim Participation." In B. Galaway & J. Hudson (eds.), *Criminal Justice, Restitution, and Reconciliation* (pp. 177–182). Monsey, NY: Criminal Justice Press.

Gendreau, P. & D.A. Andrews (2001). *The Correctional Program Assessment Inventory—2000 (CPAI 2000)*. Saint John: University of New Brunswick.

Gendreau, P., D.A. Andrews, C. Goggin & F. Chanteloupe (1992). "The Development of Clinical and Policy Guidelines for the Prediction of Criminal Behavior in Criminal Justice Settings." Unpublished manuscript available from the Department of Psychology, University of New Brunswick, St. John, New Brunswick.

Gendreau, P., F.T. Cullen & J. Bonta (1994). "Intensive Rehabilitation Supervision: The Next Generation in Community Corrections?" *Federal Probation*, 58, 72–78.

Gendreau, P., C. Goggin & F.T. Cullen (1999). *The Effects of Prison Sentences on Recidivism*. Ottawa: Solicitor General Canada. See http://www.sgc.gc.ca.

Gendreau, P., C. Goggin, S. French & P. Smith (2006). "Practicing Psychology in Correctional Settings." In I.B. Weiner & A.K. Hess (eds.), *The Handbook of Forensic Psychology*, 3rd ed. (pp. 722–750). Hoboken, NJ: Wiley.

Gendreau, P., C. Goggin & P. Smith (1999). "The Forgotten Issue in Effective Correctional Treatment: Program Implementation." *International Journal of Offender Therapy and Comparative Criminology*, 43, 180–187.

Gendreau, P., C. Goggin & P. Smith (2001). "Implementation Guidelines for Correctional Programs in the 'Real World.'" In G.A. Bernfeld, D.P. Farrington & A.W. Leschied (eds.), *Offender Rehabilitation in Practice* (pp. 247–268). Chichester, UK: John Wiley & Sons.

Gendreau, P., C. Goggin & P. Smith (2002). "Is the PCL-R Really the 'Unparalleled' Measure of Offender Risk? A Lesson in Knowledge Cumulation." *Criminal Justice and Behavior*, 29, 397–426.

Gendreau, P., T. Little & C. Goggin (1996). "A Meta-analysis of the Predictors of Adult Offender Recidivism: What Works!" *Criminology*, 34, 575–607.

Gendreau, P. & R.R. Ross (1979). "Effective Correctional Treatment: Bibliotherapy for Cynics." *Crime & Delinquency*, 25, 463–489.

Gendreau, P. & R.R. Ross (1981). "Correctional Potency: Treatment and Deterrence on Trial." In R. Roesch & R.R. Corrado (eds.), *Evaluation and Criminal Justice Policy* (pp. 29–57). Beverly Hills, CA: Sage.

Gendreau, P. & R.R. Ross (1987). "Revivication of Rehabilitation: Evidence from the 1980s." *Justice Quarterly*, 4, 349–408.

Gendreau, P., P. Smith & C. Goggin (2001). "Treatment Programs in Corrections." In J.A. Winterdyk (ed.), *Corrections in Canada: Social Reactions to Crime* (pp. 238–263). Toronto: Prentice Hall.

Gensheimer, L.K., J.P. Mayer, R. Gottschalk & W.S. Davidson (1986). "Diverting Youth from the Juvenile Justice System: A Meta-analysis of Intervention Efficacy." In S.J. Apter & A. Goldstein (eds.), *Youth Violence: Programs and Prospects* (pp. 39–57). Elmsford, NY: Pergamon.

Gershoff, E.T. (2002). "Corporal Punishment by Parents and Associated Child Behaviors and Experiences: A Meta-Analytic and Theoretical Review." *Psychological Bulletin*, 128, 539–579.

Gibbs, J.C., K.D. Arnold, H.H. Ahlborn & F.L. Cheesman (1984). "Facilitation of Sociomoral Reasoning in Delinquents." *Journal of Consulting and Clinical Psychology*, 52, 37–45.

Gilchrest, E., R. Johnson, R. Takriti, S. Weston, A. Beech & M. Kebbell (2003). *Domestic Violence Offenders: Characteristics and Offending Related Needs*. London: Home Office.

Ginsburg, J.I.D., R.E. Mann, F. Rotgers & J.R. Weekes (2002). "Using Motivational Interviewing with Criminal Justice Populations." In W.R. Miller & S. Rollnick (eds.), *Motivational Interviewing: Preparing People for Change* (pp. 333–346). New York: Guilford.

Girard, L. & S.J. Wormith (2004). "The Predictive Validity of the Level of Service Inventory—Ontario Revision on General and Violent Recidivism among Various Offender Groups." *Criminal Justice and Behavior*, 31, 150–181.

Gjone, H. & J. Stevenson (1997). "A Longitudinal Twin Study of Temperament and Behavior Problems: Common Genetic or Environmental Influences?" *Journal of the American Academy of Adolescent Psychiatry*, 36, 1148–1456.

Glaser, D. (1974). "Remedies for the Key Deficiency in Criminal Justice Evaluation Research." *Journal of Research in Crime and Delinquency*, 10, 144–154.

Glasman, L.R. & D. Albarracín (2006). "Forming Attitudes That Predict Future Behavior: A Meta-Analysis of the Attitude-Behavior Relation." *Psychological Bulletin*, 132, 778–822.

Glass, G.V., B. McGraw & L. Smith (1981). *Meta-analysis in Social Research*. Beverly Hills, CA: Sage.

Glaze, L.E. & T.P. Bonczar (2007). "Probation and Parole in the United States, 2006." *Bureau of Justice Statistics Bulletin*, December. Washington, DC: U.S. Department of Justice.

Glaze, L.E. & S. Palla (2005). "Probation and Parole in the United States, 2004." *Bureau of Justice Statistics Bulletin*, November. Washington, DC: U.S. Department of Justice.

Glenn, A.L., A. Raine, P.H. Venables & S.A. Mednick (2007). "Early Temperamental and Psychophysiological Precursors of Adult Psychopathic Personality." *Journal of Abnormal Psychology*, 116, 508–518.

Glueck, S. & E.T. Glueck (1950). *Unraveling Juvenile Delinquency*. Cambridge, MA: Harvard University Press.

Goggin, C. & P. Gendreau (in press). "The Implementation and Maintenance of Quality Services in Offender Rehabilitation Programs." In C.R. Hollin & E.J. Palmer (eds.), *Offending Behaviour Programs: Development, Application, and Controversies*. Chichester, UK: Wiley.

Golden, C.J., M.L. Jackson, A. Peterson-Rohne & S.T. Gontkovsky (1996). "Neuropsychological Correlates of Violence and Aggression: A Review of the Clinical Literature." *Aggression and Violent Behavior*, 1, 3–25.

Goldstein, A.P. (1986). "Psychological Skill Training and the Aggressive Adolescent." In S. Apter & A. Goldstein (eds.), *Youth Violence: Program and Prospects* (pp. 89–119). New York: Pergamon Press.

Goldstein, A.P. & B. Glick (1987). *Aggression Replacement Training: A Comprehensive Intervention for Aggressive Youth*. Champaign, IL: Research Press.

Goldstein, A.P. & B. Glick (1994). *The Prosocial Gang: Implementing Aggression Replacement Training*. Thousand Oaks, CA: Sage.

Goldstein, A.P. & B.G. Glick (2001). "Aggression Replacement Training: Application and Evaluation Management." In G.A. Bernfeld, D.P. Farrington & A.W. Leschied (eds.), *Offender Rehabilitation in Practice: Implementing and Evaluating Effective Programs* (pp. 121–148). New York: Wiley.

Goleman, D. (1995). *Emotional Intelligence*. New York: Bantam Books.

Gondolf, E.W. (2002). *Batterer Intervention Systems: Issues, Outcomes, Recommendations*. Thousand Oaks, CA: Sage.

Goodman, G. (1972). *Companionship Therapy*. San Francisco: Jossey-Bass.

Goodman, L.A., M.A. Dutton & L. Bennett (2000). "Predicting Repeat Abuse among Arrested Batterers: Use of the Danger Assessment Scale in the Criminal Justice System." *Journal of Interpersonal Violence*, 15, 63–74.

Gonnerman, J. (2004). "Million-dollar Blocks." *The Village Voice*. See http://www.village-voice.com/issues/0446/gonnerman.php.

Gontkovsky, S.T. (2005). "Neurobiological Bases and Neuropsychological Correlates of Aggression and Violence." In J.P. Morgan (ed.), *Psychology of Aggression* (pp. 101–116). Hauppauge, NY: Nova Science.

Gordon, D.A. (1995). "Functional Family Therapy for Delinquents." In R.R. Ross, D.H. Antonowicz & G. K. Dhaliwal (eds.), *Going Straight: Effective Delinquency Prevention and Offender Rehabilitation* (pp. 163–178). Ottawa: Air Training and Publications.

Gordon, D.A., D.A. Andrews, J. Hill & J. Kurkowsky (1992). "Therapeutic Integrity and the Effectiveness of Family Therapy: A Meta-analysis." Unpublished manuscript available from D.A. Andrews, Carleton University, Ottawa, Ontario.

Gordon, D.A., K. Graves & J. Arbuthnot (1995). "The Effect of Functional Family Therapy for Delinquents on Adult Criminal Behavior." *Criminal Justice and Behavior*, 22, 60–73.

Gordon, D.A., G. Jurkovic & J. Arbuthnot (1998). "Treatment of the Juvenile Offender." In R.M. Wettstein (ed.), *Treatment of Offenders with Mental Disorders* (pp. 365–428). New York: Guilford.

Gordon, D.A., G. Jurkovic & J. Arbuthnot (1998). "Treatment of the Juvenile Offender." In R.M. Wettstein (ed.), *Treatment of Offenders with Mental Disorders* (pp. 365–428). New York: Guilford.

Gordon, R.A., B.B. Lahey, E. Kawai, R. Loeber, M. Stouthamer-Loeber & D.P. Farrington (2004). "Antisocial Behavior and Youth Gang Membership: Selection and Socialization." *Criminology*, 42, 55–87.

Goring, C. (1913). *The English Convict*. London: His Majesty's Stationery Office.

Gossner, D. & J.S. Wormith (2007). "The Prediction of Recidivism Among Young Offenders in Saskatchewan." *The Canadian Journal of Police & Security Services*, 5, 1–13.

Gossop, M., D. Stewart & J. Marsden (2007). "Attendance at Narcotics Anonymous and Alcoholics Anonymous Meetings, Frequency of Attendance and Substance Use Outcomes After Residential Treatment for Drug Dependence: A 5-Year Follow-Up Study." *Addiction*, 103, 119–125.

Gottfredson, D.C. & M.L. Exum (2002). "The Baltimore City Drug Treatment Court: One-year Results from a Randomized Study." *Journal of Research in Crime and Delinquency*, 39, 337–356.

Gottfredson, D.M. & H.N. Snyder (2005). *The Mathematics of Risk Classification: Changing Data into Valid Instruments for Juvenile Courts*. Washington, DC: National Center for Juvenile Justice (July).

Gottfredson, M.R. (1979). "Treatment Destruction Techniques." *Journal of Research in Crime & Delinquency*, 16, 39–54.

Gottfredson, M.R. & T. Hirschi (1990). *A General Theory of Crime*. Stanford, CA: Stanford University Press.

Götz, M.J., E.C. Johnstone & S.G. Ratcliffe (1999). "Criminality and Antisocial Behaviour in Unselected Men with Sex Chromosome Abnormalities." *Psychological Medicine*, 29, 953–962.

Gough, H.G. (1965). "Cross-cultural Validation of a Measure of Asocial Behavior." *Psychological Reports*, 17, 379–387.

Graham, I.-J. & M.V. Van Dieten (1999). *Counter-Point: A Program for Attitude and Behavior Change*. Ottawa: John Howard Society of Ottawa and Correctional Service of Canada.

Granic, I. & G.R. Patterson (2006). "Toward a Comprehensive Model of Antisocial Development: A Dynamic Systems Approach." *Psychological Review*, 113, 101–131.

Grant, B.F., D.A. Dawson, F.S. Stinson, S.P. Chou, M.C. Dufour & R.P. Pickering (2006). "The 12-Month Prevalence and Trends in DSM-IV Alcohol Abuse and Dependence." *Alcohol Research & Health*, 29, 79–91.

Grant, B.F., D.S. Hasin, F.S. Stinson, D.A. Dawson, S.P. Chou, W.J. Ruan & R.P. Pickering (2004). "Prevalence, Correlates, and Disability of Personality Disorders in the U.S.: Results for the National Epidemiologic Survey on Alcohol and Related Conditions." *Journal of Clinical Psychiatry*, 65, 948–958.

Grant, J.D. (1965). "Delinquency Treatment in an Institutional Setting." In H.C. Quay (ed.), *Juvenile Delinquency: Research and Theory*. Princeton, NJ: Van Nostrand.

Grant, J.D. & M.Q. Grant (1959). "A Group Dynamics Approach to the Treatment of Nonconformists in the Navy." *Annals of the American Academy of Political and Social Science*, 322, 126–135.

Grasmick, H.G., C.R. Tittle, R.J. Bursik Jr. & B.J. Arneklev (1993). "Testing the Core Empirical Implications of Gottfredson and Hirschi's General Theory of Crime." *Journal of Research in Crime and Delinquency*, 30, 5–29.

Graves, E.T. & L.D. Vellani (2000). *Sentencing Information and Judicial Decision Making*. Raleigh, NC: North Carolina Administrative Office of the Courts.

Gray, N.S., R.J. Snowden, S. MacCulloch, H. Phillips, J. Taylor & M.J. MacCulloch (2004). "Relative Efficacy of Criminological, Clinical, and Personality Measures of Future Risk of Offending in Mentally Disordered Offenders: A Comparative Study of HCR-20, PCL: SV, and OGRS." *Journal of Consulting and Clinical Psychology*, 72, 523–530.

Gray, N.S., A. Watt, S. Hassan & M.J. MacCulloch (2003). "Behavioral Indicators of Sadistic Sexual Murder Predict the Presence of Sadistic Sexual Fantasy in a Normative Sample." *Journal of Interpersonal Violence*, 18, 1018–1034.

Green, L. & M.A. Campbell (2006). "Gender Influences and Methodological Considerations in Adolescent Risk-Need Assessment: A Meta-Analysis." A PowerPoint file from the Centre for Criminal Justice, University of New Brunswick, Saint John, New Brunswick.

Greenfeld, L.A. & M.A. Henneberg (2001). "Victim and Offender Self-Reports of Alcohol Involvement in Crime." *Alcohol Research & Health*, 25, 20–31.

Greenwood, P.W. (1982). *Selective Incapacitation*. Santa Monica, CA: RAND.

Greenwood, P.W., S.S. Everingham, E. Chen, A.F. Abrahamse, N. Merritt & J. Chiesa (1998). *Three Strikes Revisited: An Early Assessment of Implementation and Effects*. Santa Monica, CA: RAND.

Greenwood, P.W. & S. Turner (1987). *Selective Incapacitation Revisited: Why the High-Rate Offenders are Hard to Predict*. Santa Monica, CA: RAND.

Greeven, P.G.J. & C. De Ruiter (2004). "Personality Disorders in a Dutch Forensic Psychiatric Sample: Changes with Treatment." *Criminal Behaviour and Mental Health*, 14, 280–290.

Gresswell, D.M. & C.R. Hollin (1994). "Multiple Murder: A Review." *British Journal of Criminology*, 34, 1–14.

Gretton, H., R.D. Hare & R.E.H. Catchpole (2004). "Psychopathy and Offending from Adolescence to Adulthood: A Ten-year Follow-up." *Journal of Consulting and Clinical Psychology*, 72, 636–645.

Gretton, H., M. McBride, R.D. Hare, R. O'Shaughnessy & G. Kumka (2001). "Psychopathy and Recidivism in Adolescent Sex Offenders." *Criminal Justice and Behavior*, 28, 427–449.

Griffin, K.W., G.J. Botvin, J., L.M. Scheier, T. Diaz & N. Miller (2000). "Parenting Practices as Predictors of Substance Abuse, Delinquency, and Aggression among Urban Minority Youth: Moderating Effects of Family Structure and Gender." *Psychology of Addictive Behaviors*, 14, 174–184.

Groh, D.R., L.A. Jason & C.B. Keys (2008). "Social Network Variables in Alcoholics Anonymous: A Literature Review." *Clinical Psychology Review*, 28, 430–450.

Gross, A.L. & M. Sroga (2008). "Establishing the Needs of aboriginal Offenders Using the Level of Service Inventory-Ontario Revision." Paper presented at the Annual Meeting of the Canadian Psychological Association, Halifax, Nova Scotia.

Grove, W.M., E.D. Eckert, L. Heston, T.J. Bouchard, Jr., N. Segal & D.T. Lykken (1990). "Heritability of Substance Abuse and Antisocial Behavior: A Study of Monozygotic Twins Reared Apart." *Biological Psychiatry*, 27, 1293–1304.

Grove, W.M. & P.E. Meehl (1996). "Comparative Efficiency of Informal (Subjective, Impressionistic) and Formal (Mechanical, Algorithmic) Prediction Procedures: The Clinical-statistical Controversy." *Psychology, Public Policy, and Law*, 2, 293–323.

Grove, W.M., D.H. Zald, B.S. Lebow, B.E. Snitz & C. Nelson (2000). "Clinical versus Mechanical Prediction: A Meta-analysis." *Psychological Assessment*, 12, 19–30.

Guay, J.-P., J. Ruscio & R.A. Knight (2006). "Is More Simply More? A Taxometric Investigation of Psychopathy in Women." Paper presented at the Annual Meeting of the American Society of Criminology, Los Angeles, California, November.

Guay, J.-P., J. Ruscio & R.A. Knight (2007). "A Taxometric Analysis of the Latent Structure of Psychopathy: Evidence for Dimensionality." *Journal of Abnormal Psychology*, 116, 701–716.

Guo, G., M.E. Roettger & T. Cai (2008). "The Integration of Genetic Propensities into Social-control Models of Delinquency and Violence Among Male Youths." *American Sociological Review*, 73, 543–598.

Guo, G., M.E. Roettger & J.C. Shih (2007). "Contributions of the DAT1 and DRD2 Genes to Serious and Violent Delinquency Among Adolescents and Young Adults." *Human Genetics*, 121, 125–136.

Gurling, H.M.D., B.E. Oppenheim & R.M. Murray (1984). "Depression, Criminality and Psychopathology Associated with Alcoholism: Evidence from a Twin Study." *Acta Geneticae Medicae Gemellologiae: Twin Research*, 33, 333–339.

Gutierrez, L. (2008). "A Meta-analysis of the Drug Treatment Court Literature: Assessing Study and Treatment Quality." Unpublished Honours Thesis, Psychology Department, Carleton University, Ottawa, Ontario.

Gutierrez, L. & G. Bourgon (2009). "Study Quality in Drug Treatment Court Evaluations: Clouding the Water." Paper presented at the Annual Meeting of the Canadian Psychological Association, Montreal, Quebec.

Guttridge, P., W.F. Gabrielli Jr., S.A. Mednick & K.T. Van Dusen (1983). "Criminal Violence in a Birth Cohort." In K.T. Van Dusen & S.A. Mednick (eds.), *Prospective Studies of Crime and Delinquency* (pp. 211–224). Hingham, MA: Kluwer Nijhoff.

Haapasalo, J. & E. Pokela (1999). "Child-rearing and Child Abuse Antecedents of Criminality." *Aggression and Violent Behavior*, 4, 107–127.

Haas, H., D.P. Farrington, M. Killias & G. Sattar (2004). "The Impact of Different Family Configurations on Delinquency." *British Journal of Criminology*, 44, 520–532.

Haas, S.M. & K.A. DeTardo-Bora (2009). "Inmate Reentry and the Utility of the LSI-R in Case Planning." *Corrections Compendium*, Spring, 11–16, 49–54.

Haberstick, B., J. Lessem, C. Hopfer, A. Smolen, M.A. Ehringer, D. Timberlake & J.K. Hewitt (2005). "Monoamine Oxidase A (MAOA) and Antisocial Behavior in the Presence of Childhood and Adolescent Maltreatment." *American Journal of Medical Genetics: Neuropsychiatric Genetics*, 135, 59–64.

Hackler, J.C. (1966). "Boys, Blisters, and Behavior: The Impact of a Work Program in an Urban Central Area." *Journal of Research in Crime and Delinquency*, 4, 155–164.

Hackler, J.C. (1978). *The Prevention of Delinquency: The Great Stumble Forward*. Toronto: Methuen.

Hagan, J. (1989). *Structural Criminology*. New Brunswick, NJ: Rutgers University Press.

Hagan, J., A.R. Gillis & J. Simpson (1985). "The Class Structure of Gender and Delinquency: Toward a Power-Control Theory of Common Delinquent Behavior." *American Journal of Sociology*, 90, 1151–1177.

Hall, C. (1954). *A Primer of Freudian Psychology*. Cleveland, OH: World.

Hall, J.R. & S.D. Benning (2006). "The 'Successful' Psychopath: Adaptive and Subclinical Manifestations of Psychopathy in the General Population." In C.J. Patrick (ed.), *Handbook of Psychopathy* (pp. 459–478). New York: Guilford.

Hamm, M.S. & J.C. Kite (1991). "The Role of Offender Rehabilitation in Family Violence Policy: The Batterers Anonymous Experiment." *Criminal Justice Review*, 16, 227–248.

Haney, C. (2006). *Reforming Punishment: Psychological Limits to the Pains of Imprisonment, the Law and Public Policy*. Washington, DC: American Psychological Association.

Hannah-Moffat, K. (2009). "Gridlock or Mutability: Reconsidering 'Gender' and Risk Assessment." *Criminology & Public Policy*, 8, 209–219.

Hannah-Moffat, K. & M. Shaw (2001). *Taking Risks: Incorporating Gender and Culture into the Classification and Assessment of Federally Sentenced Women in Canada*. Policy Research Report. Ottawa: Status of Women Canada.

Hanson, R.K. (1996). "Evaluating the Contribution of Relapse Prevention Theory to the Treatment of Sex Offenders." *Sexual Abuse: A Journal of Research and Treatment*, 8, 201–208.

Hanson, R.K. (1997a). *The Development of a Brief Actuarial Risk Scale for Sexual Offense Recidivism*. Ottawa: Solicitor General Canada. See http://www.sgc.gc.ca.

Hanson, R.K. (1997b). "Invoking Sympathy—Assessment and Treatment of Empathy Deficits among Sexual Offenders." In B.K. Schwartz & H.R. Cellini (eds.), *The Sex Offender: New Insights, Treatment Innovations and Legal Developments* (pp. 1.1.–1.12). Kingston, NJ: Civic Research Institute.

Hanson, R.K. (2006). "Stability and Change: Dynamic Risk Factors for Sexual Offenders." In W.L. Marshall, Y.M. Fernandez, L.E. Marshall & G.A. Sarran (eds.), *Sexual Offender Treatment: Controversial Issues* (pp. 17–31). New York: Wiley.

Hanson, R.K. (in press). "The Psychological Assessment of Risk for Crime and Violence." *Canadian Psychology*.

Hanson, R.K., G. Bourgon, L. Helmus & S. Hodgson (in press). "The Principles of Effective Correctional Treatment Also Apply to Sexual Offenders: A Meta-Analysis." *Criminal Justice and Behavior*.

Hanson, R.K., I. Broom & M. Stephenson (2004). "Evaluating Community Sex Offender Treatment Programs: A 12-year Follow-up of 724 Offenders." *Canadian Journal of Behavioural Science*, 36, 87–96.

Hanson, R.K. & M.T. Bussière (1998). "Predicting Relapse: A Meta-analysis of Sexual Offender Recidivism Studies." *Journal of Consulting and Clinical Psychology*, 66, 348–362.

Hanson, R K., O. Cadsky, A. Harris & C. Lalonde (1997). "Correlates of Battering among 997 Men: Family History, Adjustment, and Attitudinal Differences." *Violence and Victims*, 12, 191–208.

Hanson, R.K., A. Gordon, A.J.R. Harris, J.K. Marques, W. Murphy, V.L. Quinsey & M.C. Seto (2002). "First Report of the Collaborative Outcome Data Project on the Effectiveness of Psychological Treatment for Sex Offenders." *Sexual Abuse: A Journal of Research and Treatment*, 14, 167–192.

Hanson, R.K. & A.J.R. Harris (2000). "Where Should We Intervene? Dynamic Predictors of Sexual Offense Recidivism." *Criminal Justice and Behavior*, 27, 6–35.

Hanson, R.K., A.J. R. Harris, T.-L. Scott & L. Helmus (2007). *Assessing the Risk of Sexual Offenders on Community Supervision: The Dynamic Supervision Project* (User Report 2007–05). Ottawa: Public Safety Canada.

Hanson, R.K., L. Helmus & D. Thornton (2009). "Predicting Recidivism among Sexual Offenders: A Multi-site Study of Static-2002." *Law and Human Behavior*.

Hanson, R.K., L. Helmus & G. Bourgon (2007). *The Validity of Risk Assessments for Intimate Partner Violence: A Meta-analysis* (User Report 2007-07). Ottawa: Public Safety Canada.

Hanson, R.K., K.E. Morton & A.J.R. Harris (2003). "Sexual Offender Recidivism Risk: What We Know and What We Need to Know." *Annals of the New York Academy of Sciences*, 989, 154–166.

Hanson, R.K. & K. Morton-Bourgon (2004). *Predictors of Sexual Recidivism: An Up-dated Meta-analysis* (User Report 2004-02). Ottawa: Public Safety and Emergency Preparedness Canada.

Hanson, R.K. & K. Morton-Bourgon (2005). "The Characteristics of Persistent Sexual Offenders: A Meta-analysis of Recidivism Studies." *Journal of Consulting and Clinical Psychology*, 73, 1154–1163.

Hanson, R.K. & K. Morton-Bourgon (2009). "The Accuracy of Recidivism Risk for Sexual Offenders: A Meta-analysis of 118 Prediction Studies." *Psychological Assessment*, 21, 1–21.

Hanson, R.K. & H. Scott (1996). "Social Networks of Sexual Offenders." *Psychology, Crime and Law*, 2, 249–258.

Hanson, R.K., H. Scott & R.A. Steffy (1995). "Comparison of Child Molesters and Nonsexual Criminals: Risk Predictors and Long-term Recidivism." *Journal of Research in Crime and Delinquency*, 32, 325–337.

Hanson, R.K. & D. Thornton (2000). "Improving Risk Assessments for Sex Offenders: A Comparison of Three Actuarial Scales." *Law and Human Behavior*, 24, 119–136.

Hanson, R.K. & D. Thornton (2003). *Notes on the Development of Static-2002* (User Report 2003-01). Ottawa: Public Safety Canada.

Hanson, R.K. & S. Wallace-Capretta (2000). *Predicting Recidivism among Male Batterers* (User Report 2000–06). Ottawa: Solicitor General Canada.

Hare, R.D. (1980). "A Research Scale for the Assessment of Psychopathy in Criminal Populations." *Personality and Individual Differences*, 1, 111–119.

Hare, R.D. (1990). *The Hare Psychopathy Checklist–Revised*. Toronto: Multi-Health Systems.

Hare, R.D. (1993). *Without Conscience: The Disturbing World of the Psychopaths Among Us*. New York: Pocket Books.

Hare, R.D. (1996). "Psychopathy: A Clinical Construct Whose Time Has Come." *Criminal Justice and Behavior*, 23, 25–54.

Hare, R.D. (1998). "Psychopaths and Their Nature: Implications for the Mental Health and Criminal Justice Systems." In T. Millon, E. Simonsen, M. Birket-Smith & R.D. Davis (eds.), *Psychopathy: Antisocial, Criminal, and Violent Behavior* (pp. 188–212). New York: Guilford.

Hare, R.D. (2003). *The Hare Psychopathy Checklist-Revised*, 2nd. ed. Toronto: Multi-Health Systems.

Hare, R.D., D. Clark, M. Grann & D. Thornton (2000). "Psychopathy and the Predictive Validity of the PCL-R: An International Perspective." *Behavioral Sciences and the Law*, 18, 623–645.

Hare, R.D., T.J. Harpur, A.R. Hakstian, A.E. Forth, S.D. Hart & J.P. Newman (1990). "The Revised Psychopathy Checklist: Reliability and Factor Structure." *Psychological Assessment: A Journal of Consulting and Clinical Psychology*, 2, 338–341.

Hare, R.D. & C.S. Neumann (2005). "Structural Models of Psychopathy." *Current Psychiatric Reports*, 7, 57–64.

Hare, R.D. & C.S. Neuman (2006). "The PCL-R Assessment of Psychopathy: Development, Structural Properties, and New Directions." In C.J. Patrick (ed.), *Handbook of Psychopathy* (pp. 58–88). New York: Guilford.

Hare, R.D. & C.S. Neumann (2008). "Psychopathy as a Clinical and Empirical Construct." *Annual Review of Clinical Psychology*, 4, 217–246.

Harford, T.C., B.F. Grant, H. Yi & C.M. Chen (2005). "Patterns of DSM-IV Alcohol Abuse and Dependence Criteria Among Adolescents and Adults: Results from the 2001 National Household Survey on Drug Abuse." *Alcoholism: Clinical and Experimental Research*, 29, 810–828.

Harper, R. & S. Hardy (2000). "An Evaluation of Motivational Interviewing as a Method of Intervention with Clients in a Probation Setting." *British Journal of Social Work*, 30, 393–400.

Harpur, T.J., A.R. Hakstian & R.D. Hare (1988). "Factor Structure of the Psychopathy Checklist." *Journal of Consulting and Clinical Psychology*, 62, 387–397.

Harris, A., & A.J. Lurigio (2007). "Mental Illness and Violence: A Brief Review of Research and Assessment Strategies." *Aggression and Violent Behavior*, 12, 542–551.

Harris, G.T., Z.N. Hilton, M.E. Rice & A.W. Eke (2007). "Children Killed by Genetic Parents versus Step-parents." *Evolution and Human Behavior*, 28, 85–95.

Harris, G.T. & M.E. Rice (1997). "Mentally Disordered Offenders: What Research Says about Effective Service." In C.D. Webster & M.A. Jackson (eds.), *Impulsivity Theory: Assessment and Treatment* (pp. 361–393). New York: Guilford.

Harris, G.T. & M.E. Rice (2006). "Treatment of Psychopathy: A Review of Empirical Findings." In C.J. Patrick (ed.), *Handbook of Psychopathy* (pp. 555–572). New York: Guilford.

Harris, G.T., M.R. Rice & C.A. Cormier (1989). "Violent Recidivism among Psychopaths and Nonpsychopaths Treated in a Therapeutic Community." Research report from the Penetanguishene Mental Health Centre VI(1), April, Penetanguishene, Ontario.

Harris, G.T., M.E. Rice & C.A. Cormier (1994). "Psychopaths: Is a Therapeutic Community Therapeutic?" *Therapeutic Communities*, 15, 283–299.

Harris, G.T., M.E. Rice & V.L. Quinsey (1993). "Violent Recidivism of Mentally Disordered Offenders: The Development of a Statistical Prediction Instrument." *Criminal Justice and Behavior*, 20, 315–335.

Harris, G.T., M.E. Rice & V.L. Quinsey (1994). "Psychopathy as a Taxon: Evidence that Psychopaths are a Discrete Class." *Journal of Consulting and Clinical Psychology*, 62, 387–397.

Harrison, P.M. & A.J. Beck (2005). "Prisoners in 2004." *Bureau of Justice Statistics Bulletin*, October. Washington, DC: U.S. Department of Justice.

Hartung, F.E. (1965). "A Vocabulary of Motives for Law Violations." In F.E. Hartung (ed.), *Crime, Law and Society* (pp. 62–83). Detroit: Wayne State University Press.

Hasin, D. (2003). "Classification of Alcohol Use Disorders." *Alcohol Research & Health*, 27, 5–17.

Hatcher, R.M., E.J. Palmer, J. McGuire, J.C. Hounsome, C.A.L. Bilby & C.R. Hollin (2008). "Aggression Replacement Training with Adult Male Offenders Within Community Settings: A Reconviction Analysis." *The Journal of Forensic Psychiatry & Psychology*, 19, 517–532.

Hawes, D.J. & M.R. Dadds (2005). "The Treatment of Conduct Problems in Children with Callous-Unemotional Traits." Journal of Consulting and Clinical Psychology, 73, 737–741.

Hay, C. & M.M. Evans (2006). "Has *Roe v. Wade* Reduced U.S. Crime Rates? Examining the Link between Mothers' Pregnancy Intentions and Children's Later Involvement in Law-violating Behavior." *Journal of Research in Crime and Delinquency*, 43, 36–66.

Haynie, D.L., P.C. Giordano, W.D. Manning & M.A. Longmore (2005). "Adolescent Romantic Relationships and Delinquency Involvement." *Criminology*, 43, 177–210.

Heaven, P. (1996). "Personality and Self-reported Delinquency: Analysis of the 'Big Five' Personality Dimensions." *Personality and Individual Differences*, 20, 47–54.

Hemphill, J.F., R.D. Hare & S. Wong (1998). "Psychopathy and Recidivism: A Review." *Legal and Criminological Psychology*, 3, 139–170.

Hendricks, B., T. Werner, L. Shipway & G.J. Turinetti (2006). "Recidivism among Spousal Abusers: Predictions and Program Evaluation." *Journal of Interpersonal Violence*, 21, 703–716.

Henggeler, S.W., W.G. Clingempeel, M.J. Brondino & S.G. Pickrel (2002). "Four-year Follow-up of Multisystemic Therapy with Substance Abusing and Dependent Juvenile Offenders." *Journal of the American Academy of Child and Adolescent Psychiatry*, 41, 695–711.

Henggeler, S.W., C.A. Halliday-Boykins, P.B. Cunningham, J. Randall, S.B. Shapiro & J.E. Chapman (2006). "Juvenile Drug Court: Enhancing Outcomes by Integrating Evidence-Based Treatments." *Journal of Consulting and Clinical Psychology*, 74, 42–54.

Henggeler, S.W., G.B. Melton & L.A. Smith (1992). "Family Preservation Using Multisystemic Therapy: An Effective Alternative to Incarcerating Serious Juvenile Offenders." *Journal of Consulting and Clinical Psychology*, 60, 953–961.

Henggeler, S.W., G.B. Melton, L.A. Smith, S.K. Schoenwald & J.H. Hanley (1993). "Family Preservation Using Multisystemic Therapy: Long-term Follow-up to a Clinical Trial with Serious Juvenile Offenders." *Journal of Child and Family Studies*, 2, 283–293.

Henggeler, S.W., S.K. Schoenwald, C.M. Borduin, M.D. Rowland & P.B. Cunningham (2009). *Multisystemic Treatment of Antisocial Behavior in Children and Adolescents*, 2nd ed. New York: Guilford.

Henning, K.R. & B.C. Frueh (1996). "Cognitive-Behavioral Treatment of Incarcerated Offenders." *Criminal Justice and Behavior*, 23, 523–541.

Henning, K., & R. Holdford (2006). "Minimization, Denial, and Victim Blaming by Batterers: How Much Does the Truth Matter?" *Criminal Justice and Behavior*, 33, 110–130.

Hepburn, J.R. (2005). "Recidivism among Drug Offenders Following Exposure to Treatment." *Criminal Justice Policy Review*, 16, 237–259.

Herrnstein, R.J. & C. Murray (1994). *The Bell Curve: Intelligence and Class Structure in American Life*. New York: Free Press.

Hersen, M. & D.H. Barlow (1976). *Single Case Experimental Designs: Strategies for Studying Behavioral Change*. New York: Pergamon Press.

Hettema, J., J. Steele & W.R. Miller (2005). "Motivational Interviewing." *Annual Review of Clinical Psychology*, 1, 91–111.

Hiatt, K.D. & J.P. Newman (2006). "Understanding Psychopathy: The Cognitive Side." In C.J. Patrick (ed.), *Handbook of Psychopathy* (pp. 334–352). New York: Guilford.

Hickey, E.W. (2006). *Serial Murderers and their Victims*, 4th ed. Toronto: Thomson Wadsworth.

Hicks, B.M., K.E. Markon, C.J. Patrick, R.F. Krueger & J.P. Newman (2004). "Identifying Psychopathy Subtypes on the Basis of Personality Structure." *Psychological Assessment*, 16, 276–288.

Hill, J., D.A. Andrews & R.D. Hoge (1991). "Meta-analysis of Treatment Programs for Young Offenders: The Effect of Clinically Relevant Treatment on Recidivism with Controls for Various Methodological Variables." *Canadian Journal of Program Evaluation*, 6, 97–109.

Hill, K., J.C. Howell, D.J. Hawkins, D.J. & S.R. Battin-Pearson (1999). "Childhood Risk Factors for Adolescent Gang Membership: Results from the Seattle Social Development Project." *Journal of Research in Crime and Delinquency*, 36, 300–322.

Hilton, Z.N. & G.T. Harris (2005). "Predicting Wife Assault: A Critical Review and Implications for Policy and Practice." *Trauma, Violence, and Abuse*, 6, 3–23.

Hilton, Z.N. & G.T. Harris (2005). "Predicting Wife Assault: A Critical Review and Implications for Policy and Practice." *Trauma, Violence, and Abuse*, 6, 3–23.

Hilton, Z.N., G.T. Harris & M.E. Rice (2006). "Sixty-Six Years of Research on the Clinical Versus Actuarial Prediction of Violence." *The Counseling Psychologist*, 34, 400–409.

Hilton, Z.N., G.T. Harris & M.E. Rice (2007). "The Effect of Arrest on Wife Assault Recidivism: Controlling for Pre-Arrest Risk." *Criminal Justice and Behavior*, 34, 1334–1344.

Hilton, Z.N., G.T. Harris, M.E. Rice, R.E. Houghton & A.W. Eke (2008). "An Indepth Assessment for Wife Assault Recidivism: The Ontario Domestic Violence Risk Appraisal Guide." *Law and Human Behavior*, 32, 150–163.

Hilton, Z.N., G.T. Harris, M.E. Rice, C. Lang, C.A. Cormier & K.J. Lines (2004). "A Brief Actuarial Assessment for the Prediction of Wife Assault Recidivism: The Ontario Domestic Assault Risk Assessment." *Psychological Assessment*, 16, 267–275.

Hindelang, M.J. (1981). "Variations in Sex-Race-Age-Specific Incidence Rates of Offending." *American Sociological Review*, 46, 461–474.

Hipwell, A.E., D.A. Pardini, R. Loeber, M., Sembower, K. Keenan & M. Stouthamer-Loeber (2007). "Callous-Unemotional Behaviors in Young Girls: Shared and Unique Effects Relative to Conduct Problems." *Journal of Clinical Child and Adolescent Psychiatry*, 36, 293–304.

Hirschfield, P.J. (2008). "The Declining Significance of Delinquent Labels in Disadvantaged Urban Communities." *Sociological Forum*, 23, 575–601.

Hirschi, T. (1969). *Causes of Delinquency*. Berkeley, CA: University of California Press.

Hirschi, T. (2004). "Self-Control and Crime." In R.F. Baumeister & K.D. Vohs (eds.), *Handbook of Self-regulation: Research, Theory and Applications* (pp. 537–552). New York: Guilford.

Hirschi, T. & M.R. Gottfredson (2000). "In Defense of Self-control." *Theoretical Criminology*, 4, 55–69.

Hirschi, T. & M.J. Hindelang (1977). "Intelligence and Delinquency: A Revisionist Review." *American Sociological Review*, 42, 571–587.

HM Prison Service and National Probation Directorate (2002). *The Offender Assessment System: User Manual*. London: Home Office.

Hobson, J., J. Shine & R. Roberts (2000). "How Do Psychopaths Behave in a Prison Therapeutic Community?" *Psychiatry, Crime and Law*, 6, 139–154.

Hodgins, S. & G. Cote (1990). "Prevalence of Mental Disorders among Penitentiary Inmates in Quebec." *Canada's Mental Health*, 38, 1–4.

Hodgins, S., U.L. Hiscoke & R. Freese (2003). "The Antecedents of Aggressive Behavior among Men with Schizophrenia: A Prospective Investigation of Patients in Community Treatment." *Behavioral Sciences and the Law*, 21, 523–546.

Hoffman, P.B. (1994). "Twenty Years of Operational Use of a Risk Prediction Instrument: The United States Parole Commission's Salient Factor Score." *Journal of Criminal Justice*, 22, 477–494.

Hoffman, P.B. & J.L. Beck (1984). "Burnout—Age at Release from Prison and Recidivism." *Journal of Criminal Justice*, 12, 617–623.

Hoge, R.D. (2009). "Youth Level of Service/Case Management Inventory." In R.K. Otto and K. Douglas (eds.), *Handbook of Violence Risk Assessment Tools*. New York: Routledge.

Hoge, R.D. & D.A. Andrews (2002). *Youth Level of Service/Case Management Inventory: User's Manual*. Toronto: Multi-Health Systems.

Hollin, C.R. & E.J. Palmer (2001). "Skills Training." In C.R. Hollin (ed.), *Handbook of Offender Assessment and Treatment* (pp. 269–280). Chichester, UK: John Wiley & Sons.

Hollin, C.R. & E.J. Palmer (2006). "The Level of Service Inventory–Revised Profile of English Prisoners: Risk and Reconviction Analysis." *Criminal Justice and Behavior*, 33, 347–280.

Hollin, C.R., E.J. Palmer & D. Clark (2003). "The Level of Service Inventory–Revised Profile of English Prisoners: A Needs Analysis." *Criminal Justice and Behavior*, 30, 422–440.

Holloway, K., T.H. Bennett & D.P. Farrington (2008). *Effectiveness of Treatment in Reducing Drug-Related Crime*. Stockholm: National Council on Crime Prevention.

Holmes, R.M. (1989). *Profiling Violent Crimes: An Investigative Tool*. Newbury Park, CA: Sage.

Holmes, R.M. & S.T. Holmes (1998). *Serial Murder*, 2nd ed. Thousand Oaks, CA: Sage.

Holmes, S.T., E. Hickey & R.M. Holmes (1998). "Female Serial Murderesses: The Unnoticed Terror." In R.M. Holmes & S.T. Holmes (eds.), *Contemporary Perspectives on Serial Murder* (pp. 59–70). Thousand Oaks, CA: Sage.

Holsinger, A. M., C.T. Lowenkamp & E.J. Latessa (2006). "Exploring the Validity of the Level of Service Inventory-Revised with Native American Offenders." *Journal of Criminal Justice*, 34, 331–337.

Holtfreter, K. & R. Cupp (2007). "Gender and Risk Assessment: The Empirical Status of the LSI-R for Women." *Journal of Contemporary Criminology*, 23, 363–382.

Holtfreter, K., M.D. Reisig & M. Morash (2004). "Poverty, State Capital, and Recidivism among Women Offenders." *Criminology and Public Policy*, 3, 185–208.

Holtzworth-Munroe, A. & J.C. Meehan (2004). "Typologies of Men who are Maritally Violent: Scientific and Clinical Implications." *Journal of Interpersonal Violence*, 19, 1369–1389.

Honig, W.K. (1966). *Operant Behavior: Areas of Research and Application*. East Norwalk, CT: Appleton-Century-Crofts.

Hooten, E.A. (1939). *Crime and the Man*. Cambridge, MA: Harvard University Press.

Howell, J.C. (1998). "Recent Gang Research: Program & Policy Implications." *Crime & Delinquency*, 40, 495–515.

Howitt, D. (2004). "What is the Role of Fantasy in Sex Offending?" *Criminal Behaviour and Mental Health*, 14, 182–188.

Hubbard, D.J. & J. Pealer (2009). "The Importance of Responsivity Factors in Predicting Reductions in Antisocial Attitudes and Cognitive Distortions Among Adult Male Offenders." *The Prison Journal*, 89, 79–98.

Hubbard, D.J. & T.C. Pratt (2002). "A Meta-Analysis of the Prediction of Delinquency Among Girls." *Journal of Offender Rehabilitation*, 34, 1–13.

Hucker, S.J. (1997). "Sexual Sadism: Psychopathology and Theory." In D.R. Laws & W. O'Donohue (eds.), *Sexual Deviance: Theory, Assessment, and Treatment* (pp. 194–224). New York: Guilford.

Hucker, S.J. & J. Bain (1990). "Androgenic Hormones and Sexual Assault." In W.L. Marshall, D.R. Laws & H.E. Barbaree (eds.), *Handbook of Sexual Assault: Issues, Theories, and Treatment of the Offender* (pp. 93–102). New York: Plenum.

Huey, S.J., Jr., S.W. Henggeler, M.J. Brondino & S.G. Pickrel (2000). "Mechanisms of Change in Multisystemic Therapy: Reducing Delinquent Behavior through Therapist Adherence and Improved Family and Peer Functioning." *Journal of Consulting and Clinical Psychology*, 68, 451–467.

Huessman, R.L. & C.-L. Podolski (2003). "Punishment: A Psychological Perspective." In S. McConville (ed.), *The Use of Punishment* (pp. 55–88). Devon, UK: Willan.

Huff, R.C. (1998). *Comparing the Criminal Behavior of Youth Gangs and At-Risk Youths*. Research in Brief. Washington, DC: National Institute of Justice.

Hunt, D.E. & R.H. Hardt (1965). "Developmental Stage, Delinquency, and Differential Treatment." *Journal of Research in Crime and Delinquency*, 2, 20–31.

Hunt, G.M. & N.H. Azrin (1973). "A Community-Reinforcement Approach to Alcoholism." *Behavior Research and Therapy*, 11, 91–104.

Huss, M.T. & J. Langhinrichsen-Rohling (2000). "Identification of the Psychopathic Batterer: The Clinical, Legal, and Policy Implications." *Aggression and Violent Behavior*, 5, 403–422.

Ike, N. (2000). "Current Thinking on XYY Syndrome." *Psychiatric Annals*, 30, 91–95.

Inada, T., F. Minagawa, S. Iwashita & T. Tokui (1995). "Mentally Disordered Criminal Offenders: Five Years' Data from the Tokyo District Public Prosecutor's Office." *International Journal of Law and Psychiatry*, 18, 221–230.

Indian and Northern Affairs Canada (2008). *Resolution Sector*. Retrieved February 20, 2009, from http://www.ainc-inac.gc.ca/ai/rqpi/index-eng.asp.

Interstate Commission for Adult Offender Supervision. (2007). *SO Assessment Information Survey 4–2007*. See http: //www.interstatecompact.org/resources/surveys/survey_results/SexOffender_Assessment_042007.pdf.

Irvin, J.E., C.A. Bowers, M.E. Dunn & M.C. Wang (1999). "Efficacy of Relapse Prevention: A Meta-analytic Review." *Journal of Consulting and Clinical Psychology*, 67, 563–570.

Ito, T.A., N. Miller & V.E. Pollock (1996). "Alcohol and Aggression: A Meta-Analysis on the Moderating Effects of Inhibitory Cues, Triggering Events, and Self-Focused Attention." *Psychological Bulletin*, 120, 60–82.

Jackson, A. (2009). "The Impact of Restorative Justice on the Development of Guilt, Shame, and Empthy Among Participants in a Victim Impact Training Program." *Victims and Offenders*, 4, 1–24.

Jackson, A., S.L. Lucas & A.G. Blackburn (2009). "Externalization and Victim-Blaming Among a Sample of Incarcerated Females." *Journal of Offender Rehabilitation*, 48, 1–22.

Jacobs, P.A., M. Brunton, H.M. Melville, R.P. Brittain & W.F. McClermont (1965). "Aggressive Behavior, Mental Subnormality and the XYY Male." *Nature*, 208, 1351–1352.

Jacobson, N.S., J.M. Gottman, E. Gortner, S. Berns & J.W. Shortt (1996). "Psychological Factors in the Longitudinal Course of Battering: When Do Couples Split Up? When Does the Abuse Decrease?" *Violence and Victims*, 11, 371–392.

Jaffe, S.R., J. Belsky, H. Harrington, A. Caspi & T.E. Moffitt (2006). "When Parents Have a History of Conduct Disorder: How is the Caregiving Environment Affected?" *Journal of Abnormal Psychology*, 115, 309–319.

Jaffe, S.R., T.E. Moffitt, A. Caspi & A. Taylor (2003). "Life With (or Without) Father: The Benefits of Living with Two Biological Parents Depend on the Father's Antisocial Behavior." *Child Development*, 74, 109–126.

James, D.V., P.E. Mullen, J.R. Meloy, M.T. Pathé, F.R. Farnham L. Preston & B. Darnley (2007). "The Role of Mental Disorder in Attacks on European Politicians 1990–2004." *Acta Psychiatrica Scandinavia*, 116, 334–344.

James, D.V., P.E. Mullen, J.R. M.T. Pathé, J.R. Meloy, F.R. Farnham, L. Preston & B. Darnley (2008). "Attacks on the British Royal Family: The Role of Psychotic Illness." *Journal of the American academy of Psychiatry*, 36, 59–67.

Jang, K.L., R.R. McCrae, A. Angleitner, R. Riemann & W.J. Livesley (1998). "Heritability of Facet-level Traits in a Cross-cultural Twin Sample: Support for a Hierarchical Model of Personality." *Journal of Personality and Social Psychology*, 74, 1556–1565.

Jarvik, L.F., V. Klodin & S.S. Matsuyama (1973). "Human Aggression and the Extra Y Chromosome." *American Psychologist*, 28, 674–682.

Jarvis, B. (2007). "Monsters Inc.: Serial Killers and Consumer Culture." *Crime, Media, Culture*, 3, 326–344.

Jeffery, C.R. (1979). *Biology and Crime*. Beverly Hills, CA: Sage.

Jenkins, P. (1998). "African-Americans and Serial Homicide." In R.M. Holmes & S.T. Holmes (eds.), *Contemporary Perspectives on Serial Murder* (pp. 17–32). Thousand Oaks, CA: Sage.

Jensen, E.L., J. Gerber & C. Mosher (2004). "Social Consequences of the War on Drugs: The Legacy of Failed Policy." *Criminal Justice Policy Review*, 15, 100–121.

Jenson, G.F. (1972). "Parents, Peers and Delinquent Action: A Test of the Differential Association Perspective." *American Journal of Sociology*, 78, 562–575.

Jesness, C.F. (1971). "The Preston Typology Study: An Experiment with Differential Treatment in an Institution." *Journal of Research in Crime and Delinquency*, 8, 38–52.

Jessor, R. & S. L. Jessor (1977). *Problem Behavior and Psychosocial Development: A Longitudinal Study of Youth*. New York: Academic Press.

Jessor, R., S.L. Jessor & J. Finney (1973). "A Social Psychology of Marijuana Use: Longitudinal Studies of High School and College Youth." *Journal of Personality and Social Psychology*, 26, 1–15.

Johnson, J.G., E. Smailes, P. Cohen, S. Kasen & J.S. Brook (2004). "Anti-social Parental Behaviour, Problematic Parenting and Aggressive Offspring Behaviour During Adulthood: A 25-year Investigation." *British Journal of Criminology*, 44, 915–930.

Johnson, R.E. (1979). *Juvenile Delinquency and its Origins: An Integrative Theoretical Approach*. Cambridge, UK: Cambridge University Press.

Johnston, J.M. (1972). "Punishment of Human Behavior." *American Psychologist*, 27, 1033–1054.

Joiner, T.E. & K.D. Wagner (1995). "Attribution Style and Depression in Children and Adolescents: A Meta-analytic Review." *Clinical Psychology Review*, 15, 777–798.

Jones, M.B. & D.R. Offord (1989). "Reduction of Antisocial Behavior in Poor Children by Nonschool Skill Development." *Journal of Child Psychology and Psychiatry and Allied Disciplines*, 30, 737–750.

Jones, P.R. (1996). "Risk Prediction in Criminal Justice." In A.T. Harland (ed.), *Choosing Correctional Options that Work: Defining the Demand and Evaluating the Supply* (pp. 33–68). Thousand Oaks, CA: Sage.

Juby, H. & D.P. Farrington (2001). "Disentangling the Link between Disrupted Families and Delinquency." *British Journal of Criminology*, 41, 22–40.

Kanin, E.J. (1967). "Reference Groups and Sex Conduct Norm Violations." *The Sociological Quarterly*, 8, 495–504.

Karberg, J.C. & D.J. James (2005). *Substance Dependence, Abuse, and Treatment of Jail Inmates, 2000*. Washington, DC: Bureau of Justice Statistics.

Kassebaum, G., D. Ward & D. Wilner (1971). *Prison Treatment and Parole Survival: An Empirical Assessment*. New York: Wiley and Sons.

Kassin, S.M., A.V. Tubb, H.H. Hosch & A. Memon (2001). "On the 'General Acceptance' of Eyewitness Testimony Research." American Psychologist, 56, 405–416.

Katz, J. & W.J. Chambliss (1995). "Biology and Crime." In J.F. Sheley (ed.), *Criminology: A Contemporary Handbook* (pp. 275–303). Belmont, CA: Wadsworth.

Kaufman, A.S. & J.C. Kaufman (2001). "Emotional Intelligence as an Aspect of General Intelligence: What Would David Wechsler Say?" *Emotion*, 1, 258–264.

Kazemian, L. & M. Le Blanc (2004). "Exploring Patterns of Perpetration of Crime Across the Life Course: Offense and Offender-Based Viewpoints." *Journal of Contemporary Criminal Justice*, 9, 383–398.

Keeney, B.T. & K.M. Heide (1994). "Gender Differences in Serial Murders: A Preliminary Analysis." *Journal of Interpersonal Violence*, 9, 383–398.

Keller, J. & K. Wagner-Steh (2005). "A Guttman Scale for Empirical Prediction of Level of Domestic Violence." *Journal of Forensic Psychology Practice*, 5, 37–48.

Kelly, C.E. & W.N. Welsh (2008). "The Predictive Validity of the Level of Service Inventory-Revised for Drug-Involved Offenders." *Criminal Justice and Behavior*, 35, 819–831.

Kelly, W.R., T.S. Macy & D.P. Mears (2005). "Juvenile Referrals in Texas: An Assessment of Criminogenic Needs and the Gap between Needs and Services." *The Prison Journal*, 85, 467–489.

Kempinen, C.A. & M.C. Kurlychek (2003). "An Outcome Evaluation of Pennsylvania's Boot Camp: Does Rehabilitative Programming within a Disciplinary Setting Reduce Recidivism?" *Crime & Delinquency*, 49, 581–602.

Kennedy, S. & R. Serin (1999). "Examining Offender Readiness to Change and the Impact on Treatment Outcome." In P.M. Harris (ed.), *Research to Results: Effective Community Corrections* (pp. 215–230). Lanham, MD: American Correctional Association.

Kernberg, O.F. (1998). "The Psychotherapeutic Management of Psychopathic, Narcissistic, and Paranoid Transferences." In T. Millon, E. Simonsen, M. Birket-Smith & R.D. Davis (eds.), *Psychopathy: Violence, Criminal, and Violent Behavior*. New York: Guilford.

Kessler, R.C., B.E. Molnar, I.D. Feurer & M. Applebaum (2001). "Patterns and Mental Health Predictors of Domestic Violence in the United States: Results from the National Comorbidity Survey." *International Journal of Law and Psychiatry*, 24, 4–5.

Keyes, K.M. & D.S. Hasin (2008). "Socio-economic Status and Problem Alcohol Use: The Positive Relationship Between Income and the DSM-IV Alcohol Abuse Diagnosis." *Addiction*, 103, 1120–1130.

Kienlen, K.K. (1995). "An Obsessive and Potentially Dangerous Pursuit: A Case Study Approach to the Phenomenon of Stalking." Unpublished doctoral dissertation, Minnesota School of Professional Psychology, Minneapolis, MN.

Kiger, K. (1990). "The Darker Figure of Crime: The Serial Murder Enigma." In S. Egger (ed.), *Serial Murder: An Elusive Phenomenon* (pp. 35–52). New York: Praeger.

Kiloh, L.G. (1978). "The Neural Basis of Aggression and its Treatment by Psychosurgery." *Australian and New Zealand Journal of Psychiatry*, 12, 21–28.

Kimonis, E.R., P.J. Frick & C.T. Barry (2004). "Callous-Unemotional Traits and Delinquent Peer Affiliation." *Journal of Consulting and Clinical Psychology*, 72, 956–966.

Kimonis, E.R., P.J. Frick, N.W. Boris, A.T. Smyke, A.H. Cornell, J.M. Farrell & C.H. Zeanah (2006). "Callous-Unemotional Features, Behavioral Inhibition, and Parenting: Independent Predictors of Aggression in a High-Risk Preschool Sample." *Journal of Child and Family Studies*, 15, 745–756.

King, R.S., M. Mauer & M.C. Young (2005). *Incarceration and Crime: A Complex Relationship*. Washington, DC: The Sentencing Project.

Kirby, B.C. (1954). "Measuring Effects of Treatment of Criminals and Delinquents." *Sociology and Social Research*, 38, 368–374.

Kitzman, K.M., N.K. Gaylord, A.R. Holt & E.D. Kenny (2003). "Child Witnesses to Domestic Violence: A Meta-analytic Review." *Journal of Consulting and Clinical Psychology*, 71, 339–352.

Kivetz, R. & Y. Zheng (2006). "Determinants of Justification and Self-Control." *Journal of Experimental Psychology: General*, 135, 752–587.

Klag, S., F. O'Callaghan & P. Creed (2005). "The Use of Legal Coercion in the Treatment of Substance Abusers: An Overview and Critical Analysis of Thirty Years of Research." *Substance Use & Misuse*, 40, 1777–1795.

Klein, A.R. (1996). "Re-Abuse in a Population of Court-restrained Male Batterers: Why Restraining Orders Don't Work." In E.S. Buzawa & C.G. Buzawa (eds.), *Do Arrests and Restraining Orders Work?* (pp. 192–213). Thousand Oaks, CA: Sage.

Klein, A.R. & A. Crowe (2008). "Findings From an Outcome Examination of Rhode Island's Specialized Domestic Violence Probation Supervision Program: Do Specialized Supervision Programs of Batterers Reduce Reabuse?" *Violence Against Women*, 14, 226–246.

Klein, A.R. & T. Tobin (2008). "A Longitudinal Study of Arrested Batterers, 1995–2005: Career Criminals." *Violence Against Women*, 14, 136–157.

Klein, M.W. (1971). *Street Gangs and Street Workers*. Englewood Cliffs, NJ: Prentice Hall.

Klein, N.C., J.F. Alexander & B.V. Parsons (1977). "Impact of Family Systems Intervention on Recidivism and Sibling Delinquency: A Model of Primary Prevention and Program Evaluation." *Journal of Consulting and Clinical Psychology*, 3, 469–474.

Knack, W.A. (2009). "Psychotherapy and Alcoholics Anonymous: An Integrated Approach." *Journal of Psychotherapy Integration*, 19, 86–109.

Kohlberg, L. (1958). "The Development of Modes of Moral Thinking and Choice in the Years Ten to Sixteen." Unpublished doctoral dissertation, University of Chicago, IL.

Kohlberg, L. & D. Candee (1984). "The Relationship of Moral Judgment to Moral Action." In L. Kohlberg (ed.), *Essays in Moral Development, Vol. 2: The Psychology of Moral Development* (pp. 498–581). New York: Harper & Row.

Konty, M. (2005). "Microanomie: The Cognitive Foundations of the Relationship between Anomie and Deviance." *Criminology*, 43, 107–132.

Kraus, R.T. (1995). "An Enigmatic Personality: Case Report of a Serial Killer." *Journal of Orthomolecular Medicine*, 10, 11–24.

Kraus, S.J. (1995). "Attitudes and the Prediction of Behavior: A Meta-analysis of the Empirical Literature." *Personality and Social Psychology Bulletin*, 21, 58–75.

Krebs, D.L. & K. Denton (2005). "Toward a More Pragmatic Approach to Morality: A Critical Evaluation of Kohlberg's Model." *Psychological Review*, 112, 629–649.

Krentzman, A.R. (2007). "The Evidence Base of the Effectiveness of Alcoholics Anonymous: Implications for Social Work Practice." *Journal of Social Work Practice in Addictions*, 7, 27–48.

Kristofferson, K. (1977). "Me and Bobby McGee."

Kroner, D.G. & J.F. Mills (2001). "The Accuracy of Five Risk Appraisal Instruments in Predicting Institutional Misconduct and New Convictions." *Criminal Justice and Behavior*, 28, 471–489.

Kropp, P.R. (2004). "Some Questions Regarding Spousal Assault Risk Assessment." *Violence Against Women*, 10, 676–697.

Kropp, P.R. & S.D. Hart (2000). "The Spousal Assault Risk Assessment (SARA) Guide: Reliability and Validity in Adult Male Offenders." *Law and Human Behavior*, 24, 101–118.

Kropp, P.R., S.D. Hart, C.D. Webster & D. Eaves (1995). *Manual for the Spousal Assault Risk Assessment Guide*, 2nd ed. Vancouver: British Columbia Institute of Family Violence.

Krueger, R.F., T.E. Moffitt, A. Caspi, A. Bleske & P.A. Silva (1998). "Assortative Mating for Antisocial Behavior: Developmental and Methodological Implications." *Behavior Genetics*, 28, 173–186.

Kruttschnitt, C. & M. Dornfeld (1993). "Exposure to Family Violence: A Partial Explanation for Initial and Subsequent Levels of Delinquency?" *Criminal Behaviour and Mental Health*, 3, 61–75.

Kurki, L. (2000). "Restorative and Community Justice in the United States." In M. Tonry (ed.), *Crime and Justice: A Review of Research*, Vol. 27 (pp. 235–303). Chicago: University of Chicago Press.

Kuther, T.L. & S.A. Wallace (2003). "Community Violence and Sociomoral Development: An African American Cultural Perspective." *American Journal of Orthopsychiatry*, 73, 177–189.

Lab, S.P. & J.T. Whitehead (1990). "From 'Nothing Works' to 'The Appropriate Works': The Latest Stop on the Search for the Secular Grail." *Criminology*, 28, 405–417.

Labriola, M., M. Rempel & R.C. Davis (2008). "Do Batterer Programs Reduce Recidivism? Results from a Randomized Trial in the Bronx." *Justice Quarterly*, 25, 252–1282.

Lacourse, E., D.S. Nagin, F. Vitaro, S. Coté, L. Aresenault & R.E. Tremblay (2006). "Prediction of Early-Onset Deviant Peer Group Affiliation: A 12-Year Longitudinal Study." *Archives of General Psychiatry*, 63, 562–568.

Lahey, B.B., R.R. Gordon, R. Loeber, M. Stouthamer-Loeber & D.P. Farrington (1999). "Boys Who Join Gangs: A Prospective Study of Predictors of First Gang Entry." *Journal of Abnormal Child Psychology*, 27, 261–276.

Lahey, B.B., R. Loeber, J.D. Burke & B. Applegate (2005). "Predicting Future Antisocial Personality Disorder in Males from a Clinical Assessment in Childhood." *Journal of Consulting and Clinical Psychology*, 73, 389–399.

Lalumière, M.L. & V.L. Quinsey (1996). "Sexual Deviance, Antisociality, Mating Effort, and the Use of Sexually Coercive Behaviors." *Personality and Individual Differences*, 21, 33–38.

Landenberger, N.A. & M.W. Lipsey (2005). "The Positive Effects of Cognitive-Behavioral Programs for Offenders: A Meta-Analysis of Factors Associated with Effective Treatment." *Journal of Experimental Criminology*, 1, 451–476.

Lane, J., S. Turner, T. Fain & A. Sehgal (2005). "Evaluating an Experimental Intensive Juvenile Probation Program: Supervision and Official Outcomes." *Crime & Delinquency*, 51, 26–52.

Lange, J. (1929). *Crime as Destiny* (translated 1931). London: Unwin.

Langevin, R. (2003). "A Study of Psychosexual Characteristics of Sex Killers: Can We Identify Them Before It Is Too Late?" *International Journal of Offender Therapy and Comparative Criminology*, 47, 366–382.

Langevin, R. & S. Curnoe (2004). "The Use of Pornography During the Commission of Sexual Offenses". *International Journal of Offender Therapy and Comparative Criminology*, 48, 572–586.

Langevin, R., R.A. Lang & S. Curnoe (1998). "The Prevalence of Sex Offenders with Deviant Fantasies." *Journal of Interpersonal Violence*, 13, 315–327.

Langhinrichsen-Rohling, J. (2005). "Top 10 Greatest 'Hits': Important Findings and Future Directions for Intimate Partner Violence Research." *Journal of Interpersonal Violence*, 20, 108–118.

Lanier, C.S. & J.R. Acker (2004). "Capital Punishment, the Moratorium Movement, and Empirical Questions." *Psychology, Public Policy, and Law*, 10, 577–617.

Larsen, R.J. & Z. Prizmic (2004). "Affect Regulation." In R. Baumeister and K. Vohs (eds.), *Handbook of Self-regulation Research* (pp. 40–60). New York: Guilford.

Larsson, H., E. Viding & R. Plomin (2008). "Callous-Unemotional Traits and Antisocial Behavior: Genetic, Environmental and Early Parenting Characteristics." *Criminal Justice and Behavior*, 35, 197–211.

Latessa, E.J., F.T. Cullen & P. Gendreau (2002). "Beyond Correctional Quackery—Professionalism and the Possibility of Effective Treatment." *Federal Probation*, 66, 43–49.

Latimer, J. (2001). "A Meta-analytic Examination of Youth Delinquency, Family Treatment, and Recidivism." *Canadian Journal of Criminology*, 43, 237–253.

Latimer, J., C. Dowden & D. Muise (2005). "The Effectiveness of Restorative Justice Practices: A Meta-analysis." *The Prison Journal*, 85, 127–144.

Latimer, J., K. Morton-Bourgon & J. Chrétien (2006). *A Meta-Analytic Examination of Drug Treatment Courts: Do They Reduce Recidivism?* Ottawa: Department of Justice Canada.

Laub, J.H. & R.J. Sampson (1988). "Unraveling Families and Delinquency: A Reanalysis of the Gluecks' Data." *Criminology*, 26, 355–380.

Laub, J.H. & G.E. Vaillant (2000). "Delinquency and Mortality: A 50-Year Follow-Up Study of 1,000 Delinquent and Nondelinquent Boys." *American Journal of Psychiatry*, 157, 96–102.

LaViolette, A.D. & O.W. Barnett (2000). *It Could Happen to Anyone: Why Battered Women Stay*, 2nd ed. Thousand Oaks, CA: Sage.

Leary, M.R., E.S. Tambor, S. K. Terdal & D.L. Downs (1995). "Self-Esteem as an Interpersonal Monitor: The Sociometer Hypothesis." *Journal of Personality and Social Psychology*, 68, 518–530.

Le Blanc, M. & N. Lanctôt (1998). "Social and Psychological Characteristics of Gang Members According to the Gang Structure and It's Subcultural and Ethnic Make-up." *Journal of Gang Research*, 5, 15–28.

Le Blanc, M. & R. Loeber (1998). "Developmental Criminology Updated." In M. Tonry (ed.), *Crime and Justice: A Review of Research*, Vol. 23 (pp. 115–198). Chicago: University of Chicago Press.

Le Blanc, M., M. Ouimet & R.E. Tremblay (1988). "An Integrative Control Theory of Delinquent Behavior: A Validation 1976–1985." *Psychiatry*, 51, 164–176.

Lee, M. & N.M. Prentice (1988). "Interrelations of Empathy, Cognition, and Moral Reasoning with Dimensions of Juvenile Delinquency." *Journal of Abnormal Child Psychology*, 16, 127–139.

Leiber, M.J. & K.C. Fox (2005). "Race and the Impact of Detention on Juvenile Decision Making." *Crime & Delinquency*, 51, 470–497.

Leistico, A.-M., R.T. Salekin, J. DeCoster & R. Rogers (2008). "A Large-Scale Meta-Analysis Relating the Hare Measures of Psychopathy to Antisocial Conduct." *Law and Human Behavior*, 32, 28–45.

Leitenberg, H. (1976). *Handbook of Behavior Modification and Behavior Therapy*. New York: Prentice Hall.

LeMarquand, D. & R.E. Tremblay (2001). "Delinquency Prevention in Schools." In C.R. Hollin (ed.), *Handbook of Offender Assessment and Treatment* (pp. 237–258). Chichester, UK: John Wiley & Sons.

Lenton, R.L. (1995). "Power versus Feminist Theories of Wife Abuse." *Canadian Journal of Criminology*, 37, 305–330.

Leschied, A.W., D. Chiodo, E. Nowicki & S. Rodger (2008). "Childhood Predictors of Adult Criminality: A Meta-Analysis Drawn from the Prospective Longitudinal Literature." *Canadian Journal of Criminology and Criminal Justice*, 50, 435–467.

Leschied, A.W. & A. Cunningham (2002). *Seeking Effective Interventions for Serious Young Offenders: Interim Results of a Four-year Randomized Study of Multisystemic Therapy in Ontario, Canada*. London, Ontario: Centre for Children and Families in the Justice System.

Leve, L.D. & P. Chamberlain (2005). "Association with Delinquent Peers: Intervention Effects for Youth in the Juvenile Justice System." *Journal of Abnormal Child Psychology*, 33, 339–347.

Leve, L.D., P. Chamberlain & J.B. Reid (2005). "Intervention Outcomes for Girls Referred from Juvenile Justice: Effects on Delinquency." *Journal of Consulting and Clinical Psychology*, 73, 1181–1185.

Leventhal. T. & J. Brooks-Gunn (2000). "The Neighborhoods They Live In: The Effects of Neighborhood Residence on Child and Adolescent Outcomes." *Psychological Bulletin*, 126, 309–337.

Leyton, E. (1986). *Hunting Humans*. Toronto: McClelland and Stewart.

Leyton, E. (2005). *Hunting Humans: The Rise of the Modern Multiple Murderer*. Toronto: McClelland and Stewart.

Lickliter, R. & H. Honeycutt (2003). "Developmental Dynamics: Toward a Biologically Plausible Evolutionary Psychology." *Psychological Bulletin*, 129, 819–835.

Lightfoot, E. & M. Umbreit (2004). "An Analysis of State Statutory Provisions for Victim-Offender Mediation." *Criminal Justice Policy Review*, 15, 418–436.

Linden, R. & K. Fillmore (1981). "A Comparative Study of Delinquency Involvement." *Canadian Review of Sociology and Anthropology*, 18, 343–361.

Lindesmith, A.R. (1947). *Opiate Addiction*. Bloomington, IN: Principles Press.

Link, B.G., H. Andrews & F.T. Cullen (1992). "The Violent and Illegal Behavior of Mental Patients Reconsidered." *American Sociological Review*, 57, 275–292.

Link, B. & C. Steuve (1994). "Psychotic Symptoms and the Violent/illegal Behavior of Mental Patients Compared to Community Controls." In J. Monahan & H. Steadman (eds.), *Violence and Mental Disorder* (pp. 137–159). Chicago: University of Chicago Press.

Link, B.G., A. Steuve & J. Phelan (1998). "Psychotic Symptoms and Violent Behaviors: Probing the Components of 'Threat/Control-Override' Symptoms." *Social Psychiatry and Psychiatric Epidemiology*, 33, S55–S60.

Lipsey, M.W. (1989, November). "The Efficacy of Intervention for Juvenile Delinquency: Results from 400 Studies." Paper presented at the 41st annual meeting of the American Society of Criminology, Reno, Nevada.

Lipsey, M.W. (1995). "What Do We Learn from 400 Research Studies on the Effectiveness of Treatment with Juvenile Delinquency? In J. McGuire (ed.), *What Works: Reducing*

Reoffending, Guidelines from Research to Practice (pp. 63–78). West Sussex, UK: John Wiley & Sons.

Lipsey, M.W. (1999). "Can Rehabilitative Programs Reduce the Recidivism of Juvenile Offenders? An Inquiry into the Effectiveness of Practical Programs." *Virginia Journal of Social Policy and the Law*, 6, 611–641.

Lipsey, M.W. & J.H. Derzon (1998). "Predictors of Violent or Serious Delinquency in Adolescence and Early Adulthood: A Synthesis of Longitudinal Research." In R. Loeber & D.P. Farrington (eds.), *Serious and Violent Juvenile Offenders: Risk Factors and Successful Interventions* (pp. 86–105). Thousand Oaks, CA: Sage.

Lipsey, M.W. & D.B. Wilson (1998). "Effective Intervention for Serious Juvenile Offenders: A Synthesis of Research." In R. Loeber & D. P. Farrington (eds.), *Serious and Violent Juvenile Offenders: Risk Factors and Successful Interventions* (pp. 313–345). Thousand Oaks, CA: Sage.

Lipsey, M.W., D.B. Wilson, M.A. Cohen & J.H. Derzon (1997). "Is There a Causal Relationship Between Alcohol Use and Violence? A Synthesis of Evidence." In M. Galanter (ed.), *Recent Developments in Alcoholism, Vol. 13: Alcoholism and Violence*. New York: Plenum Press.

Lipton, D., R. Martinson & J. Wilks (1975). *The Effectiveness of Correctional Treatment: A Survey of Treatment Evaluation Studies*. New York: Praeger.

Listwan, S.J. (2009). "Reentry for Serious and Violent Offenders: An Analysis of Program Attrition." *Criminal Justice Policy Review*, 20, 154–169.

Listwan, S.J., J.L. Sundt, A.M. Holsinger & E J. Latessa (2003). "The Effect of Drug Court Programming on Recidivism: The Cincinnati Experience." *Crime & Delinquency*, 49, 389–411.

Litt, M.D., R.M. Kadden, E. Kabela-Cormier & N.M. Petry (2009). "Changing Network Support for Drinking: Network Support Project 2-Year Follow-Up." *Journal of Consulting and Clinical Psychology*, 77, 229–242.

Llewellyn, J.J. & R. Howse (1999). *Restorative Justice: A Conceptual Framework*. Ottawa: Law Commission of Canada.

Loeber, R., D.L. Homish, E.H. Wei, D. Pardini, A.M. Crawford, D.P. Farrington, M. Stouthamer-Loeber., J. Creemers, S.A. Koehler & R. Rosenfeld (2005). "The Prediction of Violence and Homicide in Young Men." *Journal of Consulting and Clinical Psychology*, 73, 1074–1088.

Loeber, R. & M. Stouthamer-Loeber (1987). "Prediction." In H.C. Quay (ed.), *Handbook of juvenile Delinquency* (pp. 325–382). New York: Wiley

Loeber, R. & M. Stouthamer-Loeber (1996). The Development of Offending." *Criminal Justice and Behavior*, 23, 12–24.

Logan, C.H. (1972). "Evaluation Research in Crime and Delinquency: A Reappraisal." *Journal of Criminal Law, Criminology and Police Science*, 63, 378–387.

Logan, C.H. & G.G. Gaes (1993). "Meta-analysis and the Rehabilitation of Punishment." *Justice Quarterly*, 10, 245–263.

Logan, C.H., G.G. Gaes, M. Harer, C.A. Innes, L. Karacki & W.G. Saylor (1991). *Can Meta-analysis Save Correctional Rehabilitation?* Washington, DC: Federal Bureau of Prisons.

Lombroso, C. (1895/2004). "Criminal Anthropology: Its Origin and Application." In D. M. Horton & K.E. Rich (eds.), *The Criminal Anthropological Writings of Cesare Lombroso*

Published in the English Language Periodical Literature During the Late 19th and Early 20th Centuries (pp. 63–82). Lewiston, NY: Edwin Mellen Press.

Lombroso, C. & W. Ferrero (1895/1980). *The Female Offender*. Littleton, CO: Fred B. Rothman & Co.

Longshore, D., A. Hawken, D. Urada & M.D. Anglin (2006). *SACPA Cost Analysis Report (First and Second Years)*. Sacramento: California Department of Alcohol and Drug Programs.

Longshore, D., S. Turner & J.A. Stein (1996). "Self-Control in a Criminal Sample: An Examination of Construct Validity." *Criminology*, 43, 209–228.

Looman, J., J. Abracen & T.P. Nicholaichuk (2000). "Recidivism among Treated Sexual Offenders and Matched Controls: Data from the Regional Treatment Centre (Ontario)." *Journal of Interpersonal Violence*, 15, 279–290.

Looman, J., I. Dickie & J. Abracen (2005). "Responsivity Issues in the Treatment of Sexual Offenders." *Trauma, Violence, and Abuse*, 6, 330–353.

Lorber, M.F. (2004). "Psychophysiology of Aggression, Psychopathy, and Conduct Problems: A Meta-analysis." *Psychological Bulletin*, 130, 531–552.

Lösel, F. (1995). "The Efficacy of Correctional Treatment: A Review and Synthesis of Meta-evaluations." In J. McGuire (ed.), *What Works: Reducing Reoffending* (pp. 79–111). Chichester, UK: John Wiley & Sons.

Lösel, F. & M. Schmucker (2005). "The Effectiveness of Treatment for Sexual Offenders: A Comprehensive Meta-analysis." *Journal of Experimental Criminology*, 1, 117–146.

Lovell, D., G.J. Gagliardi & P. Phipps (2005). *Washington's Dangerous Mentally Ill Offender Law: Was Community Safety Increase?* Olympia: Washington State Institute for Public Policy.

Lovins, B., C.T. Lowenkamp & E.J. Latessa (2009). "Applying the Risk Principle to Sex Offenders: Can Treatment Make Some Offenders Worse?" *The Prison Journal*, 89, 344–357.

Lowenkamp, C.T. (2004). "Correctional Program Integrity and Treatment Effectiveness: A Multi-site, Program-level Analysis." Unpublished doctoral dissertation, University of Cincinnati, Cincinnati, Ohio.

Lowenkamp, C.T. & K. Bechtel (2007). "The Predictive Validity of the LSI-R on a Sample of Offenders Drawn from the Records of the Iowa Department of Corrections Data Management System." *Federal Probation*, 71, 25–29.

Lowenkamp, C.T., A.M. Holsinger, L. Brusman-Lovins & E.J. Latessa (2004). "Assessing the Inter-rater Agreement of the Level of Service Inventory-Revised." *Federal Probation*, 68, 34–38.

Lowenkamp, C.T., A.M. Holsinger & E.J. Latessa (2005). "Are Drug Courts Effective: A Meta-analytic Review." *Journal of Community Corrections*, Fall, 5–10, 28.

Lowenkamp, C.T., D. Hubbar, M.D. Makarios & E.J. Latessa (2009). "A Quasi-Experimental Evaluation of Thinking for a Change: A 'Real World' Application." *Criminal Justice and Behavior*, 36, 137–146.

Lowenkamp, C.T., E.J. Latessa & A.M. Holsinger (2004). "Empirical Evidence on the Importance of Training and Experience in Using the Level of Service Inventory–Revised." *Topics in Community Corrections—2004*. Washington, DC: National Institute of Corrections.

Lowenkamp, C.T., E.J. Latessa & A.M. Holsinger (2006). "The Risk Principle in Action: What Have We Learned from 13,676 Offenders and 97 Correctional Programs?" *Crime & Delinquency*, 52, 77–93.

Lowenkamp, C.T., E.J. Latessa & P. Smith (2006). "Does Correctional Program Quality Really Matter? The Impact of Adhering to the Principles of Effective Interventions?" *Criminology & Public Policy*, 5, 575–594.

Loza, W. & A. Loza-Fanous (2001). "The Effectiveness of the Self-appraisal Questionnaire in Predicting Offenders' Postrelease Outcome: A Comparison Study." *Criminal Justice and Behavior*, 28, 105–121.

Loza, W., A. MacTavish & A. Loza-Fanous (2007). "A Nine-Year Follow-Up Study on the Predictive Validity of the Self-appraisal Questionnaire for Predicting Violent and Nonviolent Recidivism." *Journal of Interpersonal Violence*, 22, 1144–1155.

Luo, S. & E.C. Klohnen (2005). "Assortative Mating and Marital Quality in Newlyweds: A Couple-centered Approach." *Journal of Personality and Social Psychology*, 88, 304–326.

Luong, D. (2007). "Risk Assessment and Community Management: The Relationship Between Implementation Quality and Recidivism." Master's Dissertation, Department of Psychology, University of Saskatchewan, Saskatoon, Saskatchewan.

Lurigio, A.J., Y.I. Cho, J.A. Swartz, T.P. Johnson, I. Graf & L. Pickup (2003). "Standardized Assessment of Substance-related, Other Psychiatric, and Comorbid Disorders among Probationers." *International Journal of Offender Therapy and Comparative Criminology*, 47, 630–652.

Lussier, P., J. Proulx & M. Le Blanc (2005). "Criminal Propensity, Deviant Sexual Interests and Criminal Activity of Sexual Aggressors against Women: A Comparison of Explanatory Models." *Criminology*, 43, 249–281.

Lykken, D.T. (1995). *The Antisocial Personalities*. Hillsdale, NJ: Lawrence Erlbaum.

Lynam, D.R. (1997). "Pursuing the Psychopath: Capturing the Fledgling Psychopath in the Nomological Net." *Journal of Abnormal Psychology*, 106, 425–438.

Lynam, D.R., A. Caspi, T.E. Moffitt, P.-O. H. Wikström, R. Loeber & S. Novak (2000). "The Interaction between Impulsivity and Neighborhood Context on Offending: The Effects of Impulsivity in Poorer Neighborhoods." *Journal of Abnormal Psychology*, 109, 563–574.

Lynam, D.R. & K.J. Derefinko (2006). "Psychopathy and Personality." In C.J. Patrick (ed.), *Handbook of Psychopathy* (pp. 133–155). New York: Guilford.

Lynam, D.R., R. Loeber & M. Stouthamer-Loeber (2008). "The Stability of Psychopathy from Adolescence into Adulthood." *Criminal Justice and Behavior*, 35, 228–243.

MacKenzie, D.L. & G.S. Armstrong (eds.) (2004). *Correctional Boot Camps: Military Basic Training or a Model for Corrections?* Thousand Oaks, CA: Sage.

MacKenzie, D.L., R. Brame, D. McDowall & C. Souryal (1995). "Boot Camp Prisons and Recidivism in Eight States." *Criminology*, 33, 327–357.

MacLean, B.D. (1986). "Critical Criminology and Some Limitations of Traditional Inquiry." In B.D. MacLean (ed.), *The Political Economy of Crime* (pp. 1–20). Scarborough, Ontario: Prentice Hall.

Maes, H. H., J.L. Silberg, M.C., Neale & L.J. Eaves (2007). "Genetic and Cultural Transmission of Antisocial Behavior: An Extended Twin Parent Model." *Twin Research and Human Genetics*, 10, 136–150.

Magdol, L., T.E. Moffitt, A. Caspi., D.L. Newman, J. Fagan & P.A. Silva (1997). "Gender Differences in Partner Violence in a Birth Cohort of 21-year-olds: Bridging the Gap between Clinical and Epidemiological Approaches." *Journal of Consulting and Clinical Psychology*, 65, 68–78.

Mair, G. (2005). "Electronic Monitoring in England and Wales: Evidenced-based or Not?" *Criminal Justice*, 5, 257–277.

Mair, G., L. Burke & S. Taylor (2006). " 'The Worst Tax Form You've Ever Seen?' Probation Officers' Views about OASys." *Probation Journal*, 53, 7–23.

Mak, A.S. (1990). "Testing a Psychological Control Theory of Delinquency." *Criminal Justice and Behavior*, 17, 215–230.

Makkai, T. & J. Payne (2005). "Illicit Drug Use and Offending Histories: A Study of Male Incarcerated Offenders in Australia." *Probation Journal*, 52, 153–168.

Maletzky, B.W. (1991). *Treating the Sexual Offender*. Newbury Park, CA: Sage.

Maletzky, B.M., A. Tolan & B. McFarland (2006). "The Oregon Depo-Provera Program: A Five Year Follow-Up." *Sexual Abuse*, 18, 303–316.

Malouff, J.M., S.E. Rooke & N.S. Schutte (2008). "The Heritability of Human Behavior: Results of Aggregating Meta-analyses." *Current Psychology*, 27, 153–161.

Manchak, S.M., J.L. Skeem & K.S. Douglas (2008). "Utility of the Revised Level of Service Inventory (LSI-R) in Predicting Recidivism After Long-Term Incarceration." *Law and Human Behavior*, 32, 477–488.

Manchak, S.M., J.L. Skeem, K.S. Douglas & M. Siranosian (2008). "Does Gender Moderate the Predictive Utility of the Revised Level of Service Inventory (LSI-R) for Serious Violent Offenders?" *Criminal Justice and Behavior*, 36, 425–442.

Mann, K. (2004). "Pharmacotherapy of Alcohol Dependence: A Review of the Clinical Data." *CNS Drugs*, 18, 485–504.

Mannheim, H. (1965). *Comparative Criminology*. Boston: Houghton Mifflin.

Marcus, D.K., S.L. John & J.F. Edens (2004). "A Taxometric Analysis of Psychopathic Personality." *Journal of Abnormal Psychology*, 113, 626–635.

Mark, V.H. & F.R. Ervin (1970). *Violence and the Brain*. Hagerstown, MD: Harper & Row.

Marlatt, A. & J. Gordon (1980). "Determinants of Relapse: Implications for the Maintenance of Behavior Change." In P.O. Davidson & S.M. Davidson (eds.), *Behavioral Medicine: Changing Health Lifestyles* (pp. 410–452). New York: Bruner-Mazel.

Marlowe, D.B., D.S. Festinger, P.A. Lee, K.L. Dugosh & K.M. Benasutti (2006). "Matching Judicial Supervision in Clients' Risk Status in Drug Court." *Crime & Delinquency*, 52, 52–76.

Marques, J.K., M. Wiederanders, D.M. Day, C. Nelson & A. van Ommeren (2005). "Effects of a Relapse Prevention Program on Sexual Recidivism: Final Results from California's Sex Offender Treatment and Evaluation Project (SOTEP)." *Sexual Abuse: A Journal of Research and Treatment*, 17, 79–107.

Marshall, T.F. & S. Merry (1990). *Crime and Victim Accountability: Victim/Offender Mediation in Practice*. London: Home Office.

Marshall, W.L. (1996). "Assessment, Treatment, and Theorizing about Sex Offenders: Developments During the Past Twenty Years and Future Directions." *Criminal Justice and Behavior*, 23, 162–199.

Marshall, W.L. & H. Barbaree (1990). "Outcome of Comprehensive Cognitive-Behavioral Treatment Programs." In W.L. Marshall, D.R. Laws & H.E. Barbaree (eds.), *Handbook of Sexual Assault: Issues, Theories, and Treatment of the Offender* (pp. 363–385). New York: Plenum.

Marshall, W.L., R. Jones, T. Ward, P. Johnston & H.E. Barbaree (1991). "Treatment Outcome with Sex Offenders." *Clinical Psychology Review*, 11, 465–485.

Martens, W.H. & G.B. Palermo (2005). "Loneliness and Associated Violent Antisocial Behavior: Analysis of the Case Reports of Jeffrey Dahmer and Dennis Nilsen." *International Journal of Offender Therapy and Comparative Criminology*, 49, 298–307.

Martin, C., E. Player & S. Liriano (2003). "Results of Evaluations of RAPt Drug Treatment Programme." In M. Ramsay (ed.)., *Prisoner Drug Use and Treatment: Seven Research Studies, Home Office Research Study 267* (pp. 97–112). London: Home Office.

Martin, S.E., K. Bryant & N. Fitzgerald (2001). "Self-Reported Alcohol Use and Abuse by Arrestees in the 1998 Arrestee Drug Abuse Monitoring Program." *Alcohol Research & Health*, 25, 72–79.

Martinson, R. (1974). "What Works?—Questions and Answers about Prison Reform." *The Public Interest*, 35, 22–54.

Martinson, R. (1976). "California Research at the Crossroads." *Crime & Delinquency*, 22, 178–191.

Martinson, R. (1979). "New Findings, New Views: A Note of Caution Regarding Prison Reform." *Hofstra Law Review*, 7, 243–258.

Maruna, S. (2001). *Making Good: How Ex-convicts Reform and Rebuild Their Lives*. Washington, DC: American Psychological Association.

Maruna, S. & H. Copes (2005). "What Have We Learned from Five Decades of Neutralization Research?" In M. Tonry (ed.), *Crime and Justice: A Review of Research*, Vol. 32 (pp. 221–320). Chicago: University of Chicago Press.

Mason, D.A. & P.J. Frick (1994). "The Heritability of Antisocial Behavior: A Meta-analysis of Twin and Adoption Studies." *Journal of Psychopathology and Behavioral Assessment*, 16, 301–323.

Mathiesen, T. (1998). "Selective Incapacitation Revisited." *Law and Human Behavior*, 22, 455–469.

Matseuda, R.L. (1982). "Testing Control Theory and Differential Association: A Causal Modeling Approach." *American Sociological Review*, 47, 489–504.

Matseuda, R.L. & K. Anderson (1998). "The Dynamics of Delinquent Peers and Delinquent Behavior." *Criminology*, 36, 269–308.

Matson, J.L. & A.E. Kazdin (1981). "Punishment in Behavior Modification: Pragmatic, Ethical, and Legal Issues." *Clinical Psychology Review*, 1, 197–210.

Matthews, S.K. & R. Agnew (2008). "Extending Deterrence Theory: Do Delinquent Peers Condition the Relationship between Perceptions of Getting Caught and Offending?" *Journal of Research in Crime and Delinquency*, 45, 91–118.

Matza, D. (1964). *Delinquency and Drift*, 2nd ed. New York: Wiley.

Maung, N.A. & N. Hammond (2000). *Risk of Re-offending and Needs Assessment: The User's Perspective*. Home Office Research Study 216. London: Home Office.

Maxwell, C., J.H. Garner & J.A. Fagan (2001). *The Effects of Arrest on Intimate Partner Violence: New Evidence for the Spouse Assault Replication Program*. Washington, DC: U.S. National Institute of Justice.

Maxwell, G.M. & A. Morris (1994). "The New Zealand Model of Family Group Conferences." In C. Adler & J. Wundersitz (eds.), *Family Conferencing and Juvenile Justice: The Way Forward or Misplaced Optimism?* (pp. 15–43). Canberra: Australian Institute of Criminology.

Maxwell, G., A. Morris & H. Hayes (2006). "Conferencing and Restorative Justice." In D. Sullivan & L. Tifft (eds.), *Handbook of Restorative Justice* (pp. 151–160). New York: Routledge.

Mayer, J.D. (2005). "A Tale of Two Visions: Can a New View of Personality Help Integrate Psychology?" *American Psychologist*, 60, 294–307.

Mayer, R.R. (1972). *Social Planning and Social Change*. Englewood Cliffs, NJ: Prentice Hall.

Mazerolle, P., R. Brame, R. Paternoster, A. Piquero & C. Dean (2000). "Onset Age, Persistence, and Offending Versatility: Comparisons across Gender." *Criminology*, 38, 1143–1172.

McClennen, J.C. (2005). "Domestic Violence between Same-gender Partners: Recent Findings and Future Research." *Journal of Interpersonal Violence*, 20, 149–154.

McCloskey, L.A., A.J. Figueredo & M.P. Koss (1995). "The Effects of Systemic Family Violence on Children's Mental Health." *Child Development*, 66, 1239–1261.

McCold, P. (2000). "Toward a Holistic Vision of Restorative Juvenile Justice: A Reply to the Maximalist Model." *Contemporary Justice Review*, 3, 357–414.

McCold, P. (2006). "The Recent History of Restorative Justice: Mediations, Circles, and Conferencing." In D. Sullivan & L. Tifft (eds.), *Handbook of Restorative Justice* (pp. 23–51). New York: Routledge.

McCold, P. & B. Wachtel (1998). *Restorative Policing Experiment: The Bethlehem Pennsylvania Police Family Group Conferencing Project*. Pipersville, PA: Community Service Foundation.

McCord, J. (1997). "Discipline and the Use of Sanctions." *Aggression and Violent Behavior*, 2, 313–319.

McCord, J. (1999). "Interventions: Punishment, Diversion, and Alternative Routes to Crime Prevention." In AK. Hess & I.B. Weiner (eds.), *The Handbook of Forensic Psychology*, 2nd ed. (pp. 559–579). New York: Wiley.

McCrady, B.S., E.E. Epstein & C.W. Kahler (2004). "Alcoholics Anonymous and Relapse Prevention as Maintenance Strategies after Conjoint Behavioral Alcohol Treatment for Men: 19-month Outcomes." *Journal of Consulting and Clinical Psychology*, 72, 870–878.

McCrae, R.R. & P.T. Costa Jr. (1999). "A Five-factor Theory of Personality." In L. Pervin & O.P. John (eds.), *Handbook of Personality*, 2nd ed. (pp. 139–153). New York: Guilford.

McCrae, R.R., P.T. Costa Jr., F. Ostendorf, A., M. Hrebickova, M.D. Avia, J. Sanz, M.L. Sanchez-Bernardos, M.E. Kusdil, R. Woodfield, P.R. Saunders & P.B. Smith (2000). "Nature over Nurture: Temperament, Personality, and Life Span Development." *Journal of Personality and Social Psychology*, 78, 173–176.

McEwan, T., P.E. Mullen & R. Purcell (2007). "Identifying Risk Factors in Stalking: A Review of Current Research." *International Journal of Law and Psychiatry*, 30, 1–9.

McEwan, T., P.E. Mullen & R. MacKenzie (2007). "Anti-Stalking Legislation in Practice: Are We Meeting Community Needs?" *Psychiatry, Psychology and Law*, 14, 207–217.

McEwan, T., P.E. Mullen & R. MacKenzie (2009). "A Study of the Predictors of Persistence in Stalking Situations" *Law and Human Behavior* , 33, 149–158.

McGloin, J.M. & L. O'Neill Shermer (2009). "Self-Control and Deviant Peer Network Structure." *Journal of Research in Crime and Delinquency*, 46, 35–72.

McGuire, J. (2001). "Methods to Reduce the Risk of Re-offending: International Perspectives." Invited Address to the "What Works" Seminar, Helsinki, Finland, October.

McGuire, J. (2002). "Integrating Findings from Research Reviews." In J. McGuire (ed.), *Offender Rehabilitation and Treatment: Effective Programmes and Policies to Reduce Reoffending* (pp. 3–38). West Sussex, UK: John Wiley & Sons.

McGuire, J. (2004). *Understanding Psychology and Crime: Perspectives on Theory and Action*. Berkshire, UK: Open University Press.

McGuire, J., C.A.L. Bilby, R.M. Hatcher, C.R. Hollin, J. Hounsome & E.J. Palmer (2008). "Evaluation of Structured Cognitive-Behavioural Treatment Programmes in Reducing Criminal Recidivism." *Journal of Experimental Criminology*, 4, 21–40.

McMurran, M. (2009). "Motivational Interviewing with Offenders: A Systematic Review." *Legal and Criminological Psychology*, 14, 83–100.

Mears, D.P. (2003). "Research and Interventions to Reduce Domestic Violence Revictimization." *Trauma, Violence and Abuse*, 4, 127–147.

Mednick, S.A. (1977). "A Bio-social Theory of the Learning of Law-abiding Behavior." In S. A. Mednick & K. O. Christiansen (eds.), *Biosocial Basis of Criminal Behavior* (pp. 1–8). New York: Gardner.

Mednick, S.A., W.F. Gabrielli & B. Hutchings (1983). "Genetic Influences in Criminal Convictions: Evidence from an Adoption Cohort." In K.T. Van Dusen & S.A. Mednick (eds.), *Prospective Studies of Crime and Delinquency* (pp. 39–56). Hingham, MA: Kluwer Nijhoff.

Mednick, S.A., W.F. Gabrielli & B. Hutchings (1984). "Genetic Influences in Criminal Convictions: Evidence from an Adoption Cohort." *Science*, 234, 891–894.

Mednick, S.A., W F. Gabrielli & B. Hutchings (1987). "Genetic Factors in the Etiology of Criminal Behavior." In S.A. Mednick, T.E. Moffitt & S.A. Stack (eds.), *The Causes of Crime: New Biological Approaches* (pp. 74–91). Cambridge, UK: Cambridge University Press.

Meehan, K.E. (2000). "California's Three-strikes Law: The First Six Years." *Corrections Management Quarterly*, 4, 22–33.

Megargee, E.I. (1982). "Psychological Determinants and Correlates of Criminal Violence." In M.E. Wolfgang & N.A. Weinder (eds.), *Criminal Violence* (pp. 81–170). Beverly Hills, CA: Sage.

Meichenbaum, D.A. (1977). *Cognitive-Behavior Modification: An Integrative Approach*. New York: Plenum.

Meier, M.H., W.S. Slutske, S. Arndt & R.J. Cadoret (2008). "Impulsive and Callous Traits Are More Strongly Associated With Delinquent Behavior in Higher Risk Neighborhoods Among Boys and Girls." *Journal of Abnormal Psychology*, 117, 377–385.

Meloy, J.R. (1992). "Discussion of 'On the Predictability of Violent Behavior: Considerations and Guidelines.'" *Journal of Forensic Sciences*, 37, 949–950.

Meloy, J.R. (1996). "Stalking (Obsessional Following): A Review of Some Preliminary Studies." *Aggression and Violent Behavior*, 1, 147–162.

Meloy, J.R. (ed.) (1998). *The Psychology of Stalking: Clinical and Forensic Perspectives*. New York: Academic Press.

Merritt, N., T. Fain & S. Turner (2006). "Oregon's Get Tough Sentencing Reform: A Lesson in Justice System Adaptation." *Criminology & Public Policy*, 5, 5–36.

Merton, R.K. (1938). "Social Structure and Anomie." *American Sociological Review*, 3, 672–682.

Merton, R.K. (1957). *Social Theory and Social Structure*. New York: Free Press.

Messina, N., D. Farabee & R. Rawson (2003). "Treatment Responsivity of Cocaine-Dependent Patients with Antisocial Personality Disorder to Cognitive-Behavioral and Contingency Management Interventions." *Journal of Consulting and Clinical Psychology*, 71, 320–329.

Meyers, R.J. & J.E. Smith (1995). *Clinical Guide to Alcohol Treatment: The Community Reinforcement Approach*. New York: Guilford.

Mikulincer, M. (1994). *Human Learned Helplessness: A Coping Perspective*. New York: Plenum.

Miller, J.D. & D.R. Lynam (2001). "Structural Models of Personality and their Relation to Antisocial Behavior: A Meta-analytic Review." *Criminology*, 39, 765–792.

Miller, J.D., D.R. Lynam & C. Leukefeld (2003). "Examining Antisocial Behavior Through the Lens of the Five Factor Model of Personality." *Aggressive Behavior*, 29, 497–514.

Miller, W.B. (1958). "Lower Class Culture as a Generating Milieu of Gang Delinquency." *Journal of Social Issues*, 14, 5–19.

Miller, W.R. & K.M. Carroll (2006). *Rethinking Substance Abuse: What the Science Shows, and What We Should Do about It*. New York: Guilford.

Miller, W.R., R.J. Meyers & J.S. Tonigan (1999). "Engaging the Unmotivated in Treatment for Alcohol Problems: A Comparison of Three Strategies for Intervention Through Family Members." *Journal of Consulting and Clinical Psychology*, 67, 688–697.

Mills, J.F., D. Anderson & D.G. Kroner (2004). "The Antisocial Attitudes and Associates of Sex Offenders." *Criminal Behaviour and Mental Health*, 14, 134–145.

Mills, J.F. & D.G. Kroner (2006). "Impression Management and Self-Report among Violent Offenders." *Journal of Interpersonal Violence*, 21, 178–192.

Mills, J.F., D.G. Kroner & T. Hemmati (2005). "The Measures of Criminal Attitudes and Associates (MCAA): The Prediction of General and Violent Recidivism." *Criminal Justice and Behavior*, 32, 656–585.

Minor, W.W. (1981). "Techniques of Neutralization: A Reconceptualization and Empirical Examination." *Research in Crime and Delinquency*, 18, 295–318.

Mischel, W. (1968). *Personality and Assessment*. New York: Wiley.

Mischel, W. (2004). "Toward an Integrative Science of the Person." *Annual Review of Psychology*, 55, 1–22.

Mischel, W. & O. Ayduk (2002). "Self-regulation in a Cognitive-Affective Personality System: Attentional Control in the Service of the Self." *Self and Identity*, 1, 113–120.

Mischel, W. & Y. Shoda (1998). "Reconciling Processing Dynamics and Personality Dispositions." *Annual Review of Psychology*, 49, 229–258.

Mischel, W. & Y. Shoda (2006). "Applying Meta-Theory to Achieve Generalisability and Precision in Personality Science." *Applied Psychology: An International Review*, 55, 439–452.

Mischel, W., Y. Shoda & R. Mendoza-Denton (2002). "Situation-Behavior Profiles as a Locus of Consistency in Personality." *Current Directions in Psychological Science*, 11, 50–54.

Mitchell, O. (2005). "A Meta-analysis of Race and Sentencing Research: Explaining the Inconsistencies." *Journal of Quantitative Criminology*, 21, 439–466.

Mobley, M.J. (1999). "Psychotherapy with Criminal Offenders." In A.K. Hess & I.B. Weiner (eds.), *The Handbook of Forensic Psychology*, 2nd ed. (pp. 603–639). New York: Wiley.

Moffitt, T.E. (1983). "The Learning Theory Model of Punishment: Implications for Delinquency Deterrence." *Criminal Justice and Behavior*, 10, 131–158.

Moffitt, T.E. (1987). "Parental Mental Disorder and Offspring Criminal Behavior: An Adoption Study." *Psychiatry*, 50, 346–360.

Moffitt, T.E. (1990). "The Neuropsychology of Juvenile Delinquency." In M. Tonry & N. Morris (eds.), *Crime and Justice: A Review of Research*, Vol. 8 (pp. 99–169). Chicago: University of Chicago Press.

Moffitt, T.E. (1993). " 'Life-Course-Persistent' and 'Adolescent-Limited' Antisocial Behavior: A Developmental Taxonomy." *Psychological Review*, 100, 674–701.

Moffitt, T.E. (1997). "Adolescence-Limited and Life-Course-Persistent Offending: A Complementary Pair of Developmental Theories." In T.P. Thornberry (ed.), *Developmental Theories of Criminal Behavior* (pp. 11–54). New Brunswick, NJ: Transaction.

Moffitt, T.E. (2003). "Life-Course-Persistent and Adolescence-Limited Antisocial Behavior: A 10-year Research Review and a Research Agenda." In B.A. Lahey, T.E. Moffitt & A. Caspi (eds.), *Causes of Conduct Disorder and Juvenile Delinquency*. New York: Guilford.

Moffitt, T.E., A. Caspi, N. Dickson, P. Silva & W. Stanton (1996). "Childhood-Onset versus Adolescent-Onset Antisocial Conduct Problems in Males: Natural History from Ages 3 to 18 Years." *Development and Psychopathology*, 8, 399–424.

Moffitt, T.E., A. Caspi, H. Harrington & B.J. Milne (2002). "Males on the Life-Course-Persistent and Adolescent-Limited Antisocial Pathways: Follow-up at Age 26 years." *Development and Psychopathology*, 14, 179–207.

Moffitt, T.E., D.R. Lynam & P.A. Silva (1994). "Neuropsychological Tests Predicting Persistent Male Delinquency." *Criminology*, 32, 277–300.

Moffitt, T.E. & P.A. Silva (1988). "IQ and Delinquency: A Direct Test of the Differential Detection Hypothesis." *Journal of Abnormal Psychology*, 97, 330–333.

Monahan, J. (ed.) (1980). *Who is the Client?: The Ethics of Psychological Intervention in the Criminal Justice System*. Washington, DC: American Psychological Association.

Montmarquette, C. & M. Nerlove (1985). "Deterrence and Delinquency: An Analysis of Individual Data." *Journal of Quantitative Criminology*, 1, 37–58.

Moody, C.E. & T.B. Marvell (1996). "The Uncertain Timing of Innovations in Time Series: Minnesota Sentencing Guidelines and Jail Sentences—A Comment." *Criminology*, 34, 257–267.

Moos, R.H. (2008). "Active Ingredients of Substance Use-Focused Self-Help Groups." *Addiction*, 103, 387–396.

Morash, M. (2009). "A Great Debate Over Using the Level of Service Inventory-Revised (LSI-R with Women Offenders." *Criminology & Public Policy*, 8, 173–181.

Morgan, R., D. Flora, D. Kroner, J. Mills, F. Varghese & J. Stefan (2007). "Treatment of Mentally Disordered Offenders: A Research Synthesis." Paper presented at the North American Conference of Correctional and Criminal Justice Psychology, Ottawa, Ontario, June.

Morris, A. & G. Maxwell (1998). "Restorative Justice in New Zealand: Family Group Conferences as a Case Study." *Western Criminology Review*, 1. See http://wcr.sonoma.edu/v1n1/morris.html.

Morris, N. & M. Tonry (1990). *Between Prison and Probation: Intermediate Punishment in a Rational Sentencing System*. New York: Oxford University Press.

Moskowitz, A. (2004). "Dissociation and Violence: A Review of the Literature." *Trauma, Violence, and Abuse*, 5, 21–46.

Mossman, D. (1994). "Assessing Predictions of Violence: Being Accurate about Accuracy." *Journal of Consulting and Clinical Psychology*, 62, 783–792.

Motiuk, L.L., J. Bonta & D.A. Andrews (1986). "Classification in Correctional Halfway Houses: The Relative and Incremental Predictive Criterion Validities of the Megargee-MMPI and LSI Systems." *Criminal Justice and Behavior*, 13, 33–46.

Motiuk, L.L., J. Bonta & D.A. Andrews (1990). "Dynamic Predictive Criterion Validity in Offender Assessment." Paper presented at the Canadian Psychological Association Annual Convention, Ottawa, Ontario, June.

Mullen, P.E. (2006). "Schizophrenia and Violence: From Correlations to Preventive Strategies." *Advances in Psychiatric Treatment*, 12, 239–248.

Mullen, P.E. (2009). "Stalking." In M. Gelder, J. Lopez-Ibor, N. Andreasen & J. Geddes (eds.), *New Oxford Textbook of Psychiatry*, 2nd ed. (Part II, Section 5.3, pp. 22–28). New York: Oxford University Press.

Mullen, P.E., D.V. James, J.R. Meloy, M.T. Pathé, F.R. Farnham, L. Preston & B. Darnley (2008). "The Role of Psychotic Illnesses in Attacks on Public Figures." In J.R. Meloy, L. Sheridan & J. Hoffmann (eds.), *Stalking, Threatening, and Attacking Public Figures* (pp. 55–82). New York: Oxford University Press.

Mullen, P.E., R. MacKenzie, J.R.P. Ogloff, M. Pathé, T. McEwan & R. Purcell (2006). "Assessing and Managing the Risks in the Stalking Situation." *Journal of the American Academy of Psychiatry and the Law*, 34, 439–450.

Mullen, P.E. & M. Pathé (2002). "Stalking." In M. Tonry (ed.), *Crime and Justice: A Review of Research*, Vol. 29 (pp. 273–318). Chicago: University of Chicago Press.

Müller-Isberner, R. & S. Hodgins (2000). "Evidence-based Treatment for Mentally Disordered Offenders." In S. Hodgins & R. Müller-Isberner (eds.), *Violence, Crime and Mentally Disordered Offenders* (pp. 7–38). New York: Wiley.

Murphy, B.C. (1972). *A Quantitative Test of the Effectiveness of an Experimental Treatment Program for Delinquent Opiate Addicts*. Ottawa: Information Canada.

Murphy, W.D. & J.M. Peters (1992). "Profiling Child Sexual Abusers: Psychological Considerations." *Criminal Justice and Behavior*, 19, 24–37.

Mustard, S., D.C. May & D.W. Phillips (2006). "Prevalence and Predictors of Cheating on Antabuse: Is Antabuse a Cure or Merely an Obstacle? *American Journal of Criminal Justice*, 31, 51–63.

Nagin, D.S. & G. Pogarsky (2004). "Time and Punishment: Delayed Consequences and Criminal Behavior." *Journal of Quantitative Criminology*, 20, 295–317.

Nelson, R.J. & B.C. Trainor (2007). "Neural Mechanisms of Aggression." *Nature Reviews/ Neuroscience*, 8, 536–546.

Neo, L.H., C. Misir & P. Lee (eds., 2006). *Correctional Research Compendium, 2006.* Singapore: Singapore Prison Service.

Nesovic, A. (2003). "Psychometric Evaluation of the Correctional Program Assessment Inventory (CPAI)." Unpublished doctoral dissertation, Carleton University, Ottawa, Ontario.

Newman, G. (1976). *Comparative Deviance: Perception and Law in Six Cultures.* New York: Elsevier.

Neves, A.C. & R.A. Gonçalves (2008). "Criminal Recidivism and Violation of Conditional Release: A Comparative Study of the LSI-R and the HCR-20 in Portuguese Probationers/ Parolees." Paper presented at the IAFMHS Eighth Annual Conference, Vienna, Austria.

Newcomb, M.D. & T.B. Loeb (1999). "Poor Parenting as an Adult Problem Behavior: General Deviance, Deviant Attitudes, Inadequate Family Support and Bonding, or Just Bad Parents?" *Journal of Family Psychology*, 13, 175–193.

Newman, G. (1995). *Just and Painful: A Case for the Corporal Punishment of Criminals*, 2nd ed. New York: Harrow and Heston.

Newsom, C., J.E. Flavell & A. Rincover (1983). "The Side Effects of Punishment." In S. Axelrod & J. Apsche (eds.), *The Effects of Punishment on Human Behavior* (pp. 285–316). New York: Academic.

Newton, M. (2000). *The Encyclopedia of Serial Killers.* New York: Checkmark.

Nicholson-Crotty, S. (2004). "The Impact of Sentencing Guidelines on State-level Sanctions: An Analysis Over Time." *Crime & Delinquency*, 50, 395–411.

Nieuwbeerta, P. & A.R. Piquero (2008). "Mortality Rates and Causes of Death of Convicted Dutch Criminals 25 Years Later." *Journal of Research in Crime and Delinquency*, 45, 256–286.

Novaco, R. (1975). *Anger Control: The Development and Evaluation of an Experimental Treatment.* Lexington, MA: Lexington Books.

Novaco, R.W. (2000). "Anger." In A. E. Kazdin (ed.), *Encyclopedia of Psychology*, Vol. 1 (pp. 170–174). New York: American Psychological Association.

Nuffield, J. (1982). *Parole Decision-making in Canada.* Ottawa: Solicitor General of Canada.

Nuffield, J. (1997). *Evaluation of the Adult Victim-Offender Mediation Program Saskatoon Community Mediation Services.* Regina: Saskatchewan Justice.

Nugent, W.R. & J.B. Paddock (1995). "The Effect of Victim-Offender Mediation on Severity of Reoffense." *Mediation Quarterly*, 12, 353–367.

Odgers, C.L., B.J. Milne, A. Caspi, R. Crump, R. Poulton, R. & T.E. Moffitt (2007). "Predicting Prognosis for Conduct-problem Boy: Can Family History Help?" *Journal of the American Academy of Child & Adolescent Psychiatry*, 46, 1240–1249.

Odgers, C.L., T.E. Moffitt, J.M. Broadbent, N. Dickson, R.J. Hancox, H. Harrington, R. Poulton, M.R. Sears, W.M. Thomson & A. Caspi (2008). "Female and Male Antisocial Trajectories: From Childhood Origins to Adult Outcomes." *Developmental Psychopathology*, 20, 673–716.

Office of National Drug Control Policy (2000). *Drug-related Crime*. Washington, DC: Drug Policy Information Clearinghouse.

Ogloff, J.R.P. (2006). "Psychopathy/Antisocial Personality Disorder Conundrum." *Australian and New Zealand Journal of Psychiatry*, 40, 519–528.

Ogloff, J.R.P. & M.R. Davis (2004). "Advances in Offender Assessment and Rehabilitation: Contributions of the Risk-Need-Responsivity Approach." *Psychology: Crime and Law*, 10, 229–242.

Ogloff, J.R.P., S. Wong & A. Greenwood (1990). "Treating Criminal Psychopaths in a Therapeutic Community Program." *Behavioral Sciences and the Law*, 8, 181–190.

O'Leary, K.D., J. Malone & A. Tyree (1994). "Physical Aggression in Early Marriage: Prerelationship and Relationship Effects." *Journal of Consulting and Clinical Psychology*, 62, 594–602.

Olver, M.E., K.C. Stockdale & J.S. Wormith (2009). "Risk Assessment with Young Offenders: A Meta-Analysis of Three Assessment Measures." *Criminal Justice and Behavior*, 36, 329–353.

Olver, M.E. & S.C.P. Wong (2009). "Therapeutic Responses of Psychopathic Sexual Offenders: Treatment Attrition, Therapeutic Change, and Long-Term Recidivism." *Journal of Consulting and Clinical Psychology*, 77, 328–336.

Olver, M.E., S.C.P. Wong & T.P. Nicholaichuk (2009). "Outcome Evaluation of a High-Intensity Inpatient Sex Offender Treatment Program." *Journal of Interpersonal Violence*, 24, 522–536.

Onifade, E., W. Davidson, C. Campbell, G. Turke, J. Malinowski & K. Turner (2008). "Predicting Recidivism in Probationers with the Youth Level of Service Case Management Inventory (YLS/CMI)." *Criminal Justice and Behavior*, 35, 474–483.

Osgood, D.W. & A.L. Anderson (2004). "Unstructured Socializing and Rates of Delinquency." *Criminology*, 42, 519–549.

Osofsky, J. (2003). "Prevalence of Children's Exposure to Domestic Violence and Child Maltreatment: Implications for Prevention and Intervention." *Clinical Child and Family Psychology Review*, 6, 161–170.

Padgett, K.G., W.D. Bales & T.G. Blomberg (2006). "Under Surveillance: An Empirical Test of the Effectiveness and Consequences of Electronic Monitoring." *Criminology & Public Policy*, 5, 61–92.

Palarea, R.E., M.A. Zona, J.C. Lane & J. Langhinrichsen-Rohling (1999). "The Dangerous Nature of Intimate Relationship Stalking: Threats, Violence, and Associated Risk Factors." *Behavioral Sciences and the Law*, 17, 269–283.

Palker-Corell, A. & D.K. Marcus (2004). "Partner Abuse, Learned Helplessness, and Trauma Symptoms." *Journal of Social and Clinical Psychology*, 23, 445–462.

Palmer, E.J. (2003). *Offending Behaviour: Moral Reasoning, Criminal Conduct and the Rehabilitation of Offenders*. Cullompton, UK: Willan.

Palmer, T. (1974). "The Youth Authority's Community Treatment Project." *Federal Probation*, (March): 3–14.

Palmer, T. (1975). "Martinson Revisited." *Journal of Research in Crime and Delinquency*, 12, 133–152.

Palmer, T. (1983). "The Effectiveness Issue Today: An Overview." *Federal Probation*, 46, 3–10.

Palmer, T. (1992). *The Re-emergence of Correctional Intervention*. Newbury Park, CA: Sage.

Pan, H.S., P.H. Neidig & K.D. O'Leary (1994). "Predicting Mild and Severe Husband-to-Wife Physical Aggression." *Journal of Consulting and Clinical Psychology*, 62, 975–981.

Paparozzi, M.A. & P. Gendreau (2005). "An Intensive Supervision Program That Worked: Service Delivery, Professional Orientation, and Organizational Supportiveness." *The Prison Journal*, 85, 445–466.

Parent, D.G., M. Chaiken & W. Logan (1989). *Shock Incarceration: An Overview of Existing Programs*. Washington, DC: Office of Justice Programs, U.S. Department of Justice.

Parhar, K.K., J.S. Wormith, D.M. Derkzen & A.M. Beauregard (2008). "Offender Coercion in Treatment: A Meta-analysis of Effectiveness." *Criminal Justice and Behavior*, 35, 1109–1135.

Parker, K.F. & S.R. Maggard (2005). "Structural Theories and Race-specific Drug Arrests: What Structural Factors Account for the Rise in Race-specific Drug Arrests Over Time?" *Crime & Delinquency*, 51, 521–547.

Patrick, C.J. (ed.), (2006) *Handbook of Psychopathy*. New York: Guilford.

Patrick, C.J., J.J. Curtin & A. Tellegen (2002). "Development and Validation of a Brief Form of the Multidimensional Personality Questionnaire." *Psychological Assessment*, 14, 150–163.

Patterson, G.R. (1982). *Coercive Family Process*. Eugene, OR: Castalia.

Patterson, G.R. (1997). "Performance Models for Parenting: A Social Interactional Perspective." In J.E. Grusec & L. Kuczynski (eds.), *Parenting and Children's Internalization of Values: A Handbook of Contemporary Theory* (pp. 193–226). New York: Wiley.

Patterson, G.R., D.S. DeGarmo & N. Knutson (2000). "Hyperactive and Antisocial Behaviors: Comorbid or Two Points in the Same Process?" *Development and Psychopathology*, 12, 91–106.

Patterson, G.R. & K. Yoerger (1999). "Intraindividual Growth in Covert Antisocial Behaviour: A Necessary Precursor to Chronic Juvenile and Adult Arrests?" *Criminal Behaviour and Mental Health*, 9, 24–38.

Payne, D.C. & Cornwell, B. (2007). "Reconsidering Peer Influences on Delinquency: Do Less Proximate Contacts Matter?" *Journal of Quantitative Criminology*, 23, 127–149.

Peachy, D.E. (1989). "The Kitchener Experiment." In M. Wright & B. Galaway (eds.), *Mediation and Criminal Justice: Victims, Offenders and Community* (pp. 14–26). Newbury Park, CA: Sage.

Pearson, F.S. & D.S. Lipton (1999). "A Meta-analytic Review of the Effectiveness of Corrections-based Treatments for Drug Abuse." *The Prison Journal*, 79, 384–410.

Pearson, F.S., D.S. Lipton & C.M. Cleland (1996). "Some Preliminary Findings from the CDATE Project." Paper presented at the Annual Meeting of the American Society of Criminology, Chicago, Illinois, November.

Pendergast, M.L., D. Podus & E. Chang (2000). "Program Factors and Treatment Outcomes in Drug Dependence Treatment: An Examination Using Meta-Analysis." *Substance Use & Misuse*, 35, 1931–1965.

Perez, C. (1993). "Stalking: When Does Obsession Become a Crime?" *American Journal of Criminal Law*, 20, 263–280.

Perkins, D. (1991). "Clinical Work with Sex Offenders in Secure Settings." In C.R. Hollins & K. Howells (eds.), *Clinical Approaches to Sex Offenders and Their Victims* (pp. 151–177). Chichester, UK: Wiley.

Perkins, D. (1993). "Psychological Perspectives on Working with Sex Offenders." In J.M. Ussher & C.D. Baker (eds.), *Psychological Perspectives on Sexual Problems: New Directions in Theory and Practice* (pp. 168–205). London: Routledge.

Pernanen, K., M.-M. Cousineau, S. Brochu & F. Sun (2002). *Proportions of Crimes Associated with Alcohol and Other Drugs in Canada*. Ottawa: Canadian Centre on Substance Abuse.

Perry, D. (2001). "What Works in England and Wales." Invited address to the International Congress on the Effectiveness of Criminal Justice Sanctions, Amsterdam, The Netherlands, October.

Perry, L., T. Lajeunesse & A. Woods (1987). *Mediation Services: An Evaluation*. Winnipeg: Manitoba Attorney General.

Petersilia, J. & S. Turner (1993). *Evaluating Intensive Supervision Probation/Parole: Results of a Nationwide Experiment*. Research in Brief. Washington, DC: National Institute of Justice.

Petrides, K.V. (2006). "Trait Emotional Intelligence and Children's Peer Relations at School." *Social Development*, 15, 537–547.

Petrosino, A. & H. Soydan (2005). "The Impact of Program Developers as Evaluators on Criminal Recidivism: Results from Meta-Analyses of Experimental and Quasi-Experimental Research." *Journal of Experimental Criminology*, 1, 435–450.

Petrosino, A., C. Turpin-Petrosino & J.O. Finckenauer (2000). "Well-meaning Programs Have Harmful Effects! Lessons from Experiments of Programs Such as Scared Straight." *Crime & Delinquency*, 46, 354–379.

Pettit, B. & B. Western (2004). "Mass Imprisonment and the Life Course: Race and Class Inequality in U.S. Incarceration." *American Sociological Review*, 69: 151–169.

Pew Charitable Trusts (2008). *One in 100: Behind Bars in America*. Retrieved May 8, 2008, from http://www.pewcenteronthestates.org.

Pew Charitable Trusts (2009). *One in 31: The Long Reach of American Corrections*. Washington, DC: The Pew Charitable Trusts.

Phillips, H.K., N.S. Gray, S.I. MacCulloch, J. Taylor, S.C. Moore; P. Huckle & M. MacCulloch (2005). "Risk Assessment in Offenders with Mental Disorders: Relative Efficacy of Personal Demographic, Criminal History, and Clinical Variables." *Journal of Interpersonal Violence*, 20, 833–847.

Phillips, K.A. & J.G. Gunderson (1999). "Personality Disorders." In R.E. Hales, S.C. Yudofsky & J.A. Talbot (eds.), *Textbook of Psychiatry*, 3rd ed. (pp. 795–805). Washington, DC: American Psychiatric Press.

Phillips, S., J. Matusko & E. Tomasovic (2007). "Reconsidering the Relationship Between Alcohol and Lethal violence." *Journal of Interpersonal Violence*, 22, 66–84.

Pichot, P. (1978). "Psychopathic Behavior: A Historical Overview." In R.D. Hare & D. Schalling (eds.), *Psychopathic Behavior* (pp. 55–70). New York: Wiley.

Pilliavin, I., C. Thornton, R. Gartner & R.L. Matsueda (1986). "Crime, Deterrence, and Rational Choice." *American Sociological Review*, 51, 101–119.

Piquero, A. (2001). "Testing Moffitt's Neuropsychological Variation Hypothesis for the Prediction of Life-Course-Persistent Offending." *Psychology, Crime and Law*, 7, 193–215.

Piquero, A.R. (2008). "Taking Stock of Developmental Trajectories of Criminal Activity Over the Life Course." In A.M. Liberman (ed.), *The Long View of Crime* (pp. 23–78). New York: Springer.

Piquero, A.R. & A. Blumstein (2007). "Does Incapacitation Reduce Crime?" *Journal of Quantitative Criminology*, 23, 267–285.

Piquero, A.R., T. Brezina & M. Turner (2005). "Testing Moffitt's Account of Delinquency Abstention." *Journal of Research in Crime and Delinquency*, 42, 27–54.

Piquero, A.R., L.E. Daigle, C. Gibson, N.L. Piquero & S.G. Tibbetts (2007). "Are Life-Course-Persistent Offenders at Risk for Adverse Health Outcomes?" *Journal of Research in Crime and Delinquency*, 44, 185–207.

Piquero, A.R., D.P. Farrington, B. Welsh, R. Tremblay & W. Jennings (2009). "Effects of Early Family/Parent Training Programs on Antisocial Behavior and Delinquency." *Journal of Experimental Criminology*, 5, 83–120.

Piquero, A.R. & G. Pogarsky (2002). "Beyond Stafford and Warr's Reconceptualization of Deterrence: Personal and Vicarious Experiences, Impulsivity, and Offending." *Journal of Research in Crime and Delinquency*, 39, 153–186.

Platt, J.J. & M.F. Prout (1987). "Cognitive-Behavioral Theory and Interventions for Crime and Delinquency." In E.K. Morris & C.J. Braukmann (eds.), *Behavioral Approaches to Crime and Delinquency: A Handbook of Applications, Research, and Concepts* (pp. 477–497). New York: Plenum.

Plomin, R. (1989). "Environment and Genes: Determinants of Behavior." *American Psychologist*, 44, 105–111.

Pogarsky, G. (2007). "Deterrence and Individual Differences Among Convicted Offenders." *Journal of Quantitative Criminology*, 25, 59–74.

Pogarsky, G., A.J. Lizotte & T.P. Thornberry (2003). "The Delinquency of Children Born to Young Mothers: Results from the Rochester Youth Development Study." *Criminology*, 41, 1249–1286.

Pogarsky, G. & A. Piquero (2003). "Can Punishment Encourage Offending? Investigating the 'Resetting' Effect." *Journal of Research in Crime and Delinquency*, 40, 95–120.

Polaschek, D.L.L., N.J. Wilson, M.R. Townsend & L.R. Daly (2005). "Cognitive-Behavioral Rehabilitation for High-risk Violent Offenders: An Outcome Evaluation of the Violence Prevention Unit." *Journal of Interpersonal Violence*, 20, 1611–1627.

Porter, S. (1996). "Without Conscience or Without Active Conscience? The Etiology of Psychopathy Revisited." *Aggression and Violent Behavior*, 1, 179–189.

Pratt, T.C. (1998). "Race and Sentencing: A Meta-analysis of Conflicting Empirical Research Results." *Journal of Criminal Justice*, 26, 513–523.

Pratt, T.C. & F.T. Cullen (2000). "The Empirical Status of Gottfredson and Hirschi's General Theory of Crime: A Meta-analysis." *Criminology*, 38, 931–964.

Pratt, T.C. & F.T. Cullen (2005). "Assessing Macro-level Predictors and Theories of Crime: A Meta-analysis." In M. Tonry (ed.), *Crime and Justice: A Review of Research*, Vol. 32 (pp. 373–450). Chicago: University of Chicago Press.

Prendergast, M.L., D. Farabee, J. Cartier & S. Henkin (2006). "Involuntary Treatment within a Prison Setting: Impact on Psychosocial Change during Treatment." In C.R. Bartol & A. M. Bartol (eds.), *Current Perspectives in Forensic Psychology and Criminal Justice* (pp. 231–238). Thousand Oaks, CA: Sage.

Prendergast, M.L., E.A. Hall, H.K. Wexler, G. Melnick & Y. Cao (2004). "Amity Prison-based Therapeutic Community: 5-year Outcomes." *The Prison Journal*, 84, 36–60.

Prentky, R.A., A.W. Burgess, F. Rokous, A. Lee, C. Hartman, R. Ressler & J. Douglas (1989). "The Presumptive Role of Fantasy in Serial Sexual Homicide." *American Journal of Psychiatry*, 146, 887–891.

Prochaska, J.O., C.C. DiClemente & J.C. Norcross (1992). "In Search of How People Change: Applications to Addictive Behaviors." *American Psychologist*, 47, 1102–1114.

Provost, M.P., C. Kormos, G. Kosakoski & V.L. Quinsey (2006). "Sociosexuality in Women and Preference for Facial Masculinization and Somatotype in Men." *Archives of Sexual Behavior*, 35, 305–312.

Purcell, R., M. Pathé & P.E. Mullen (2004). "Stalking: Defining and Prosecuting a New Category of Offending." *International Journal of Law and Psychiatry*, 27, 157–169.

Quay, H.C. (1965). "Psychopathic Personality as Pathological Stimulus-seeking." *American Journal of Psychiatry*, 122, 180–183.

Quay, H.C. (1977). "The Three Faces of Evaluation: What Can Be Expected to Work." *Criminal Justice and Behavior*, 4, 341–354.

Quigely, B.M. & K.E. Leonard (1996). "Desistance of Husband Aggression in the Early Years of Marriage." *Violence and Victims*, 11, 355–370.

Quinet, K. (2007). "The Missing Missing: Toward a Quantification of Serial Murder Victimization in the United States." *Homicide Studies*, 11, 319–339.

Quinsey, V.L. (2002). "Evolutionary Theory and Criminal Behavior." *Legal and Criminological Psychology*, 7, 1–13.

Quinsey, V.L., A. Book & T.A. Skilling (2004). "A Follow-up of Deinstitutionalized Men with Intellectual Disabilities and Histories of Antisocial Behaviour." *Journal of Applied Research in Intellectual Disabilities*, 17, 243–253.

Quinsey, V.L., G. Coleman, B. Jones & I.F. Altrows (1997). "Proximal Antecedents of Eloping and Reoffending among Mentally Disordered Offenders." *Journal of Interpersonal Violence*, 12, 794–813.

Quinsey, V.L., G.T. Harris, M.E. Rice & C.A. Cormier (1998). *Violent Offenders: Appraising and Managing Risk*. Washington, DC: American Psychological Association.

Quinsey, V.L., G.T. Harris, M.E. Rice & C.A. Cormier (2006). *Violent Offenders: Appraising and Managing Risk*, 2nd ed. Washington, DC: American Psychological Association.

Quinsey, V.L., T.A. Skilling, M.L. Lalumière & W.M. Craig (2004). *Juvenile Delinquency: Understanding the Origins of Individual Differences*. Washington, DC: American Psychological Association.

Rafter, N. (2004). "Earnest A. Hooten the Biological Tradition in American Criminology." *Criminology*, 42, 735–771.

Rafter, N. (2008). "Criminology's Darkest Hour: Biocriminology in Nazi Germany." *Australian and New Zealand Journal of Criminology*, 41, 287–306.

Raine, A. (1997). "Antisocial Behavior and Psychophysiology: A Biosocial Perspective and a Prefrontal Dysfunction Hypothesis." In D.M. Stoff, J. Breiling & J.D. Maser (eds.), *Handbook of Antisocial Behavior* (pp. 289–304). New York: Wiley.

Raine, A., T. Lencz, S. Bihrle, L. LaCasse & P. Colletti (2000). "Reduced Prefrontal Gray Matter Volume and Reduced Autonomic Activity in Antisocial Personality Disorder." *Archives of General Psychiatry*, 57, 119–129.

Raine, A., T.E. Moffitt, A. Caspi, R. Loeber, M. Stouthamer-Loeber & D. Lynam (2005). "Neurocognitive Impairments in Boys on the Life-Course-Persistent Antisocial Path." *Journal of Abnormal Psychology*, 114, 38–49.

Raine, A., C. Reynolds, P.H. Venables & S.A. Mednick (2002). "Stimulation Seeking and Intelligence: A Prospective Longitudinal Study." *Journal of Personality and Social Psychology*, 82, 663–674.

Raine, A., P.H. Venables & M. Williams (1996). "Better Autonomic Conditioning and Faster Electrodermal Half-recovery Time at Age 15 Years as Possible Protective Factors against Crime at Age 29 Years." *Developmental Psychology*, 32, 624–630.

Rajkumar A.S. & M.T. French (1997). "Drug Abuse, Crime Costs, and the Economic Benefits of Treatment." *Journal of Quantitative Criminology*. 13, 291–323.

Ramirez, I.L. (2005). "Criminal History and Assaults on Intimate Partners by Mexican American and Non-Mexican White College Students." *Journal of Interpersonal Violence*, 20, 1628–1647.

Rand, M.R. (2008). *Criminal Victimization, 2007*. Washington, DC: Bureau of Justice Statistics.

Rankin, J.H. & R. Kern (1994). "Parental Attachments and Delinquency." *Criminology*, 32, 495–515.

Ratchford, M. & K.M. Beaver (2009). "Neuropsychological Deficits, Low Self-Control, and Delinquent Involvement." *Criminal Justice and Behavior*, 36, 147–162.

Raynor, P. (2007). "Risk and Need Assessment in British Probation: The Contribution of the LSI-R." *Psychology, Crime, and Law*, 13, 125–138.

Raynor, P. (2008). "Community Penalties and Home Office Research: On the Way Back to "Nothing Works"?" *Criminology & Criminal Justice*, 8, 73–87.

Raynor, P., J. Kynch, C. Roberts & S. Merrington (2000). *Risk and Need Assessment in Probation Services: An Evaluation*. Home Office Research Study No. 211. London: Home Office.

Raynor, P. & G. Robinson (2005). *Rehabilitation, Crime and Justice*. Swansea, Wales: Palgrave Macmillan.

Rebellon, C.J. (2002). "Reconsidering the Broken Homes/Delinquency Relationship and Exploring Its Mediating Mechanism(s)." *Criminology*, 40, 103–135.

Rebellon, C.J., M.A. Strauss & R. Medeiros (2008). "Self-Control in Global Perspective: An Empirical Assessment of Gottfredson and Hirschi's General Theory Within and Across 32 National Settings." *European Journal of Criminology*, 5, 331–362.

Reckless, W.C. (1967). *The Crime Problem*. New York: Appleton-Century-Crofts.

Reckless, W.C. & S. Dinitz (1972). *The Prevention of Delinquency.* Columbus: Ohio State University Press.

Redondo, S., V. Garrido & J. Sanchez-Meca (1999). "The Influence of Treatment Programs on the Recidivism of Juvenile and Adult Offenders: A European Meta-analytic Review." *Psychology, Crime, and Law,* 5, 251–278.

Rehm, L.P., A.L. Wagner & C. Ivens-Tyndal (2001). "Mood Disorders: Unipolar and Bipolar." In P.B. Sutker & H.E. Adams (eds.), *Comprehensive Handbook of Psychopathology,* 3rd ed. (pp. 277–308). New York: Kluwer Academic.

Reid, W.H. & C. Gacono (2000). "Treatment of Antisocial Personality, Psychopathy, and Other Characterologic Antisocial Syndromes." *Behavioral Sciences and the Law,* 18, 647–662.

Reisig, M.D., K. Holtfreter & M. Morash (2006). "Assessing Recidivism Risk Across Female Pathways to Crime." *Justice Quarterly,* 23, 384–405.

Reitsma-Street, M. "Differential Treatment of Young Offenders: A Review of the Conceptual Level Matching Model." *Canadian Journal of Criminology,* 26, 2, 199–215.

Reitzel-Jaffe, D. & D. Wolfe (2001). "Predictors of Relationship Abuse among Young Men." *Journal of Interpersonal Violence,* 16, 99–115.

Rempel, M., M. Labriola & R.C. Davis (2008). "Does Judicial Monitoring Deter Domestic Violence Recidivism? Results from a Quasi-Experimental Comparison in the Bronx." *Violence Against Women,* 14, 185–207.

Renzema, M. & E. Mayo-Wilson (2005). "Can Electronic Monitoring Reduce Crime for Moderate to High-risk Offenders?" *Journal of Experimental Criminology,* 1, 215–237.

Rettinger, L.J. (1998). "A Recidivism Follow-up Study Investigating Risk and Need Within a Sample of Provincially Sentenced Women." Unpublished doctoral dissertation, Carleton University, Ottawa, Ontario.

Rhee, S.H. & I.D. Waldman (2002). "Genetic and Environmental Influences on Antisocial Behavior: A Meta-analysis of Twin and Adoption Studies." *Psychological Bulletin,* 128, 490–529.

Rhule-Louie, D.M. & R.J. McMahon (2007). "Problem Behavior and Romantic Relationships: Assortative Mating, Behavior Contagion, and Desistance." *Clinical Child and Family Psychology Review,* 10, 53–100.

Rice, M.E., T.C. Chaplin, G.T. Harris & J. Coutts (1994). "Empathy for the Victim and Sexual Arousal among Rapists and Nonrapists." *Journal of Interpersonal Violence,* 9, 435–449.

Rice, M.E. & G.T. Harris (1997). "Cross Validation and Extension of the Violence Risk Appraisal Guide with Child Molesters and Rapists." *Law and Human Behavior,* 21, 231–241.

Rice, M.E. & G.T. Harris (2005). "Comparing Effect Sizes in Follow-up Studies: ROC Area, Cohen's d, and r." *Law and Human Behavior,* 29, 615–620.

Rigakos, G.S. (1999). "Risk Society and Actuarial Criminology: Prospects for Critical Discourse." *Canadian Journal of Criminology,* 41, 137–151.

Rimmele, C.T., M.O. Howard & M.L. Hilfrink (1995). "Aversion Therapies." In R.K. Hester & W.R. Miller (eds.), *Handbook of Alcoholism Treatment Approaches: Effective Alternatives,* 2nd ed (pp. 134–147). Boston: Allyn & Bacon.

Ring, J. & R. Svensson (2007). "Social Class and Criminality among Young People: A Study Considering the Effects of School Achievement as a Mediating Factor on the Basis of Swedish Register and Self-Report Data." *Journal of Scandinavian Studies in Criminology and Crime Prevention*, 8, 210–233.

Roberts, D.W. (2009). "Intimate Partner Homicide: Relationships to Alcohol and Firearms." *Journal of Contemporary Criminal Justice*, 25, 67–68.

Roberts, J.V. (2003). "Public Opinion and Mandatory Sentencing: A Review of International Findings." *Criminal Justice and Behavior*, 30, 483–508.

Roberts, K.A. (2005). "Women's Experience of Violence During Stalking by Former Romantic Partners." *Violence Against Women*, 11, 89–114.

Robinson, D. & F.J. Porporino (2001). "Programming in Cognitive Skills: The Reasoning and Rehabilitation Programme." In C.R. Hollin (ed.), *Handbook of Offender Assessment and Treatment* (pp. 179–193). Chichester, UK: John Wiley & Sons.

Robinson, G. & J. Shapland (2008). "Reducing Recidivism: A Task for Restorative Justice?" *British Journal of Criminology*, 48, 337–358.

Rogers, C. (1961). *On Becoming a Person*. Boston: Houghton Mifflin.

Rogers, S. (1981). *Factors Related to Recidivism Among Adult Probationers in Ontario*. Toronto: Ontario Ministry of Correctional Services.

Rosenfeld, B. (2004). "Violence Risk Factors in Stalking and Obsessional Harassment: A Review and Preliminary Meta-analysis." *Criminal Justice and Behavior*, 31, 9–36.

Rhoner, R.P. (2004). "The Parental 'Acceptance-Rejection Syndrome': Universal Correlates of Perceived Rejection." *American Psychologist*, 59, 830–840.

Rooke, S.E., D.W. Hine & E.B. Thorsteinsson (2008). "Implicit Cognition and Substance Use: A Meta-Analysis." *Addictive Behaviors*, 33, 1314–1328.

Rooney, J. & R.K. Hanson (2001). "Predicting Attrition from Treatment Programs for Abusive Men." *Journal of Family Violence*, 16, 131–149.

Roozen, H.G., J.J. Boulogne, M.W. van Tulder, W. van den Brink, C.A. De Jong & A. Kerkhof (2004). "A Systematic Review of the Effectiveness of the Community Reinforcement Approach in Alcohol, Cocaine and Opioid Addiction." *Drug and Alcohol Dependence*, 74, 1–13.

Roper v. Simmons (2005, March). Supreme Court of the United States. See http://www.supremecourtus.gov/opinions/04pdf/03–633.pdf

Rosenthal, R. (1984). *Meta-analytic Procedures for Social Research*. Beverly Hills, CA: Sage.

Ross, R.R. (1995). "The Reasoning and Rehabilitation Program for High-risk Probationers and Prisoners." In R.R. Ross, D.H. Antonowicz & G.K. Dhaliwal (eds.), *Going Straight: Effective Delinquency Prevention and Offender Rehabilitation* (pp. 195–222). Ottawa: Air Training and Publications.

Ross, R.R. & E.A. Fabiano (1985). *Time to Think: A Cognitive Model of Delinquency Prevention and Offender Rehabilitation*. Johnson City, TN: Institute of Social Science and Arts.

Ross, R.R. & P. Gendreau (eds.) (1980). *Effective Correctional Treatment*. Toronto: Butterworth.

Ross, S.M. (1996). "Risk of Physical Abuse to Children of Spouse Abusing Parents." *Child Abuse and Neglect*, 20, 589–598.

Rowe, D.C. (1983). "Biometrical Models of Self-Reported Criminal Behavior: A Twin Study." *Behavior Genetics*, 13, 473–489.

Rowe, D.C. & D.P. Farrington (1997). "The Familial Transmission of Criminal Convictions." *Criminology*, 35, 177–201.

Rowe, D.C. & D.W. Osgood (1984). "Heredity and Sociological Theories of Delinquency: A Reconsideration." *American Sociological Review*, 49, 526–540.

Rowe, R.C. (2008). "Proximal Antecedents to Criminal Offending in a Young Offender Sample." Paper presented at the annual Meeting of the Canadian Psychological Association, Halifax, Nova Scotia.

Rubak, S., A. Sandbaek, T. Lauritzen & B. Christensen (2005). "Motivational Interviewing: A Systematic Review and Meta-Analysis." *British Journal of General Practice*, 55, 305–312.

Rubington, E. & M.S. Weinberg (1973). *Deviance: The Interactionist Perspective*. New York: Macmillan.

Rushton, J.P. (1988). "Race Differences in Behaviour: A Review and Evolutionary Analysis." *Personality and Individual Differences*, 9, 1009–1024.

Rushton, J.P. & C.D. Ankney (1996). "Brain Size and Cognitive Ability: Correlations with Age, Sex, Social Class, and Race." *Psychonomic Bulletin and Review*, 3, 21–36.

Rushton, J.P. & A.R. Jensen (2005). "Thirty Years of Research on Race Differences in Cognitive Ability." *Psychology, Public Policy, and Law*, 11, 235–294.

Rushton, J.P. & A.R. Jensen (2006). "The Totality of Evidence Shows the Race IQ Gap Still Remains." *Psychological Science*, 17, 921–922.

Rushton, J.P. & A.R. Jensen (2008). "James Watson's Most Inconvenient Truth: Race, Realism and Moralistic Fallacy." *Medical Hypotheses*, 71, 629–640.

Rutter, M., T.E. Moffitt & A. Caspi (2006). "Gene-Environment Interplay and Psychopathology: Multiple Varieties but Real Effects." *Journal of Child Psychology and Psychiatry*, 47, 226–261.

Ryan, J.P. & M.F. Testa (2005). "Child Maltreatment and Juvenile Delinquency: Investigating the Role of Placement and Placement Instability." *Children and Youth Services Review*, 227–249.

Salekin, R.T. (2006). "Psychopathy in Children and Adolescents: Key Issues in Conceptualization and Assessment." In C.J. Patrick (ed.), *Handbook of Psychopathy* (pp. 389–414). New York: Guilford.

Salekin, R.T., D.A. Brannen, A.A. Zalot, A. Leistico & C.S. Neumann (2006). "Factor Structure of Psychopathy in Youth: Testing the Applicability of the New Four-Factor Model." *Criminal Justice and Behavior*, 33, 135–157.

Salekin, R.T., R. Roger & K.W. Sewell (1996). "A Review and Meta-analysis of the Psychopathy Checklist and Psychopathy Checklist-Revised: Predictive Validity of Dangerousness." *Clinical Psychology: Science and Practice*, 3, 203–215.

Sampson, R.J. & J.H. Laub (1990). "Crime and Development over the Life Course: The Salience of Adult Social Bonds." *American Sociological Review*, 55, 609–627.

Sampson, R.J. & J.H. Laub (1993). *Crime in the Making: Pathways and Turning Points through Life*. Cambridge, MA: Harvard University Press.

Sampson, R.J. & J.H. Laub (2003). "Life-course Desisters? Trajectories of Crime among Delinquent Boys Followed to Age 70." *Criminology*, 41, 555–592.

Sampson, R.J., J.H. Laub & C. Wimer (2006). "Does Marriage Reduce Crime? A Counterfactual Approach to Within-Individual Causal Effects." *Criminology*, 44, 465–504.

Sampson, R.J. & S.W. Raudenbush (2001). *Disorder in Urban Neighborhoods—Does it Lead to Crime?* Research in Brief. Washington, DC: National Institute of Justice.

Samuels, J., O.J. Bienvenu, B. Cullen, P.T. Costa Jr., W.W. Eaton & G. Nestadt (2004). "Personality Dimensions and Criminal Arrest." *Comprehensive Psychiatry*, 45, 275–280.

Sandberg A.A., G.F. Koepf, T. Ishihara & T.S. Hauschka (1961). "An XYY Human Male." *Lancet*, 278, 488–489.

Saudino, K.J. (2005). "Behavioral Genetics and Child Temperament." *Journal of Developmental and Behavioral*, 26, 214–223.

Saudino, K.J., S. McGuire, D. Reiss, M.E. Hetherington & R. Plomin (1995). "Parent Ratings of EAS Temperaments in Twins, Full Siblings, Half Siblings, and Step Siblings." *Journal of Personality and Social Psychology*, 68, 723–733.

Saunders, D.G. (1995). "Prediction of Wife Assault." In J.C. Campbell (ed.), *Assessing Dangerousness: Violence by Sexual Offenders, Batterers, and Child Abusers* (pp. 68–95). Thousand Oaks, CA: Sage.

Saunders, D.G. (1996). "Feminist-Cognitive-Behavioral and Process-Psychodynamic Treatment for Men Who Batter: Interaction of Abuser Traits and Treatment Models." *Violence and Victims*, 11, 393–414.

Saunders, D.G. & S.T. Azar (1989). "Treatment Programs for Family Violence." In L. Ohlin & M. Tonry (eds.), *Family Violence* (pp. 481–546). Chicago: University of Chicago Press.

Scalora, M.J., J.V. Baumgartner, W. Zimmerman, D. Callaway, M.A. Hatch Maillette, C.N. Covell, R.E. Palarea, J.A. Crebs & D.O. Washington (2002). "Risk Factors for Approach Behavior toward the U.S. Congress." *Journal of Threat Assessment*, 2, 35–55.

Scarpa, A. & A. Raine (2007). "Biosocial Basis of Violence." In D.J. Flannery, A.T. Vazsonyi & I.D. Waldman (eds.), *The Cambridge Handbook of Violent Behavior and Aggression* (pp. 151–169). Cambridge, UK: Cambridge University Press.

Schaeffer, C.M. & C.M. Borduin (2005). "Long-term Follow-up to a Randomized Clinical Trial of Multisystemic Therapy with Serious and Violent Juvenile Offenders." *Journal of Consulting and Clinical Psychology*, 73, 445–453.

Schachter, S. & B. Latane (1964). "Crime, Cognition and the Autonomic Nervous System." In D. Levine (ed.), *Nebraska Symposium on Motivation* (pp. 221–273). Lincoln, NE: University of Nebraska Press.

Schirmer, S., A. Nellis & M. Mauer (2009). *Incarcerated Parents and Their Children: Trends 1991–2007*. Washington, DC: The Sentencing Project.

Schlager, M.D. & D.J. Simourd (2007). "Validity of the Level of Service Inventory–Revised (LSI-R) Among African American and Hispanic Male Offenders." *Criminal Justice and Behavior*, 34, 545–554.

Schmidt, J.D. & L.W. Sherman (1996). "Does Arrest Deter Domestic Violence?" In E.S. Buzawa & C.G. Buzawa (eds.), *Do Arrests and Restraining Orders Work?* (pp. 43–53). Thousand Oaks, CA: Sage.

Schmitt, D.P., A. Realo, M. Voracek & J. Allik (2008). "Why Can't a Man Be More Like a Woman? Sex Differences in Big Five Personality Traits Across 55 Cultures." *Journal of Personality and Social Psychology*, 94, 168–182.

Schneider, A.L., L. Ervin & Z. Snyder-Joy (1996). "Further Exploration of the Flight from Discretion: The Role of Risk/Need Instruments in Probation Supervision Decisions." *Journal of Criminal Justice*, 24, 109–121.

Schneider, B.H., L. Atkinson & C. Tardiff (2001). Child-parent Attachment and Children's Peer Relations: A Quantitative Review." *Developmental Psychology*, 37, 86–100.

Schuessler, K.F. & D.R. Cressy (1950). "Personality Characteristics of Criminals." *American Journal of Sociology*, 55, 476–484.

Schur, E.M. (1973). *Radical Nonintervention: Rethinking the Delinquency Problem.* Englewood Cliffs, NJ: Prentice Hall.

Schwalbe, C.S. (2008). "A Meta-Analysis of Juvenile Risk Assessment Instruments: Predictive Validity by Gender." *Criminal Justice and Behavior*, 35, 1367–1381.

Schwartz, C.E., N. Snidman & J. Kagan (1996). "Early Childhood Temperament as a Determinant of Externalizing Behavior in Adolescence." *Development and Psychopathology*, 8, 527–537.

Schweinhart, L.J. & D.P. Weikart (1995). "The High/Scope Perry Preschool Study through Age 27. In R.R. Ross, D.H. Antonowicz & G.K. Dhaliwal (eds.), *Going Straight: Effective Delinquency Prevention and Offender Rehabilitation* (pp. 57–75). Ottawa: Air Training Publications.

Séguin, J.R., B. Boulerice, P.H. Harden, R.E. Tremblay & R.O. Pihl (1999). "Executive Functions and Physical Aggression after Controlling for Attention Deficit Hyperactivity Disorder, General Memory, and IQ." *Journal of Child Psychology and Psychiatry*, 8, 1197–1208.

Seligman, M.E.P. (1975). *Helplessness: On Depression, Development, and Death.* San Francisco: Freeman.

Sellin, J.T. (1980). *The Penalty of Death, 1980.* Beverly Hills: Sage.

Serin, R.C. (1996). "Violent Recidivism in Criminal Psychopaths." *Law and Human Behavior*, 20, 207–217.

Serin, R.C., R. Gobeil & D.L. Preston (2009). "Evaluation of the Persistently Violent Offender Treatment Program." *International Journal of Offender Therapy and Comparative Criminology*, 53, 57–73.

Serin, R.C., R.D. Peters & H.E. Barbaree (1990). "Predictors of Psychopathy and Release Outcome in a Criminal Population." *Psychological Assessment: A Journal of Consulting and Clinical Psychology*, 2, 419–422.

Seto, M.C., A. Maric & H.E. Barbaree (2001). "The Role of Pornography in the Etiology of Sexual Aggression." *Aggression and Violent Behavior*, 6, 35–53.

Shaw, D.S. & J.I. Vondra (1995). "Infant Attachment Security and Maternal Predictors of Early Behavior Problems: A Longitudinal Study of Low-income Families." *Journal of Abnormal Child Psychology*, 23, 335–357.

Shearer, R.A. (2003). "Court-ordered Counseling: An Ethical Minefield for Psychotherapists." *Annals of the American Psychotherapy Association*, 6, 8–11.

Sheeran, P., C. Abraham & S. Orbell (1999). "Psychosocial Correlates of Heterosexual Condom Use: A Meta-analysis." *Psychological Bulletin*, 125, 90–132.

Sheldon, W.H. (1942). *The Varieties of Temperament: A Psychology of Constitutional Differences.* New York: Harper.

Sherman, L.W. & R.A. Berk (1984). "The Specific Deterrent Effect of Arrest for Domestic Assault." *American Sociological Review*, 49, 261–272.

Sherman, L.W. & H. Strang (2007). *Restorative Justice: The Evidence*. London: The Smith Institute.

Shields, I.W. & M. Ball (1990). "Neutralization in a Population of Incarcerated Young Offenders." Paper presented at the Annual Meeting of the Canadian Psychological Association, Ottawa, Ontario.

Shields, I.W. & D.J. Simourd (1991). "Predicting Predatory Behavior in a Population of Incarcerated Young Offenders." *Criminal Justice and Behavior*, 18, 180–194.

Shields, I.W. & G.C. Whitehall (1994). "Neutralizations and Delinquency among Teenagers." *Criminal Justice and Behavior*, 21, 223–235.

Shoda, Y. & W. Mischel (2006). "Applying Meta-Theory to Achieve Generalisability and Precision in Personality Science." *Applied Psychology: An International Review*, 55, 439–452.

Short, J.F., Jr. (1957a). "Differential Association and Delinquency." *Social Problems*, 4, 233–239.

Short, J.F., Jr. (1991). "Poverty, Ethnicity, and Crime: Change and Continuity in U.S. Cities." *Journal of Research in Crime and Delinquency*, 28, 501–518.

Shortt, J.W., D.M. Capaldi, T.J. Dishion, L. Bank & L.D. Owen (2003). "The Role of Adolescent Friends, Romantic Partners, and Siblings in the Emergence of the Adult Antisocial Lifestyle." *Journal of Family Psychology*, 17, 521–533.

Silver, E. & L.L. Miller (2005). "Sources of Informal Social Control in Chicago Neighborhoods." *Criminology*, 551–583.

Silver, E., W.R. Smith & S. Banks (2000). "Constructing Actuarial Devices for Predicting Recidivism: A Comparison of Methods." *Criminal Justice and Behavior*, 27, 733–764.

Simonoff, E., J. Elander, J. Holmshaw, A. Pickles, R. Murray & M. Rutter (2004). "Predictors of Antisocial Personality: Continuities from Childhood to Adult Life." *British Journal of Psychiatry*, 184, 118–127.

Simons, R.L., C. Johnson, R.D. Conger & G. Elder (1998). "A Test of Latent Trait versus Life Course Perspectives on the Stability of Adolescent Antisocial Behavior." *Criminology*, 36, 217–244.

Simons, R.L., L.G. Simons, Y. Chen, G.H. Brody, and K. Lin (2007). "Identifying the Psychological Factors that Mediate the Association between Parenting Practices and Delinquency." *Criminology*, 45, 451–518.

Simourd, D.J. (1997). "The Criminal Sentiments Scale-Modified and Pride in Delinquency Scale: Psychometric Properties and Construct Validity of Tow Measures of Criminal Attitudes." *Criminal Justice and Behavior*, 24, 52–70.

Simourd, D.J. & R.D. Hoge (2000). "Criminal Psychopathy: A Risk-and-Need Perspective." *Criminal Justice and Behavior*, 27, 256–272.

Simourd, D.J. & J.M. Mamuza (2000). "The Hostile Interpretations Questionnaire: Psychometric Properties and Construct Validity." *Criminal Justice and Behavior*, 27, 645–663.

Simourd, D.J. & M. Olver (2002). "The Future of Criminal Attitude Research and Practice." *Criminal Justice and Behavior*, 29, 427–446.

Simourd, D.J. & J. Van De Ven (1999). C7 Assessment of Criminal Attitudes: Criterion-related Validity of the Criminal Sentiments Scale-Modified and Pride in Delinquency Scale." *Criminal Justice and Behavior*, 26, 90–106.

Simourd, L. & D.A. Andrews (1994). "Correlates of Delinquency: A Look at Gender Differences." *Forum on Corrections Research*, 6, 26–31.

Sims, B. (ed.) (2005). *Substance Abuse Treatment with Correctional Clients: Practical Implications for Institutional and Correctional Settings*. New York: Haworth.

Sirdifield, C., D. Gojkovic, C. Brooker & M. Ferriter (2009). "A Systematic Review of Research on the Epidemiology of Mental Health Disorders in Prison Populations: A Summary of Findings." *The Journal of Forensic Psychiatry & Psychology*, 20, S78–S101.

Sisson, R.W. & N.H. Azrin (1989). "The Community Reinforcement Approach." In R.K. Hester & W.R. Miller (eds.), *Handbook of Alcoholism Treatment Approaches: Effective Alternatives* (pp. 242–258). Elmsford, NY: Pergamon Press.

Sjöstedt, G. & N. Långström (2000). "Actuarial Assessment of Risk for Criminal Recidivism among Sex Offenders Released from Swedish Prison 1993–1997." Paper presented at the 19th Annual ATSA Research and Treatment Conference, San Diego, California, November.

Skeem, J.L. (2008). "Probationers and Parolees with Mental Illness: What Works!" Presentation available from skeem@uci.edu.

Skeem, J.L. & D.J. Cooke (in press). "Is Criminal Behavior a Central Component of Psychopathy? Conceptual Directions for Resolving the Debate." *Psychological Assessment*.

Skeem, J.L., J.E. Louden, D. Polaschek & J. Camp (2007). "Assessing Relationship Quality in Mandated Community Treatment: Blending Care with Control." *Psychological Assessment*, 19, 397–410.

Skeem, J.L., S. Manchak & J.K. Peterson (in press). "Smart Sentencing for Offenders with Mental Illness: Moving Beyond the One-Dimensional Focus to Reduce Recidivism." *Law and Human Behavior*.

Skilling, T.A., G.T. Harris, M. Rice & V.L. Quinsey (2002). "Identifying Persistently Antisocial Offenders Using the Hare Psychopathy Checklist and DSM Antisocial Personality Disorder Criteria." *Psychological Assessment*, 14, 27–38.

Skilling, T.A., V.L. Quinsey & W.M. Craig (2001). "Evidence of a Taxon Underlying Serious Antisocial Behavior in Boys." *Criminal Justice and Behavior*, 28, 450–470.

Skinner, B.F. (1953). *Science and Human Behavior*. New York: Macmillan.

Skinner, W.F. & A.M. Fream (1997). "A Social Learning Theory Analysis of Computer Crime among College Students." *Journal of Research in Crime and Delinquency*, 34, 495–518.

Smith, C. & T.P. Thornberry (1995). "The Relationship between Childhood Maltreatment and Adolescent Involvement in Delinquency." *Criminology*, 33, 451–481.

Smith, C.A. & D.P. Farrington (2004). "Continuities in Antisocial Behavior and Parenting across Three Generations." *Journal of Child Psychology and Psychiatry*, 45, 230–247.

Smith, P., F.T. Cullen & E.J. Latessa (2009). "Can 14,373 Women be Wrong? A Meta-Analysis of the LSI-R and Recidivism for Female Offenders." *Criminology & Public Policy*, 8, 183–208.

Smith, P., P. Gendreau & K. Swartz (2009). "Validating the Principles of Effective Intervention: A Systematic Review of the Contributions of Meta-Analysis in the Field of Corrections." *Victims & Offenders*, 4, 148–169.

Smith, P., C. Goggin & P. Gendreau (2002). *The Effects of Prison Sentences and Intermediate Sanctions on Recidivism: General Effects and Individual Differences* (User Report 2002-01). Ottawa: Public Safety and Emergency Preparedness Canada.

Smith, P.H., G.E. Thornton, R. DeVellis, J. Earp & A.L. Coker (2002). "A Population-based Study of the Prevalence and Distinctiveness of Battering, Physical Assault, and Sexual Assault in Intimate Relationships." *Violence Against Women*, 8, 1208–1232.

Smith Stover, C. (2005). "Domestic Violence Research: What Have We Learned and Where Do We Go from Here?" *Journal of Interpersonal Violence*, 20, 448–454.

Snell, T.L. (2008). *Capital Punishment, 2007—Statistical Tables*. Retrieved February 15, 2009, from http://www.ojp.usdoj.gov/bjs/pub/html/cp/2007/cp07st.pdf.

Snyder, H.N. (1998). "Serious, Violent, and Chronic Juvenile Offenders—An Assessment of the Extent of and Trends in Officially Recognized Serious Criminal Behavior in a Delinquent Population." In R. Loeber & D.P. Farrington (eds.), *Serious & Violent Juvenile Offenders: Risk Factors and Successful Interventions* (428–444). Thousand Oaks, CA: Sage.

Sobell, L.C. & M.B. Sobell (1972). "Effects of Alcohol on the Speech of Alcoholics." *Journal of Speech and Hearing Research*, 15, 861–868.

Solomon, R.L. (1964). "Punishment." *American Psychologist*, 19, 239–253.

Somers, J.M., E.M. Goldner, P. Waraich & L. Hsu (2004). "Prevalence Studies of substance-Related Disorders: A Systematic Review of the Literature." *Canadian Journal of Psychiatry*, 49, 373–383.

Soothill, K., B. Francis, B. Sanderson & E. Ackerley (2000). "Sex Offenders: Specialists, Generalists—Or Both?" *British Journal of Criminology*, 40, 56–67.

Sorensen, J. & D. Stemen (2002). "The Effect of State Sentencing Policies on Incarceration Rates." *Crime & Delinquency*, 48, 456–474.

Spelman, W. (2000). "What Recent Studies Do (and Don't) Tell Us About Imprisonment and Crime." In M. Tonry (ed.), *Crime and Justice: A Review of Research*, Vol. 27 (pp. 419–494). Chicago: University of Chicago Press.

Sprott, J.B. & A.N. Doob (2000). "Bad, Sad, and Rejected: The Lives of Aggressive Children." *Canadian Journal of Criminology*, 42, 123–133.

Stadtland, C., M. Hollweg, N. Kleindienst, J. Dietl, U. Reich & N. Nedopil (2005). "Risk Assessment and Prediction of Violent and Sexual Recidivism in Sex Offenders: Long-term Predictive Validity of Four Risk Assessment Instruments." *The Journal of Forensic Psychiatry and Psychology*, 16, 92–108.

Stauffer, A.R., M.D. Smith, J.K. Cochran, S.J. Fogel & B. Bjerregaard (2006). "The Interaction Between Victim Race and Gender on Sentencing Outcomes in Capital Murder Trials: A Further Exploration." *Homicide Studies*, 10, 98–117.

Steadman, H.J. & J.J. Cocozza (1974). *Careers of the Criminally Insane: Excessive Social Control of Deviance*. Lexington, MA: Lexington Books.

Steinberg, L. & E.S. Scott (2003). "Less Guilty by Reason of Adolescence: Developmental Immaturity, Diminished Responsibility, and the Juvenile Death Penalty." *American Psychologist*, 58, 1009–1018.

Stemen, D. (2007). *Reconsidering Incarceration: New Directions for Reducing Crime*. New York: Vera Institute of Justice. See http://www.vera.org/publications.

Stephenson, R.M. & F.R. Scarpitti (1974). *Group Interaction as Therapy: The Use of the Small Group in Corrections*. Westport, CT: Greenwood.

Sternberg, R.J. (2005). "There Are No Public-Policy Implications: A Reply to Rushton and Jensen (2005)." *Psychology, Public Policy, and Law*, 11, 295–301.

Stevens, A., D. Berto, W. Heckman, V. Kerschl, K. Oeuvray, M. van Ooyen, E. Steffan & A. Uchtenhagen (2005). "Quasi-compulsory Treatment of Drug Dependent Offenders: An International Literature Review." *Substance Use and Misuse*, 40, 269–283.

Stevenson, H.E. & S.J. Wormith (1987). *Psychopathy and the Level of Supervision Inventory* (User Report #1987–25). Ottawa: Solicitor General Canada.

Stewart, E.A., C.J. Schreck & R.L. Simons (2006). "'I Ain't Gonna Let No One Disrespect Me': Does the Code of the Street Reduce or Increase Violent Victimization among African American Adolescents?" *Journal of Research in Crime and Delinquency*, 43, 427–458.

Stith, S.M., N.M. Green, D.B. Smith & D.B. Ward (2008). "Marital Satisfaction and Marital Discord as Risk Markers for Intimate Partner Violence: A Meta-Analytic Review." *Journal of Family Violence*, 23, 149–160.

Stolzenberg, L. & S.J. D'Alessio (1997). "'Three Strikes and You're Out': The Impact of California's New Mandatory Sentencing Law on Serious Crime Rates." *Crime & Delinquency*, 43, 457–469.

Stomp, T. & G. Ortwein-Swoboda (2004). "Schizophrenia, Delusional Symptoms, and Violence: The Threat/Control-Override Concept Reexamined." *Schizophrenia Bulletin*, 30, 31–44.

Stouthamer-Loeber, M., R. Loeber, E. Wei, D.P. Farrington & P.H. Wikstrom (2002). "Risk and Promotive Effects in the Explanation of Persistent Serious Delinquency in Boys." *Journal of Consulting and Clinical Psychology*, 70, 111–123.

Stover, S. (2005), "Domestic Violence Research: What Have We Learned and Where Do We Go from Here?" *Journal of Interpersonal Violence*, 20, 448–454.

Strang, H., L. Sherman, C.M. Angel, D.J. Woods, S. Bennett, D. Newbury-Birch &. N. Inkpen (2006). "Victim Evaluations of Face-to-Face Restorative Justice Conferences: A Quasi-Experimental Analysis." *Journal of Social Issues*, 62, 281–306.

Straus, M.A. (1996). "Identifying Offenders in Criminal Justice Research on Domestic Assault." In E.S. Buzawa & C.G. Buzawa (eds.), *Do Arrests and Restraining Orders Work?* (pp. 14–29). Thousand Oaks, CA: Sage.

Straus, M.A. & G.K. Kantor (1994). "Corporal Punishment of Adolescents by Parents: A Risk Factor in the Epidemiology of Depression, Suicide, Alcohol Abuse, Child Abuse, and Wife Beating." *Adolescence*, 29, 543–561.

Stuart, B. (1996). "Circle Sentencing: Turning Swords into Ploughshares." In B. Galaway & J. Hudson (eds.), *Restorative Justice: International Perspectives* (pp. 193–206). Monsey, NY: Criminal Justice Press.

Stuart, B. & K. Pranis (2006). "Peacemaking Circles: Reflections on Principle Features and Primary Outcomes." In D. Sullivan & L. Tifft (eds.), *Handbook of Restorative Justice* (pp. 121–133). New York: Routledge.

Studer, L.H., A.S. Aylwin & J.R. Reddon (2005). "Testosterone, Sexual Offense Recidivism, and Treatment Effect among Adult Male Sex Offenders." *Sexual Abuse: A Journal of Research and Treatment*, 17, 171–181.

Substance Abuse and Mental Health Services Administration (2005). *Overview of Findings from the 2004 National Survey on Drug Use and Health*. Washington, DC: Department of Health and Human Services.

Sullivan, D. & L. Tifft (2005). *Restorative Justice: Healing the Foundations of Our Everyday Lives*, 2nd ed. Monsey, NY: Willow Tree.

Sullivan, D. & L. Tifft (2006). *Handbook of Restorative Justice*. New York: Routledge.

Sundell, K., K. Hansson, C.A. Löfholm, T. Olsson, L.-H. Gustle & C. Kadesjö (2008). "The Transportability of Multisystemic Therapy to Sweden: Short-Term Results From a Randomized Trial of Conduct-Disordered Youths." *Journal of Family Psychology*, 22, 550–560.

Sutherland, E.H. (1939). *Principles of Criminology*, 3rd ed. Philadelphia: Lippincott.

Sutherland, E.H. (1947). *Principles of Criminology*, 4th ed. Philadelphia: Lippincott.

Sutherland, E.H. & D.R. Cressey (1970). *Principles of Criminology*, 6th ed. New York: Lippincott.

Svrakic, N.M., D.M. Svrakic & C.R. Cloninger (1996). "A General Quantitative Theory of Personality Development: Fundamentals of a Self-organizing Psychobiological Complex." *Development and Psychopathology*, 8, 247–272.

Swanson, J.W., R. Borum, M.S. Swartz, V.A. Hiday, H.R. Wagner & B.J. Burns (2001). "Can Involuntary Outpatient Commitment Reduce Arrests among Persons with Severe Mental Illness?" *Criminal Justice and Behavior*, 28, 156–189.

Swanson, J.W., R. Borum, M.S. Swartz & J. Monahan (1996). "Psychotic Symptoms and the Risk of Violent Behaviour in the Community." *Criminal Behaviour and Mental Health*, 6, 309–329.

Swartz, J.A., A.J. Lurigio & S.A. Slomka (1996). "The Impact of IMPACT: An Assessment of the Effectiveness of a Jail-based Treatment Program." *Crime & Delinquency*, 42, 553–573.

Sweeten, G., S.D. Bushway & R. Paternoster (2009). "Does Dropping Out of School Mean Dropping into Delinquency?" *Criminology*, 47, 47–91.

Swenson, C.C., S.W. Henggeler & S.K. Schoenwald (2001). "Family-based Treatments." In C.R. Hollin (ed.), *Handbook of Offender Assessment and Treatment* (pp. 205–221). New York: Wiley.

Swogger, M.T., Z. Walsh & D.S. Kosson (2007). "Domestic Violence and Psychopathic Traits: Distinguishing the Antisocial Batterer from Other Antisocial Offenders." *Aggressive Behaviour*, 33, 253–260.

Sykes, G.M. & D. Matza (1957). "Techniques of Neutralization: A Theory of Delinquency." *American Sociological Review*, 22, 664–670.

Tanasichuk, C. & S.J. Wormith (2009). "The Predictive Validity of the Level of Service Inventory-Ontario Revision (LSI-OR) with Aboriginal Offenders." Paper presented at the Annual Meeting of the Canadian Psychological Association, Montreal, Quebec.

Taylor, I., P. Walton & J. Young (1973). *The New Criminology: For a Social Theory of Deviance*. London: Routledge and Kegan Paul.

Taylor, K.N. & K. Blanchette (2009). "The Women Are Not Wrong: It Is the Approach that Is Debatable." *Criminology & Public Policy*, 8, 221–229.

Tehrani, J.A., P.A. Brennan, S. Hodgins & S.A. Mednick (1998). "Mental Illness and Criminal Violence." *Social Psychiatry and Psychiatric Epidemiology*, 33, 81–85.

Tehrani, J.A. & S.A. Mednick (2000). "Genetic Factors and Criminal Behavior." *Federal Probation*, 64, 24–27.

Temcheff, C., L. Serbin, A. Martin-Storey, D. Stack, S. Hodgins, J. Ledingham & A. Shwartzman (2008). "Continuity and Pathways from Aggression in Childhood to Family Violence in Adulthood: A 30-Year Longitudinal Study." *Journal of Family Violence*, 23, 231–242.

Tennenbaum, D.J. (1977). "Personality and Criminality: A Summary and Implications of the Literature." *Journal of Criminal Justice*, 5, 225–235.

Teplin, L.A. (1984). "Criminalizing Mental Disorder: The Comparative Arrest Rate of the Mentally Ill." *American Psychologist*, 39, 794–803.

Teplin, L.A. & J. Swartz (1989). "Screening for Severe Mental Disorder in Jails." *Law and Human Behavior*, 13, 1–18.

Thistlethwaite, A., J. Wooldredge & D. Gibbs (1998). "Severity of Dispositions and Domestic Violence Recidivism." *Crime & Delinquency*, 1998, 44, 388–398.

Thomas, A. & S. Chess (1977). *Temperament and Development*. New York: Brunner/Mazel.

Thomas, A., S. Chess, H.G. Birch, M.E. Hertzig & S. Korn (1963). *Behavioral Individuality in Early Childhood*. New York: New York University Press.

Thomas, S.D.M., M. Daffern, T. Martin, J.R.P. Ogloff, L.D.G. Thomson, & M. Ferguson (2009). "Harm Associated with Stalking Victimization." *Australian and New Zealand Journal of Psychiatry*, 42, 800–806.

Thomas, S.D.M., R. Purcell, M. Pathé & P.E. Mullen (2008). "Factors Associated with Seclusion in a Statewide Forensic Psychiatric Service in Australia Over a 2-Year Period." *International Journal of Mental Health Nursing*, 18, 2–9.

Thompson, M.P., L.E. Saltzman & H. Johnson (2001). "Risk Factors for Physical Injury among Women Assaulted by Current or Former Spouses." *Violence Against Women*, 7, 886–899.

Thornberry, T.P., D. Huizinga & R. Loeber (2004). "The Causes and Correlates Studies: Findings and Policy Implications." *Juvenile Justice*, 9, 3–19.

Thornberry, T.P. & J.E. Jacoby (1979). *The Criminally Insane: A Community Follow-up of Mentally Ill Offenders*. Chicago: University of Chicago Press.

Thornberry, T.P., M.D. Krohn, A.J. Lizotte, C.A. Smith & K. Tobin (2003). *Gangs and Delinquency in Developmental Perspective*. Cambridge, UK: Cambridge University Press.

Thornberry, T.P., C.A. Smith, C. Rivera, D. Huizinga & M. Stouthamer-Loeber (1999). "Family Disruption and Delinquency." *Juvenile Justice Bulletin*. Washington, DC: Office of Juvenile Justice and Delinquency Prevention, U.S. Department of Justice.

Thornton, D. & C. Blud (2007). "The Influence of Psychopathic Traits on Response to Treatment. In H. Huges & J.C. Yuille (eds.), *The Psychopath: Theory, Research and Practice* (pp. 505–539). Mahwah, NJ: Lawrence Erlbaum.

Thorstad, D. (1991). "Man/Boy Love and the American Gay Movement." *Journal of Homosexuality*, 20, 251–274.

Tierney, D.W. & M.P. McCabe (2001). "The Assessment of Denial, Cognitive Distortions, and Victim Empathy among Pedophilic Sex Offenders: An Evaluation of the Utility of Self-report Measures." *Trauma, Violence, and Abuse*, 2, 259–270.

Timmons-Mitchell, J., M.B. Bender, M.A. Kishna & C.C. Mitchell (2006). "An Independent Effectiveness Trial of Multisystemic Therapy with Juvenile Justice Youth." *Journal of Clinical Child and Adolescent Psychology*, 35, 227–236.

Tittle, C.R. & R.F. Meier (1990). "Specifying the SES/Delinquency Relationship." *Criminology*, 28, 271–299.

Tittle, C.R. & R.F. Meier (1991). "Specifying the SES/Delinquency Relationship by Social Characteristics of Contexts." *Journal of Research in Crime and Delinquency*, 28, 430–455.

Tittle, C.R., W.J. Villimez & D.A. Smith (1978). "The Myth of Social Class and Criminality: An Empirical Assessment of the Empirical Evidence." *American Sociological Review*, 43, 643–656.

Tjaden, P. & N. Thoennes (2006). *Extent, Nature, and Consequences of Rape Victimization: Findings from the National Violence Against Women Survey*. Washington, DC: U.S. Department of Justice, Office of Justice Programs.

Tolan, P.H., D. Gorman-Smith & D.B. Henry (2003). "The Developmental Ecology of Urban Males' Youth Violence." *Developmental Psychology*, 39, 274–291.

Tomada, G. & B.H. Schneider (1997). "Relational Aggression, Gender, and Peer Acceptance: Invariance across Culture, Stability over Time, and Concordance among Informants." *Developmental Psychology*, 33, 601–609.

Tong, J.L.S. & D. Farrington (2006). "How Effective is the 'Reasoning and Rehabilitation' Programme in Reducing Reoffending? A Meta-analysis of Evaluations in Four Countries." *Psychology, Crime and Law*, 12, 3–24.

Tonigan, J.S., G.J. Connors & W.R. Miller (1996). "Special Populations in Alcoholics Anonymous" *Alcohol Health & Research World*, 22, 281–285.

Tonigan, J.S., R. Toscova & W.R. Miller (1996). "Meta-analysis of the Literature on Alcoholics Anonymous: Sample and Study Characteristics, Moderate Findings." *Journal of Studies on Alcohol*, 57, 65–72.

Tonry, M. (2004). *Thinking about Crime: Sense and Sensibility in American Penal Culture*. New York: Oxford University Press.

Tonry, M. (2008). "Learning from the Limitations of Deterrence Research." In M. Tonry (ed.), *Crime and Justice: A Review of Research*, Vol. 37 (pp. 279–311). Chicago: Chicago University Press.

Tonry, M. (2009). "Explanations of American Punishment Policies: A National History." *Punishment & Society*, 11, 377–394.

Tonry, M. & M. Lynch (1996). "Intermediate Sanctions." In M. Tonry (ed.), *Crime and Justice: A Review of Research*, Vol. 20 (pp. 99–144). Chicago: University of Chicago Press.

Toon, J. (2005). "Fourth European conference: Analysis of EM Programs." *The Journal of Offender Monitoring*, 18, 16–18.

Travis, L.F., III & F.T. Cullen (1984). "Radical Nonintervention: The Myth of Doing No Harm." *Federal Probation*, 48, 28–32.

Tremblay, R.E. (2000). "The Origins of Youth Violence." *ISUMA*, 1, 19–24.

Tremblay, P. (2002). "Social Interactions among Paedophiles." Unpublished paper available from the School of Criminology, University of Montreal, Quebec, Montreal.

Tremblay, P. (2006). "Convergence Settings for Non-predatory "Boy Lovers." *Crime Prevention Studies*, 19, 145–168.

Tremblay, R.E. (2008). "Understanding Development and Prevention of Chronic Physical Aggression: Towards Experimental Epigenetic Studies." *Philosophical Transactions of the Royal Society*, 363, 2613–2622.

Tremblay, P. & P.-P. Paré (2003). "Crime and Destiny: Patterns in Serious Offenders' Mortality Rates." *Canadian Journal of Criminology and Criminal Justice*, 45, 299–326.

Trotter, C. (1999). *Working with Involuntary Clients: A Guide to Practice*. Thousand Oaks, CA: Sage.

Trotter, C. (2006). *Working with Involuntary Clients: A Guide to Practice*, 2nd ed. Crows Nest, Australia: Allen & Unwin.

Trzesniewski, K.E., M.B. Donnellan, T.E. Moffitt, R.W. Robins, R. Poulton & A. Caspi (2006). "Low Self-Esteem During Adolescence Predicts Poor Health, Criminal Behavior, and Limited Economic Prospects During Adulthood." *Developmental Psychology*, 42, 381–390.

Truax, C.B., D.G. Wargo & N. R. Volksdorf (1970). "Antecedents to Outcome in Group Counseling with Institutionalized Juvenile Delinquents." *Journal of Abnormal Psychology*, 76, 235–242.

Turner, S., P.W. Greenwood, E. Chen & T. Fain (1999). "The Impact of Truth-in-sentencing and Three-strikes Legislation: Prison Populations, State Budgets, and Crime Rates." *Stanford Law and Policy Review*, 11, 75–91.

Tuvblad, C., M. Grann & P. Lichtenstein (2006). "Heritability for Adolescent Antisocial Behavior Differs with Socioeconomic Status: Gene-Environment Interaction." *Journal of Child Psychology and Psychiatry*, 47, 734–743.

Twenge, J.M., R.F. Baumeister, C.N. DeWall, N.J. Ciarocco & J.M. Bartels (2007). "Social Exclusion Decreases Prosocial Behavior." *Journal of Personality and Social Psychology*, 92, 56–66.

Twenge, J.M., R. F. Baumeister, D.M. Tice & T.S. Stucke (2001). "If You Can't Join Them, Beat Them: Effects of Social Exclusion on Aggressive Behavior." *Journal of Personality and Social Psychology*, 81, 1058–1069.

Ullmann, L. & L. Krasner (1976). *A Psychological Approach to Abnormal Behavior*, 2nd ed. Englewood Cliffs, NJ: Prentice Hall.

Ullrich, S., D.P. Farrington & J.W. Coid (2008). "Psychopathic Personality Traits and Life-Success." *Personality and Individual Differences*, 44, 1162–1171.

Umbreit, M.S. (1988). "Mediation of Victim-Offender Conflict." *Journal of Dispute Resolutions*, 85–105.

Umbreit, M.S. (1995). *Mediation of Criminal Conflict: An Assessment of Programs in Four Canadian Provinces*. St. Paul, MN: Center for Restorative Justice and Mediation.

Umbreit, M.S. & R.B. Coates (1992). *Victim Offender Mediation: An Analysis of Programs in Four States of the U.S.* Minneapolis: Citizens Council Mediation Services.

Umbreit, M.S. & A.W. Roberts (1996). *Mediation of Criminal Conflict in England: An Assessment of Services in Coventry and Leeds*. St. Paul, MN: Center for Restorative Justice and Mediation.

Umbreit, M.S. & B. Vos (2000). "Homicide Survivors Meet the Offender Prior to Execution." *Homicide Studies*, 4, 63–87.

Underwood, R.C., P.C. Patch, G.G. Cappelletty & R.W. Wolfe (1999). "Do Sexual Offenders Molest When Other Persons are Present? A Preliminary Investigation." *Sexual Abuse: Journal of Research and Treatment*, 11, 243–247.

United States General Accounting Office (1997). *Drug Courts: An Overview of Growth, Characteristics, and Results*. Washington, DC: U.S. Government Printing Office.

Vaillant, G.E. & T.J. Davis (2000). "Social/emotional Intelligence and Midlife Resilience in Schoolboys with Low Tested Intelligence." *American Journal of Orthopsychiatry*, 70, 215–222.

Valdez, A., C.D. Kaplan & E. Codina (2000). "Psychopathy among Mexican American Gang Members: A Comparative Study." *International Journal of Offender Therapy and Comparative Criminology*, 44, 46–58.

van Dam, C., J.M.A.M. Janssens & E.E.J. De Bruyn (2005). "PEN, Big Five, Juvenile Delinquency and Criminal Recidivism." *Personality and Individual Differences*, 39, 7–19.

Van De Rakt, M., P. Nieuwbeerta & N.D. De Graf (2008). "The Relationships between Conviction Trajectories of Fathers and Their Sons and Daughters." *British Journal of Criminology*, 48, 538–556.

Van Dieten, M. (1991). *Individual, Family, and Community Correlates of Child Problematic Behaviour in Disadvantaged Families*. Unpublished doctoral dissertation, University of Ottawa, Ottawa, Ontario.

Van Dusen, K.T. & S.A. Mednick (eds.) (1983). *Prospective Studies of Crime and Delinquency*. Hingham, MA: Kluwer Nijhoff.

Van Houten, R. (1983). "Punishment: From the Animal Laboratory to the Applied Setting." In S. Axelrod & J. Apsche (eds.), *The Effects of Punishment on Human Behavior* (pp. 13–44). New York: Academic Press.

van IJzendoorn, M.H. (1997). "Attachment, Emergent Morality, and Aggression: Toward a Developmental Socioemotional Model of Antisocial Behaviour." *International Journal of Behavioral Development*, 21, 703–727.

Van Ness, D.W. & K.H. Strong (2010). *Restoring Justice: An Introduction to Restorative Justice*, 4th ed. New Providence, NJ: LexisNexis Matthew Bender.

Van Voorhis, P. (1994). *Psychological Classification of the Adult Male Prison Inmate*. Albany: State University of New York Press.

Van Voorhis, P. (2009). "An Overview of Offender Classification Systems." In P. Van Voorhis, M. Braswell & D. Lester (eds.), *Correctional Counseling and Rehabilitation*, 7th ed. (pp. 133–161). New Providence, NJ: LexisNexis Matthew Bender.

Van Voorhis, P., E. Salisbury, E. Wright & A. Bauman (2008). *Achieving Accurate Pictures of Risk and Identifying Gender Responsive Needs: Two New Assessments for Women Offenders*. Retrieved April 30, 2009, from http://www.uc.edu/womenoffenders/NIC%20 Summary%20Report.pdf.

Vasilaki, E., S.G. Hosier & W.M. Cox (2006). "The Efficacy of Motivational Interviewing as a Brief Intervention for Excessive Drinking: A Meta-Analytic Review." *Alcohol & Alcoholism*, 41, 328–335.

Vazsonyi, A.T., H.H. Cleveland & R.P. Wiebe (2006). "Does the Effect of Impulsivity on Delinquency Vary by Level of Neighborhood Disadvantage?" *Criminal Justice and Behavior*, 33, 511–541.

Ventura, L.A. & G. Davis (2005). "Domestic Violence: Court Case Conviction and Recidivism." *Violence Against Women*, 11, 255–277.

Viding, E., A.P. Jones, P.J. Frick, T.E. Moffitt & R. Plomin (2008). "Heritability of Antisocial Behavior at 9: Do Callous-Unemotional Traits Matter?" *Developmental Science*, 11, 17–22.

Vieraitis, L.M., T.V. Kovandzic & T.B. Marvell (2007). "The Criminogenic Effects of Imprisonment: Evidence from State Panel Data, 1974–2002." *Criminology and Public Policy*, 6, 589–622.

Villa-Vicencio, C. (1999). "A Different Kind of Justice: The South African Truth and Reconciliation Commission." *Contemporary Justice Review*, 1, 407–428.

Vincent, G.M., M.J. Vitacco, T. Grisso & R.R. Corrado (2003). "Subtypes of Adolescent Offenders: Affective Traits and Antisocial Behavior Patterns." *Behavioral Sciences and the Law*, 21, 695–712.

Visher, C.A. (1986). The Rand Inmate Survey: A Reanalysis." In A. Blumstein, J. Cohen, J.A. Roth & C.A. Christy (eds.), *Criminal Careers and Career Offenders*. Washington, DC: National Academy Press.

Visher, C.A., A. Harrell, L. Newmark & J. Yahner (2008). "Reducing Intimate Partner Violence: An Evaluation of a Comprehensive Justice System-Community Collaboration." *Criminology & Public Policy*, 7, 495–523.

Vohs, K.D., R.F. Baumeister, B.J. Schmeichel, J.M. Twenge, N.M. Nelson & D.M. Tice (2008). "Making Choices Impairs Subsequent Self-control: A Limited-Resource Account of Decision Making, Self-Regulation, and Active Initiative." *Personality Processes and Individual Differences*, 94, 883–898.

Vold, G.B. & T.J. Bernard (1986). *Theoretical Criminology*, 3rd ed. New York: Oxford University Press.

Volavka, J. (2002). *Neurobiology of Violence*, 2nd ed. Washington, DC: American Psychiatric Association.

von Hirsch, A. (1976). *Doing Justice: The Choice of Punishments*. New York: Hill and Wang.

von Hirsch, A. (1987). *Past or Future Crimes: Deservedness and Dangerousness in the Sentencing of Criminals*. New Brunswick, NJ: Rutgers University Press.

von Hirsch, A., A.E. Bottoms, E. Burney & P.-O. Wikström. (1999). *Criminal Deterrence and Sentence Severity: An Analysis of Recent Research*. Oxford, UK: Hart.

Vose, B., F.T. Cullen & P. Smith (2008). "The Empirical Status of the Level of Service Inventory." *Federal Probation*, 72, 22–29.

Vrana, G.C. & M. Sroga (2008). "Predictive Validity of the LSI-OR Among a Sample of Adult Male Sexual Assaulters." Paper presented at the Annual Meeting of the Canadian Psychological Association, Halifax, Nova Scotia.

Waldo, G.P. & S. Dinitz (1967). "Personality Attributes of the Criminal: An Analysis of Research Studies, 1950–1965." *Journal of Research in Crime and Delinquency*, 4, 185–202.

Waldron, H.B. & C.W. Turner (2008). "Evidence-Based Psychosocial Treatments for Adolescent Substance Abuse." *Journal of Clinical Child & Adolescent Psychology*, 37, 238–261.

Walker, P.A., W.J. Meyer, L.E. Emory & A.L. Ruben (1984). "Antiandrogen Treatment of the Paraphilias." In H.C. Stancer, P.E. Garfinkel & V.M. Rakoff (eds.), *Guidelines for the Use of Psychotropic Drugs: A Clinical Handbook* (pp. 427–444). New York: SP Medical & Scientific Books.

Wallace, D.S., R.M. Paulson, C.G. Lord & C.F. Bond Jr. (2005). "Which Behaviors Do Attitudes Predict? Meta-Analyzing the Effects of Social Pressure and Perceived Difficulty." *Review of General Psychology*, 9, 214–227.

Walmsely, R. (2008). *World Prison Population List*, 8th ed. London: International Centre for Prison Studies.

Walsh, A. (2000). "Behavior Genetics and Anomie/Strain Theory." *Criminology*, 38, 1075–1108.

Walsh, A. (2005). "African Americans and Serial Killing in the Media." *Homicide Studies*, 9, 271–291.

Walters, G.D. (1992). "A Meta-analysis of the Gene-Crime Relationship." *Criminology*, 30, 595–613.

Walters, G.D. (1996). "The Psychological Inventory of Criminal Thinking Styles: Part III. Predictive Validity." *International Journal of Offender Therapy and Comparative Criminology*, 40, 105–112.

Walters, G.D. (2003). "Predicting Criminal Justice Outcomes with the Psychopathy Checklist and Lifestyle Criminality Screening Form: A Meta-analytic Comparison." *Behavioral Sciences and the Law*, 21, 89–102.

Walters, G.D. (2006a). *Lifestyle Theory: Past, Present, and Future*. Hauppauge, NY: Nova.

Walters, G.D. (2006b). "Risk-Appraisal Versus Self-Report in the Prediction of Criminal Justice Outcomes: A Meta-Analysis." *Criminal Justice and Behavior*, 33, 279–304.

Walters, S.T., M.D. Clark, R. Gingerich & M.L. Meltzer (2007). *A Guide for Probation and Parole: Motivating Offenders to Change*. Washington, DC: National Institute of Corrections.

Wampold, B.E. (2007). "Psychotherapy: The Humanistic (and Effective) Treatment." *American Psychologist*, 62, 857–873.

Wanberg, K.W. & H.B. Milkman (1995). *Strategies for Self-improvement and Change: A Cognitive Behavioral Approach for Treatment of the Substance Abusing Offender*. Denver: Center for Interdisciplinary Studies.

Ward, A. & J. Dockerill (1999). "The Predictive Accuracy of the Violent Offender Treatment Program Risk Assessment Scale." *Criminal Justice and Behavior*, 26, 125–140.

Ward, T.A. (2000). "Sexual Offenders' Cognitive Distortions as Implicit Theories." *Aggression and Violent Behavior*, 5, 491–507.

Ward, T. & A. Beech (2006). "An Integrated Theory of Sexual Offending." *Aggression and Violent Behavior*, 11, 44–63.

Ward, T. & L. Eccleston (2004). "Risk, Responsivity, and the Treatment of Offenders: Introduction to the Special Issue." *Psychology, Crime, and Law*, 10, 223–227.

Ward, T., J. Melzer & P. Yates (2007). "Reconstructing the Risk Need Responsivity Model: A Theoretical Elaboration and Evaluation." *Aggression and Violent Behavior*, 12, 208–228.

Ward, T., D.L.L. Polaschek & A.R. Beech (2006). *Theories of Sexual Offending*. New York: Wiley.

Ward, T. & C. Stewart (2003). "Criminogenic Needs and Human Needs: A Theoretical Model." *Psychology, Crime, and Law*, 9, 125–143.

Warr, M. (1998). "Life-course Transitions and Desistance from Crime." *Criminology*, 36, 183–216.

Warren, L.J., P.E. Mullen, S.D.M. Thomas, J.R.P. Ogloff & P.M. Burgess (2008). "Threats to Kill: A Follow-up Study." *Psychological Medicine*, 38, 599–605.

Washington State Institute for Public Policy (2003). *Washington Offender Accountability Act: Update and Progress Report on the Act's Evaluation*. Olympia: Washington State Institute for Public Policy.

Washington State Institute for Public Policy (2004). *Outcome Evaluation of Washington State's Research-based Programs for Juvenile Offenders*. Olympia: Washington State Institute for Public Policy.

Washington State Institute for Public Policy (2006). *Sex Offender Sentencing in Washington State: Predicting Recidivism Based on the LSI-R*. Olympia: Washington State Institute for Public Policy.

Wasserman, D. & R. Wachbroit (eds.) (2001). *Genetics and Criminal Behavior*. New York: Cambridge University Press.

Weatherburn, D., J. Hua & S. Moffatt (2006). "How Much Crime Does Prison Stop? The Incapacitation Effect of Prison on Burglary." *Crime and Justice Bulletin*, Number 93, New South Wales Bureau of Crime, Australia.

Webster, C.D., K.S. Douglas, D. Eaves & S.D. Hart (1997). *The HCR-20: Assessing Risk for Violence (Version 2)*. Burnaby, BC: Simon Fraser University.

Webster, C.D. & M.A. Jackson (eds.) (1997). *Impulsivity: Theory, Assessment, and Treatment*. New York: Guilford.

Webster, C.D., R.J. Menzies, M.D. Butler & R.E. Turner (1982). "Forensic Psychiatric Assessment in Selected Canadian Cities." *Canadian Journal of Psychiatry*, 27, 455–462.

Weekes, J., R. Mugford, G. Bourgon & S. Price. (2007). *Drug Treatment Courts FAQs*. Retrieved April 13, 2008, from http://www.ccsc.ca/NR/rdonlyres/FFBA90ED-2E2F-408D-A6C9–4F9E9F9B9155/0/ccsa00113482007.pdf.

Weis, R.D., S.S. O'Malley, J.D. Hosking, J.S. LoCastro & R. Swift (2008). "Do Patients with Alcohol Dependence Respond to Placebo? Results From the COMBINE Study." *Journal of Studies on Alcohol and Drugs*, 69, 878–884.

Weis, R., S.M. Whitemarsh & N.L. Wilson (2005). "Military-style Residential Treatment for Disruptive Adolescents: Effective for Some Girls, All Girls, When, and Why?" *Psychological Services*, 2, 105–122.

Wellford, C. (1975). "Labeling Theory and Criminology: An Assessment." *Social Problems*, 22, 332–345.

Wells, L.E. & J.H. Rankin (1991). "Families and Delinquency: A Meta-analysis of the Impact of Broken Homes." *Social Problems*, 38, 71–93.

Welsh, B.C. & D.P. Farrington (2000a). "Monetary Costs and Benefits of Crime Prevention Programs." In M. Tonry (ed.), *Crime and Justice: A Review of Research*, Vol. 27 (pp. 305–361). Chicago: University of Chicago Press.

Welsh, B.C. & D.P. Farrington (2000b). "Correctional Intervention Programs and Cost-benefit Analysis." *Criminal Justice and Behavior*, 27, 115–133.

Welsh, W.N. & G. Zajac (2004). "A Census of Prison-based Drug Treatment Programs: Implications for Programming, Policy, and Evaluation." *Crime & Delinquency*, 50, 108–133.

Werner, E.E. (1987). "Vulnerability and Resiliency in Children at Risk for Delinquency: A Longitudinal Study from Birth to Adulthood." In J.D. Burchard and S.N. Burchard (eds.), *Prevention of Delinquent Behavior* (pp. 16–43). Beverly Hills, CA: Sage.

West, D.J. & D.P. Farrington (1977). *Who Becomes Delinquent?* London: Heinemann Educational Books.

Whitaker, D.J., B. Le, R.K. Hanson, C. Baker, G. Ryan, P. McMahon, A. Klein & D.D. Rice (2008). "Risk Factors for the Perpetration of Child Sexual Abuse: A Review and Meta-Analysis." *Child Abuse & Neglect*, 32, 529–548.

White, J., R.M. Kowalski, A. Lyndon & S. Valentine (2000). "An Integrative Contextual Developmental Model of Male Stalking." *Violence and Victims*, 15, 373–388.

Whiteacre, K. (2004). "Case Manager Experiences with the LSI-R at a Federal Community Corrections Center." *Corrections Compendium*, 29, 1–5, 32–35.

Whiteacre, K. (2006). "Testing the Level of Service Inventory-Revised (LSI-R) for Racial/Ethnic Bias." *Criminal Justice Policy Review*, 17, 330–342.

Whitefield, D. (1999). "Electronic Monitoring in Europe: A Conference Report." *The Journal of Offender Monitoring*, 12, 15, 18–19.

Whitehead, J.T. & S.P. Lab (1989). "A Meta-analysis of Juvenile Correctional Treatment." *Journal of Research in Crime and Delinquency*, 26, 276–295.

Whiteside, M.F. & B.J. Becker (2000). "Parental Factors and the Young Child's Postdivorce Adjustment: A Meta-analysis with Implications for Parenting Arrangements." *Journal of Family Psychology*, 14, 5–26.

Widiger, T.A. (2006). "Psychopathy and DSM-IV Psychopathology." In C.J. Patrick (ed.), *Handbook of Psychopathy* (pp. 156–171). New York: Guilford.

Widiger, T.A., R. Cadoret, R.D. Hare, L. Robins, M. Rutherford, M. Zanarini, A. Alterman, M. Apple, E. Corbitt, A.E. Forth, S.D. Hart, J. Kultermann, G. Woody & A. Frances (1996). "DSM-IV Antisocial Personality Disorder Field Trial." *Journal of Abnormal Psychology*, 105, 3–16.

Widiger, T.A. & D.B. Samuel (2005). "Evidence-based Assessment of Personality Disorders." *Psychological Assessment*, 17, 278–287.

Widiger, T.A. & T.J. Trull (2007). "Plate Teutonics in the Classification of Personality Disorder: Shifting to a Dimensional Model." *American Psychologist*, 62, 71–83.

Widom, C.S. (1977). "A Methodology for Studying Non-institutional Psychopaths." *Journal of Consulting and Clinical Psychology*, 45, 674–683.

Widom, C.S. & M.G. Maxfield (2001). *An Update on the "Cycle of Violence."* Research in Brief. Washington, DC: National Institute of Justice.

Widom, C.S. & J.P. Newman (1985). "Characteristics of Non-institutional Psychopaths." In D.P. Farrington & J. Gunn (eds.), *Aggression and Dangerousness* (pp. 57–80). New York: Wiley.

Wiebe, R.P. (2004). "Delinquent Behavior and the Five-Factor Model: Hiding in the Adaptive Landscape?" *Individual Differences Research*, 2, 38–62.

Wiederanders, M.R., D.L. Bromley & P.A. Choate (1997). "Forensic Conditional Release Programs and Outcomes in Three States." *International Journal of Law and Psychiatry*, 20, 249–257.

Wikström, P-O.H. & R. Loeber (2000). "Do Disadvantaged Neighborhoods Cause Well-adjusted Children to Become Adolescent Delinquents? A Study of Male Juvenile Serious Offending, Individual Risk and Protective Factors, and Neighborhood Context." *Criminology*, 38, 1109–1142.

Wilcox, A., R. Young & C. Hoyle (2004). *An Evaluation of the Impact of Restorative Cautioning: Findings from a Reconviction Study*. London: Home Office Online Report 57/04.

Wilson, D.B., L.A. Bouffard & D.L. MacKenzie (2005). "A Quantitative Review of Structured, Group-oriented, Cognitive-Behavioral Programs for Offenders." *Criminal Justice and Behavior*, 32, 172–204.

Wilson, D.B., C.A. Gallagher, M.B. Coggeshall & D.L. MacKenzie (1999). "A Quantitative Review and Description of Corrections-based Education, Vocation, and Work Programs." *Corrections Management Quarterly*, 3, 8–18.

Wilson, D.B., O. Mitchell & D.L. MacKenzie (2006). "A Systematic Review of Drug Court Effects on Recidivism." *Journal of Experimental Criminology*, 4, 459–487.

Wilson, J.A. & R.C. Davis (2006). "Good Intentions Meet Hard Realities: An Evaluation of the Project Greenlight Reentry Program." *Criminology & Public Policy*, 5, 303–338.

Wilson, J.Q. & A. Abrahamse (1992). "Does Crime Pay?" *Justice Quarterly*, 9, 359–377.

Wilson, M. & M. Daly (1992). "Who Kills Whom in Spouse Killings? On the Exceptional Sex Ratio of Spousal Homicides in the United States." *Criminology*, 30, 189–215.

Wilson, P.W.F., R.B. D'Agostino, D. Levy, A.M. Belanger, H. Silbershatz & W.B. Kannel (1998). "Prediction of Coronary Heart Disease Using Risk Factor Categories." *Circulation*, 97, 1837–1847.

Wilson, R.J. & M. Barrett (1999). "Responsivity and Motivation to Change in Sexual Offenders." Paper presented at the annual conference of the American Society of Criminology, Toronto, Ontario, November.

Wilson, R.J. & J.E. Picheca (2005). "Circles of Support and Accountability—Engaging the Community in Sexual Offender Management." In B. Schwartz (ed.), *The Sex Offender*, Vol. 5. New York: Civic Research Institute.

Wilson, S.J. & M.W. Lipsey (2007). "School-Based Interventions for Aggressive and Disruptive Behavior." *American Journal of Preventative Medicine*, 33, S130–S143.

Wilson, S.J., M.W. Lipsey & J.H. Derzon (2003). "The Effects of School-based Intervention Programs on Aggressive Behavior: A Meta-analysis." *Journal of Consulting and Clinical Psychology*, 71, 136–149.

Wilson, T., D. Goldiner & P. Mickle (1993). "Prisoner Finds Rehab a Drag." *The Trentonian*, April 13.

Wintour, P. (2008). "Labour Plans to Toughen Up on Offenders." *The Guardian*, June 16.

Witbrodt, J., J. Bond, L.A. Kaskutas & C. Weisner (2007). "Day Hospital and Residential Addiction Treatment: Randomized and Nonrandomized Managed Care Clients." *Journal of Consulting and Clinical Psychology*, 75, 947–959.

Witkin, H.A., S.A. Mednick, F. Schulsinger, E. Bakkestrom, K.O. Christiansen, D.R. Goodenough, K. Hirschhorn, D. Lundsteen, D.R. Owen, J. Philip, D.B. Rubin & M. Stocking (1976). "XYY and XXY Men: Criminality and Aggression." *Science*, 193, 547–555.

Witte, T.D., C. Di Placido, D. Gu & S.C.P. Wong (2006). "An Investigation of the Validity and Reliability of the Criminal Sentiments Scale in a Sample of Treated Sex Offenders." *Sexual Abuse*, 18, 249–258.

Wolfe, D.A., C.V. Crooks, V. Lee, A. McIntyre-Smith & P.G. Jaffe (2003). "The Effects of Children's Exposure to Domestic Violence: A Meta-analysis and Critique." *Clinical Child and Family Psychology Review*, 6, 171–187.

Wolfgang, M. (1983). "Delinquency in Two Birth Cohorts." In K.T. Van Dusen & S.A. Mednick (eds.), *Prospective Studies in Crime and Delinquency* (pp. 7–16). Hingham, MA: Kluwer Nijhoff.

Wolfgang, M., R.M. Figlio & T. Sellin (1972). *Delinquency in a Birth Cohort*. Chicago: University of Chicago Press.

Wong, S. (2000). "Psychopathic Offenders." In S. Hodgins & R. M9Fller-Isberner (eds.), *Violence, Crime and Mentally Disordered Offenders* (pp. 87–112). Chichester, UK: John Wiley & Sons.

Wong, S. & A. Gordon (2006). "The Validity and Reliability of the Violence Risk Scale: A Treatment-Friendly Violence Risk Assessment Tool." *Psychology, Public Policy, and Law*, 12, 279–309.

Wong, S. & R.D. Hare (2005). *Guidelines for a Psychopathy Treatment Program*. Toronto: Multi-Health Systems.

Wood, P.B. & G. Dunaway (2003). "Consequences of Truth-in-Sentencing: The Mississippi Case." *Punishment and Society*, 5, 139–154.

Wood, P.R., W.R. Gove, J.A. Wilson & J.K. Cochran (1997). "Nonsocial Reinforcement and Habitual Criminal Conduct: An Extension of Learning Theory." *Criminology*, 35, 335–366.

Woodward, L.J., D.M. Fergusson & L.J. Horwood (2002). *Journal of Child Psychology and Psychiatry*, 43, 177–190.

Wooldredge, J. & A. Thistlethwaite (2005). "Court Disposition and Rearrest for Intimate Assault." *Crime & Delinquency*, 51, 75–102.

Worden, R.E., T.S. Bynum & J. Frank (1994). "Police Crackdowns on Drug Abuse and Trafficking." In D.L. Mackenzie & C.D. Uchida (eds.), *Drugs and Crime: Evaluating Public Policy Initiatives* (pp. 95–113). Thousand Oaks, CA: Sage.

Worling, J.R. & T. Curwen (2000). "Adolescent Sexual Offender Recidivism: Success of Specialized Treatment and Implications for Risk Prediction." *Child Abuse and Neglect*, 24, 965–982.

Wormith, J.S. (1984). "Attitude and Behavior Change of Correctional Clientele: A Three Year Follow-up." *Criminology*, 22, 595–618.

Wormith, J.S. & M. Olver (2002). "Offender Treatment Attrition and its Relationship with Risk, Responsivity and Recidivism." *Criminal Justice and Behavior*, 29, 447–471.

Wright, B.R.E., A. Caspi, T.E. Moffitt & R. Paternoster (2004). "Does the Perceived Risk of Punishment Deter Criminally Prone Individuals? Rational Choice, Self-control, and Crime." *Journal of Research in Crime and Delinquency*, 41, 180–213.

Wright, B.R.E., A. Caspi, T.E. Moffitt & P.A. Silva (2001). "The Effects of Social Ties on Crime Vary by Criminal Propensity: A Life-course Model of Interdependence." *Criminology*, 39, 321–352.

Wright, J.A., A.G. Burgess, A.W. Burgess, A.T. Laszlo, G.O. McCrary & J.E. Douglas (1996). "A Typology of Interpersonal Stalking." *Journal of Interpersonal Violence*, 11, 487–502.

Wright, J.P. & F.T. Cullen (2004). "Employment, Peers, and Life-course Transitions." *Justice Quarterly*, 21, 183–205.

Wright, J.P., F.T. Cullen & N. Williams (1997). "Working While in School and Delinquent Involvement: Implications for Social Policy." *Crime & Delinquency*, 43, 203–221.

Wright, K.A., T.C. Pratt & M. DeLisi (2008). "Examining Offending Specialization in a Sample of Male Multiple Homicide Offenders." *Homicide Studies*, 12, 381–398.

Wyrick, P.A. & J.C. Howell (2004). "Strategic Risk-based Response to Youth Gangs." *Juvenile Justice*, 9, 20–29.

Yang, B. & D. Lester (2008). "The Deterrent Effect of Executions: A Meta-Analysis Thirty Years After Ehrlich." *Journal of Criminal Justice*, 36, 453–460.

Yates, P.M. & T. Ward (2007). "Treatment of Sexual Offenders: Relapse Prevention and Beyond." In K. Witkiewitz & G.A. Marlatt (eds.), *Therapist's Guide to Evidence-Based Relapse Prevention* (pp. 215–234). Burlington, MA: Elsevier.

Yessine, A.K. & J. Bonta (2009). "The Offending Trajectories of Youthful Aboriginal Offenders." *Canadian Journal of Criminology and Criminal Justice*, 51, 435–472.

Yessine, A.K. & D.G. Kroner (2004). *Altering Antisocial Attitudes Among Federal Male Offenders on Release: A Preliminary Analysis of the Counter-Point Community Program (R-152)*. Ottawa: Correctional Service of Canada.

Yochelson, S. & S.E. Samenow (1976). *The Criminal Personality, Vol. 1: A Profile for Change.* New York: Jason Aronson.

Zamble, E. & V.L. Quinsey (1997). *The Criminal Recidivism Process.* New York: Cambridge University Press.

Zedlewski, E.W. (1987). *Making Confinement Decisions.* Research in Brief. Washington, DC: National Institute of Justice.

Zehr, H. & H. Mika (1998). "Fundamental Concepts of Restorative Justice." *Contemporary Justice Review*, 1, 47–57.

Zhang, Z. (2003). *Drug and Alcohol Use and Related Matters Among Arrestees 2003.* Retrieved March 27, 2009, from http://www.ojp.usdoj.gov/nij/topics/drugs/adam.htm.

Zimring, F.E. & G. Hawkins (1988). "The New Mathematics of Imprisonment." *Crime & Delinquency*, 34, 425–436.

Zinger, I. (2004). "Actuarial Risk Assessment and Human Rights: A Commentary." *Canadian Journal of Criminology and Criminal Justice*, 46, 607–620.

Zinger, I. & A.E. Forth (1998). "Psychopathy and Canadian Criminal Proceedings: The Potential for Human Rights Abuse." *Canadian Journal of Criminology*, 40, 237–277.

Zion, J.W. & R. Yazzie (2006). "Navajo Peacemaking: Original Dispute Resolution and a Life Way." In D. Sullivan & L. Tifft (eds.), *Handbook of Restorative Justice* (pp. 91–107). New York: Routledge.

Zlotnick, C., D.M. Johnson & R. Kohn (2006). "Intimate Partner Violence and Long-term Psychosocial Functioning in a National Sample of American Women." *Journal of Interpersonal Violence*, 21, 262–275.

Zona, M.A., K.K. Sharma & J. Lane (1993). "A Comparative Study of Erotomanic and Obsessional Subjects in a Forensic Sample." *Journal of Forensic Sciences*, 38, 894–903.

Zuckerman, M. (1984). "Sensation Seeking: A Comparative Approach to a Human Trait." *Behavioral and Brain Sciences*, 7, 413–471.

Zuckerman, M. (1993). "P-impulsive Sensation Seeking and its Behavioral, Psychophysiological and Biochemical Correlates." *Neuropsychobiology*, 28, 30–36.

Index to Selected Acronyms

GPCSL	General Personality and Cognitive Social Learning
GPS	Global Positioning Satellite
GREAT	Gang Resistance Education and Training
GST	General Strain Theory
ICCA	International Community Corrections Association
ICPS	Interpersonal Cognitive Problem Solving
IDS	Inventory of Drinking Situations
IPAT	Interpersonal Anxiety Test
ISP	Intensive Supervision Programs
LCSF	Lifestyle Criminality Screening Forum
LS/CMI	Level of Service/Case Management Inventory
LSI-R	Level of Service Inventory–Revised
MDO	Mentally Disordered Offender
MI	Motivational Interviewing
MMPI	Minnesota Multiphasic Personality Inventory
MPA	Medroxyprogesterone
MRT	Moral Reconation Therapy
MST	Multisystemic Therapy
MTFC	Multidimensional Treatment Foster Care
MZ	Monozygotic
NGRI	Not Guilty by Reason of Insanity
NIC	National Institute of Corrections
NYS	National Youth Survey
OCLC	Oregon Social Learning Center
ODARA	Ontario Domestic Assault Risk Assessment
OGRS	Offender Group Reconviction Scale
PAS	Propensity for Abusiveness Scale
PCB	Psychology of Criminal Behavior
PCC	Psychology of Criminal Conduct
PCL-R	Psychopathy Checklist–Revised
PCL:YV	Psychopathy Checklist: Youth Version
PICO	Pilot Intensive Counseling Organization

PIC-R	Personal, Interpersonal, and Community-Reinforcement
PIQ	Performance IQ
ROC	Receiver Operating Characteristic
R&R	Reasoning and Rehabilitation
RNR	Risk, Need, Responsivity
RRASOR	Rapid Risk Assessment for Sexual Offence Recidivism
SAI	Special Alternative Incarceration
SARA	Spousal Assault Risk Assessment
SCJ	Structured Clinical Judgment
SES	Socioeconomic Status
SFS	Salient Factor Score
SIR	Statistical Information on Recidivism
STICS	Strategic Training Initiative in Community Supervision
TCO	Threat/Control-Override
VIQ	Verbal IQ
VORP	Victim Offender Reconciliation Program
VRAG	Violence Risk Appraisal Guide

Subject Index

Name Index

Abracen, J., 483–484
Abraham, C., 183
Abrahamse, A., 447, 451
Abrams, K.M., 488
Accordino, M.P., 268
Acker, J.R., 441, 454
Ackerley, E., 479
Adams, Stuart, 352
Addison, O.W., 257
Agee, V.L., 388
Ageton, S.S., 124
Ægisdóttier, S., 312, 343
Agnew, Robert, 18, 116, 146, 151, 153,
    203, 240, 262–263, 265, 445, 515
Aguirre, A., 441
Ajzen, I., 19, 79, 123, 134, 235,
    237, 515
Akers, R.L., 19, 80, 123–125, 132, 137,
    151, 153, 202, 515
Alarid, L.F., 202
Albarracin, D., 237
Alder, C., 479
Alexander, J.F., 255–256
Alexy, E.M., 479
Allik, J., 195
Allrucker, K.W., 252
Altrows, I.F., 27
Amato, P.R., 250
Amell, J.W., 174
Anderson, A.L., 228
Anderson, D., 240–241
Anderson, K., 230
Anderson, L.A., 312
Andrews, D.A., 21–22, 27, 31, 40–41,
    47–49, 56, 59, 62–63, 67, 71, 80, 82,
    121, 123, 125, 132, 153, 185, 226,
    240, 244, 277, 279, 286, 288,
    309–310, 313–318, 328, 332, 334, 343,
    355–356, 359–360, 362–366, 371–374,
    377, 381, 384, 386, 388–390, 397,
    402, 404, 407–408, 457, 504, 505,
    508, 513, 515, 531–532, 535, 542
Andrews, D.W., 231
Andrews, H., 473
Andrews, K.H., 153
Angel, C.M., 454
Angus, G., 339

Ankney, C.D., 181
Annis, H.M., 288
Antonowicz, D., 288
Aos, S., 261, 287, 292, 363, 424, 433
Appelbaum, P.S., 74
Applegate, B.K., 433–434, 437, 439
Arbuthnot, J., 235, 256–257
Archer, J., 462
Argyle, Michael, 234
Arkowitz, H., 290
Armstrong, B., 288, 318, 364
Armstrong, G.S., 437, 459
Arndt, S., 171
Arnekley, B.J., 202
Arnold, T., 316, 333
Arthur, M.W., 267
Asch, Solomon, 234
Ashford, J.B., 241, 477
Atkinson, L., 252, 273
Au, A., 466
Auerhahn, K., 434
Austin, J., 429–431, 434, 440
Ayduk, O., 136
Aylwin, A.S., 482
Azar, S.T., 469
Azrin, N.H., 146, 280, 281–282, 443, 446,
    450, 459, 515

Babcock, J., 391, 469
Babiak, P., 214
Baborm T.F., 276
Bailey, Walter, 70, 348–349, 351–352
Bain, J., 482
Bains, P., 283
Baird, C., 515
Baird, S.C., 48, 314
Baker, C., 479
Baker, D.V., 441
Baker, J.R., 173
Baker, T. 479
Bales, R.F., 381
Bales, W.D., 268, 439
Ball, M., 49
Ball, R.A., 239–240
Bandura, Albert, 18–19, 79–80, 109, 119,
    124, 134, 148, 238, 449, 515
Bank, L., 231, 254

Deluty, M.Z., 444
DeMatteo, D., 213, 333
Dembo, R., 252
Demuth, S., 250–251
Dennison, S.M., 485
Denton, K., 238
Derefinko, K.J., 220
Derkzen, D.M., 291
Derzon, J.H., 230, 251, 264, 279
de Salvo, Albert (Boston Strangler), 470
De Tardo-Bora, K.A., 338
DeWall, C.N., 229
DeYoung, C.G., 167–168
Dickie, I., 484
Dickson, N., 160, 332
DiClemente, C.C., 51, 289
DiClemente, D., 510
Diefenbach, D.L., 470
Dieten, M., 408
Dietz, P.E., 486, 490
Digman, J.M., 19, 58, 194
Dilillio, D., 462
Dillingham, D., 515
Dinitz, S., 153, 198
Dinsmoor, J.A., 444, 446
Di Placido, C., 233, 240
Dishion, T.J., 174, 231, 409
Dobash, R.E., 469
Dobash, R.P., 469
Dockerill, J., 335
Dodge, A., 171
Dodge, J.E., 448
Dolan, M., 334
Doll, H., 283
Dollard, J., 18–19, 111–112, 130, 151, 515
Donahue, J.J., 183
Donato, P., 424
Donnellan, M.B., 228
Doob, A.N., 227, 434
Doob, L., 111, 515
Dooley, M., 457
Dornfeld.M., 462
Douglas, K.S., 212, 216, 334–335, 487, 488
Dowden, C., 48, 56, 71, 244, 279, 283, 288, 294, 309, 334, 343, 365, 371–373, 377, 391, 454–455, 457, 501–502, 513, 515
Downs, D.L., 229
Drake, E., 287, 292, 363, 433
D'Silva, K., 215
Dugdale, R.L., 161, 227
Duggan, C., 215
Dunaway, G., 440
Dunaway, R.G., 185, 202
Durrett, C., 195
Dutra, L., 288, 391

Dutton, D.G., 462, 465–466, 468–469, 487, 488
Dutton, M.A., 466

Eamon, M.K.., 269–270
Eaves, L.J., 162, 168
Eddy, M.J., 254
Edens, J.F., 210, 212, 216–217, 220
Edwards, D.L., 261
Egan, V., 481
Egley, A., 231
Ehrensaft, M.K., 462
Eitle, D., 467
Eke, A.W., 182
Elbogen, E.B., 473
Elliott, D.S., 124, 202
Ellis, L., 41, 168, 171, 180–182, 191, 525, 531, 538
Else-Quest, N.M., 172
Engel, R.S., 473
Epstein, E.E., 281
Epstein, M.E., 216
Erickson, M.L., 126, 388
Erickson, S., 478
Erikson, M., 149
Ervin, Frank, 169
Ervin, L., 338
Erwin, B.S., 428, 437
Esbensen, F.-A., 231–233
Evans, S.C., 462
Evans, T.D., 202
Exum, M.L., 292
Eysenck, H.J., 38, 94, 153, 173, 175, 195–196, 215, 447, 515
Ezell, M.E., 438

Fabiano, E.A., 136, 359, 399, 515
Factor, D., 441
Fagan, J.A., 285, 465, 467
Fain, T., 438, 440
Fals-Stewart, W., 464
Farabee, D., 283, 286, 291, 397
Farbring, A.C., 291
Farrington, D.P., 9–10, 23, 39, 161–162, 173, 183, 186, 202, 214, 250, 253, 285–286, 356, 392, 424, 437, 515
Farver, J.A.M., 270
Fass, T.L., 333, 432
Favell, J.E., 448
Fazel, J.E., 209
Fazel.S., 283
Fein, R.A., 486
Ferguson, A.M., 334
Ferguson, C.J., 183
Fergusson, D.M., 268

Jensen, Arthur, 181
Jensen, E.L., 432
Jenson, G.F., 153
Jesness, C.F., 50
Jesseman, R., 454
Jessor, R., 11, 80, 124, 137, 151, 515
Jessor, S.L., 11, 80, 124, 137, 151, 515
John, O.P., 222
Johnson, D.M., 462
Johnson, H., 466
Johnson, J.G., 253
Johnson, R.E., 132, 153
Johnson, S.C., 473
Johnson, W.R., 291
Johnston, J.M., 443
Johnstone, E.C., 166
Joiner, T.E., 448
Jolliffee, D., 161
Jones, A.P., 173
Jones, B., 27
Jones, M.B., 267
Jones, P.R., 312
Jongsma, A.E., 390
Juby, H., 250
Juke, M., 161
Jurkovic G., 256

Kabela-Cormier, E., 281
Kadden, R.M., 281
Kagan, J., 174
Kahler, C.W., 281
Kandel, D.B., 153
Kanin, E.J., 479
Kantor, G.K., 462
Kaplan, C., 233
Karberg, L.E., 283
Kaskutas, L.A., 281
Kassebaum, G., 384, 393
Katz, J., 166
Kavanagh, B., 481
Kazdin, A.E., 443
Kazemian, L., 279
Keeney, R.T., 489
Keller, J., 462
Kelly, C.E., 315, 334
Kelly, W.K., 285
Kemper, Edmund, 491
Kempinen, C.A., 438
Kennedy, R., 249, 252
Kennedy, S., 51
Kern, Roger, 251
Kernberg, O.F., 215
Kessler, R.C., 462, 465
Keyes, K.M., 276
Keys, C.B., 281

Kienlen, K.K., 485, 488
Kiessling, J.J., 48–49, 128, 359, 381, 389
Kiger, K., 489
Kiloh, L.G., 169
Kim, S.Y., 269
Kimonis, E.R., 175, 228
King, R.S., 431–432
Kirby, B.C., 70, 347–349
Kishna, M.A., 259
Kite, J.C., 469
Kitzman, K.M., 462
Kivetz, R., 219, 239
Klag, S., 291
Klebold, Dylan, 488
Klein, A.R., 464–465, 468
Klein, M.W., 384–386
Klein, N., 256
Klodin, V., 166
Klohnen, E.C., 162
Knack, W.A., 281
Knight, R.A., 210
Knutson, N.., 174
Koepf, G.F., 166
Kohlberg, L., 235
Kohn, R., 462
Kohnfeld, C.W., 436
Konty, M., 203
Kormos, C., 182
Korn, S., 172
Kornick, M., 388
Kosakoski, G., 182
Koss, M.P., 462
Kosson, D.S., 216, 465
Kovandzic, T.V., 433
Kramer, S.P., 478
Krasner, L., 11–12
Kraus, R.T., 491
Kraus, S.J., 237
Krebs, D.L., 238
Krentzman, A.R., 281
Kringlen, E., 163
Kristofferson, K., 247
Kroner, D.G., 241, 315, 335
Kropp, P.R., 466–467
Krueger, J.I., 227
Krueger, R.F., 162, 196
Kruttschnitt, C., 462
Kurki, L., 454
Kurkowsky, K., 373
Kurlychek, M.C., 438
Kuther, T.L., 270

Lab, S.P., 357, 362–364, 370–372
Labriola, M., 468–469
Lacourse, E., 227, 253